To the Glory of God

and in honour of

Blessed Edmund,

King & Martyr

This book is presented to

St. Edmund's Church

Hunstanton

in memory of

....

THE
ENGLISH HYMNAL

WITH TUNES

1933

LONDON
OXFORD UNIVERSITY PRESS
A. R. MOWBRAY & CO., LTD.

Oxford University Press, Ely House, London W. 1

GLASGOW NEW YORK TORONTO MELBOURNE WELLINGTON
CAPE TOWN IBADAN NAIROBI DAR ES SALAAM LUSAKA ADDIS ABABA
DELHI BOMBAY CALCUTTA MADRAS KARACHI DACCA
KUALA LUMPUR SINGAPORE HONG KONG TOKYO

The First Edition was issued in 1906
A New Edition was first published in 1933
Nineteenth Impression 1976

Printed in Great Britain
at the University Press, Oxford
by Vivian Ridler
Printer to the University

PREFACE[1]

THE ENGLISH HYMNAL is a collection of the best hymns in the English language, and is offered as a humble companion to the Book of Common Prayer for use in the Church. It is not a party-book, expressing this or that phase of negation or excess, but an attempt to combine in one volume the worthiest expressions of all that lies within the Christian Creed, from those 'ancient Fathers' who were the earliest hymn-writers down to contemporary exponents of modern aspirations and ideals.

We therefore offer the book to all broad-minded men, in the hope that every one will find within these pages the hymns which he rightly wants. At the same time, since literary, musical, and religious standards vary, a really inclusive collection must of necessity be larger than the needs of each particular individual: hymn books, indeed, afford special facilities in this respect, because those who use them can select according to their requirements. Such a method of selection we have ourselves suggested in the Musical Edition by a List of simple hymns, which may satisfy the ordinary needs of many parishes; while we have also arranged a Table of hymns for all the Sundays and Holy-days of the year, which covers the whole ground. Thus we have endeavoured to produce a book that shall suit the needs of learned and simple alike, and shall at the same time exhibit the characteristic virtue of hymnody, — its witness, namely, to the fact that in the worship of God Christians are drawn the closer together as they are drawn more closely to the one Lord. In Christian song Churches have forgotten their quarrels and men have lost their limitations, because they have reached the higher ground where the soul is content to affirm and to adore. The hymns of Christendom show more clearly than anything else that there is even now such a thing as the unity of the Spirit.

Little explanation is needed of the principles which governed the selection and arrangement of the hymns. The new work, inserted

[1] *Reprinted from the 1906 Edition. For General Note on the 1933 Edition see p.* **xx**.

PREFACE

in every case to fill an acknowledged gap or to introduce a tune of special excellence, must stand or fall on its merits. One feature, however, requires a word of comment. Hymns are printed, whereever possible, as their authors wrote them. To many it will be a surprise to find that the ascription of a hymn to this or that author, when it was given at all in hymnals of the last century, was very often misleading. The public now has the opportunity of comparing many originals with their altered versions; and few, we venture to predict, will deny that they had been altered for the worse. Occasionally, indeed, the music requires the removal of an extra word if a hymn is to be used at all, as for instance in Neale's hymn, No. 137 (The Day of Resurrection), and in Milton's, No. 532 (Let us, with a gladsome mind); but although these hymns are marked as altered, none of their characteristic epithets have been changed. Sometimes alterations are justified for other reasons; and some translations are the work of several hands. But, apart from such exceptional cases, the efforts, so often made in the past to improve the work of competent authors, have had the inevitable result. The freshness and strength of the originals have been replaced by stock phrases and commonplace sentiments; and injury has been done to the quality of our public worship as well as to the memory of great hymn-writers.

A Hymn Book that is offered as a companion to the Book of Common Prayer must provide adequately not only for Sundays but also for all those other Holy-days which in the Prayer Book are ordered to be observed precisely in the same way as Sundays. The Office Hymns for the Saints' Days 'to be observed' are therefore given, as well as many suitable modern hymns: to these have been added the hymns for the Minor Saints' Days of the Anglican Calendar (since it is a common practice to sing a hymn as a memorial of such days), although we recognize the fact that as there is no Office for such days in the Prayer Book they can have no Office Hymn in the strict sense of the word.

The Hymns marked 'Office Hymn' are translations from those appointed in the ancient choir-services of the English Church. In suggesting these as specially suitable, by placing them out of the

PREFACE

alphabetical order under a special heading, we have followed the example of the Reformers, who went to the same source for our present Offices of Morning and Evening Prayer. Very many of these hymns are already well known, thanks to the good work of former hymnals; but there remained many Sundays and other days for which the proper hymns were not provided. There is indeed no need for all the hymns of all the ancient services, such as the hymns for both Mattins and Lauds on every occasion; but there is a legitimate demand for all those hymns which belong to the services of Morning and Evening Prayer, according to the Prayer Book Calendar. The need has long been felt of such a complete set of these ancient hymns, which in their Scriptural simplicity and sober dignity represent the deep Christian experience of more than a thousand years. This need we have now supplied, endeavouring where new translations were required to convey as faithfully as possible the spirit of the originals, so that in these hymns also the authors should speak for themselves.

Thus we have made complete provision for the liturgical requirements of Churchmen, while we have at the same time added many modern hymns of the first rank which have not hitherto been at their disposal. In so doing we have attempted to redress those defects in popular hymnody which are deeply felt by thoughtful men; for the best hymns of Christendom are as free as the Bible from the self-centred sentimentalism, the weakness and unreality which mark inferior productions. The great hymns, indeed, of all ages abound in the conviction that duty lies at the heart of the Christian life—a double duty to God and to our neighbour; and such hymns, like the Prayer Book, are for all sorts and conditions of men.

EXPLANATORY NOTES

The book is divided into twelve parts, and the hymns are arranged alphabetically in each part or section, so that they may be readily found. In Parts I to III, the Office Hymns for each occasion are placed first, and after them the other hymns follow in alphabetical order. Part X is divided into two sections: the first consists of

PREFACE

hymns and prayers arranged so that processions may be definite acts of prayer and worship, after the manner of the Prayer Book Litany and the older processions upon which it is based; the second contains other hymns that are suitable for use in processions. The Metrical Litanies in Part XI are similarly arranged, so that they form complete acts of prayer. Part XII consists of liturgical prose pieces, which are arranged in their natural order.

The heading 'OFFICE HYMN' shows that the original was the Office Hymn for the corresponding service in the Salisbury service-books, except in the case of No. 175, which is taken from those of York. The letters 'E.' and 'M.' stand for Evensong and Mattins, the first Evensong being that on the day before the festival. When these letters occur twice for the same festival or season ('E.' and 'M.,' 'M.' and 'E.'), the first 'E' denotes the hymn for the first Evensong, and the second 'E.' the Evensong on the day itself; while the first 'M.' shows that the hymn anciently belonged to Mattins only, and the second 'M.' stands over the hymn that belonged to Lauds: as our present Mattins occupies the place of the older Mattins and Lauds, either hymn is equally suitable.

The names and dates of all authors are given, in so far as they are known. Initials only are provided in the case of living translators, whose names are given in the Index of Authors, and in the case of a few living authors. The letters '*Tr.*' are prefixed to the names of all translators. The number of the Psalm (*Ps.*) is given in the case of paraphrases, though it must be remembered that some paraphrases are extremely free, while others are based upon one or two verses only of a Psalm.

Where the author's or translator's name has no mark, the hymn is unaltered or has been revised by the author himself. The sign † shows that an alteration has been made in one line only; the sign ‡ denotes alterations in two or three lines. To hymns that are the work of more than one writer a second name is given, or the words '*and others*' are added. Translations which have no one special source are marked '*Tr. cento.*' Alterations in spelling are not marked, nor is any note made of the omission of verses, nor do the statements as to authorship refer to the doxologies.

PREFACE

In the case of long hymns and of hymns with slow tunes, the sign * is prefixed to those verses which may be most conveniently omitted. It does not follow that verses so marked are considered in any way inferior, but only that they can be omitted without doing violence to the context.

Choruses and refrains are printed once for all in italic. 'Amen' is only printed with doxologies. In the case of other hymns its use is sometimes appropriate and sometimes not; but in the Musical Edition it is given with its musical setting in every case except that of sequences, so that it can be sung when desired. The verses are numbered, and in order to show when the last verse of a hymn is reached at the bottom of a page, a full point is in every case printed after the number of the last verse.

The Introits are given in Part XII, and as in some churches other Scriptural passages from the older Liturgy are occasionally used, these also are for convenience given in full. They follow the Introit, and are marked by letters which are explained in a note at the head of this Part.

We desire to express our warmest thanks to the authors who have aided us by writing or translating hymns specially for this Hymnal, i.e. Rev. Maurice F. Bell; Rev. Dr. C. Bigg, Professor of Ecclesiastical History, Oxford; Mr. F. C. Burkitt, Norrisian Professor of Divinity, Cambridge; Mr. G. K. Chesterton; Rev. G. Gillett; Mr. Laurence Housman; Miss H. Packer; Rev. E. S. Palmer; Rev. Canon Rawnsley; Mr. R. Ellis Roberts.

1933

The names of those concerned in the original production of the English Hymnal in 1906 are:—

W. J. BIRKBECK	D. C. LATHBURY
A. HANBURY-TRACY	ARTHUR REYNOLDS
W. H. H. JERVOIS	ATHELSTAN RILEY
T. A. LACEY	PERCY DEARMER
	(General Editor)

PREFACE

THE MUSIC[1]

The music of this hymnal is divided into two main sections; the plainsong melodies and the comparatively modern music. The modern music only is dealt with here. The plainsong is discussed separately.

The Choice of Material.

The music is intended to be essentially congregational in character, and this end has been kept in view both in the choice of tunes and in the manner of setting them out. Fine melody rather than the exploitation of a trained choir has been the criterion of selection: the pitch of each tune has been kept as low as is consistent with the character of the melody.

Where there is congregational singing it is important that familiar melodies should be employed, or at least those which have stood the test of time: therefore the 'specially composed tune'—that bane of many a hymnal—has been avoided as far as possible. There are already many hundreds of fine tunes in existence, so many indeed that it is impossible to include more than a small part of them in any one collection.

The task of providing congregations with familiar tunes is difficult; for, unfortunately, many of the tunes of the present day which have become familiar and, probably merely from association, popular with congregations are quite unsuitable to their purpose. More often than not they are positively harmful to those who sing and hear them. The committee were therefore placed in the hard position of having to decide whether they should risk momentary unpopularity by discarding certain tunes, or whether they should sacrifice the greater ultimate good for the lesser and more immediate advantage. The problem, however, solved itself in a happy and unforeseen manner because the insertion of several of the tunes in question was not allowed by the owners of the copyright. Thus the committee, while regretting that they are not able for a few years to

[1] *Reprinted from the 1906 edition. For 1933 revision see p.* xv *and General Note on p.* xx

PREFACE

include such beautiful tunes as Dykes' 'Dominus regit me' or Stainer's 'In Memoriam', yet feel that nothing but gain can result from the exclusion of certain other tunes, which are worthy neither of the congregations who sing them, the occasions on which they are sung, nor the composers who wrote them.

The committee believe that many clergymen and organists are now realizing their responsibility in this matter, and will welcome a tune-book in which enervating tunes are reduced to a minimum. The usual argument in favour of bad music is that the fine tunes are doubtless 'musically correct', but that the people want 'something simple'. Now the expression 'musically correct' has no meaning; the only 'correct' music is that which is beautiful and noble. As for simplicity, what could be simpler than 'St. Anne' or 'The Old Hundredth', and what could be finer?

It is indeed a moral rather than a musical issue. No doubt it requires a certain effort to tune oneself to the moral atmosphere implied by a fine melody; and it is far easier to dwell in the miasma of the languishing and sentimental hymn tunes which so often disfigure our services. Such poverty of heart may not be uncommon, but at least it should not be encouraged by those who direct the services of the Church; it ought no longer to be true anywhere that the most exalted moments of a church-goer's week are associated with music that would not be tolerated in any place of secular entertainment.

There are, however, many who recognize this bad state of things, but are timid about removing old favourites. Those who have this fear should remember that most of our 'old favourites' are of very recent growth, dating at the earliest from the year 1861— a very short life for a hymn tune; also that it does not take more than a couple of years to make a tune which congregations like into an 'old favourite', and furthermore that it is not by any means necessarily bad music which is popular. The average congregation likes fine melody when it can get it, but it is apt to be undiscriminating, and will often take to bad melody when good is not forthcoming. Is it not worth while making a vigorous effort to-day

PREFACE

for the sake of establishing a good tradition? Especially should this be the case with children's hymns. Children at all events have no old association with any particular tune, and incalculable good or harm may be done by the music which they sing in their most impressionable years.

An attempt has been made to set a minimum standard in the music selected for this work. This does not mean that austerity has been unduly sought, or that difficult and colourless music has been preferred to that which is vigorous and bright. A tune has no more right to be dull than to be demoralizing. Indeed, anxiety to ensure the co-operation of the congregation may have caused the boundary to be occasionally overstepped, so that a few tunes have been retained which ought to have been rejected, but on this borderland individual tastes must necessarily differ, and the committee have done their best to select the most suitable tune for each hymn. To make the possibilities of selection wider, numerous cross-references have been given, which should be freely used, and a short appendix is added of alternative tunes to certain hymns for the use of those who do not agree with the choice of the musical editor.

The Manner of Performance.

(a) *Pitch.*—The pitch of all the tunes has been fixed as low as possible for the sake of mixed congregations. Except in the case of tunes with an extended compass the highest note is not above D or E. Some choirmasters may object to this on the ground that it places the hymns in the worst part of the boy-chorister's voice, and that it takes the basses and altos rather low. The obvious answer is that hymns are essentially for the congregation; the choir have their opportunity elsewhere, but in the hymn they must give way to the congregation, and it is a great mistake to suppose that the result will be inartistic. A large body of voices singing together makes a distinctly artistic effect, though that of each individual voice might be the opposite. And it may be added that a desire to parade a trained choir often accompanies a debased musical taste.

PREFACE

Where a tune occurs twice in the book it is usually given in two different keys, and in one or two cases a higher version of certain well-known tunes is given in the appendix. If this is not sufficient it is always possible to transpose the tunes to a higher key. Where a tune is only given once it is obvious why it should be printed in a lower key. Such a key is particularly suitable for village churches where the organist is rarely able to transpose. On the other hand, in churches where it is desired to give the first consideration to a trained choir, the organist will certainly be competent to transpose at sight into the key desired.

(b) *Unison singing.*—Every hymn is so arranged that it can be sung in unison accompanied by the organ. Certain verses are marked as being specially suitable for unison singing, and it is suggested that the first verse of most hymns should be sung in unison as well as all the doxologies. In any case the congregation must *always* sing the melody, and the *melody only.*

In these circumstances it has been thought advisable occasionally to introduce harmonizations (especially those of J. S Bach) rather more elaborate than usual. These will no doubt add greatly to the beauty and the popularity of the tunes. If some choirs find them difficult the tunes can be sung in unison accompanied by the organ; the organist will find no difficulty in playing them, if they are taken at the proper speed. It is a great mistake to suppose that untrained musicians are insensible to fine harmony. They may not be able to analyse the effect, but there can be no doubt that a well-harmonized tune makes a more powerful appeal than one in which the harmonies are bad or unsuitable. Choirs would be much better occupied in learning these beautiful settings of Bach (which are not hard if practised a little) than in rehearsing vulgar anthems by indifferent composers.

(c) *Choir and people.*—There are churches in which the experiment has been successfully tried of making choir and people sing some hymns antiphonally. By this means the people are given a distinct status in the services, and are encouraged to take an intelligent

PREFACE

interest in the music they sing, while the eternal war between choir and congregation, each considering the other an unnecessary appendage to the services of the church, is done away with.

The congregation might be encouraged to sing and appreciate the finer melodies if a system of monthly congregational practices were held, at which the less known tunes could be made familiar in some such way as the following:—The first two verses might be sung by the choir alone, or some body of singers with good voices who already knew the melody: at the third verse the congregation would be invited to join in, and would finally sing a verse unaided by the trained singers. A *hymn recital*, at which some of the less familiar hymns might be sung by the choir, would also be a pleasant variety from the Sunday evening organ recital.

(*d*) *Speed.*—The custom in English churches is to sing many hymns much too fast. It is distressing to hear 'Nun Danket' or 'St. Anne' raced through at about twice the proper speed. Metronome marks are added to each hymn, which, the editor believes, indicate the proper speed in a fairly large building with a congregation of average size. The speed indications should not be judged at the pianoforte.

Another painful experience is to hear an organist trying to play through a C M. or L. M. tune in absolutely strict time, regardless of the slight pauses which the congregation, with unconscious artistic insight, are inclined to make at the end of every line. Pauses have been marked wherever they should be made, and a sign ⸲ has also been extensively used to designate a very short break, less than the ordinary pause (⁀). Sometimes ⁀ and ⸲ are used together, signifying a pause as well as a complete break in the sound.

Some of the hymns are marked to be sung 'in free rhythm'. This direction is especially applicable to unmeasured tunes, but all hymn tunes should be sung more or less freely; at all events a stiff clock-work rendering should be avoided. If this is borne in mind, and the hymns are not sung too fast, the bad effect will be largely

PREFACE

avoided of those false accents which inevitably occur when several verses of a hymn are sung to the same tune.

(e) *Expression.*—Expression marks have been altogether omitted, as it is considered that subtleties of expression are entirely unsuitable for congregational singing. The organist can use his own judgement as to the general dynamics of each verse, and convey his idea to the congregation by his registering. All sudden 'pianos' or small 'crescendos' and 'diminuendos' should be avoided as destroying the broad and massive effect which congregational singing should convey.

(f) *Notation.*—Both minims and crotchets have been employed, the former for the slower and more solemn hymns and the latter for those of a brighter nature. The point of division has been fixed at M. 85 for hymns in duple time, and 100 in triple time in the more ordinary hymns, but special rules have been framed to govern special cases.

Sources of the Melodies.

No particular country, period, or school has been exclusively drawn upon to supply material, but an attempt has been made to include the best specimens of every style. In settling the form which each melody shall take, no rules have been made, but each case has been decided on its merits. The object has been to print the finest version of every tune, not necessarily the earliest. Thus the later forms of 'Wachet Auf', 'Nun Danket', and 'London New', to give a few examples, have been preferred to the originals. But the old method of mutilating tunes to suit new metres has been as far as possible avoided—only in one or two cases have a composer's rhythms been very slightly adapted, and then for some very special purpose. In cases where such a slight adaptation from a composer's rhythm is made the general outline is never destroyed, so that the original can at any time be restored without disturbing a congregation. But adaptations already made have been occasionally retained when the result is a fine and popular tune: thus 'Dix', 'Narenza', and 'Ravenshaw' have not been discarded, though the

PREFACE

fact of their adaptation is duly acknowledged. On the other hand the committee are glad to be able to restore the true metres of such tunes as 'Innsbruck', 'Weimar', or 'Les commandemens', which have been disfigured into dullness in so many hymnals.

The original rhythms of many of the old psalter tunes have also been restored, especially the long initial on the first syllable, which gives such a broad and dignified effect to these tunes. Attempts to adapt them to the procrustean bed of the nineteenth century hymn tune have merely taken away their character and made them appear dull. For the same reason no attempt has been made to square the irregular times of some tunes. These irregularities are always easy to sing by ear—and this is the way in which a hymn melody should be learnt – so that choirmasters should not let the fear of what may appear to be irregular deter them from using many splendid and essentially congregational melodies.

The following classification shows the chief sources from which the tunes come:—

A. GERMAN.—(1) Lutheran chorale tunes 16th and 17th centuries. (2) Tunes from the 16th and 17th century Catholic song books (chiefly Leisentritt's, 1567, and the Andernach *Gesangbuch*, 1608). (3) Tunes of the 18th century, chiefly by Bach and Freylinghausen. (4) Modern German tunes. (5) German traditional melodies.

B. FRENCH AND SWISS.—(1) Tunes from the Genevan Psalters of the 16th century. 2) Ecclesiastical melodies from the *paroissiens* of various French uses (chiefly those of Rouen and Angers). (3) French and Swiss traditional melodies.

C. ITALIAN, SPANISH, FLEMISH, DUTCH. – Ecclesiastical, traditional, and other melodies from these countries are also included.

D. AMERICAN.— Among American tunes may be mentioned Lowell Mason's tunes, certain tunes from 'Sacred Songs and Solos' and a few 'Western melodies' in use in America as hymn tunes.

E. BRITISH ISLES.—I. *Ireland*. (1) Irish traditional melodies. (2) Tunes by Irish composers.

PREFACE

II. *Scotland.* (1) Melodies from the Scottish Psalters of the 16th and 17th centuries. (2) Melodies from the Scottish tune-books of the 18th and 19th centuries. (3) Scottish traditional melodies.

III. *Wales.* (1) Archdeacon Prys' Psalter, which contains the famous tune 'St. Mary'. (2) Welsh traditional melodies. (3) Tunes by 18th and 19th century Welsh composers, which partake decidedly of the nature of their traditional melodies.

IV. *England.* (1) Tunes from Day's, Damon's, Este's, Ravenscroft's, and Playford's Psalters of the 16th and 17th centuries (the original versions of these, with the melody in the tenor, are occasionally included as alternatives to the modern version. (2) Tunes by Tallis, Gibbons, Lawes, &c., from their own collections. (3) Tunes from 18th century books—especially those by J. Clark and Dr. Croft. 4) English carol, and other traditional melodies. (5) Tunes by 19th and 20th century composers.

1933[1]

THE Musical Editor wishes to renew his thankful acknowledgement of the help and advice given him, in the preparation of the original edition, by the following:—Sir H. P. Allen, Rev. A. M. Y. Baylay, Professor W. H. Bell, Rev. Maurice F. Bell, the late Rev. J. B. Croft, Rev. Hugh Davies, Mr. T. F. Dunhill, Dr. N. C. Gatty, Mr. E. W. Goldsmith, Dr. W. H. Harris, Mr. Gustav Holst, Dr. J. N. Ireland, the late Rev. Dr. G. H. Palmer, the late Mr. Arthur Reynolds, and Rev. W. L. Richards.

The Musical Editor further wishes to thank Dr. Martin Shaw for allowing the results of his knowledge and research as shown in *Songs of Praise* to be made use of in this new edition of the *English Hymnal*. He also wishes to thank Mr. J. H. Arnold, not only for undertaking the revision of the Plainsong, but for much help and advice in the book as a whole.

His thanks are due too to Mr. E. Noel Burghes for untiring patience in the production of this revision.

R. VAUGHAN WILLIAMS
Musical Editor.

[1] *An outline of the method and scope of the 1933 revision will be found on p.* **xx**

PREFACE

THE PLAINSONG MELODIES
(1933)
SOURCES.

THE plainsong melodies contained in this book were selected under the guidance of the late Mr. W. J. Birkbeck and have, as far as possible, been taken from English sources. Those for the Office Hymns are, without exception, taken from the MS. versions of the Sarum Antiphoner[1]. Those in Part X are taken from the Sarum *Processionale*, as is also the music of No. 737. Of other plainsong melodies contained in the book, 10, 22, and 130 are taken from the Sarum *Graduale*, 155 and 351 from the Gradual edited by the Benedictines of Solesmes and printed in Tournai in 1883, and 317 from the Ghent *Graduale*. The rest (172, 253, 735, 736, 739, 740) are taken from various more or less ancient sources, mostly French. The transcriptions of the three Reproaches (at No. 737) and the Respond 'Hail our Monarch' (Appendix, No. 3) were made by the late Dr. George H. Palmer, in close collaboration with whom Mr. Birkbeck carried out his work, and whose scholarship, judgement, and influence in the field of plainsong is widely known.

EXECUTION.

The singing of the plainsong hymn melodies should be light, smooth, and fairly rapid. Staccato effects, violence of contrast, and extremes of loud and soft singing are all alien to the character of the music; so on the other hand is a lifeless and unrhythmic monotony. It should be borne in mind that though all notes, whatever their shape, are equal in time value (except at cadences), they are not equal in weight, and it is of first importance that the natural verbal pulse which would be felt in careful reading aloud should be felt through the music, without being exaggerated. In fact, the rhythm and pace of good reading will form a reasonably safe standard for singing the simple syllabic hymns. It will be the background, too, of the more ornate hymns in which grouped notes occur freely, though the presence of the groups naturally complicates the rhythmic scheme slightly.

[1] Additional melodies from Sarum books are given at No. 191 and Appendix No. 6. A melody from the Barking hymnal has been added at No. 229, one from Guisborough at No. 56, one from Hereford at No. 180, and one from York at No. 249; also another English tune at No. 61, and one from the Roman Antiphoner at No. 237.

PREFACE

In such tunes it must be remembered that all notes, whether single or grouped, remain equal in time value, but that independently of the natural verbal accentuation, which should never fail quietly to emerge, the first note [1] of each group should receive a gentle stress—hardly more than a mental 'touch'—and the other note or notes within the group should flow easily from the first [2]; care will be needed not to hurry the group.

It frequently happens that a group of two notes allied to a verbally weak syllable is immediately preceded by a single note allied to a verbally strong syllable, e.g.

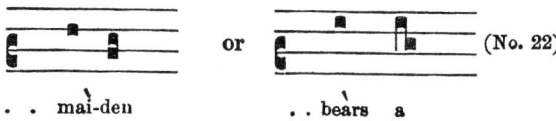

In such cases the relative intensity of volume of the three notes might be roughly expressed in some such gradation as 3 : 2 : 1, or 6 : 5 : 4; the contrasts will be slight, but in that order. Constant care will be needed neither to prolong the single note nor to hurry either of the grouped notes.

Bar-lines are introduced into these melodies to indicate pauses varying in degree with the size of the sign. The general scheme of barring a four-line tune is—

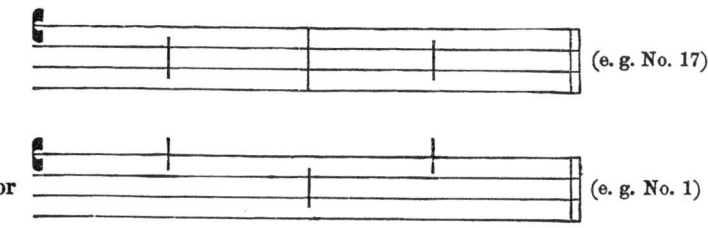

---

[1] For the treatment of two exceptional groups—the rising 5th group DABb (e.g. in No. 14), and groups containing a *pressus* (the conjunction of two notes on the same degree within a group, e.g. in No. 123, Part II)—see the rhythmic implications of the accompaniments provided for them in this book.

[2] It may be useful to bear in mind that a group coinciding with a verbal accent will naturally be more prominent than one allied to a weak syllable.

PREFACE

The latter is usually reserved for the syllabic hymns which tend to move a little more rapidly than the more ornamented melodies, and in which it may be found desirable to link lines one and two together without a breath, similarly lines three and four. The quarter-bar will thus be interpreted in the sense of an indication merely to dwell momentarily on the note immediately before it, and carry over. The half-bar may generally be taken as a sign to double the length of the note before it and take a quick breath—out of the doubled time value. The whole bar (the place of repose) will naturally call for a more pronounced pause and a full breath; in all cases the pairing of lines will be observed, so that the rhythmic unity of the pair may not be broken.

It is characteristic of this music that the cadences which the bar-lines mark are softened. A common type of cadence which is frequently maltreated, in one direction or the other, is what may loosely be called the feminine cadence, i.e. one in which the final note is rhythmically weak, either (a) because it is the second note of a group of two, or (b) because it is a single note allied to a verbally weak syllable. In the first instance (a) the broad rule is to double the length of both notes, softening the second; in the other instance (the 'syllabic spondee') it is generally accounted best to prolong only the last note, *softly*, thus:—

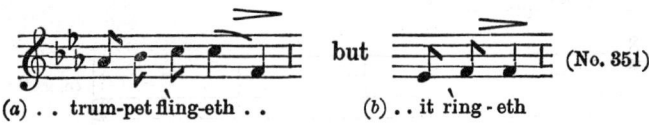

(a) .. trum-pet fling-eth ..   (b) .. it ring - eth   (No. 351)

The natural *ritardando* before a double-bar, however, would involve a slight slackening of tempo before the final note is reached.

According to ancient custom the hymn was sung from side to side of the choir, only Amen being sung by all. The alternate verses are now commonly sung in contrast either of volume or of pitch, e. g. a chanter (or two) alternating with the full choir, or men with boys. In either case it is usual for the chanter to precent the first line of the first verse, and for the first and last verses and Amen to be sung full.

PREFACE

ACCOMPANIMENT.

Anything in the nature of a heavy accompaniment tends to cloud and clog the supple movement of the voices. Lightness of texture, or even delicacy, should mark the organ part rather than weight; this by no means implies that the accompaniment need be dull. The 16-ft. pedal should be used only sparingly, and seldom if ever when accompanying sopranos or chanters alone. Sometimes it is good to omit the melody line of the accompaniment, playing merely the lower parts. In the few cases in this book where the suggested accompaniment has been allowed to rise above the melody line, it is of the utmost importance that the registration should be extremely light.

Thanks are due to the Church Music Society for kind permission to use the accompaniment of the Advent Prose (No. 735).

J. H. ARNOLD

[*The Plainsong accompaniments are the copyright of the Proprietors of* The English Hymnal.]

NOTE ON THE MUSIC OF THE 1933 EDITION

In order to eliminate the possibility of confusion or inconvenience to those using the older edition, the revision has been confined to the enrichment of the music. The hymns themselves remain as they were in 1906 except that, during subsequent years, in rare instances a few words have been altered at the request of authors.

No tune found in the 1906 book has been omitted, but over a hundred tunes have been added. This has been made possible by (a) the removal of duplications and (b) the placing of certain tunes in an Appendix, and by filling such vacancies with new tunes.

Congregations will not be affected, and choirs will have the opportunity of enlarging their repertory, while they can still, if it is preferred, sing any particular hymn to the former tune, since in every case a cross-reference will make it easy for the old tune to be found quickly in another part of the book.

A new Preface has been written for the Plainsong tunes, all of which are now provided with new accompaniments.

NOTE FOR CHOIR-MASTERS

Since the original edition was issued in 1906, more correct versions of the following tunes have been discovered, involving a slight alteration to the melody:

Nos. 134 (i), 184, 212, 247*, 413*, 438*, 461, 488*, 514*, 538*, 613.

In those marked thus * the harmony has been slightly changed, and the lower parts also of Nos. 19, 217, 277, 283, and 398 have been altered in details.

It has not been considered necessary to enumerate alterations in the harmonies of purely unison melodies.

The following Plainsong melodies have been slightly adjusted:—
22, 50, 67, 69, 123 Pt. I (and 124 Pt. I), 154, 213, 264 (i), 624 (and 628, 630, 634), 737 (the psalm), 740. Another transcription of the Reproaches has been used, and the Easter Grail omitted.

R. V. W.

In this revision, tunes have been substituted or added at the following numbers:—

18 mod.	180 mod.	271	386	535
33	186	273	391	539
46	191 pl.	274 (i)	396	541
54 mod.	195	276	400	542
56 pl.	198	279	414 (ii)	545
56 mod.	201	280	415	548
58 mod.	202	282	417	554
61 pl.	205	285	419 (i)	556
67 mod.	206	304	427	563
75 (ii)	210	307	429	578
81	211	309	430	587
91	214 mod.	314	439	602
99	222	320	440	609
111	223 mod	322	445 (ii)	615
115 (iii)	227	334	456	616
122 mod.	229 pl.	347	478	629
127	233 pl.	356	481	633
136	233 mod.	368	482	638 (iii)
141 mod.	237 pl.	371	492	638 (iv)
144	237 mod.	373	497	645
157	246	376	503	649
158	249 pl.	381 (i)	509	652
164 mod.	263	381 (ii)	510	Ap. 3
177	265	382	525 (ii)	,, 6
180 pl.	270	383	531	,, 7
				,, 11

mod. = modern tune　　　　　pl. = plainsong tune

ACKNOWLEDGEMENTS

(WORDS OF HYMNS)

THANKS are due to the following for permission to include their copyright hymns, viz.: The Rev. the Abbot, Mount Saint Bernard's Abbey, Coalville, Leicester, 416, 417; Miss E. Alexander, 112, 117, 212, 227; Exors. of the late Bishop Bickersteth, 468; Miss K. Blacker, 10, 636; Mr. E. M. Butler, 429; the Representatives of the late Mr. A. W. Chatfield, 77; Rev. Dudley Clark, 648, 651; Exors. of the late Rev. V. S. S. Coles, 190, 218, 334; Mrs. Coote, 222; Mrs. Creighton, 347; Mr. R. F. Davis and Messrs. J. M. Dent & Co. Ltd., 613; Mr. Gerald Gurney, 346; Mr. F. D. How, 294, 565, 588, 597; Mr. C. W. Humphreys, 310, 329; Miss Mary Elizabeth Julian and Mr. W. H. Hortin, 386; The Rev. the Warden and Council of Keble College, Oxford, 240, 302; Mr. Rudyard Kipling and Messrs. Methuen & Co. Ltd., from *The Five Nations*, 558; Hon. Mrs. A. Lowry, 529; Mrs. Mason, 179; Miss Mary Maude, 344; The Mothers' Union, 530; Mrs. Grace M. Muirhead, 488; Mr. G. Murray-Smith, 121; The National Sunday School Union, 595; Mrs. Louie Newell, 211; Messrs. Novello & Co. Ltd., 29, 225, 539, 559; Oxford University Press, 18, 116, 207, 209, 248, 271, 277, 345, 520, 528, 545; Sir Isaac Pitman & Sons, Ltd., 322; Rev. R. Martin Pope and Messrs. J. M. Dent & Co. Ltd., 54, 55; Messrs. Reid Bros., Ltd., 607; Messrs. A. W. Ridley & Co., 136, 503, 568, 592, 603, 643; Very Rev. J. Armitage Robinson, 236; Mr. W. H. C. Romanis, 232, 272; the Representatives of Miss Christina Rossetti, and Messrs. Macmillan & Co. Ltd., 25; the Representatives of the late Rev. Dr. W. Chalmers Smith, 407; Society for Promoting Christian Knowledge, 548; Society of St. John the Evangelist, Oxford, 189; Mr. Leonard G. P. Thring, 448, 527, 615; Lt.-Col. W. H. Turton, 324; Mr. A. Cyprian Bourne Webb, 319.

The following copyright owners have passed away since they gave permission for their hymns to be included in the book, viz.: Dr. Robert Bridges, 50, 52, 70, 102, 154, 200, 269, 278, 398, 438, 442, 475, 564, from the *Yattendon Hymnal*; Rev. Dr. John Brownlie, 349, 454, 650, 652; Mr. William Canton, 403, 609; Miss A. C. Hankey, 583,

ACKNOWLEDGEMENTS

586; Rev. L. Hensley, 554; Rev. Dr. F. L. Hosmer, 463, 504, 538; Rev. J. S. Jones, 282; Archbishop Maclagan, 113, 120; Rev. F. Pott, 73, 625; also the Rev. J. B. Croft for hymns Nos. 328 and 335 by Rev. W. H. H. Jervois.

The following hymns are controlled by the Proprietors of *The English Hymnal*, viz.: Nos. 2, 8, 11, 12, 16, 34, 38, 49, 58, 60, 66, 67, 68, 69, 95, 97, 104, 114, 118, 123, 124, 126, 142, 150, 151, 160, 165, 172, 174, 180, 185, 186, 188, 191, 193, 194, 195, 208, 213, 215, 219, 220, 221, 223, 224, 226, 228, 229, 230, 231, 233, 234, 237, 239, 242, 247, 249, 308, 313, 321, 325, 329, 352, 353 (2), 356, 357, 360, 402, 423, 519, 531, 543, 544, 562, 598, 604, 611, 621, 624, 628, 630, 634, 744.

Music Acknowledgements

Thanks are due to the following for permission to include their copyright tunes and arrangements, viz.: The Very Rev. the Abbot of Downside, 44, 120, 150 (Mod.), 213 (Mod.), 346, App. 44, App. 49, App. 60; Mr. G. E. P. Arkwright, 16; Mr. W. H. Bell, 225, 546; Dr. P. C. Buck, 136, 141–142 (Mod.), 307, 633; Messrs. J. Curwen & Sons, Ltd., 99, 205, 376, 415, 427, 481, 503, 535, 602 from Curwen Edition No. 6300; also 587 from Curwen Edition No. 80629; Sir H. Walford Davies, 454; Mr. T. F. Dunhill, 650; Dr. David Evans, 222, 270, 334, 430, 539, 563; Messrs. W. Gwenlyn Evans & Son, 108; Rev. W. H. Ferguson, 276; Mr. J. A. Fuller-Maitland, 641 (2); Dr. Nicholas Gatty, 22 (Mod.), 146; Hon. Mrs. W. H. Gladstone, App. 34, App. 50; Mr. E. W. Goldsmith, 387, 626 (1); Sir W. H. Hadow, 359; Dr. Basil Harwood, 214–215 (Mod.), 545; Rev. A. J. Hodson, 169–170 (Mod.); Mr. G. Holst, 25, 310, 571; the Misses Horder, App. 48; Messrs. Hughes & Son, 87; Dr. J. N. Ireland, 520; Dr. Ernest Jones, 56–57 (Mod.); Mr. W. Percy Merrick, 275; Mr. E. J. Moeran, 638 (3) melody; Messrs. Marshall, Morgan & Scott, Ltd., App. 22; Messrs. Novello & Co. Ltd., 24, 26, 48, 383, 559, 585, 643 (2), 744, App. 17, App. 19, App. 20, App. 32, App. 69; the Exors. of the late Sir Walter Parratt, App. 37; Mr. R. N. Quaile, App. 72; Messrs. A. W. Ridley & Co., 315 (1), 591 (2), 603; Professor Julius Röntgen, 145; Rev. Canon G. C. E. Ryley, 34; the Exors. of the late Cecil J. Sharp, 355, 389, 498, 656 (1), 656 (2); Dr. Geoffrey Shaw,

ACKNOWLEDGEMENTS

54-55 (Mod.), 186, 274, 279, 309, 373, 445 (2), 497; Society for Promoting Christian Knowledge, App. 63; Sir Arthur Somervell, 522, 590; Messrs. Stainer & Bell, Ltd., 212 (1), 490; the Editor of '*A Students' Hymnal*', 227; Sir Richard Terry, 233 (Mod.); Mr. W. R. Waghorne, App. 66; Rev. Canon H. van de Wattyne, 308; Rev. W. J. Whitwell, 592; Rev. Canon David F. R. Wilson, 609; Rev. G. R. Woodward, 82, 371 from *Songs of Syon*; 14 (Mod.), 610; Mr. J. Yoakley, App. 57.

The following copyright owners have passed away since they gave permission for their tunes to be included in the book: Rev. C. Bicknell, 619; Dr. Robert Bridges, 180 (Mod.) from the *Yattendon Hymnal*; Rev. Dr. E. W. Bullinger, App. 18; Rev. R. F. Dale, App. 65; Rev. R. S. Genge, 410; the Viscountess Hawarden (Caroline Maude), 569; Mr. H. A. Jeboult, 112; Archbishop Maclagan, App. 33, App. 43; Major G. E. Wyndham Malet, App. 47; Rev. W. G. Whinfield, 409, 342, App. 56.

The following tunes and arrangements are the copyright of the Oxford University Press: 17, 46, 117, 122 (Mod.), 198, 221, 238, 271, 294, 316, 344, 366, 379, 390, 400, 419, 482, 488, 509, 531, 574, 599, 601, 606, 615, 624, 651, App. 40.

The following tunes and arrangements are the copyright of the Musical Editors of the enlarged edition of *Songs of Praise*: 67 (Mod.), 75 (2), 91, 127, 144, 157, 164 (Mod.), 202, 206, 211, 223-224 (Mod.), 246, 273, 277, 285, 304, 314, 356, 368, 381, 439, 525 (2), 541, 548, 578, 638 (3), 638 (3 alt.), 645, 649.

The following tunes and arrangements are the copyright of the Proprietors of *The English Hymnal*: 2 (Mech.), 8, 15, 18 (Mod.), 23, 38 (Mod.), 51 (Mod.), 58-59-60 (Mod.), 65 (Mod.), 115 (3), 123 (Mod.), 125 (Mod.), 129, 151 (Mod.), 152, 154 (Mech.), 159 (Mod.), 165 (Mod.), 176 (Mod.), 181 (Mod.), 188 (Mod.), 191 (Mod.), 208 (Mod.), 239, 242 (Mod.), 280, 295, 299, 301, 311, 326, (Mech.), 331, 385, 396, 402, 440, 480, 519, 521, 524, 525 (1), 562, 566, 572, 593, 594, 595, 597, 607, 611, 624 (Mod.), 629, 641, 652, 653, App. 7, App. 16, App. 71.

Other settings (including the plainsong accompaniments) that have been specially harmonized for *The English Hymnal* belong to the Proprietors of *The English Hymnal*.

CONTENTS

PART I

	HYMNS
THE CHRISTIAN YEAR	1–173
Advent to Trinity	1–165
Ember Days	166–168
Dedication, &c.	169–173

PART II

SAINTS' DAYS AND OTHER HOLY DAYS	174–253
General	174–204
Apostles and Evangelists	174–179
Martyrs	180–187
Confessors	188–190
Virgins	191, 192
Matrons	193
Vigil	194
Patronal Festival	195
Any Saint	196–204
Proper (St. Andrew to All Saints)	205–253

PART III

TIMES AND SEASONS	254–299
Morning	254–260
Noon	261–263
Evening	264–281
Saturday Evening	282
Sunday	283, 284
New Year	285, 286
Spring	287
Summer	288
Harvest	289–293
Autumn	294
Winter	295
Seasons: General	296–299

CONTENTS

HYMNS

PART IV

SACRAMENTS AND OTHER RITES	300–360
Holy Communion	300–335
Holy Baptism	336–339
Confirmation	340–344
Marriage	345–348
The Sick	349
The Departed	350–360

PART V

GENERAL HYMNS	361–519

PART VI

SPECIAL OCCASIONS	520–543
Absent Friends	520
Almsgiving	521, 522
Beginning and End of Term	523
Farewell	524
Hospitals	525–527
Societies: Friendly	528
,, General	529
,, Mothers'	530
,, Temperance	531
Thanksgiving	532–537
Time of Trouble	538
,, ,, War	539
,, ,, Rough Weather	540, 541
Use at Sea	542, 543

PART VII

CHURCH AND PEOPLE	544–566
The Church	544, 545
Home and Foreign Missions	546–554
Church Work	555, 556
National	557–566

PART VIII

MISSION SERVICES	567–585

CONTENTS

PART IX
                                                              HYMNS

AT CATECHISM 586–612

PART X

PROCESSIONAL 613–646
    Christmas to Trinity 613–633
    Dedication 634–637
    Saint's Day 638–640
    Suitable for Use in Procession 641–646

PART XI

LITANIES, &c. 647–656
    The Advent 647
    Penitence 648
    The Passion 649
    Rogationtide 650
    The Church 651
    Evening 652
    The Blessed Sacrament 653
    Children 654
    Commendatory 655
    Story of the Cross 656

PART XII

INTROITS, &c. 657–744
    Introits, Grails, &c. 657–733
    Advent Antiphons, The Reproaches, &c. . . 734–744

                                                              PAGES
APPENDIX 901–984

INDEXES, &c. 985–1040
    Table of Office Hymns for Saints' Days . . 985
    Hymns Arranged for Sundays and Holy Days . 987
    Metrical Index of Tunes 997
    Alphabetical Index of Tunes 1004
        „   „ Composers and Sources . 1010
        „   „ Authors, &c. 1014
    Index of Original First Lines of Translated Hymns . 1019
    General Index 1023

NOTE

The harmonies in the following hymns are intended for the ORGANIST *and* CHOIR. *The congregation should sing the* MELODY ONLY.

Part I
THE CHRISTIAN YEAR
ADVENT

1

Mode iv.   *arr.* J. H. A.

If a modern tune is required for this hymn it may be sung to ANGEL'S SONG (*No.* 259) *or* O AMOR QUAM ECSTATICUS (*No.* 215).

OFFICE HYMN. E.   Conditor alme siderum.   *7th cent.*   *Tr.* J. M. Neale.

CREATOR of the stars of night,
Thy people's everlasting light,
Jesu, Redeemer, save us all,
And hear thy servants when they call.

2 Thou, grieving that the ancient curse
Should doom to death a universe,
Hast found the medicine, full of grace,
To save and heal a ruined race.

3 Thou cam'st, the Bridegroom of the bride,
As drew the world to evening-tide;
Proceeding from a virgin shrine,
The spotless Victim all divine:

4 At whose dread name, majestic now,
All knees must bend, all hearts must bow;
And things celestial thee shall own,
And things terrestrial, Lord alone.

5 O thou whose coming is with dread
To judge and doom the quick and dead,
Preserve us, while we dwell below,
From every insult of the foe.

6. To God the Father, God the Son,
And God the Spirit, Three in One,
Laud, honour, might, and glory be
From age to age eternally. Amen.

A - men.

1

THE CHRISTIAN YEAR

2

Mode ii.   arr. J. H. A.

OFFICE HYMN. M.   *c.* 10*th cent.*   *Tr. Charles Bigg.*
Verbum supernum prodiens.

HIGH Word of God, who once didst come,
   Leaving thy Father and thy home,
To succour by thy birth our kind,
When, towards thy advent, time declined,

2 Pour light upon us from above,
   And fire our hearts with thy strong love,
That, as we hear thy Gospel read,
All fond desires may flee in dread;

3 That when thou comest from the skies,
   Great Judge, to open thine assize,
To give each hidden sin its smart,
And crown as kings the pure in heart,

4 We be not set at thy left hand,
   Where sentence due would bid us stand,
But with the Saints thy face may see,
For ever wholly loving thee.

ADVENT

2
MECHLIN MELODY

VERBUM SUPERNUM. (L. M.)
In free rhythm: to be sung in unison.
Mode viii.

*From the Processionale Ritibus Romanae Ecclesiae,
Mechlin, 1851. arr. J. H. A.*

5. Praise to the Father and the Son,
   Through all the ages as they run;
   And to the holy Paraclete
   Be praise with them and worship meet.   Amen.

THE CHRISTIAN YEAR

3

SECOND MODE MELODY. (D. C. M.)
Moderately slow, dignified ♩ = 69.

T. TALLIS, c. 1515–1585.

Horologion. c. 8th cent. Tr. G. Moultrie.

Ἰδοὺ ὁ Νυμφίος ἔρχεται.

BEHOLD the Bridegroom cometh in the middle of the night,
And blest is he whose loins are girt, whose lamp is burning bright;
But woe to that dull servant, whom the Master shall surprise
With lamp untrimmed, unburning, and with slumber in his eyes.

2 Do thou, my soul, beware, beware, lest thou in sleep sink down,
Lest thou be given o'er to death, and lose the golden crown;
But see that thou be sober, with a watchful eye, and thus
Cry—'Holy, holy, holy God, have mercy upon us.'

ADVENT

3

ALTERNATIVE VERSION (melody in the tenor)

TALLIS' *Original Version.*

[*This version may be used, in connexion with the other, for one or more verses; it is intended for the* CHOIR ALONE *and must be sung without the organ. This version should only be attempted by good choirs.*]

'KINGSFOLD' (*No.* 574) *is also suitable to this hymn.*

3 That day, the day of fear, shall come; my soul, slack not thy toil,
But light thy lamp, and feed it well, and make it bright with oil;
Who knowest not how soon may sound the cry at eventide,
'Behold, the Bridegroom comes! Arise! Go forth to meet the bride.'

4. Beware, my soul; beware, beware, lest thou in slumber lie,
And, like the Five, remain without, and knock, and vainly cry;
But watch, and bear thy lamp undimmed, and Christ shall gird thee on
His own bright wedding-robe of light—the glory of the Son

A - men.

THE CHRISTIAN YEAR

4

LUTHER'S HYMN (NUN FREUT EUCH). (87.87.887.)
Slow ♩ = 50.

Present form of melody in 'Geistliche Lieder' (Wittenberg), 1535.

Unison.

Anon. (1802), *W. B. Collyer* (1812), *T. Cotterill* (1819), *and others.*

GREAT God, what do I see and hear!
  The end of things created:
The Judge of mankind doth appear,
  On clouds of glory seated;
The trumpet sounds, the graves restore
The dead which they contained before:
  Prepare, my soul, to meet him!

2 The dead in Christ shall first arise
    At that last trumpet's sounding,
  Caught up to meet him in the skies,
    With joy their Lord surrounding;
  No gloomy fears their souls dismay;
  His presence sheds eternal day
    On those prepared to meet him.

3 The ungodly, filled with guilty fears,
    Behold his wrath prevailing;
  For they shall rise, and find their tears
    And sighs are unavailing:
  The day of grace is past and gone;
  Trembling they stand before his throne,
    All unprepared to meet him.

4. Great Judge, to thee our prayers we pour,
    In deep abasement bending;
  O shield us through that last dread hour,
    Thy wondrous love extending.
  May we, in this our trial day,
  With faithful hearts thy word obey,
    And thus prepare to meet thee.

A - men.

ADVENT

5

MERTON. (8 7. 8 7.)
Moderately slow ♩ = 66.

W. H. MONK, 1828-1889.

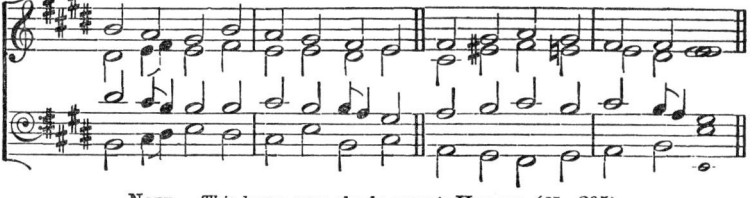

NOTE.—*This hymn may also be sung to* HERALD (*No.* 205).

6th cent. Tr. E. Caswall †.

Vox clara ecce intonat.

HARK! a herald voice is calling:
'Christ is nigh,' it seems to say;
'Cast away the dreams of darkness,
O ye children of the day!'

2 Startled at the solemn warning,
Let the earth-bound soul arise;
Christ, her Sun, all sloth dispelling,
Shines upon the morning skies.

3 Lo! the Lamb, so long expected,
Comes with pardon down from heaven;
Let us haste, with tears of sorrow,
One and all to be forgiven;

4 So when next he comes with glory,
Wrapping all the earth in fear,
May he then as our defender
On the clouds of heaven appear.

Unison. 5. Honour, glory, virtue, merit,
To the Father and the Son,
With the co-eternal Spirit,
While unending ages run. Amen.

A - men.

THE CHRISTIAN YEAR

6

BRISTOL. (C.M.)
Moderately slow ♩ = 69.

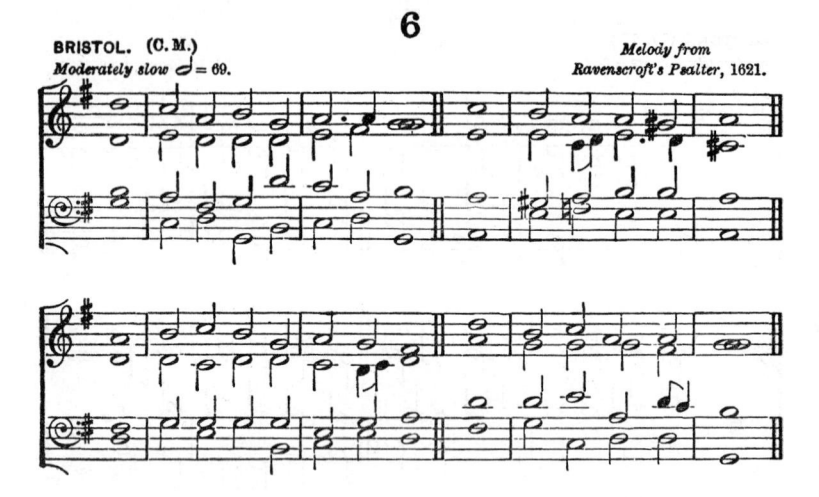

Melody from Ravenscroft's Psalter, 1621.

P. Doddridge, 1702-51.

HARK the glad sound! the Saviour comes,
　The Saviour promised long!
Let every heart prepare a throne,
　And every voice a song.

2 He comes the prisoners to release
　　In Satan's bondage held;
　The gates of brass before him burst,
　　The iron fetters yield.

3 He comes the broken heart to bind,
　　The bleeding soul to cure,
　And with the treasures of his grace
　　To enrich the humble poor.

4. Our glad hosannas, Prince of peace,
　　Thy welcome shall proclaim,
　And heaven's eternal arches ring
　　With thy belovèd name.

A - men.

ADVENT

6

ALTERNATIVE VERSION

Harmonized by T. RAVENSCROFT, *in his Psalter.*

to en - rich . . the hum - ble poor.

[*This version may be used in connexion with the other for verse 3, the people singing the melody as usual.*]

THE CHRISTIAN YEAR

7

HELMSLEY. (87.87.47.)
Moderately slow, very dignified ♩ = 69.

English Melody of the 18th century.

[*May be sung in unison throughout.*]

This hymn is sometimes sung to St. Thomas (*No.* 623).

ADVENT

C. Wesley (1758) *and J. Cennick* (1750.)

LO! he comes with clouds descending,
Once for favoured sinners slain;
Thousand thousand Saints attending
Swell the triumph of his train:
Alleluya!
God appears, on earth to reign.

2 Every eye shall now behold him
Robed in dreadful majesty;
Those who set at nought and sold him,
Pierced and nailed him to the tree,
Deeply wailing
Shall the true Messiah see.

3 Those dear tokens of his passion
Still his dazzling body bears,
Cause of endless exultation
To his ransomed worshippers:
With what rapture
Gaze we on those glorious scars!

Unison. 4. Yea, amen! let all adore thee,
High on thine eternal throne;
Saviour, take the power and glory:
Claim the kingdom for thine own:
O come quickly!
Alleluya! Come, Lord, come!

THE CHRISTIAN YEAR

VENI EMMANUEL. (8 8. 8 8. 8 8.)   **8**   *Melody adapted by* T. HELMORE
'from a French Missal.'
arr. J. H. A.

In free rhythm: to be sung in unison.

Another accompaniment is given in the Appendix (No. 24).

Veni, veni, Emmanuel.   18*th cent.* *Tr.* T. A. L.

1. O COME, O come, Emmanuel!
Redeem thy captive Israel,
That into exile drear is gone
Far from the face of God's dear Son.

   Rejoice! Rejoice! Emmanuel
   Shall come to thee, O Israel.

2. O come, thou Branch of Jesse! draw
The quarry from the lion's claw;
From the dread caverns of the grave,
From nether hell, thy people save.

3. O come, O come, thou Dayspring bright!
Pour on our souls thy healing light;
Dispel the long night's lingering gloom,
And pierce the shadows of the tomb.

4. O come, thou Lord of David's Key!
The royal door fling wide and free;
Safeguard for us the heavenward road,
And bar the way to death's abode.

ADVENT

5. O come, O come, Adonaï,
   Who in thy glorious majesty
   From that high mountain clothed with awe
   Gavest thy folk the elder law.

WINCHESTER NEW. (L. M.)   **9**   *Adapted from Chorale in the 'Musikalisches Hand-Buch,' Hamburg, 1690.*
Slow and dignified ♩ = 56.

C. Coffin, 1676–1749.   Tr. J. Chandler.
Jordanis oras praevia.

ON Jordan's bank the Baptist's cry
Announces that the Lord is nigh;
Come then and hearken, for he brings
Glad tidings from the King of kings.

2 Then cleansed be every Christian breast,
And furnished for so great a guest!

Yea, let us each our hearts prepare
For Christ to come and enter there.

Unison.

3 For thou art our salvation, Lord,
Our refuge and our great reward;
Without thy grace our souls must fade,
And wither like a flower decayed.

4 Stretch forth thine hand, to heal our sore,
And make us rise to fall no more;
Once more upon thy people shine,
And fill the world with love divine.

Unison. 5. All praise, eternal Son, to thee
Whose advent sets thy people free,
Whom, with the Father, we adore,
And Holy Ghost, for evermore. Amen.

THE CHRISTIAN YEAR

10

Sequence. Salus aeterna. *Before 11th cent. Tr. M. J. Blacker ‡.*

Mode vii. *arr.* J. H. A.

1 Sa - viour e - ter - nal! * Health and life of the world un - fail - ing,
2 Light ev - er - last - ing! And in ve - ri - ty our re - demp - tion,

3 Griev-ing that the a - ges of men must per-ish Thro' the temp-ter's sub-tle - ty,
4 Still in heav'n a-bid-ing, thou cam-est earth-ward Of thine own great cle-men-cy:

5 Then free - ly and gra-cious-ly Deign-ing to as - sume hu-man - i - ty,

14

ADVENT

10 (*continued*)

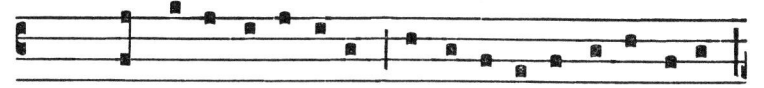

6 To lost ones and per-ish-ing Gav-est thou thy free de-liv-er-ance,

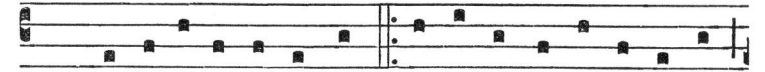

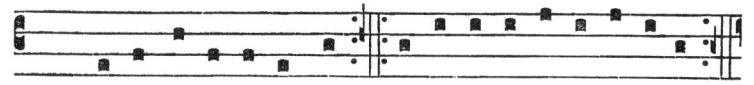

Fill-ing all the world with joy. 7 O Christ, our souls and bo-dies cleanse
8 That we as tem-ples pure and bright

By thy per-fect sa-cri-fice; 9 By thy for-mer ad-vent jus-ti-fy,
Fit for thine a-bode may be. 10 By thy se-cond grant us lib-er-ty:

THE CHRISTIAN YEAR

10 (*continued*)

11 That when in the might of glo - ry Thou de-scend-est, Judge of all,

12. We in rai - ment un - de - fi - led, Bright may shine, and ev - er

fol - low, Lord, thy foot - steps blest, where - 'er they lead us.

ADVENT

ST. THOMAS. (S. M.)
In moderate time ♩ = 72.

11

A. Williams' *New Universal Psalmodist*, 1770.

This hymn can also be sung to FRANCONIA (*No.* 370).

Instantis adventum Dei.

C. Coffin, 1676–1749. *Tr. H. P*

THE advent of our God
  With eager prayers we greet,
And singing haste upon his road
  His glorious gift to meet.

2 The everlasting Son
  Scorns not a Virgin's womb;
That we from bondage may be won
  He bears a bondsman's doom.

3 Daughter of Sion, rise
  To meet thy lowly king;
Let not thy stubborn heart despise
  The peace he deigns to bring.

Unison. 4 In clouds of awful light,
  As Judge he comes again,
His scattered people to unite,
  With them in heaven to reign.

5 Let evil flee away
  Ere that dread hour shall dawn,
Let this old Adam day by day
  God's image still put on.

Unison. 6 Praise to the Incarnate Son,
  Who comes to set us free,
With God the Father, ever one,
  To all eternity. Amen.

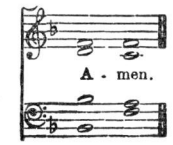

A - men.

THE CHRISTIAN YEAR

12

WACHET AUF! (898. 898. 664. 88.)
Very slow and solemn $\d = 39$ ($\d = 78$).

Melody attributed to P. NICOLAI, 1556–1608.
Adapted and harmonized by J. S. BACH.

ADVENT

12 (*continued*)

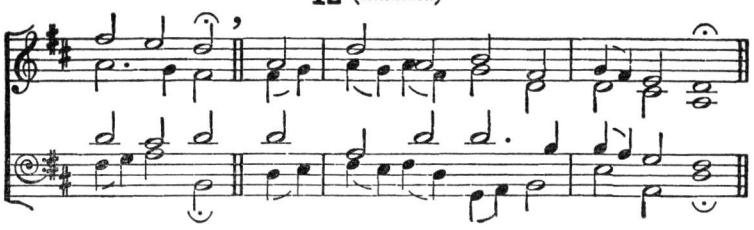

P. Nicolai, 1556–1608. *Tr. F. C. B.*

Wachet auf.

WAKE, O wake! with tidings thrilling
The watchmen all the air are filling,
　　Arise, Jerusalem, arise!
Midnight strikes! no more delaying,
'The hour has come!' we hear them saying.
　　　　Where are ye all, ye virgins wise?
　　　　　The Bridegroom comes in sight,
　　　　　Raise high your torches bright!
　　　　　　　Alleluya!
　　　　　The wedding song
　　　　　Swells loud and strong:
　　　　Go forth and join the festal throng.

2 Sion hears the watchmen shouting,
　Her heart leaps up with joy undoubting,
　　　She stands and waits with eager eyes;
　See her Friend from heaven descending,
　Adorned with truth and grace unending!
　　　　　Her light burns clear, her star doth rise.
　　　　　　Now come, thou precious Crown,
　　　　　　Lord Jesu, God's own Son!
　　　　　　　　Hosanna!
　　　　　　Let us prepare
　　　　　　To follow there,
　　　　　Where in thy supper we may share.

Unison.　3. Every soul in thee rejoices;
　　From men and from angelic voices
　　　　Be glory given to thee alone!
　　Now the gates of pearl receive us,
　　Thy presence never more shall leave us,
　　　　　We stand with Angels round thy throne.
　　　　　　Earth cannot give below
　　　　　　The bliss thou dost bestow.
　　　　　　　　Alleluya!
　　　　　　Grant us to raise,
　　　　　　To length of days,
　　　　　The triumph-chorus of thy praise.

Ver. 2, line 9, must run: Ho - san - na.

A - men.

THE CHRISTIAN YEAR

WALSALL. (C. M.)

13

From 'A Choice Collection of Psalm Tunes,'
W. ANCHORS, c. 1721.

J. Anstice, 1808-36.

WHEN came in flesh the incarnate Word,
    The heedless world slept on,
And only simple shepherds heard
    That God had sent his Son.

2 When comes the Saviour at the last,
    From east to west shall shine
The awful pomp, and earth aghast
    Shall tremble at the sign.

ADVENT

3 Then shall the pure of heart be blest;
    As mild he comes to them,
As when upon the Virgin's breast
    He lay at Bethlehem:

4 As mild to meek-eyed love and faith,
    Only more strong to save;
Strengthened by having bowed to death,
    By having burst the grave.

5 Lord, who could dare see thee descend
    In state, unless he knew
Thou art the sorrowing sinner's friend,
    The gracious and the true?

6. Dwell in our hearts, O Saviour blest;
    So shall thine advent's dawn
'Twixt us and thee, our bosom-guest,
    Be but the veil withdrawn.

A - men.

The following are also suitable

374 Christian, seek not yet repose.
404 How shall I sing
420 Jesus shall reign.
462 O quickly come, dread Judge of all.
492 The Lord will come and not be slow.
495 The world is very evil.
504 Thy kingdom come! on bended knee.
518 Ye servants of the Lord.
553 Thou whose almighty Word.
734 The Advent Antiphons.
735 Drop down ye heavens.

THE CHRISTIAN YEAR

14

Mode i.   *arr.* J. H. A.

A - men.

CHRISTMAS EVE

OFFICE HYMN. E.   *St. Ambrose, 340-97. Tr. J. M. Neale and others.*
Veni, Redemptor gentium.

COME, thou Redeemer of the earth,
   And manifest thy virgin-birth:
Let every age adoring fall;
Such birth befits the God of all.

2 Begotten of no human will,
But of the Spirit, thou art still
The Word of God in flesh arrayed,
The promised fruit to man displayed.

CHRISTMAS EVE

14 (MODERN TUNE)

PUER NOBIS NASCITUR. (L. M.)
In moderate time ♩ = 144.

Melody adapted by
M. PRAETORIUS, 1571–1621.
Harmonized by G. R. WOODWARD.

[*May be sung in unison throughout.*]

3 The virgin womb that burden gained
With virgin honour all unstained;
The banners there of virtue glow;
God in his temple dwells below.

4 Forth from his chamber goeth he,
That royal home of purity,
A giant in twofold substance one,
Rejoicing now his course to run.

5 From God the Father he proceeds,
To God the Father back he speeds;
His course he runs to death and hell,
Returning on God's throne to dwell.

6 O equal to thy Father, thou !
Gird on thy fleshly mantle now;
The weakness of our mortal state
With deathless might invigorate.

7 Thy cradle here shall glitter bright,
And darkness breathe a newer light,
Where endless faith shall shine serene,
And twilight never intervene.

8. All laud to God the Father be,
All praise, eternal Son, to thee:
All glory, as is ever meet,
To God the Holy Paraclete.

A - men.

23

THE CHRISTIAN YEAR

15

FOREST GREEN. (D. C. M. Words irreg.)
In moderate time ♩ = 80.
English Traditional Melody.

Suitable till Candlemas.

Bp. Phillips Brooks, 1835-93.

O LITTLE town of Bethlehem,
  How still we see thee lie!
Above thy deep and dreamless sleep
  The silent stars go by.
Yet in thy dark streets shineth
  The everlasting light;
The hopes and fears of all the years
  Are met in thee to-night.

2 O morning stars, together
  Proclaim the holy birth,
And praises sing to God the King,
  And peace to men on earth;
For Christ is born of Mary;
  And, gathered all above
While mortals sleep, the angels keep
  Their watch of wondering love.

3 How silently, how silently,
  The wondrous gift is given!
So God imparts to human hearts
  The blessings of his heaven.
No ear may hear his coming;
  But in this world of sin, [still
Where meek souls will receive him,
  The dear Christ enters in.

4 Where children pure and happy
  Pray to the blessèd Child,
Where misery cries out to thee,
  Son of the mother mild;
Where charity stands watching
  And faith holds wide the door,
The dark night wakes, the glory breaks,
  And Christmas comes once more.

CHRISTMAS EVE

5. O holy Child of Bethlehem,
    Descend to us, we pray;
    Cast out our sin, and enter in,
    Be born in us to-day.
    We hear the Christmas Angels
    The great glad tidings tell:
    O come to us, abide with us,
    Our Lord Emmanuel.

A - men.

16

NEWBURY. (C.M.)
In moderate time ♩ = 92.

English Traditional Melody.

Suitable till Candlemas.

Laurence Housman. 1865–1959

THE Maker of the sun and moon,
  The Maker of our earth,
Lo! late in time, a fairer boon,
  Himself is brought to birth!

2 How blest was all creation then,
    When God so gave increase;
  And Christ, to heal the hearts of men,
    Brought righteousness and peace!

3 No star in all the heights of heaven
    But burned to see him go;
  Yet unto earth alone was given
    His human form to know.

4 His human form, by man denied,
    Took death for human sin:
  His endless love, through faith descried,
    Still lives the world to win.

5. O perfect Love, outpassing sight,
    O Light beyond our ken,
  Come down through all the world to-night,
    And heal the hearts of men!

A - men.

25

THE CHRISTIAN YEAR

17

Mode i.   *arr.* J. H. A.

[*Copyright*, 1931, *by Oxford University Press.*]

CHRISTMAS DAY

See also: 613 Of the Father's heart begotten.
614 O come all ye faithful (*in full*).

OFFICE HYMN. M.   Christe Redemptor omnium.   *6th cent.* *Tr. J. M. Neale.*

JESU, the Father's only Son, [won;
  Whose death for all redemption
Before the worlds, of God most high
Begotten all ineffably:

2 The Father's light and splendour thou,
Their endless hope to thee that bow;
Accept the prayers and praise to-day
That through the world thy servants [pay.

3 Salvation's author, call to mind
How, taking form of humankind,
Born of a Virgin undefiled,
Thou in man's flesh becam'st a child.

CHRISTMAS

17 (Modern Tune)

VOM HIMMEL HOCH. (L. M.)
Very slow and dignified ♩ = 46.

Later form of melody in SCHUMANN'S *Gesangbuch*, 1539.

Another harmonization of this tune will be found in the Appendix (No. 35).

4 Thus testifies the present day,
   Through every year in long array,
   That thou, salvation's source alone,
   Proceededst from the Father's throne.

5 Whence sky, and stars, and sea's abyss,
   And earth, and all that therein is,
   Shall still, with laud and carol meet,
   The Author of thine advent greet.

6 And we who, by thy precious blood
   From sin redeemed, are marked for God,
   On this the day that saw thy birth,
   Sing the new song of ransomed earth :

7. For that thine advent glory be,
   O Jesu, virgin-born, to thee ;
   With Father, and with Holy Ghost,
   From men and from the heavenly host.
                      Amen.

A - men.

THE CHRISTIAN YEAR

18

Mode iii.　　　　　　　　　　　　　　　　　　　　　　　arr. J. H. A.

Other texts have A B C D ♩♩ ♩♩ instead.

OFFICE HYMN. M., E.　　　　　　　　*Coelius Sedulius, c.* 450.　Tr. *J. Ellerton.*

A solis ortus cardine.

F ROM east to west, from shore to shore,
　Let every heart awake and sing
The holy Child whom Mary bore,
　The Christ, the everlasting King.

2 Behold, the world's Creator wears
　The form and fashion of a slave;
Our very flesh our Maker shares,
　His fallen creature, man, to save.

28

CHRISTMAS

18 (MODERN TUNE)

ROUEN. (L. M.)
In moderate time ♩ = 144.

*Rouen Church Melody.
Harmonized by R. V. W.*

To be sung in unison.

NOTE.—*This hymn may also be sung to* ST. VENANTIUS (*No.* 38).

3 For this how wondrously he wrought!
   A maiden, in her lowly place,
Became in ways beyond all thought,
   The chosen vessel of his grace.

4 She bowed her to the Angel's word
   Declaring what the Father willed,
And suddenly the promised Lord
   That pure and hallowed temple filled.

5 He shrank not from the oxen's stall,
   He lay within the manger-bed,
And he, whose bounty feedeth all,
   At Mary's breast himself was fed.

6 And while the Angels in the sky
   Sang praise above the silent field,
To shepherds poor the Lord most high,
   The one great Shepherd, was revealed.

7. All glory for this blessèd morn
   To God the Father ever be;
All praise to thee, O Virgin-born,
   All praise, O Holy Ghost, to thee. Amen.

A - men.

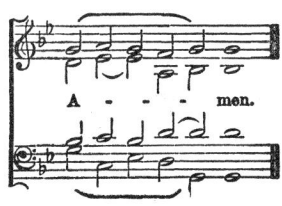

A - - - men.

THE CHRISTIAN YEAR
19

ES IST EIN' ROS' ENTSPRUNGEN. (7 6. 7 6. 6 7 6.)
In moderate time ♩ = 100.

Old German Melody,
harmony by M. PRAETORIUS, 1571–1621.

A full and ho ly cure!

And peace on earth to men.

[*The barring of this tune is necessarily irregular; but its performance will be found to be easy if it is remembered that the time-value of a crotchet is the same throughout.*]

Suitable till Candlemas.

St. Germanus, 634–734. Tr. J. M. Neale †.

Μέγα καὶ παράδοξον θαῦμα.

A GREAT and mighty wonder,
  A full and holy cure!
The Virgin bears the Infant
  With virgin-honour pure.

  Repeat the hymn again!
  'To God on high be glory,
  And peace on earth to men!'

2 The Word becomes incarnate
  And yet remains on high!
  And Cherubim sing anthems
  To shepherds from the sky.

3 While thus they sing your Monarch,
  Those bright angelic bands,
  Rejoice, ye vales and mountains,
  Ye oceans clap your hands.

4 Since all he comes to ransom,
  By all be he adored,
  The Infant born in Bethl'em,
  The Saviour and the Lord.

5 And idol forms shall perish,
  And error shall decay,
  And Christ shall wield his sceptre,
  Our Lord and God for ay.

A - men.

CHRISTMAS

20

THIS ENDRIS NYGHT. (C. M.)

Moderately slow ♩ = 120.

Ancient English Carol. 15th cent.

Suitable till Candlemas.

T. Pestel, 1584–1659.

BEHOLD the great Creator makes
  Himself a house of clay,
A robe of Virgin flesh he takes
  Which he will wear for ay.

2 Hark, hark, the wise eternal Word,
    Like a weak infant cries!
  In form of servant is the Lord,
    And God in cradle lies.

3 This wonder struck the world amazed,
    It shook the starry frame;
  Squadrons of spirits stood and gazed,
    Then down in troops they came.

4 Glad shepherds ran to view this sight;
    A choir of Angels sings,
  And eastern sages with delight
    Adore this King of kings.

5. Join then, all hearts that are not stone,
     And all our voices prove,
   To celebrate this holy One
     The God of peace and love.

A - men.

THE CHRISTIAN YEAR
21

YORKSHIRE or STOCKPORT. (10 10. 10 10. 10 10.)
In moderate time, dignified ♩ = 100.

J. WAINWRIGHT, 1723–68.

CHRISTMAS

John Byrom, 1692-1763.

CHRISTIANS, awake, salute the happy morn,
Whereon the Saviour of the world was born;
Rise to adore the mystery of love,
Which hosts of Angels chanted from above;
With them the joyful tidings first begun
Of God incarnate and the Virgin's Son :

2 Then to the watchful shepherds it was told,
Who heard the angelic herald's voice, 'Behold,
I bring good tidings of a Saviour's birth
To you and all the nations upon earth;
This day hath God fulfilled his promised word,
This day is born a Saviour, Christ the Lord.'

Unison. 3 He spake; and straightway the celestial choir
In hymns of joy, unknown before, conspire.
The praises of redeeming love they sang,
And heaven's whole orb with Alleluyas rang:
God's highest glory was their anthem still,
Peace upon earth, and mutual goodwill.

4 To Bethlehem straight the enlightened shepherds ran,
To see the wonder God had wrought for man,
And found, with Joseph and the blessèd Maid,
Her Son, the Saviour, in a manger laid;
Amazed the wondrous story they proclaim,
The first apostles of his infant fame.

5. * Like Mary let us ponder in our mind
God's wondrous love in saving lost mankind;
Trace we the Babe, who hath retrieved our loss,
From his poor manger to his bitter cross;
Then may we hope, angelic thrones among,
To sing, redeemed, a glad triumphal song.

THE CHRISTIAN YEAR

22

Christmas Sequence, and Candlemas Office Hymn
Mode v.

Laetabundus

11th cent. or earlier.
arr. J. H. A.

1 Come re - joic - ing, ✻ Faith - ful men, with rap - ture sing - ing
2 Mon - arch's Mon - arch, From a ho - ly mai - den spring - ing,

Al - le - lu - ya! 3 An - gel of the Coun - sel here,
Migh - ty won - der! 4 He a sun who knows no night,

Sun from star, he doth ap - pear, Born of mai - den:
She a star whose pa - ler light Fad - eth ne - ver.

CHRISTMAS

22 (*continued*)

5 As a star its kind-red ray, Ma-ry doth her Child dis-play,
6 Still un-dimmed the star shines on, And the mai-den bears a Son,

Like in na-ture; 7 Le-ba-non his ce-dar tall
Pure as e-ver. 8 From the high-est, him we name

To the hys-sop on the wall Low-ly bend-eth;
Word of God, to hu-man frame Now de-scend-eth.

THE CHRISTIAN YEAR

22 (continued)

9 Yet the syn-a-gogue de-nied What E-sai-as had de-scried:
10 If her pro-phets speak in vain, Let her heed a Gen-tile strain,

Blind-ness fell up-on the guide, Proud, un-heed-ing.
And, from mys-tic Sy-bil, gain Light and lead-ing.

11 No long-er then de-lay, Hear what the Scrip-tures say,
12. Turn and this Child be-hold, That ve-ry Son, of old

CHRISTMAS

22 (continued)

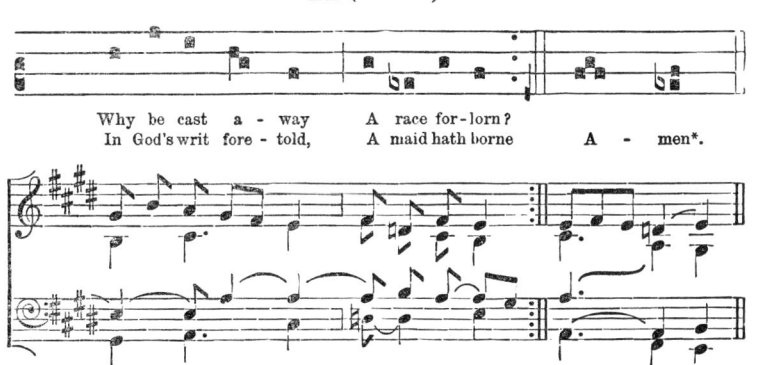

Why be cast a - way A race for-lorn?
In God's writ fore - told, A maid hath borne A - men*.

* *Amen is sung only when the Hymn is used as an Office Hymn, not as a Sequence.*

22 (Modern Tune)

LAETABUNDUS. (Irreg.)

In moderate time, majestically ♩ = 76.

NICHOLAS GATTY.

To be sung in unison.

1 Come re-joic-ing, Faith-ful men, with rap-ture sing-ing Al - - le - lu - - - ya! (2) Mon-arch's Mon-arch, From a ho-ly mai-den spring-ing,

THE CHRISTIAN YEAR

22 (*continued*)

Might-y won-der!
3 An-gel of the Coun-sel here,
5 As a star its kin-dred ray,
7 Le-ba-non his ce-dar tall

Sun from star, he doth ap-pear, Born of mai-den:
Ma-ry doth her Child dis-play, Like in na-ture;
To the hys-sop on the wall Low-ly bend-eth;

(4) He a sun who knows no night, She a star whose pa-ler light
(6) Still undimmed the star shines on, And the mai-den bears a Son,
(8) From the high-est, him we name Word of God, to hu-man frame

Fad-eth ne-ver.
Pure as e-ver. 9 Yet the sy-na-gogue de-nied
Now de-scend-eth.

CHRISTMAS

22 (*continued*)

What E-sai-as had de-scried: Blind-ness fell up-on the guide, Proud, un-heed - - - ing. (10) If her pro-phets speak in vain, Let her heed a Gen-tile strain, And, from mys-tic Sy-bil, gain Light and lead - - - ing. 11 No lon-ger then de-

THE CHRISTIAN YEAR

22 (*continued*)

CHRISTMAS

23

DENT DALE. (7 7.7 7.)
Moderately fast ♩=100.

English Traditional Melody.

C. Wesley, 1707–88.

1 HARK, how all the welkin rings!
'Glory to the King of kings,
Peace on earth and mercy mild,
God and sinners reconciled.'

2 Joyful, all ye nations, rise,
Join the triumph of the skies;
Universal nature say
'Christ the Lord is born to-day.

3 Christ, by highest heaven adored,
Christ, the everlasting Lord,
Late in time behold him come
Offspring of a Virgin's womb.

4 Veiled in flesh, the Godhead see!
Hail the incarnate Deity!
Pleased as man with men to appear
Jesus, our Emmanuel here!

Unison. 5 Hail the heavenly Prince of peace!
Hail the Sun of righteousness!
Light and life to all he brings,
Risen with healing in his wings.

6 Mild he lays his glory by,
Born that man no more may die,
Born to raise the sons of earth,
Born to give them second birth!

7 Come, Desire of nations, come,
Fix in us thy humble home;
Rise, the woman's conquering Seed,
Bruise in us the serpent's head.

Unison. 8. Now display thy saving power,
Ruined nature now restore,
Now in mystic union join
Thine to ours, and ours to thine.

A - men.

THE CHRISTIAN YEAR

24

MENDELSSOHN. (7777.7777.77.)
In moderate time ♩ = 92.

Adapted from a Chorus by
F. MENDELSSOHN-BARTHOLDY, 1809-47.

Unison.

Organ pedals.

[*By permission of Novello & Co., Ltd.*]

CHRISTMAS

C. Wesley (1743), *G. Whitefield* (1758), *M. Madan*
(1760), *and others.*

HARK! the herald Angels sing
 Glory to the new-born King;
Peace on earth and mercy mild,
God and sinners reconciled:
Joyful all ye nations rise,
Join the triumph of the skies,
With the angelic host proclaim,
Christ is born in Bethlehem.

> *Hark! the herald Angels sing*
> *Glory to the new-born King.*

2 Christ, by highest heaven adored,
Christ, the everlasting Lord,
Late in time behold him come
Offspring of a Virgin's womb!
Veiled in flesh the Godhead see,
Hail the incarnate Deity!
Pleased as man with man to dwell,
Jesus, our Emmanuel.

3. Hail the heaven-born Prince of peace!
Hail the Sun of Righteousness!
Light and life to all he brings,
Risen with healing in his wings;
Mild he lays his glory by,
Born that man no more may die,
Born to raise the sons of earth,
Born to give them second birth.

A - men.

THE CHRISTIAN YEAR

25

CRANHAM. (Irreg.)
In moderate time ♩ = 100.

G. HOLST.

[*The metre of this hymn is peculiar. The music as printed is that of the first verse, and it can easily be adapted to the others.*]

Verses 2 and 3 run:

Our God, heaven can-not hold him Nor .. earth sus-tain;
Heaven and earth shall flee a-way When he comes to reign: In the bleak mid-

E-nough for him, whom Che-ru-bim Wor-ship night and day, A
breast-ful of milk, And a man-ger-ful of hay; E-nough for him, whom &c.

CHRISTMAS

Christina G. Rossetti, 1830-94.

IN the bleak mid-winter
Frosty wind made moan,
Earth stood hard as iron,
Water like a stone;
Snow had fallen, snow on snow,
Snow on snow,
In the bleak mid-winter,
Long ago.

2 Our God, heaven cannot hold him
Nor earth sustain;
Heaven and earth shall flee away
When he comes to reign:
In the bleak mid-winter
A stable-place sufficed
The Lord God Almighty
Jesus Christ.

3 Enough for him, whom Cherubim
Worship night and day,
A breastful of milk,
And a mangerful of hay;
Enough for him, whom Angels
Fall down before,
The ox and ass and camel
Which adore.

4 Angels and Archangels
May have gathered there,
Cherubim and Seraphim
Thronged the air—
But only his mother
In her maiden bliss
Worshipped the Belovèd
With a kiss.

5. What can I give him
Poor as I am?
If I were a shepherd
I would bring a lamb;
If I were a wise man
I would do my part;
Yet what I can I give him—
Give my heart.

A - men.

THE CHRISTIAN YEAR

26

NOEL. (D.C.M.)
In moderate time ♩ = 92.

Traditional Air, adapted by
A. SULLIVAN, 1842-1900.

Other occasions also.

[By permission of Novello & Co. Ltd.]

E. H. Sears, 1810-76.

IT came upon the midnight clear,
  That glorious song of old,
From Angels bending near the earth
  To touch their harps of gold:
'Peace on the earth, good-will to men,
  From heaven's all-gracious King!'
The world in solemn stillness lay
  To hear the Angels sing.

CHRISTMAS

2 Still through the cloven skies they come,
   With peaceful wings unfurled;
And still their heavenly music floats
   O'er all the weary world;
Above its sad and lowly plains
   They bend on hovering wing;
And ever o'er its Babel sounds
   The blessèd Angels sing.

3 Yet with the woes of sin and strife
   The world has suffered long;
Beneath the Angel-strain have rolled
   Two thousand years of wrong;
And man, at war with man, hears not
   The love-song which they bring:
O hush the noise, ye men of strife,
   And hear the Angels sing!

4 * And ye, beneath life's crushing load,
   Whose forms are bending low,
Who toil along the climbing way
   With painful steps and slow,
Look now! for glad and golden hours
   Come swiftly on the wing;
O rest beside the weary road,
   And hear the Angels sing!

5. For lo! the days are hastening on,
   By prophet-bards foretold,
When, with the ever-circling years,
   Comes round the age of gold;
When peace shall over all the earth
   Its ancient splendours fling,
And the whole world send back the song
   Which now the Angels sing.

A - men.

THE CHRISTIAN YEAR

27

ST. MICHAEL (OLD 134TH). (S.M.)
In moderate time ♩ = 69.
Adapted from L. BOURGEOIS'
Genevan Psalter, 1551.

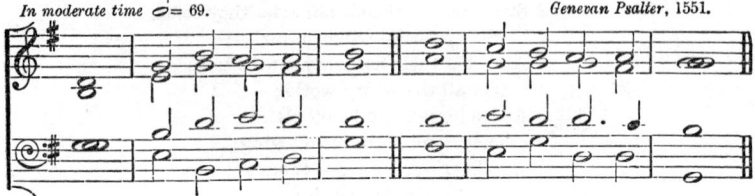

C. Coffin, 1676-1749. Tr. W. J. Blew.

Jam desinant suspiria.

LET sighing cease and woe,
  God from on high hath heard,
Heaven's gate is opening wide, and lo!
  The long-expected Word.

2 Peace! through the deep of night
  The heavenly choir breaks forth,
Singing, with festal songs and bright,
  Our God and Saviour's birth.

3 The cave of Bethlehem
  Those wakeful shepherds seek:
Let us too rise and greet with them
  That infant pure and meek.

4 We enter—at the door
  What marvel meets the eye?
A crib, a mother pale and poor,
  A child of poverty.

5 Art thou the eternal Son,
  The eternal Father's ray?
Whose little hand, thou infant one,
  Doth lift the world alway?

6 Yea—faith through that dim cloud,
  Like lightning, darts before,
And greets thee, at whose footstool bowed
  Heaven's trembling hosts adore.

7 Chaste be our love like thine,
  Our swelling souls bring low,
And in our hearts, O Babe divine
  Be born, abide, and grow.

8. So shall thy birthday morn,
  Lord Christ, our birthday be,
Then greet we all, ourselves new-born,
  Our King's nativity.

A - men.

CHRISTMAS

ADESTE FIDELES. (Irreg.)
Very slow ♩ = 72.

28

Composer unknown. Probably 18th cent.

Without pedals.

Pedals.

18th cent. Tr. F. Oakeley ‡, 1802–80.
[For the Complete Version, see No. 614.]

Adeste, fideles.

O COME, all ye faithful,
   Joyful and triumphant,
O come ye, O come ye to Bethlehem;
Come and behold him,
   Born the King of Angels:

O come, let us adore him,
O come, let us adore him,
O come, let us adore him, Christ the Lord.

2 God of God,
   Light of Light,
Lo! he abhors not the Virgin's womb;
Very God,
   Begotten not created:

3 Sing, choirs of Angels,
   Sing in exultation,
Sing, all ye citizens of heaven above,
   Glory to God
   In the highest:

Unison. 4. Yea, Lord, we greet thee,
   Born this happy morning,
Jesu, to thee be glory given;
   Word of the Father,
   Now in flesh appearing:

A - men.

THE CHRISTIAN YEAR
29

A VIRGIN UNSPOTTED. (11 11. 11 11. and refrain.)

Moderately slow ♩ = 96.

English Traditional Carol.

(*Small notes for verse 6, line 2*).

Refrain.

[*In one or more verses the first part of this tune may be sung as a solo.*]

CHRISTMAS

Suitable till Candlemas.   *H. R. Bramley*, 1833–1917.

THE great God of heavèn is come down to earth,
His mother a Virgin, and sinless his birth;
The Father eternal his Father alone:
He sleeps in the manger; he reigns on the throne:

> *Then let us adore him, and praise his great love:*
> *To save us poor sinners he came from above.*

2 A Babe on the breast of a Maiden he lies,
Yet sits with the Father on high in the skies;
Before him their faces the Seraphim hide,
While Joseph stands waiting, unscared, by his side:

3 Lo! here is Emmanuel, here is the Child,
The Son that was promised to Mary so mild;
Whose power and dominion shall ever increase,
The Prince that shall rule o'er a kingdom of peace:

4 The Wonderful Counsellor, boundless in might,
The Father's own image, the beam of his light;
Behold him now wearing the likeness of man,
Weak, helpless, and speechless, in measure a span:

5 O wonder of wonders, which none can unfold:
The Ancient of days is an hour or two old;
The Maker of all things is made of the earth,
Man is worshipped by Angels, and God comes to birth:

6. The Word in the bliss of the Godhead remains,
Yet in flesh comes to suffer the keenest of pains;
He is that he was, and for ever shall be,
But becomes that he was not, for you and for me.

A - men.

THE CHRISTIAN YEAR
30

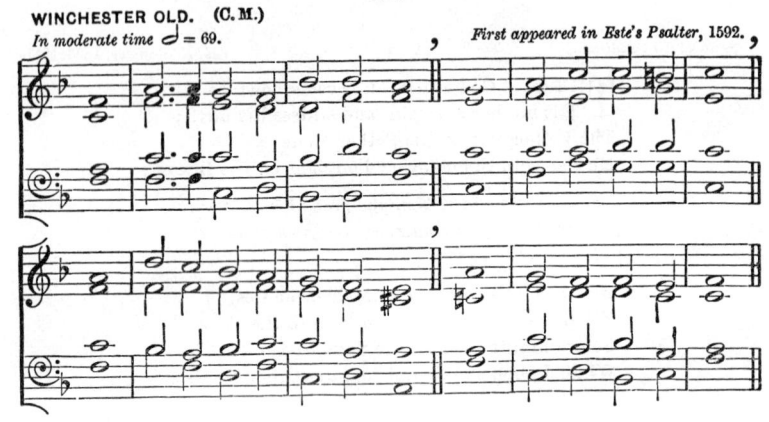

WINCHESTER OLD. (C.M.)
In moderate time ♩ = 69.

First appeared in Este's Psalter, 1592.

Nahum Tate, 1652–1715.

WHILE shepherds watched their flocks by night,
    All seated on the ground,
The Angel of the Lord came down,
    And glory shone around.

2 'Fear not,' said he (for mighty dread
    Had seized their troubled mind);
'Glad tidings of great joy I bring
    To you and all mankind.

3 'To you in David's town this day
    Is born of David's line
A Saviour, who is Christ the Lord;
    And this shall be the sign:

4 'The heavenly Babe you there shall find
    To human view displayed,
All meanly wrapped in swathing bands,
    And in a manger laid.'

5 Thus spake the Seraph; and forthwith
    Appeared a shining throng
Of Angels praising God, who thus
    Addressed their joyful song:

6. 'All glory be to God on high,
    And on the earth be peace;
Good-will henceforth from heaven to men
    Begin and never cease'

CHRISTMAS
30
ALTERNATIVE VERSION

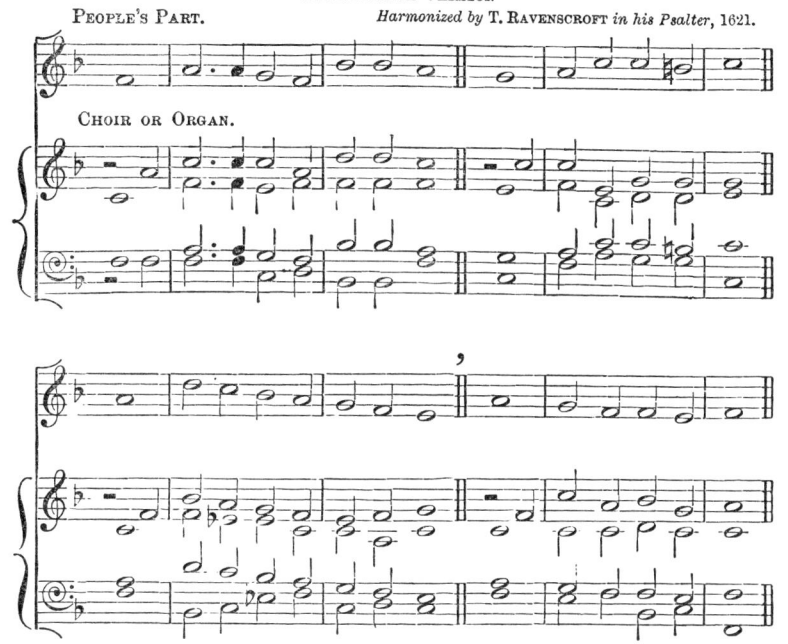

PEOPLE'S PART. *Harmonized by* T. RAVENSCROFT *in his Psalter*, 1621.

CHOIR OR ORGAN.

[*It is suggested that this version be used either by the Choir alone, or with the people singing the melody, to verses* 2, 3, *and* 4. *The tenor part which has the melody should be made prominent.*]

NOTE.—*It is impossible to print all the tunes which are traditionally sung to this hymn. The tune often used in Cornwall is printed in the Appendix* (No. 8).
UNIVERSITY (*No.* 93) *and* CROWLE (*No.* 463) *are sometimes sung to this hymn.*

A - men.

THE CHRISTIAN YEAR

31

Mode ii.   *arr.* J. H. A.

ST. STEPHEN'S DAY

OFFICE HYMN. M. *and* E.   10*th*–16*th cent.*   *Tr.* J. M. Neale

Sancte Dei pretiose.

SAINT of God, elect and precious,
   Protomartyr Stephen, bright
With thy love of amplest measure,
   Shining round thee like a light;
Who to God commendedst, dying,
   Them that did thee all despite:

54

ST. STEPHEN'S DAY

31 (Modern Tune)

ST. THOMAS. (87. 87. 87.)
Moderately slow, dignified ♩ = 66.

Melody from S. Webbe's
'Motetts or Antiphons,' 1792,
and *An Essay on the Church Plain Chant*, 1782.

2 Glitters now the crown above thee,
   Figured in thy sacred name :
O that we, who truly love thee,
   May have portion in the same ;
In the dreadful day of judgement
   Fearing neither sin nor shame.

3. Laud to God, and might, and honour,
   Who with flowers of rosy dye
Crowned thy forehead, and hath placed thee
   In the starry throne on high :
He direct us, he protect us
   From death's sting eternally.   Amen.

A - men.

A - men.

THE CHRISTIAN YEAR

32

WOHLAUF, THUT NICHT VERZAGEN. (7 6. 7 6. D.)

B. HELDER, 1585-1635.
Harmonized by G. H. PALMER.

In moderate time ♩ = 69.

Anatolius, c. 800.   Tr. J. M. Neale.

Τῷ Βασιλεῖ καὶ Δεσπότῃ.

THE Lord and King of all things
   But yesterday was born;
And Stephen's glorious offering
   His birth-tide shall adorn:
No pearls of orient splendour,
   No jewels can he show;
But with his own true heart's blood
   His shining vestments glow.

2 Come, ye that love the Martyrs,
   And pluck the flowers of song.
And weave them in a garland
   For this our suppliant throng;
And cry, 'O thou that shinest
   In grace's brightest ray,
Christ's valiant Protomartyr,
   For peace and favour pray!'

3. Thou first of all confessors,
   Of all the deacons crown,
Of every following athlete
   The glory and renown:
Make supplication, standing
   Before Christ's royal throne,
That he would give the kingdom,
   And for our sins atone!

A - men.

ST. JOHN THE EVANGELIST

33

GRAFTON. (87. 87. 87.)
Moderately slow ♩ = 66.

*French Church Melody,
from Chants Ordinaires de l'Office Divin* (Paris, 1881).

NOTE.—*This hymn may also be sung to* TANTUM ERGO (*No.* 63).
(*Office Hymns,* 174–6.)

J. Keble, 1792–1866.

WORD supreme, before creation
  Born of God eternally,
Who didst will for our salvation
  To be born on earth. and die;
Well thy Saints have kept their station,
  Watching till thine hour drew nigh.

2 Now 'tis come, and faith espies thee;
  Like an eaglet in the morn,
One in steadfast worship eyes thee,
  Thy beloved, thy latest born:
In thy glory he descries thee
  Reigning from the tree of scorn.

3 * He first hoping and believing
  Did beside the grave adore;
Latest he, the warfare leaving,
  Landed on the eternal shore;
And his witness we receiving
  Own thee Lord for evermore.

4 * Much he asked in loving wonder,
  On thy bosom leaning, Lord!
In that secret place of thunder,
  Answer kind didst thou accord,
Wisdom for thy Church to ponder
  Till the day of dread award.

5 Lo! heaven's doors lift up, revealing
  How thy judgements earthward move;
Scrolls unfolded, trumpets pealing,
  Wine-cups from the wrath above,
Yet o'er all a soft voice stealing—
  'Little children, trust and love!'

6. Thee, the Almighty King eternal,
  Father of the eternal Word;
Thee, the Father's Word supernal,
  Thee, of both, the Breath adored:
Heaven, and earth, and realms infernal
  Own, one glorious God and Lord. Amen.

A - men.

THE CHRISTIAN YEAR

34

SARRATT. (L. M.)
Moderately slow ♩=112.
G. C. E. RYLEY.

NOTE.—*This hymn may also be sung to the Rouen Melody, No. 38.*

THE INNOCENTS' DAY

(*Office Hymns*, 182, 183.) *Prudentius, b.* 348. *Tr. A. R.*

Salvete, flores martyrum.

ALL hail, ye little Martyr flowers,
  Sweet rosebuds cut in dawning hours!
When Herod sought the Christ to find
Ye fell as bloom before the wind.

2 First victims of the Martyr bands,
  With crowns and palms in tender hands,
  Around the very altar, gay
  And innocent, ye seem to play.

3 What profited this great offence?
  What use was Herod's violence?
  A Babe survives that dreadful day,
  And Christ is safely borne away.

4. All honour, laud, and glory be,
  O Jesu, virgin-born, to thee;
  All glory, as is ever meet
  To Father and to Paraclete.
                                Amen.

35

WER DA WONET. (D. L. M.)
In moderate time ♩=120.
Melody in 'St. Gall Gesangbuch,' 1863,
from VEHE's *Gesangbüchlein*, 1537.

INNOCENTS' DAY

35 (continued)

The Venerable Bede, 673-735. Tr. J. M. Neale.
Hymnum canentes martyrum.

THE hymn for conquering Martyrs raise,
The victor Innocents we praise,
Whom in their woe earth cast away,
But heaven with joy received to-day;
Whose Angels see the Father's face
World without end, and hymn his grace;
And, while they chant unceasing lays,
The hymn for conquering Martyrs raise.

2 A voice from Ramah was there sent,
A voice of weeping and lament,
When Rachel mourned the children's care
Whom for the tyrant's sword she bare.
Triumphal is their glory now,
Whom earthly torments could not bow,
What time, both far and near that went,
A voice from Ramah was there sent.

3 * Fear not, O little flock and blest,
The lion that your life opprest!
To heavenly pastures ever new
The heavenly Shepherd leadeth you;
Who, dwelling now on Sion's hill,
The Lamb's dear footsteps follow still;
By tyrant there no more distrest,
Fear not, O little flock and blest.

4 * And every tear is wiped away
By your dear Father's hands for ay:
Death hath no power to hurt you more,
Whose own is life's eternal store.
Who sow their seed, and sowing weep,
In everlasting joy shall reap,
What time they shine in heavenly day,
And every tear is wiped away.

5. O city blest o'er all the earth,
Who gloriest in the Saviour's birth,
Whose are his earliest Martyrs dear,
By kindred and by triumph here;
None from henceforth may call thee small,
Of rival towns thou passest all:
In whom our Monarch had his birth,
O city blest o'er all the earth!

A - men.

The following is also suitable: 611 When Christ was born.

THE CHRISTIAN YEAR

DAS WALT' GOTT VATER. (L. M.) **36**

Very slow and solemn ♩ = 46.

Later form of melody by
D. Vetter, *d. c.* 1730
Harmony from J. S. Bach.

THE CIRCUMCISION OF CHRIST

(*Office Hymns, E. M.* 18, *M.* 17.)   S. Besnault, *d.* 1724. Tr. J. Chandler.

Felix dies quem proprio.

1. O HAPPY day, when first was poured
The blood of our redeeming Lord!
O happy day, when first began
His sufferings for sinful man!

2. Just entered on this world of woe,
His blood already learned to flow;
His future death was thus expressed,
And thus his early love confessed.

3. From heaven descending to fulfil
The mandates of his Father's will,
E'en now behold the victim lie,
The Lamb of God, prepared to die!

4. Lord, circumcise our hearts, we pray,
Our fleshly natures purge away;
Thy name, thy likeness may they bear:
Yea, stamp thy holy image there!

5. O Lord, the virgin-born, to thee
Eternal praise and glory be,
Whom with the Father we adore,
And Holy Ghost for evermore. Amen.

A - men.

THE CIRCUMCISION OF CHRIST

INNOCENTS. (7 7.7 7.)
Moderately fast ♩ = 100.

Composed or adapted by
J. SMITH, 1800–73.

Victis sibi cognomina.

c. 1736. Tr. *J. Chandler*‡.

CONQUERING kings their titles take
　From the lands they captive make :
Jesu, thine was given thee
For a world thou madest free.

2 Not another name is given
Power possessing under heaven,
Strong to call dead souls to rise
And exalt them to the skies.

3 That which Christ so hardly wrought,
That which he so dearly bought,
That salvation, mortals, say,
Will ye madly cast away ?

4 Rather gladly for that name
Bear the Cross, endure the shame ;
Joyfully for him to die
Is not death but victory.

5 Jesu, if thou condescend
To be called the sinner's Friend,
Ours the joy and glory be
Thus to make our boast of thee.

6. Glory to the Father be,
Glory, Virgin-born, to thee,
Glory to the Holy Ghost,
Ever from the heavenly host.　Amen.

For the New-Year's Day hymns, see 285–6.

A - men.

THE CHRISTIAN YEAR

38

Mode iii.   arr. J. H. A.

* *For this group other texts have* A B C D ♩ ♩ *instead.*

NOTE.—*A simpler form of this tune is given at No. 18.*

If an easier alternative is needed, that given at No. 56 may be suitable.

See also   615 From the eastern mountains.
               616 Hail thou Source of every blessing.

THE EPIPHANY

ST. VENANTIUS. (L. M.)   **38** (Modern Tune)

In moderate time ♩ = 144.
To be sung in unison.

Rouen Church Melody.
Harmonized by R. V. W.

Office Hymn. E. *and* M.   *C. Sedulius, c.* 450.   Tr. **P. D.**
Hostis Herodes impie.

WHY, impious Herod, shouldst thou fear
Because the Christ is come so near?
He who doth heavenly kingdoms grant
Thine earthly realm can never want.

2 Lo, sages from the East are gone
To where the star hath newly shone:
Led on by light to Light they press,
And by their gifts their God confess.

3 The Lamb of God is manifest
Again in Jordan's water blest,
And he who sin had never known
By washing hath our sins undone.

4 Yet he that ruleth everything
Can change the nature of the spring,
And gives at Cana this for sign—
The water reddens into wine.

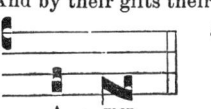

5 Then glory, Lord, to thee we pay
For thine Epiphany to-day;
All glory through eternity
To Father, Son, and Spirit be.   Amen.

A - men.

A - - men.

THE CHRISTIAN YEAR

39

DIX. (7.7. 7 7. 7 7.)
In moderate time ♩ = 96.

Abridged from a Chorale, 'Treuer Heiland,' by C. Kocher, 1786–1872.

W. Chatterton Dix, 1837–98.

AS with gladness men of old
   Did the guiding star behold,
As with joy they hailed its light,
Leading onward, beaming bright,
So, most gracious God, may we
Evermore be led to thee.

2 As with joyful steps they sped,
   To that lowly manger-bed,
There to bend the knee before
Him whom heaven and earth adore,
So may we with willing feet
Ever seek thy mercy-seat.

3 As they offered gifts most rare
   At that manger rude and bare,
So may we with holy joy,
Pure, and free from sin's alloy,
All our costliest treasures bring,
Christ, to thee our heavenly King.

4 Holy Jesu, every day
   Keep us in the narrow way;
And, when earthly things are past,
Bring our ransomed souls at last
Where they need no star to guide,
Where no clouds thy glory hide.

5. In the heavenly country bright
   Need they no created light;
Thou its Light, its Joy, its Crown,
Thou its Sun which goes not down:
There for ever may we sing
Alleluyas to our King.

A - men.

THE EPIPHANY

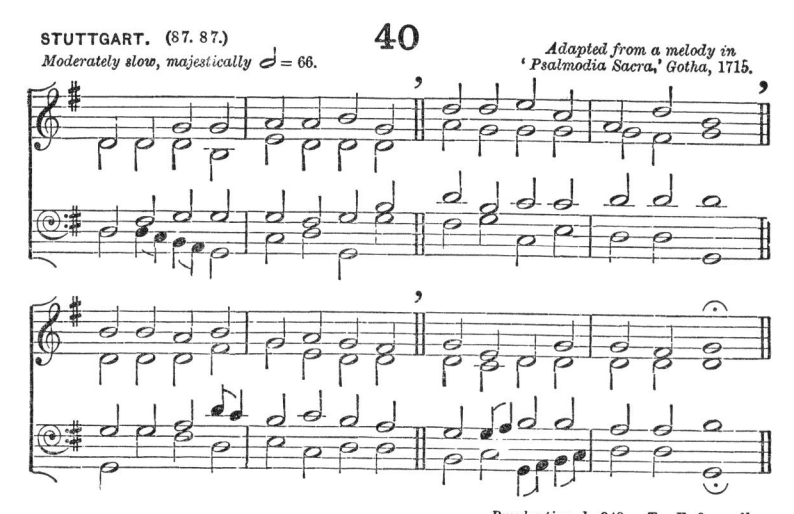

STUTTGART. (87. 87.)
Moderately slow, majestically ♩ = 66.

40

Adapted from a melody in
'Psalmodia Sacra,' Gotha, 1715.

Prudentius, b. 348.   *Tr. E. Caswall.*

O sola magnarum urbium.

BETHLEHEM, of noblest cities
  None can once with thee compare;
Thou alone the Lord from heaven
  Didst for us incarnate bear.

2 Fairer than the sun at morning
    Was the star that told his birth;
  To the lands their God announcing,
    Hid beneath a form of earth.

3 By its lambent beauty guided
    See the eastern kings appear;
  See them bend, their gifts to offer,
    Gifts of incense, gold and myrrh.

4 Solemn things of mystic meaning:
    Incense doth the God disclose,
  Gold a royal child proclaimeth,
    Myrrh a future tomb foreshows.

Unison. 5. Holy Jesu, in thy brightness
    To the Gentile world displayed,
  With the Father and the Spirit
    Endless praise to thee be paid.   Amen.

A - men.

THE CHRISTIAN YEAR

LIEBSTER IMMANUEL. (11 10. 11 10.)
Slow ♩ = 72.

Later form of melody from 'Himmels-Lust,' 1679.

NOTE.—*A major tune for this hymn will be found in the Appendix (No. 9).*

Bishop R. Heber, 1783–1826.

BRIGHTEST and best of the sons of the morning,
  Dawn on our darkness and lend us thine aid;
Star of the East, the horizon adorning,
  Guide where our infant Redeemer is laid.

2 Cold on his cradle the dew-drops are shining,
   Low lies his head with the beasts of the stall:
 Angels adore him in slumber reclining,
   Maker and Monarch and Saviour of all.

3 Say, shall we yield him, in costly devotion,
   Odours of Edom and offerings divine?
 Gems of the mountain and pearls of the ocean,
   Myrrh from the forest or gold from the mine?

4 Vainly we offer each ample oblation,
   Vainly with gifts would his favour secure;
 Richer by far is the heart's adoration,
   Dearer to God are the prayers of the poor.

Unison. 5. Brightest and best of the sons of the morning,
   Dawn on our darkness and lend us thine aid;
 Star of the East, the horizon adorning,
   Guide where our infant Redeemer is laid.

A - men.

THE EPIPHANY

WAS LEBET, WAS SCHWEBET. (13 10. 13 10.) **42**

Moderately slow ♩ = 80.

From the 'Rheinhardt MS.,' Üttingen, 1754.

Notes in small type are for the first and last verses only.

Suitable till Septuagesima.   *J. S. B. Monsell, 1811–75.*

O WORSHIP the Lord in the beauty of holiness!
  Bow down before him, his glory proclaim;
With gold of obedience, and incense of lowliness,
  Kneel and adore him, the Lord is his name!

2 Low at his feet lay thy burden of carefulness,
  High on his heart he will bear it for thee,
Comfort thy sorrows, and answer thy prayerfulness,
  Guiding thy steps as may best for thee be.

3 Fear not to enter his courts in the slenderness
  Of the poor wealth thou wouldst reckon as thine:
Truth in its beauty, and love in its tenderness,
  These are the offerings to lay on his shrine.

4 These, though we bring them in trembling and fearfulness,
  He will accept for the name that is dear;
Mornings of joy give for evenings of tearfulness,
  Trust for our trembling and hope for our fear.

5. O worship the Lord in the beauty of holiness!
  Bow down before him, his glory proclaim;
With gold of obedience, and incense of lowliness,
  Kneel and adore him, the Lord is his name!

A - men.

THE CHRISTIAN YEAR

43

DUNDEE. (C. M.)
Moderately slow ♩ = 66.

Scottish Psalter, 1615, as given in Ravenscroft's Psalter, 1621.

Suitable till Septuagesima.   J. Morison, 1749–98 (*Scottish Paraphrases*).

THE race that long in darkness pined
  Have seen a glorious light;
The people dwell in day, who dwelt
  In death's surrounding night.

2 To hail thy rise, thou better Sun,
    The gathering nations come,
  Joyous as when the reapers bear
    The harvest-treasures home.

3 To us a Child of hope is born,
    To us a Son is given;
  Him shall the tribes of earth obey,
    Him all the hosts of heaven.

4 His name shall be the Prince of Peace,
    For evermore adored;
  The Wonderful, the Counsellor,
    The great and mighty Lord.

Unison. 5. His power increasing still shall spread;
    His reign no end shall know:
  Justice shall guard his throne above,
    And peace abound below.

A - men.

THE EPIPHANY

43
ALTERNATIVE VERSION

Harmonized by RAVENSCROFT.

PEOPLE'S PART.

CHOIR OR ORGAN.

[*This version may be used in connexion with the other for one or more verses, the people singing the melody as usual.*]

THE CHRISTIAN YEAR

EIN KIND GEBOR'N. (L. M.) **44**
Moderately fast ♩ = 152.   *Old German Carol.*

C. Coffin, 1676–1749. Tr. J. Chandler†.
Quae stella sole pulchrior.

1. WHAT star is this, with beams so bright,
  More lovely than the noonday light?
  'Tis sent to announce a new-born King,
  Glad tidings of our God to bring.

2. 'Tis now fulfilled what God decreed,
  'From Jacob shall a star proceed';
  And lo! the eastern sages stand,
  To read in heaven the Lord's command.

3. While outward signs the star displays,
  An inward light the Lord conveys,
  And urges them, with force benign,
  To seek the giver of the sign.

4. True love can brook no dull delay:
  Through toils and dangers lies their way;
  And yet their home, their friends, their all,
  They leave at once, at God's high call.

5. O, while the star of heavenly grace
  Invites us, Lord, to seek thy face,
  May we no more that grace repel,
  Or quench that light which shines so well!

6. To God the Father, God the Son,
  And Holy Spirit, Three in One,
  May every tongue and nation raise
  An endless song of thankful praise!

A . men.

FROM THE EPIPHANY TILL SEPTUAGESIMA

CRÜGER. (7 6. 7 6. D.) **45**   *Adapted by* W. H. MONK *from a Chorale by* J. CRÜGER, 1598–1662.
Slow and dignified ♩ = 56.

70

FROM EPIPHANY TILL SEPTUAGESIMA

45 (continued)

Unison.   *J. Montgomery*, 1771–1854.

HAIL to the Lord's Anointed!
   Great David's greater Son;
Hail, in the time appointed,
   His reign on earth begun!
He comes to break oppression,
   To let the captive free;
To take away transgression,
   And rule in equity.

2 He comes with succour speedy
   To those who suffer wrong;
To help the poor and needy,
   And bid the weak be strong;
To give them songs for sighing,
   Their darkness turn to light,
Whose souls, condemned and dying,
   Were precious in his sight.

3 He shall come down like showers
   Upon the fruitful earth,
And love, joy, hope, like flowers,
   Spring in his path to birth:

Before him on the mountains
   Shall peace the herald go;
And righteousness in fountains
   From hill to valley flow.

4 * Arabia's desert-ranger
   To him shall bow the knee;
The Ethiopian stranger
   His glory come to see;
With offerings of devotion
   Ships from the isles shall meet,
To pour the wealth of ocean
   In tribute at his feet.

5 Kings shall fall down before him,
   And gold and incense bring;
All nations shall adore him,
   His praise all people sing;
To him shall prayer unceasing
   And daily vows ascend;
His kingdom still increasing,
   A kingdom without end.

Unison. 6. * O'er every foe victorious,
   He on his throne shall rest,
From age to age more glorious,
   All-blessing and all-blest:
The tide of time shall never
   His covenant remove;
His name shall stand for ever;
   That name to us is Love.

A - men.

THE CHRISTIAN YEAR

46

CORNHILL. (C. M.)
In moderate time ♩ = 96.

HAROLD E. DARKE.

[*Copyright, 1931, by Oxford University Press.*]
NOTE.—*This hymn may also be sung to* TALLIS' ORDINAL (*No.* 453).

J.-B. de Santeüil, 1630-97. Tr. J. Chandler.

Divine, crescebas Puer.

1. IN stature grows the heavenly Child,
   With death before his eyes;
   A Lamb unblemished, meek and mild,
   Prepared for sacrifice.

2. The Son of God his glory hides
   With parents mean and poor;
   And he who made the heaven abides
   In dwelling-place obscure.

3. Those mighty hands that stay the sky
   No earthly toil refuse;
   And he who set the stars on high
   An humble trade pursues.

4. He before whom the angels stand,
   At whose behest they fly,
   Now yields himself to man's command,
   And lays his glory by.

5. Jesu, the Virgin's holy Son,
   We praise thee and adore,
   Who art with God the Father one,
   And Spirit evermore.   Amen.

47

ST. EDMUND. (7 7. 7 7. D.)
Moderately fast ♩ = 100.

C. STEGGALL, 1826-1905.

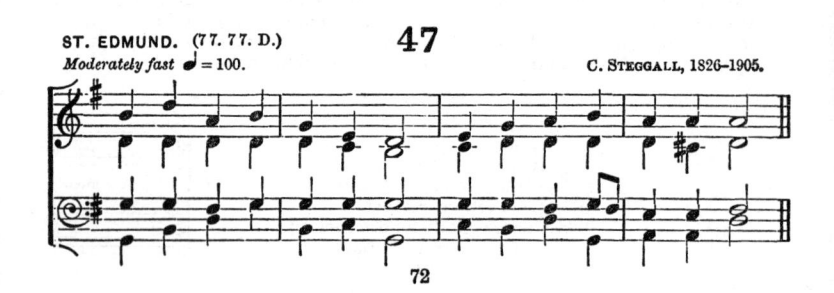

FROM EPIPHANY TILL SEPTUAGESIMA

Bishop Chr. Wordsworth, 1807–85.

1. SONGS of thankfulness and praise,
Jesu, Lord, to thee we raise,
Manifested by the star
To the sages from afar;
Branch of royal David's stem
In thy birth at Bethlehem;
Anthems be to thee addrest,
God in Man made manifest.

2 Manifest at Jordan's stream,
Prophet, Priest, and King supreme;
And at Cana wedding-guest
In thy Godhead manifest;
Manifest in power divine,
Changing water into wine;
Anthems be to thee addrest,
God in Man made manifest.

3 Manifest in making whole
Palsied limbs and fainting soul;
Manifest in valiant fight,
Quelling all the devil's might;
Manifest in gracious will,
Ever bringing good from ill;
Anthems be to thee addrest,
God in Man made manifest.

4* Sun and moon shall darkened be,
Stars shall fall, the heavens shall flee;
Christ will then like lightning shine,
All will see his glorious sign;
All will then the trumpet hear,
All will see the Judge appear;
Thou by all wilt be confest,
God in Man made manifest.

5. Grant us grace to see thee, Lord,
Mirrored in thy holy word;
May we imitate thee now,
And be pure, as pure art thou;
That we like to thee may be
At thy great Epiphany,
And may praise thee, ever blest,
God in Man made manifest.

A - men.

73

THE CHRISTIAN YEAR

48

CANTATE DOMINO. (D. L. M.)

Slow ♩ = 56.

J. BARNBY, 1838–96.

(By permission of Novello & Co. Ltd.)

FROM EPIPHANY TILL SEPTUAGESIMA

A. P. Stanley, 1815–81.

THE Lord is come! On Syrian soil,
  The child of poverty and toil;
The Man of Sorrows, born to know
Each varying shade of human woe:
  His joy, his glory, to fulfil,
  In earth and heaven, his Father's will;
On lonely mount, by festive board,
On bitter Cross, despised, adored.

2 The Lord is come! In him we trace
  The fullness of God's truth and grace;
Throughout those words and acts divine
Gleams of the eternal splendour shine;
  And from his inmost Spirit flow,
  As from a height of sunlit snow,
The rivers of perennial life,
To heal and sweeten Nature's strife.

3. The Lord is come! In every heart
  Where truth and mercy claim a part;
In every land where right is might,
And deeds of darkness shun the light;
  In every Church where faith and love
  Lift earthward thoughts to things above
In every holy, happy home,
We bless thee, Lord, that thou hast come.

The following are also suitable:

364 All hail the power of Jesu's name.
380 Come, ye faithful, raise the anthem.
381 Crown him with many crowns.
384 Eternal Ruler of the ceaseless round.
395 God of mercy, God of grace.
419 Jesu, the very thought of thee.
420 Jesus shall reign where'er the sun.
423 Judge eternal, throned in splendour,
459 O Love, how deep, how broad, how high.
481 Songs of praise the angels sang.
514 Who is this so weak and helpless.

FROM THE OCTAVE OF THE EPIPHANY TILL LENT

OFFICE HYMN. *Saturday*, E.
St. Ambrose, 340–97. Tr. C. B.

Deus Creator omnium.

CREATOR of the earth and sky,
　Ruling the firmament on high,
Clothing the day with robes of light,
Blessing with gracious sleep the night,

2 That rest may comfort weary men,
　And brace to useful toil again,
　And soothe awhile the harassed mind,
　And sorrow's heavy load unbind:

3 Day sinks; we thank thee for thy gift;
　Night comes; and once again we lift
　Our prayer and vows and hymns that
　Against all ills may shielded be. [we

4 Thee let the secret heart acclaim,
　Thee let our tuneful voices name,
　Round thee our chaste affections cling,
　Thee sober reason own as King.

FROM THE EPIPHANY TILL LENT

49 (MODERN TUNE)

ST. GREGORY (ZEUCH MEINEN GEIST). (L. M.) *From KÖNIG's Choralbuch (1738)*
Slow and solemn ♩ = 50. *(slightly altered).*

5 That when black darkness closes day,
And shadows thicken round our way,
Faith may no darkness know, and night
From faith's clear beam may borrow light.

6 Rest not, my heaven-born mind and will;
Rest, all ye thoughts and deeds of ill;
May faith its watch unwearied keep,
And cool the dreaming warmth of sleep.

7 From cheats of sense, Lord, keep me free,
And let my heart's depth dream of thee;
Let not my envious foe draw near,
To break my rest with any fear.

8. Pray we the Father and the Son,
And Holy Ghost: O Three in One,
Blest Trinity, whom all obey,
Guard thou thy sheep by night and day. Amen.

THE CHRISTIAN YEAR

50

Mode iv.   arr. J. H. A.

* *In some texts the B is flattened.*

OFFICE HYMN. *Sunday*, M.   *Ascribed to St. Gregory the Great,*
              Primo dierum omnium.   *6th cent. Tr. Y. H.*

THIS day the first of days was made,
   When God in light the world arrayed;
Or when his Word arose again,
And, conquering death, gave life to men.

2 Slumber and sloth drive far away;
   Earlier arise to greet the day;
   And ere its dawn in heaven unfold
   The heart's desire to God be told:

FROM THE EPIPHANY TILL LENT

ANDERNACH. (L. M.)   **50** (MODERN TUNE)

In moderate time, dignified ♩ = 78.
To be sung in unison.

Andernach Gesangbuch, 1608.

This tune is set in the Andernach Gesangbuch to the hymn 'Vexilla Regis' (No. 94).

3 Unto our prayer that he attend,
His all-creating power extend,
And still renew us, lest we miss
Through earthly stain our heavenly
    bliss.

4 That us, who here this day repair
To keep the Apostles' time of prayer,
And hymn the quiet hours of morn,
With blessèd gifts he may adorn.

5 For this, Redeemer, thee we pray
That thou wilt wash our sins away,
And of thy loving-kindness grant
Whate'er of good our spirits want:

6 That exiles here awhile in flesh
Some earnest may our souls refresh
Of that pure life for which we long,
Some foretaste of the heavenly song.

7. O Father, that we ask be done,
Through Jesus Christ, thine only Son;
Who, with the Holy Ghost and thee,
Doth live and reign eternally. Amen.

A - men.

THE CHRISTIAN YEAR

51

Mode viii.   arr. J. H. A.

* *In some texts the B is not flattened.*

OFFICE HYMN. *Sunday*, E.   *6th cent.* Tr. J. M. Neale.

Lucis Creator optime.

O BLEST Creator of the light,
  Who mak'st the day with radiance bright,
And o'er the forming world didst call
The light from chaos first of all;

2 Whose wisdom joined in meet array
  The morn and eve, and named them Day:
Night comes with all its darkling fears;
Regard thy people's prayers and tears,

FROM THE EPIPHANY TILL LENT

51 (Modern Tune)

LUCIS CREATOR. (L. M.)
In moderate time ♩ = 144. Unison.

Angers Church Melody.
Harmonized by Martin Shaw.

3 Lest, sunk in sin, and whelm'd with strife,
　They lose the gift of endless life;
　While thinking but the thoughts of time,
　They weave new chains of woe and crime.

4 But grant them grace that they may strain
　The heavenly gate and prize to gain:
　Each harmful lure aside to cast,
　And purge away each error past.

5. O Father, that we ask be done,
　Through Jesus Christ, thine only Son;
　Who, with the Holy Ghost and thee,
　Doth live and reign eternally.　Amen.

A - men.

A - - men.

THE CHRISTIAN YEAR

52, 53

Mode i.   arr. J. H. A.

WAREHAM. (L. M.)   (MODERN TUNE)   *Later version of melody by*
Very slow and dignified ♩ = 63.   W. KNAPP, 1698(?)–1768.

FROM THE EPIPHANY TILL LENT

52

OFFICE HYMN. St. Ambrose, 340–97. Tr. Y. H.
Monday Morning. Splendor paternae gloriae.

O SPLENDOUR of God's glory bright,
O thou that bringest light from light,
O Light of light, light's living spring,
O Day, all days illumining,

2 O thou true Sun, on us thy glance
Let fall in royal radiance,
The Spirit's sanctifying beam
Upon our earthly senses stream.

3 The Father, too, our prayers implore,
Father of glory evermore;
The Father of all grace and might,
To banish sin from our delight:

4 To guide whate'er we nobly do,
With love all envy to subdue,
To make ill-fortune turn to fair,
And give us grace our wrongs to bear.

5 Our mind be in his keeping placed,
Our body true to him and chaste,
Where only faith her fire shall feed,
To burn the tares of Satan's seed.

6 And Christ to us for food shall be,
From him our drink that welleth free,
The Spirit's wine, that maketh whole,
And, mocking not, exalts the soul.

7 Rejoicing may this day go hence,
Like virgin dawn our innocence,
Like fiery noon our faith appear,
Nor know the gloom of twilight drear.

8 Morn in her rosy car is borne;
Let him come forth our perfect morn,
The Word in God the Father one,
The Father perfect in the Son.

9. All laud to God the Father be,
All praise, eternal Son, to thee;
All glory, as is ever meet,
To God the holy Paraclete. Amen.

53

OFFICE HYMN. *Prudentius, b. 348. Tr. J. M. Neale.*
Tuesday Morning. Ales diei nuntius.

THE wingèd herald of the day
Proclaims the morn's approaching ray:
And Christ the Lord our souls excites,
And so to endless life invites.

2 Take up thy bed, to each he cries,
Who sick or wrapt in slumber lies;
And chaste and just and sober stand,
And watch: my coming is at hand.

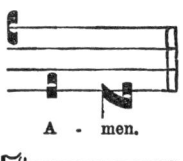

3 With earnest cry, with tearful care,
Call we the Lord to hear our prayer;
While supplication, pure and deep,
Forbids each chastened heart to sleep.

4 Do thou, O Christ, our slumbers wake;
Do thou the chains of darkness break;
Purge thou our former sins away,
And in our souls new light display.

5. All laud to God the Father be,
All praise, eternal Son, to thee;
All glory, as is ever meet,
To God the holy Paraclete. Amen.

A - men.

THE CHRISTIAN YEAR

54, 55

Mode i.   *arr.* J. H. A.

GAUDE, REGINA GLORIAE. (L.M.) (MODERN TUNE)   *Bohemian Brethren's Gesangbuch,*
In moderate time ♩ = 60.   1544. *Arr.* GEOFFREY SHAW.

NOTE.—*This hymn may also be sung to* WAREHAM (*No.* 52).

FROM THE EPIPHANY TILL LENT

54

OFFICE HYMN. *Prudentius, b. 348. Tr. R. M. P.*
Wednesday Morning. Nox et tenebrae et nubila.

YE clouds and darkness, hosts of night,
That breed confusion and affright,
Begone! o'erhead the dawn shines clear,
The light breaks in and Christ is here.

2 Earth's gloom flees broken and dispersed,
By the sun's piercing shafts coerced:
The day-star's eyes rain influence bright,
And colours glimmer back to sight.

3 Thee, Christ, alone we know; to thee
We bend in pure simplicity;
Our songs with tears to thee arise,
Prove thou our hearts with thy clear eyes.

4 Though we be stained with blots within,
Thy quickening rays shall purge our sin;
Light of the Morning Star, thy grace
Shed on us from thy cloudless face.

   5. All laud to God the Father be,
    All praise, eternal Son, to thee;
    All glory, as is ever meet,
    To God the holy Paraclete. Amen.

55

OFFICE HYMN. *Prudentius, b. 348. Tr. R. M. P.*
Thursday Morning. Lux ecce surgit aurea.

LO! golden light rekindles day:
Let paling darkness steal away,
Which all too long o'erwhelmed our gaze
And led our steps by winding ways.

2 We pray thee, rising Light serene,
E'en as thyself our hearts make clean;
Let no deceit our lips defile,
Nor let our souls be vexed by guile.

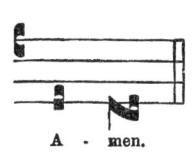

   3 O keep us, as the hours proceed,
    From lying word and evil deed;
    Our roving eyes from sin set free,
    Our body from impurity.

   4 For thou dost from above survey
    The converse of each fleeting day;
    Thou dost foresee from morning light
    Our every deed, until the night.

   5. All laud to God the Father be,
    All praise, eternal Son, to thee;
    All glory, as is ever meet,
    To God the holy Paraclete. Amen.

THE CHRISTIAN YEAR

56, 57

Mode iv.

Melody from the Guisborough Hymnal.
arr. J. H. A.

The proper Sarum melody is that given at No. 52.

RICHARD. (L. M.)   (MODERN TUNE)

Moderately slow ♩ = 63.

MORFYDD OWEN, 1892–1918.

NOTE.—*This hymn may also be sung to* WAREHAM (*No.* 52).

FROM THE EPIPHANY TILL LENT

56

OFFICE HYMN. *Friday Morning.* Aeterna caeli gloria. *6th cent. Tr. J. M. Neale.*

ETERNAL Glory of the sky,
Blest hope of frail humanity,
The Father's sole-begotten One,
Yet born a spotless Virgin's Son!

2 Uplift us with thine arm of might,
And let our hearts rise pure and bright,
And, ardent in God's praises, pay
The thanks we owe him every day.

3 The day-star's rays are glittering clear,
And tell that day itself is near:
The shadows of the night depart;
Thou, holy Light, illume the heart!

4 Within our senses ever dwell,
And worldly darkness thence expel;
Long as the days of life endure,
Preserve our souls devout and pure.

5 The faith that first must be possest,
Root deep within our inmost breast;
And joyous hope in second place,
Then charity, thy greatest grace.

6. All laud to God the Father be,
All praise, eternal Son, to thee;
All glory, as is ever meet,
To God the holy Paraclete. **Amen.**

57

OFFICE HYMN. *Saturday Morning.* Aurora jam spargit polum. *Before 8th cent. Tr. E. Caswall.*

THE dawn is sprinkling in the east
Its golden shower, as day flows in;
Fast mount the pointed shafts of light:
Farewell to darkness and to sin!

2 Away, ye midnight phantoms all!
Away, despondence and despair!
Whatever guilt the night has brought
Now let it vanish into air.

3 So, Lord, when that last morning breaks,
Looking to which we sigh and pray,
O may it to thy minstrels prove
The dawning of a better day.

4. To God the Father glory be,
And to his sole-begotten Son;
Glory, O Holy Ghost, to thee
While everlasting ages run. **Amen.**

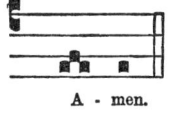

THE CHRISTIAN YEAR
58, 59, 60

Mode ii.
arr. J. H. A.

(MODERN TUNE)

O INVIDENDA MARTYRUM. (L. M.)
In moderate time ♩ = 144. To be sung in unison.

Dijon Church Melody.
Harmonized by R. V. W.

NOTE.—*This hymn may also be sung to* ILLSLEY (No. 61).

FROM THE EPIPHANY TILL LENT

58

OFFICE HYMN.
Monday Evening.   Immense caeli Conditor.   *c. 6th cent.*   *Tr. G. G.*

O BOUNDLESS Wisdom, God most
O Maker of the earth and sky, [high,
Who bid'st the parted waters flow
In heaven above, on earth below:

2 The streams on earth, the clouds in heaven, [given,
By thee their ordered bounds were
Lest 'neath the untempered fires of day
The parchèd soil should waste away.

3 E'en so on us who seek thy face
Pour forth the waters of thy grace;
Renew the fount of life within,
And quench the wasting fires of sin.

4 Let faith discern the eternal Light
Beyond the darkness of the night,
And through the mists of falsehood see
The path of truth revealed by thee.

5. O Father, that we ask be done,
Through Jesus Christ, thine only Son;
Who, with the Holy Ghost and thee,
Doth live and reign eternally. Amen.

59

OFFICE HYMN.
Tuesday Evening.   Telluris ingens Conditor.   *c. 7th cent.*   *Tr. Anon.* (1854).

EARTH'S mighty Maker, whose command
Raised from the sea the solid land,
And drove each billowy heap away,
And bade the earth stand firm for aye:

2 That so, with flowers of golden hue,
The seeds of each it might renew;
And fruit-trees bearing fruit might yield—
And pleasant pasture of the field;

3 Our spirit's rankling wounds efface
With dewy freshness of thy grace:
That grief may cleanse each deed of ill,
And o'er each lust may triumph still.

4 Let every soul thy law obey,
And keep from every evil way;
Rejoice each promised good to win
And flee from every mortal sin.

5. O Father, that we ask be done,
Through Jesus Christ, thine only Son;
Who, with the Holy Ghost and thee,
Doth live and reign eternally. Amen.

60

OFFICE HYMN.
Wednesday Evening.   Caeli Deus sanctissime.   *4th or 5th cent.*   *Tr. M. F. B.*

MOST holy Lord and God of heaven,
Who to the glowing sky hast given
The fires that in the east are born
With gradual splendours of the morn;

2 Who, on the fourth day, didst reveal
The sun's enkindled flaming wheel,
Didst set the moon her ordered ways,
And stars their ever-winding maze;

3 That each in its appointed way
Might separate the night from day,
And of the seasons through the year
The well-remembered signs declare:

4 Illuminate our hearts within, [sin;
And cleanse our minds from stain of
Unburdened of our guilty load
May we unfettered serve our God.

5. O Father, that we ask be done,
Through Jesus Christ, thine only Son;
Who, with the Holy Ghost and thee,
Doth live and reign eternally. Amen.

A - men.

A - - men.

THE CHRISTIAN YEAR

61, 62

Source uncertain; probably English.
arr. J. H. A.

Mode ii.

The Sarum proper melody is given at No. 58.

ILLSLEY. (L.M.)   (MODERN TUNE)   J. BISHOP, *c.* 1665–1737.
Slow ♩ = 56.

FROM THE EPIPHANY TILL LENT

61

OFFICE HYMN.   *6th or 7th cent.*   *Tr. J. M. Neale* ‡.
Thursday Evening.   Magnae Deus potentiae.

1. ALMIGHTY God, who from the flood
Didst bring to light a twofold brood;
Part in the firmament to fly,
And part in ocean's depths to lie;

2. Appointing fishes in the sea,
And fowls in open air to be,
That each, by origin the same,
Its separate dwelling-place might claim:

3. Grant that thy servants, by the tide
Of Blood and water purified,
No guilty fall from thee may know,
Nor death eternal undergo.

4. Be none submerged in sin's distress,
None lifted up in boastfulness;
That contrite hearts be not dismayed,
Nor haughty souls in ruin laid.

5. O Father, that we ask be done,
Through Jesus Christ, thine only Son;
Who, with the Holy Ghost and thee,
Doth live and reign eternally. Amen.

62

OFFICE HYMN.   *c. 7th cent.*   *Tr. J. D. Chambers* ‡.
Friday Evening.   Plasmator hominis, Deus.

1. MAKER of man, who from thy throne
Dost order all things, God alone;
By whose decree the teeming earth
To reptile and to beast gave birth:

2. The mighty forms that fill the land,
Instinct with life at thy command,
Are given subdued to humankind
For service in their rank assigned.

3. From all thy servants drive away
Whate'er of thought impure to-day
Hath been with open action blent,
Or mingled with the heart's intent.

4. In heaven thine endless joys bestow,
And grant thy gifts of grace below;
From chains of strife our souls release,
Bind fast the gentle bands of peace.

5. O Father, that we ask be done,
Through Jesus Christ, thine only Son;
Who, with the Holy Ghost and thee,
Doth live and reign eternally. Amen.

(*Until Candlemas the Doxology of No.* 36 *may be used for Nos.* 50–62.)

THE CHRISTIAN YEAR

TANTUM ERGO. (8 7. 8 7. 8 7.) **63**
Moderately slow, dignified ♩ = 66.

Melody from S. WEBBE'S
'*Motetts or Antiphons*', 1792.

THE WEEK BEFORE SEPTUAGESIMA

Before 11th cent. Tr. J. M. Neale.

Alleluya, dulce carmen.

ALLELUYA, song of sweetness,
  Voice of joy, eternal lay;
Alleluya is the anthem
  Of the choirs in heavenly day,
Which the Angels sing, abiding
  In the house of God alway.

2 Alleluya, thou resoundest,
  Salem, mother, ever blest;
Alleluyas without ending,
  Fit yon place of gladsome rest;
Exiles we, by Babel's waters,
  Sit in bondage and distrest.

3 Alleluya we deserve not
  Here to chant for evermore:
Alleluya our transgressions
  Make us for awhile give o'er;
For the holy time is coming,
  Bidding us our sins deplore.

4. Trinity of endless glory,
  Hear thy people as they cry;
Grant us all to keep thy Easter
  In our home beyond the sky;
There to thee our Alleluya
  Singing everlastingly. Amen.

SEPTUAGESIMA TO LENT

DUNFERMLINE. (C. M.)
Moderately slow ♩ = 66.

64

Scottish Psalter, 1615.

C. Coffin, 1676-1749.   *Tr. J. M. Neale.*

Te laeta, mundi Conditor.

MAKER of earth, to thee alone
   Perpetual rest belongs;
And the bright choirs around thy throne
   May pour their endless songs.

2 But we,—ah holy now no more!
   Are doomed to toil and pain;
Yet exiles on an alien shore
   May sing their country's strain.

3 Father, whose promise binds thee still
   To heal the suppliant throng,
Grant us to mourn the deeds of ill
   That banish us so long;

4 And, while we mourn, in faith to rest
   Upon thy love and care,
Till thou restore us with the blest
   The song of heaven to share.

5. O God the Father, God the Son,
   And God the Holy Ghost,
To thee be praise, great Three in One,
   From thy created host.   Amen.

A - men.

The following are also suitable:

459 O Love, how deep, how broad, how high.
470 Praise, my soul, the King.
497 There is a book who runs may read.

THE CHRISTIAN YEAR

65

Mode ii.   *arr.* J. H. A.

A - men.

LENT

OFFICE HYMN. E.   *Till Lent* iii.   *c. 6th cent.*   *Tr.* J. M. Neale.
Ex more docti mystico.

1 THE fast, as taught by holy lore,
    We keep in solemn course once
      more:
The fast to all men known, and bound
In forty days of yearly round.

2 The law and seers that were of old
   In divers ways this Lent foretold,
Which Christ, all seasons' King and
    guide,
In after ages sanctified.

LENT

JESU CORONA. (L. M.)
In moderate time ♩ = 144.
To be sung in unison.

65 (MODERN TUNE)

Rouen Church Melody.
Harmonized by R. V. W.

3 More sparing therefore let us make
  The words we speak, the food we take,
  Our sleep and mirth,—and closer barred
  Be every sense in holy guard.

4 In prayer together let us fall,
  And cry for mercy, one and all,
  And weep before the Judge's feet,
  And his avenging wrath entreat.

5 Thy grace have we offended sore,
  By sins, O God, which we deplore;
  But pour upon us from on high,
  O pardoning One, thy clemency.

6 Remember thou, though frail we be,
  That yet thine handiwork are we;
  Nor let the honour of thy name
  Be by another put to shame.

7 Forgive the sin that we have wrought;
  Increase the good that we have sought;
  That we at length, our wanderings o'er,
  May please thee here and evermore.

8. We pray thee, Holy Trinity,
  One God, unchanging Unity,
  That we from this our abstinence
  May reap the fruits of penitence. Amen.

A . . . men.

THE CHRISTIAN YEAR

66

Mode ii. arr. J. H. A.

A - men.

Office Hymn. M. *Till Lent* iii.　　Asc. to St. *Gregory the Great, 6th cent.* Tr. *T. A. L.*
Audi, benigne Conditor.

O KIND Creator, bow thine ear
　To mark the cry, to know the tear
Before thy throne of mercy spent
In this thy holy fast of Lent.

2 Our hearts are open, Lord, to thee:
　Thou knowest our infirmity;
　Pour out on all who seek thy face
　Abundance of thy pardoning grace.

LENT

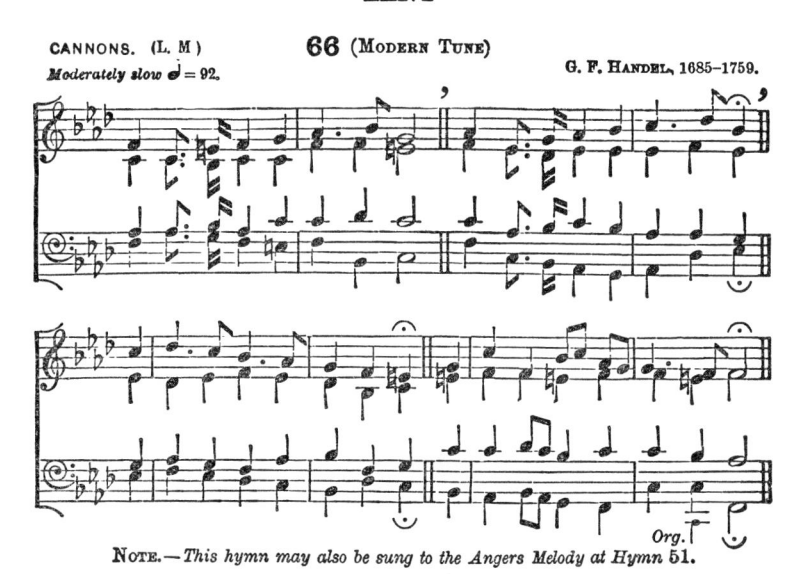

CANNONS. (L. M.)   **66** (MODERN TUNE)

Moderately slow ♩ = 92.

G. F. HANDEL, 1685–1759.

NOTE.—*This hymn may also be sung to the Angers Melody at Hymn* 51.

3 Our sins are many, this we know;
Spare us, good Lord, thy mercy show;
And for the honour of thy name
Our fainting souls to life reclaim.

4 Give us the self-control that springs
From discipline of outward things,
That fasting inward secretly
The soul may purely dwell with thee.

5. We pray thee, Holy Trinity,
One God, unchanging Unity,
That we from this our abstinence
May reap the fruits of penitence. Amen.

A - men.

THE CHRISTIAN YEAR

67

Mode iii. arr. J. H. A.

A - men.

Office Hymn. E. *Lent iii. till Passion Sunday.* Before 12th cent. Tr. T. A. L.
Ecce tempus idoneum.

1. NOW is the healing time decreed
For sins of heart, of word or deed,
When we in humble fear record
The wrong that we have done the Lord;

2. Who, alway merciful and good,
Has borne so long our wayward mood.
Nor cut us off unsparingly
In our so great iniquity.

LENT

67 (MODERN TUNE)

JENA (DAS NEUGEBORNE KINDELEIN). (L. M.)

In moderate time ♩ = 69.   Later form of melody from VULPIUS' *Gesangbuch* (Jena, 1609).

NOTE.—*This hymn may also be sung to* BABYLON'S STREAMS (*No.* 487).

3 Therefore with fasting and with prayer,
Our secret sorrow we declare;
With all good striving seek his face,
And lowly hearted plead for grace.

4 Cleanse us, O Lord, from every stain,
Help us the meed of praise to gain,
Till with the Angels linked in love
Joyful we tread thy courts above.

5. Father and Son and Spirit blest,
To thee be every prayer addrest,
Who art in threefold Name adored,
From age to age, the only Lord.
    Amen.

A - men.

THE CHRISTIAN YEAR

68

Mode ii.   arr. J. H. A.

A- men.

OFFICE HYMN.   M.   *Lent iii. till Passion Sunday.*   *Ascr. to St. Gregory the Great,*
                                                                                         6th cent.   *Tr. M. F. B.*

Clarum decus jejunii.

THE glory of these forty days
   We celebrate with songs of praise;
For Christ, by whom all things were made,
Himself has fasted and has prayed.

LENT

68 (MODERN TUNE)

ERHALT' UNS, HERR. (L.M.)
Very slow and solemn ♩ = 46.

Later form of melody from Klug, Geistliche Lieder, 1547.
Harmony from J. S. Bach.

NOTE.—*This hymn may also be sung to the Rouen Melody at Hymn 65.*

2 Alone and fasting Moses saw
The loving God who gave the Law;
And to Elijah, fasting, came
The steeds and chariots of flame.

3 So Daniel trained his mystic sight,
Delivered from the lions' might;
And John, the Bridegroom's friend, became
The herald of Messiah's name.

4 Then grant us, Lord, like them to be
Full oft in fast and prayer with thee;
Our spirits strengthen with thy grace,
And give us joy to see thy face.

5. Father and Son and Spirit blest,
To thee be every prayer addrest,
Who art in threefold Name adored,
From age to age, the only Lord. Amen.

A - men.

THE CHRISTIAN YEAR

69

Mode iv.   *   arr. J. H. A.

A . men.

* *In some texts the B is flattened.*

OFFICE HYMN.   M.   *Lent* iii. *till Passion Sunday.*   c. 9th cent.   Tr. T. A. L.

Jesu, quadragenariae.

1. O JESU Christ, from thee began
This healing for the soul of man,
By fasting sought, by fasting found,
Through forty days of yearly round;

2. That he who fell from high delight,
Borne down to sensual appetite,
By dint of stern control may rise
To climb the hills of Paradise.

LENT

69 (MODERN TUNE)

PLAISTOW. (L. M.)
Slow ♩ = 58.

From 'Magdalen Hymns,' 1760 (?).

3 Therefore behold thy Church, O Lord,
And grace of penitence accord
To all who seek with generous tears
Renewal of their wasted years.

4 Forgive the sin that we have done,
Forgive the course that we have run,
And show henceforth in evil day
Thyself our succour and our stay.

5 But now let every heart prepare,
By sacrifice of fast and prayer,
To keep with joy magnifical
The solemn Easter festival.

6. Father and Son and Spirit blest,
To thee be every prayer addrest,
Who art in threefold Name adored,
From age to age, the only Lord.
     Amen.

A - men.

THE CHRISTIAN YEAR

HERZLIEBSTER JESU. (11 11. 11 5.) **70**
Very slow and solemn ♩ = 46.

Melody by J. CRÜGER, 1598–1662.

[*May be sung in unison throughout.*]

J. Heermann, 1585–1647. Tr. Y. H.

Herzliebster Jesu.

AH, holy Jesu, how hast thou offended,
That man to judge thee hath in hate pretended?
By foes derided, by thine own rejected,
   O most afflicted.

2 Who was the guilty? Who brought this upon thee?
Alas, my treason, Jesu, hath undone thee.
'Twas I, Lord Jesu, I it was denied thee:
   I crucified thee.

A - men.

LENT

70 (ALTERNATIVE VERSION)

*Harmonized by J. S. BACH in the
'Passion according to St. Matthew.'*

[*This version may be used in connexion with the other in those verses only where the* CHOIR SINGS ALONE. *This version should only be attempted by good choirs.*]

3 Lo, the good Shepherd for the sheep is offered;
The slave hath sinnèd, and the Son hath suffered;
For man's atonement, while he nothing heedeth,
                God intercedeth.

4 For me, kind Jesu, was thy incarnation,
Thy mortal sorrow, and thy life's oblation;
Thy death of anguish and thy bitter passion,
                For my salvation.

5. Therefore, kind Jesu, since I cannot pay thee,
I do adore thee, and will ever pray thee,
Think on thy pity and thy love unswerving,
                Not my deserving.

THE CHRISTIAN YEAR

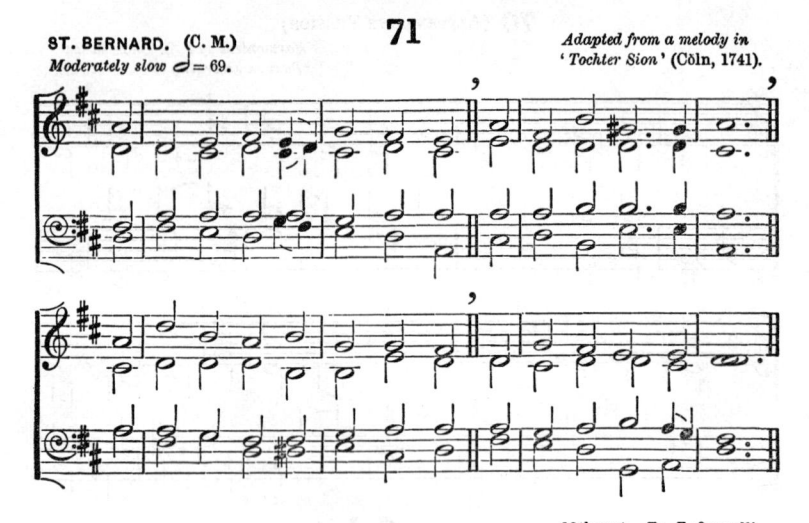

ST. BERNARD. (C. M.)
Moderately slow ♩= 69.

71

Adapted from a melody in
'Tochter Sion' (Cöln, 1741).

18th cent. Tr. E. Caswall‡.

Quicumque certum quaeritis.

ALL ye who seek a comfort sure
  In trouble and distress,
Whatever sorrow vex the mind,
  Or guilt the soul oppress,

2 Jesus, who gave himself for you
    Upon the Cross to die,
  Opens to you his sacred Heart;
    O to that Heart draw nigh.

3 Ye hear how kindly he invites;
    Ye hear his words so blest—
  'All ye that labour come to me,
    And I will give you rest.'

4 O Jesus, joy of Saints on high,
    Thou hope of sinners here,
  Attracted by those loving words
    To thee I lift my prayer.

5. Wash thou my wounds in that dear Blood
    Which forth from thee doth flow;
  New grace, new hope inspire, a new
    And better heart bestow.

A - men.

LENT

72

GUTE BÄUME BRINGEN. (6 5. 6 5. D.)
Moderately fast ♩ = 108.

Later form of melody by
P. SOHREN, *d. c.* 1692.

J. M. Neale, 1818–66. *From the Greek.*

CHRISTIAN, dost thou see them
　On the holy ground,
How the troops of Midian
　Prowl and prowl around?
Christian, up and smite them,
　Counting gain but loss;
Smite them by the merit
　Of the holy Cross.

2 Christian, dost thou feel them,
　　How they work within,
　Striving, tempting, luring,
　　Goading into sin?
　Christian, never tremble;
　　Never be down-cast;
　Smite them by the virtue
　　Of the Lenten fast.

3 Christian, dost thou hear them,
　　How they speak thee fair?
　'Always fast and vigil?
　　Always watch and prayer?'
　Christian, answer boldly,
　　'While I breathe, I pray:'
　Peace shall follow battle,
　　Night shall end in day.

4. 'Well I know thy trouble,
　　O my servant true;
　Thou art very weary,—
　　I was weary too;
　But that toil shall make thee
　　Some day all mine own,—
　But the end of sorrow
　　Shall be near my throne.'

A - men.

107

THE CHRISTIAN YEAR

73

AUS DER TIEFE. (77. 77.)
Slow ♩ = 54.

Probably by MARTIN HERBST, 1654–81.

G. H. Smyttan, 1825–70, and F. Pott.

FORTY days and forty nights
  Thou wast fasting in the wild;
Forty days and forty nights
  Tempted, and yet undefiled:

2 Sunbeams scorching all the day;
  Chilly dew-drops nightly shed;
Prowling beasts about thy way;
  Stones thy pillow, earth thy bed.

3 Shall not we thy watchings share,
  And from earthly joys abstain,
Fasting with unceasing prayer,
  Glad with thee to suffer pain?

4 And if Satan, vexing sore,
  Flesh or spirit should assail,
Thou, his vanquisher before,
  Grant we may not faint nor fail.

5 So shall we have peace divine;
  Holier gladness ours shall be;
Round us too shall Angels shine,
  Such as ministered to thee.

6. Keep, O keep us, Saviour dear,
  Ever constant by thy side;
That with thee we may appear
  At the eternal Eastertide.

A - men.

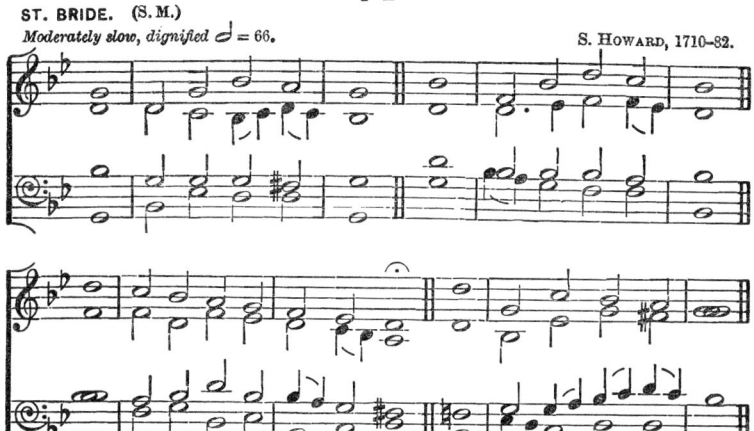

LENT

74

ST. BRIDE. (S.M.)
Moderately slow, dignified ♩ = 66.

S. HOWARD, 1710-82.

Ps. 51. N. Tate and N. Brady. (New Version, 1698.)

HAVE mercy, Lord, on me,
As thou wert ever kind;
Let me, opprest with loads of guilt,
Thy wonted mercy find.

2 Wash off my foul offence,
And cleanse me from my sin;
For I confess my crime, and see
How great my guilt has been.

3 The joy thy favour gives
Let me again obtain,
And thy free Spirit's firm support
My fainting soul sustain.

4. To God the Father, Son,
And Spirit glory be,
As 'twas, and is, and shall be so
To all eternity. Amen.

A - men.

THE CHRISTIAN YEAR

75 (First Tune)

ST. RAPHAEL. (8 7. 8 7. 4 7.)
In moderate time ♩ = 69.
E. J. Hopkins, 1818–1901.

J. J. *Cummins* ‡, 1795–1867.

JESU, Lord of life and glory,
  Bend from heaven thy gracious ear;
While our waiting souls adore thee,
  Friend of helpless sinners, hear:
    By thy mercy,
  O deliver us, good Lord.

2*Taught by thine unerring Spirit
    Boldly we draw nigh to God,
  Only in thy spotless merit,
    Only through thy precious Blood:
      By thy mercy,
    O deliver us, good Lord.

3 From the depth of nature's blindness,
    From the hardening power of sin,
  From all malice and unkindness,
    From the pride that lurks within:
      By thy mercy,
    O deliver us, good Lord.

4 When temptation sorely presses,
    In the day of Satan's power,
  In our times of deep distresses,
    In each dark and trying hour:
      By thy mercy,
    O deliver us, good Lord.

LENT

75 (Second Tune)

LLANILAR. (8 7. 8 7. 4 7.)
Moderately slow ♩ = 63.
Welsh Hymn Melody.

5* In the weary hours of sickness,
  In the times of grief and pain,
When we feel our mortal weakness,
  When the creature's help is vain :
    By thy mercy,
    O deliver us, good Lord.

6 In the solemn hour of dying,
  In the awful judgement day,
May our souls, on thee relying,
  Find thee still our rock and stay :
    By thy mercy,
    O deliver us, good Lord.

7. Jesu, may thy promised blessing
  Comfort to our souls afford ;
May we now, thy love possessing,
  And at length our full reward,
    Ever praise thee,
    Thee, our ever-glorious Lord.

A - men.

A - men.

THE CHRISTIAN YEAR

76

HEILIGER GEIST (BERLIN). (7.7.7.)
Very slow and solemn ♩ = 63.

J. CRÜGER, 1598–1662.

Ped. in vv. 4 and 5.

NOTE.—*Another tune for this hymn will be found in the Appendix (No. 10).*

Isaac Williams‡, 1802–65.

LORD, in this thy mercy's day,
　Ere it pass for ay away,
On our knees we fall and pray.

2 Holy Jesu, grant us tears,
　Fill us with heart-searching fears,
　Ere that awful doom appears.

3 Lord, on us thy Spirit pour,
　Kneeling lowly at the door,
　Ere it close for evermore.

4 By thy night of agony,
　By thy supplicating cry,
　By thy willingness to die;

5 By thy tears of bitter woe
　For Jerusalem below,
　Let us not thy love forgo.

6. Grant us 'neath thy wings a place,
　Lest we lose this day of grace,
　Ere we shall behold thy face.

A - men.

LENT

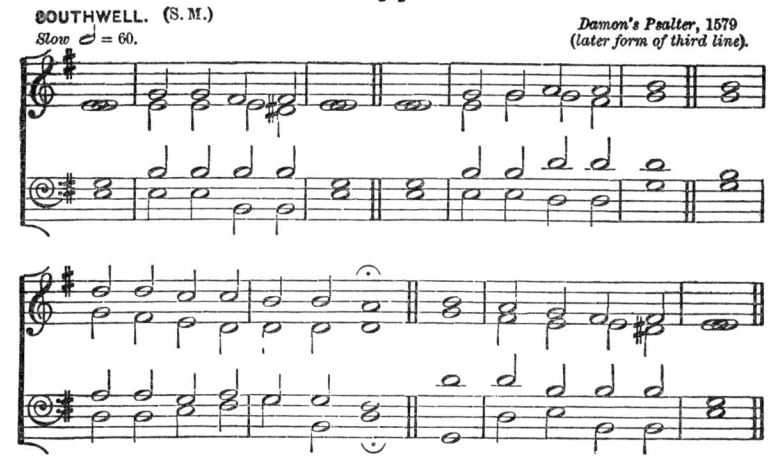

77

SOUTHWELL. (S. M.)
Slow ♩ = 60.

Damon's Psalter, 1579
(later form of third line).

Bp. Synesius, 375-430. Tr. A. W. Chatfield.

Μνώεο, Χριστέ.

LORD Jesus, think on me,
  And purge away my sin;
From earthborn passions set me free,
  And make me pure within.

2 Lord Jesus, think on me,
    With care and woe opprest;
  Let me thy loving servant be,
    And taste thy promised rest.

3 Lord Jesus, think on me,
    Amid the battle's strife;
  In all my pain and misery
    Be thou my health and life.

4 Lord Jesus, think on me,
    Nor let me go astray;
  Through darkness and perplexity
    Point thou the heavenly way.

5 Lord Jesus, think on me,
    When flows the tempest high:
  When on doth rush the enemy
    O Saviour, be thou nigh.

6. Lord Jesus, think on me,
    That, when the flood is past,
  I may the eternal brightness see,
    And share thy joy at last.

A - men.

THE CHRISTIAN YEAR

78

FIRST MODE MELODY. (D.C.M.)
Moderately slow ♩=84.

T. TALLIS, *c.* 1510-85.
Harmony slightly adapted.

NOTE.—*This hymn may also be sung to a* C. M. *tune.* WINDSOR (*No.* 332) *or* ST. PETER (*No.* 405) *are suitable.*

J. Montgomery, 1771-1854.

LORD, teach us how to pray aright
With reverence and with fear;
Though dust and ashes in thy sight,
We may, we must draw near.

2 We perish if we cease from prayer;
O grant us power to pray;
And when to meet thee we prepare,
Lord, meet us by the way.

3 God of all grace, we come to thee
With broken contrite hearts;
Give, what thine eye delights to see,
Truth in the inward parts;

4 Faith in the only sacrifice
That can for sin atone;
To cast our hopes, to fix our eyes,
On Christ, on Christ alone;

5 Patience to watch, and wait, and weep,
Though mercy long delay;
Courage our fainting souls to keep,
And trust thee though thou slay.

6. Give these, and then thy will be done;
Thus, strengthened with all might,
We, through thy Spirit and thy Son,
Shall pray, and pray aright.

LENT

79

HUNNYS. (C. M.)
Moderately slow ♩ = 80.

Melody in 'Seven Sobs of a Sorrowful Soul,' 1585.

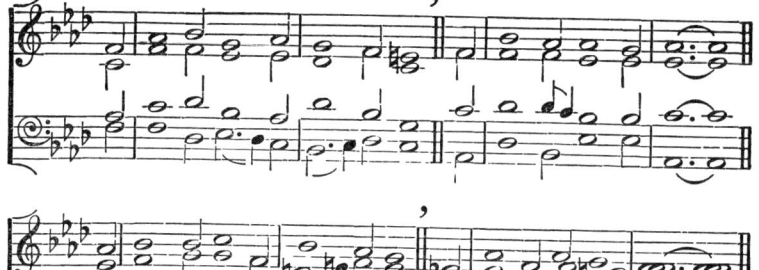

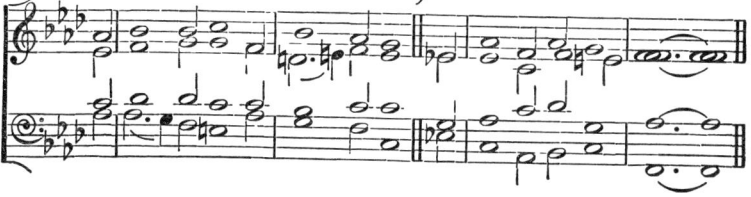

J. D. Carlyle, 1758–1804.

LORD, when we bend before thy throne,
   And our confessions pour,
Teach us to feel the sins we own,
   And hate what we deplore.

2 Our broken spirits pitying see,
   And penitence impart;
Then let a kindling glance from thee
   Beam hope upon the heart.

3 When we disclose our wants in prayer
   May we our wills resign,
And not a thought our bosom share
   That is not wholly thine.

4. Let faith each meek petition fill,
   And waft it to the skies;
And teach our hearts 'tis goodness still
   That grants it or denies.

A - men.

THE CHRISTIAN YEAR

80

SOLOMON. (C.M.)
In moderate time ♩ = 72.

Adapted from the Air 'What tho' I trace.'
G. F. HANDEL, 1685–1759.

O Deus, ego amo te.   *17th cent. Tr. E. Caswall†*

MY God, I love thee; not because
  I hope for heaven thereby,
Nor yet because who love thee not
  Are lost eternally.

2 Thou, O my Jesus, thou didst me
    Upon the Cross embrace;
  For me didst bear the nails and spear,
    And manifold disgrace,

3 And griefs and torments numberless,
    And sweat of agony;
  E'en death itself; and all for one
    Who was thine enemy.

4 Then why, O blessèd Jesu Christ,
    Should I not love thee well,
  Not for the sake of winning heaven,
    Or of escaping hell;

5 Not with the hope of gaining aught,
    Not seeking a reward;
  But as thyself hast lovèd me,
    O ever-loving Lord!

6. E'en so I love thee, and will love,
    And in thy praise will sing,
  Solely because thou art my God,
    And my eternal King.

A - men.

LENT

81

ST. BARTHOLOMEW. (L. M.)
In moderate time ♩ = 92.

HENRY DUNCALF (1762).

The proper plainsong tune for this hymn is given in the Appendix, No. 1.
NOTE.—*This hymn may also be sung to* ALFRETON (*No.* 240).

Compline.

Christe qui lux es et dies.

Before 800. *Tr. W. J. Copeland and others.*

O CHRIST, who art the Light and Day,
   Thou drivest darksome night away!
We know thee as the Light of light,
Illuminating mortal sight.

2 All-holy Lord, we pray to thee,
   Keep us to-night from danger free;
Grant us, dear Lord, in thee to rest,
So be our sleep in quiet blest.

3 And while the eyes soft slumber take,
   Still be the heart to thee awake;
Be thy right hand upheld above
Thy servants resting in thy love.

4 Yea, our Defender, be thou nigh
   To bid the powers of darkness fly;
Keep us from sin, and guide for good
Thy servants purchased by thy Blood.

5 Remember us, dear Lord, we pray,
   While in this mortal flesh we stay:
'Tis thou who dost the soul defend—
Be present with us to the end.

6 Blest Three in One and One in Three,
   Almighty God, we pray to thee
That thou wouldst now vouchsafe to bless
Our fast with fruits of righteousness. Amen.

A - men.

THE CHRISTIAN YEAR

82

STOCKTON. (C. M.)
In moderate time ♩=76.

T. WRIGHT, 1763–1829.

C. Wesley, 1707–88

O FOR a heart to praise my God,
 A heart from sin set free;
A heart that always feels thy Blood
 So freely spilt for me:

2 A heart resigned, submissive, meek,
 My dear Redeemer's throne;
Where only Christ is heard to speak,
 Where Jesus reigns alone:

3 A humble, lowly, contrite heart,
 Believing, true, and clean,
Which neither life nor death can part
 From him that dwells within:

4 A heart in every thought renewed,
 And full of love divine;
Perfect, and right, and pure, and good,
 A copy, Lord, of thine.

5 My heart, thou know'st, can never rest
 Till thou create my peace;
Till of mine Eden repossest,
 From self, and sin, I cease.

6. Thy nature, gracious Lord, impart,
 Come quickly from above;
Write thy new name upon my heart,
 Thy new best name of love.

A - men.

LENT

BEDFORD. (C. M.) — **83** — *Original form of melody by*
Very slow and dignified ♩ = 63. W. WEALE, d. 1727.

NOTE.—*This tune is sometimes sung in duple time. To effect this all the semibreves must be counted as minims.*

H. H. Milman, 1791-1868.

O HELP us, Lord; each hour of need
   Thy heavenly succour give;
Help us in thought, and word, and deed,
   Each hour on earth we live.

2 O help us, when our spirits bleed
   With contrite anguish sore,
And when our hearts are cold and dead,
   O help us, Lord, the more.

3 O help us through the prayer of faith
   More firmly to believe;
For still the more the servant hath,
   The more shall he receive.

4. O help us, Jesu, from on high,
   We know no help but thee;
O help us so to live and die
   As thine in heaven to be.

A - men.

THE CHRISTIAN YEAR

84

ST. MARY. (C.M.)
Slow ♩ = 56.

Prys' Psalter, 1621
(as given in Playford's 'Psalms,' 1677).

J. Marckant (Old Version, 1560).

O LORD, turn not away thy face
  From him that lies prostrate,
Lamenting sore his sinful life
  Before thy mercy-gate;

2 Which gate thou openest wide to those
    That do lament their sin:
  Shut not that gate against me, Lord,
    But let me enter in.

3 And call me not to mine account
    How I have livèd here;
  For then I know right well, O Lord,
    How vile I shall appear.

4 So come I to thy mercy-gate,
    Where mercy doth abound,
  Requiring mercy for my sin
    To heal my deadly wound.

5. Mercy, good Lord, mercy I ask,
    This is the total sum;
  For mercy, Lord, is all my suit:
    Lord, let thy mercy come.

A - men.

LENT

HARINGTON (RETIREMENT). (C. M.) **85**

Moderately slow ♩ = 80.

H. HARINGTON, 1727–1816.

T. Haweis, 1732–1820, and others.

O THOU from whom all goodness flows,
  I lift my heart to thee;
In all my sorrows, conflicts, woes,
  Dear Lord, remember me.

2 When on my poor distressèd heart
    My sins lie heavily,
  Thy pardon grant, new peace impart:
    Dear Lord, remember me.

3 When trials sore obstruct my way,
    And ills I cannot flee,
  O let my strength be as my day:
    Dear Lord, remember me.

4 If, for thy sake, upon my name
    Shame and reproaches be,
  All hail reproach and welcome shame:
    Dear Lord, remember me.

5 If worn with pain, disease, or grief
    This feeble spirit be;
  Grant patience, rest, and kind relief:
    Dear Lord, remember me.

6. And O, when in the hour of death
    I wait thy just decree,
  Be this the prayer of my last breath:
    Dear Lord, remember me.

A - men.

THE CHRISTIAN YEAR

86

INNSBRUCK. (776.778.)
Very slow and solemn ♩ = 42.

Traditional German Melody.
Adapted and harmonized by J. S. BACH.

LENT

J. W. Hewett and others. Based on
Summi largitor praemii, *c. 6th cent.*

O THOU who dost accord us
　The highest prize and guerdon,
　　Thou hope of all our race,
Jesu, do thou afford us
　The gift we ask of pardon
　　For all who humbly seek thy face.

2 With whispered accusation
　　Our conscience tells of sinning
　　　In thought, and word, and deed;
Thine is our restoration,
　　The work of grace beginning
　　　For souls from every burthen freed.

3 For who, if thou reject us,
　　Shall raise the fainting spirit?
　　　'Tis thine alone to spare:
If thou to life elect us,
　　With cleansèd hearts to near it,
　　　Shall be our task, our lowly prayer.

4. O Trinity most glorious,
　　Thy pardon free bestowing,
　　　Defend us evermore;
That in thy courts victorious,
　　Thy love more truly knowing,
　　　We may with all thy Saints adore.

THE CHRISTIAN YEAR

ABERYSTWYTH. (77.77. D.) **87**
Slow ♩ = 58.
JOSEPH PARRY, 1841-1903.

[By permission of Messrs. Hughes & Son, Wrexham.]
Sir R. Grant, 1785-1838.

SAVIOUR, when in dust to thee
Low we bow the adoring knee;
When repentant, to the skies
Scarce we lift our weeping eyes:
O, by all thy pains and woe,
Suffered once for man below,
Bending from thy throne on high,
Hear our solemn Litany.

2 By thy helpless infant years,
By thy life of want and tears,
By thy days of sore distress
In the savage wilderness,
By the dread mysterious hour
Of the insulting tempter's power:
Turn, O turn a favouring eye,
Hear our solemn Litany.

3 By the sacred griefs that wept
O'er the grave where Lazarus slept;
By the boding tears that flowed
Over Salem's loved abode;
By the anguished sigh that told
Treachery lurked within thy fold:
From thy seat above the sky
Hear our solemn Litany.

LENT

4 By thine hour of dire despair,
 By thine agony of prayer,
 By the Cross, the nail, the thorn,
 Piercing spear and torturing scorn;
 By the gloom that veiled the skies
 O'er the dreadful Sacrifice:
 Listen to our humble cry,
 Hear our solemn Litany.

5. By thy deep expiring groan,
 By the sad sepulchral stone,
 By the vault whose dark abode
 Held in vain the rising God;
 O! from earth to heaven restored,
 Mighty reascended Lord,
 Listen, listen to the cry
 Of our solemn Litany.

88

TUNBRIDGE. (77.77.)
Moderately slow ♩ = 63.

J. Clark, 1670–1707.

J. S. B. Monsell, 1811–75.

SINFUL, sighing to be blest;
 Bound, and longing to be free;
Weary, waiting for my rest:
 God, be merciful to me.

2 Holiness I've none to plead,
 Sinfulness in all I see,
 I can only bring my need:
 God, be merciful to me.

3 Broken heart and downcast eyes
 Dare not lift themselves to thee;
 Yet thou canst interpret sighs:
 God, be merciful to me.

4 From this sinful heart of mine
 To thy bosom I would flee;
 I am not mine own, but thine:
 God, be merciful to me.

5 There is One beside thy throne,
 And my only hope and plea
 Are in him and him alone:
 God, be merciful to me.

6. He my cause will undertake,
 My interpreter will be;
 He's my all, and for his sake,
 God, be merciful to me.

THE CHRISTIAN YEAR
89

ANIMA CHRISTI. (7 7. 7 7. D.)
Slow ♩ = 83. To be sung in unison.   *Adapted from an English Traditional Melody.*

Paraphrase of Anima Christi, sanctifica me.

14th cent. Anon. ‡ 1855.

1. SOUL of Jesus, make me whole,
   Meek and contrite make my soul;
   Thou most stainless Soul Divine,
   Cleanse this sordid soul of mine,
   Hallow this my contrite heart,
   Purify my every part;
   Soul of Jesus, hallow me,
   Miserere Domine.

2. Save me, Body of my Lord,
   Save a sinner, vile, abhorred;
   Sacred Body, wan and worn, [torn,
   Bruised and mangled, scourged and
   Piercèd hands, and feet, and side.
   Rent, insulted, crucified:
   Save me—to the Cross I flee,
   Miserere Domine.

LENT

3 Blood of Jesus, stream of life,
Sacred stream with blessings rife,
From thy broken Body shed
On the Cross, that altar dread;
Given to be our drink Divine,
Fill my heart and make it thine;
Blood of Christ, my succour be,
Miserere Domine.

4 Holy Water, stream that poured
From thy riven side, O Lord,
Wash thou me without, within,
Cleanse me from the taint of sin,
Till my soul is clean and white,
Bathed, and purified, and bright
As a ransomed soul should be,
Miserere Domine.

5 Jesu, by the wondrous power
Of thine awful Passion hour,
By the unimagined woe
Mortal man may never know;
By the curse upon thee laid,
By the ransom thou hast paid,
By thy Passion comfort me,
Miserere Domine.

6 Jesu, by thy bitter Death,
By thy last expiring breath,
Give me the eternal life,
Purchased by that mortal strife;
Thou didst suffer death that I
Might not die eternally;
By thy dying quicken me,
Miserere Domine.

7. *Miserere;* let me be
Never parted, Lord, from thee;
Guard me from my ruthless foe,
Save me from eternal woe;
When the hour of death is near,
And my spirit faints for fear,
Call me with thy voice of love,
Place me near to thee above,
With thine Angel host to raise
An undying song of praise,
Miserere Domine.

THE CHRISTIAN YEAR

90
DE PROFUNDIS. (88.77.)
Slow ♩ = 72.
Adapted from an English Traditional Melody.

Ps. 86.   *Joseph Bryan (c. 1620).*

TO my humble supplication,
  Lord, give ear and acceptation;
Save thy servant, that hath none
Help nor hope but thee alone.

2 Send, O send, relieving gladness
  To my soul opprest with sadness,
Which, from clog of earth set free,
Winged with zeal, flies up to thee;

    3 To thee, rich in mercies' treasure,
      And in goodness without measure,
    Never-failing help to those
    Who on thy sure help repose.

    4. Heavenly Tutor, of thy kindness,
      Teach my dullness, guide my blindness,
    That my steps thy paths may tread,
    Which to endless bliss do lead.

A - men.

91
VALOR. (10 10. 10 10.)
In moderate time ♩ = 60.
Adapted from a Traditional Melody.

LENT

91 (continued)

NOTE.—*This hymn may also be sung to* DALKEITH (*Appendix, No.* 25).

S. J. Stone, 1839–1900.

WEARY of earth and laden with my sin,
I look at heaven and long to enter in;
But there no evil thing may find a home,
And yet I hear a voice that bids me 'Come.'

2 So vile I am, how dare I hope to stand
In the pure glory of that holy land?
Before the whiteness of that throne appear?
Yet there are hands stretched out to draw me near.

3 The while I fain would tread the heavenly way,
Evil is ever with me day by day;
Yet on mine ears the gracious tidings fall,
'Repent, confess, thou shalt be loosed from all.

4 It is the voice of Jesus that I hear,
His are the hands stretched out to draw me near,
And his the Blood that can for all atone,
And set me faultless there before the throne.

Part 2.

5 O great Absolver, grant my soul may wear
The lowliest garb of penitence and prayer,
That in the Father's courts my glorious dress
May be the garment of thy righteousness.

6 Yea, thou wilt answer for me, righteous Lord;
Thine all the merits, mine the great reward;
Thine the sharp thorns, and mine the golden crown;
Mine the life won, and thine the life laid down.

7. Naught can I bring, dear Lord, for all I owe,
Yet let my full heart what it can bestow;
Like Mary's gift, let my devotion prove,
Forgiven greatly, how I greatly love.

A - men.

THE CHRISTIAN YEAR

92

THIRD MODE MELODY. (D.C.M.)
Slow ♩ = 84 (𝅗𝅥 = 42).

T. TALLIS, c. 1515-85
(*rhythm slightly simplified*).

J. Addison, 1672-1719.

WHEN, rising from the bed of death,
    O'erwhelmed with guilt and fear,
I see my Maker face to face,
    O how shall I appear?

2 If yet, while pardon may be found,
    And mercy may be sought,
My heart with inward horror shrinks,
    And trembles at the thought;

3 When thou, O Lord, shalt stand dis-
    In majesty severe,   [closed
And sit in judgement on my soul,
    O how shall I appear?

4 But thou hast told the troubled mind
    Who does her sins lament,
The timely tribute of her tears
    Shall endless woe prevent.

5 Then see the sorrow of my heart,
    Ere yet it be too late;
And hear my Saviour's dying groans,
    To give those sorrows weight.

6. For never shall my soul despair
    Her pardon to procure,
Who knows thine only Son has died
    To make her pardon sure.

LENT

92

ALTERNATIVE VERSION (melody in the tenor) *Tallis' Original Version (rhythm slightly simplified).*

[This version may be used, in connexion with the other, for one verse; it is intended for the CHOIR ALONE and must be sung without the organ. It should only be attempted by good choirs.]

NOTE.—*This tune is founded on the alternation of $\frac{3}{1}$ and $\frac{6}{2}$ times. This can be easily learnt by a congregation, who will sing the melody by ear. However, should a C. M. tune be thought preferable, CHESHIRE (No. 109) or MARTYRS (No. 449) are also suitable.*

The following are also suitable, among others:

107 When I survey.	430 Lighten the darkness.	483 Strong Son of God.
378 Come, O thou Traveller.	439 My faith looks up.	484 Take up thy cross.
385 Father, hear the prayer.	456 O Lord, and Master.	495 The world is very evil.
397 Guide me, O thou great.	474 Prayer is the soul's.	510 We sing the praise.
418 Jesu, name all names.	477 Rock of Ages.	515 Wilt thou forgive.
422 Jesus, where'er thy.	482 Still will we trust.	736 Lent Prose.

A - men.

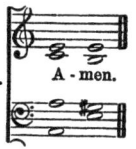

131

THE CHRISTIAN YEAR

93

UNIVERSITY. (C. M.)
Moderately fast ♩ = 100.

Probably by J. RANDALL, 1715–99.

REFRESHMENT SUNDAY

Ps. 23. (Suitable also for general use.)　　　　　George Herbert, 1598–1632.

1. THE God of love my Shepherd is,
   And he that doth me feed;
   While he is mine and I am his,
   What can I want or need?

2. He leads me to the tender grass,
   Where I both feed and rest;
   Then to the streams that gently pass:
   In both I have the best.

3. Or if I stray, he doth convert,
   And bring my mind in frame,
   And all this not for my desert,
   But for his holy name.

4. Yea, in death's shady black abode
   Well may I walk, not fear;
   For thou art with me, and thy rod
   To guide, thy staff to bear.

5. Surely thy sweet and wondrous love
   Shall measure all my days;
   And as it never shall remove
   So neither shall my praise.

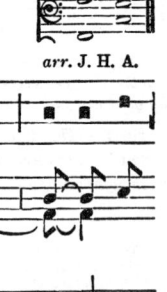

A - men.

94

Mode i.　　　　　　　　　　　　　　　　　　　　　arr. J. H. A.

PASSIONTIDE

If a modern tune is required for this hymn it may be sung to that at Hymn 50 which was originally proper to VEXILLA REGIS.

PASSIONTIDE

OFFICE HYMN (*in full*). E. *Passion Sunday, and daily till Maundy Thursday.* Vexilla Regis prodeunt.

1–5 *Bishop Venantius Fortunatus, 530–609.* Tr. *J. M. Neale.*

THE royal banners forward go;
The Cross shines forth in mystic glow;
Where he in flesh, our flesh who made,
Our sentence bore, our ransom paid:

2 Where deep for us the spear was dyed,
Life's torrent rushing from his side,
To wash us in that precious flood,
Where mingled Water flowed, and Blood.

Part 2.

3 Fulfilled is all that David told
In true prophetic song of old;
Amidst the nations, God, saith he,
Hath reigned and triumphed from the tree.

4 O Tree of beauty, Tree of light!
O Tree with royal purple dight!
Elect on whose triumphal breast
Those holy limbs should find their rest:

5 On whose dear arms, so widely flung,
The weight of this world's ransom hung:
The price of humankind to pay,
And spoil the spoiler of his prey.

6*O Cross, our one reliance, hail!
So may thy power with us avail
To give new virtue to the saint,
And pardon to the penitent.

7. To thee, eternal Three in One,
Let homage meet by all be done:
Whom by the Cross thou dost restore,
Preserve and govern evermore. Amen.

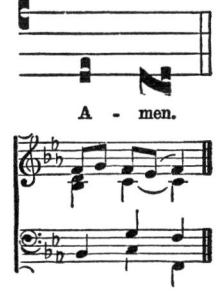

A - men.

F

THE CHRISTIAN YEAR
95, 96

Mode iii.   *arr.* J. H. A.

95

OFFICE HYMN. M. *Passion Sunday and daily till Maundy Thursday.*   *Bishop Venantius Fortunatus, 530–609. Tr. P. D.*

Pange, lingua, gloriosi proelium certaminis.

SING, my tongue, the glorious battle,
  Sing the ending of the fray;
Now above the Cross, the trophy,
  Sound the loud triumphant lay:
Tell how Christ, the world's Redeemer,
  As a Victim won the day.

2 God in pity saw man fallen,
  Shamed and sunk in misery,
When he fell on death by tasting
  Fruit of the forbidden tree;
Then another tree was chosen [free.
  Which the world from death should

PASSIONTIDE

3 Thus the scheme of our salvation
　Was of old in order laid,
　That the manifold deceiver's
　　Art by art might be outweighed,
　And the lure the foe put forward
　　Into means of healing made.

4 Therefore when the appointed fullness
　Of the holy time was come,
　He was sent who maketh all things
　　Forth from God's eternal home;
　Thus he came to earth, incarnate,
　　Offspring of a maiden's womb.

5. To the Trinity be glory
　　Everlasting, as is meet;
　Equal to the Father, equal
　　To the Son and Paraclete:
　Trinal Unity, whose praises
　　All created things repeat. Amen.

96

OFFICE HYMN (*in full*). M. *Passion Sunday and daily till Maundy Thursday.*

Bishop Venantius Fortunatus, 530-609. Tr. J. M. Neale.

Lustra sex qui jam peracta.

THIRTY years among us dwelling,
　His appointed time fulfilled,
Born for this, he meets his Passion,
　For that this he freely willed,
On the Cross the Lamb is lifted
　Where his life-blood shall be spilled.

2 He endured the nails, the spitting,
　Vinegar, and spear, and reed;
From that holy Body broken
　Blood and water forth proceed:
Earth, and stars, and sky, and ocean
　By that flood from stain are freed.

Part 2.

3 Faithful Cross! above all other,
　One and only noble tree!
None in foliage, none in blossom,
　None in fruit thy peer may be;
Sweetest wood and sweetest iron!
　Sweetest weight is hung on thee.

4 Bend thy boughs, O Tree of Glory!
　Thy relaxing sinews bend;
For awhile the ancient rigour
　That thy birth bestowed, suspend;
And the King of heavenly beauty
　On thy bosom gently tend!

5 Thou alone wast counted worthy
　　This world's ransom to uphold;
　For a shipwreck'd race preparing
　　Harbour, like the Ark of old;
　With the sacred Blood anointed
　　From the smitten Lamb that rolled.

6. To the Trinity be glory
　　Everlasting, as is meet;
　Equal to the Father, equal
　　To the Son, and Paraclete:
　Trinal Unity, whose praises
　　All created things repeat. **Amen.**

A - men.

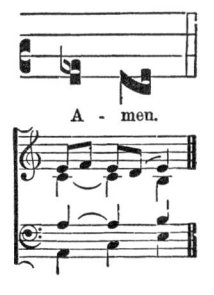

NOTE.—*Nos. 95 and 96 may also be sung to* ST. THOMAS (*No.* 31), TANTUM ERGO (*No.* 63), *the Mechlin Melody at* 326, *or* ORIEL (*No.* 507).

THE CHRISTIAN YEAR

DAS IST MEINE FREUDE. (76.76.776.) **97**

Moderately slow ♩ = 60.

Melody by
J. A. FREYLINGHAUSEN, 1670–1739.

PASSIONTIDE

14th or 15th cent. Tr. A. R.

Si vis vere gloriari.

DOST thou truly seek renown
   Christ his glory sharing?
Wouldst thou win the heavenly crown
   Victor's meed declaring?
Tread the path the Saviour trod,
Look upon the crown of God,
   See what he is wearing.

2 This the King of heaven bore
   In that sore contending;
This his sacred temples wore,
   Honour to it lending;
In this helm he faced the foe,
On the Rood he laid him low,
   Satan's kingdom ending.

3 Christ upon the Tree of Scorn,
   In salvation's hour,
Turned to gold these pricks of thorn
   By his Passion's power;
So on sinners, who had earned
Endless death, from sin returned,
   Endless blessings shower.

4. When in death's embrace we lie.
   Then, good Lord, be near us;
With thy presence fortify,
   And with victory cheer us;
Turn our erring hearts to thee,
That we crowned for ay may be:
   O good Jesu, hear us!

A - men.

THE CHRISTIAN YEAR
98

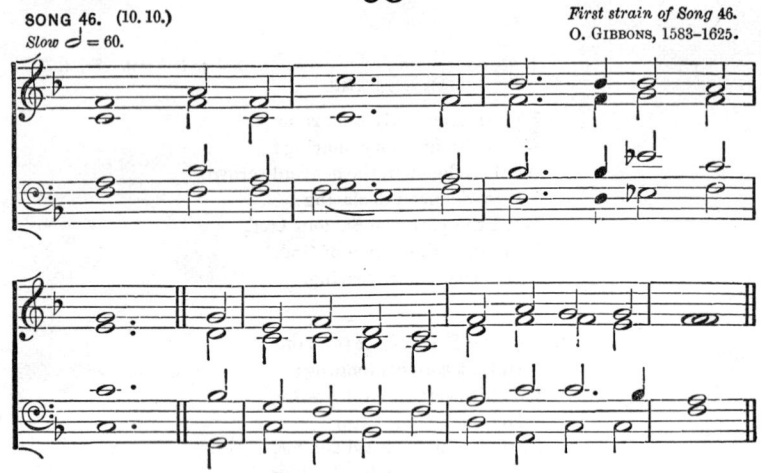

SONG 46. (10.10.)
Slow ♩ = 60.

First strain of Song 46.
O. GIBBONS, 1583–1625.

Phineas Fletcher, 1582–1650.

DROP, drop, slow tears,
   And bathe those beauteous feet,
Which brought from heaven
   The news and Prince of peace.

2 Cease not, wet eyes,
   His mercies to entreat;
To cry for vengeance
   Sin doth never cease.

3. In your deep floods
   Drown all my faults and fears;
Nor let his eye
   See sin, but through my tears.

A - men.

PASSIONTIDE

99

BOUNDARY. (6 5. 6 5.)
In moderate time ♩ = 120.
MARTIN SHAW.

[Copyright 1915, by J. Curwen & Sons, Ltd.]

NOTE.—*This hymn may also be sung to* CASWALL (WEM IN LEIDENSTAGEN) (*No.* 315).

18th cent. *Tr. E. Caswall.*

Viva! Viva! Gesù.

GLORY be to Jesus,
   Who, in bitter pains,
Poured for me the life-blood
   From his sacred veins.

2 Grace and life eternal
   In that Blood I find;
Blest be his compassion,
   Infinitely kind.

3 Blest through endless ages
   Be the precious stream,
Which from endless torment
   Doth the world redeem.

4 Abel's blood for vengeance
   Pleaded to the skies;
But the Blood of Jesus
   For our pardon cries.

5 Oft as it is sprinkled
   On our guilty hearts,
Satan in confusion
   Terror-struck departs.

6 Oft as earth exulting
   Wafts its praise on high,
Hell with terror trembles
   Heaven is filled with joy.

Unison. 7. Lift ye then your voices;
   Swell the mighty flood;
Louder still and louder
   Praise the precious Blood.

A - men.

THE CHRISTIAN YEAR

NICHT SO TRAURIG. (77. 77. 77.) **100**

Slow and dignified ♩ = 50.

J. S. BACH, 1685–1750.

NOTE.—*This hymn may also be sung to* REDHEAD 76 (*No.* 477).

J. *Montgomery*, 1771–1854.

GO to dark Gethsemane,
   Ye that feel the Tempter's power;
Your Redeemer's conflict see,
   Watch with him one bitter hour:
Turn not from his griefs away,
Learn of Jesus Christ to pray.

2 See him at the judgement-hall,
   Beaten, bound, reviled, arraigned;
See him meekly bearing all!
   Love to man his soul sustained.
Shun not suffering, shame, or loss,
Learn of Christ to bear the Cross.

3. Calvary's mournful mountain view;
   There the Lord of Glory see,
Made a sacrifice for you,
   Dying on the accursèd tree:
'It is finished!' hear him cry;
Trust in Christ and learn to die.

A - men.

PASSIONTIDE

101

DER TAG BRICHT AN. (L. M.)
Slow and solemn ♩ = 84 (𝅗𝅥 = 42).

Melody probably by M. VULPIUS, 1560–1616?

NOTE.—*This hymn may also be sung to* ST. CRISPIN (*Appendix, No.* 36).

F. W. Faber, 1814–63.

MY God! my God! and can it be
That I should sin so lightly now,
And think no more of evil thoughts
Than of the wind that waves the bough?

2 I walk the earth with lightsome step,
Smile at the sunshine, breathe the air,
Do my own will, nor ever heed
Gethsemane and thy long prayer.

3 Shall it be always thus, O Lord?
Wilt thou not work this hour in me
The grace thy Passion merited,
Hatred of self, and love of thee!

4 Ever when tempted, make me see,
Beneath the olives' moon-pierced shade,
My God, alone, outstretched, and bruised,
And bleeding, on the earth he made;

5. And make me feel it was my sin,
As though no other sins there were,
That was to him who bears the world
A load that he could scarcely bear.

A - men.

THE CHRISTIAN YEAR

102

PASSION CHORALE. (7 6. 7 6. D.)
Very slow and solemn ♩=42.

Melody by H. L. HASSLER, 1564–1612.
Adapted and harmonized by J. S. BACH.

P. Gerhardt, 1607–76, based on Salve caput cruentatum (ascribed to St. Bernard). Tr. Y. H.

O Haupt voll Blut und Wunden.

O SACRED head, sore wounded,
  Defiled and put to scorn;
O kingly head, surrounded
  With mocking crown of thorn:
What sorrow mars thy grandeur?
  Can death thy bloom deflower?
O countenance whose splendour
  The hosts of heaven adore.

2 Thy beauty, long-desirèd,
  Hath vanished from our sight;
Thy power is all expirèd,
  And quenched the light of light.
Ah me! for whom thou diest,
  Hide not so far thy grace:
Show me, O Love most highest,
  The brightness of thy face.

3 * I pray thee, Jesus, own me,
  Me, Shepherd good, for thine;
Who to thy fold hast won me,
  And fed with truth divine.
Me guilty, me refuse not,
  Incline thy face to me,
This comfort that I lose not,
  On earth to comfort thee.

A - men.

PASSIONTIDE

102 (ALTERNATIVE VERSION) *Harmonized by J. S. BACH.*
In the 'Passion according to St. Matthew.'

[*This version may be used, in connexion with the other, for verse 4, and must be sung by the* CHOIR ALONE. *This version should only be attempted by good choirs.*]

4 In thy most bitter passion
  My heart to share doth cry,
With thee for my salvation
  Upon the Cross to die.
Ah, keep my heart thus movèd
  To stand thy Cross beneath,
To mourn thee, well-belovèd,
  Yet thank thee for thy death.

5.* My days are few, O fail not,
  With thine immortal power,
To hold me that I quail not
  In death's most fearful hour:
That I may fight befriended,
  And see in my last strife
To me thine arms extended
  Upon the Cross of life.

THE CHRISTIAN YEAR

103

ALLEIN GOTT IN DER HÖH SEI EHR. (87.87.887.)

Slow and dignified ♩ = 50.

Adapted (1524) from Easter plainsong 'Gloria in excelsis (later form of the melody).

PASSIONTIDE

103 (*continued*)

c. 17*th cent.* *Tr. J. M. Neale and others.*
Attolle paulum lumina.

1. O SINNER, raise the eye of faith,
 To true repentance turning,
Consider well the curse of sin,
 Its shame and guilt discerning :
Upon the Crucified One look,
So shalt thou learn, as in a book,
 What well is worth thy learning.

2. Look on the head, with such a crown
 Of bitter thorns surrounded;
Look on the blood that trickles down
 The feet and hands thus wounded;
And see his flesh with scourges rent:
Mark how upon the Innocent
 Man's malice hath abounded.

3.* But though upon him many a pain
 Its bitterness is spending,
Yet more, O how much more! his heart
 Man's wickedness is rending!
Such is the load for sinners borne,
As Mary's Son in woe forlorn
 His life for us is ending.

4. None ever knew such pangs before,
 None ever such affliction,
As when his people brought to pass
 The Saviour's crucifixion.
He willed to bear for us the throes,
For us the unimagined woes,
 Of death's most fell infliction.

5.* O sinner, stay and ponder well
 Sin's fearful condemnation;
Think on the wounds that Christ endured
 In working thy salvation;
For if thy Lord had never died,
Nought else could sinful man betide
 But utter reprobation.

6. Lord, give us sinners grace to flee
 The death of evil-doing,
To shun the gloomy gates of hell,
 Thine awful judgement viewing
So thank we thee, O Christ, to-day,
And so for life eternal pray,
 The holy road pursuing.

A - men.

THE CHRISTIAN YEAR
104

NUN LASST UNS GEH'N. (7.7.7.7.)
Moderately slow ♩ = 80.

'*Kirchen- und Haus-Buch,*' *Dresden*, 1694.

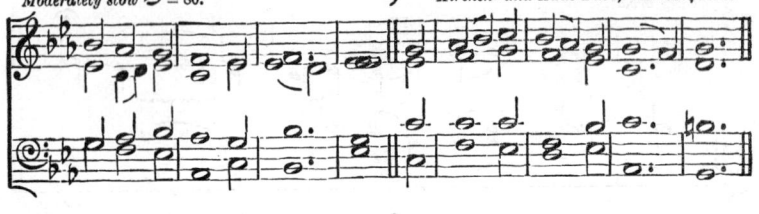

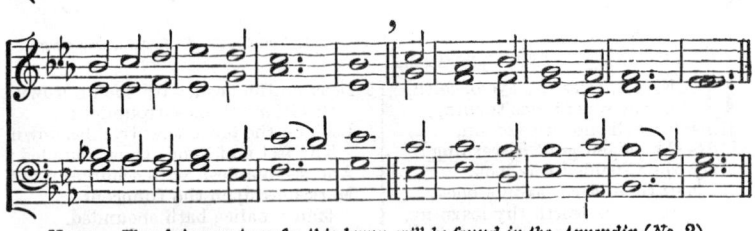

NOTE.—*The plainsong tune for this hymn will be found in the Appendix (No. 2).*

Compline.   **Cultor Dei, memento.**   *Prudentius, b.* 348.   Tr. *T. A. L.*

SERVANT of God, remember
  The stream thy soul bedewing,
The grace that came upon thee
  Anointing and renewing.

2 When kindly slumber calls thee,
  Upon thy bed reclining,
Trace thou the Cross of Jesus,
  Thy heart and forehead signing.

3 The Cross dissolves the darkness,
  And drives away temptation;
It calms the wavering spirit
  By quiet consecration.

4 Begone, begone, the terrors
  Of vague and formless dreaming;
Begone, thou fell deceiver,
  With all thy boasted scheming.

5 Begone, thou crookèd serpent,
  Who, twisting and pursuing,
By fraud and lie preparest
  The simple soul's undoing;

6 Tremble, for Christ is near us,
  Depart, for here he dwelleth,
And this, the Sign thou knowest,
  Thy strong battalions quelleth.

7 Then while the weary body
  Its rest in sleep is nearing,
The heart will muse in silence
  On Christ and his appearing.

8. To God, eternal Father,
  To Christ, our King, be glory,
And to the Holy Spirit,
  In never-ending story. Amen.

A - men.

PASSIONTIDE

105

BATTY. (87.87.)
Moderately slow ♩ = 60.

Adapted from Chorale 'Ringe recht' in
'Erbaulicher musikalischen Christenschatz,' 1745.

W. Shirley, 1725-86, *and others.*

SWEET the moments, rich in blessing,
    Which before the Cross I spend,
Life, and health, and peace possessing
    From the sinner's dying Friend.

2 Here I stay, for ever viewing
    Mercy streaming in his Blood;
Precious drops, my soul bedewing,
    Plead and claim my peace with God.

3 Truly blessèd is this station,
    Low before his Cross to lie,
While I see divine compassion
    Floating in his languid eye.

4. Lord, in ceaseless contemplation
    Fix our hearts and eyes on thee,
Till we taste thy full salvation,
    And unveiled thy glories see.

A - men.

THE CHRISTIAN YEAR

106

HORSLEY. (C. M.)
Moderately slow ♩ = 88.

W. Horsley, 1774–1858.

Mrs. C. F. Alexander, 1823-95.

THERE is a green hill far away,
    Without a city wall,
Where the dear Lord was crucified
    Who died to save us all.

2 We may not know, we cannot tell,
    What pains he had to bear,
But we believe it was for us
    He hung and suffered there.

3*He died that we might be forgiven,
    He died to make us good;
That we might go at last to heaven,
    Saved by his precious Blood.

4*There was no other good enough
    To pay the price of sin;
He only could unlock the gate
    Of heaven, and let us in.

5. O, dearly, dearly has he loved,
    And we must love him too,
And trust in his redeeming Blood.
    And try his works to do.

A - men.

PASSIONTIDE

107

CATON OR ROCKINGHAM. (L.M.)
Very slow ♩ = 63.

Adapted by E. MILLER, 1731-1807.
Harmony chiefly from S. WEBBE
(A Collection of Psalm Tunes, 1820).

NOTE.—*A different harmonization of this tune will be found in the Appendix (No. 45).*

I. Watts, 1674-1748.

WHEN I survey the wondrous Cross,
   On which the Prince of glory died,
My richest gain I count but loss,
   And pour contempt on all my pride.

2 Forbid it, Lord, that I should boast
   Save in the death of Christ my God;
All the vain things that charm me most,
   I sacrifice them to his Blood.

3 See from his head, his hands, his feet,
   Sorrow and love flow mingled down;
Did e'er such love and sorrow meet,
   Or thorns compose so rich a crown?

4*His dying crimson like a robe,
   Spreads o'er his body on the Tree;
Then am I dead to all the globe,
   And all the globe is dead to me.

5. Were the whole realm of nature mine,
   That were a present far too small;
Love so amazing, so divine,
   Demands my soul, my life, my all.

* *Webbe's original version of this passage is:*

A - men.

THE CHRISTIAN YEAR
108

EBENEZER (TON-Y-BOTEL). (87. 87. D.)
Very slow ♩ = 48. [*This tune may be sung throughout in unison.*]   *Welsh Hymn Melody.*

(By permission of W. Gwenlyn Evans, Carnarvon.)

NOTE.—*This hymn may also be sung to* ZUM FRIEDEN (*No.* 499).

Bishop A. Cleveland Coxe, 1818-96.

WHO is this with garments gory,
   Triumphing from Bozrah's way;
This that weareth robes of glory,
   Bright with more than victory's ray?
Who is this unwearied comer
   From his journey's sultry length,
Travelling through Idumè's summer
   In the greatness of his strength?

2 Wherefore red in thine apparel
   Like the conquerors of earth,
And arrayed like those who carol
   O'er the reeking vineyard's mirth?

Who art thou, the valleys seeking
   Where our peaceful harvests wave?
'I, in righteous anger speaking,
   I, the mighty One to save;

3 'I, that of the raging heathen
   Trod the winepress all alone,
Now in victor-garlands wreathen
   Coming to redeem mine own:
I am he with sprinkled raiment,
   Glorious for my vengeance-hour,
Ransoming, with priceless payment,
   And delivering with power.'

HOLY WEEK

Unison. 4. Hail! All hail! Thou Lord of Glory!
　　Thee, our Father, thee we own;
　Abram heard not of our story,
　　Israel ne'er our name hath known.
　But, Redeemer, thou hast sought us,
　　Thou hast heard thy children's wail,
　Thou with thy dear Blood hast bought us:
　　Hail! Thou mighty Victor, hail!

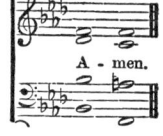

The following are also suitable, in addition to several of the Lent hymns:

118 It is finished.	416 Jesu, meek and lowly.
305 Bread of the world.	418 Jesu, name all names above.
409 In the Cross of Christ I glory.	477 Rock of ages.

HOLY WEEK

Passiontide Office Hymns till Maundy Thursday. No Office Hymns from Maundy Thursday till Low Sunday.

CHESHIRE. (C. M.)

109

Slow ♩ = 56.　　　　　　　　　　　　　　Este's Psalter, 1592.

J. M. Neale, 1818–66 ; (4.) W. Denton.

O THOU who through this holy week
　Didst suffer for us all,
The sick to cure, the lost to seek,
　To raise up them that fall:

2 We cannot understand the woe
　Thy love was pleased to bear;
O Lamb of God, we only know
　That all our hopes are there.

3 Thy feet the path of suffering trod;
　Thy hand the victory won:
What shall we render to our God
　For all that he hath done?

4 O grant us, Lord, with thee to die,
　With thee to rise anew;
Grant us the things of earth to fly,
　The things of heaven pursue.

PALM SUNDAY

See
619 Come, faithful people, come away.
620 Ride on! ride on in majesty!
621 Glory and praise and dominion.
622 All glory, laud, and honour.
623 Now, my soul, thy voice upraising.

MAUNDY THURSDAY

The following are suitable :
300 According to thy gracious word.
317 Laud, O Sion, thy salvation.
326 Of the glorious Body telling.
330 The Word of God proceeding forth

THE CHRISTIAN YEAR

110

NUN KOMM, DER HEIDEN HEILAND. (7 7. 7 7.)

Very slow ♩ = 46.

Melody in Walther's *'Gesangbüchlein,'* 1524.
Harmony from J. S. BACH.

NOTE.— *This hymn may also be sung to* REDHEAD NO. 47 (*No.* 513).

GOOD FRIDAY

See also 737 The Reproaches.

Bishop R. Mant, 1776–1848.

SEE the destined day arise!
  See, a willing sacrifice,
To redeem our fatal loss,
Jesus hangs upon the Cross!

2 Jesu, who but thou had borne,
  Lifted on that Tree of scorn,
Every pang and bitter throe,
Finishing thy life of woe?

3 Who but thou had dared to drain,
  Steeped in gall, the cup of pain,
And with tender body bear
Thorns, and nails, and piercing spear?

4 Thence, poured forth, the water flowed,
  Mingled from thy side with blood,—
Sign to all attesting eyes
Of the finished Sacrifice.

5 Holy Jesu, grant us grace
  In that Sacrifice to place
All our trust for life renewed,
Pardoned sin, and promised good.

Unison. 6. Grant us grace to sing to thee,
  In the Trinal Unity,
Ever with the sons of light,
Blessing, honour, glory, might. Amen.

A - men.

PASSIONTIDE: GOOD FRIDAY

111

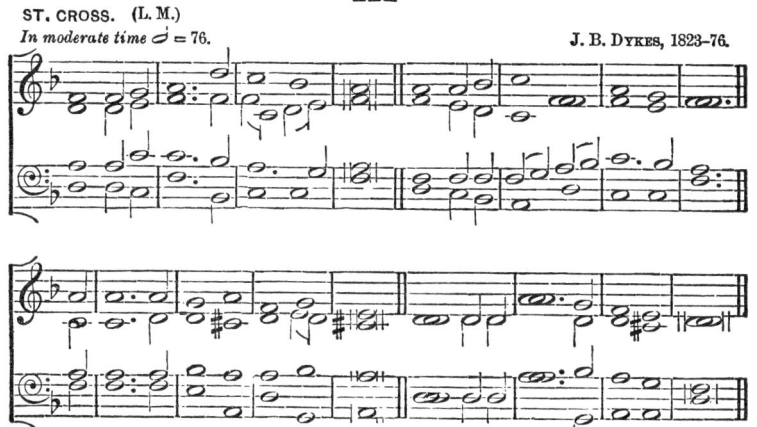

ST. CROSS. (L. M.)
In moderate time ♩ = 76.

J. B. DYKES, 1823-76.

NOTE.—*This hymn may also be sung to* DAS LEIDEN DES HERRN (*Appendix, No.* 11), *of which there is another harmony at No.* 387.

F. W. Faber, 1814-63.

1. O COME and mourn with me awhile;
See Mary calls us to her side;
O come and let us mourn with her:
Jesus, our Love, is crucified.

2. Have we no tears to shed for him,
While soldiers scoff and Jews deride?
Ah, look how patiently he hangs:
Jesus, our Love, is crucified.

3.* How fast his hands and feet are tied;
nailed;
His blessèd tongue with thirst is
His failing eyes are blind with blood:
Jesus, our Love is crucified.

4.* His Mother cannot reach his face;
She stands in helplessness beside;
Her heart is martyred with her Son's:
Jesus, our Love, is crucified.

5. Seven times he spoke, seven words of love;
And all three hours his silence cried
For mercy on the souls of men:
Jesus, our Love, is crucified.

6.* O break, O break, hard heart of mine;
Thy weak self-love and guilty pride
His Pilate and his Judas were:
Jesus, Our Love, is crucified.

7.* A broken heart, a fount of tears,
Ask, and they will not be denied;
A broken heart love's cradle is:
Jesus, our Love, is crucified.

8. O Love of God! O sin of Man!
In this dread act your strength is tried;
And victory remains with Love:
For he, our Love, is crucified.

A - men.

Or the following:

97 Dost thou truly seek renown.
484 Take up thy cross.

THE CHRISTIAN YEAR

112

ST. MARY MAGDALENE. (7 6. 7 6.)
Slow ♩ = 56.
H. A. JEBOULT, 1871–1925.

NOTE.—*This hymn may also be sung to* CHRISTUS DER IST MEIN LEBEN (*No. 232*).

Mrs. C. F. Alexander, 1818–95.

'Father, forgive them, for they know not what they do.'

'FORGIVE them, O my Father,
    They know not what they do:'
The Saviour spake in anguish,
    As the sharp nails went through.

2 No pained reproaches gave he
    To them that shed his Blood,
But prayer and tenderest pity
    Large as the love of God.

3 For me was that compassion,
    For me that tender care;
I need his wide forgiveness
    As much as any there.

4*It was my pride and hardness
    That hung him on the Tree;
Those cruel nails, O Saviour,
    Were driven in by me.

5 And often I have slighted
    Thy gentle voice that chid;
Forgive me too, Lord Jesus;
    I knew not what I did.

6. O depth of sweet compassion!
    O love divine and true!
Save thou the souls that slight thee,
    And know not what they do.

A - men.

Or the following: 416 Jesu, meek and lowly.

113

SONG 4. (10 10. 10 10.)
Moderately slow ♩ = 63.
O. GIBBONS, 1583–1625.

PASSIONTIDE: GOOD FRIDAY

113 (*continued*)

Note.—*This hymn may also be sung to* All Souls (*Appendix, No. 57*).

Archbishop W. D. Maclagan, 1826–1910.

'Verily I say unto thee, To-day shalt thou be with me in Paradise.'

'LORD, when thy kingdom comes, remember me;'
   Thus spake the dying lips to dying ears;
O faith, which in that darkest hour could see
   The promised glory of the far-off years!

2 No kingly sign declares that glory now,
   No ray of hope lights up that awful hour;
A thorny crown surrounds the bleeding brow,
   The hands are stretched in weakness, not in power.

3 Hark! through the gloom the dying Saviour saith,
   'Thou too shalt rest in Paradise to-day;'
O words of love to answer words of faith!
   O words of hope for those that live to pray!

4 Lord, when with dying lips my prayer is said,
   Grant that in faith thy kingdom I may see;
And, thinking on thy Cross and bleeding head,
   May breathe my parting words, 'Remember me.'

5 Remember me, but not my shame or sin;
   Thy cleansing Blood hath washed them all away;
Thy precious death for me did pardon win;
   Thy Blood redeemed me in that awful day.

6. Remember me; and, ere I pass away,
   Speak thou the assuring word that sets us free,
And make thy promise to my heart, 'To-day
   Thou too shalt rest in Paradise with me.'

A - men.

THE CHRISTIAN YEAR

114

OLD 124TH. (10. 10. 10. 10. 10.)
Slow ♩ = 66.

*English form of
Melody in Genevan Psalter, 1551.*

T. A. Lacey, 1853-1931.

THE dying robber raised his aching brow
   To claim the dying Lord for company;
And heard, in answer to his trembling vow,
The promise of the King: Thou—even thou—
   To-day shalt be in Paradise with me.

2 We too the measure of our guilt confess,
   Knowing thy mercy, Lord, our only plea;
That we, like him, through judgement and distress,
For all the weight of our unworthiness,
   May win our way to Paradise with thee.

PASSIONTIDE: GOOD FRIDAY
114
ALTERNATIVE VERSION (melody in the tenor)

Harmony by W. PARSONS (*slightly altered*) *in Day's Psalter*, 1563.

[*This version may be used in connexion with the other in those verses only where the* CHOIR SINGS ALONE. *It is not suitable when the hymn is sung at a Three Hours' Service, but may be used on other occasions, and also for No.* 352.]

  3 But so bewildered is our failing heart,
    So dim the lustre of thy royalty,
  We hardly know thee, Lord, for what thou art,
  Till we begin to take the better part
    And lose ourselves in Paradise with thee.

  4. Then lift our eyes, dear Lord, from this poor dross,
    To see thee reigning in humility,
  The King of love; that, wresting gain from loss,
  We too may climb the ladder of the Cross,
    To find our home in Paradise with thee.

A - men.

Or the following: 477 **Rock of ages.**

THE CHRISTIAN YEAR

115

STABAT MATER. (887. D.)
Slow and solemn ♩ = 50.

French Church Melody.

A-men.

Ascribed to Jacopone da Todi, d. 1306.
Tr. Bishop Mant, Aubrey de Vere, and others.

'Behold thy Mother.'
Stabat mater dolorosa.

1. AT the Cross her station keeping,
   Stood the mournful Mother weeping,
   Close to Jesus at the last,
   Through her soul, of joy bereavèd,
   Bowed with anguish, deeply grievèd,
   Now at length the sword hath passed.

2.* O, that blessèd one, grief-laden,
   Blessèd Mother, blessèd Maiden,
   Mother of the all-holy One;
   O that silent, ceaseless mourning,
   O those dim eyes, never turning
   From that wondrous, suffering Son.

3. Who on Christ's dear Mother gazing,
   In her trouble so amazing,
   Born of woman, would not weep?
   Who on Christ's dear Mother thinking,
   Such a cup of sorrow drinking,
   Would not share her sorrow deep?

4. For his people's sins, in anguish,
   There she saw the victim languish,
   Bleed in torments, bleed and die:
   Saw the Lord's anointed taken;
   Saw her Child in death forsaken;
   Heard his last expiring cry.

5.* In the Passion of my Maker,
   Be my sinful soul partaker,
   May I bear with her my part;
   Of his Passion bear the token,
   In a spirit bowed and broken
   Bear his death within my heart.

6.* May his wounds both wound and heal me,
   He enkindle, cleanse, anneal me,
   Be his Cross my hope and stay.
   May he, when the mountains quiver,
   From that flame which burns for ever
   Shield me on the judgement day.

7. Jesu, may thy Cross defend me,
   And thy saving death befriend me,
   Cherished by thy deathless grace;
   When to dust my dust returneth,
   Grant a soul that to thee yearneth
   In thy Paradise a place.

PASSIONTIDE: GOOD FRIDAY

115 (Alternative Tunes)

CHRISTI MUTTER STUND VOR SCHMERZEN. (887. D.)

Very slow and solemn ♩ = 58.

G. Corner,
Gesangbuch, 1625.

A-men.

STABAT MATER DOLOROSA.
Unison. In free rhythm.

Melody from the Mechlin Gradual.
arr. J. H. A.

A - men.

Or the following:
510 We sing the praise of him who died.

THE CHRISTIAN YEAR

116

ARFON. (7.7.7.7.7.7.)
Moderately slow ♩ = 66.

Welsh Hymn Melody.

NOTE —*This hymn may also be sung to* REDHEAD 76 (*No. 477*).

J. Ellerton, 1826–93.

'My God, my God, why hast thou forsaken me?'

THRONED upon the awful Tree,
King of grief, I watch with thee;
Darkness veils thine anguished face,
None its lines of woe can trace,
None can tell what pangs unknown
Hold thee silent and alone;

2 Silent through those three dread hours,
Wrestling with the evil powers,
Left alone with human sin,
Gloom around thee and within,
Till the appointed time is nigh,
Till the Lamb of God may die.

3 Hark that cry that peals aloud
Upward through the whelming cloud!
Thou, the Father's only Son,
Thou his own anointed One,
Thou dost ask him—can it be?—
'Why hast thou forsaken me?'

4. Lord, should fear and anguish roll
Darkly o'er my sinful soul,
Thou, who once wast thus bereft
That thine own might ne'er be left,
Teach me by that bitter cry
In the gloom to know thee nigh.

A - men.

Or the following:
103 O sinner, raise the eye of faith.

PASSIONTIDE: GOOD FRIDAY

SAFFRON WALDEN. (8 8. 8 6.)   **117**

Slow ♩ = 76.

A. H. Brown, 1830–1926.

Mrs. C. F. Alexander, 1818–95.

'I thirst.'

HIS are the thousand sparkling rills
   That from a thousand fountains burst,
And fill with music all the hills:
   And yet he saith, 'I thirst.'

2 All fiery pangs on battlefields,
   On fever beds where sick men toss,
Are in that human cry he yields
   To anguish on the Cross.

3 * But more than pains that racked him then
   Was the deep longing thirst divine
That thirsted for the souls of men:
   Dear Lord! and one was mine.

4. O Love most patient, give me grace;
   Make all my soul athirst for thee:
That parched dry lip, that fading face,
   That thirst, were all for me.

A - men.

Or the following:
106 There is a green hill far away.

THE CHRISTIAN YEAR
118

JESU MEINES GLAUBENS ZIER. (7 8. 8 7. 8 7. 8 7.)

Very slow and solemn ♩ = 46.

Melody from FREYLINGHAUSEN'S *Gesangbuch*, 1714.
Harmony from J. S. BACH, 1685–1750.

Other occasions also.   'It is finished.'   *Gabriel Gillett*, 1873–1948.

IT is finished! Christ hath known
All the life of men wayfaring,
Human joys and sorrows sharing,
Making human needs his own.
Lord, in us thy life renewing,
Lead us where thy feet have trod,
Till, the way of truth pursuing,
Human souls find rest in God.

2 It is finished! Christ is slain,
On the altar of creation,
Offering for a world's salvation
Sacrifice of love and pain.
Lord, thy love through pain revealing,
Purge our passions, scourge our vice,
Till, upon the Tree of Healing,
Self is slain in sacrifice.

3. It is finished! Christ our King
Wins the victor's crown of glory;
Sun and stars recite his story,
Floods and fields his triumph sing.
Lord, whose praise the world is telling,
Lord, to whom all power is given,
By thy death, hell's armies quelling,
Bring thy Saints to reign in heaven.

Or the following: **107** When I survey the wondrous Cross.

PASSIONTIDE: GOOD FRIDAY

ZU MEINEM HERRN. (11. 10. 11. 10.) **119**

Moderately slow ♩ = 72.

J. SCHICHT, 1753-1823.

Mrs. E. S. Alderson, 1818-88.

'Father, into thy hands I commend my Spirit.'

AND now, belovèd Lord, thy soul resigning
    Into thy Father's arms with conscious will,
Calmly, with reverend grace, thy head inclining,
    The throbbing brow and labouring breast grow still.

2 O Love! o'er mortal agony victorious,
    Now is thy triumph! now that Cross shall shine
To earth's remotest age revered and glorious,
    Of suffering's deepest mystery the sign.

3 My Saviour, in mine hour of mortal anguish,
    When earth grows dim, and round me falls the night,
O breathe thy peace, as flesh and spirit languish;
    At that dread eventide let there be light.

4. To thy dear Cross turn thou mine eyes in dying;
    Lay but my fainting head upon thy breast;
Those outstretched arms receive my latest sighing;
    And then, O! then, thine everlasting rest.

A - men.

Or the following: **102** O sacred head, sore wounded.

The following are also suitable:

80 My God, I love thee; not because.
95 Sing, my tongue, the glorious battle.
471 Praise to the Holiest in the height.

THE CHRISTIAN YEAR
120

OMNI DIE. (87.87.)
Very slow and solemn ♩ = 46 (♩ = 92).

Melody in
CORNER'S 'Gesangbuch,' 1631.
Arranged by W. S. ROCKSTRO.

GOOD FRIDAY EVENING AND EASTER EVEN

Archbishop W. D. Maclagan, 1826–1910.

IT is finished! Blessèd Jesus,
   Thou hast breathed thy latest sigh,
Teaching us the sons of Adam
   How the Son of God can die.

2 Lifeless lies the piercèd Body,
   Resting in its rocky bed;
Thou hast left the Cross of anguish
   For the mansions of the dead.

3 In the hidden realms of darkness
   Shines a light unseen before,
When the Lord of dead and living
   Enters at the lowly door.

4 * Lo! in spirit, rich in mercy
   Comes he from the world above,
Preaching to the souls in prison
   Tidings of his dying love.

5 * Lo! the heavenly light around him,
   As he draws his people near;
All amazed they come rejoicing
   At the gracious words they hear.

6 Patriarch and Priest and Prophet
   Gather round him as he stands,
In adoring faith and gladness
   Hearing of the piercèd hands.

7 There in lowliest joy and wonder
   Stands the robber by his side,
Reaping now the blessèd promise
   Spoken by the Crucified.

8. Jesus, Lord of our salvation,
   Let thy mercy rest on me;
Grant me too, when life is finished,
   Rest in Paradise with thee.

A - men.

GOOD FRIDAY AND EASTER EVEN

121

O MENSCH SIEH. (888.)   *Bohemian Brethren 'Gesangbuch,' 1566,*
Very slow ♩ = 66.   *slightly adapted.*

Isaac Gregory Smith, 1826–1920.

BY Jesus' grave on either hand,
While night is brooding o'er the land,
The sad and silent mourners stand.

2 At last the weary life is o'er,
The agony and conflict sore
Of him who all our sufferings bore.

3 Deep in the rock's sepulchral shade
The Lord, by whom the world was made,
The Saviour of mankind, is laid.

4. O hearts bereaved and sore distrest,
Here is for you a place of rest;
Here leave your griefs on Jesus' breast.

A - men.

EASTER

See also: 624 Hail thee, Festival Day.
625 The strife is o'er, the battle done.
626 Ye sons and daughters of the King.
627 The Lord is risen indeed.

There is no Office Hymn till Low Sunday, but 738 This is the day *may be sung in the place of the Office Hymn at Evensong on Easter-Day and till the Saturday following.*

THE CHRISTIAN YEAR

122

Mode iii.   arr. J. H. A.

A - men.

OFFICE HYMN. *Saturday evenings:*   St. Fulbert of Chartres, c. 1000.
i.e. 1st E. of Sundays after Easter.   Tr. J. M. Neale.
Chorus novae Jerusalem.

YE choirs of new Jerusalem,
  To sweet new strains attune your theme;
The while we keep, from care released,
With sober joy our Paschal feast:

EASTERTIDE

122 (Modern Tune)

MONTESANO. (L. M.)
In moderate time ♩ = 108.

JOHN LAW.

[*Copyright*, 1931, *by Oxford University Press.*]

NOTE.—*This hymn may also be sung to* BROCKHAM (*No.* 220).

2 When Christ, unconquer'd Lion, first
The dragon's chains by rising burst:
And while with living voice he cries,
The dead of other ages rise.

3 Engorged in former years, their prey
Must death and hell restore to-day:
And many a captive soul, set free,
With Jesus leaves captivity.

4 Right gloriously he triumphs now,
Worthy to whom should all things bow;
And joining heaven and earth again,
Links in one commonweal the twain.

5 And we, as these his deeds we sing,
His suppliant soldiers, pray our King,
That in his palace, bright and vast,
We may keep watch and ward at last.

6. Long as unending ages run,
To God the Father, laud be done:
To God the Son, our equal praise,
And God the Holy Ghost, we raise.
                    Amen.

A - men.

THE CHRISTIAN YEAR

123 (Part I)

Mode viii. *arr. J. H. A.*

Office Hymn (*in full*). *Low Sunday till Ascension*, M.

4th or 5th cent. Tr. T. A. L.

Aurora lucis rutilat.

THE day draws on with golden light,
　Glad songs go echoing through the height,
The broad earth lifts an answering cheer,
The deep makes moan with wailing fear.

2 For lo, he comes, the mighty King,
　To take from death his power and sting,
　To trample down his gloomy reign
　And break the weary prisoner's chain.

3 Enclosed he lay in rocky cell,
　With guard of armèd sentinel;
　But thence returning, strong and free,
　He comes with pomp of jubilee.

Note.—*Verses 6 and 7 may follow.*

EASTERTIDE

123 (PART II)

Mode iv. *arr.* J. H. A.

On Feasts of Apostles in Eastertide. On Feasts of Apostles in Ascensiontide Tune 142 is used.

Part 2.

4 The sad Apostles mourn him slain,
  Nor hope to see their Lord again;
  Their Lord, whom rebel thralls defy,
  Arraign, accuse, and doom to die.

5 But now they put their grief away,
  The pains of hell are loosed to-day;
  For by the grave, with flashing eyes,
  ' Your Lord is risen,' the Angel cries.

6 Maker of all, to thee we pray,
  Fulfil in us thy joy to-day;
  When death assails, grant, Lord, that we
  May share thy Paschal victory.

7. To thee who, dead, again dost live,
  All glory, Lord, thy people give;
  All glory, as is ever meet,
  To Father and to Paraclete. Amen.

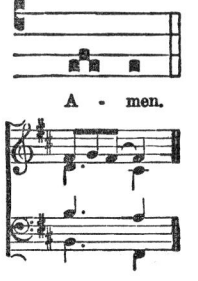

A - men.

THE CHRISTIAN YEAR

123 (Modern Tune)

SOLEMNIS HAEC FESTIVITAS. (L. M.)

With vigour ♩ = 150.
To be sung in unison.

Angers Church Melody.
Harmonized by R. V. W.

1 The day draws on with gold - en light, Glad songs go echo - ing through the height, The broad earth lifts an an - swer - ing cheer, The deep makes moan with wail - ing fear.

2 For lo, he comes, the migh - ty King, To take from

EASTERTIDE

123 (*continued*)

death his pow - er and sting, To tram - ple down his gloom - y reign, And break the wea - ry prison - er's chain.

3 En - closed he lay in rock - y cell, With guard of arm - ed sen - ti - nel; But thence re - turn - ing, strong and free, He comes with pomp of ju - bi - lee.

THE CHRISTIAN YEAR

123 (*continued*)

(Part 2)

4 The sad Apostles mourn him slain, Nor hope to see their Lord again; Their Lord, whom rebel thralls defy, Arraign, accuse, and doom to die.

5 But now they put their grief away, The pains of hell are loosed to-day; For by the grave, with

✱ NOTE.—*This verse must be played through twice when accompanying Hymn* 124.

EASTERTIDE

123 (*continued*)

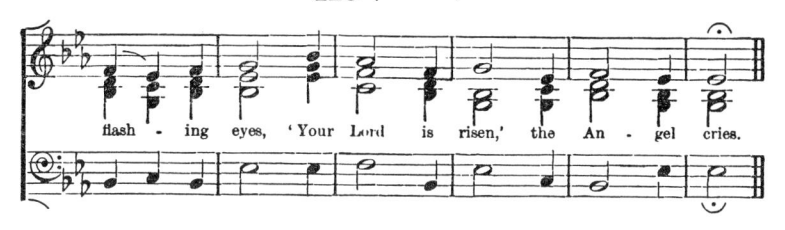

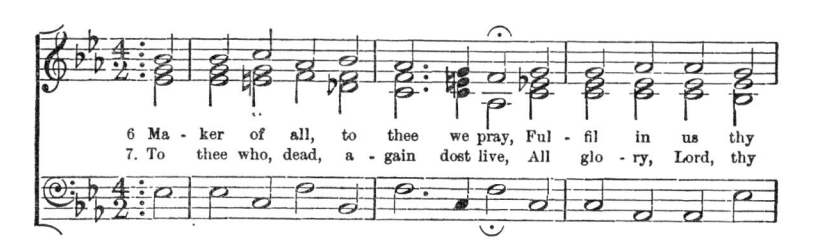

flash-ing eyes, 'Your Lord is risen,' the An-gel cries.

6. Ma-ker of all, to thee we pray, Ful-fil in us thy
7. To thee who, dead, a-gain dost live, All glo-ry, Lord, thy

joy to-day; When death as-sails, grant, Lord, that we May
peo-ple give; All glo-ry, as is ev-er meet, To

share thy Pas-chal vic-to-ry.
Fa-ther and to Pa-ra-clete. A - - - men.

NOTE.—*The whole hymn may be sung to the melody of verse 1, 4, or 5 if preferred.*

THE CHRISTIAN YEAR

124 (PART I)

Mode viii.   *arr.* J. H. A.

A - men.

OFFICE HYMN (*in full*). Low Sunday till Ascension, M.   4th or 5th cent. *Tr.* T. A. L.

Sermone blando Angelus.

H IS cheering message from the grave
  An Angel to the women gave:
'Full soon your Master ye shall see:
He goes before to Galilee.'

2 But while with flying steps they press
  To bear the news, all eagerness,
Their Lord, the living Lord, they meet,
And prostrate fall to kiss his feet.

3 So when his mourning followers heard
  The tidings of that faithful word,
Quick went they forth to Galilee,
Their loved and lost once more to see.

NOTE.—*Verses* 7 *and* 8 *may follow*

EASTERTIDE

124 (Part II)

On Feasts of Apostles in Eastertide.   On Feasts of Apostles in Ascensiontide Tune 142 is used.
Part 2.

4 On that fair day of Paschal joy
　The sunshine was without alloy,
　When to their very eyes restored
　They looked upon the risen Lord.

5 The wounds before their eyes displayed
　They see in living light arrayed,
　And that they see they testify
　In open witness fearlessly.

6 O Christ, the King of gentleness,
　Our several hearts do thou possess,
　That we may render all our days
　Thy meed of thankfulness and praise.

7 Maker of all, to thee we pray,
　Fulfil in us thy joy to-day;
　When death assails, grant, Lord, that we
　May share thy Paschal victory.

8 To thee who, dead, again dost live,
　All glory, Lord, thy people give;
　All glory, as is ever meet,
　To Father and to Paraclete.   Amen.

THE CHRISTIAN YEAR

124 (Modern Tune)

SOLEMNIS HAEC FESTIVITAS. (L. M.) *Angers Church Melody*
With vigour ♩ = 150. (♮) *(same melody as preceding hymn).*

1 His cheer-ing mes-sage from the grave
An An-gel to the wo-men gave:
'Full soon your Mas-ter ye shall see;
He goes be-fore to Ga-li-lee.'

2 But while with fly-ing steps they press
To bear the news, all ea-ger-ness,
Their Lord, the liv-ing Lord, they meet,
And pros-trate fall to kiss his feet.

3 So when his mourn-ing follow-ers heard
The tid-ings of that faith-ful word,
Quick went they forth to Ga-li-lee,
Their loved and lost once more to see.

EASTERTIDE

124 (continued)

(Part 2)

4 On that fair day of Pas - chal joy, The sun - shine was with - out al - loy, When to their ve - ry eyes re - stored They looked up - on the ris - en Lord.

5 The wounds be - fore their eyes dis - played They see in liv - ing light ar - rayed, And that they see they tes - ti - fy In o - pen wit - ness fear - less - ly.

6 O Christ, the King of gen - tle - ness, Our sev' - ral hearts do thou pos - sess, That we may ren - der all our days Thy meed of thank - ful - ness and praise.

7 Ma - ker of all, to thee we pray, Ful - fil in us thy joy to - day; When death as - sails, grant, Lord, that we May share thy Pas - chal vic - to - ry. A - - - men.

8. To thee who, dead, a - gain dost live, All glo - ry, Lord, thy peo - ple give; All glo - ry as is e - ver meet, To Fa - ther and to Pa - ra - clete.

NOTE.— *The melody only is given for this hymn. The organ accompaniment will be the same as that of the preceding hymn (No. 123).*

THE CHRISTIAN YEAR

Mode viii. **125** *arr.* J. H. A.

A - men.

NOTE.—*On Sundays, tune 123, part 2, was anciently used for this hymn.*

OFFICE HYMN. *Low Sunday till Ascension,* E.

Ad cenam Agni providi.

7th cent. Tr. J. M. Neale.

THE Lamb's high banquet we await
In snow-white robes of royal state;
And now, the Red Sea's channel past,
To Christ, our Prince, we sing at last.

EASTERTIDE

REX GLORIOSE. (L. M.)   **125** (Modern Tune)

In moderate time ♩ = 144.
To be sung in unison.

French Church Melody.
Harmonized by R. V. W.

Note.—*Another tune to this hymn will be found in the Appendix, No. 26.*

2 Upon the altar of the Cross
His Body hath redeemed our loss;
And tasting of his roseate Blood
Our life is hid with him in God.

3 That Paschal eve God's arm was bared;
The devastating Angel spared:
By strength of hand our hosts went free
From Pharaoh's ruthless tyranny.

4 Now Christ our Paschal Lamb is slain,
The Lamb of God that knows no stain;
The true Oblation offered here,
Our own unleavened Bread sincere.

5 O thou from whom hell's monarch flies,
O great, O very Sacrifice,
Thy captive people are set free,
And endless life restored in thee.

6 For Christ, arising from the dead,
From conquered hell victorious sped;
He thrusts the tyrant down to chains,
And Paradise for man regains.

7 Maker of all, to thee we pray,
Fulfil in us thy joy to-day;
When death assails, grant, Lord, that we
May share thy Paschal victory.

8. To thee who, dead, again dost live,
All glory, Lord, thy people give;
All glory, as is ever meet,
To Father and to Paraclete. Amen.

THE CHRISTIAN YEAR

126

NUN LASST UNS GOTT DEM HERREN. (7 7. 7 7.)
In moderate time ♩=120.

Later form of melody in
Selnecker's 'Christliche Psalmen,' 1587.

A - men.

P. D.

A BRIGHTER dawn is breaking,
  And earth with praise is waking;
For thou, O King most highest,
The power of death defiest;

2 And thou hast come victorious,
  With risen Body glorious,
  Who now for ever livest,
  And life abundant givest.

3 O free the world from blindness,
  And fill the world with kindness,
  Give sinners resurrection,
  Bring striving to perfection;

4. In sickness give us healing,
   In doubt thy clear revealing,
   That praise to thee be given
   In earth as in thy heaven.

127

WÜRZBURG. (8 7. 8 7. D.)
In moderate time ♩ = 100.

Melody from Andächtige und auserlesene Gesänger,
WÜRZBURG, 1705.

EASTERTIDE

127 (continued)

NOTE.—*This hymn may also be sung to* EVERTON (*Appendix, No. 27*).

Bishop Chr. Wordsworth, 1807–85.

ALLELUYA! Alleluya!
 Hearts to heaven and voices raise;
Sing to God a hymn of gladness,
 Sing to God a hymn of praise;
He who on the Cross a victim
 For the world's salvation bled,
Jesus Christ, the King of glory,
 Now is risen from the dead.

2 Christ is risen, Christ the first-fruits
 Of the holy harvest field,
Which will all its full abundance
 At his second coming yield;
Then the golden ears of harvest
 Will their heads before him wave,
Ripened by his glorious sunshine
 From the furrows of the grave.

3 Christ is risen, we are risen;
 Shed upon us heavenly grace,
Rain, and dew, and gleams of glory
 From the brightness of thy face;
That we, Lord, with hearts in heaven
 Here on earth may fruitful be,
And by angel-hands be gathered,
 And be ever safe with thee.

4. Alleluya! Alleluya!
 Glory be to God on high;
To the Father. and the Saviour,
 Who has gained the victory;
Glory to the Holy Spirit,
 Fount of love and sanctity;
Alleluya! Alleluya!
 To the Triune Majesty. **Amen.**

A - men.

THE CHRISTIAN YEAR

128

SALZBURG. (77. 77. D.)
Moderately slow, dignified ♩ = 66.

Melody from J. Hintze, 1622-1702.
Harmony from J. S. Bach.

EASTERTIDE

R. Campbell ‡, 1814–68. Based on Ad regias Agni dapes.

AT the Lamb's high feast we sing
Praise to our victorious King:
Who hath washed us in the tide
Flowing from his piercèd side;
Praise we him whose love Divine
Gives the guests his Blood for wine,
Gives his Body for the feast,
Love the Victim, Love the Priest.

2 * Where the Paschal blood is poured,
Death's dark angel sheathes his sword;
Israel's hosts triumphant go
Through the wave that drowns the foe.
Christ, the Lamb whose Blood was shed,
Paschal victim, Paschal bread!
With sincerity and love
Eat we Manna from above.

3 Mighty Victim from on high,
Powers of hell beneath thee lie;
Death is broken in the fight,
Thou hast brought us life and light.
Now thy banner thou dost wave,
Conquering Satan and the grave.
See the prince of darkness quelled;
Heaven's bright gates are open held.

4. Paschal triumph, Paschal joy,
Only sin can this destroy;
From sin's death do thou set free,
Souls re-born, dear Lord, in thee.
Hymns of glory, songs of praise,
Father, unto thee we raise.
Risen Lord, all praise to thee,
Ever with the Spirit be.

THE CHRISTIAN YEAR

ORIENTIS PARTIBUS. (77.77.4.) **129**

In moderate time ♩=144.
To be sung in unison.

Mediaeval French Melody.
Harmonized by R. V. W.

Al - le - lu - ya!

NOTE.—*Another tune to this hymn will be found in the Appendix, No. 12.*

Christus ist erstanden.

Michael Weisse, c. 1480–1534.
Tr. C. Winkworth.

CHRIST the Lord is risen again!
  Christ hath broken every chain!
Hark, the angels shout for joy,
Singing evermore on high,
    Alleluya!

2 He who gave for us his life,
Who for us endured the strife,
Is our Paschal Lamb to-day!
We too sing for joy, and say
    Alleluya!

3 He who bore all pain and loss
Comfortless upon the Cross,
Lives in glory now on high,
Pleads for us, and hears our cry.
    Alleluya!

4 He whose path no records tell,
Who descended into hell; [bound,
Who the strong man armed hath
Now in highest heaven is crowned.
    Alleluya!

5 Now he bids us tell abroad
How the lost may be restored,
How the penitent forgiven,
How we too may enter heaven.
    Alleluya!

6. Thou, our Paschal Lamb indeed,
Christ, to-day thy people feed;
Take our sins and guilt away,
That we all may sing for ay,
    Alleluya!

Harmony.

A - men.

184

EASTERTIDE

130

Sequence.   Victimae Paschali.   *Ascribed to Wipo, c.* 1030.   ***Tr. cento.***

Mode i.   *arr.* J. H. A.

1 Chris-tians, to the Pas-chal Vic - tim   *   Of - fer your thank-ful prai - ses!

2 A Lamb the sheep re - deem - eth: Christ, who on - ly is sin - less,

Re-con-cil-eth sin-ners to the Fa-ther; 3 Death and life have con-tend-ed

THE CHRISTIAN YEAR

130 (*continued*)

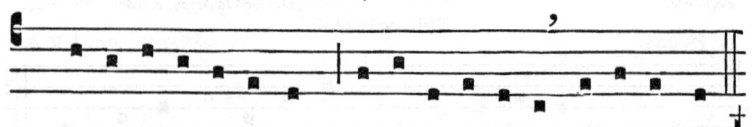

In that com-bat stu-pen-dous: The Prince of Life, who died, reigns im-mor-tal.

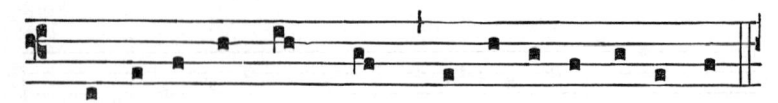

4 Speak Ma-ry, de-clar-ing What thou saw-est way-far-ing:

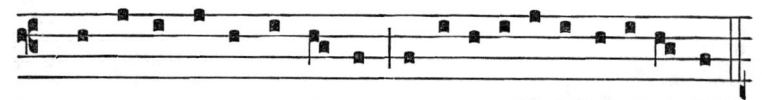

5 'The Tomb of Christ, who is liv-ing, The glo-ry of Je-su's Re-sur-rec-tion:

EASTERTIDE

130 (continued)

6 Bright an-gels at-test-ing, The shroud and nap-kin rest-ing.

7 Yea, Christ my hope is a-ris-en: To Ga-li-lee he goes be-fore you.'

8 Hap-py they who hear the wit-ness, Ma-ry's word be-liev-ing A-bove the tales of Jew-ry de-ceiv-ing.

9. Christ in-deed from death is ris-en, Our new life ob-tain-ing. Have mer-cy, vic-tor King, ev-er reign-ing!

THE CHRISTIAN YEAR

AVE VIRGO VIRGINUM. (7 6. 7 6. D.) **131**   Leisentritt's '*Gesangbuch*,' 1584
In moderate time ♩ = 100.   (*rhythm of bar 7 slightly simplified*).

Αἴσωμεν πάντες λαοί.

St. John Damascene, c. 750.
Tr. J. M. Neale.

COME, ye faithful, raise the strain
  Of triumphant gladness;
God hath brought his Israel
  Into joy from sadness;
Loosed from Pharaoh's bitter yoke
  Jacob's sons and daughters;
Led them with unmoistened foot
  Through the Red Sea waters.

2 'Tis the Spring of souls to-day;
  Christ hath burst his prison,
And from three days' sleep in death
  As a Sun hath risen;
All the winter of our sins,
  Long and dark, is flying
From his Light, to whom we give
  Laud and praise undying.

3 Now the Queen of seasons, bright
  With the Day of splendour,
With the royal Feast of feasts,
  Comes its joy to render;
Comes to glad Jerusalem,
  Who with true affection
Welcomes in unwearied strains
  Jesu's Resurrection.

4. Neither might the gates of death,
  Nor the tomb's dark portal,
Nor the watchers, nor the seal,
  Hold thee as a mortal;
But to-day amidst the twelve
  Thou didst stand, bestowing
That thy peace which evermore
  Passeth human knowing.

A - men.

EASTERTIDE

GOTT DES HIMMELS. (87.87.77.) **132**
In moderate time ♩ = 120.

H. ALBERT, 1604–51.

Mrs. C. F. Alexander, 1823–95.

HE is risen, he is risen:
Tell it with a joyful voice;
He has burst his three days' prison;
Let the whole wide earth rejoice.
Death is conquered, man is free,
Christ has won the victory.

2 Come, ye sad and fearful-hearted,
    With glad smile and radiant brow;
Lent's long shadows have departed,
    All his woes are over now,
And the passion that he bore:
Sin and pain can vex no more.

3. Come, with high and holy hymning,
    Chant our Lord's triumphant lay;
Not one darksome cloud is dimming
    Yonder glorious morning ray,
Breaking o'er the purple East,
Brighter far our Easter-feast.

A - men.

THE CHRISTIAN YEAR

EASTER HYMN. (7 4. 7 4. D.)
Slow ♩ = 58.

133

Altered from melody in Lyra Davidica, 1708.

NOTE.—*A higher setting of this tune will be found in the Appendix* (No. 13).

Lyra Davidica (1708), *and the Supplement* (1816).
Based partly on Surrexit Christus hodie.
c. 14th cent.

JESUS Christ is risen to-day, Alleluya!
  Our triumphant holy day, Alleluya!
Who did once, upon the Cross, Alleluya!
Suffer to redeem our loss. Alleluya!

EASTERTIDE

133 (ORIGINAL VERSION)

Slow ♩ = 58.   *Lyra Davidica, 1708.*

NOTE.—*Either of these two versions may be used, not, of course, together. The second (original) version may also be sung to the words of Hymn* **143**.

2 Hymns of praise then let us sing,   Alleluya!
Unto Christ, our heavenly King,   Alleluya!
Who endured the Cross and grave,   Alleluya!
Sinners to redeem and save.   Alleluya!

3. But the pains that he endured   Alleluya!
Our salvation have procured;   Alleluya!
Now above the sky he's King,   Alleluya!
Where the angels ever sing.   Alleluya!

A - men.

THE CHRISTIAN YEAR

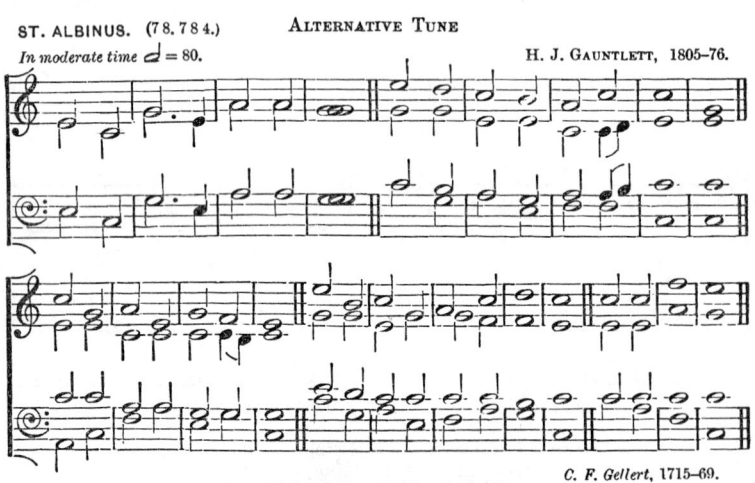

CHRIST IST ERSTANDEN. (7 8. 7 8 4.) **134**
Moderately slow, very dignified ♩ = 69.
To be sung in unison.

German melody, about 12th cent.

NOTE.—*The above tune is appropriate to this hymn, being anciently connected with Eastertide. An alternative tune is given below.*

ST. ALBINUS. (7 8. 7 8 4.)   ALTERNATIVE TUNE

In moderate time ♩ = 80.

H. J. GAUNTLETT, 1805–76.

Jesus lebt, mit ihm auch ich.   *Tr. Frances E. Cox and others.*

C. F. Gellert, 1715–69.

JESUS lives! thy terrors now
  Can, O Death, no more appal us;
Jesus lives! by this we know
  Thou, O grave, canst not enthral us.
               Alleluya!

2 Jesus lives! henceforth is death
  But the gate of life immortal;
This shall calm our trembling breath,
  When we pass its gloomy portal.
               Alleluya!

EASTERTIDE

3 Jesus lives! for us he died;
  Then, alone to Jesus living,
  Pure in heart may we abide,
    Glory to our Saviour giving,
                Alleluya!

4 Jesus lives! our hearts know well
    Nought from us his love shall sever;
  Life, nor death, nor powers of hell
    Tear us from his keeping ever.
                Alleluya!

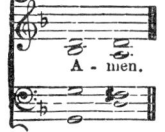

5. Jesus lives! to him the throne
    Over all the world is given;
   May we go where he is gone,
    Rest and reign with him in heaven.
                Alleluya!

A - men.

A - men.

135

SAVANNAH (OR HERRNHUT). (7.7.7.7.)
Moderately fast ♩ = 100.

Melody from a MS. Choralbuch
(Herrnhut, c. 1740) as given in
J. WESLEY'S '*Foundery Collection*,' 1742.

C. *Wesley*, 1707–88.

LOVE'S redeeming work is done;
  Fought the fight, the battle won:
Lo, our Sun's eclipse is o'er!
Lo, he sets in blood no more!

2 Vain the stone, the watch, the seal,
  Christ has burst the gates of hell;
  Death in vain forbids his rise;
  Christ has opened Paradise.

3 Lives again our glorious King;
  Where, O Death, is now thy sting?
  Dying once, he all doth save;
  Where thy victory, O grave?

4 Soar we now where Christ has led,
  Following our exalted Head;
  Made like him, like him we rise;
  Ours the cross, the grave, the skies.

5. Hail the Lord of earth and heaven!
    Praise to thee by both be given:
   Thee we greet triumphant now;
   Hail, the Resurrection thou!

A - men.

THE CHRISTIAN YEAR

136

RESURRECTION MORNING. (87.83.)   P. C. BUCK.
With some freedom, but not too fast ♩=100.

NOTE.—*This hymn may also be sung to* HORNSEY (*Appendix, No.* 28).

S. *Baring-Gould,* 1834–1924.

1 ON the Resurrection morning
    Soul and body meet again;
No more sorrow, no more weeping,
        No more pain!

2*Here awhile they must be parted,
    And the flesh its Sabbath keep,
Waiting in a holy stillness,
        Wrapt in sleep.

3*For a while the wearied body
    Lies with feet toward the morn;
Till the last and brightest Easter
        Day be born.

4*But the soul in contemplation
    Utters earnest prayer and strong,
Bursting at the Resurrection
        Into song.

5 Soul and body reunited
    Thenceforth nothing shall divide,
Waking up in Christ's own likeness
        Satisfied.

6 O the beauty, O the gladness
    Of that Resurrection day,
Which shall not through endless ages
        Pass away!

7 On that happy Easter morning
    All the graves their dead restore;
Father, sister, child, and mother
        Meet once more.

8. To that brightest of all meetings
    Bring us, Jesu Christ, at last,
By thy Cross, through death and judgement,
        Holding fast.

A-men.

EASTERTIDE

137

ELLACOMBE. (76. 76. D.)
Brightly ♩ = 116.

Mainz Gesangbuch, 1833.

This hymn may also be sung to ACH GOTT VON HIMMELREICHE (*No. 179*).

’Αναστάσεως ἡμέρα.

St. John Damascene, c. 750.
Tr. J. M. Neale ‡.

THE Day of Resurrection!
  Earth, tell it out abroad;
The Passover of gladness,
  The Passover of God!
From death to life eternal,
  From earth unto the sky,
Our Christ hath brought us over
  With hymns of victory.

2 Our hearts be pure from evil,
  That we may see aright
The Lord in rays eternal
  Of resurrection-light;
And, listening to his accents,
  May hear so calm and plain
His own 'All hail,' and, hearing,
  May raise the victor strain.

3. Now let the heavens be joyful,
    And earth her song begin,
  The round world keep high triumph,
    And all that is therein;
  Let all things seen and unseen
    Their notes of gladness blend,
  For Christ the Lord hath risen,
    Our Joy that hath no end.

A - men.

THE CHRISTIAN YEAR

MACH'S MIT MIR GOTT. (8 7. 8 7. 8 8.) **138**

Very slow and solemn ♩ = 46.

Melody by J. H. Schein, 1586-1630.
Harmony from J. S. Bach.

NOTE.—*An adaptation of this tune to the L. M. measure is found at Hymn 459 (EISENACH). Those who think it inadvisable to use two versions of the same tune can sing the present hymn to the tune on the following page.*

Αὕτη ἡ κλητή.

St. John Damascene, c. 750
Tr. J. M. Neale.

THOU hallowed chosen morn of praise,
    That best and greatest shinest:
Lady and queen and day of days,
    Of things divine, divinest!
On thee our praises Christ adore
For ever and for evermore.

2 Come, let us taste the Vine's new fruit,
    For heavenly joy preparing;
To-day the branches with the Root
    In Resurrection sharing:
Whom as true God our hymns adore
For ever and for evermore.

EASTERTIDE

138 (Alternative Tune)

DIES IST DER TAG. (87 87. 88.)
In moderate time ♩ =120.

Melody by P. Sohren, c. 1676
(rhythm slightly adapted).

3 Rise, Sion, rise! and looking forth,
   Behold thy children round thee!
From east and west, from south and north,
   Thy scattered sons have found thee;
And in thy bosom Christ adore
   For ever and for evermore.

4. O Father, O co-equal Son,
   O co-eternal Spirit,
In persons Three, in substance One,
   And One in power and merit;
In thee baptized, we thee adore
   For ever and for evermore. Amen.

A - men.

A - men.

THE CHRISTIAN YEAR

139

ST. FULBERT. (C. M.)
Moderately slow ♩ = 66.

H. J. GAUNTLETT, 1805–76.

St. Fulbert of Chartres, c. 1000.
Tr. R. Campbell.

Chorus novae Jerusalem.

YE choirs of new Jerusalem,
  Your sweetest notes employ,
The Paschal victory to hymn
  In strains of holy joy.

2 How Judah's Lion burst his chains,
  And crushed the serpent's head;
And brought with him, from death's domains,
  The long-imprisoned dead.

EASTERTIDE

3 From hell's devouring jaws the prey
   Alone our Leader bore;
His ransomed hosts pursue their way
   Where he hath gone before.

4 Triumphant in his glory now
   His sceptre ruleth all,
Earth, heaven, and hell before him bow,
   And at his footstool fall.

5 While joyful thus his praise we sing,
   His mercy we implore,
Into his palace bright to bring
   And keep us evermore.

6. All glory to the Father be,
   All glory to the Son,
All glory, Holy Ghost, to thee,
   While endless ages run. Alleluya! Amen.

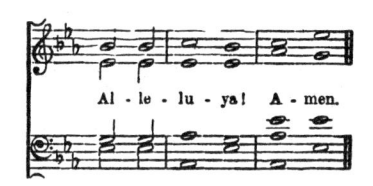

The following are also suitable:

 93 The God of love my Shepherd is.
319 Lord, enthroned in heavenly splendour.
380 Come, ye faithful, raise the anthem.
461 O praise our great and gracious Lord.
490 The King of love my Shepherd is.
491 The Lord my pasture shall prepare.
494 The strain upraise of joy and praise.
534 Praise the Lord of heaven.
535 Praise the Lord! ye heavens, adore him.
536 Praise to the Lord

THE CHRISTIAN YEAR

140

LINCOLN. (C. M.)
Moderately slow ♩ = 66.

Ravenscroft's Psalter, 1621.

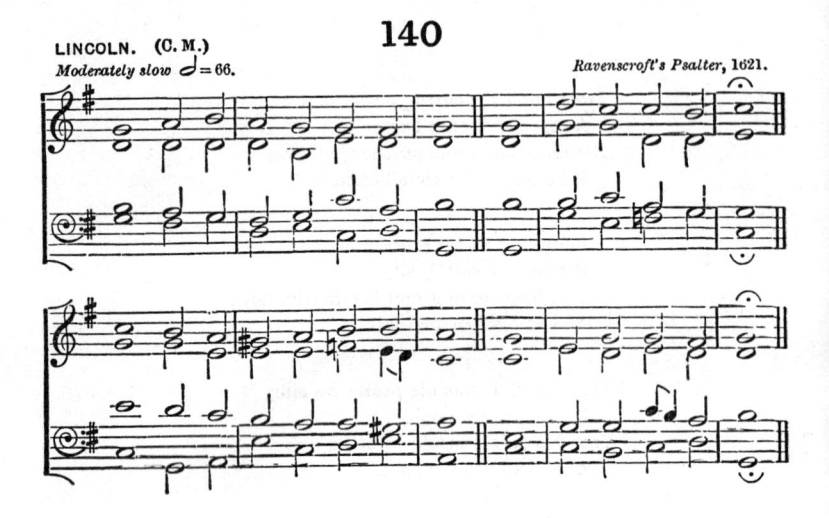

ROGATION DAYS

J. Keble, 1792-1866.

LORD, in thy name thy servants plead,
   And thou hast sworn to hear;
Thine is the harvest, thine the seed,
   The fresh and fading year.

2 Our hope, when autumn winds blew wild,
   We trusted, Lord, with thee;
And still, now spring has on us smiled,
   We wait on thy decree.

3 The former and the latter rain,
   The summer sun and air,
The green ear, and the golden grain,
   All thine, are ours by prayer

4 Thine too by right, and ours by grace,
   The wondrous growth unseen,
The hopes that soothe, the fears that brace,
   The love that shines serene.

5. So grant the precious things brought forth
   By sun and moon below,
That thee in thy new heaven and earth
   We never may forgo.

A - men.

ROGATION DAYS

140 (ALTERNATIVE VERSION)

Harmonised by W. Harrison in Ravenscroft's Psalter.

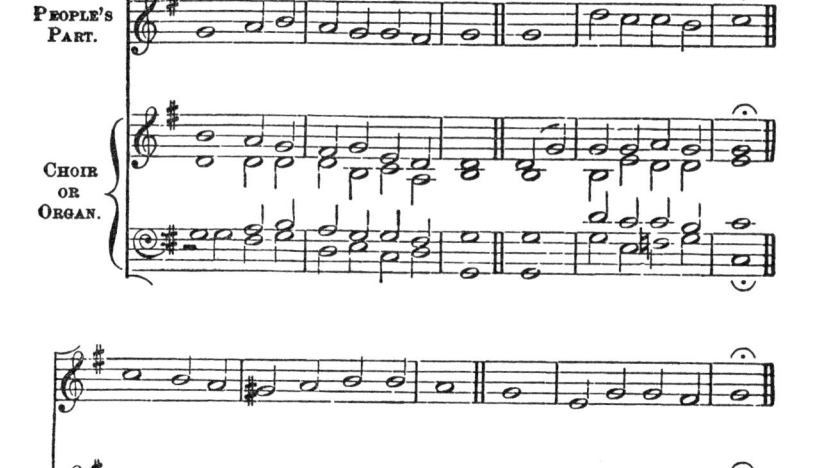

PEOPLE'S PART.

CHOIR OR ORGAN.

[*This version may be used in connexion with the other for one or more verses, the people singing the melody as usual.*]

The following are also suitable:

384 Eternal Ruler of the ceaseless round.
423 Judge eternal, throned in splendour.
447 O God of Bethel, by whose hand.
475 Rejoice, O land, in God thy might.
492 The Lord will come and not be slow.
528 Father of men.
558 God of our fathers.
564 The King, O God.
650 Litany for Rogationtide.

For the Rogation Procession the Proses at Nos. 785 or 786 may be useful; also the Prayer-book Litany, and Benedicite.

THE CHRISTIAN YEAR

141, 142

Mode viii.   arr. J. H. A.

NOTE.—*If a simpler melody is needed, that given at No. 61 may be found suitable.*

ASCENSIONTIDE

See also: 628 Hail thee, Festival Day.   629 O King most high of earth and sky.

OFFICE HYMN. *Till Whitsun Even,* E.

141

Aeterne Rex altissime.   *c. 5th cent.*   Tr. J. M. Neale.

ETERNAL Monarch, King most high,
Whose Blood hath brought redemption nigh,
By whom the death of Death was wrought,
And conquering Grace's battle fought:

2 Ascending to the throne of might,
And seated at the Father's right,
All power in heaven is Jesu's own,
That here his manhood had not known.

ASCENSIONTIDE
141, 142 (Modern Tune)

GONFALON ROYAL. (L. M.)
With movement ♩ = 120. Unison.
P. C. BUCK.

NOTE.—*This hymn may also be sung to* DEUS TUORUM MILITUM (*No.* 181).

3 That so, in nature's triple frame,
Each heavenly and each earthly name,
And things in hell's abyss abhorred,
May bend the knee and own him Lord.

4 Yea, Angels tremble when they see
How changed is our humanity;
That flesh hath purged what flesh had stained,
And God, the Flesh of God, hath reigned.

5 Be thou our joy and strong defence,
Who art our future recompense:
So shall the light that springs from thee
Be ours through all eternity.

6. O risen Christ, ascended Lord,
All praise to thee let earth accord,
Who art, while endless ages run,
With Father and with Spirit One.
Amen.

142

OFFICE HYMN. M.
Tu Christe nostrum gaudium.
c. 5th cent. Tr. L. H.

O CHRIST, our joy, to whom is given
A throne o'er all the thrones of heaven,
In thee, whose hand all things obey,
The world's vain pleasures pass away.

2 So, suppliants here, we seek to win
Thy pardon for thy people's sin,
That, by thine all-prevailing grace,
Uplifted, we may seek thy face.

3 And when, all heaven beneath thee bowed,
Thou com'st to judgement throned in cloud,
Then from our guilt wash out the stain
And give us our lost crowns again.

4 Be thou our joy and strong defence,
Who art our future recompense:
So shall the light that springs from thee
Be ours through all eternity.

5 O risen Christ, ascended Lord,
All praise to thee let earth accord,
Who art, while endless ages run,
With Father and with Spirit One.
Amen.

THE CHRISTIAN YEAR
143

LLANFAIR. (7 4. 7 4. D.)
In moderate time, dignified ♩ = 80.
Melody by R. WILLIAMS, 1817.

Voices in unison.

Org.

NOTE.—*This hymn may also be sung to the* ORIGINAL *version of* EASTER HYMN (*No.* 133).

C. *Wesley*, 1707-88, *and T. Cotterill* † (1820).

HAIL the day that sees him rise Alleluya!
Glorious to his native skies; Alleluya!
Christ, awhile to mortals given, Alleluya!
Enters now the highest heaven! Alleluya!

2 There the glorious triumph waits; Alleluya!
Lift your heads, eternal gates! Alleluya!
Christ hath vanquished death and sin; Alleluya!
Take the King of glory in. Alleluya!

3* See! the heaven its Lord receives, Alleluya!
Yet he loves the earth he leaves: Alleluya!
Though returning to his throne, Alleluya!
Still he calls mankind his own. Alleluya!

4* See! he lifts his hands above; Alleluya!
See! he shows the prints of love: Alleluya!
Hark! his gracious lips bestow Alleluya!
Blessings on his Church below. Alleluya!

5* Still for us he intercedes; Alleluya!
His prevailing death he pleads; Alleluya!
Near himself prepares our place, Alleluya!
Harbinger of human race. Alleluya!

ASCENSIONTIDE

Unison. 6 Lord, though parted from our sight,   **Alleluya!**
    Far above yon azure height,   **Alleluya!**
    Grant our hearts may thither rise,   **Alleluya!**
    Seeking thee beyond the skies.   Alleluya!

Unison. 7. There we shall with thee remain,   **Alleluya!**
    Partners of thine endless reign;   Alleluya!
    There thy face unclouded see,   Alleluya!
    Find our heaven of heavens in thee.   Alleluya!

144

BROMSGROVE. (C. M.)
In moderate time ♩ = 84.
Later form of melody from Psalmodia Evangelica, 1789.

NOTE.—*This hymn may also be sung to* METZLER'S REDHEAD No. 66 (*Appendix*, *No.* 29).

Compline.   Jesu nostra redemptio.   *c.* 8*th cent.*   *Tr.* J. *Chandler* †.

O CHRIST, our hope, our hearts'
    desire,
Redemption's only spring;
Creator of the world art thou,
    Its Saviour and its King.

2 How vast the mercy and the love
    Which laid our sins on thee,
And led thee to a cruel death
    To set thy people free.

3 But now the bonds of death are burst,
    The ransom has been paid;
And thou art on thy Father's throne
    In glorious robes arrayed.

4 O may thy mighty love prevail
    Our sinful souls to spare;
O may we come before thy throne,
    And find acceptance there!

5 O Christ, be thou our present joy,
    Our future great reward;
Our only glory may it be
    To glory in the Lord.

6 All praise to thee, ascended Lord;
    All glory ever be
To Father, Son, and Holy Ghost,
    Through all eternity. Amen.

THE CHRISTIAN YEAR
145

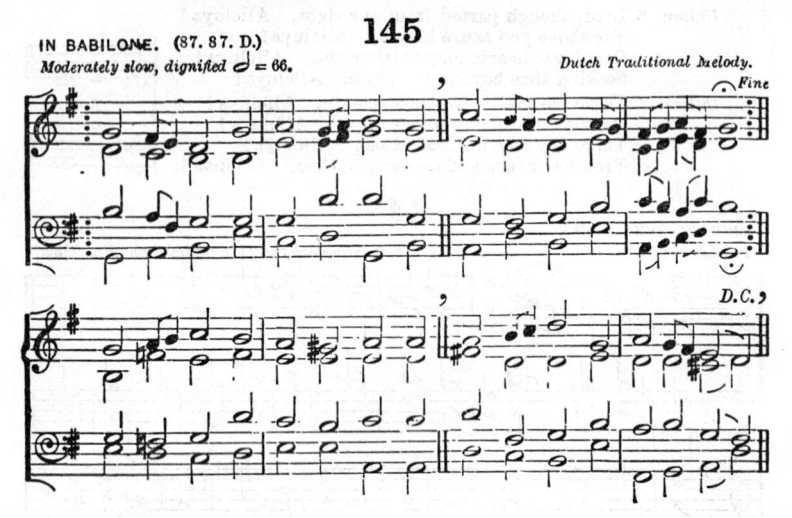

IN BABILONE. (87. 87. D.)
Moderately slow, dignified ♩ = 66.

Dutch Traditional Melody.

Bishop Chr. Wordsworth, 1807–85.

SEE the Conqueror mounts in triumph,
   See the King in royal state
Riding on the clouds his chariot
   To his heavenly palace gate;
Hark! the choirs of angel voices
   Joyful Alleluyas sing,
And the portals high are lifted
   To receive their heavenly King.

Unison. 2 Who is this that comes in glory,
   With the trump of jubilee?
Lord of battles, God of armies,
   He has gained the victory;
He who on the Cross did suffer,
   He who from the grave arose,
He has vanquished sin and Satan,
   He by death has spoiled his foes.

3 Thou hast raised our human nature
   In the clouds to God's right hand;
There we sit in heavenly places,
   There with thee in glory stand;
Jesus reigns, adored by Angels;
   Man with God is on the throne;
Mighty Lord, in thine Ascension
   We by faith behold our own.

ASCENSIONTIDE

Unison. 4. Glory be to God the Father;
 Glory be to God the Son,
Dying, risen, ascending for us,
 Who the heavenly realm has won;
Glory to the Holy Spirit;
 To One God in persons Three;
Glory both in earth and heaven,
 Glory, endless glory, be. Amen.

Part 2.

5 Holy Ghost, Illuminator,
 Shed thy beams upon our eyes,
Help us to look up with Stephen,
 And to see beyond the skies,
Where the Son of Man in glory
 Standing is at God's right hand,
Beckoning on his Martyr army,
 Succouring his faithful band;

6 See him, who is gone before us,
 Heavenly mansions to prepare,
See him, who is ever pleading
 For us with prevailing prayer,
See him, who with sound of trumpet
 And with his angelic train,
Summoning the world to judgement,
 On the clouds will come again.

Unison. 7. Glory be to God the Father;
 Glory be to God the Son,
Dying, risen, ascending for us,
 Who the heavenly realm has won;
Glory to the Holy Spirit;
 To One God in persons Three;
Glory both in earth and heaven,
 Glory, endless glory, be. Amen.

THE CHRISTIAN YEAR

146

TUGWOOD. (L.M.)
In moderate time, very dignified ♩ = 76.

NICHOLAS GATTY.

NOTE.—*This hymn can also be sung to* BEATA NOBIS (*No.* 185).

Hymnum canamus gloriae.

The Venerable Bede, 673–735.
Tr. B. Webb.

Unison.

1. SING we triumphant hymns of praise,
New hymns to heaven exulting raise:
Christ, by a road before untrod,
Ascendeth to the throne of God.

2. The holy apostolic band
Upon the Mount of Olives stand,
And with the Virgin-mother see
Jesu's resplendent majesty.

3. To whom the Angels, drawing nigh,
'Why stand and gaze upon the sky?
This is the Saviour!' thus they say,
'This is his noble triumph-day!'

4. 'Again shall ye behold him, so
As ye to-day have seen him go;
In glorious pomp ascending high,
Up to the portals of the sky.'

5.* O grant us thitherward to tend,
And with unwearied hearts ascend
Toward thy kingdom's throne, where thou,
As is our faith, art seated now.

6.* Be thou our joy and strong defence,
Who art our future recompense:
So shall the light that springs from thee
Be ours through all eternity.

Unison. 7. O risen Christ, ascended Lord,
All praise to thee let earth accord,
Who art, while endless ages run,
With Father and with Spirit One.
Amen.

A - men.

208

ASCENSIONTIDE
147

ST. MAGNUS (NOTTINGHAM). (C.M.)
Moderately slow ♩ = 60.

J. CLARK, 1670-1707.

T. Kelly, 1769-1854.

THE head that once was crowned with thorns
  Is crowned with glory now:
A royal diadem adorns
  The mighty Victor's brow.

2 The highest place that heaven affords
    Is his, is his by right,
  The King of kings and Lord of lords,
    And heaven's eternal Light;

3 The joy of all who dwell above,
    The joy of all below,
  To whom he manifests his love,
    And grants his name to know.

4 To them the Cross, with all its shame,
    With all its grace is given:
  Their name an everlasting name,
    Their joy the joy of heaven.

5 They suffer with their Lord below,
    They reign with him above,
  Their profit and their joy to know
    The mystery of his love.

6. The Cross he bore is life and health,
    Though shame and death to him;
  His people's hope, his people's wealth,
    Their everlasting theme.

A - men.

THE CHRISTIAN YEAR

148

NUN FREUT EUCH. (87. 87. 887.)
Slow and dignified ♩ = 50.

Christliche Lieder (Wittenberg, 1524).
Adapted and harmonized by J. S. BACH.

A. T. Russell, 1806–74, and others.

1. THE Lord ascendeth up on high,
   Loud anthems round him swelling;
   The Lord hath triumphed gloriously,
   In power and might excelling:
   Hell and the grave are captive led;
   Lo, he returns, our glorious Head,
   To his eternal dwelling.

2. The heavens with joy receive their Lord;
   O day of exultation!
   By Saints, by Angel-hosts adored
   For his so great salvation:
   O earth, adore thy glorious King,
   His Rising, his Ascension sing
   With grateful adoration.

Unison. 3. By Saints in earth and Saints in heaven,
   With songs for ever blended,
   All praise to Christ our King be given,
   Who hath to heaven ascended:
   To Father, Son, and Holy Ghost,
   The God of heaven's resplendent host,
   In bright array extended. Amen.

ASCENSIONTIDE

149

OLD 25TH. (D.S.M.)
In moderate time ♩ = 72.

Day's Psalter, 1563
(rhythm slightly adapted).

Mrs. E. Toke, 1812-72.

THOU art gone up on high,
   To mansions in the skies,
And round thy throne unceasingly
   The songs of praise arise;
But we are lingering here,
   With sin and care opprest:
Lord, send thy promised Comforter,
   And lead us to thy rest.

2 Thou art gone up on high;
   But thou didst first come down,
Through earth's most bitter misery
   To pass unto thy crown;
And girt with griefs and fears
   Our onward course must be;
But only let that path of tears
   Lead us at last to thee.

3. Thou art gone up on high;
   But thou shalt come again,
With all the bright ones of the sky
   Attendants in thy train.
O, by thy saving power
   So make us live and die,
That we may stand in that dread hour
   At thy right hand on high.

A - men.

The following are also suitable:

301 Alleluya, sing to Jesus.
364 All hail the power of Jesu's name.
368 At the name of Jesus.
380 Come, ye faithful, raise the anthem.

424 King of glory.
470 Praise, my soul.
476 Rejoice, the Lord is King.

THE CHRISTIAN YEAR

150

Mode i.   arr. J. H. A.

A - men.

WHITSUNTIDE

OFFICE HYMN. *Whitsun Eve,*
E.: *and daily till Trinity*
Sunday. M.

Jam Christus astra ascenderat.

c. 4th cent.   Tr. P. D.

W̲HEN Christ our Lord had passed once more
    Into the heaven he left before,
He sent a Comforter below
The Father's promise to bestow.

WHITSUNTIDE

150 (Modern Tune)

MONTE CASSINO. (L.M.)
In moderate time ♩ = 72.
Italian Hymn Melody.

Note.—*This hymn may also be sung to the Grenoble Melody at Hymn 181.*

2 The solemn time was soon to fall
Which told the number mystical;
For since the Resurrection day
A week of weeks had passed away.

3 At the third hour a rushing noise
Came like the tempest's sudden voice,
And mingled with the Apostles' prayer,
Proclaiming loud that God was there.

4 From out the Father's light it came,
That beautiful and kindly flame,
To kindle every Christian heart,
And fervour of the Word impart.

5 As then, O Lord, thou didst fulfil,
Each holy heart to do thy will,
So now do thou our sins forgive
And make the world in peace to live.

6. To God the Father, God the Son,
And God the Spirit, praise be done;
May Christ the Lord upon us pour
The Spirit's gift for evermore.
                          Amen.

A - men.

See also:

630 Hail thee, Festival Day.
631 Spirit of mercy, truth, and love.

THE CHRISTIAN YEAR

151

Mode i.   arr. J. H. A.

OFFICE HYMN. *Daily till Trinity Sunday.* E.   *c. 4th cent.* Tr. R. E. R.
Beata nobis gaudia.

REJOICE! the year upon its way
Has brought again that blessèd day,
When on the chosen of the Lord
The Holy Spirit was outpoured.

WHITSUNTIDE

151 (Modern Version)

AETERNA CHRISTI MUNERA (ROUEN). (L. M.)
In moderate time ♩ = 144. May be sung in unison.

Rouen Church Melody.
Harmonized by Martin Shaw.

Note.—*This hymn may also be sung to* Beata Nobis (*No. 185*).

2 On each the fire, descending, stood
In quivering tongues' similitude—
Tongues, that their words might ready
    prove,   [love.
And fire, to make them flame with

3 To all in every tongue they spoke;
Amazement in the crowd awoke,
Who mocked, as overcome with wine,
Those who were filled with power
    divine.

4 These things were done in type that day,
When Eastertide had passed away,
The number told which once set free
The captive at the jubilee.

5 And now, O holy God, this day
Regard us as we humbly pray,
And send us, from thy heavenly seat,
The blessings of the Paraclete.

6. To God the Father, God the Son,
And God the Spirit, praise be done;
May Christ the Lord upon us pour
The Spirit's gift for evermore. Amen.

THE CHRISTIAN YEAR

152

DOWN AMPNEY. (6 6. 11. D.)
Moderately slow ♩ = 88 (♩ = 44).

R. Vaughan Williams.

Bianco da Siena, d. 1434. Tr. R. F. Littledale.
Discendi, Amor santo.

COME down, O Love divine,
  Seek thou this soul of mine,
And visit it with thine own ardour glowing;
  O Comforter, draw near,
  Within my heart appear,
And kindle it, thy holy flame bestowing.

2 O let it freely burn,
  Till earthly passions turn
To dust and ashes in its heat consuming;
  And let thy glorious light
  Shine ever on my sight,
And clothe me round, the while my path illuming.

3 Let holy charity
  Mine outward vesture be,
And lowliness become mine inner clothing;
  True lowliness of heart,
  Which takes the humbler part,
And o'er its own shortcomings weeps with loathing.

4. And so the yearning strong,
  With which the soul will long,
Shall far outpass the power of human telling;
  For none can guess its grace,
  Till he become the place
Wherein the Holy Spirit makes his dwelling.

A - men.

WHITSUNTIDE

153

VENI CREATOR. (L. M.)
Slow ♩ = 58.

Attributed to T. TALLIS, *c.* 1515–85.

Last two lines (to be sung in unison).

Praise to thy e-ter-nal me-rit, Fa-ther, Son, and Ho-ly Spi-rit. A-men.

NOTE.—*This hymn may be also sung to the Mechlin Melody at Hymn* 154 *or to Attwood's Melody at Hymn* 156.

Bishop J. Cosin, 1594–1672. Based on
Veni, Creator Spiritus.

COME, Holy Ghost, our souls inspire,
And lighten with celestial fire;
Thou the anointing Spirit art,
Who dost thy sevenfold gifts impart:

2 Thy blessèd unction from above
Is comfort, life, and fire of love;
Enable with perpetual light
The dullness of our blinded sight:

3 Anoint and cheer our soilèd face
With the abundance of thy grace:
Keep far our foes, give peace at home;
Where thou art guide no ill can come.

4. Teach us to know the Father, Son,
And thee, of Both, to be but One;
That through the ages all along
This may be our endless song,
  Praise to thy eternal merit,
  Father, Son, and Holy Spirit. Amen.

THE CHRISTIAN YEAR

154

Mode viii.   arr. J. H. A.

* *In some texts the B is flattened.*

Terce.   *Before 10th cent. Tr. and rev. Y. H.*

Veni, Creator Spiritus.

COME, O Creator Spirit, come,
  And make within our hearts thy home;
To us thy grace celestial give,
Who of thy breathing move and live.

WHITSUNTIDE

154 (Mechlin Version)

VENI CREATOR. (L. M.)
In free rhythm: to be sung in unison.

Melody from 'Vesperale Romanum'
(Mechlin) Mode viii; arr. J. H. A.

Another accompaniment is given in the Appendix (No. 30).

2 O Comforter, that name is thine,
Of God most high the gift divine;
The well of life, the fire of love,
Our souls' anointing from above.

3 Thou dost appear in sevenfold dower
The sign of God's almighty power;
The Father's promise, making rich
With saving truth our earthly speech.

4 Our senses with thy light inflame,
Our hearts to heavenly love reclaim;
Our bodies' poor infirmity
With strength perpetual fortify.

5 Our mortal foe afar repel,
Grant us henceforth in peace to dwell;
And so to us, with thee for guide,
No ill shall come, no harm betide.

6. May we by thee the Father learn,
And know the Son, and thee discern,
Who art of both; and thus adore
In perfect faith for evermore. Amen.

If this tune is used for Hymn No. 153, the last two lines will begin thus:

Praise to thy e - ter - nal mer - it, Fa - ther, &c.

# THE CHRISTIAN YEAR

155

The Golden Sequence.
Veni, sancte Spiritus.

Mode i.

13th cent. Ascribed to Abp. Stephen Langton.
Tr. J. M. Neale.
arr. J. H. A.

1 Come, thou holy Paraclete, ✶ And from thy celestial seat Send thy light and brilliancy: 3 Come, of comforters the best, Of the soul the sweetest guest,

2 Father of the poor, draw near; Giver of all gifts, be here; Come, the soul's true radiancy: 4 Thou in labour rest most sweet, Thou art shadow from the heat,

220

WHITSUNTIDE

155 (*continued*)

Come in toil re - fresh - ing - ly: 5 O thou Light, most
Com - fort in ad - ver - si - ty. 6 Where thou art not,

pure and blest, Shine with - in the in - most breast Of thy
man hath nought; Ev - 'ry ho - ly deed and thought Comes from

faith - ful com - pa - ny. 7 What is soil - ed,
thy Di - vi - ni - ty. 8 What is ri - gid,

THE CHRISTIAN YEAR

155 (continued)

make thou pure; What is wound-ed, work its cure; What is parch-ed, fruc-ti-fy;
gent-ly bend; What is fro-zen, warm-ly tend; Straight-en what goes err-ing-ly.

9 Fill thy faithful, who con-fide In thy power to guard and guide, With thy seven-fold Mys-te-ry.

10. Here thy grace and vir-tue send: Grant sal-va-tion in the end, And in heaven fe-li-ci-ty.

WHITSUNTIDE

155 (Modern Tune)

VENI SANCTE SPIRITUS. (7 7 7. D.)

Slow ♩ = 58.

S. WEBBE the elder, 1740–1816.

The Golden Sequence.
Veni, sancte Spiritus.

13th cent. *Tr. J. M. Neale.*

COME, thou holy Paraclete,
And from thy celestial seat
  Send thy light and brilliancy:
Father of the poor, draw near;
Giver of all gifts, be here;
  Come, the soul's true radiancy:

2 Come, of comforters the best,
Of the soul the sweetest guest,
  Come in toil refreshingly:
Thou in labour rest most sweet,
Thou art shadow from the heat,
  Comfort in adversity.

3 O thou Light, most pure and blest,
Shine within the inmost breast
  Of thy faithful company.
Where thou art not, man hath nought;
Every holy deed and thought
  Comes from thy Divinity.

4 What is soilèd, make thou pure;
What is wounded, work its cure;
  What is parchèd, fructify;
What is rigid, gently bend;
What is frozen, warmly tend;
  Straighten what goes erringly.

5. Fill thy faithful, who confide
In thy power to guard and guide,
  With thy sevenfold Mystery.
Here thy grace and virtue send:
Grant salvation in the end,
  And in heaven felicity.

A - men.

THE CHRISTIAN YEAR

156

VENI CREATOR (ATTWOOD). (8 8. 8 8. 8 8.)

Moderately slow ♩ = 69.

T. ATTWOOD, 1765–1838.

WHITSUNTIDE

156 (*continued*)

NOTE.—*This tune can also be used for* COME, HOLY GHOST (*Hymn* 153). *In this case each verse will be six lines, instead of four.*

This hymn may also be sung to FALKLAND (*No.* 219).

J. Dryden, 1631-1701.
Based on Veni, Creator Spiritus.

CREATOR Spirit, by whose aid
The world's foundations first were laid,
Come, visit every pious mind;
Come, pour thy joys on human kind;
From sin and sorrow set us free,
And make thy temples worthy thee.

2 O Source of uncreated light,
The Father's promised Paraclete,
Thrice holy Fount, thrice holy Fire,
Our hearts with heavenly love inspire;
Come, and thy sacred unction bring
To sanctify us while we sing.

3 Plenteous of grace, descend from high
Rich in thy sevenfold energy;
Make us eternal truths receive,
And practise all that we believe;
Give us thyself, that we may see
The Father and the Son by thee.

4. Immortal honour, endless fame,
Attend the almighty Father's name;
The Saviour Son be glorified,
Who for lost man's redemption died;
And equal adoration be,
Eternal Paraclete, to thee. Amen.

THE CHRISTIAN YEAR

157

WICKLOW. (8 6. 8 4.)
In moderate time ♩ = 100.

Irish Traditional Melody (slightly adapted).

NOTE.—*This hymn may also be sung to* ST. CUTHBERT (*Appendix, No.* 31).

Harriet Auber, 1773-1862.

OUR blest Redeemer, ere he breathed
His tender last farewell,
A Guide, a Comforter, bequeathed
With us to dwell.

2 He came in tongues of living flame,
To teach, convince, subdue;
All-powerful as the wind he came,
As viewless too.

3 He came sweet influence to impart,
A gracious, willing Guest,
While he can find one humble heart
Wherein to rest.

4 And his that gentle voice we hear,
Soft as the breath of even,
That checks each fault, that calms each fear,
And speaks of heaven.

5 And every virtue we possess,
And every victory won,
And every thought of holiness,
Are his alone.

6. Spirit of purity and grace,
Our weakness, pitying, see:
O make our hearts thy dwelling-place,
And worthier thee.

A - men.

WHITSUNTIDE

158

STROUDWATER. (C. M.)
Moderately slow ♩ = 90.

The Psalter in Metre, 1899.
Attributed there to Wilkins' Psalmody (c. 1750).

NOTE.—*This hymn may also be sung to* WINCHESTER OLD (*No.* 30).

J. Keble, 1792–1866.

WHEN God of old came down from heaven,
In power and wrath he came;
Before his feet the clouds were riven,
Half darkness and half flame:

2 But when he came the second time,
He came in power and love;
Softer than gale at morning prime
Hovered his holy Dove.

3 The fires that rushed on Sinai down
In sudden torrents dread,
Now gently light, a glorious crown,
On every sainted head.

Unison.
4 And as on Israel's awe-struck ear
The voice exceeding loud,
The trump, that Angels quake to hear,
Thrilled from the deep dark cloud;

5 So, when the Spirit of our God
Came down his flock to find,
A voice from heaven was heard abroad,
A rushing mighty wind.

Unison. 6 It fills the Church of God; it fills
The sinful world around;
Only in stubborn hearts and wills
No place for it is found.

7. Come Lord, come Wisdom, Love, and Power,
Open our ears to hear;
Let us not miss the accepted hour;
Save, Lord, by love or fear.

A - men.

The following are also suitable:

145 (Pt. 2) Holy Ghost, Illuminator.
384 Eternal Ruler of the ceaseless round.
393 Glorious things of thee are spoken.
396 Gracious Spirit, Holy Ghost.
438 Love of the Father.
453 O Holy Spirit, Lord of grace.
452 O King enthroned on high.
458 O Lord of hosts, all heaven possessing.

159

TRINITY SUNDAY

See also: 632 Eternal Light, Divinity.   633 All hail, adorèd Trinity.

OFFICE HYMN. E. *and* M.   *c. 10th cent.   Tr. J. M. Neale.*

Adesto, sancta Trinitas.

BE present, Holy Trinity,
Like splendour, and one Deity:
Of things above, and things below,
Beginning, that no end shall know.

TRINITY SUNDAY

159 (Modern Tune)

ADESTO SANCTA TRINITAS. (L. M.)

In moderate time ♩ = 144. *To be sung in unison.*

Chartres Church Melody.
Harmonized by R. V. W.

2 Thee all the armies of the sky
  Adore, and laud, and magnify;
  And Nature, in her triple frame,
  For ever sanctifies thy name.

3 And we, too, thanks and homage pay,
  Thine own adoring flock to-day;
  O join to that celestial song
  The praises of our suppliant throng!

4 Light, sole and one, we thee confess,
  With triple praise we rightly bless;
  Alpha and Omega we own,
  With every spirit round thy throne.

5. To thee, O unbegotten One,
  And thee, O sole-begotten Son,
  And thee, O Holy Ghost, we raise
  Our equal and eternal praise.
                    Amen.

THE CHRISTIAN YEAR

160

Mode iv.   *arr.* J. H. A.

* *In some texts the B is not flattened.*

OFFICE HYMN. M.   *c.* 10*th cent.* *Tr.* P. D.

O Pater sancte.

FATHER most holy, merciful and tender;
Jesus our Saviour, with the Father reigning;
Spirit all-kindly, Advocate, Defender,
Light never waning;

2 Trinity sacred, Unity unshaken;
Deity perfect, giving and forgiving,
Light of the Angels, Life of the forsaken,
Hope of all living;

TRINITY SUNDAY

160 (Modern Tune)

CHRISTE DU BEISTAND. (11 11, 11 5.)
Very slow ♩ = 42. [May be sung in unison throughout.]

M. A. von LÖWENSTERN,
1594–1648.

Slightly slower.

Light ne - ver wan - ing, Light ne - ver wan - ing;

NOTE.—*This hymn may also be sung to the Rouen Melody at Hymn 636.*

3 Maker of all things, all thy creatures praise thee;
   Lo, all things serve thee through thy whole creation:
   Hear us, Almighty, hear us as we raise thee
      Heart's adoration.

Unison.
4. To the all-ruling triune God be glory:
   Highest and greatest, help thou our endeavour;
   We too would praise thee, giving honour worthy,
      Now and for ever. Amen.

A - men.

THE CHRISTIAN YEAR

161

ST. FLAVIAN. (C. M.)
Moderately slow ♩ = 66.

Adapted from Psalm 132
in 'Day's Psalter,' 1566.

Suitable also for other occasions.

F. W. Faber, 1814-68.

HAVE mercy on us, God most high,
Who lift our hearts to thee;
Have mercy on us, worms of earth,
Most holy Trinity.

Part 2.

2 Most ancient of all mysteries,
Before thy throne we lie;
Have mercy now, most merciful,
Most holy Trinity.

3 When heaven and earth were yet unmade,
When time was yet unknown,
Thou in thy bliss and majesty
Didst live and love alone.

4 Thou wert not born; there was no fount
From which thy Being flowed;
There is no end which thou canst reach;
But thou art simply God.

5 How wonderful creation is,
The work which thou didst bless,
And O! what then must thou be like,
Eternal loveliness!

6 How beautiful the Angels are,
The Saints how bright in bliss;
But with thy beauty, Lord, compared,
How dull, how poor is this!

A - men.

TRINITY SUNDAY

161 (ALTERNATIVE VERSION)

Harmonized by T. Ravenscroft in his Psalter, 1621 (rhythm slightly simplified).

[*This version may be used in connexion with the other for one or more verses, the people singing the melody as usual.*]

7 O listen then, most pitiful,
   To thy poor creature's heart:
  It blesses thee that thou art God,
   That thou art what thou art.

8. Most ancient of all mysteries,
   Still at thy throne we lie:
  Have mercy now, most merciful,
   Most holy Trinity.

THE CHRISTIAN YEAR
162

NICAEA. (11 12, 12 10.)
Very slow ♩ = 42.
Slightly faster ♩ = 50.
J. B. DYKES, 1823-76.

NOTE.—*This hymn is marked to be sung at a much slower rate than usual, it may, if preferred, be sung at the more usual rate of ♩ = 63 and the pauses may be omitted.*

A higher setting of this tune will be found in the Appendix (No. 14).

Suitable also for other occasions.   *Bishop R. Heber, 1783-1826.*

HOLY, Holy, Holy! Lord God Almighty!
   Early in the morning our song shall rise to thee;
Holy, Holy, Holy! Merciful and mighty!
   God in three Persons, blessèd Trinity!

2 Holy, Holy, Holy! all the Saints adore thee,
   Casting down their golden crowns around the glassy sea;
Cherubim and Seraphim falling down before thee,
   Which wert, and art, and evermore shalt be.

3 Holy, Holy, Holy! though the darkness hide thee,
   Though the eye of sinful man thy glory may not see,
Only thou art holy, there is none beside thee
   Perfect in power, in love, and purity.

Unison. 4. Holy, Holy, Holy! Lord God Almighty!
   All thy works shall praise thy name, in earth, and sky, and sea;
Holy, Holy, Holy! Merciful and mighty!
   God in three Persons, blessèd Trinity! Amen.

A - men.

TRINITY SUNDAY

163

OLD 22ND (D. C. M.)
In moderate time, very dignified ♩ = 76 (𝅗𝅥 = 38).

Melody from Este's Psalter, 1592
(also in Day's Psalter, 1563).

Τριφεγγὴς μονὰς θεαρχική.

Metrophanes, Bishop of Smyrna,
c. 900. Tr. J. M. Neale.

O UNITY of threefold light,
　Send out thy loveliest ray,
And scatter our transgressions' night,
　And turn it into day;
Make us those temples pure and fair
　Thy glory loveth well,
The spotless tabernacles, where
　Thou may'st vouchsafe to dwell.

2 The glorious hosts of peerless might,
　That ever see thy face,
Thou mak'st the mirrors of thy light,
　The vessels of thy grace.
Thou, when their wondrous strain they weave,
　Hast pleasure in the lay:
Deign thus our praises to receive,
　Albeit from lips of clay.

3. And yet thyself they cannot know,
　Nor pierce the veil of light
That hides thee from the Thrones below,
　As in profoundest night.
How then can mortal accents frame
　Due tribute to their King?
Thou, only, while we praise thy name,
　Forgive us as we sing.

A-men.

The following are also suitable:

372 Bright the vision that delighted.
384 Eternal Ruler.
387 Father of heaven, whose love profound.

404 How shall I sing.
407 Immortal, invisible, God only wise.

235

THE CHRISTIAN YEAR

164

Mode viii. — arr. J. H. A.

A - men.

TRINITY TO ADVENT

164 (Modern Tune)

HILARITER (DIE GANZE WELT). (L. M.)
Rather fast ♩ = 144.

Melody from Cölner Gesangbuch, 1623.
Harmonized by MARTIN SHAW.

NOTE.—*This hymn may also be sung to* ILLSLEY (*No. 61*); *to the Chartres Melody at Hymn* 159; *or to* DEO GRACIAS (*No* 249).

FROM TRINITY SUNDAY TO ADVENT

OFFICE HYMN. *Saturdays.* E.   *St. Ambrose*, 340-97.   Tr. J. M. Neale.

O Lux beata Trinitas.

O TRINITY of blessèd light,
O Unity of princely might,
The fiery sun now goes his way;
Shed thou within our hearts thy ray.

2 To thee our morning song of praise,
To thee our evening prayer we raise;
Thy glory suppliant we adore
For ever and for evermore.

3. All laud to God the Father be;
All praise, eternal Son, to thee;
All glory, as is ever meet,
To God the holy Paraclete. **Amen.**

THE CHRISTIAN YEAR

165

Mode vi.   *arr.* J. H. A.

OFFICE HYMN. *Sundays and week-days.* M.   Nocte surgentes.   *Ascr. to St. Gregory the Great. 6th cent. Tr. P. D.*

FATHER, we praise thee, now the night is over,
   Active and watchful, stand we all before thee;
Singing we offer prayer and meditation:
      Thus we adore thee.

2 Monarch of all things, fit us for thy mansions;
   Banish our weakness, health and wholeness sending;
Bring us to heaven, where thy Saints united
      Joy without ending.

TRINITY TO ADVENT

165 (MODERN TUNE)

CHRISTE SANCTORUM. (11 11. 11 5.)

In moderate time ♩ = 96.
To be sung in unison.

Melody from LA FEILLÉE,
'*Methode du plain-chant*,' 1782.
Harmonized by R. V. W.

3. All-holy Father, Son and equal Spirit,
   Trinity blessèd, send us thy salvation;
   Thine is the glory, gleaming and resounding
           Through all creation. Amen.

A - - - men.

The evening Office Hymn for Sunday, and for every day except Saturday is:
51 O blest Creator of the light.

THE CHRISTIAN YEAR

166

ST. DAVID. (C.M.)
Moderately slow ♩ = 69.

Later form of melody in Ravenscroft's Psalter, 1621.

EMBER DAYS

J. M. Neale, 1818–66

CHRIST is gone up; yet ere he passed
From earth, in heaven to reign,
He formed one holy Church to last
Till he should come again.

2 His twelve Apostles first he made
His ministers of grace;
And they their hands on others laid,
To fill in turn their place

3 So age by age, and year by year,
His grace was handed on;
And still the holy Church is here,
Although her Lord is gone.

4. Let those find pardon, Lord, from thee,
Whose love to her is cold:
And bring them in, and let there be
One Shepherd and one Fold.

167

DUKE STREET. (L.M.)
In moderate time ♩ = 76.

J. Hatton, d. 1793.

EMBER DAYS

J. Montgomery †, 1771–1854.

POUR out thy Spirit from on high;
  Lord, thine assembled servants bless;
Graces and gifts to each supply,
  And clothe thy priests with righteousness.

2 Within the temple when they stand,
  To teach the truth, as taught by thee,
Saviour, like stars in thy right hand
  May all thy Church's pastors be.

3 Wisdom, and zeal, and faith impart,
  Firmness with meekness, from above,
To bear thy people in their heart,
  And love the souls whom thou dost love:

4 To watch, and pray, and never faint,
  By day and night, strict guard to keep,
To warn the sinner, cheer the saint,
  Nourish thy lambs, and feed thy sheep.

5. Then, when their work is finished here,
  May they in hope their charge resign;
When the Chief Shepherd shall appear,
  O God, may they and we be thine.

A - men.

MANCHESTER. (C.M.)
Slow ♩ = 80.

168

ROBERT WAINWRIGHT, 1748–82.

J. M. Neale, 1818–66.

THE earth, O Lord, is one great field
  Of all thy chosen seed;
The crop prepared its fruit to yield;
  The labourers few indeed.

2 We therefore come before thee now
  By fasting and by prayer,
Beseeching of thy love that thou
  Wouldst send more labourers there.

3 Not for our land alone we pray,
  Though that above the rest;
The realms and islands far away,
  O let them all be blest.

4 Endue the bishops of thy flock
  With wisdom and with grace,
Against false doctrine, like a rock,
  To set the heart and face:

5 To all thy priests thy truth reveal,
  And make thy judgements clear;
Make thou thy deacons full of zeal
  And humble and sincere:

6. And give their flocks a lowly mind
  To hear and not in vain;
That each and all may mercy find
  When thou shalt come again.

A - men.

THE CHRISTIAN YEAR

169, 170

Mode ii. *arr. J. H. A.*

DEDICATION FESTIVAL

See also: 634 Hail thee, Festival Day.
635 Eternal Power, whose high abode.
636 Only-begotten, Word of God eternal.
637 Lo! God is here! let us adore.

DEDICATION FESTIVAL

169

Office Hymn. E. *and* M.
c. 7th cent. Tr. J. M. Neale ‡.

Urbs beata Jerusalem.

BLESSÈD City, heavenly Salem,
Vision dear of peace and love,
Who, of living stones upbuilded,
Art the joy of heaven above,
And, with Angel cohorts circled,
As a bride to earth dost move!

2 From celestial realms descending,
Bridal glory round her shed,
To his presence, decked with jewels,
By her Lord shall she be led:
All her streets, and all her bulwarks,
Of pure gold are fashionèd.

3 Bright with pearls her portals glitter,
They are open evermore;
And, by virtue of his merits,
Thither faithful souls may soar,
Who for Christ's dear name in this
Pain and tribulation bore. [world

4 Many a blow and biting sculpture
Fashioned well those stones elect,
In their places now compacted
By the heavenly Architect,
Who therewith hath willed for ever
That his palace should be decked.

5. Laud and honour to the Father;
Laud and honour to the Son;
Laud and honour to the Spirit;
Ever Three, and ever One:
Consubstantial, co-eternal,
While unending ages run. Amen.

170

Office Hymn. M. *and* E.
c. 7th cent. Tr. J. M. Neale.

Angularis fundamentum.

CHRIST is made the sure Foundation,
And the precious Corner-stone,
Who, the two walls underlying,
Bound in each, binds both in one,
Holy Sion's help for ever,
And her confidence alone.

2 All that dedicated City,
Dearly loved by God on high,
In exultant jubilation
Pours perpetual melody:
God the One, and God the Trinal,
Singing everlastingly.

3 To this temple, where we call thee,
Come, O Lord of Hosts, to-day;
With thy wonted loving-kindness
Hear thy people as they pray;
And thy fullest benediction
Shed within its walls for ay.

4 Here vouchsafe to all thy servants
What they supplicate to gain;
Here to have and hold for ever
Those good things their prayers
And hereafter in thy glory [obtain,
With thy blessèd ones to reign.

5. Laud and honour to the Father;
Laud and honour to the Son;
Laud and honour to the Spirit;
Ever Three and ever One:
Consubstantial, co-eternal,
While unending ages run. Amen.

A - men.

THE CHRISTIAN YEAR

169, 170 (Modern Tune)

URBS COELESTIS. (87.87.87.)
In moderate time ♩ = 104 (𝅗𝅥 = 52).

No. XVI from 'The Golden Legend,' 1880.
By H. E. Hodson, 1842-1917.

DEDICATION FESTIVAL

169

OFFICE HYMN. E. and M.
c. 7th cent. Tr. J. M. Neale ‡.

Urbs beata Jerusalem.

BLESSÈD City, heavenly Salem,
Vision dear of peace and love,
Who, of living stones upbuilded,
Art the joy of heaven above,
And, with Angel cohorts circled,
As a bride to earth dost move!

2 From celestial realms descending,
Bridal glory round her shed,
To his presence, decked with jewels,
By her Lord shall she be led :
All her streets, and all her bulwarks,
Of pure gold are fashionèd.

3 Bright with pearls her portals glitter,
They are open evermore;
And, by virtue of his merits,
Thither faithful souls may soar,
Who for Christ's dear name in this
Pain and tribulation bore. [world

4 Many a blow and biting sculpture
Fashioned well those stones elect,
In their places now compacted
By the heavenly Architect,
Who therewith hath willed for ever
That his palace should be decked.

Unison.
5. Laud and honour to the Father;
Laud and honour to the Son;
Laud and honour to the Spirit;
Ever Three, and ever One:
Consubstantial, co-eternal,
While unending ages run. Amen.

170

OFFICE HYMN. M. and E.
c. 7th cent. Tr. J. M. Neale.

Angularis fundamentum.

CHRIST is made the sure Foundation,
And the precious Corner-stone,
Who, the two walls underlying,
Bound in each, binds both in one,
Holy Sion's help for ever,
And her confidence alone.

2 All that dedicated City,
Dearly loved by God on high,
In exultant jubilation
Pours perpetual melody:
God the One, and God the Trinal,
Singing everlastingly.

3 To this temple, where we call thee,
Come, O Lord of Hosts, to-day;
With thy wonted loving-kindness
Hear thy people as they pray;
And thy fullest benediction
Shed within its walls for ay.

4 Here vouchsafe to all thy servants
What they supplicate to gain;
Here to have and hold for ever
Those good things their prayers
And hereafter in thy glory [obtain,
With thy blessèd ones to reign.

Unison.
5. Laud and honour to the Father;
Laud and honour to the Son;
Laud and honour to the Spirit;
Ever Three and ever One:
Consubstantial, co-eternal,
While unending ages run. Amen.

THE CHRISTIAN YEAR

171

ST. EDMUND. (S.M.)
Moderately slow ♩ = 90.

Adapted from Hymn Melody by
E. GILDING, d. 1782.

C. *Guiet*, 1601–64. Tr. *I. Williams*‡.

Patris aeterni suboles coaeva.

O WORD of God above,
   Who fillest all in all,
Hallow this house with thy sure love,
   And bless our festival.

2* Grace in this font is stored
   To cleanse each guilty child;
The Spirit's blest anointing poured
   Brightens the once defiled.

3 Here Christ of his own Blood
   Himself the chalice gives,
And feeds his own with Angels' food,
   On which the spirit lives.

4 For guilty souls that pine
   Sure mercies here abound,
And healing grace with oil and wine
   For every secret wound.

5 God from his throne afar,
   Comes in this house to dwell:
And prayer, beyond the evening star,
   Builds here her citadel.

Unison 6. All might, all praise be thine.
   The God whom all adore;
The Father, Son, and Spirit divine,
   Both now and evermore. Amen.

DEDICATION FESTIVAL

Sequence.
Mode v.

172
Jerusalem et Sion filiae.

Ascr. to Adam of St. Victor, c. 1170.
Tr. G. G.
Arr. J. H. A.

1 Si-on's daugh-ters! Sons of Je - ru - sa - lem! All ye hosts of hea - ven - ly
5 Not more fair the moon in her love - li - ness! Not more bright the sun in his

chi - val - ry! Lift your voi - ces, sing-ing right mer - ri - ly
ma - jes - ty! Like an ar - my splen-did and ter - ri - ble,

Al - le - lu - ya! 2 Christ our Sa - viour weds on this fes - ti - val
Ranged for bat - tle— 6 So the Church shines forth on her pil - grim - age,

247

THE CHRISTIAN YEAR

172 (continued)

Ho - ly Church, the Pat - tern of Right - eous - ness, Whom from depths of ut - ter - most mi - se - ry He hath res - cued. 3 Now the Bride re - ceiv - eth his be - ni - son, Tast - eth now the joys of the Pa - ra - clete;

Signed with Jor - dan's wa - ters of pe - ni - tence, Drawn to hear the wis - dom of So - lo - mon, From the world's end. 7 *So, fore - told by fi - gures and pro - phe - cies, Clothed in nup - tial ves - ture of cha - ri - ty,

DEDICATION FESTIVAL

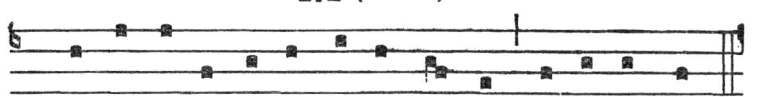

172 (*continued*)

Kings and queens with ju - bi - lant me - lo - dy Call her bless - ed.
Joined with Christ, o'er hea - ven's glad ci - ti - zens Now she reign - eth.

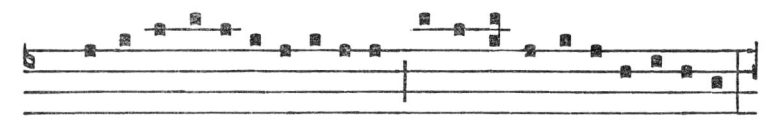

4 Mo-ther meet for sin - ful hu - ma - ni - ty, Life's sure ha - ven, rest for the sor-row-ful,
8*Welcome! feast of light and fe - li - ci - ty, Bride to Bridegroom join-ing in u - ni - ty;

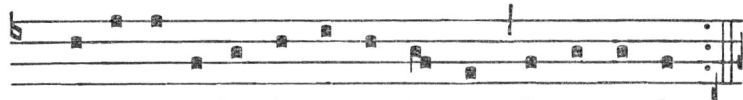

Strong pro - tect - ress, born in a mys - te - ry Ev - er won - drous.
In her mys - tic mar - riage is ty - pi - fied Our sal - va - tion.

THE CHRISTIAN YEAR

172 (continued)

9. Christ, whose joys we joy-ful-ly ce-le-brate, Grant us all a place with thy cho-sen ones, True de-lights, in-ef-fa-ble hap-pi-ness, Rest e-ter-nal.

Another melody for this Sequence is given in the Appendix, No. 7.

The above hymns are suitable for a Dedication Festival only. For a Patronal Festival see Nos. 195—204 and the Proper Saints' Day Hymns.

DEDICATION OR RESTORATION OF A CHURCH

173

HERR JESU CHRIST. (L. M.)
Very slow and dignified ♩ = 46.
Melody from 'Pensum Sacrum' (Görlitz, 1648).

NOTE.—*This hymn may also be sung to* LLANGOLLEN (*No.* 556).

DEDICATION OR RESTORATION OF A CHURCH

J. G. Whittier, 1807–92.

ALL things are thine; no gift have we,
Lord of all gifts, to offer thee:
And hence with grateful hearts to-day
Thine own before thy feet we lay.

2 Thy will was in the builders' thought;
Thy hand unseen amidst us wrought;
Through mortal motive, scheme and plan,
Thy wise eternal purpose ran.

3 In weakness and in want we call
On thee for whom the heavens are small;
Thy glory is thy children's good,
Thy joy thy tender Fatherhood.

Unison. 4. O Father, deign these walls to bless;
Fill with thy love their emptiness;
And let their door a gateway be
To lead us from ourselves to thee.

A - men.

For a Dedication Festival, or *for a Special Service of Dedication, the following
are also suitable:*

450 O God, our help in ages past.
472 Pray that Jerusalem may have.
489 The Church's one foundation.
508 We love the place, O God.
533 Now thank we all our God.
534 Praise the Lord of heaven; praise him in the height.
535 Praise the Lord! ye heavens, adore him.
536 Praise to the Lord, the Almighty.
557 Rejoice to-day with one accord.
544 O Faith of England, taught of old.

Part II
SAINTS' DAYS: GENERAL
APOSTLES AND EVANGELISTS

174

Mode i.   arr. J. H. A.

See also for Procession on any Saint's Day:
638 Jerusalem, my happy home.   639 The Church triumphant in thy love.   641 For all the Saints.

APOSTLES AND EVANGELISTS
174 (Modern Tune)

ANNUE CHRISTE. (12 12. 12 12.)
In moderate time ♩ = 96 (𝅗𝅥 = 48).
To be sung in unison.

Melody from LA FEILLÉE,
'*Méthode du plain-chant*,' 1782.

OFFICE HYMN. *Common of Apostles and Evangelists.* E. and M.

Before 11th cent. Tr. T. A. L.

Annue Christe, saeculorum Domine.

LORD of Creation, bow thine ear, O Christ. to hear
The intercession of thy servant true and dear,
That we unworthy, who have trespassed in thy sight,
May live before thee where he dwells in glorious light.

2 O God our Saviour, look on thine inheritance,
Sealed by the favour shining from thy countenance;
That no false spirit bring to nought the souls of price
Bought by the merit of thy perfect Sacrifice.

3 We bear the burden of our guilt and enmity,
Until thy pardon lift the heart from slavery;
Then through the spending of thy life-blood, King of grace,
Grant us unending triumph in thy holy place.

4. To thee the glorious Christ, our Saviour manifest,
All wreaths victorious, praise and worship be addrest,
Whom with the living Father humbly we adore,
And the life-giving Spirit, God for evermore. Amen.

A - men.

Harmony.

A - men.

SAINTS' DAYS: GENERAL

175

Mode iii.   *arr.* J. H. A.

OFFICE HYMN. *Common of Apostles and Evangelists.* (*York*) M.   *Before 11th cent.* Tr. J. M. Neale.

Aeterna Christi munera.

THE eternal gifts of Christ the King,
 The Apostles' glorious deeds, we sing;
And while due hymns of praise we pay,
Our thankful hearts cast grief away.

APOSTLES AND EVANGELISTS

175 (Modern Tune)

AETERNA CHRISTI MUNERA. (L.M.)

In free rhythm ♩ = 90.

To be sung in unison.

Melody from GUIDETTI,
'*Directorium Chori*,' 1582.

NOTE.— *This hymn may also be sung to the Chartres Melody at Hymn* 159 *or to*
DEO GRACIAS (*No.* 249).

2 The Church in these her princes boasts,
These victor chiefs of warrior hosts;
The soldiers of the heavenly hall,
The lights that rose on earth for all.

3 'Twas thus the yearning faith of Saints,
The unconquered hope that never faints,
The love of Christ that knows not shame,
The prince of this world overcame.

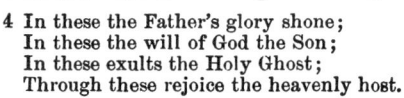

4 In these the Father's glory shone;
In these the will of God the Son;
In these exults the Holy Ghost;
Through these rejoice the heavenly host.

5 Redeemer, hear us of thy love,
That, with this glorious band above,
Hereafter, of thine endless grace,
Thy servants also may have place.
Amen.

SAINTS' DAYS: GENERAL

Mode viii. **176** *arr. J. H. A.*

A - - men.

Office Hymn. *Common of Apostles and Evangelists. M. and E.* *c.* 10th cent. Tr. *Bishop R. Mant* ‡.

Exultet caelum laudibus.

LET the round world with songs rejoice;
Let heaven return the joyful voice;
All mindful of the Apostles' fame,
Let heaven and earth their praise proclaim.

256

APOSTLES AND EVANGELISTS
176 (Modern Tune)

AUCTORITATE SAECULI. (L. M.)
In moderate time ♩ = 144. Unison.

Angers Church Melody.
Harmonized by J. H. Arnold.

2 Ye servants who once bore the light
Of Gospel truth o'er heathen night,
Still may your work that light impart,
To glad our eyes and cheer our heart.

3 O God, by whom to them was given
The key that shuts and opens heaven,
Our chains unbind, our loss repair,
And grant us grace to enter there;

4 For at thy will they preached the word
Which cured disease, which health conferred:
O may that healing power once more
Our souls to grace and health restore:

5 That when thy Son again shall come,
And speak the world's unerring doom,
He may with them pronounce us blest,
And place us in thy endless rest.

6. To thee, O Father; Son, to thee;
To thee, blest Spirit, glory be!
So was it ay for ages past,
So shall through endless ages last. Amen.

Office Hymn for Apostles and Evangelists during Eastertide. E. and M. 123, Part 2; and for M. and E. 124, Part 2.

SAINTS' DAYS: GENERAL

177

MARTS. (7 7. 7 7.)
In moderate time ♩ = 72.

B. MILGROVE, 1781-1810.

NOTE.—*This hymn may also be sung to* UNIVERSITY COLLEGE (*No.* 467).

Apostles.
Caelestis aulae principes.

J.-B. de Santeüil, 1630-97.
Tr. Sir H. W. Baker.

CAPTAINS of the saintly band,
    Lights who lighten every land,
Princes who with Jesus dwell,
Judges of his Israel:

2 On the nations sunk in night
Ye have shed the Gospel light;
Sin and error flee away;
Truth reveals the promised day.

3 Not by warrior's spear and sword,
Not by art of human word,
Preaching but the Cross of shame,
Rebel hearts for Christ ye tame.

4 Earth, that long in sin and pain
Groaned in Satan's deadly chain,
Now to serve its God is free
In the law of liberty.

5 Distant lands with one acclaim
Tell the honour of your name,
Who, wherever man has trod,
Teach the mysteries of God.

Unison. 6. Glory to the Three in One
While eternal ages run,
Who from deepest shades of night
Called us to his glorious light. Amen.
(*See also* No. 239).

A - men.

178

OLD 104TH. (5 5. 5 5. 6 5. 6 5.)
Slow and dignified ♩ = 69.

Ravenscroft's Psalter, 1621.

258

APOSTLES AND EVANGELISTS

178 (continued)

Supreme, quales, Arbiter.

J.-B. de Santeüil, 1630–97.
Tr. I. Williams ‡.

DISPOSER supreme, and Judge of the earth,
   Who choosest for thine the weak and the poor;
To frail earthen vessels, and things of no worth,
   Entrusting thy riches which ay shall endure;

2 Those vessels soon fail, though full of thy light,
   And at thy decree are broken and gone;
Then brightly appeareth the arm of thy might,
   As through the clouds breaking the lightnings have shone.

Unison. 3 Like clouds are they borne to do thy great will,
   And swift as the winds about the world go;
All full of thy Godhead, while earth lieth still,
   They thunder, they lighten, the waters o'erflow.

4*Their sound goeth forth, 'Christ Jesus is Lord!'
   Then Satan doth fear, his citadels fall:
As when the dread trumpets went forth at thy word,
   And one long blast shattered the Canaanites' wall.

5 O loud be their trump, and stirring the sound,
   To rouse us, O Lord, from sin's deadly sleep;
May lights which thou kindlest in darkness around
   The dull soul awaken her vigils to keep!

Unison. 6. All honour and praise, dominion and might,
   To thee, Three in One, eternally be,
Who pouring around us thy glorious light,
   Dost call us from darkness thy glory to see.
                               Amen.

SAINTS' DAYS: GENERAL
179

ACH GOTT VON HIMMELREICHE. (7 6, 7 6, D.)

Brightly ♩ = 168.

Melody by
M. PRÆTORIUS, 1571–1621.

Sequence. Evangelists.

Plausu chorus laetabundo.

Adam of St. Victor, c. 1170.
Tr. Jackson Mason.

COME sing, ye choirs exultant,
   Those messengers of God,
Through whom the living Gospels
   Came sounding all abroad!
Whose voice proclaimed salvation
   That poured upon the night,
And drove away the shadows,
   And flushed the world with light.

APOSTLES AND EVANGELISTS

2 He chose them, our Good Shepherd,
   And, tending evermore
His flock through earth's four quarters.
   In wisdom made them four;
True Lawgiver, he bade them
   Their healing message spread,
One charter for all nations,
   One glorious title-deed.

3 * In one harmonious witness
   The chosen Four combine,
While each his own commission
   Fulfils in every line;
As, in the Prophet's vision,
   From out the amber flame
In form of visage diverse
   Four living creatures came.

4 * Lo, these the wingèd chariots
   That bring Emmanuel nigh;
The golden staves uplifting
   The ark of God on high;
And these the fourfold river
   Of Paradise above,
Whence flow for all the nations
   New mysteries of love.

Unison. 5. Foursquare on this foundation
   The Church of Christ remains,
A house to stand unshaken
   By floods or winds or rains.
O glorious happy portion
   In this safe home to be,
By God, true Man, united
   With God eternally!

SAINTS' DAYS: GENERAL

180

Mode iv.

Melody from the Hereford Hymnal.
arr. J. H. A.

The proper Sarum melody is that given at No. 151.

This hymn is sung during Christmastide to No. 17, *and during Eastertide to* No. 128, *Part* 2.

MARTYRS

OFFICE HYMN.   *Common of one Martyr.*   *c. 10th cent.*   *Tr. P. D.*
E. and M.
                   Martyr Dei qui unicum.

MARTYR of God, whose strength was steeled
   To follow close God's only Son,
Well didst thou brave thy battlefield,
   And well thy heavenly bliss was won!

2 Now join thy prayers with ours, who pray
   That God may pardon us and bless;
For prayer keeps evil's plague away,
   And draws from life its weariness.

MARTYRS

180 (Modern Tune)

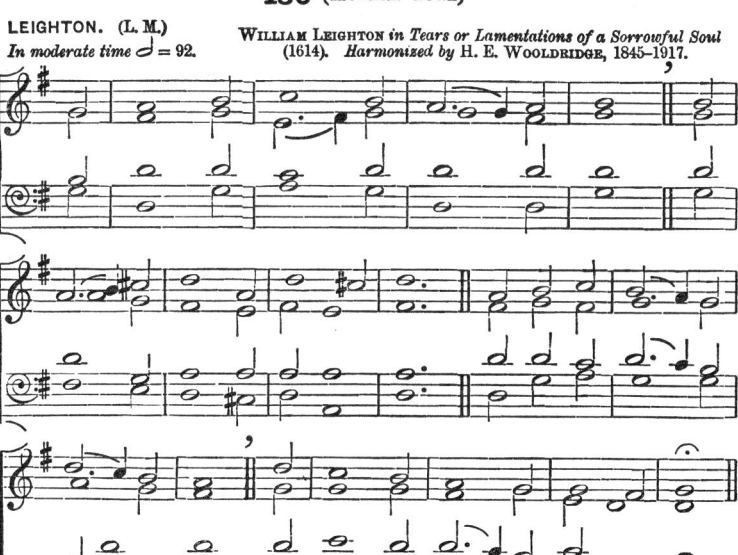

LEIGHTON. (L.M.)
In moderate time ♩ = 92.

WILLIAM LEIGHTON in *Tears or Lamentations of a Sorrowful Soul*
(1614). *Harmonized by* H. E. WOOLDRIDGE, 1845–1917.

NOTE.—*This hymn may also be sung to the Grenoble Melody at Hymn* 181; *or to* WHITEHALL (*No.* 234).

3 Long, long ago, were loosed the chains
    That held thy body once in thrall;
For us how many a bond remains!
    O Love of God release us all.

4. All praise to God the Father be,
    All praise to thee, eternal Son;
All praise, O Holy Ghost, to thee,
    While never-ending ages run.
                      Amen.

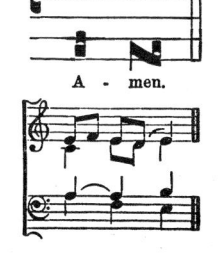

A - men.

A - men.

SAINTS' DAYS: GENERAL

Mode viii.   **181**   arr. J. H. A.

This hymn is sung during Christmastide to No. 18, and during Eastertide to No. 123, Part 2.

OFFICE HYMN. *Common of one Martyr.* M. and E.   *Deus, tuorum militum.*   6th cent. *Tr. J. M. Neale.*

O GOD, thy soldiers' crown and guard,
    And their exceeding great reward;
From all transgressions set us free,
Who sing thy Martyr's victory.

MARTYRS
181 (MODERN TUNE)

DEUS TUORUM MILITUM. (L. M.)

In moderate time ♩ = 144.
To be sung in unison.

Grenoble Church Melody.
Harmonized by R. V. W.

2 The pleasures of the world he spurned,
From sin's pernicious lures he turned;
He knew their joys imbued with gall,
And thus he reached thy heavenly hall.

3 For thee through many a woe he ran,
In many a fight he played the man;
For thee his blood he dared to pour,
And thence hath joy for evermore.

4 We therefore pray thee, full of love,
Regard us from thy throne above;
On this thy Martyr's triumph day,
Wash every stain of sin away.

5. O Christ, most loving King, to thee,
With God the Father, glory be;
Like glory, as is ever meet,
To God the holy Paraclete.

Amen.

SAINTS' DAYS: GENERAL

182

Mode vii. *arr. J. H. A.*

Office Hymn. *Common of many Martyrs. E. and M.*
Sanctorum meritis.
8th cent. *Tr. J. M. Neale.*

THE merits of the Saints,
　Blessèd for evermore,
Their love that never faints,
　The toils they bravely bore—
For these the Church to-day
Pours forth her joyous lay—
These victors win the noblest bay.

2 They, whom this world of ill,
　While it yet held, abhorred;
Its withering flowers that still
　They spurned with one accord—
They knew them short-lived all,
And followed at thy call,
King Jesu, to thy heavenly hall.

MARTYRS

182 (Modern Tune)

DAS HERRLICH HOHE FEST. (66. 66. 668.)

Slow and dignified ♩ = 100.

C. PETER, c. 1674.

3 Like sheep their blood they poured;
   And without groan or tear,
They bent before the sword
   For that their King most dear:
Their souls, serenely blest,
In patience they possest,
And looked in hope towards their rest.

4 What tongue may here declare,
   Fancy or thought descry,
The joys thou dost prepare
   For these thy Saints on high!
Empurpled in the flood
Of their victorious blood,
They won the laurel from their God.

5. To thee, O Lord most high,
   One in Three Persons still,
To pardon us we cry,
   And to preserve from ill:
Here give thy servants peace,
Hereafter glad release,
And pleasures that shall never cease.
                      Amen.

A - men.

A - men.

SAINTS' DAYS: GENERAL

Mode viii.   **183**   *arr.* J. H. A.

A - - men.

NOTE.—*This hymn is sung during Christmastide to No. 18.*

OFFICE HYMN. *Common of many*   *c. 6th cent.*
Martyrs. M. and E.   Rex gloriose Martyrum.   *Tr. R. F. Littledale and others*

O GLORIOUS King of Martyr hosts,
  Thou Crown that each Confessor boasts,
Who leadest to celestial day
The Saints who cast earth's joys away:

MARTYRS

REX GLORIOSE. (L. M.) **183** (Modern Tune) *Proper melody from Andernach Gesangbuch, 1608.*
Moderately slow ♩ = 66

2 Thine ear in mercy, Saviour, lend,
  While unto thee our prayers ascend;
  And as we count their triumphs won,
  Forgive the sins that we have done.

3 Martyrs in thee their triumphs gain,
  Confessors grace from thee obtain;
  We sinners humbly seek to thee,
  From sin's offence to set us free.

4. All laud to God the Father be,
  All praise, eternal Son, to thee;
  All glory, as is ever meet,
  To God the holy Paraclete. Amen.

A - men.

NOTE.—*This hymn may also be sung to the French Melody at Hymn* 125.

SAINTS' DAYS: GENERAL

184

ALTA TRINITA BEATA. (87.87. D.)
In moderate time ♩ = 66 (♩ = 112).
To be sung in unison.

*Adapted from a melody in
Laudi Spirituali, 14th cent., Florence.*

MARTYRS

Sequence.   *Before 12th cent. Tr. J. M. Neale.*

O beata beatorum.

BLESSÈD Feasts of blessèd Martyrs,
   Saintly days of saintly men,
With affection's recollections
   Greet we your return again.

2 Mighty deeds they wrought, and wonders,
   While a frame of flesh they bore;
We with meetest praise and sweetest
   Honour them for evermore.

3 Faith unblenching, hope unquenching,
   Well-loved Lord, and single heart,—
Thus they glorious and victorious
   Bore the Martyr's happy part.

4*Blood in slaughter poured like water,
   Torments long and heavy chain,
Flame, and axe, and laceration,
   They endured, and conquered pain.

5*While they passed through divers tortures,
   Till they sank by death opprest,
Earth's rejected were elected
   To have portion with the blest.

6 By contempt of worldly pleasures,
   And by mighty battles done,
Have they merited with Angels
   To be knit for ay in one.

7 Wherefore made co-heirs of glory,
   Ye that sit with Christ on high,
Join to ours your supplications,
   As for grace and peace we cry;

8. That, this weary life completed,
   And its many labours past,
We may merit to be seated
   In our Father's home at last.

SAINTS' DAYS: GENERAL

185

BEATA NOBIS GAUDIA. (L. M.)
In free rhythm ♩ = 96.

Melody from
'Psalterium Chorale,' Constance, 1510.

To be sung in unison.

NOTE.—*This hymn may also be sung to the Angers Melody at Hymn* 176.

Beate Martyr, prospera.   *Prudentius, b.* 348.   *Tr. A. R.*

BLEST Martyr, let thy triumph-day
God's favouring grace to us convey; [flowed
The day on which thy life-blood
And he thy crown in meed bestowed.

2 Thy soul to heavenly mansions sped
While this world's gloomy shadows fled;
The judge and torturer o'erthrown,
Christ claimed the victor for his own.

3 Now consort of the Angels bright
Thou shinest clothed in robes of white;
Robes thou hast washed in streams of blood,
A dauntless Martyr for thy God.

4 Be thou on this thy holy-day
Our strong upholder; while we pray
That from our guilt we may be freed,
Stand thou before the throne and plead.

5 All laud to God the Father be,
All praise, eternal Son, to thee;
All glory, as is ever meet,
To God the holy Paraclete. Amen.

A — — men.

MARTYRS

186

BALFOUR. (C.M.)
Moderately slow ♩ = 72.

Melody by G. J. KNOWLES (1750–1789).
Harmonized by GEOFFREY SHAW.

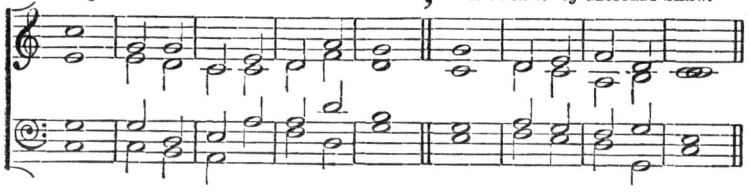

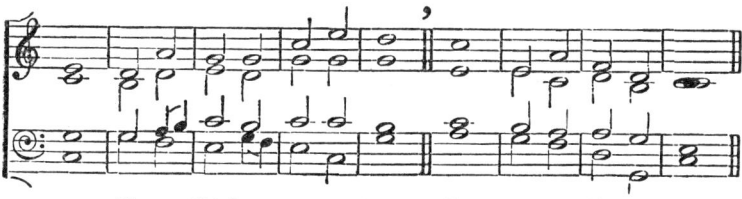

NOTE.—*This hymn may also be sung to* RODMELL (*No.* 611).

A. R.

COME, let us join the Church above
   The Martyr's praise to sing,
That soldier true who gave to-day
   His life-blood for his King.

2 To-day through heaven the cry rang out,
   'Great God, the fight is done!
Room for the Victor! lo, his crown
   Christ's valiant Saint hath won!'

3 The Martyr's triumph shall endure,
   His fame time cannot dim:
See how he calls on one and all
   To rise and follow him!

4 We know that in our Saviour Christ
   The blest our troubles heed,
That Saints in heaven to saints on earth
   Are very near indeed.

Unison. 5 The cloud of witnesses look down,
   They cheer us on to fight;
To God their prayers go up that he
   May lead their friends aright.

6 Brave Martyr, we will follow till
   To God we yield our breath;
And learn from thee to spurn the world
   And mock at pain and death!

Unison. 7. To Christ, for whom the Martyrs die,
   All laud and glory be,
With Father, and with Holy Ghost,
   To all eternity. Amen.

A - men.

SAINTS' DAYS: GENERAL

187

WEIMAR. (7 6. 7 6. D.)
Very slow and dignified ♩ = 48.

Later form of melody by
M. VULPIUS, 1560–1616.

MARTYRS

St Joseph the Hymnographer, d. 883
Tr. J. M. Neale.

Τῶν ἱερῶν ἀθλοφόρων.

LET our choir new anthems raise,
  Wake the morn with gladness;
God himself to joy and praise
  Turns the Martyrs' sadness:
This the day that won their crown,
  Opened heaven's bright portal,
As they laid the mortal down
  And put on the immortal.

2 Never flinched they from the flame,
  From the torture never;
Vain the foeman's sharpest aim,
  Satan's best endeavour:
For by faith they saw the land
  Decked in all its glory,
Where triumphant now they stand
  With the victor's story.

Unison. 3. Up and follow, Christian men!
  Press through toil and sorrow;
Spurn the night of fear, and then,
  O, the glorious morrow!
Who will venture on the strife?
  Who will first begin it?
Who will grasp the land of life?
  Warriors, up and win it!

SAINTS' DAYS: GENERAL

188

Mode ii.   arr. J. H. A.

NOTE.—*This tune is proper to Evensong. The proper to Mattins is No.* 191.

FOR A CONFESSOR

OFFICE HYMN. *Common of a Confessor.*   8*th cent.*   *Tr.* L. H.
E. and M.   Iste Confessor.

H E, whose confession God of old accepted,
   Whom through the ages all now hold in honour,
Gaining his guerdon this day came to enter
      Heaven's high portal.

CONFESSORS
188 (Modern Tune)

ISTE CONFESSOR. (11 11. 11 5.)
In moderate time ♩ = 96. *Unison.*

Angers Church Melody.
Harmonised by MARTIN SHAW.

2 God-fearing, watchful, pure of mind and body,
  Holy and humble, thus did all men find him;
  While, through his members, to the life immortal
        Mortal life called him.

3 Thus to the weary, from the life enshrinèd,
  Potent in virtue, flowed humane compassion;
  Sick and sore laden, howsoever burdened,
        There they found healing.

4 So now in chorus, giving God the glory,
  Raise we our anthem gladly to his honour,
  That in fair kinship we may all be sharers
        Here and hereafter.

5. Honour and glory, power and salvation,
  Be in the highest unto him who reigneth
  Changeless in heaven over earthly changes,
        Triune, eternal.
            Amen.

A - men.

A - men.

277

SAINTS' DAYS: GENERAL

Mode viii.   **189**   *arr.* J. H. A.

This hymn is sung during Christmastide to No. 17, during Eastertide to No. 123, Part 2, and during Ascensiontide to No. 141.

The Modern Tune for this hymn is the Angers Melody at Hymn 176.

OFFICE HYMN. *Common of a Confessor (in full).*
M. and E.
Part 2. *For a Matron.* (*York.*)   Jesu, Redemptor omnium.

8th cent.   *Tr. R. M. B.*

O THOU whose all-redeeming might
  Crowns every chief in faith's true
On this commemoration day   [fight,
Hear us, good Jesu, while we pray.

2 In faithful strife for thy dear name
  Thy servant earned the saintly fame,
Which pious hearts with praise revere
In constant memory year by year.

Part 2.

3 Earth's fleeting joys *he* counted nought,
  For higher, truer joys *he* sought,
And now, with Angels round thy throne,
Unfading treasures are *his* own.

4 O grant that we, most gracious God,
  May follow in the steps *he* trod;
And, freed from every stain of sin,
As *he* hath won may also win.

5. To thee, O Christ, our loving King.
  All glory, praise, and thanks we bring;
Whom with the Father we adore
And Holy Ghost for evermore. Amen.

A - men.

CONFESSORS

190

CARLISLE. (S. M.)
Moderately slow, dignified ♩ = 60.

C. LOCKHART, 1745-1815.

For a Bishop.　　　　　　　　　　　　　　　　　　　　　V. S. S. C.

1 O SHEPHERD of the sheep,
　　High Priest of things to come,
Who didst in grace thy servant keep,
　　And take him safely home:

2 Accept our song of praise
　　For all his holy care, [of days,
His zeal unquenched through length
　　The trials that he bare.

3 Chief of thy faithful band,
　　He held himself the least, [hand,
Though thy dread keys were in his
　　O everlasting Priest.

4 So, trusting in thy might,
　　He won a fair renown;
So, waxing valiant in the fight,
　　He trod the lion down;

5 Then rendered up to thee
　　The charge thy love had given,
And passed away thy face to see
　　Revealed in highest heaven.

6 On all our bishops pour
　　The Spirit of thy grace;
That, as he won the palm of yore,
　　So they may run their race;

7. That when this life is done,
　　They may with him adore
The ever-blessèd Three in One,
　　In bliss for evermore.

A - men.

SAINTS' DAYS: GENERAL

191

Mode viii. *arr. J. H. A.*

This tune is proper to Mattins. The proper to Evensong is No. 188.

FOR A VIRGIN

OFFICE HYMN. *Common of a Virgin*
 (in full). E. and M.
 Part 2. *For a Matron.* (York.)   Virginis Proles.   *8th cent.* **Tr. L. H.**

S ON of a Virgin, Maker of thy mother,
 Thou, Rod and Blossom from a Stem unstainèd,
Now while a Virgin fair of fame we honour,
 Hear our devotion!

VIRGINS

191 (MODERN TUNE)

UT QUEANT LAXIS. (11 11. 11 5.)
Moderately fast ♩ = 96. Unison.

Rouen Church Melody.
Harmonized by J. H. ARNOLD.

2 Lo, on thy handmaid fell a twofold blessing,
Who, in her body vanquishing the weakness,
In that same body, grace from heaven obtaining,
   Bore the world witness.

3 Death, nor the rending pains of death appalled her
Bondage and torment found her undefeated:
So by the shedding of her life attained she
   Heavenly guerdon.

Part 2.

4 Fountain of mercy, hear the prayers she offers;
Purge our offences, pardon our transgressions,
So that hereafter we to thee may render
   Praise with thanksgiving.

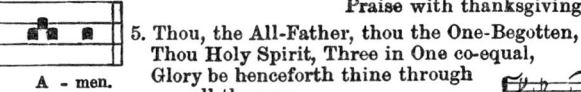

5. Thou, the All-Father, thou the One-Begotten,
Thou Holy Spirit, Three in One co-equal,
Glory be henceforth thine through
 all the ages,
   World without ending.
   Amen.

A - men.

A - - men.

SAINTS' DAYS: GENERAL

192

Mode viii.   *arr.* J. H. A.

The tune here given is that which is used at Evensong. At Matins it is sung to No. 14. During Christmastide it is sung (M. and E.) to 17, and during Eastertide to 123, Part 2.

The Modern Tune to this hymn will be found on the opposite page (St. Ambrose).

OFFICE HYMN. *Common of a Virgin.*   *St. Ambrose*, 340–97.
M. and E.   Jesu, Corona Virginum.   *Tr. J. M. Neale.*

1. JESU, the Virgins' Crown, do thou
Accept us as in prayer we bow;
Born of that Virgin whom alone
The Mother and the Maid we own.

2. Amongst the lilies thou dost feed,
With Virgin choirs accompanied—
With glory decked, the spotless brides
Whose bridal gifts thy love provides.

3. They, wheresoe'er thy footsteps bend,
With hymns and praises still attend;
In blessèd troops they follow thee,
With dance, and song, and melody.

4. We pray thee therefore to bestow
Upon our senses here below
Thy grace, that so we may endure
From taint of all corruption pure.

5. All laud to God the Father be,
All praise, eternal Son, to thee;
All glory, as is ever meet,
To God the holy Paraclete. Amen.

A - men.

MATRONS: VIGILS

193, 194

ST. AMBROSE. (L. M.)
In moderate time ♩ = 72.

From LA FEILLÉE,
'*Méthode du plain-chant,*' 1782.

[*May be sung in unison throughout.*]

NOTE.—*Hymns* 193 *and* 194 *may also be sung to* ALFRETON (*No.* 240) *or to any suitable* L. M. *tune.*

FOR A MATRON
193

Silvio Antoniano, b. 1540. *Tr. A. R.*
Fortem, virili pectore.

THE praises of that Saint we sing,
  To whom all lands their tribute bring,
Who with indomitable heart [part.
  Bore throughout life true woman's

2 Restraining every froward sense
  By gentle bonds of abstinence,
With prayer her hungry soul she fed,
  And thus to heavenly joys hath sped.

3 King Christ, from whom all virtue springs,
  Who only doest wondrous things,
As now to thee she kneels in prayer,
  In mercy our petitions hear.

4. All praise to God the Father be,
  All praise, eternal Son, to thee;
Whom with the Spirit we adore
  For ever and for evermore. Amen.

FOR A VIGIL
194

St. Ephraim the Syrian, d. 373. *Tr. F. C. B.*

ܡܕܠܚ ܡܢܐ ܚܕܗܢ ܕܠ

RECEIVE, O Lord, in heaven above
  Our prayers and supplications pure;
Give us a heart all full of love
  And steady courage to endure.

2 Thy holy name our mouths confess,
  Our tongues are harps to praise thy grace;
Forgive our sins and wickedness,
  Who in this vigil seek thy face.

3 Let not our song become a sigh,
  A wail of anguish and despair;
In loving-kindness, Lord most high,
  Receive to-night our evening prayer.

4. O raise us in that day, that we
  May sing, where all thy Saints adore,
Praise to thy Father, and to thee,
  And to thy Spirit, evermore. Amen.

A - men.

SAINTS' DAYS: GENERAL

195

BREMEN. (7 6. 7 6. D.)
In moderate time ♩ = 72.

Melody adapted from STORL'S
Wurtemberg Gesangbuch, 1710.

NOTE.—*This hymn may also be sung to* WOHLAUF, THUT NICHT VERZAGEN (*No.* 32).

FOR A PATRONAL FESTIVAL

Ecce dies nobis.

St. Paulinus of Nola,
353–431. *Tr. A. R.*

ANOTHER year completed,
  The day comes round once more
Which with our patron's radiance
  Is bright as heretofore.
Now, strong in hope, united
  His festival we greet;
He will present our troubles
  Before the mercy-seat.

2 The Scriptures tell how Moses
  Did for the people pray,
Appeased the Judge eternal,
  And turned his wrath away;
Elijah's prayer had power,
  To close and open heaven:
Such Saints as were aforetime,
  Such Saints to us are given.

3 O Saint of God, belovèd,
  And placed on his right hand,
Thy prayers be like a rampart
  As 'gainst the foe we stand;
For Abraham's God is thy God,
  And Isaac's God is thine,
Thine is the God of Jacob,
  The Lord of power benign.

4. For forty years his Israel
  He fed with Angels' food;
The flinty rock he opened
  The streams of water flowed.
Entreat that Christ his people
  May lead to victory:
The God of Joshua's triumph
  The Lord thy God is he.

A - men.

FOR ANY SAINT'S DAY

196

MOUNT EPHRAIM. (S. M.).
Slow ♩ = 69.

B. MILGROVE, 1731–1810.

NOTE.—*This hymn may also be sung to* ST. MICHAEL (*No.* 27).

FOR ANY SAINT'S DAY

Bishop R. Mant, 1776–1848.

FOR all thy Saints, O Lord,
  Who strove in thee to live,
Who followed thee, obeyed, adored,
  Our grateful hymn receive.

2 For all thy Saints, O Lord,
  Accept our thankful cry,
Who counted thee their great reward,
  And strove in thee to die.

3 They all in life and death,
  With thee their Lord in view,
Learned from thy Holy Spirit's breath
  To suffer and to do.

4 For this thy name we bless,
  And humbly beg that we
May follow them in holiness,
  And live and die in thee;

5. With them the Father, Son,
  And Holy Ghost to praise,
As in the ancient days was done,
  And shall through endless days.
        Amen.

SAINTS' DAYS: GENERAL

197
SONG 67. (C. M.)
In moderate time ♩ = 72.
Melody by O. GIBBONS, 1583–1625.

I. Watts, 1674–1748.

GIVE me the wings of faith to rise
  Within the veil, and see
The Saints above, how great their joys,
  How bright their glories be.

2 Once they were mourning here below,
  And wet their couch with tears;
They wrestled hard, as we do now,
  With sins and doubts and fears.

3 I ask them whence their victory came;
  They, with united breath,
Ascribe their conquest to the Lamb,
  Their triumph to his death.

4 They marked the footsteps that he trod,
  His zeal inspired their breast,
And, following their incarnate God,
  Possess the promised rest.

5. Our glorious Leader claims our praise
  For his own pattern given
While the long cloud of witnesses
  Show the same path to heaven.

A - men.

198
VISION. (8 7. 8 7. D.)
Moderately fast ♩ = 120.
S. MASON.

FOR ANY SAINTS' DAY
198 (continued)

[Copyright, 1925, by Oxford University Press.]

NOTE.—*This hymn may also be sung to* IN BABILONE (*No.* 145) *or to* DEERHURST (*Appendix, No.* 32).

Bishop Chr. Wordsworth, 1807–85.

HARK! the sound of holy voices,
  Chanting at the crystal sea,
Alleluya, Alleluya,
  Alleluya, Lord, to thee:
Multitude, which none can number,
  Like the stars in glory stands,
Clothed in white apparel, holding
  Palms of victory in their hands.

2 Patriarch, and holy Prophet,
  Who prepared the way of Christ,
King, Apostle, Saint, Confessor,
  Martyr, and Evangelist,
Saintly Maiden, godly Matron,
  Widows who have watched to prayer,
Joined in holy concert, singing
  To the Lord of all, are there.

3 They have come from tribulation,
  And have washed their robes in blood,
Washed them in the Blood of Jesus;
  Tried they were, and firm they stood;

Mocked, imprisoned, stoned, tormented.
  Sawn asunder, slain with sword,
They have conquered death and Satan
  By the might of Christ the Lord.

4 Marching with thy Cross their banner,
  They have triumphed following
Thee, the Captain of salvation,
  Thee, their Saviour and their King;
Gladly, Lord, with thee they suffered;
  Gladly, Lord, with thee they died,
And by death to life immortal
  They were born, and glorified.

5 Now they reign in heavenly glory,
  Now they walk in golden light,
Now they drink, as from a river,
  Holy bliss and infinite,
Love and peace they taste for ever,
  And all truth and knowledge see
In the beatific vision
  Of the blessèd Trinity.

6. God of God, the One-begotten,
  Light of light, Emmanuel,
In whose Body joined together
  All the Saints for ever dwell;
Pour upon us of thy fullness,
  That we may for evermore
God the Father, God the Son, and
  God the Holy Ghost adore. Amen.

A - men.

SAINTS' DAYS: GENERAL

199

BALLERMA. (C. M.)
In moderate time ♩ = 116.

Probably by F. Barthélémon, 1741–1808.

Verse 4, line 1, should be sung:

Hun-ger and thirst are felt no more,

I. Watts and others, 18th cent.

How bright these glorious spirits shine!
Whence all their white array?
How came they to the blissful seats
Of everlasting day?

Unison.
2 Lo! these are they from sufferings great
Who came to realms of light,
And in the Blood of Christ have washed
Those robes that shine so bright.

3 Now with triumphal palms they stand
Before the throne on high,
And serve the God they love amidst
The glories of the sky.

4 Hunger and thirst are felt no more,
Nor sun with scorching ray;
God is their sun, whose cheering beams
Diffuse eternal day.

5 The Lamb, which dwells amid the throne,
Shall o'er them still preside,
Feed them with nourishment divine,
And all their footsteps guide.

6. In pastures green he'll lead his flock
Where living streams appear;
And God the Lord from every eye
Shall wipe off every tear.

200

PSALM 42. (87. 87. 77. 88.)
In moderate time, majestically ♩ = 120.

Composed or adapted by L. Bourgeois
for Genevan Psalter, 1551.

FOR ANY SAINT'S DAY

200 (continued)

** Note.—When this tune is sung to Hymn 127 (ALLELUYA! ALLELUYA!)
♩ ♩ must be substituted for 𝅗𝅥 here.*

Sequence.   Suitable also for other festivals.   Adam of St. Victor, c. 1150.   Tr. Y. H.
Supernae matris gaudia.

Unison.

JOY and triumph everlasting
  Hath the heavenly Church on high;
For that pure immortal gladness
  All our feast-days mourn and sigh:
Yet in death's dark desert wild
Doth the mother aid her child,
Guards celestial thence attend us,
Stand in combat to defend us.

2 Here the world's perpetual warfare
  Holds from heaven the soul apart;
Legioned foes in shadowy terror
  Vex the Sabbath of the heart.
O how happy that estate
Where delight doth not abate;
For that home the spirit yearneth,
Where none languisheth nor mourneth.

Unison.

3 There the body hath no torment,
  There the mind is free from care,
There is every voice rejoicing,
  Every heart is loving there.
Angels in that city dwell;
Them their King delighteth well:
Still they joy and weary never,
More and more desiring ever.

4*There the seers and fathers holy,
  There the prophets glorified,
All their doubts and darkness ended,
  In the Light of light abide.
There the Saints, whose memories old
We in faithful hymns uphold,
Have forgot their bitter story
In the joy of Jesu's glory.

Unison.

5.*There from lowliness exalted
  Dwelleth Mary, Queen of grace,
Ever with her presence pleading
  'Gainst the sin of Adam's race.
To that glory of the blest,
By their prayers and faith confest,
Us, us too, when death hath freed us,
Christ of his good mercy lead us.

SAINTS' DAYS: GENERAL

201

BOYCE. (7 7. 7 7.)
In moderate time ♩ = 116.

W. BOYCE, 1710–79.

NOTE.—*This hymn may also be sung to* PALMS OF GLORY (*Appendix, No. 33*).

J. Montgomery, 1771–1854.

PALMS of glory, raiment bright,
  Crowns that never fade away,
Gird and deck the Saints in light,
  Priests, and kings, and conquerors they.

2 Yet the conquerors bring their palms
    To the Lamb amidst the throne,
  And proclaim in joyful psalms
    Victory through his Cross alone.

3 Kings for harps their crowns resign,
    Crying, as they strike the chords,
  'Take the kingdom, it is thine,
    King of kings, and Lord of lords.'

4 Round the altar priests confess,
    If their robes are white as snow,
  'Twas the Saviour's righteousness,
    And his Blood, that made them so.

5. They were mortal too like us;
    Ah! when we like them must die,
  May our souls translated thus
    Triumph, reign, and shine on high.

A - men.

FOR ANY SAINT'S DAY

202

STETTIN (NUN SEHT). (D. C. M.)
Not too slow ♩ = 112.

Later form of melody from the Song Book of the Bohemian Brethren, 1566.

NOTE.—*This hymn may also be sung to* ST. ANNE (*No.* 450) *or* OLD 81ST (*No.* 461).

Bishop R. Heber, 1783–1826.

THE Son of God goes forth to war,
   A kingly crown to gain;
His blood-red banner streams afar!
   Who follows in his train?

2 Who best can drink his cup of woe,
   Triumphant over pain,
Who patient bears his cross below,
   He follows in his train.

3*The Martyr first, whose eagle eye
   Could pierce beyond the grave;
Who saw his Master in the sky,
   And called on him to save.

4*Like him, with pardon on his tongue
   In midst of mortal pain,
He prayed for them that did the wrong!
   Who follows in his train?

Unison.
5*A glorious band, the chosen few
   On whom the Spirit came,
Twelve valiant Saints, their hope they knew,
   And mocked the cross and flame.

6*They met the tyrant's brandish'd steel,
   The lion's gory mane,
They bowed their necks the death to feel;
   Who follows in their train?

Unison.
7 A noble army, men and boys,
   The matron and the maid,
Around the Saviour's throne rejoice
   In robes of light arrayed.

8. They climbed the steep ascent of heaven
   Through peril, toil, and pain;
O God, to us may grace be given
   To follow in their train.

SAINTS' DAYS: GENERAL

203

YMDAITH MWNGC. (Irreg.)
In moderate time ♩ = 96.

Christina G. Rossetti, 1830–94.
Welsh Traditional Melody.

Voices in unison.

1 What are ... these that glow from a-far, These that lean o - ver the gol - den bar, ... Strong as the li - on, pure as the dove, With o - pen arms, and
2 What are ... these that fly as a cloud, With flash - ing heads and fa - ces bowed; In their .. mouths a vic - to - rious psalm, In their hands a
3 Light a - bove .. light, and bliss be - yond bliss, Whom words can - not ut - ter, lo, who is this? As a King with .. ma - ny crowns he stands, And our names are grav'n up -
4 God the ... Fa - ther give us grace To walk in the light of Je - sus' face; ... God the Son give us a part In the hi - ding-place of

FOR ANY SAINT'S DAY

203 *(continued)*

hearts of love? They the bless-èd ones gone be - fore,
robe and a palm? Wel - com-ing An - gels these that shine,
- on his hands; As a Priest, with God-up-lift-ed eyes, He
Je - su's heart; God the Spi - rit so hold us up That

They the bles-sèd for e - ver - more; Out of great tri - bu -
Your own An - gel, and yours, and mine; Who have hedged us, both
off - ers for us his Sac - ri - fice; As the Lamb of God, for
we may drink of Je - su's cup; God Al - migh - ty,

- la - tion they went Home to their home of heaven con-tent.
day and night On the left hand and on the right.
sin - ners slain, That we too may live, he lives a - gain.
God Three in One, God Al - migh - ty, God a - lone. A - men.

SAINTS' DAYS: GENERAL
204

ALL SAINTS. (87. 87. 77.)
Moderately slow, dignified ♩ = 66.

Darmstadt Gesangbuch, 1698
(slightly adapted).

Wer sind die vor Gottes Throne.

H. T. Schenk, 1656–1727.
Tr. F. E. Cox.

1 WHO are these, like stars appearing,
   These before God's throne who stand?
Each a golden crown is wearing;
   Who are all this glorious band?
     Alleluya, hark! they sing,
     Praising loud their heavenly King.

2 Who are these of dazzling brightness,
   These in God's own truth arrayed,
Clad in robes of purest whiteness,
   Robes whose lustre ne'er shall fade,
     Ne'er be touched by time's rude hand—
     Whence comes all this glorious band?

3 These are they who have contended
   For their Saviour's honour long,
Wrestling on till life was ended,
   Following not the sinful throng;
     These, who well the fight sustained,
     Triumph through the Lamb have gained.

4 These are they whose hearts were riven,
   Sore with woe and anguish tried,
Who in prayer full oft have striven
   With the God they glorified;
     Now, their painful conflict o'er,
     God has bid them weep no more.

5 These like priests have watched and waited,
   Offering up to Christ their will,
Soul and body consecrated,
   Day and night to serve him still:
     Now, in God's most holy place
     Blest they stand before his face.

A-men.

The following is also suitable: 641 For all the Saints who from their labours rest.

SAINTS' DAYS: ST. ANDREW

205

HERALD. (8 7. 8 7.)
In moderate time ♩ = 104.

MARTIN SHAW.

[*Copyright*, 1915, *by J. Curwen & Sons, Ltd.*]
NOTE.—*This hymn may also be sung to* MERTON (*No. 5*).

SAINTS' DAYS: PROPER

ST. ANDREW

(O. H., 174–6.)

Mrs. C. F. Alexander, 1818–95.

JESUS calls us!—o'er the tumult
　Of our life's wild restless sea
Day by day his sweet voice soundeth,
　Saying, 'Christian, follow me':

2 As of old Saint Andrew heard it
　　By the Galilean lake,
Turned from home, and toil, and kindred,
　Leaving all for his dear sake.

3 Jesus calls us from the worship
　Of the vain world's golden store,
From each idol that would keep us,
　Saying, 'Christian, love me more.'

4 In our joys and in our sorrows,
　　Days of toil and hours of ease,
Still he calls, in cares and pleasures,
　'Christian, love me more than these.'

5 Jesus calls us!—by thy mercies,
　Saviour, may we hear thy call,
Give our hearts to thy obedience,
　Serve and love thee best of all.

A - men.

The following is also suitable:
383 Dear Lord and Father.

SAINTS' DAYS: ST. THOMAS

206

CREDITON. (C.M.)
In moderate time ♩ = 84.

THOMAS CLARK, 1775–1859.
Harmonized by MARTIN SHAW.

NOTE.—*This hymn may also be sung to* DUNDEE (*No. 43*).

ST. THOMAS

(O. H., 174-6.)

Mrs. E. Toke, 1812–72, and W. Denton.

O THOU, who didst with love untold
  Thy doubting servant chide,
Bidding the eye of sense behold
  Thy wounded hands and side:

2 Grant us, like him, with heartfelt awe
  To own thee God and Lord,
And from his hour of darkness draw
  Faith in the incarnate Word.

3 And while that wondrous record now
  Of unbelief we hear,
O let us only lowlier bow
  In self-distrusting fear;

4 And grant that we may never dare
  Thy loving heart to grieve,
But, at the last, their blessing share
  Who see not, yet believe.

A - men.

SAINTS' DAYS: ST. PAUL

207

LLANGLOFFAN. (76. 76. D.)
In moderate time ♩ = 76.
Welsh Hymn Melody.

NOTE.—*This hymn may also be sung to* AURELIA (*No.* 489).

ST. PAUL

(*O. H.*, 174-6.)   *J. Ellerton*, 1826-93.

WE sing the glorious conquest
  Before Damascus' gate,
When Saul, the Church's spoiler,
  Came breathing threats and hate;
The ravening wolf rushed forward
  Full early to the prey;
But lo! the Shepherd met him,
  And bound him fast to-day!

2 O Glory most excelling
  That smote across his path!
O Light that pierced and blinded
  The zealot in his wrath!
O Voice that spake within him
  The calm reproving word!
O Love that sought and held him
  The bondman of his Lord!

3 O Wisdom, ordering all things
  In order strong and sweet,
What nobler spoil was ever
  Cast at the Victor's feet?
What wiser master-builder
  E'er wrought at thine employ,
Than he, till now so furious
  Thy building to destroy?

4. Lord, teach thy Church the lesson,
  Still in her darkest hour
Of weakness and of danger
  To trust thy hidden power.
Thy grace by ways mysterious
  The wrath of man can bind,
And in thy boldest foeman
  Thy chosen Saint can find!

A - men.

THE PURIFICATION

208

Mode i.   *arr.* J. H. A.

THE PURIFICATION

OFFICE HYMN E.   *Ascribed to Archbishop Rabanus*
(M. 214 *or* 215.)   Quod chorus vatum.   *Maurus, 9th cent. Tr.* T. A. L.

ALL prophets hail thee, from of old announcing,
    By the inbreathèd Spirit of the Father,
God's Mother, bringing prophecies to fullness,
        Mary the maiden.

THE PURIFICATION

208 (Modern Tune)

DIVA SERVATRIX. (11 11. 11 5.)
In moderate time ♩ = 96. To be sung in unison.

Bayeux Church Melody.
Harmonized by R. V. W.

2 Thou the true Virgin Mother of the Highest,
  Bearing incarnate God in awed obedience,
  Meekly acceptest for a sinless offspring
                Purification.

3 In the high temple Simeon receives thee,
  Takes to his bent arms with a holy rapture
  That promised Saviour, vision of redemption,
                Christ long awaited.

4 Now the fair realm of Paradise attaining,
  And to thy Son's throne, Mother of the Eternal,
  Raisèd all glorious, yet in earth's devotion
                Join with us always.

5 Glory and worship to the Lord of all things
  Pay we unresting, who alone adorèd,
  Father and Son and Spirit, in the highest
                Reigneth eternal. Amen.

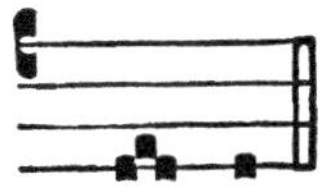

A - men.

See also (for 2nd E.):
22 Come rejoicing.

A . . . men.

THE PURIFICATION

209

OLD 120TH. (66. 66. 66.)
Moderately slow ♩= 66.

Melody from *Damon's Psalter*, 1579,
and *Este's Psalter*, 1592,
rhythm slightly adapted.

J. Ellerton, 1826-93.

1 HAIL to the Lord who comes,
  Comes to his temple gate!
Not with his Angel host,
  Not in his kingly state;
No shouts proclaim him nigh,
  No crowds his coming wait;

2 But borne upon the throne
  Of Mary's gentle breast,
Watched by her duteous love,
  In her fond arms at rest;
Thus to his Father's house
  He comes, the heavenly Guest.

3 There Joseph at her side
  In reverent wonder stands;
And, filled with holy joy,
  Old Simeon in his hands
Takes up the promised Child,
  The glory of all lands.
Unison.

4 Hail to the great First-born
  Whose ransom-price they pay!
The Son before all worlds,
  The Child of man to-day,
That he might ransom us
  Who still in bondage lay.

5. O Light of all the earth,
  Thy children wait for thee!
Come to thy temples here,
  That we, from sin set free,
Before thy Father's face
  May all presented be!

A - men.

SAINTS' DAYS: ST. MATTHIAS

210

JACKSON. (C. M.)
In moderate time ♩ = 72.

T. JACKSON, 1715-81.

NOTE.—*This hymn may also be sung to* ST. JAMES (*No.* 341).

ST. MATTHIAS

(*O. H.,* 174-6.)

H. Alford, 1810-71.

THE highest and the holiest place
    Guards not the heart from sin;
The Church that safest seems without
    May harbour foes within.

2 Thus in the small and chosen band,
    Beloved above the rest,
One fell from his apostleship,
    A traitor-soul unblest.

3 But not the great designs of God
    Man's sins shall overthrow;
Another witness to the truth
    Forth to the lands shall go.

4 The soul that sinneth, it shall die;
    Thy purpose shall not fail;
The word of grace no less shall sound,
    The truth no less prevail.

5. Righteous, O Lord, are all thy ways;
    Long as the worlds endure,
From foes without and foes within
    Thy Church shall stand secure.

A - men.

SAINTS' DAYS: ST. DAVID

211

OLD 44TH. (D. C. M.)
In moderate time ♩ = 72.

Anglo-Genevan Psalter, 1556.
Melody as in *Este's Psalter,* 1592.

NOTE.—*This hymn may also be sung to* OLD 81ST (*No.* 461) *or* STETTIN (*No.* 202).

ST. DAVID

E. J. Newell, 1853–1916.

1. WE praise thy name, all-holy Lord,
  For him, the beacon-light
That shone beside our western sea
  Through mists of ancient night;
Who sent to Ireland's fainting Church
  New tidings of thy word:
For David, prince of Cambrian Saints,
  We praise thee, holy Lord.

2. For all the saintly band whose prayers
  Still gird our land about,
Of whom, lest men disdain their praise,
  The voiceless stones cry out;
Our hills and vales on every hand
  Their names and deeds record:
For these, thy ancient hero host,
  We praise thee, holy Lord.

3. Grant us but half their burning zeal,
  But half their iron faith,
But half their charity of heart,
  And fortitude to death;
That we with them and all thy Saints
  May in thy truth accord,
And ever in thy holy Church
  May praise thee, holy Lord.

A - men.

302

SAINTS' DAYS: ST. PATRICK

212

ST. PATRICK (March 17th).

St. Patrick's Breastplate.

Suitable also for general occasions.

Ascribed to *St. Patrick, 372–466.*
Tr. *Mrs. C. F. Alexander.*

Atomriuɼ inoiu

ST. PATRICK. (D. L. M.)*
Slow and dignified ♩ = 72.

*From an Ancient
Irish Hymn Melody.*

Voices in unison.

1 I bind un-to my-self to-day The strong name of the Trin-i-ty, By in-vo-ca-tion of the same, The Three in One, and One in Three.

* *This refers to the complete tune only as given for verses 2–7.*

SAINTS' DAYS: ST. PATRICK

212 (continued)

2* I bind	this	day	to	me	for ev-er,	By power of
3* I bind	un-to	my-self	the power	Of	the great
4 I bind	un-to	my-self	to-day	The	vir-tues
5 I bind	un-to	my-self	to-day	The	power of
6* A-gainst	the de-mon	snares	of	sin,	The	vice that
7* A-gainst	all Sa-tan's	spells	and	wiles,	A-gainst false

faith,	Christ's In-car-nation;	His	bap - - tism	in
love	of Cher-u-bim;	The	sweet 'Well done'	in
of	the star-lit heaven,	The	glo-rious sun's	life-
God	to hold and lead,	His	eye to watch,	his
gives	tempt-a-tion force,	The	na-tural lusts	that
words	of he-re-sy,	A-gainst	the know-ledge

SAINTS' DAYS: ST. PATRICK

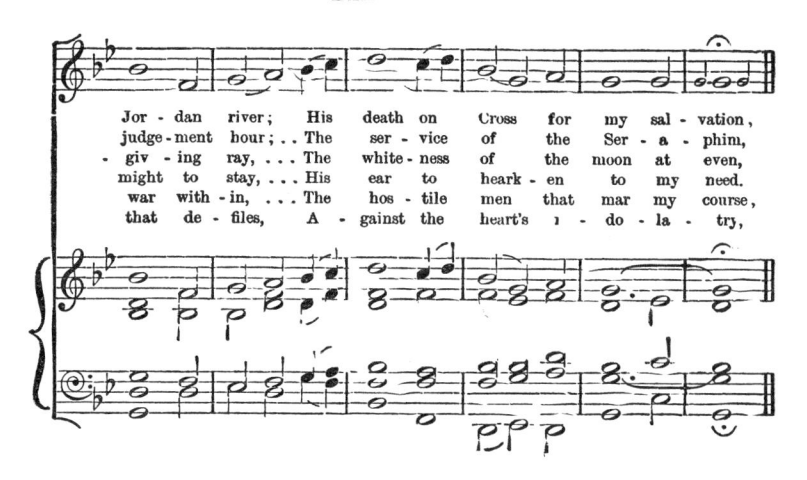

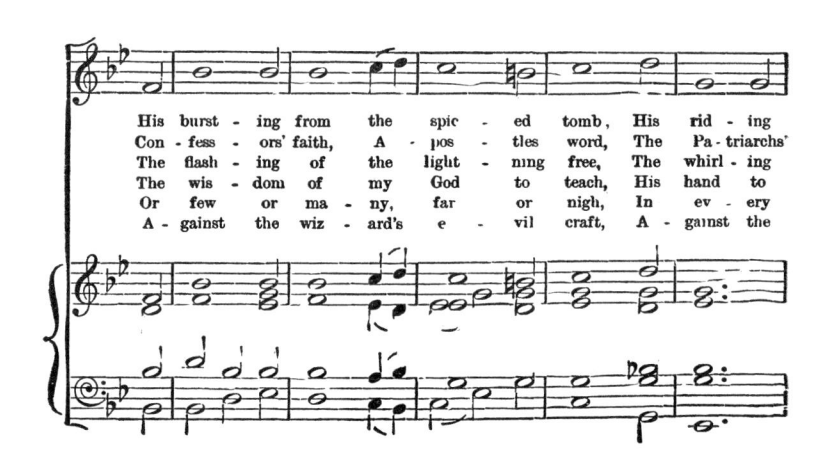

212 (continued)

Jor - dan river; His death on Cross for my sal - vation,
judge - ment hour; .. The ser - vice of the Ser - a - phim,
- giv - ing ray, ... The white - ness of the moon at even,
might to stay, ... His ear to heark - en to my need.
war with - in, ... The hos - tile men that mar my course,
that de - files, A - gainst the heart's i - do - la - try,

His burst - ing from the spic - ed tomb, His rid - ing
Con - fess - ors' faith, A - pos - tles word, The Pa - triarchs'
The flash - ing of the light - ning free, The whirl - ing
The wis - dom of my God to teach, His hand to
Or few or ma - ny, far or nigh, In ev - ery
A - gainst the wiz - ard's e - vil craft, A - gainst the

SAINTS' DAYS: ST PATRICK

212 (*continued*)

up the heaven - ly way; His com - ing at the day of
prayers, the Pro - phets' scrolls, All good deeds done un - to the
wind's tem - pes - tuous shocks, The sta - ble earth, the deep salt
guide, his shield to ward; The word of God to give me
place, and in all hours, A - gainst their fierce hos - ti - li -
death - wound and the burn-ing, The chok - ing wave, the poi-soned

doom; .. I bind un - to my - self to - day.
Lord, .. And pu - ri - ty of vir - gin souls.
sea, .. A - round the old e - ter - nal rocks.
speech, .. His heaven - ly host to be my guard.
- ty, ... I bind to me these ho - ly powers.
shaft, ... Pro - tect me, Christ, till thy re - turn-ing.

SAINTS' DAYS: ST. PATRICK

212 (continued)

DEIRDRE. (8 8. 8 8.)
In Harmony.
Part 2.
Adapted from an Ancient Irish Melody.

8 Christ be with me, Christ with-in me, Christ be-hind me, Christ be-fore me,

Christ be-side me, Christ to win me, Christ to com-fort and re-store me,

Christ be-neath me, Christ a-bove me, Christ in qui-et, Christ in dan-ger,

Christ in hearts of all that love me, Christ in mouth of friend and stranger.

SAINTS' DAYS: ST. PATRICK

212 *(continued)*

Doxology to either Part.

9. I bind un-to my self the name, The strong name of the Trin-i-ty; By in-vo-ca-tion of the same, The Three in One, and One in Three.

SAINTS' DAYS: ST. PATRICK

212 (continued)

Of whom all nature hath cre - a - tion; E - ter - nal Fa - ther, Spi - rit, Word: Praise to the Lord of my sal - va - tion, Sal - va - tion is of Christ the Lord.

Harmony.

A - men.

THE ANNUNCIATION
213

Mode i. *arr.* J. H. A.

* *For this group some texts have* DEFEDC ♪♪♪♪ *instead.*

THE ANNUNCIATION

See also : **640** Virgin-born! we bow before thee.

OFFICE HYMN. E. *Conception, Annunciation, Nativity, B.V.M.* c. 9th cent. Tr. A. R.

Ave, maris Stella.

HAIL, O Star that pointest
  Towards the port of heaven,
Thou to whom as maiden
  God for Son was given.

2 When the salutation
    Gabriel had spoken,
  Peace was shed upon us,
    Eva's bonds were broken.

3 Bound by Satan's fetters,
    Health and vision needing,
  God will aid and light us
    At thy gentle pleading.

THE ANNUNCIATION

AVE MARIS STELLA. (6 6. 6 6.) **213** (Modern Tune)

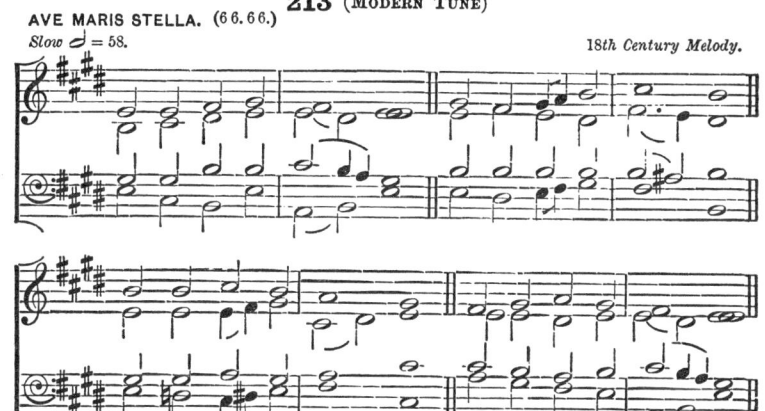

Slow ♩ = 58.

18th Century Melody.

Note.—*This hymn may also be sung to* St. Martin (*No.* 416) *which was originally composed for it.*

4 Jesu's tender Mother,
   Make thy supplication
Unto him who chose thee
   At his Incarnation;

5 That, O matchless Maiden,
   Passing meek and lowly,
Thy dear Son may make us
   Blameless, chaste and holy.

6 So, as now we journey,
   Aid our weak endeavour,
Till we gaze on Jesus,
   And rejoice for ever.

A - men.

7. Father, Son and Spirit,
   Three in One confessing,
Give we equal glory,
   Equal praise and blessing. Amen.

Another version.

SAINTS' DAYS: ST. MARY THE VIRGIN
214, 215

Mode ii.   *arr.* J. H. A.

A - men.

SAINTS' DAYS : ST. MARY THE VIRGIN

214, 215 (Modern Tune)

O AMOR QUAM ECSTATICUS. (L. M.)
In moderate time ♩ = 144. Unison.

Old French Melody (?). Mode I.
Set by BASIL HARWOOD.

NOTE.—*These hymns may also be sung to* PUER NOBIS NASCITUR (*No.* 14) *or* ST. AMBROSE (*No.* 193).

214

OFFICE HYMN. M. *Conception,* c. 9th cent.
Annunciation, Nativity, B.V.M. Tr. J. M. Neale.

Quem terra, pontus, aethera.

THE God whom earth, and sea, and sky,
    Adore, and laud, and magnify,
Who o'er their threefold fabric reigns,
The Virgin's spotless womb contains.

2 The God whose will by moon and sun
   And all things in due course is done,
Is borne upon a Maiden's breast,
By fullest heavenly grace possest.

3 How blest that Mother, in whose shrine
   The great Artificer Divine,
Whose hand contains the earth and sky,
Vouchsafed, as in his ark, to lie!

4 Blest, in the message Gabriel brought;
   Blest, by the work the Spirit wrought:
From whom the Great Desire of earth
Took human flesh and human birth.

5. All honour, laud, and glory be,
   O Jesu, Virgin-born, to thee!
All glory, as is ever meet,
To Father and to Paraclete.
                  Amen.

215

OFFICE HYMN. M. *Conception,* c. 9th cent.
Annunciation, Nativity, B.V.M. Tr. P. D.

O gloriosa Femina.

O GLORIOUS Maid, exalted far
   Beyond the light of burning star,
From him who made thee thou hast
   Grace to be Mother of his Son. [won

2 That which was lost in hapless Eve
Thy holy Scion did retrieve:
The tear-worn sons of Adam's race
Through thee have seen the heavenly place.

3 Thou wast the gate of heaven's high Lord.
The door through which the light hath poured.
Christians rejoice, for through a Maid
To all mankind is life conveyed!

4. All honour, laud, and glory be,
O Jesu, Virgin-born, to thee!
All glory, as is ever meet,
To Father and to Paraclete. Amen.

A - men.

SAINTS' DAYS: ST. MARY THE VIRGIN

216

ST. ALBAN. (8 8 6. D.)
Moderately slow ♩ = 108.

St. Alban's Tune Book, 1865.

NOTE.—*This hymn may also be sung to* MAGDALEN COLLEGE (*No.* 457).

J. Keble, 1792–1866.

1 AVE Maria! blessèd Maid!
   Lily of Eden's fragrant shade!
  Who can express the love
That nurtured thee, so pure and sweet,
Making thy heart a shelter meet
  For Jesus' holy Dove!

2 Ave Maria! Mother blest,
  To whom, caressing and caressed,
   Clings the eternal Child;
Favoured beyond Archangels' dream,
When first on thee with tenderest gleam
   Thy new-born Saviour smiled.

3 Thou wept'st meek Maiden, Mother mild,
  Thou wept'st upon thy sinless Child,
   Thy very heart was riven:
And yet, what mourning matron here
Would deem thy sorrows bought too dear
  By all on this side heaven!

4 A Son that never did amiss,
  That never shamed his Mother's kiss,
   Nor crossed her fondest prayer:
E'en from the Tree he deign'd to bow
For her his agonized brow,
  Her, his sole earthly care.

5. Ave Maria! thou whose name
  All but adoring love may claim,
   Yet may we reach thy shrine;
For he, thy Son and Saviour, vows
To crown all lowly lofty brows
  With love and joy like thine.

A - men.

SAINTS' DAYS: ST. MARY THE VIRGIN

FARLEY CASTLE. (10 10. 10 10.) **217**
In moderate time ♩ = 72.

H. Lawes, 1596–1662.

Bishop T. Ken, 1637–1711.

HER Virgin eyes saw God incarnate born,
   When she to Bethl'em came that happy morn;
How high her raptures then began to swell,
None but her own omniscient Son can tell.

2 As Eve when she her fontal sin reviewed,
   Wept for herself and all she should include,
Blest Mary with man's Saviour in embrace
Joyed for herself and for all human race.

3 All Saints are by her Son's dear influence blest,
   She kept the very Fountain at her breast;
The Son adored and nursed by the sweet Maid
A thousandfold of love for love repaid.

4. Heaven with transcendent joys her entrance graced,
   Next to his throne her Son his Mother placed;
And here below, now she's of heaven possest,
All generations are to call her blest.

A - men.

SAINTS' DAYS: ST. MARY THE VIRGIN

DEN DES VATERS SINN GEBOREN. (8 7. 8 7. 8 7. 6.)

218

Melody by
J. A. FREYLINGHAUSEN, 1670–1789.
Harmony from 'Zions Harfe' (1855).

Moderately slow ♩ = 66.

NOTE.—*By omitting the refrain of each verse this hymn may be sung to* TANTUM ERGO (*No. 63*).

V. S. S. C.

YE who own the faith of Jesus
  Sing the wonders that were done,
When the love of God the Father
  O'er our sin the victory won,
When he made the Virgin Mary
  Mother of his only Son.
    Hail Mary, full of grace.

SAINTS' DAYS: ST. MARY THE VIRGIN

2 Blessèd were the chosen people
    Out of whom the Lord did come,
Blessèd was the land of promise
    Fashioned for his earthly home;
But more blessèd far the Mother
    She who bare him in her womb.

3 Wherefore let all faithful people
    Tell the honour of her name,
Let the Church in her foreshadowed
    Part in her thanksgiving claim;
What Christ's Mother sang in gladness
    Let Christ's people sing the same.

4 Let us weave our supplications,
    She with us and we with her,
For the advancement of the faithful,
    For each faithful worshipper,
For the doubting, for the sinful,
    For each heedless wanderer.

5 * May the Mother's intercessions
    On our homes a blessing win,
That the children all be prospered,
    Strong and fair and pure within,
Following our Lord's own footsteps,
    Firm in faith and free from sin.

6 * For the sick and for the agèd,
    For our dear ones far away,
For the hearts that mourn in secret,
    All who need our prayers to-day,
For the faithful gone before us,
    May the holy Virgin pray.

7. Praise, O Mary, praise the Father,
    Praise thy Saviour and thy Son,
Praise the everlasting Spirit,
    Who hath made thee ark and throne
O'er all creatures high exalted,
    Lowly praise the Three in One.
                Amen.

SAINTS DAYS: ST. GEORGE

219

FALKLAND. (88.88.88.)
Moderately slow, dignified ♩ = 66.

Melody by H. Lawes, 1596–1662.

ST. GEORGE

Laurence Housman.

LORD God of Hosts, within whose hand
Dominion rests on sea and land,
Before whose word of life or death
The strength of nations is but breath:
O King, enthroned all thrones above,
Give strength unto the land we love.

2 Thou Breath of Life since time began,
Breathing upon the lips of man,
Hast taught each kindred race to raise
United word to sound thy praise:
So, in this land, join, we beseech,
All hearts and lips in single speech.

3 To George our Saint thou gavest grace
Without one fear all foes to face,
And to confess by faithful death
That Word of Life which was his breath.
O help us, Helper of Saint George,
To fear no bonds that man can forge.

Unison. 4. Arm us like him, who in thy trust
Beat down the dragon to the dust;
So that we too may tread down sin
And with thy Saints a crown may win.
Help us, O God, that we may be
A land acceptable to thee.

A - men.

SAINTS' DAYS: ST. MARK

BROCKHAM. (L. M.)
Moderately fast ♩ = 104.

220

J. CLARK, 1670-1707.

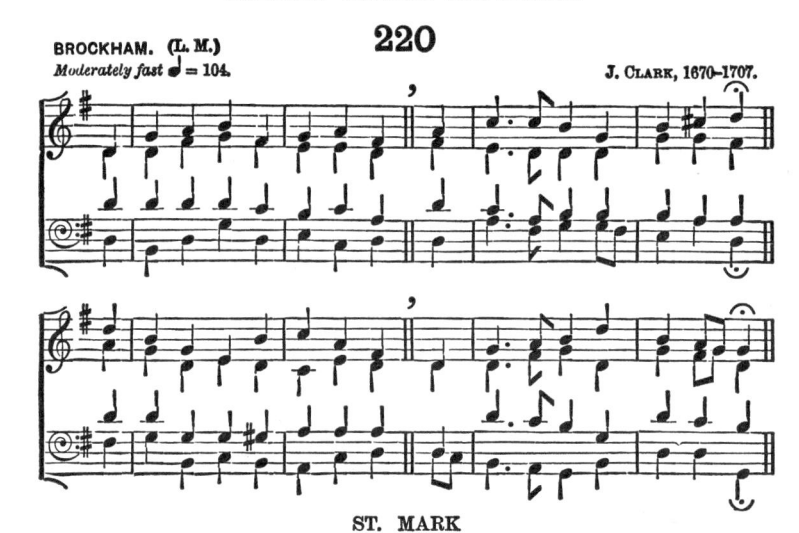

ST. MARK

(*O. H.*, 123, *Pt.* 2; 124, *Pt.* 2.)

Laurence Housman, 1865-1959.

THE Saint who first found grace to pen
The Life which was the Life of men,
And shed abroad the Gospel's ray,
His fame we celebrate to-day.

2 Lo, drawn by Pentecostal fire,
His heart conceived its great desire,
When pure of mind, inspired, he heard
And with his hand set forth the Word.

3 Then, clearly writ, the Godhead shone
Serene and fair to look upon;
And through that record still comes power
To lighten souls in death's dark hour.

4 O holy mind, for wisdom fit
Wherein that Life of lives stood writ,
May we through minds of like accord
Show forth the pattern of our Lord.

5 And so may all whose minds are dark
Be led to truth by good Saint Mark,
And after this our earthly strife
Stand written in the Book of Life.

6. Praise God who made the world so fair,
And sent his Son our Saviour there,
And by his Holy Spirit wist
To teach the first Evangelist. Amen.

A - men.

SAINTS' DAYS: ST. PHILIP AND ST. JAMES

221

KING'S LANGLEY. (C.M., Irreg.)
In moderate time ♩=92.
English Traditional May-Day Carol.

ST. PHILIP AND ST. JAMES

(*O. H.*, 123, *Pt.* 2; 124, *Pt.* 2)   P. D.

THE winter's sleep was long and deep,
   But earth is awakened and gay;
For the life ne'er dies that from God doth rise,
   And the green comes after the grey.

2*So God doth bring the world to spring;
   And on their holy day
Doth the Church proclaim her Apostles' fame,
   To welcome the first of May.

3 Two Saints of God went by the road
   That leadeth on to light;
And they gave up all at their Master's call,
   To work in their Master's sight.

4 Would Philip's mind the Father find?
   Lo, he hath found the Way;
For to know the Son is to know the One
   Whom the earth and the heavens obey.

5 And, James, 'twas thine by grace divine
   To preach the Christian life,
Where our faith is shown by our works alone,
   And love overcometh strife.

6. Lord, grant that we may brethren be—
   As Christians live in deed;
For it is but so we can learn to know
   The truth that to thee doth lead.

A - men.

SAINTS' DAYS: ST. BARNABAS

222

RHYDDID. (7 6. 7 6. D.)
In moderate time ♩ = 72.
Welsh Hymn Melody.

A-men.

NOTE.—*This hymn may also be sung to* AURELIA (*No.* 489).

ST. BARNABAS

(*O. H.*, 174-6, *if after Ascensiontide*).   *Mrs. Coote.*

THE Son of Consolation!
  Of Levi's priestly line,
Filled with the Holy Spirit
  And fervent faith divine,
With lowly self-oblation,
  For Christ an offering meet,
He laid his earthly riches
  At the Apostles' feet.

2 The Son of Consolation!
  O name of soothing balm!
It fell on sick and weary
  Like breath of heaven's own calm!
And the blest Son of Comfort
  With fearless loving hand
The Gentiles' great Apostle
  Led to the faithful band.

Unison.

3 The Son of Consolation!
  Drawn near unto his Lord,
He won the Martyr's glory,
  And passed to his reward;
With him is faith now ended,
  For ever lost in sight,
But love, made perfect, fills him
  With praise, and joy, and light.

4 The Son of Consolation!
  Lord, hear our humble prayer,
That each of us thy children
  This blessèd name may bear;
That we, sweet comfort shedding
  O'er homes of pain and woe,
'Midst sickness and in prisons,
  May seek thee here below.

5. The Sons of Consolation!
  O what their bliss will be
When Christ the King shall tell them,
  'Ye did it unto me!'
The merciful and loving
  The Lord of life shall own,
And as his priceless jewels
  Shall set them round his throne.

SAINTS' DAYS: ST. JOHN BAPTIST

223, 224

Mode ii.   *arr.* J. H. A.

ST. JOHN BAPTIST
223

OFFICE HYMN E.   *Paulus Diaconus, 8th cent.*   Tr. R. E. R.
Ut queant laxis

LET thine example, holy John, remind us,
  Ere we can meetly sing thy deeds of wonder,
Hearts must be chastened, and the bonds that bind us
          Broken asunder'

SAINTS' DAYS: ST. JOHN BAPTIST

223, 224 (Modern Tune)

HERR, DEINEN ZORN. (11 11. 11 5.)

In moderate time, not too fast ♩ = 92.   *Later form of melody by* J. CRÜGER, 1598-1662.

Unison Amen.

NOTE.—*This hymn may also be sung to* ISTE CONFESSOR *(No.* 188

2 Lo' a swift Angel, from the skies descending,
                  naming;
Tells to thy father what shall be thy
All thy life's greatness to its bitter
    ending
            Duly proclaiming.

3 But when he doubted what the Angel
    told him,
                        story;
Came to him dumbness to confirm the
At thine appearing, healed again behold
    him,
            Chanting thy glory!

4 Oh' what a splendour and a revelation
Came to each mother, at thy joyful
    leaping,
Greeting thy Monarch, King of every
                        nation,
    In the womb sleeping.

5. Angels in orders everlasting praise
    thee,
                            dous;
God, in thy triune Majesty tremen
Hark to the prayers we, penitents
    upraise thee
        Save and defend us. Amen.

224

OFFICE HYMN. M.   *Paulus Diaconus* 8th cent   *Tr* R E.R.
                              Antra desert

E'EN in thy childhood, 'mid the desert places,
    Thou hadst a refuge from the city gainèd,
Far from all slander and its bitter traces
        Living unstained.

2 Often had prophets in the distant ages
Sung to announce the Daystar and to name him;
But as the Saviour, last of all the sages,
        Thou didst proclaim him.

A - men.

3 Than John the Baptist, none of all Eve's daughters
E'er bore a greater, whether high or lowly
He was thought worthy, washing in the waters
        Jesus the holy.

4. Angels in orders everlasting praise thee.
God, in thy triune Majesty tremendous;
Hark to the prayers we, penitents, upraise thee:
        Save and defend us. Amen.

SAINTS' DAYS: ST. JOHN BAPTIST

HAIL HARBINGER OF MORN. (6 6. 10. D.) **225**

In moderate time ♩ = 80.

W. H. BELL.

The Venerable Bede, 678–735.
Tr. *C. S. Calverley* †.

Praecursor altus luminis.

HAIL, harbinger of morn:
　Thou that art this day born,
And heraldest the Word with clarion voice!
　Ye faithful ones, in him
　Behold the dawning dim
Of the bright day, and let your hearts rejoice.

SAINTS' DAYS: ST. JOHN BAPTIST

    2   John;—by that chosen name
         To call him, Gabriel came
     By God's appointment from his home on high:
         What deeds that babe should do
         To manhood when he grew,
     God sent his Angel forth to testify.

Unison. 3   There is none greater, none,
         Than Zachariah's son;
     Than this no mightier prophet hath been born:
         Of prophets he may claim
         More than a prophet's fame;
     Sublimer deeds than theirs his brow adorn.

    4   'Lo, to prepare thy way,'
         Did God the Father say,
     'Before thy face my messenger I send,
         Thy coming to forerun;
         As on the orient sun
     Doth the bright daystar morn by morn attend.'

Unison. 5. Praise therefore God most high;
         Praise him who came to die
     For us, his Son that liveth evermore;
         And to the Spirit raise,
         The Comforter, like praise,
     While time endureth, and when time is o'er.
                         Amen.

A - men.

(*No. 9 is also suitable.*)

SAINTS' DAYS: ST. PETER
226

Mode i.

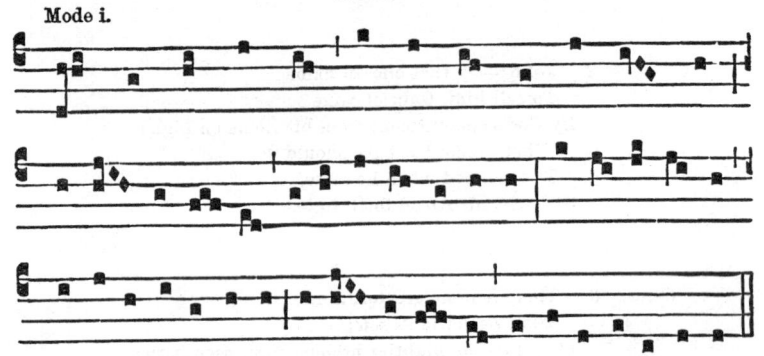

NOTE.—*The accompaniment to this plainsong melody, and also the modern tune to this hymn is the same as that of No. 174.*

ST. PETER

OFFICE HYMN (*St. Peter and St. Paul*). E. and M.

Aurea luce.

*Ascribed to Elpis, c. 500.
Tr. T. A. L.*

WITH golden splendour and with roseate hues of morn,
  O gracious Saviour, Light of light, this day adorn,
Which brings to ransomed sinners hopes of that far home
Where saints and angels sing the praise of martyrdom.

2 Lo, the Keybearer, lo, the Teacher of mankind,
Lights of the world and judges sent to loose and bind,
Alike triumphant or by cross or sword-stroke found,
In life's high Senate stand with victor's laurel crowned.

3 Good Shepherd, Peter, unto whom the charge was given
To close or open ways of pilgrimage to heaven,
In sin's hard bondage held may we have grace to know
The full remission thou wast granted to bestow.

4 O noble Teacher, Paul, we trust to learn of thee
Both earthly converse and the flight of ecstasy;
Till from the fading truths that now we know in part
We pass to fulness of delight for mind and heart.

5 Twin olive branches, pouring oil of gladness forth,
Your prayers shall aid us, that for all our little worth,
Believing, hoping, loving, we for whom ye plead,
This body dying, may attain to life indeed.

6. Now to the glorious Trinity be duly paid
Worship and honour, praise and service unafraid,
Who in unchanging Unity, one Lord sublime,
Hath ever lived as now and to unending time. Amen.

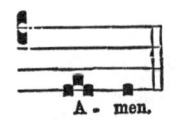

(*Or for O. H., M. 175 or 176.*)

SAINTS' DAYS: ST. PETER

CHILDHOOD. (8 8. 8 6.) **227**

In moderate time ♩ = 100. 'University of Wales' (Students' Hymnal), 1923.

NOTE.—*This hymn may also be sung to* ERSKINE (*Appendix, No.* 34).

Mrs. C. F. Alexander, 1818–95.

FORSAKEN once, and thrice denied,
  The risen Lord gave pardon free,
Stood once again at Peter's side,
  And asked him, 'Lov'st thou me?'

2 How many times with faithless word
  Have we denied his holy name,
How oft forsaken our dear Lord,
  And shrunk when trial came!

3 Saint Peter, when the cock crew clear,
  Went out, and wept his broken faith;
Strong as a rock through strife and fear,
  He served his Lord till death.

4 How oft his cowardice of heart
  We have without his love sincere,
The sin without the sorrow's smart,
  The shame without the tear!

5 O oft forsaken, oft denied,
  Forgive our shame, wash out our sin;
Look on us from thy Father's side
  And let that sweet look win.

6. Hear when we call thee from the deep,
  Still walk beside us on the shore,
Give hands to work, and eyes to weep,
  And hearts to love thee more.

A - men.

THE VISITATION

228

Mode ii.　　　　　　　　　　　　　　　　　　　　　　　　　　*arr.* J. H. A.

THE VISITATION

OFFICE HYMN. E.　　　　　　　　　　　　　　　　　　　15th cent.　*Tr.* L. H.

Festum Matris gloriosae.

николаи

NOW in holy celebration
　Sing we of that Mother blest,
In whose flesh for men's salvation
　God incarnate deigned to rest,
When a kindred salutation
　Named in faith the mystic Guest.

2* Lo, the advent Word confessing,
　Spake for joy the voice yet dumb,
Through his mother's lips addressing
　Her, of motherhood the sum,—
Bower of beauty, blest and blessing,
　Crowned with fruit of Life to come.

THE VISITATION

ORIEL. (8 7. 8 7. 8 7.)   **228** (MODERN TUNE)
Moderately slow ♩ = 66.
C. ETT, '*Cantica Sacra*,' 1840.

3 'Whence,' she cried, at that fair meeting,
  'Comes to me this great reward?
For when first I heard the greeting
  Of the Mother of my Lord,
In my womb, the joy repeating,
  Leapt my babe in sweet accord!'

4 Lo. at that glad commendation
  Joy found voice in Mary's breast
While in holy exultation
  She her Maker's power confest,
At whose word each generation
  Now henceforward names her blest.

5. Triune Godhead, health supplying,
  Ruler of eternity,
On the Fount of grace relying,
  We uplift our hearts to thee,
Praying that in realms undying
  We at one with Life may be. **Amen.**

A - men.

A - men.

THE VISITATION
229, 230

Mode viii.

Melody from the Barking Hymnal.
arr. J. H. A.

The Sarum proper melody was No. 169.

229

Office Hymn. M.

Mundi salus affutura.

15th cent. Tr. L. H.

PORTAL of the world's salvation,
  Lo, a virgin pure and mild,
Humble-hearted, high in station,
  Form of beauty undefiled,
Crown of earth's anticipation,
  Comes the Mother-maid with child.

2* Here, the serpent's power subduing,
  See the Bush unburned by fire,
Gideon's Fleece of heaven's imbuing,
  Aaron's Rod of bright attire,
Fair, and pure, and peace-ensuing,
  Spouse of Solomon's desire.

SAINTS' DAYS: ST. MARY MAGDALENE

3 * Jesse's Branch received its Flower,
  Mother of Emmanuel,
Portal sealed and mystic Bower
  Promised by Ezekiel,
Rock of Daniel's dream, whose power
  Smote, and lo, the image fell!

4 See in flesh so great a wonder
  By the power of God ordained,—
Him, whose feet all worlds lay under,
  In a Virgin's womb contained;—
So on earth, her bonds to sunder,
  Righteousness from heaven hath rained.

5 Virgin sweet, with love o'erflowing,
  To the hills in haste she fares;
On a kindred heart bestowing
  Blessing from the joy she bears;
Waiting while with mystic showing
  Time the sacred birth prepares.

6 What fair joy o'ershone that dwelling,
  Called so great a guest to greet;
What her joy whose love compelling
  Found a rest for Mary's feet,
When, the bliss of time foretelling,
  Lo, the Voice and Word did meet!

7. God most high, the heaven's Foundation,
  Ruler of eternity;
Jesu, who for man's salvation
  Came in flesh to make us free;
Spirit, moving all creation,
  Evermore be praise to thee! Amen.

230

ST. MARY MAGDALENE

OFFICE HYMN. E.   *Philippe de Grève, d. 1236.*
Collaudemus Magdalenae.   *Tr. L. H.*

SING we all the joys and sorrows
  Which in Mary's heart were found;
To her fame our voices raising
  Let consenting praise abound:
So do birds of night and morning
  Make their mingled songs resound.

2 Through the guest-throng at the banquet
  Undismayed she sought her Lord;
Cleansing tears and salving ointments
  Lowly on his feet she poured,—
Wiped them with her hair, obtaining
  By her love the great reward.

3 * Deigns the Cleanser to be cleansed;
  Stoops the Source to find the flow;
Drains the Flower in outpoured fragrance
  Perfume which its heart let go:
Heavens which have rained their bounty
  Drink the dew from earth below!

4 There in box of alabaster,
  Bearing nard of fragrance pure,
She with gift of outpoured sweetness
  Bids the mystic sign endure:
Seeking from anointment healing,
  Lo, the sick anoints the Cure!

5 Dearly then for that dear offering
  Did our Lord in love repay:
Since so perfect her devotion,
  All her sins he put away:
Made her be his own forerunner
  On his Resurrection day.

6. Now be glory, laud, and honour
  Unto him the Paschal Host,
Who, in war with Death a Lion,
  As a Lamb gave up the ghost,
And the third day rose a Victor
  Crowned with spoils that Death had lost.

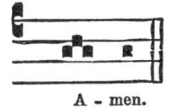

A - men.

THE VISITATION

229, 230 (Modern Tune)

COLLAUDEMUS. (87. 87. 87.)
In moderate time ♩ = 126.
French Carol.

229

Office Hymn. M.   *Mundi salus affutura.*   15th cent. Tr. L. H.

PORTAL of the world's salvation,
  Lo, a virgin pure and mild,
Humble-hearted, high in station,
  Form of beauty undefiled,
Crown of earth's anticipation,
  Comes the Mother-maid with child.

2 * Here, the serpent's power subduing,
  See the Bush unburned by fire,
Gideon's Fleece of heaven's imbuing,
  Aaron's Rod of bright attire,
Fair, and pure, and peace-ensuing,
  Spouse of Solomon's desire.

3 * Jesse's Branch received its Flower,
  Mother of Emmanuel,
Portal sealed and mystic Bower
  Promised by Ezekiel,
Rock of Daniel's dream, whose power
  Smote, and lo, the image fell!

4 See in flesh so great a wonder
  By the power of God ordained,—
Him, whose feet all worlds lay under,
  In a Virgin's womb contained;—
So on earth, her bonds to sunder,
  Righteousness from heaven hath rained.

SAINTS' DAYS: ST. MARY MAGDALENE

5 Virgin sweet, with love o'erflowing,
   To the hills in haste she fares;
On a kindred heart bestowing
   Blessing from the joy she bears;
Waiting while with mystic showing
   Time the sacred birth prepares.

6 What fair joy o'ershone that dwelling,
   Called so great a guest to greet;
What her joy whose love compelling
   Found a rest for Mary's feet,
When, the bliss of time foretelling,
   Lo, the Voice and Word did meet!

7. God most high, the heaven's Foundation,
   Ruler of eternity;
Jesu, who for man's salvation
   Came in flesh to make us free;
Spirit, moving all creation,
   Evermore be praise to thee! Amen.

230

ST. MARY MAGDALENE

OFFICE HYMN. E.
Collaudemus Magdalenae.
Philippe de Grève, d. 1236.
Tr. L. H.

SING we all the joys and sorrows
   Which in Mary's heart were found;
To her fame our voices raising
   Let consenting praise abound:
So do birds of night and morning
   Make their mingled songs resound.

2 Through the guest-throng at the banquet
   Undismayed she sought her Lord;
Cleansing tears and salving ointments
   Lowly on his feet she poured,—
Wiped them with her hair, obtaining
   By her love the great reward.

3 * Deigns the Cleanser to be cleansed;
   Stoops the Source to find the flow;
Drains the Flower in outpoured fragrance
   Perfume which its heart let go:
Heavens which have rained their bounty
   Drink the dew from earth below!

4 There in box of alabaster,
   Bearing nard of fragrance pure,
She with gift of outpoured sweetness
   Bids the mystic sign endure:
Seeking from anointment healing,
   Lo, the sick anoints the Cure!

5 Dearly then for that dear offering
   Did our Lord in love repay:
Since so perfect her devotion,
   All her sins he put away:
Made her be his own forerunner
   On his Resurrection day.

6. Now be glory, laud, and honour
   Unto him the Paschal Host,
Who, in war with Death a Lion,
   As a Lamb gave up the ghost,
And the third day rose a Victor
   Crowned with spoils that Death had lost.

A - men.

SAINTS' DAYS: ST. MARY MAGDALENE

231

Mode ii.   *arr.* J. H. A.

NOTE.—*If a Modern Tune is required for this hymn, it may be sung to* ORIEL (*No.* 228) *or* COLLAUDEMUS (*No.* 230).

OFFICE HYMN. M. *and* E.
               O Maria, noli flere.
                                      Philippe de Grève, d. 1236.
                                                        Tr. L. H.

MARY, weep not, weep no longer,
   Now thy heart hath gained its goal;
Here, in truth, the Gardener standeth,
   But the Gardener of thy soul,
Who within thy spirit's garden
   By his love hath made thee whole.

2 Now from grief and lamentation
   Lift thy drooping heart with cheer;
While for love of him thou mournest,
   Lo, thy Lord regained is here!
Fainting for him, thou hast found him;
   All unknown, behold him near!

SAINTS' DAYS: ST. MARY MAGDALENE

3* Whence thy sorrow, whence thy weeping,
Since with thee true bliss abides?
In thy heart, though undiscovered,
Balm of consolation hides:
Holding all, thou canst no longer
Lack the cure that Health provides.

4 Nay, no wonder if she knows not
Till the Sower's seed be sown,
Till from him, the Word eternal,
Light within her heart is thrown.
Lo, he calls her; lo, 'Rabboni,'
She in turn her Lord doth own.

5 Faith that washed the feet of Jesus,
Fed with dew the Fount of Grace,
Win for us a like compassion,
That, with all the ransomed race,
At the glory of his rising
We may see him face to face!

6. Glory be to God and honour,
Who, preferring sacrifice,
Far above the rich man's bounty,
Sweetness found in Mary's sighs,
Who for all, his love foretasting,
Spreads the banquet of the skies.

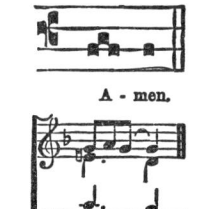

CHRISTUS DER IST MEIN LEBEN. (7 6. 7 6.)

232

Melody by MELCHIOR VULPIUS, 1560-1616. *Adapted and harmonized by* J. S. BACH.

Slow ♩ = 50.

A-men.

NOTE.—*Another harmonization of this tune, in a lower key, will be found at Hymn* 360.

(*O. H.*, 174-6.)   ST. JAMES   *W. Romanis*, 1824-99.

LORD, who shall sit beside thee,
Enthroned on either hand,
When clouds no longer hide thee,
'Mid all thy faithful band?

2 Who drinks the cup of sorrow
Thy Father gave to thee
'Neath shadows of the morrow
In dark Gethsemane;

3 Who on thy Passion thinking
Can find in loss a gain,
And dare to meet unshrinking
Thy baptism of pain.

4 O Jesu, form within us
Thy likeness clear and true;
By thine example win us
To suffer or to do.

5. This law itself fulfilleth,—
Christlike to Christ is nigh,
And, where the Father willeth,
Shall sit with Christ on high.

335

THE TRANSFIGURATION

233

Mode i.   *arr.* J. H. A.

THE TRANSFIGURATION

OFFICE HYMN. E.   *Caelestis formam gloriae.*   15*th cent.*   *Tr.* R. E. R.

AN image of that heavenly light,
    The goal the Church keeps ay in sight,
Christ on the holy mount displays
Where he outshines the sun's bright [rays.

2 Let every age proclaimer be
   How, on this day, the chosen three
With Moses and Elias heard
The Lord speak many a gracious word

3 As witnesses to grace are nigh
   Those twain, the Law and Prophecy;
And to the Son, from out the cloud,
The Father's record thunders loud.

THE TRANSFIGURATION

233 (Modern Tune)

NOSTRE DIEU. (D. L. M.)
In moderate time ♩ = 85.

Melody from Calvin's Psalter, 1539.
Harmonized by R. R. Terry.

NOTE.—*This hymn may also be sung to* Vom Himmel hoch (*No.* 17, *or Appendix, No.* 35) *or to* Auctoritate Saeculi (*No.* 176).

4 With garments whiter than the snows,
  And shining face, Lord Jesus shows
  What glory for those saints shall be
  Who joy in God with piety.

5 The vision and the mystery
  Make faithful hearts beat quick and high,
  So on this solemn day of days
  The cry goes up of prayer and praise.

6. O God the Father, God the Son,
   And Holy Spirit, Three in One,
   Vouchsafe to bring us, by thy grace,
   To see thy glory face to face. Amen.

A - men.

THE TRANSFIGURATION

234

Mode viii. *arr.* J. H. A.

NOTE.—*If a simpler melody is needed, that given at No. 61 may be found suitable.*

OFFICE HYMN. M.   O nata Lux de lumine.   10*th cent.* *Tr.* L. H.

O LIGHT of light, by love inclined,
  Jesu, Redeemer of mankind,
With loving-kindness deign to hear
From suppliant voices praise and prayer.

2 Thou who to raise our souls from hell
  Didst deign in fleshly form to dwell,
Vouchsafe us, when our race is run,
In thy fair Body to be one.

3 More bright than day thy face did show,
Thy raiment whiter than the snow,
When on the mount to mortals blest
Man's Maker thou wast manifest.

THE TRANSFIGURATION

WHITEHALL. (L. M.)   **234** (Modern Tune)

In moderate time ♩ = 76.

Melody by H. Lawes, 1596–1662.

4 Two prophets, that had faith to see,
   With thine elect found company,
   Where unto each, divinely shown,
   The Godhead veiled in form was known.

5 The heavens above his glory named,
   The Father's voice the Son proclaimed;
   To whom, the King of glory now,
   All faithful hearts adoring bow.

6 May all who seek thy praise aright
   Through purer lives show forth thy light;
   So to the brightness of the skies
   By holy deeds our hearts shall rise.

7. Eternal God, to thee we raise,
    The King of kings, our hymn of praise,
    Who Three in One and One in Three
    Doth live and reign eternally.
                   Amen.

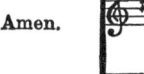

A - men.

A - men.

THE TRANSFIGURATION

235

TALLIS' LAMENTATION. (D. L. M.)
Very slow and solemn ♩ = 60.

Melody in Day's Psalter, 1562.

NOTE.—*This hymn may also be sung to* CANTATE DOMINO (*No.* 48).

Suitable also for Retreats.

A. P. Stanley †, 1815–81.

1. O MASTER, it is good to be [thee;
High on the mountain here with
Where stand revealed to mortal gaze
The great old Saints of other days;
Who once received on Horeb's height
The eternal laws of truth and right;
Or caught the still small whisper, higher [fire.
Than storm, than earthquake, or than

2. O Master, it is good to be
With thee, and with thy faithful three:
Here, where the Apostle's heart of rock
Is nerved against temptation's shock;
Here, where the Son of Thunder learns
The thought that breathes, and word that burns;
Here, where on eagle wings we move
With him whose last best creed is love.

THE TRANSFIGURATION

3*O Master, it is good to be
  Entranced, enwrapt, alone with thee;
  Watching the glistering raiment glow,
  Whiter than Hermon's whitest snow,
  The human lineaments that shine
  Irradiant with a light divine:
  Till we too change from grace to grace
  Gazing on that transfigured face.

4. O Master, it is good to be
  Here on the holy mount with thee:
  When darkling in the depths of night,
  When dazzled with excess of light,
  We bow before the heavenly voice
  That bids bewildered souls rejoice,
  Though love wax cold, and faith be dim,
  'This is my Son! O hear ye him.'

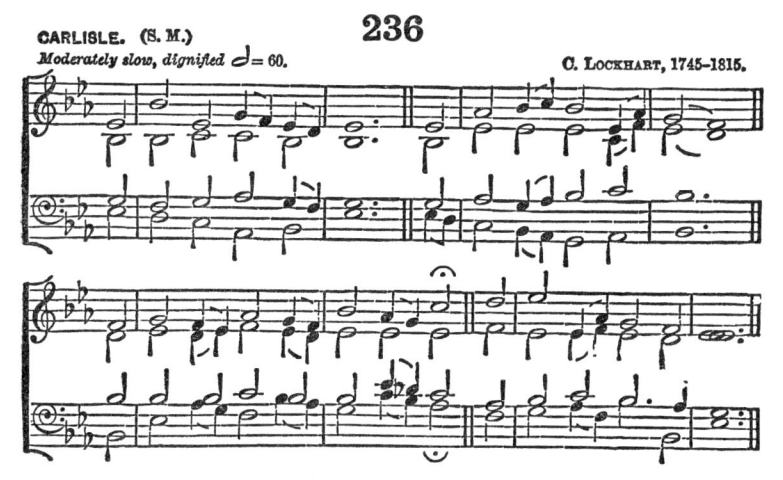

236

CARLISLE. (S. M.)
Moderately slow, dignified ♩= 60.

C. LOCKHART, 1745–1815.

Suitable also for general use.

J. *Armitage Robinson*, 1858–1933.

'TIS good, Lord, to be here!
  Thy glory fills the night;
Thy face and garments, like the sun,
  Shine with unborrowed light.

2 'Tis good, Lord, to be here,
     Thy beauty to behold,
   Where Moses and Elijah stand,
     Thy messengers of old.

3 Fulfiller of the past!
     Promise of things to be!
   We hail thy Body glorified,
     And our redemption see.

4 Before we taste of death,
     We see thy kingdom come;
   We fain would hold the vision bright,
     And make this hill our home.

5. 'Tis good, Lord, to be here!
     Yet we may not remain;
   But since thou bidst us leave the mount
     Come with us to the plain.

341

THE HOLY NAME
237

Melody from Antiphonale Romanum.
arr. J. H. A.

Mode i.

NOTE.—*The Sarum proper melody is No. 14.*

THE HOLY NAME

OFFICE HYMN. E.　　　　　　　　　　　　　　　　　　　　　　　15th cent.　Tr. P. D.

Exultet cor praecordiis.

O LET the heart beat high with bliss,
　Yea, let it triumph at the sound
Of Jesus' name, so sweet it is,
　For every joy therein is found.

2 The name that comforteth in woe,
　The name of Jesus healing sin,
The name that curbs the powers below
　And drives away the death within:

3 The name that soundeth ever sweet
　In speech or verse or holy song,
And bids us run with willing feet,
　Consoled, and comforted, and strong.

4 Then let the name of Jesus ring
　With lofty praise in every place;
Let heart and voice together sing—
　That name shall every ill efface.

THE HOLY NAME
237 (MODERN TUNE)

CROMER. (L. M.)
In moderate time ♩ = 72.
J. A. LLOYD, 1815–74.

NOTE.—*This hymn may also be sung to* TRURO (*No.* 420) *or to the Rouen Melody at Hymn* 151.

5 Ah! Jesus, health of sinful men,
    Give ear unto our loving prayer;
Guide thou our wandering feet again,
    And hold our doings in thy care.

6 Lord, may thy name supply our needs,
    And keep us all from danger free,
And make us perfect in good deeds,
    That we may lose our sins by thee.

7 To thee, O Christ, all glory be
    Who shinest with this holy name;
We worship thy divinity,
    Jesus, thou Lord of gentle fame.

8. O Jesus, of the Virgin born,
    Immortal honour be to thee;
Praise to the Father infinite,
    And Holy Ghost eternally. Amen.

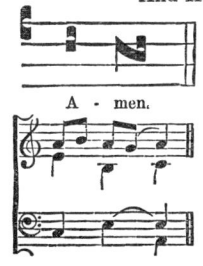

A - men.

A - men.

THE HOLY NAME

238

Mode i.

The accompaniment for this plainsong melody is given at No. 17.

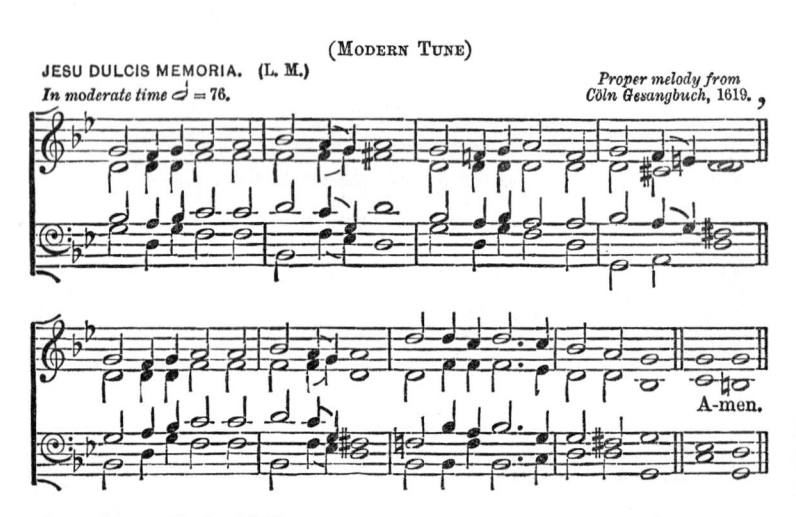

(MODERN TUNE)

JESU DULCIS MEMORIA. (L. M.)
In moderate time ♩ = 76.

Proper melody from Cöln Gesangbuch, 1619.

OFFICE HYMN. (*Pts.* 1 *and* 2) M.
Suitable also for other occasions.

11*th century.*
Tr. J. M. Neale.

Jesu, dulcis memoria.

1 JESU!—the very thought is sweet!
In that dear name all heart-joys meet;
But sweeter than the honey far
The glimpses of his presence are.

2 No word is sung more sweet than this:
No name is heard more full of bliss:
No thought brings sweeter comfort nigh,
Than Jesus, Son of God most high.

THE HOLY NAME

3 Jesu! the hope of souls forlorn!
How good to them for sin that mourn!
To them that seek thee, O how kind!
But what art thou to them that find?

4 Jesu, thou sweetness, pure and blest,
Truth's Fountain, Light of souls distrest,
Surpassing all that heart requires,
Exceeding all that soul desires!

5 No tongue of mortal can express,
No letters write its blessedness:
Alone who hath thee in his heart
Knows, love of Jesus! what thou art.

Part 2.

6 O Jesu! King of wondrous might!
O Victor, glorious from the fight!
Sweetness that may not be exprest,
And altogether loveliest!

7 Remain with us, O Lord to-day!
In every heart thy grace display:
That now the shades of night are fled,
On thee our spirits may be fed.

8. All honour, laud and glory be,
O Jesu, Virgin-born, to thee!
All glory, as is ever meet,
To Father and to Paraclete.   Amen.

238

(Alternative Setting of Parts 1 and 3)

THE ROSY SEQUENCE. (L. M.)
In speaking rhythm.   To be sung in unison.

Sarum Gradual, 1527, 1528, *and* 1532
arr. J. H. A.

Je-su!—the ve-ry thought is sweet! In that dear name all heart-joys meet;

But sweet-er than the hon-ey far The glimp-ses of . . his pre-sence are.

2 No word is sung more sweet than this: No name is heard more full of bliss:

THE HOLY NAME

238 (continued)

No thought brings sweet-er com-fort nigh, Than Je-sus, Son of God most high.

3 Je-su! the hope of souls for-lorn! How good to them for sin that mourn!

To them that seek thee, O how kind! But what art thou to them that find?

4 Je-su, thou sweetness, pure and blest, Truth's Fountain, Light of souls dis-trest,

THE HOLY NAME

238 (*continued*)

Sur-pass-ing all that heart re-quires, Ex-ceed-ing all that soul de-sires!

5 No tongue of mor-tal can ex-press, No let-ters write its bless-ed-ness:

A-lone who hath thee in his heart Knows, love of Je-sus! what thou art.

6 I seek for Je-sus in re-pose, When round my heart its cham-bers close;
7 With Ma-ry in the morn-ing gloom I seek for Je-sus at the tomb;

THE HOLY NAME

238 (continued)

A-broad, and when I shut the door, I long for Je - sus . . . ev - er - more.
For him, with love's most earnest cry, I seek with heart and . . . not with eye.

8 Je-sus, to God the Fa-ther gone, Is seat - ed on the heavenly throne;
9. We fol-low Je-sus now, and raise The voice of prayer, the hymn of praise,

My heart hath al-so passed from me, That where he is . . there it may be.
That he at last may make us meet With him to gain . the heav'nly seat.

[*Copyright, 1931, by Oxford University Press.*]

239

SUSSEX. (8 7. 8 7.) *Adapted from an English Traditional Melody.*

In moderate time ♩ = 72.

The harmony of this tune will be found at No. 385.

NOTE.—*This hymn may also be sung to* STUTTGART (*No. 40*).

ST. BARTHOLOMEW : ST. MATTHEW

(O. H., 174–6.)   ST. BARTHOLOMEW (*or any Apostle*)   A. R.

SAINTS of God! Lo, Jesu's people
  Age to age your glory tell;
In his name for us ye laboured,
  Now in bliss eternal dwell.

2 Twelve poor men, by Christ anointed,
  Braved the rich, the wise, the great,
All the world counts dear rejecting,
  Rapt in their apostolate.

3 Thus the earth their death-wounds purchased,
  Hallowed by the blood therefrom,
On her bosom bore the nations,
  Laved, illumined,—Christendom.

Unison. 4. On this feast, almighty Father,
  May we praise thee with the Son,
Evermore his love confessing,
  Who from Both with Both is One. Amen.

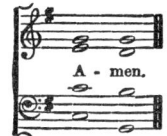

ALFRETON. (L. M.)   **240**
In moderate time ♩ = 72.   'Supplement to the NEW VERSION,' 1708.

(O. H., 174–6.)   ST. MATTHEW   W. Bright, 1824–1901.

HE sat to watch o'er customs paid,
  A man of scorned and hardening [trade;
Alike the symbol and the tool
Of foreign masters' hated rule.

2 But grace within his breast had stirred;
  There needed but the timely word;
It came, true Lord of souls, from thee,
That royal summons, 'Follow me.'

3 Enough, when thou wert passing by,
  To hear thy voice, to meet thine eye:
He rose, responsive to the call,
And left his task, his gains, his all.

4 O wise exchange! with these to part,
  And lay up treasure in thy heart;
With twofold crown of light to shine
Amid thy servants' foremost line.

5 Come, Saviour, as in days of old;
  Pass where the world has strongest hold,
And faithless care and selfish greed
Are thorns that choke the holy seed.

6. Who keep thy gifts, O bid them claim
  The steward's, not the owner's name;
Who yield all up for thy dear sake,
Let them of Matthew's wealth partake.

ST. MICHAEL AND ALL ANGELS

241

Mode ii.   *arr.* J. H. A.

MICHAELMAS

OFFICE HYMN. E. *and* M.   *Ascr. to Archbishop Rabanus Maurus,*
             Tibi, Christe, splendor Patris.   *9th cent.*   *Tr. J. M. Neale.*

THEE, O Christ, the Father's splendour,
   Life and virtue of the heart,
In the presence of the Angels
   Sing we now with tuneful art,
Meetly in alternate chorus
   Bearing our responsive part.

ST. MICHAEL AND ALL ANGELS

241 (Modern Tune)

NEANDER. (87. 87. 87.)
Moderately slow, dignified 𝅗𝅥 = 66.

From Chorale 'Unser Herrscher'
by J. Neander, 1640–80.

2 Thus we praise with veneration
    All the armies of the sky;
Chiefly him, the warrior Primate,
    Of celestial chivalry,
Michael, who in princely virtue
    Cast Abaddon from on high.

3 By whose watchful care repelling—
    King of everlasting grace—
Every ghostly adversary,
    All things evil, all things base,
Grant us of thine only goodness
    In thy Paradise a place.

4. Laud and honour to the Father,
    Laud and honour to the Son,
Laud and honour to the Spirit,
    Ever Three, and ever One,
Consubstantial, co-eternal,
    While unending ages run. Amen.

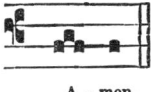

A - men.

A - men.

ST. MICHAEL AND ALL ANGELS

242

Mode i.   *arr.* J. H. A.

* In some texts the B is flattened.

OFFICE HYMN. M.   *Ascr. to Archbishop Rabanus Maurus, 9th cent.*
Christe, sanctorum decus Angelorum.   *Tr. A. R.*

CHRIST, the fair glory of the holy Angels,
   Thou who hast made us, thou who o'er us rulest,
Grant of thy mercy unto us thy servants
      Steps up to heaven.

ST. MICHAEL AND ALL ANGELS

242 (Modern Tune)

COELITES PLAUDANT. (11 11. 11 5.)
In moderate time ♩ = 96. To be sung in unison.

Rouen Church Melody.
Harmonized by R. V. W.

2 Send thy Archangel, Michael, to our succour;
Peacemaker blessèd, may he banish from us
Striving and hatred, so that for the peaceful
    All things may prosper.

3 Send thy Archangel, Gabriel, the mighty;
Herald of heaven, may he from us mortals
Spurn the old serpent, watching o'er the temples
    Where thou art worshipped.

4 Send thy Archangel, Raphael, the restorer
Of the misguided ways of men who wander,
Who at thy bidding strengthens soul and body
    With thine anointing.

5 May the blest Mother of our God and Saviour,
May the assembly of the Saints in glory,
May the celestial companies of Angels
    Ever assist us.

6. Father almighty, Son and Holy Spirit,
God ever blessèd, be thou our preserver;
Thine is the glory which the Angels worship,
    Veiling their faces. Amen.

ST. MICHAEL AND ALL ANGELS
243

SOLOTHURN. (L. M.)
In moderate time ♩ = 66 (♪ =132).
Voices in unison.

Swiss Traditional Melody.

J. M. Neale, 1818-66.

AROUND the throne of God a band
Of glorious Angels always stand;
Bright things they see, sweet harps they hold,
And on their heads are crowns of gold.

2 Some wait around him, ready still
To sing his praise and do his will;
And some, when he commands them, go
To guard his servants here below.

3 Lord, give thy Angels every day
Command to guide us on our way,
And bid them every evening keep
Their watch around us while we sleep.

4. So shall no wicked thing draw near,
To do us harm or cause us fear;
And we shall dwell, when life is past,
With Angels round thy throne at last.

Harmony.

A - men.

ST. MICHAEL AND ALL ANGELS

244

ST. MICHAEL NEW. (10 10. 6 6. 10.)
In moderate time ♩ = 85.

S. S. WESLEY, 1810–76.

Bishop R. Heber, 1783–1826, and J. Keble.

1. O GOD the Son eternal, thy dread might
Sent forth Saint Michael and the hosts of heaven,
   And from the realms of light
   Cast down in burning fight [given.
Satan's rebellious hosts, to darkness

2.*Thine Angels, Lord, we bless with thankful lays, [of sky:
Dwelling with thee above yon depths
   Who, 'mid thy glory's blaze,
   Heaven's ceaseless anthems raise,
And gird thy throne in faithful ministry.

3. We celebrate their love, whose viewless wing [high,
Hath left for us so oft their mansion
   The mercies of their King
   To mortal saints to bring,
Or guard the couch of slumbering infancy.

Unison.

4. But thee, the First and Last, we glorify,
Who, when thy world was sunk in death and sin.
   Not with thine hierarchy,
   The armies of the sky, [win.
But didst with thine own arm the battle

Unison. 5.*Therefore with Angels and Archangels we
   To thy dear love our thankful chorus raise,
      And tune our songs to thee,
      Who art, and art to be;
   And, endless as thy mercies, sound thy praise!

A - men.

ST. MICHAEL AND ALL ANGELS

245

QUEDLINBURG. (10 10. 10 10.)
Moderately slow ♩ = 80.

From a Chorale by
J. C. KITTEL, 1732–1809.

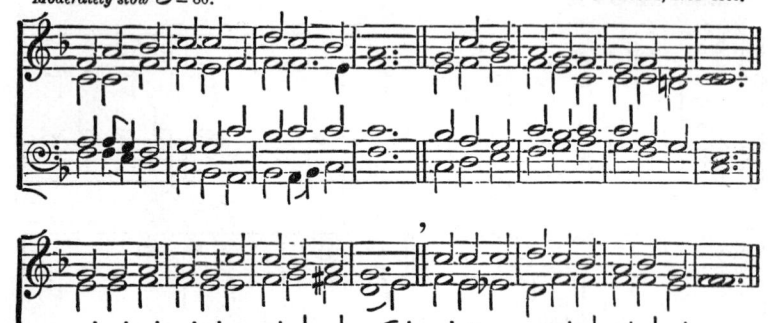

St. Joseph the Hymnographer, d. 883.
Tr. J. M. Neale.

Φωστῆρες τῆς ἀΰλου.

STARS of the morning, so gloriously bright,
Filled with celestial resplendence and light,
These that, where night never followeth day,
Raise the Trisagion ever and ay:

2 These are thy counsellors, these dost thou own,
Lord God of Sabaoth, nearest thy throne;
These are thy ministers, these dost thou send,
Help of the helpless ones! man to defend.

Unison. 3 These keep the guard amid Salem's dear bowers;
Thrones, Principalities, Virtues, and Powers;
Where, with the Living Ones, mystical Four,
Cherubim, Seraphim bow and adore.

4 * 'Who like the Lord?' thunders Michael the Chief;
Raphael, 'the cure of God,' comforteth grief;
And, as at Nazareth, prophet of peace,
Gabriel, 'the Light of God,' bringeth release.

5 Then, when the earth was first poised in mid space,
Then, when the planets first sped on their race,
Then, when were ended the six days' employ,
Then all the Sons of God shouted for joy.

Unison. 6. Still let them succour us; still let them fight,
Lord of angelic hosts, battling for right;
Till, where their anthems they ceaselessly pour,
We with the Angels may bow and adore.

A - men.

356

ST. MICHAEL AND ALL ANGELS

DANIEL. (L. M.) **246** Irish Traditional Melody.
In moderate time ♩ = 96. *Unison.* Harmonized by MARTIN SHAW.

NOTE.—*This hymn may also be sung to* ST. CRISPIN (*Appendix, No.* 36).

R. Campbell, 1814–68, and others.

THEY come, God's messengers of love,
  They come from realms of peace above,
From homes of never-fading light,
From blissful mansions ever bright.

2 They come to watch around us here,
  To soothe our sorrow, calm our fear:
Ye heavenly guides, speed not away,
God willeth you with us to stay.

3 But chiefly at its journey's end
  'Tis yours the spirit to befriend,
And whisper to the willing heart,
'O Christian soul, in peace depart.'

4 Blest Jesu, thou whose groans and tears
  Have sanctified frail nature's fears,
To earth in bitter sorrow weighed,
Thou didst not scorn thine Angel's aid.

5 To us the zeal of Angels give,
  With love to serve thee while we live;
To us an Angel-guard supply,
When on the bed of death we lie.

6. To God the Father, God the Son,
  And God the Spirit, Three in One,
From all above and all below
Let joyful praise unceasing flow. **Amen.**

A-men.

SAINTS' DAYS: ST. LUKE

247

JESUS IST DAS SCHÖNSTE LICHT (OR MEINE LIEBE LEBET NOCH). (7 8. 7 8. 7 8. 8 8.)

J. A. Freylinghausen, 1670–1739
(rhythm slightly adapted).

In moderate time ♩ = 76.

ST. LUKE

(*O. H.*, 174–6.)

H. D. Rawnsley, 1850–1920.

1. SAVIOUR, who didst healing give,
　Still in power go before us;
Thou through death didst bid men live,
　Unto fuller life restore us;
Strength from thee the fainting found,
　Deaf men heard, the blind went seeing;
At thy touch was banished sickness,
　And the leper felt new being.

2. Thou didst work thy deeds of old
　Through the loving hands of others;
Still thy mercies manifold
　Bless men by the hands of brothers;
Angels still before thy face
Go, sweet health to brothers bringing;
Still, hearts glow to tell his praises
　With whose name the Church is ringing.

3. Loved physician! for his word
　Lo, the Gospel page burns brighter,
Mission servant of the Lord,
　Painter true, and perfect writer;
Saviour, of thy bounty send
　Such as Luke of Gospel story,
Friends to all in body's prison
　Till the sufferers see thy glory.

A- men.

SAINTS' DAYS: ST. SIMON AND ST. JUDE

BRYNTIRION. (8 7. 8 7. 8 7.)   **248**
Moderately slow ♩ = 90.

H. ROTH (?).

ST. SIMON AND ST. JUDE

(O. H., 174-6.)   *J. Ellerton*, 1826-93.

1. THOU who sentest thine Apostles
   Two and two before thy face,
   Partners in the night of toiling,
   Heirs together of thy grace,
   Throned at length, their labours ended,
   Each in his appointed place:

2. Praise to thee for those thy champions
   Whom our hymns to-day proclaim;
   One, whose zeal by thee enlightened
   Burned anew with nobler flame;
   One, the kinsman of thy childhood
   Brought at last to know thy name.

Unison. 3. Praise to thee! Thy fire within them
   Spake in love, and wrought in power;
   Seen in mighty signs and wonders
   In thy Church's morning hour;
   Heard in tones of sternest warning
   When the storms began to lour.

4. God the Father, great and wondrous
   In thy works, to thee be praise;
   King of Saints, to thee be glory,
   Just and true in all thy ways;
   Praise to thee, from both proceeding,
   Holy Ghost, through endless days. **Amen.**

A - men.

SAINTS' DAYS: ALL SAINTS

249

Melody from the York Breviary.
arr. J. H. A.

Mode i.

A - men.

The Sarum proper is No. 151. If a simpler melody is needed No. 237 may be used.

ALL SAINTS

OFFICE HYMN. E. *and* M.

Jesu, Salvator saeculi.

9th cent. *Tr. T. A. L.*

O SAVIOUR Jesu, not alone
  We plead for help before thy throne;
Thy Mother's love shall aid our prayer
To win for us that healing care.

SAINTS' DAYS: ALL SAINTS

249 (Modern Tune)

DEO GRACIAS. (L.M.)
Moderately slow ♩ = 92. To be sung in unison.
English Melody, 15th cent.

2 For souls defaulting supplicate
All orders of the Angel state,
The Patriarchs in line to thee,
The Prophets' goodly company.

3 For souls in guilt ensnarèd pray
The Baptist, herald of thy way,
The wielder of the heavenly keys,
The apostolic witnesses.

4 For souls polluted intercede
Thy Martyrs, hallowed in their deed,
Confessors high in priestly power,
And they who have the virgin dower.

5 Let all who served thy Church below,
And now thy heavenly freedom know,
Give heed to help our lingering strife
And claim for us the crown of life.

6. To God the Father, God the Son,
And God the Spirit, Three in One,
All honour, praise, and glory be
From age to age eternally. Amen.

A - - - men.

SAINTS' DAYS: ALL SAINTS

250

LEWES. (87.87.87.)
In moderate time ♩ = 80.

J. RANDALL, 1715–99.

Quisquis valet numerare.
15th cent. Tr. J. M. Neale.

IF there be that skills to reckon
All the number of the blest,
He perchance can weigh the gladness
Of the everlasting rest,
Which, their earthly exile finished,
They by merit have possest.

2 Through the vale of lamentation
Happily and safely past,
Now the years of their affliction
In their memory they recast,
And the end of all perfection
They can contemplate at last.

3 There the gifts of each and single
All in common right possess;
There each member hath his portion
In the Body's blessedness;
So that he, the least in merits,
Shares the guerdon none the less.

4 *In a glass through types and riddles
Dwelling here, we see alone;
Then serenely, purely, clearly,
We shall know as we are known,
Fixing our enlightened vision
On the glory of the throne.

5 There the Trinity of Persons
Unbeclouded shall we see;
There the Unity of Essence
Perfectly revealed shall be;
While we hail the Threefold Godhead
And the simple Unity.

6.*Wherefore, man, take heart and courage,
Whatsoe'er thy present pain;
Such untold reward through suffering
Thou may'st merit to attain:
And for ever in his glory
With the Light of light to reign.

A-men.

SAINTS' DAYS: ALL SAINTS

PADERBORN. (7 6. 7 6.)
In moderate time ♩ = 100 (𝅗𝅥 = 50).

251

Melody from 'Katholische Kirchengesänge,'
Paderborn, 1616.

NOTE.—*This hymn may also be sung to* ST. ALPHEGE (*No.* 348).

Caelestis O Jerusalem.

18th cent.   *Tr. I. Williams.*

O HEAVENLY Jerusalem
   Of everlasting halls,
Thrice blessèd are the people
   Thou storest in thy walls.

2 Thou art the golden mansion,
   Where Saints for ever sing,
The seat of God's own chosen,
   The palace of the King.

3 There God for ever sitteth,
   Himself of all the Crown;
The Lamb the Light that shineth
   And never goeth down.

4 Nought to this seat approacheth
   Their sweet peace to molest;
They sing their God for ever,
   Nor day nor night they rest.

5 Calm hope from thence is leaning,
   To her our longings bend;
No short-lived toil shall daunt us
   For joys that cannot end.

6. To Christ, the Sun that lightens
   His Church above, below,
To Father, and to Spirit,
   All things created bow. Amen.

A - men.

SAINTS' DAYS: ALL SAINTS
252

AU FORT DE MA DÉTRESSE. (7 6. 7 6. D.)
In moderate time ♩ = 96 (𝅗𝅥 = 48).

Genevan Psalter, 1542
(*rhythm slightly simplified*).

A-men.

In domo Patris. 15th cent. Tr. J. M. Neale ‡.

OUR Father's home eternal,
  O Christ, thou dost prepare
With many divers mansions,
  And each one passing fair;
They are the victors' guerdon,
  Who, through the hard-won fight,
Have followed in thy footsteps,
  And reign with thee in light.

2*Amidst the happy number
  The Virgins' crown and queen,
The ever-virgin Mother
  Is first and foremost seen;
The Patriarchs in their triumph
  Thy praises nobly sing,
The Prophets of thy wisdom
  Adore the nations' King;

3*The Apostles reign in glory,
  The Martyrs joy in thee;
The Virgins and Confessors
  Thy shining brightness see;
And every patient sufferer,
  Who sorrow dared contemn,
For each especial anguish
  Hath one especial gem.

4 The holy men and women,
  Their earthly struggle o'er,
With joy put off the armour
  That they shall need no more;
For these, and all that battled
  Beneath their Monarch's eyes,
The harder was the conflict
  The brighter is the prize.

5. And every faithful servant,
  Made perfect in thy grace,
Hath each his fitting station
  'Mid those that see thy face;
The bondsman and the noble,
  The peasant and the king,
All gird one glorious Monarch
  In one eternal ring.

SAINTS' DAYS: ALL SAINTS

Sequence.

253

Modes i & ii.   Sponsa Christi quae per orbem.

J. B. De Contes, 1601-79.
Tr. W. Palmer and others.
arr. J. H. A.

1 Spouse of Christ, in arms con-tend-ing* O'er each clime be-neath the sun,
2 As the Church to-day re-joi-ces All her Saints to join on high,

Blend with prayers for help as-cend-ing Notes of praise for tri-umphs won.
So from earth let all our voi-ces Rise in so-lemn har-mo-ny.

3 First a-mid the lau-relled le-gions Prays the Mo-ther to her Son,
4 An-gels next, in due gra-da-tion Of the Spi-rit's min-is-try,

365

SAINTS' DAYS: ALL SAINTS

253 (*continued*)

Close to Christ in those fair re-gions Where high praise to him is done.
Hymn the Fa-ther of cre-a-tion, Ma-ker of the stars on high.

5 John, the he-rald-voice so-nor-ous, Head of the pro-phe-tic throng,
6 Near to Christ the Apos-tles seat-ed, Tramp-ling on the powers of hell,

Pa-tri-archs, and Seers in chor-us, Join to swell the An-gels' song.
By the pro-mise now com-ple-ted Judge the tribes of Is-ra-el.

SAINTS' DAYS: ALL SAINTS

253 (*continued*)

7 They who no-bly died be-liev-ing, Mar-tyrs pur-pled in their gore,
8 Priests and Le-vites, Gos-pel preach-ers, And Con-fes-sors num-ber-less,

Crowns of life by death re-ceiv-ing, Rest in joy for ev-er-more.
Pre-lates meek and ho-ly teach-ers, Bear the palm of right-eous-ness.

9 Vir-gin souls, by high pro-fes-sion To the Lamb de-vo-ted here,
10 All are blest to-ge-ther, prais-ing God's e-ter-nal Ma-jes-ty,

SAINTS' DAYS: ALL SAINTS

253 (*continued*)

Strew-ing flowers in gay pro-ces-sion   At the mar-riage-feast ap-pear.
Thrice re-peat-ed an-thems rais-ing   To the all-ho-ly Trin-i-ty.

11 In your heav'n-ly hab-i-ta-tions, In your bless-ed
12 E-ver prais-ing, ev-er pray-ing, Help ye thus your

home on high, Hear, ye Saints, our as-pi-ra-tions,
breth-ren here, That the will of God o-bey-ing

SAINTS' DAYS: ALL SAINTS

253 (continued)

As to God we lift our cry. 13. So may we, with hearts de-
We in peace may per-se-vere.

-vo-ted, Serve our God in ho-li-ness; So may we, by

God pro-mo-ted, Share that heaven which ye pos-sess.

SAINTS' DAYS: ALL SAINTS

GOTT WILL'S MACHEN. (8 7. 8 7.) **253** (Modern Tune)

In moderate time ♩ = 80.

J. L. Steiner, 1688–1761.

Sequence.

J.-B. De Contes, 1601–79.
Tr. W. Palmer and others.

Sponsa Christi quae per orbem.

SPOUSE of Christ, in arms contending
O'er each clime beneath the sun,
Blend with prayers for help ascending
Notes of praise for triumphs won.

2 As the Church to-day rejoices
All her Saints to join on high,
So from earth let all our voices
Rise in solemn harmony.

3 First amid the laurelled legions
Prays the Mother to her Son,
Close to Christ in those fair regions
Where high praise to him is done.

4 Angels next, in due gradation
Of the Spirit's ministry,
Hymn the Father of creation,
Maker of the stars on high.

5 John, the herald-voice sonorous,
Head of the prophetic throng,
Patriarchs, and Seers in chorus,
Join to swell the Angels' song.

6 Near to Christ the Apostles seated,
Trampling on the powers of hell,
By the promise now completed
Judge the tribes of Israel.

SAINTS' DAYS: ALL SAINTS

7 They who nobly died believing,
    Martyrs purpled in their gore,
Crowns of life by death receiving,
    Rest in joy for evermore.

8 Priests and Levites, Gospel preachers,
    And Confessors numberless,
Prelates meek and holy teachers,
    Bear the palm of righteousness.

9 Virgin souls, by high profession
    To the Lamb devoted here,
Strewing flowers in gay procession
    At the marriage-feast appear.

10 All are blest together, praising
    God's eternal Majesty,
Thrice repeated anthems raising
    To the all-holy Trinity.

11 In your heavenly habitations,
    In your blessèd home on high,
Hear, ye Saints, our aspirations,
    As to God we lift our cry.

12 Ever praising, ever praying,
    Help ye thus your brethren here,
That the will of God obeying
    We in peace may persevere.

13. So may we, with hearts devoted,
    Serve our God in holiness;
So may we, by God promoted,
    Share that heaven which ye possess.

A - men.

Nos. 250-252 are suitable also for other days.

The following are suitable for All Saints' Day:

197 Give me the wings of faith to rise.
198 Hark! the sound of holy voices.
199 How bright these glorious spirits shine.
200 Joy and triumph everlasting.
202 The Son of God goes forth to war.
203 What are these that glow from afar.
204 Who are these, like stars appearing.
401 He wants not friends that hath thy love.
486 Ten thousand times ten thousand.
519 Ye watchers and ye holy ones.
641 For all the Saints who from their labours rest.

Part III
TIMES AND SEASONS
MORNING
254

Mode viii.   arr. J. H. A.

A - men.

NOTE.—*If a Modern Tune is required for this hymn, it may be sung to* MELCOMBE (*No.* 260) *or* ST. VENANTIUS (*No.* 38).

OFFICE HYMN. *Prime.*   Jam lucis orto sidere.   5th cent. *Tr. J. M. Neale.*

NOW that the daylight fills the sky,
We lift our hearts to God on high,
That he, in all we do or say,
Would keep us free from harm to-day:

2 Would guard our hearts and tongues from strife;
From anger's din would hide our life;
From all ill sights would turn our eyes;
Would close our ears from vanities:

3 Would keep our inmost conscience pure;
Our souls from folly would secure;
Would bid us check the pride of sense
With due and holy abstinence.

4 So we, when this new day is gone,
And night in turn is drawing on,
With conscience by the world unstained
Shall praise his name for victory gained.

5. All laud to God the Father be;
All praise, eternal Son, to thee;
All glory, as is ever meet,
To God the holy Paraclete. Amen.

Anciently the Hymns for the Hours were sung with the special doxologies of the M. and E. Office Hymns during Christmastide, Epiphany, Eastertide, Ascension, and Whitsuntide.

TIMES AND SEASONS.—MORNING

Mode iv. **255** *arr.* J. H. A.

A - men.

N.B.—*On all Ferias Appendix No. 6 was used.*

NOTE.—*If a Modern Tune is required for this hymn, it may be sung to* MELCOMBE (*No.* 260) *or* ST. VENANTIUS (*No.* 88).

OFFICE HYMN. *Terce.*   *Ascribed to St. Ambrose,* 340-97.
      Nunc, Sancte, nobis, Spiritus.   *Tr. J. M. Neale.*

COME, Holy Ghost, with God the Son
And God the Father, ever one;
Shed forth thy grace within our breast,
And dwell with us a ready guest.

2 By every power, by heart and tongue,
By act and deed, thy praise be sung;
Inflame with perfect love each sense,
That others' souls may kindle thence.

3. O Father, that we ask be done,
Through Jesus Christ, thine only Son,
Who, with the Holy Ghost and thee,
Shall live and reign eternally. Amen.

On Whitsunday and the three following days, at Terce:
154 Come, O Creator Spirit, come.

373

TIMES AND SEASONS.—MORNING

256

VOLLER WUNDER. (7 7. 7 7. 7 7.)
In moderate time ♩ = 120.

J. G. Ebeling, 1620-76.

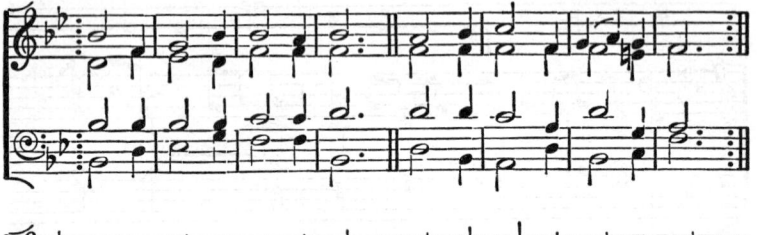

W. Bright, 1824-1901.

At thy feet, O Christ, we lay
   Thine own gift of this new day;
Doubt of what it holds in store
Makes us crave thine aid the more;
   Lest it prove a time of loss,
   Mark it, Saviour, with thy Cross.

2 If it flow on calm and bright,
   Be thyself our chief delight;
If it bring unknown distress,
Good is all that thou canst bless;
   Only, while its hours begin,
   Pray we, keep them clear of sin.

3*We in part our weakness know,
   And in part discern our foe;
Well for us, before thine eyes
All our danger open lies;
   Turn not from us, while we plead
   Thy compassions and our need.

4 Fain would we thy word embrace,
   Live each moment on thy grace,
All our selves to thee consign,
Fold up all our wills in thine,
   Think, and speak, and do, and be
   Simply that which pleases thee.

5. Hear us, Lord, and that right soon;
   Hear, and grant the choicest boon
That thy love can e'er impart,
Loyal singleness of heart;
   So shall this and all our days,
   Christ our God, show forth thy praise.

A - men.

TIMES AND SEASONS.—MORNING

MORNING HYMN. (L. M.)
In moderate time ♩ = 96.

257

F. H. Barthélémon, 1741-1808.

Note.—*The second part of this hymn may be sung to* Tallis' Canon (*No.* 267).

Bishop T. Ken, 1637-1711.

AWAKE, my soul, and with the sun
  Thy daily stage of duty run;
Shake off dull sloth, and joyful rise
To pay thy morning sacrifice.

2 Redeem thy mis-spent time that's past
  Live this day as if 'twere thy last:
  Improve thy talent with due care;
  For the great Day thyself prepare.

3 Let all thy converse be sincere,
  Thy conscience as the noon-day clear;
  Think how all-seeing God thy ways
  And all thy secret thoughts surveys.

4 By influence of the light Divine
  Let thy own light in good works shine;
  Reflect all heaven's propitious ways
  In ardent love and cheerful praise.

Part 2.

5 Wake, and lift up thyself, my heart,
  And with the Angels bear thy part,
  Who all night long unwearied sing
  High praise to the eternal King.

6 Awake, awake, ye heavenly choir,
  May your devotion me inspire,
  That I like you my age may spend,
  Like you may on my God attend.

Part 3.

7 Glory to thee, who safe hast kept
  And hast refreshed me whilst I slept;
  Grant, Lord, when I from death shall wake
  I may of endless light partake.

8 Heaven is, dear Lord, where'er thou art,
  O never then from me depart;
  For to my soul 'tis hell to be
  But for one moment void of thee.

9 Lord, I my vows to thee renew;
  Scatter my sins as morning dew;
  Guard my first springs of thought and will,
  And with thyself my spirit fill.

10 Direct, control, suggest, this day
  All I design, or do, or say; [might,
  That all my powers, with all their
  In thy sole glory may unite.

11. Praise God, from whom all blessings flow,
  Praise him, all creatures here below,
  Praise him above, ye heavenly host,
  Praise Father, Son, and Holy Ghost. Amen.

This Doxology may be sung after any Part.

A - men.

375

TIMES AND SEASONS.—MORNING
258

MINISTRES DE L'ÉTERNEL. (77. 77. 77.)
In moderate time ♩ = 66 (♪ = 112).

*Psalm 135 in the Genevan Psalter, 1562
(rhythm of line 2 slightly simplified).*

C. Wesley, 1707-88.

CHRIST, whose glory fills the skies,
  Christ, the true, the only Light,
Sun of Righteousness, arise,
  Triumph o'er the shades of night;
Dayspring from on high, be near;
Daystar, in my heart appear.

2 Dark and cheerless is the morn
    Unaccompanied by thee;
  Joyless is the day's return,
    Till thy mercy's beams I see;
  Till they inward light impart,
  Glad my eyes, and warm my heart.

3. Visit then this soul of mine,
    Pierce the gloom of sin and grief;
  Fill me, Radiancy Divine,
    Scatter all my unbelief;
  More and more thyself display,
  Shining to the perfect day.

A - men.

376

TIMES AND SEASONS.—MORNING

259

ANGEL'S SONG (SONG 34). (L. M.)
Slow ♩ = 110 (𝅗𝅥 = 55). *Slightly faster.*

Original version of melody by
O. GIBBONS, 1583-1625.

Suitable also for Mid-day Services. C. *Wesley*, 1707-88.

FORTH in thy name, O Lord, I go,
  My daily labour to pursue;
Thee, only thee, resolved to know,
  In all I think, or speak, or do.

2 The task thy wisdom hath assigned
  O let me cheerfully fulfil;
In all my works thy presence find,
  And prove thine acceptable will.

3 Preserve me from my calling's snare,
  And hide my simple heart above,
Above the thorns of choking care,
  The gilded baits of worldly love.

4 Thee may I set at my right hand,
  Whose eyes my inmost substance see,
And labour on at thy command,
  And offer all my works to thee.

5 Give me to bear thy easy yoke,
  And every moment watch and pray,
And still to things eternal look,
  And hasten to thy glorious day;

6. For thee delightfully employ
  Whate'er thy bounteous grace hath given,
And run my course with even joy,
  And closely walk with thee to heaven.

A - men.

TIMES AND SEASONS.—MORNING

260

MELCOMBE. (L. M.)
Moderately slow ♩ = 69.

S. WEBBE the elder, 1740–1816.

NOTE.—*A higher setting of this tune will be found at Hymn* 631.

J. Keble, 1792–1866.

NEW every morning is the love
  Our wakening and uprising prove;
Through sleep and darkness safely brought,
Restored to life, and power, and thought.

2 New mercies, each returning day,
Hover around us while we pray;
New perils past, new sins forgiven,
New thoughts of God, new hopes of heaven.

3*If on our daily course our mind
Be set to hallow all we find,
New treasures still, of countless price,
God will provide for sacrifice.

4 Old friends, old scenes, will lovelier be,
As more of heaven in each we see;
Some softening gleam of love and prayer
Shall dawn on every cross and care.

5 We need not bid, for cloistered cell,
Our neighbour and our work farewell,
Nor strive to wind ourselves too high
For sinful man beneath the sky:

6 The trivial round, the common task,
Would furnish all we ought to ask,—
Room to deny ourselves, a road
To bring us daily nearer God.

7.*Only, O Lord, in thy dear love
Fit us for perfect rest above;
And help us this and every day
To live more nearly as we pray.

A - men.

See also for Sunday Morning: **50** This day the first of days was made.

For other days, Hymns 52 *to* 57.

For Sundays and Week-days: **165** Father, we praise thee.

TIMES AND SEASONS.—NOON
261

Mode ii.   arr. J. H. A.

N.B.—*On all Ferias Appendix No. 6 was used.*

NOTE.—*If a Modern Tune is required for this hymn it may be sung to* MELCOMBE (*No.* 260) *or* ST. VENANTIUS (*No.* 38).

NOON

OFFICE HYMN. Sext.   *Ascribed to St. Ambrose, 340-97.*
                                                                                                     Tr. J. M. Neale.

                    Rector potens, verax Deus.

O GOD of truth, O Lord of might,
  Who orderest time and change aright,
And send'st the early morning ray,
And light'st the glow of perfect day:

2 Extinguish thou each sinful fire,
  And banish every ill desire;
And while thou keep'st the body whole,
Shed forth thy peace upon the soul.

3. O Father, that we ask be done,
  Through Jesus Christ, thine only Son;
Who, with the Holy Ghost and thee,
Doth live and reign eternally. Amen.

A - men.

TIMES AND SEASONS.—NOON

262

Mode iv.   *arr.* J. H. A.

N.B.—*On Double Feasts tune 261 was anciently used, and on all Ferias Appendix No. 6.*

NOTE.—*If a Modern Tune is required for this hymn it may be sung to* ALFRETON (*No.* 240) *or* ST. VENANTIUS (*No.* 38).

OFFICE HYMN. *None*   *Ascribed to St. Ambrose,* 340–97.
                          Rerum Deus tenax vigor.   *Tr.* J. M. Neale.

O GOD, Creation's secret force,
  Thyself unmoved, all motion's source,
Who from the morn till evening ray
Through all its changes guid'st the day:

2 Grant us, when this short life is past,
  The glorious evening that shall last;
That, by a holy death attained,
Eternal glory may be gained.

3. O Father, that we ask be done,
  Through Jesus Christ, thine only Son;
Who, with the Holy Ghost and thee,
Doth live and reign eternally. Amen.

A - men.

TIMES AND SEASONS.—NOON

263

WARRINGTON. (L. M.)
In moderate time ♩ = 96.

R. HARRISON, 1748–1810.

NOTE.—*This hymn may also be sung to* ALFRETON (*No.* 240).

William Wordsworth, 1770–1850.

BLEST are the moments, doubly blest,
That, drawn from this one hour of rest,
Are with a ready heart bestowed
Upon the service of our God!

2 * Each field is then a hallowed spot,
An altar is in each man's cot,
A church in every grove that spreads
Its living roof above our heads.

3 Look up to heaven! the industrious sun
Already half his race hath run;
He cannot halt or go astray,
But our immortal spirits may.

4 Lord, since his rising in the east,
If we have faltered or transgressed,
Guide, from thy love's abundant source,
What yet remains of this day's course;

5. Help with thy grace, through life's short day,
Our upward and our downward way;
And glorify for us the west,
When we shall sink to final rest.

A - men.

The following is also suitable for Mid-day Services:
259 Forth in thy name, O Lord, I go.

Also many of the simpler Hymns.

TIMES AND SEASONS.—EVENING
264
Tune 1 (*On Sundays and Feasts*).

Mode viii. *arr.* J. H. A.

* In some texts the B is flattened.

EVENING

Office Hymn. *Compline.*   *Before 8th cent. Tr.* J. M. Neale.
Te lucis ante terminum.

BEFORE the ending of the day,
Creator of the world, we pray
That with thy wonted favour thou
Wouldst be our Guard and Keeper now.

2 From all ill dreams defend our eyes,
From nightly fears and fantasies;
Tread under foot our ghostly foe,
That no pollution we may know.

3. O Father, that we ask be done,
Through Jesus Christ, thine only Son;
Who, with the Holy Ghost and thee,
Doth live and reign eternally. Amen.

A - men.

See also :
81 O Christ, who art the Light and Day.
104 Servant of God, remember.
134 O Christ, our hope, our hearts' desire.

For a late evening service, see also the Short Respond Nos. 739 *and* 740
Into thy hands, O Lord.

Modern Tune.

A - men.

TIMES AND SEASONS.—EVENING

264

Tune 2 (*On Ferias*)

Mode viii.

arr. J. H. A.

A - men.

264 (Modern Tune)

TE LUCIS ANTE TERMINUM. (L. M.)

Moderately slow ♩ = 69.

Proper melody from
Andernach Gesangbuch, 1608.

TIMES AND SEASONS.—EVENING
265

ST. NICHOLAS. (C. M.)
Moderately slow ♩ = 92.
Melody from HOLDROYD'S *Spiritual Man's Companion*, 1753.

NOTE.—*This hymn may also be sung to* ST. PETER (*No.* 405).

C. *Coffin*, 1676–1749.   Tr. *J. Chandler* ‡.
Labente jam solis rota.

A S now the sun's declining rays
　　At eventide descend,
E'en so our years are sinking down
　　To their appointed end.

2 Lord, on the Cross thine arms were stretched
　　To draw the nations nigh;
O grant us then that Cross to love,
　　And in those arms to die.

3. To God the Father, God the Son,
　　And God the Holy Ghost,
All glory be from saints on earth,
　　And from the Angel host. Amen.

A - men.

TIMES AND SEASONS.—EVENING
266

ANGELUS (DU MEINER SEELEN). (L. M.)
Slow ♩ = 69.

'*Cantica Spiritualia,*' 1847
(founded on a melody by G. Joseph, 1657)

H. Twells †, 1823-1900.

AT even when the sun was set
   The sick, O Lord, around thee lay;
O, in what divers pains they met!
O with what joy they went away!

2 Once more 'tis eventide, and we
   Oppressed with various ills draw near;
What if thy form we cannot see?
We know and feel that thou art here.

3 O Saviour Christ, our woes dispel;
   For some are sick, and some are sad,
And some have never loved thee well,
   And some have lost the love they had;

4*And some have found the world is vain,
   Yet from the world they break not free;
And some have friends who give them pain,
   Yet have not sought a friend in thee;

5*And none, O Lord, have perfect rest,
   For none are wholly free from sin;
And they who fain would serve thee best
   Are conscious most of wrong within.

6 O Saviour Christ, thou too art Man;
   Thou hast been troubled, tempted, tried;
Thy kind but searching glance can scan
   The very wounds that shame would hide;

7. Thy touch has still its ancient power,
   No word from thee can fruitless fall;
Hear in this solemn evening hour,
   And in thy mercy heal us all.

A - men.

TIMES AND SEASONS.—EVENING

267

TALLIS' CANON. (L. M.)
Slow and dignified ♩ = 52.

T. TALLIS, c. 1515–85.

Bishop T. Ken, 1637–1711.

1 GLORY to thee, my God, this night
For all the blessings of the light;
Keep me, O keep me, King of kings,
Beneath thy own almighty wings.

2 Forgive me, Lord, for thy dear Son,
The ill that I this day have done,
That with the world, myself, and thee,
I, ere I sleep, at peace may be.

3 Teach me to live, that I may dread
The grave as little as my bed;
Teach me to die, that so I may
Rise glorious at the awful day.

4 O may my soul on thee repose,
And with sweet sleep mine eyelids close,
Sleep that may me more vigorous make
To serve my God when I awake.

5*When in the night I sleepless lie,
My soul with heavenly thoughts supply;
Let no ill dreams disturb my rest,
No powers of darkness me molest.

6*You, my blest guardian, whilst I sleep
Close to my bed your vigils keep;
Divine love into me instil,
Stop all the avenues of ill.

7. Praise God, from whom all blessings flow,
Praise him, all creatures here below,
Praise him above, ye heavenly host,
Praise Father, Son, and Holy Ghost. Amen.

A - men.

TIMES AND SEASONS.—EVENING

267 (ALTERNATIVE VERSION)

Ravenscroft's Psalter, 1621.

PEOPLE'S PART.

CHOIR OR ORGAN.

This version may be used in connexion with the other for one or more verses, the people singing the melody as usual or the CHOIR SINGING ALONE. *Prominence should be given to the tenor part which in this version leads the canon.*

TIMES AND SEASONS.—EVENING

268

AR HYD Y NOS. (84.84.88.84.)
In moderate time ♩ = 72.

Welsh Traditional Melody.

NOTE.—*Another tune for this hymn will be found in the Appendix (No. 15).*

1. *Bishop Heber* (1827).   2. *Archbishop Whately* (1855).

GOD, that madest earth and heaven,
 Darkness and light;
Who the day for toil hast given,
 For rest the night;
May thine Angel-guards defend us,
Slumber sweet thy mercy send us,
Holy dreams and hopes attend us,
 This livelong night.

2. Guard us waking, guard us sleeping;
 And, when we die,
May we in thy mighty keeping
 All peaceful lie:
When the last dread call shall wake us,
Do not thou our God forsake us,
But to reign in glory take us
 With thee on high.

A - men.

TIMES AND SEASONS.—EVENING

NUNC DIMITTIS. (667. 667.)
Moderately slow, dignified ♩ = 66.

269

Composed or adapted by L. BOURGEOIS, *in 1549, for the Genevan Psalter. Harmony chiefly from Goudimel.*

3rd cent. or earlier. *Tr.* Y. H.

Φῶς ἱλαρόν.

O GLADSOME light, O grace
   Of God the Father's face,
The eternal splendour wearing;
   Celestial, holy, blest,
   Our Saviour Jesus Christ,
Joyful in thine appearing.

2 Now, ere day fadeth quite,
   We see the evening light,
Our wonted hymn outpouring;
   Father of might unknown,
   Thee, his incarnate Son,
And Holy Spirit adoring.

3. To thee of right belongs
   All praise of holy songs,
O Son of God, Lifegiver;
   Thee, therefore, O Most High,
   The world doth glorify,
And shall exalt for ever.

A - men.

TIMES AND SEASONS.—EVENING

270

TON-MÂN. (7 7. 7 5.)
In moderate time ♩ = 92.

DAVID EVANS (*adapted by permission*).

NOTE.—*This hymn may also be sung to* CAPETOWN (*No.* 501) *or to* HUDDERSFIELD (*Appendix, No.* 37).

R. H. Robinson, 1842–92.

HOLY Father, cheer our way
With thy love's perpetual ray;
Grant us every closing day
Light at evening time.

2 Holy Saviour, calm our fears
When earth's brightness disappears;
Grant us in our latter years
Light at evening time.

3 Holy Spirit, be thou nigh
When in mortal pains we lie;
Grant us, as we come to die,
Light at evening time.

4. Holy, blessèd Trinity,
Darkness is not dark with thee;
Those thou keepest always see
Light at evening time.

A - men.

TIMES AND SEASONS.—EVENING

271

SCHOOL HOUSE. (11 10. 11 10.)

In moderate time ♩ = 96 (𝅗𝅥 = 48). *Unison.*

THOMAS WOOD.

[*Copyright*, 1931, *by Oxford University Press.*]

NOTE —*This hymn may also be sung to* WELWYN (*No.* 346).

Ascribed to St. Ambrose, 340–97.
Tr. J. Ellerton, F. J. A. Hort.

Rerum Deus tenax vigor.

O STRENGTH and Stay upholding all creation,
  Who ever dost thyself unmoved abide,
Yet day by day the light in due gradation
  From hour to hour through all its changes guide;

2 Grant to life's day a calm unclouded ending,
  An eve untouched by shadows of decay,
The brightness of a holy death-bed blending
  With dawning glories of the eternal day.

3. Hear us, O Father, gracious and forgiving,
  Through Jesus Christ thy co-eternal Word,
Who, with the Holy Ghost, by all things living
  Now and to endless ages art adored. Amen.

A - men.

TIMES AND SEASONS.—EVENING

272

SEELENBRÄUTIGAM. (55. 88. 55.)
Slow ♩ = 100 (𝅗𝅥 = 50).

A. DRESE, 1620–1701.

W. Romanis, 1824–99.

ROUND me falls the night;
    Saviour, be my Light:
Through the hours in darkness shrouded
Let me see thy face unclouded;
    Let thy glory shine
    In this heart of mine.

2   Earthly work is done,
    Earthly sounds are none;
Rest in sleep and silence seeking,
Let me hear thee softly speaking;
    In my spirit's ear
    Whisper, 'I am near.'

3   Blessèd, heavenly Light,
    Shining through earth's night;
Voice, that oft of love hast told me;
Arms, so strong to clasp and hold me;
    Thou thy watch wilt keep,
    Saviour, o'er my sleep.

A - men.

TIMES AND SEASONS.—EVENING

273

MAGDA. (10 10. 10 10.)
In moderate time, not too slow ♩ = 96.

R. VAUGHAN WILLIAMS.

[*Copyright*, 1925, *by R. Vaughan Williams.*]

NOTE.—*This hymn may also be sung to* ELLERS (*Appendix, No.* 38).

J. *Ellerton*, 1826-93.

SAVIOUR, again to thy dear name we raise
  With one accord our parting hymn of praise.
Guard thou the lips from sin, the hearts from shame,
That in this house have called upon thy name.

2 Grant us thy peace, Lord, through the coming night;
  Turn thou for us its darkness into light;
  From harm and danger keep thy children free,
  For dark and light are both alike to thee.

3 Grant us thy peace throughout our earthly life;
  Peace to thy Church from error and from strife;
  Peace to our land, the fruit of truth and love;
  Peace in each heart, thy Spirit from above:

4. Thy peace in life, the balm of every pain;
  Thy peace in death, the hope to rise again;
  Then, when thy voice shall bid our conflict cease,
  Call us, O Lord, to thine eternal peace.

A - men.

TIMES AND SEASONS.—EVENING

274

BIRLING. (L. M.)
Not too slow ♩ = 108.

From an early 19th cent. MS.
Harmonized by GEOFFREY SHAW.

NOTE.—*This hymn may also be sung to* HURSLEY (*Appendix, No. 39*).

J. *Keble*, 1792-1866.

SUN of my soul, thou Saviour dear,
It is not night if thou be near:
O may no earth-born cloud arise
To hide thee from thy servant's eyes.

2 When the soft dews of kindly sleep
My wearied eyelids gently steep,
Be my last thought, how sweet to rest
For ever on my Saviour's breast.

3 Abide with me from morn till eve,
For without thee I cannot live;
Abide with me when night is nigh,
For without thee I dare not die.

4 If some poor wand'ring child of thine
Have spurned to-day the voice divine,
Now, Lord, the gracious work begin;
Let him no more lie down in sin.

TIMES AND SEASONS.—EVENING

274 (Alternative Tune)

HERR GOTT VATER. (L. M.)
Slow ♩ = 80.

Melody from
S. BESLER, 1574-1625.

To hide ... thee from ... thy ser - - vant's eyes.

5 Watch by the sick; enrich the poor
  With blessings from thy boundless store;
  Be every mourner's sleep to-night
  Like infant's slumbers, pure and light.

6. Come near and bless us when we wake,
   Ere through the world our way we take;
   Till in the ocean of thy love
   We lose ourselves in heaven above.

A - men.

A - men.

TIMES AND SEASONS.—EVENING

275

LODSWORTH. (88. 88. 88.)
In moderate time ♩ = 76.

English Traditional Melody.

F. W. Faber, 1814-63.

1. SWEET Saviour, bless us ere we go;
    Thy word into our minds instil;
  And make our lukewarm hearts to glow
    With lowly love and fervent will.
  Through life's long day and death's dark night,
  O gentle Jesus, be our Light.

2. The day is done, its hours have run,
    And thou hast taken count of all;
  The scanty triumphs grace hath won,
    The broken vow, the frequent fall.

3. Grant us, dear Lord, from evil ways
    True absolution and release;
  And bless us, more than in past days,
    With purity and inward peace.

4.* Do more than pardon; give us joy,
    Sweet fear and sober liberty,
  And loving hearts without alloy,
    That only long to be like thee.

5.* Labour is sweet, for thou hast toiled,
    And care is light, for thou hast cared;
  Let not our works with self be soiled,
    Nor in unsimple ways ensnared.

6. For all we love, the poor, the sad,
    The sinful,—unto thee we call;
  O let thy mercy make us glad;
    Thou art our Jesus and our All.

A - men.

TIMES AND SEASONS—EVENING

HOMINUM AMATOR. (7 6. 7 6. 8 8.) **276**

In moderate time ♩ = 116. *Unison.*

W. H. FERGUSON.

NOTE.—*This hymn may also be sung to* ST. ANATOLIUS (*Appendix, No.* 40).

Ascribed to 6th cent. Tr. **J. M. Neale.**

Τὴν ἡμέραν διελθών.

1. THE day is past and over;
　All thanks, O Lord, to thee;
I pray thee that offenceless
　The hours of dark may be:
O Jesu, keep me in thy sight,
And guard me through the coming night.

2. The joys of day are over;
　I lift my heart to thee,
And call on thee that sinless
　The hours of dark may be:
O Jesu, make their darkness light,
And guard me through the coming night.

3. The toils of day are over;
　I raise the hymn to thee,
And ask that free from peril
　The hours of dark may be:
O Jesu, keep me in thy sight,
And guard me through the coming night.

4. Be thou my soul's preserver,
　O God! for thou dost know
How many are the perils
　Through which I have to go:
Lover of men! O hear my call,
And guard and save me from them all.

A - men.

TIMES AND SEASONS.—EVENING

277

LES COMMANDEMENS DE DIEU. (9 8. 9 8.)
Moderately slow ♩ = 50 (♩ = 100).

Original form of melody composed or adapted by L. BOURGEOIS for the Genevan Psalter, 1543.

NOTE.—*Another tune for this hymn will be found in the Appendix* (No. 16).

J. Ellerton, 1826–93.

THE day thou gavest Lord, is ended,
    The darkness falls at thy behest;
To thee our morning hymns ascended,
    Thy praise shall sanctify our rest.

2 We thank thee that thy Church unsleeping,
    While earth rolls onward into light,
Through all the world her watch is keeping,
    And rests not now by day or night.

3 As o'er each continent and island
    The dawn leads on another day,
The voice of prayer is never silent,
    Nor dies the strain of praise away.

4 The sun that bids us rest is waking
    Our brethren 'neath the western sky,
And hour by hour fresh lips are making
    Thy wondrous doings heard on high.

5. So be it, Lord; thy throne shall never,
    Like earth's proud empires, pass away;
Thy kingdom stands, and grows for ever,
    Till all thy creatures own thy sway.

A - men.

278

INNSBRUCK. (7 7 6. 7 7 8.)
Very slow and solemn ♩ = 42.

*Traditional German Melody.
Adapted and harmonized by J. S. BACH.*

TIMES AND SEASONS.—EVENING

278 (*continued*)

P. Gerhardt, 1607-76.   *Tr. Y. H.*

Nun ruhen alle Wälder.

THE duteous day now closeth,
　Each flower and tree reposeth,
　　Shade creeps o'er wild and wood:
Let us, as night is falling,
On God our Maker calling,
　Give thanks to him, the Giver good.

2 Now all the heavenly splendour
　Breaks forth in starlight tender
　　From myriad worlds unknown;
And man, the marvel seeing,
Forgets his selfish being,
　For joy of beauty not his own.

3 His care he drowneth yonder,
Lost in the abyss of wonder;
　To heaven his soul doth steal:
This life he disesteemeth,
The day it is that dreameth,
　That doth from truth his vision seal.

4. Awhile his mortal blindness
May miss God's lovingkindness,
　And grope in faithless strife:
But when life's day is over
Shall death's fair night discover
　The fields of everlasting life.

A - men.

TIMES AND SEASONS—EVENING

GAZA. (8 8. 8 4.)
In moderate time ♩ = 76.

279

Adapted from an Ancient Jewish Melody.
Harmonized by GEOFFREY SHAW.

NOTE.—*This hymn may also be sung to* ST. LEONARD (*Appendix, No. 41*).

G. Thring, 1823–1903.

THE radiant morn hath passed away,
   And spent too soon her golden store;
The shadows of departing day
        Creep on once more.

2 Our life is but an autumn sun,
   Its glorious noon how quickly past;
Lead us, O Christ, our life-work done,
        Safe home at last.

3 O by thy soul-inspiring grace
   Uplift our hearts to realms on high;
Help us to look to that bright place
        Beyond the sky;—

4 Where light, and life, and joy, and peace
   In undivided empire reign,
And thronging Angels never cease
        Their deathless strain;—

5. Where Saints are clothed in spotless white,
   And evening shadows never fall,
Where thou, eternal Light of light,
        Art Lord of all.

A - men.

TIMES AND SEASONS—EVENING

SPEER (SAG WAS HILFT). (6 4. 6 6.) **280** *Melody by D. Speer, c. 1620–c. 1694, slightly adapted.*
Moderately slow ♩ = 63.

Note.—*This hymn may also be sung to* St. Columba (*Appendix, No.* 42).

Sol praeceps rapitur. *c.* 18*th cent.* *Tr. E. Caswall.*

1. THE sun is sinking fast,
    The daylight dies;
Let love awake, and pay
    Her evening sacrifice.

2 As Christ upon the Cross,
    In death reclined,
Into his Father's hands
    His parting soul resigned,

3 So now herself my soul
    Would wholly give
Into his sacred charge,
    In whom all spirits live;

4 So now beneath his eye
    Would calmly rest,
Without a wish or thought
    Abiding in the breast,

5 Save that his will be done,
    Whate'er betide,
Dead to herself, and dead
    In him to all beside.

6 Thus would I live; yet now
    Not I, but he
In all his power and love
    Henceforth alive in me—

7. One sacred Trinity,
    One Lord Divine,
Myself for ever his,
    And he for ever mine!

A - men.

401

TIMES AND SEASONS.—EVENING

281

DRETZEL. (87.87.77.)
Moderately slow ♩ = 66.

Abridged by W. H. MONK from a Chorale by C. H. DRETZEL, 1698-1775.

T. Kelly, 1769-1854

THROUGH the day thy love has spared us;
  Now we lay us down to rest;
Through the silent watches guard us,
  Let no foe our peace molest:
    Jesus, thou our Guardian be;
    Sweet it is to trust in thee.

2. Pilgrims here on earth, and strangers,
    Dwelling in the midst of foes;
  Us and ours preserve from dangers;
    In thine arms may we repose,
      And, when life's sad day is past,
      Rest with thee in heaven at last.

A - men.

See also for Saturday Evening, No. 282, on next page, and
No. 49 Creator of the earth and sky.

For other days: 51 O blest Creator of the light.

For Week days: Nos. 58-62.

TIMES AND SEASONS—SATURDAY EVENING

282

RATISBON (JESU, MEINE ZUVERSICHT). (7 7. 7 7. 7 7.)

Slow 𝅗𝅥 = 58.   *Later form of Melody attributed to* J. CRÜGER, 1598–1662.

NOTE.—*This hymn may also be sung to* HEATHLANDS (*No.* 395).

SATURDAY EVENING
John Samuel Jones.

NOW the busy week is done,
  Now the rest-time is begun;
Thou hast brought us on our way,
Kept and led us day by day;
Now there comes the first and best,
Day of worship, light and rest.

2 Hallow, Lord, the coming day!
When we meet to praise and pray,
Hear thy word, thy Feast attend,
Hours of happy service spend;
To our hearts be manifest,
Lord of labour and of rest!

3 For thy children gone before
We can trust thee and adore;
All their earthly week is past,
Sabbath-time is theirs at last;
Fold them, Father, to thy breast,
Give them everlasting rest.

4. Guide us all the days to come,
Till thy mercy call us home:
All our powers do thou employ,
Be thy work our chiefest joy;
Then, the promised land possest,
Bid us enter into rest.

A - men.

See also: 49 Creator of the earth and sky.
          164 O Trinity of blessed light.
          465 O what their joy and their glory must be.

TIMES AND SEASONS.—SUNDAY

283
SUNDAY

Morning.
FARLEY CASTLE. (10 10. 10 10.)
In moderate time ♩ = 72.

Edmund Spenser, 1553-99.
H. Lawes, 1596-1662.

1 Most glorious Lord of life, that on this day Didst make thy triumph over death and sin, And having harrowed hell, didst bring away Captivity thence captive, us to win:
2 This joyous day, dear Lord, with joy begin, And grant that we for whom thou didst die, Being with thy dear Blood clean washed from sin, May live for ever in felicity:
3 And that thy love we weighing worthily, May likewise love thee for the same again; And for thy sake, that all like dear didst buy, With love may one another entertain;
4. So let us love, dear Love, like as we ought: Love is the lesson which the Lord us taught. A-men.

TIMES AND SEASONS.—SUNDAY
284

HERZLICH THUT MICH ERFREUEN. (7 6. 7 6. D.)

In moderate time = 132.

Chorale founded on a German Mediaeval Traditional Melody.

Bishop Chr. Wordsworth, 1807-85.

O DAY of rest and gladness,
   O day of joy and light,
O balm of care and sadness,
   Most beautiful, most bright;
On thee the high and lowly,
   Through ages joined in tune,
Sing Holy, Holy, Holy,
   To the great God triune.
Unison.
2 On thee at the creation
   The light first had its birth;
On thee for our salvation
   Christ rose from depths of earth;
On thee our Lord victorious
   The Spirit sent from heaven;
And thus on thee most glorious
   A triple light was given.

3 Thou art a cooling fountain
   In life's dry dreary sand;
From thee, like Pisgah's mountain,
   We view our promised land:
A day of sweet refection,
   A day thou art of love,
A day of resurrection
   From earth to things above.

4. New graces ever gaining
   From this our day of rest,
We reach the rest remaining
   To spirits of the blest.
To Holy Ghost be praises,
   To Father, and to Son;
The Church her voice upraises
   To thee, blest Three in One. Amen.

See also Nos. 50 and 51.

TIMES AND SEASONS.—NEW YEAR

285

CHERRY TREE. (7 6. 7 6.)
In moderate time, not slow ♩ = 96.

*From a traditional English Carol Melody.
Harmonized by* MARTIN SHAW.

NOTE.—*This hymn may also be sung to* MAGDALENA (*No.* 392).

NEW YEAR

F. R. Havergal, 1836-79

ANOTHER year is dawning,
   Dear Master, let it be,
In working or in waiting,
   Another year with thee.

2 Another year of leaning
   Upon thy loving breast,
Of ever-deepening trustfulness,
   Of quiet, happy rest.

3 Another year of mercies,
   Of faithfulness and grace;
Another year of gladness
   In the shining of thy face.

4 Another year of progress,
   Another year of praise,
Another year of proving
   Thy presence all the days.

5 Another year of service,
   Of witness for thy love;
Another year of training
   For holier work above.

6. Another year is dawning,
   Dear Master, let it be,
On earth, or else in heaven,
   Another year for thee!

A - men.

TIMES AND SEASONS.—NEW YEAR

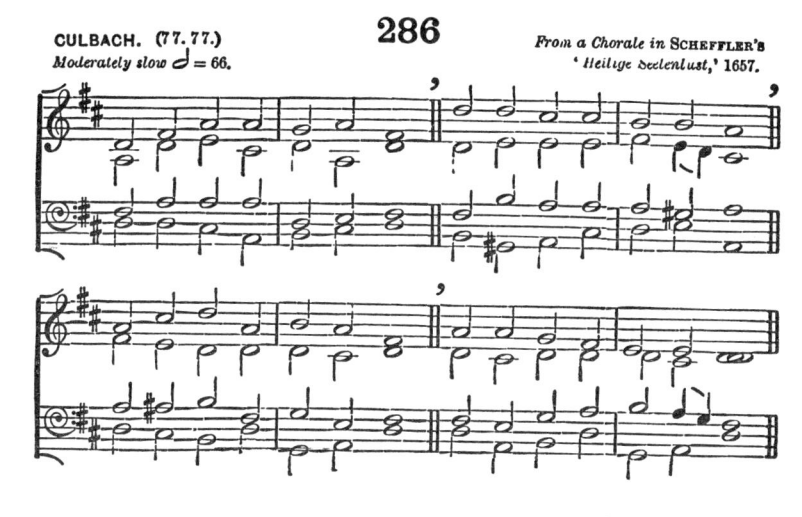

286

CULBACH. (77.77.)
Moderately slow ♩ = 66.

From a Chorale in Scheffler's 'Heilige Seelenlust,' 1657.

H. Downton, 1818-85.

FOR thy mercy and thy grace,
　Faithful through another year,
Hear our song of thankfulness,
　Father, and Redeemer, hear.

2 Lo, our sins on thee we cast,
　Thee, our perfect Sacrifice;
And, forgetting all the past,
　Press towards our glorious prize.

3 Dark the future: let the light
　Guide us, bright and Morning Star;
Fierce our foes, and hard the fight:
　Arm us Saviour, for the war.

4 In our weakness and distress,
　Rock of strength, be thou our Stay.
In the pathless wilderness
　Be our true and living Way.

5 Who of us death's awful road
　In the coming year shall tread,
With thy rod and staff. O God,
　Comfort thou his dying head.

6. Keep us faithful, keep us pure,
　Keep us evermore thine own:
Help, O help us to endure;
　Fit us for the promised crown.

A - men.

The following Hymns are also suitable for the New Year:

　　3 Behold, the Bridegroom cometh.
　365 All people that on earth.
　368 At the Name of Jesus.
　389 Fight the good fight.
　405 How sweet the name of Jesus sounds.
　426 Lead us, heavenly Father.
　450 O God, our help in ages past.
　502 Through all the changing scenes.
　503 Through the night of doubt.
　507 To the name that brings salvation.
　511 When all thy mercies.

TIMES AND SEASONS.—SPRING

DA CHRISTUS GEBOREN WAR. (7 7. 7 7.)
In moderate time ♩ = 80.

287

Melody probably by
J. F. DOLES, 1715-97.

SPRING

J. Newton †, 1725-1807.

KINDLY spring again is here,
   Trees and fields in bloom appear;
Hark! the birds with artless lays
Warble their Creator's praise.

2 Where in winter all was snow,
   Now the flowers in clusters grow;
And the corn, in green array,
Promises a harvest-day.

3 Lord, afford a spring to me,
   Let me feel like what I see;
Speak, and by thy gracious voice,
Make my drooping soul rejoice.

4. On thy garden deign to smile,
   Raise the plants, enrich the soil;
Soon thy presence will restore
Life to what seemed dead before.

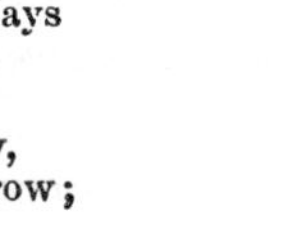

A - men.

TIMES AND SEASONS.—SUMMER

288

SOLL'S SEIN. (D.C.M.)
Slow ♩ = 88.

Melody in '*Drei schöne neue geistliche Lieder*,' München, 1637.

SUMMER

S. *Longfellow* ‡, 1819–92.

THE summer days are come again;
  Once more the glad earth yields
Her golden wealth of ripening grain,
  And breath of clover fields,
And deepening shade of summer woods,
  And glow of summer air,
And winging thoughts, and happy moods
  Of love and joy and prayer.

2. The summer days are come again;
  The birds are on the wing;
God's praises, in their loving strain,
  Unconsciously they sing.
We know who giveth all the good
  That doth our cup o'erbrim;
For summer joy in field and wood
  We lift our song to him.

A - men.

409

TIMES AND SEASONS.—HARVEST

289

ST. GEORGE. (7.7.7.7. D.)
Brightly ♩ = 100.

G. J. Elvey, 1816-93.

HARVEST

H. Alford, 1810-71.

COME, ye thankful people, come,
  Raise the song of harvest-home!
All be safely gathered in,
Ere the winter storms begin;
God, our Maker, doth provide
For our wants to be supplied;
Come to God's own temple, come;
Raise the song of harvest-home!

2 We ourselves are God's own field,
Fruit unto his praise to yield;
Wheat and tares together sown,
Unto joy or sorrow grown;
First the blade and then the ear,
Then the full corn shall appear:
Grant, O harvest Lord, that we
Wholesome grain and pure may be.

3 For the Lord our God shall come,
And shall take his harvest home;
From his field shall purge away
All that doth offend, that day;
Give his Angels charge at last
In the fire the tares to cast,
But the fruitful ears to store
In his garner evermore.

Unison. 4. Then, thou Church triumphant, come,
  Raise the song of harvest-home;
  All be safely gathered in,
  Free from sorrow, free from sin,
  There for ever purified
  In God's garner to abide:
  Come, ten thousand Angels, come,
  Raise the glorious harvest-home!

A - men.

TIMES AND SEASONS.—HARVEST

SELMA. (S. M.)
In moderate time ♩ = 80.

290

Adapted by R. A. SMITH (1780–1829)
*from a Traditional Melody
of the Isle of Arran.*

J. Hampden Gurney, 1802–62.

FAIR waved the golden corn
   In Canaan's pleasant land,
When full of joy, some shining morn,
   Went forth the reaper-band.

2   To God so good and great
     Their cheerful thanks they pour;
  Then carry to his temple-gate
     The choicest of their store.

3   Like Israel, Lord, we give
     Our earliest fruits to thee,
  And pray that, long as we shall live,
     We may thy children be.

4   Thine is our youthful prime,
     And life and all its powers;
  Be with us in our morning time,
     And bless our evening hours.

5.   In wisdom let us grow,
     As years and strength are given,
  That we may serve thy Church below,
     And join thy Saints in heaven.

A - men.

TIMES AND SEASONS.—HARVEST

291

67TH PSALM. (10 10. 10 10.)
In moderate time, with vigour ♩ = 88.

Scottish Psalter, 1615.

R. F. Littledale, 1833-90.

O SING to the Lord, whose bountiful hand
   Again doth accord his gifts to the land.
His clouds have shed down their plenteousness here,
His goodness shall crown the hopes of the year.

2 In clefts of the hills the founts he hath burst,
   And poureth their rills through valleys athirst.
The river of God the pastures hath blest,
The dry, withered sod in greenness is drest.

Unison. 3 And every fold shall teem with its sheep,
   With harvests of gold the fields shall be deep;
The vales shall rejoice with laughter and song,
And man's grateful voice the music prolong.

4. So too may he pour, the Last and the First,
   His graces in store on spirits athirst,
Till, when the great day of harvest hath come,
He takes us away to garner at home.

A - men.

TIMES AND SEASONS.—HARVEST

ST. GALL. (8 7. 8 7. D.)

292

Moderately fast ♩ = 112.

St. Gall Gesangbuch, 1863.

NOTE.—*Another tune for this hymn will be found in the Appendix* (No. 17).

W. Chatterton Dix, 1837-98.

TO thee, O Lord, our hearts we raise
  In hymns of adoration;
To thee bring sacrifice of praise
  With shouts of exultation.
Bright robes of gold the fields adorn,
  The hills with joy are ringing,
The valleys stand so thick with corn
  That even they are singing.

2 And now, on this our festal day,
  Thy bounteous hand confessing,
Upon thine altar, Lord, we lay
  The first-fruits of thy blessing;
By thee the souls of men are fed
  With gifts of grace supernal;
Thou who dost give us daily bread,
  Give us the Bread eternal.

3 We bear the burden of the day,
  And often toil seems dreary;
But labour ends with sunset ray,
  And rest is for the weary;
May we, the Angel-reaping o'er,
  Stand at the last accepted,
Christ's golden sheaves for evermore
  To garners bright elected.

Unison. 4. O, blessèd is that land of God,
  Where Saints abide for ever;
Where golden fields spread fair and broad,
  Where flows the crystal river:
The strains of all its holy throng
  With ours to-day are blending;
Thrice blessèd is that harvest-song
  Which never hath an ending.

A - men.

TIMES AND SEASONS.—HARVEST

WIR PFLÜGEN. (7 6. 7 6. 7 6. 7 6. 6 6. 8 4.) **293**

In moderate time ♩ = 100.

'*Bible Class Magazine*,' 1854, said to be arranged from
J. A. P. Schulz, 1747–1800.

A little slower.

M. *Claudius*, 1740–1815. Tr. *Jane M. Campbell.*

Wir pflügen und wir streuen.

WE plough the fields, and scatter
  The good seed on the land,
But it is fed and watered
  By God's almighty hand;
He sends the snow in winter,
  The warmth to swell the grain,
The breezes and the sunshine,
  And soft refreshing rain:
    All good gifts around us
      Are sent from heaven above,
    Then thank the Lord, O thank the Lord,
      For all his love.

2 He only is the Maker
  Of all things near and far.
He paints the wayside flower,
  He lights the evening star.
The winds and waves obey him,
  By him the birds are fed;
Much more to us, his children,
  He gives our daily bread:

3. We thank thee then, O Father,
  For all things bright and good;

TIMES AND SEASONS.—HARVEST.—AUTUMN

The seed-time and the harvest,
  Our life, our health, our food.
No gifts have we to offer
  For all thy love imparts,
But that which thou desirest,
  Our humble, thankful hearts:

A - men.

The following are also suitable:

309 For the beauty of the earth.
447 O God of Bethel, by whose hand.
475 Rejoice, O land, in God thy might.
532 Let us, with a gladsome mind.

Also the other Hymns of Thanksgiving, Nos. 533 to 537.

294

DEVONSHIRE. (7 6. 7 6.)
In moderate time ♩ = 104 (𝅗𝅥 = 52).

English Traditional Melody.

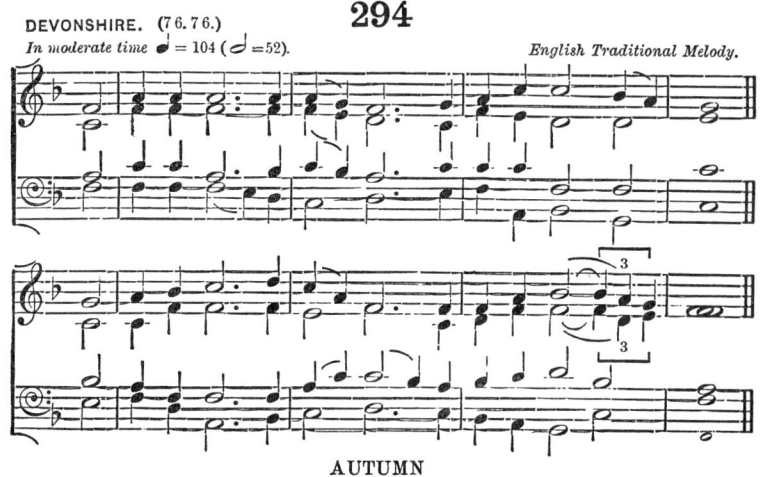

AUTUMN

Bishop W. W. How, 1823-97.

THE year is swiftly waning,
  The summer days are past;
And life, brief life, is speeding;
  The end is nearing fast.

2 The ever-changing seasons
  In silence come and go;
But thou, eternal Father,
  No time or change canst know.

3 O, pour thy grace upon us,
  That we may worthier be,
Each year that passes o'er us,
  To dwell in heaven with thee.

4 Behold the bending orchards
  With bounteous fruit are crowned;
Lord, in our hearts more richly
  Let heavenly fruits abound.

5 O, by each mercy sent us,
  And by each grief and pain,
By blessings like the sunshine,
  And sorrows like the rain,

6. Our barren hearts make fruitful
  With every goodly grace,
That we thy name may hallow,
  And see at last thy face.

A - men.

415

TIMES AND SEASONS.—WINTER

295

DANBY. (L.M.)
In moderate time ♩ = 104 (𝅗𝅥 = 52).

English Traditional Melody.

WINTER

S. Longfellow, 1819-92.

'TIS winter now; the fallen snow
  Has left the heavens all coldly clear;
Through leafless boughs the sharp winds blow,
And all the earth lies dead and drear.

2 And yet God's love is not withdrawn;
  His life within the keen air breathes;
  His beauty paints the crimson dawn,
  And clothes the boughs with glittering wreaths.

3 And though abroad the sharp winds blow,
  And skies are chill, and frosts are keen,
  Home closer draws her circle now,
  And warmer glows her light within.

4. O God! who giv'st the winter's cold,
  As well as summer's joyous rays,
  Us warmly in thy love enfold,
  And keep us through life's wintry days.

A - men.

SEASONS.—GENERAL

296

LYNE. (7 7.77.)
In moderate time ♩ = 120.

'*Magdalen Hymns*,' 1760 (?).

SEASONS.—GENERAL

J. Austin, 1613–69.

HARK, my soul, how everything
   Strives to serve our bounteous
     King;
Each a double tribute pays,
Sings its part, and then obeys.

2 Nature's chief and sweetest choir
Him with cheerful notes admire;
Chanting every day their lauds,
While the grove their song applauds.

3 Though their voices lower be,
Streams have too their melody;
Night and day they warbling run,
Never pause, but still sing on.

4 All the flowers that gild the spring
Hither their still music bring;
If heaven bless them, thankful, they
Smell more sweet, and look more gay.

5 Only we can scarce afford
   This short office to our Lord;
We, on whom his bounty flows,
All things gives, and nothing owes.

6 Wake! for shame, my sluggish heart,
Wake! and gladly sing thy part;
Learn of birds, and springs, and flowers,
How to use thy nobler powers.

7 Call whole nature to thy aid;
Since 'twas he whole nature made;
Join in one eternal song,
Who to one God all belong.

Unison. 8. Live for ever, glorious Lord!
Live by all thy works adored,
One in Three, and Three in One,
Thrice we bow to thee alone. Amen.

A - men.

SEASONS.—GENERAL

LONDON (OR ADDISON'S). (D. L. M.) **297**

In moderate time ♩ = 72.

J. SHEELES, c. 1720.

SEASONS.—GENERAL

J. Addison, 1672–1719.

THE spacious firmament on high,
With all the blue ethereal sky,
And spangled heavens, a shining frame,
Their great Original proclaim.
The unwearied sun from day to day
Does his Creator's power display,
And publishes to every land
The works of an almighty hand.

2 Soon as the evening shades prevail
The moon takes up the wondrous tale,
And nightly to the listening earth
Repeats the story of her birth;
Whilst all the stars that round her burn,
And all the planets in their turn,
Confirm the tidings, as they roll,
And spread the truth from pole to pole.

Unison. 3. What though in solemn silence all
Move round the dark terrestrial ball;
What though nor real voice nor sound
Amid their radiant orbs be found;
In reason's ear they all rejoice,
And utter forth a glorious voice;
For ever singing as they shine,
'The hand that made us is Divine.'

A - men.

SEASONS.—GENERAL

298

NEW 113TH. (8 8. 8 8. 8 8.)
Moderately slow ♩ = 88.

W. HAYES, 1706-1777.

Thomas Moore, 1779-1852.

1 THOU art, O God, the life and light
   Of all this wondrous world we see;
 Its glow by day, its smile by night,
   Are but reflections caught from thee:
 Where'er we turn, thy glories shine,
 And all things fair and bright are thine.

2 When day with farewell beam delays
   Among the opening clouds of even,
 And we can almost think we gaze
   Through golden vistas into heaven,—
 Those hues that make the sun's decline
 So soft, so radiant, Lord, are thine.

3 When night with wings of starry gloom
   O'ershadows all the earth and skies,
 Like some dark beauteous bird whose plume
   Is sparkling with unnumbered eyes,—
 That sacred gloom, those fires divine,
 So grand, so countless, Lord, are thine.

4.*When youthful spring around us breathes,
   Thy Spirit warms her fragrant sigh,
 And every flower the summer wreathes
   Is born beneath that kindling eye,—
 Where'er we turn, thy glories shine,
 And all things fair and bright are thine.

A - men.

SEASONS.—GENERAL

GOSTERWOOD. (13 13. 14 14.) **299**
In moderate time ♩ = 96.　　　　　　　　　*English Traditional Melody.*

Bishop R. Heber, 1783–1826.

WHEN spring unlocks the flowers to paint the laughing soil;
　　When summer's balmy showers refresh the mower's toil;
When winter binds in frosty chains the fallow and the flood;
In God the earth rejoiceth still, and owns his Maker good.

2 The birds that wake the morning, and those that love the shade;
　The winds that sweep the mountain, or lull the drowsy glade;
　The sun that from his amber bower rejoiceth on his way,
　The moon and stars—their Master's name in silent pomp display.

3 Shall man, the lord of nature, expectant of the sky,
　Shall man alone, unthankful, his little praise deny?
　No; let the year forsake his course, the seasons cease to be,
　Thee, Master, must we always love, and, Saviour, honour thee.

4. The flowers of spring may wither, the hope of summer fade,
　The autumn droop in winter, the birds forsake the shade;
　The winds be lulled, the sun and moon forget their old decree;
　But we, in nature's latest hour, O Lord, will cling to thee!

Part IV
SACRAMENTS AND OTHER RITES
HOLY COMMUNION

BANGOR. (C.M.)
Moderately slow ♩ = 60.

300

WILLIAM TANS'UR,
The Harmony of Zion, 1784.

J. Montgomery, 1771-1854.

ACCORDING to thy gracious word,
  In meek humility,
This will I do, my dying Lord,
  I will remember thee.

2 Thy Body, broken for my sake,
  My Bread from heaven shall be;
Thy testamental Cup I take,
  And thus remember thee.

3 Gethsemane can I forget?
  Or there thy conflict see,
Thine agony and bloody sweat,
  And not remember thee?

4 When to the Cross I turn mine eyes
  And rest on Calvary,
O Lamb of God, my Sacrifice,
  I must remember thee:

5 Remember thee, and all thy pains,
  And all thy love to me;
Yea, while a breath, a pulse remains,
  Will I remember thee.

6. And when these failing lips grow dumb,
  And mind and memory flee,
When thou shalt in thy kingdom come,
  Jesu, remember me.

A. men.

HYFRYDOL. (87. 87. D.)
Slow and dignified ♩ = 76.

301

Melody by
R. H. PRICHARD, 1811-87.

HOLY COMMUNION

W. Chatterton Dix, 1837-98.

ALLELUYA, sing to Jesus,
　His the sceptre, his the throne;
Alleluya, his the triumph,
　His the victory alone:
Hark the songs of peaceful Sion
　Thunder like a mighty flood;
Jesus, out of every nation,
　Hath redeemed us by his Blood.

2 *Alleluya, not as orphans
　Are we left in sorrow now;
Alleluya, he is near us,
　Faith believes, nor questions how;
Though the cloud from sight received him
　When the forty days were o'er,
Shall our hearts forget his promise,
　'I am with you evermore'?

3 Alleluya, Bread of angels,
　Thou on earth our Food, our Stay;
Alleluya, here the sinful
　Flee to thee from day to day;
Intercessor, Friend of sinners,
　Earth's Redeemer, plead for me,
Where the songs of all the sinless
　Sweep across the crystal sea.

Unison. 4. Alleluya, King eternal,
　Thee the Lord of lords we own;
Alleluya, born of Mary,
　Earth thy footstool, Heaven thy throne:
Thou within the veil hast entered,
　Robed in flesh, our great High Priest;
Thou on earth both Priest and Victim
　In the Eucharistic Feast.

A - men.

SACRAMENTS AND OTHER RITES

SONG 1. (10 10. 10 10. 10 10.) **302**

Moderately slow ♩ = 69.

O. GIBBONS, 1583–1625.

NOTE.—*A lower setting of this tune will be found at Hymn 384.*

At the Communion. W. Bright, 1824–1901.

AND now, O Father, mindful of the love [Calvary's Tree,
That bought us, once for all, on
And having with us him that pleads above, [forth to thee
We here present, we here spread
That only Offering perfect in thine eyes,
The one true, pure, immortal Sacrifice.

2 Look, Father, look on his anointed face,
And only look on us as found in him;
Look not on our misusings of thy grace,
Our prayer so languid, and our faith so dim: [reward
For lo! between our sins and their
We set the Passion of thy Son our Lord.

Part 2.

3 And then for those, our dearest and our best, [appeal;
By this prevailing presence we
O fold them closer to thy mercy's breast,
O do thine utmost for their souls true weal: [white and clear,
From tainting mischief keep them
And crown thy gifts with strength to persevere.

HOLY COMMUNION

4. And so we come; O draw us to thy feet,
   Most patient Saviour, who canst love us still;
And by this Food, so awful and so sweet,
   Deliver us from every touch of ill:
In thine own service make us glad and free,
And grant us never more to part with thee.

LOVELY. (66. 66. 88.) **303**
Moderately slow ♩ = 69.
J. D. EDWARDS, 1805-85.

NOTE.—*This hymn may also be sung to* DOLGELLY (*No.* 349).

C. Wesley, 1707-88.

AUTHOR of life divine,
   Who hast a table spread,
Furnished with mystic Wine
   And everlasting Bread,
Preserve the life thyself hast given,
And feed and train us up for heaven.

2. Our needy souls sustain
   With fresh supplies of love,
Till all thy life we gain,
   And all thy fullness prove,
And, strengthened by thy perfect grace,
Behold without a veil thy face.

NOTE.—*Lines 1 and 3 of the first verse may be sung:*

Au - thor of life di - vine,
Fur - nished with mys - tic Wine

SACRAMENTS AND OTHER RITES

CHRISTOPHER (IHR GESTIRN').
(7 7 7 7. 7 7.)
In moderate time ♩ = 100.

304

Later form of melody by
CHRISTOPH PETER, 1626–69
(slightly adapted).

NOTE.—*This hymn may also be sung to* NICHT SO TRAURIG (*No.* 100) *or to* BREAD OF HEAVEN (*Appendix, No.* 43).

At the Communion.   J. Conder ‡, 1789–1855.

BREAD of heaven, on thee we feed,
For thy Flesh is meat indeed;
Ever may our souls be fed
With this true and living Bread,
Day by day with strength supplied
Through the life of him who died.

2. Vine of heaven, thy Blood supplies
This blest cup of sacrifice;
'Tis thy wounds our healing give;
To thy Cross we look and live:
Thou our life! O let us be
Rooted, grafted, built on thee.

At the Communion.

RENDEZ À DIEU. (98. 98. D.)
Slow and dignified ♩ = 60.

305

Bishop R. Heber, 1783–1826.
Melody composed or adapted by
L. BOURGEOIS *for Psalm* 118
in the Genevan Psalter, 1543.

Bread of the world in mer-cy bro-ken, Wine of the soul in mer-cy

HOLY COMMUNION

shed, By whom the words of life were spo-ken, And in whose death our sins are dead: Look on the heart by sorrow bro-ken, Look on the tears by sin-ners shed, And be thy feast to us the to-ken That by thy grace our souls are fed! A-men.

[*As this hymn consists of one verse only, it is suggested that it be sung twice over; once by the* CHOIR ALONE *and again by choir and people in unison. It may also be used as a short motet for unaccompanied singing by the choir.*]

SACRAMENTS AND OTHER RITES

306

SCHMÜCKE DICH. (8 8. 8 8. D.)
Slow ♩ = 69 (𝅗𝅥 = 34)

Melody by J. Crüger, 1598-1662.

NOTE.—*The original rhythm of line 3 is as follows, and may be substituted for the above, if preferred:*

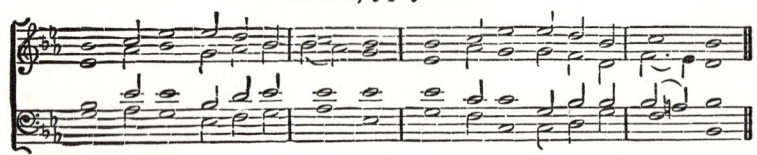

HOLY COMMUNION

Before Communion, or Preparation.   *J. Franck,* 1618–77.   *Tr. C. Winkworth.*

Schmücke dich.

DECK thyself, my soul, with gladness,
Leave the gloomy haunts of sadness,
Come into the daylight's splendour,
There with joy thy praises render
Unto him whose grace unbounded
Hath this wondrous banquet founded;
High o'er all the heavens he reigneth,
Yet to dwell with thee he deigneth.

2 * Now I sink before thee lowly,
Filled with joy most deep and holy,
As with trembling awe and wonder
On thy mighty works I ponder;
How, by mystery surrounded,
Depths no man hath ever sounded,
None may dare to pierce unbidden
Secrets that with thee are hidden.

At the Communion.   *Part 2.*

3 Sun, who all my life dost brighten;
Light, who dost my soul enlighten;
Joy, the sweetest man e'er knoweth.
Fount, whence all my being floweth.
At thy feet I cry, my Maker,
Let me be a fit partaker
Of this blessèd food from heaven,
For our good, thy glory, given.

4. Jesus, Bread of Life, I pray thee,
Let me gladly here obey thee;
Never to my hurt invited.
Be thy love with love requited :
From this banquet let me measure,
Lord, how vast and deep its treasure;
Through the gifts thou here dost give me,
As thy guest in heaven receive me.

A - men.

429

SACRAMENTS AND OTHER RITES

DRAW NIGH. (10 10. 10 10.) **307**
With free rhythm, quietly, and not too slowly ♩ = 126.
P. C. BUCK.
To be sung in unison.

NOTE.—*This hymn may also be sung to* THE SACRED HEART (*Appendix, No. 44*).

7th cent. Tr. J. M. Neale.
Sancti, venite, Christi Corpus sumite.

DRAW nigh, and take the Body of the Lord,
  And drink the holy Blood for you outpoured,
Saved by that Body, hallowed by that Blood,
Whereby refreshed we render thanks to God.

2 Salvation's giver, Christ the only Son,
By that his Cross and Blood the victory won,
Offered was he for greatest and for least:
Himself the Victim, and himself the Priest.

3*Victims were offered by the law of old,
That, in a type, celestial mysteries told.
He, Ransomer from death and Light from snade,
Giveth his holy grace his saints to aid.

4 Approach ye then with faithful hearts sincere,
And take the safeguard of salvation here.
He that in this world rules his saints and shields,
To all believers life eternal yields:

HOLY COMMUNION

5.*With heavenly Bread makes them that hunger whole,
Gives living waters to the thirsty soul.
Alpha and Omega, to whom shall bow
All nations at the Doom, is with us now.

A - men.

ADORO TE (NO. 2). (6 5. 6 5. D.)
In moderate time ♩ = 72.

308

*Melody of 'Adoro te devote,'
as given by Canon* VAN DAMME *of Ghent.*

NOTE.—*The tune at Hymn 331 can be adapted to these words by substituting ♪♪ for ♩ at the beginning of lines 1, 2, & 4, and by substituting ♪♪ for ♪ at the first note of line 3.*

At the Communion. *W. H. H. Jervois and W. B. T.*

FATHER, see thy children bending at thy throne,
  Pleading here the Passion of thine only Son,
Pleading here before thee all his dying love,
As he pleads it ever in the courts above.

2. Not for our wants only we this Offering plead,
But for all thy children who thy mercy need:
Bless thy faithful people, win thy wandering sheep,
Keep the souls departed who in Jesus sleep.

A - men.

431

SACRAMENTS AND OTHER RITES
309

ENGLAND'S LANE. (7 7. 7 7. 7 7.)
Moderately fast ♩ = 116. *Unison.*

Adapted by GEOFFREY SHAW
from an English Melody.

A-men-

[*This tune may also be sung in harmony.*]

NOTE.—*This hymn may also be sung to* RATISBON (JESU, MEINE ZUVERSICHT) (*No.* 282).

Other occasions also. F. S. Pierpoint, 1835–1917.

1. FOR the beauty of the earth,
   For the beauty of the skies,
   For the love which from our birth
   Over and around us lies:
     Christ our God, to thee we raise
     This our sacrifice of praise.

2. For the beauty of each hour
   Of the day and of the night,
   Hill and vale, and tree and flower,
   Sun and moon and stars of light:

3. For the joy of ear and eye,
   For the heart and brain's delight,
   For the mystic harmony
   Linking sense to sound and sight:

4. For the joy of human love,
   Brother, sister, parent, child,
   Friends on earth, and friends above,
   For all gentle thoughts and mild:

5. For each perfect gift of thine
   To our race so freely given,
   Graces human and divine,
   Flowers of earth and buds of heaven:

6.*For thy Bride that evermore
   Lifteth holy hands above,
   Offering up on every shore
   This pure sacrifice of love:

7.*For the Martyrs' crown of light,
   For thy Prophets' eagle eye,
   For thy bold Confessors' might,
   For the lips of infancy.

8.*For thy Virgins' robes of snow,
   For thy Maiden-mother mild,
   For thyself, with hearts aglow,
   Jesu, Victim undefiled:

HOLY COMMUNION

310

SHEEN. (14. 14. 14. 15.)
In moderate time 𝅗𝅥 = 92.

G. HOLST.

After Communion. *Liturgy of St. James.* Tr. C. W. H.

'Απὸ δόξης εἰς δόξαν πορευόμενοι.

FROM glory to glory advancing, we praise thee, O Lord;
Thy name with the Father and Spirit be ever adored.

2 From strength unto strength we go forward on Sion's highway,
To appear before God in the city of infinite day.

3 Thanksgiving, and glory and worship, and blessing and love,
One heart and one song have the Saints upon earth and above.

4. Evermore, O Lord, to thy servants thy presence be nigh;
Ever fit us by service on earth for thy service on high.

433

SACRAMENTS AND OTHER RITES

311

At the Communion.
AVE VERUM. (Irreg.) **Ave. verum Corpus natum.**
To be sung in unison, freely, but without hurry.

14th cent. Tr. H. N. Oxenham.
Proper Melody (Rouen version).
arr. J. H. A.

Hail, . . true Body, born of Ma - ry, Spot - less Vir - gin's
Thou . . who tru - ly hang-edst wea - ry On the Cross for

vir - gin birth; Thou whose sa - cred side was riv - en,
sons of earth; O may'st thou, dear Lord, be giv - en

Whence the . . Wa - ter flowed . and Blood, O . . . . most
At death's hour to be . . my food:

kind! . . O . . . gra - cious One! . . . O . . sweet - est

HOLY COMMUNION

Je - su, ho - ly Ma - ry's Son! A - men.

CONGLETON. (10 10. 10 10.)   **312**   *The Standard Psalm tune-book*, 1852
Moderately slow ♩ = 69.   (attributed there to M. WISE, c. 1648-87).

A-men.

NOTE.—*This hymn may also be sung to* ALL SOULS (*Appendix, No. 57*).

H. Bonar, 1808–89.

HERE, O my Lord, I see thee face to face; [things unseen;
Here faith would touch and handle
Here grasp with firmer hand the eternal grace, [lean.
And all my weariness upon thee

2 Here would I feed upon the Bread of God; [of heaven;
Here drink with thee the royal Wine
Here would I lay aside each earthly load; [forgiven.
Here taste afresh the calm of sin

3 I have no help but thine; nor do I need
Another arm save thine to lean upon:
It is enough, my Lord, enough indeed;
My strength is in thy might, thy might alone.

4. Mine is the sin, but thine the righteousness; [cleansing Blood;
Mine is the guilt, but thine the
Here is my robe, my refuge, and my peace,— [Lord my God.
Thy Blood, thy righteousness, O

435

SACRAMENTS AND OTHER RITES

At the Communion.
DA ZU DIR DER HEILAND KAM. (7 7. 7 7. 7 7. 4 4. 5 5.)
Very slow ♩ = 33 (♪ = 66).

313

P. D.

R. WAGNER, 1813-83.

1. Holy God, we show forth here Jesus' death our hearts to clear, Jesus' life our life to be, Jesus' love the world to free. Stay the faithful, win the strayed, Bless the living and the dead.

Pt. 2. 2. Lord, unite us every one Each to other, through thy Son; Join us truly heart to heart, Let us ne'er be drawn apart: All one Bread, one Body we, Bound by love to all and thee.

HOLY COMMUNION

Fa - ther lead us, Sa - viour feed us, Spi - rit ev - er - be our store, Now and ev - er - more.
Bles - s d Mas - ter, Bind us fas - ter; In thy love di - vine, Love we thee . . . and thine! A - men.

FREUEN WIR UNS. (7 7. 7 7.)
In moderate time ♩ = 63.

314

M. WEISSE, *c.* 1480–1534.

NOTE.—*This hymn may also be sung to* SONG 13 (*No.* 413).

T. Parnell, 1679–1717.

HOLY Jesus! God of love!
  Look with pity from above!
Shed the precious purple tide
From thine hands, thy feet, thy side;

2. Let thy streams of comfort roll,
  Let them please and fill my soul.
Let me thus for ever be,
Full of gladness, full of thee.

A - men.

SACRAMENTS AND OTHER RITES

315

Verses 1, 3, 5 Choir only.
EUDOXIA. (6 5. 6 5.)
Moderately slow ♩ = 63.

S. BARING-GOULD, 1834–1924.

Verses 2, 4, 6 full, to be sung in unison.
CASWALL (WEM IN LEIDENSTAGEN). (6 5. 6 5.)
Moderately slow ♩ = 63.

F. FILITZ, 1804–76.

After Communion.

F. W. FABER, 1814–63.

Choir only.

    JESU, gentlest Saviour,
       God of might and power,
  Thou thyself art dwelling
    In us at this hour.

Full. Unison.

2 Nature cannot hold thee,
    Heaven is all too strait
  For thine endless glory
    And thy royal state.

Choir only.

3 Out beyond the shining
    Of the furthest star
  Thou art ever stretching
    Infinitely far.

Full. Unison.

4 Yet the hearts of children
    Hold what worlds cannot,
  And the God of wonders
    Loves the lowly spot.

HOLY COMMUNION

Choir only.
5 Jesu, gentlest Saviour,
   Thou art in us now;
   Fill us full of goodness
   Till our hearts o'erflow.

Full. Unison.
6. Multiply our graces,
   Chiefly love and fear,
   And, dear Lord, the chiefest,
   Grace to persevere.

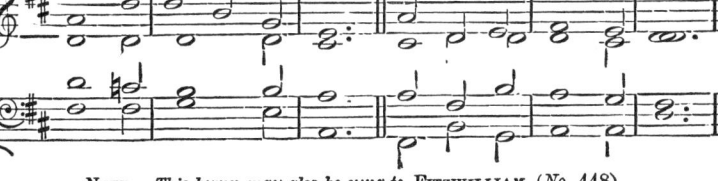

A - men

SAFFRON WALDEN. (88. 8. 6.)   **316**   A. H. Brown, 1830-1926.
Slow ♩ = 76.

NOTE.—*This hymn may also be sung to* FITZWILLIAM (*No.* 448).

Suitable also for other occasions.   *Charlotte Elliott*, 1789-1871.

JUST as I am, without one plea
   But that thy Blood was shed for me,
And that thou bidd'st me come to thee,
   O Lamb of God, I come.

2 Just as I am, though tossed about
   With many a conflict, many a doubt,
   Fightings within, and fears without,

3 Just as I am, poor, wretched, blind;
   Sight, riches, healing of the mind,
   Yea all I need, in thee to find,

4 Just as I am, thou wilt receive,
   Wilt welcome, pardon, cleanse, relieve:
   Because thy promise I believe,

5 Just as I am (thy love unknown
   Has broken every barrier down),
   Now to be thine, yea, thine alone,

6. Just as I am, of that free love
   The breadth, length, depth, and height to prove,
   Here for a season, then above,

A - men.

SACRAMENTS AND OTHER RITES

317

Sequence.
Modes vii and viii.

Lauda, Sion, Salvatorem.

St. Thomas Aquinas, 1227-74.
Tr. cento.
arr. J. H. A.

1. Laud, O Sion, thy salvation, Laud with hymns of exultation
Spend thyself, his honour raising, Who surpasseth all thy praising;
Christ, thy King and Shepherd true:

2. Sing to-day, the mystery showing
E'en the same of old provided,
Of the living, life bestowing,
Where the Twelve, divinely guided,
Bread from heaven before thee set;
At the holy Table met.

Never canst thou reach his due.

HOLY COMMUNION

317 (continued)

3 Full and clear ring out thy chant-ing, Joy nor sweet-est grace be want-ing
To thy heart and soul to-day; When we gath-er up the mea-sure
Of that Sup-per and its trea-sure, Keep-ing feast in glad ar-ray.

SACRAMENTS AND OTHER RITES

317 (*continued*)

4 Lo, the new King's Ta - ble gra - cing, This new Pass - o - ver of bless-ing
Hath ful - filled the eld - er rite: Now the new the old ef - fa - ceth,
Truth re - vealed the sha - dow chas - eth, Day is break-ing on the night.

HOLY COMMUNION

317 (continued)

5 What he did at Supper seated, Christ ordained to be repeated,

His memorial ne'er to cease: And, his word for guidance taking,

Bread and wine we hallow, making Thus our Sacrifice of peace.

SACRAMENTS AND OTHER RITES

317 (continued)

6 This the truth to Chris-tians giv-en— Bread be-comes his Flesh from hea-ven,
Wine be-comes his ho-ly Blood. Doth it pass thy com-pre-hend-ing?
Yet by faith, thy sight transcending, Won-drous things are un-der-stood.

HOLY COMMUNION

317 (continued)

7 { Yea, beneath these signs are hidden Glorious things to sight forbidden:
   Wine is poured and Bread is broken, But in either sacred token
   Look not on the outward sign.
   Christ is here by power divine. }

8 { Whoso of this Food partaketh,
   Thousands are, as one, receivers,
   Rendeth not the Lord nor breaketh: Christ is whole to all that taste.
   One, as thousands of believers, Takes the Food that cannot waste. }

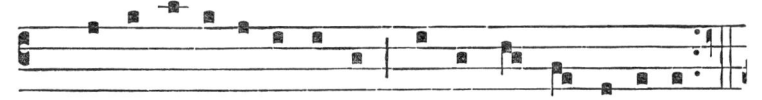

SACRAMENTS AND OTHER RITES

317 (*continued*)

9* Good and e - vil men are shar - ing One re - past, a
Doom of life or death a - ward - ed, As their days shall

doom pre - par - ing Va - ried as the heart of man; 10 When the
be re - cord - ed Which from one be - gin - ning ran Nought the

Sac - ra - ment is bro - ken, Doubt not in each sev - ered to - ken,
pre - cious Gift di - vi - deth, Break - ing but the sign be - ti - deth,

HOLY COMMUNION

317 (continued)

Hal-lowed by the word once spo-ken, Rest-eth all the true con-tent:
He him-self the same a-bi-deth, Noth-ing of his full-ness spent.

Part 2. ECCE! PANIS ANGELORUM.

11 { Lo! the An-gels' Food is giv-en To the pil-grim who hath stri-ven;
    Truth the an-cient types ful-fill-ing, I-saac bound, a vic-tim will-ing,

See the chil-dren's Bread from hea-ven,
Pas-chal lamb, its life-blood spill-ing.

SACRAMENTS AND OTHER RITES

317 (continued)

Part 3. BONE PASTOR.

Which to dogs may not be cast;
Man-na sent in a-ges past.
12 { Ve-ry Bread, good Shepherd, tend us,
Thou who all things canst and know-est,

Je-su, of thy love be-friend us,
Who on earth such Food be-stow-est,
Thou re-fresh us, thou de-fend us,
Grant us with thy Saints, tho' low-est,

Thine e-ter-nal good-ness send us
Where the heavenly Feast thou show-est,
In the land of life to see;
Fel-low-heirs and guests to be.

HOLY COMMUNION

317 (continued)

When the Ecce Panis *is sung alone the organ accompaniment may be played one tone lower as below.*

SACRAMENTS AND OTHER RITES

318

PICARDY. (87.87.87.)
Slow ♩ = 92 (𝅗𝅥 = 46). *To be sung in unison.*

French Traditional Carol.

NOTE.—*This hymn may also be sung to* ST. THOMAS (*No.* 31).

Liturgy of St. James. Tr. G. Moultrie.

Σιγησάτω πᾶσα σὰρξ βροτεία.

LET all mortal flesh keep silence, and with fear and trembling stand;
Ponder nothing earthly-minded, for with blessing in his hand,
Christ our God to earth descendeth, our full homage to demand.

2 King of kings, yet born of Mary, as of old on earth he stood,
Lord of lords, in human vesture—in the Body and the Blood—
He will give to all the faithful his own Self for heavenly Food.

3 Rank on rank the host of heaven spreads its vanguard on the way,
As the Light of light descendeth from the realms of endless day,
That the powers of hell may vanish as the darkness clears away.

4. At his feet the six-winged Seraph; Cherubim with sleepless eye,
Veil their faces to the Presence, as with ceaseless voice they cry.
Alleluya, Alleluya, Alleluya, Lord most high.

Harmony.

A - men.

HOLY COMMUNION

319

BRYN CALFARIA. (8 7. 8 7. 4 7.)
Slow ♩ = 96.
Melody by W. Owen, 1814-93.

NOTE.—*This hymn may also be sung to* BRYNTIRION *(No. 248).*

G. H. Bourne, 1840-1925.

LORD, enthroned in heavenly splendour,
　First-begotten from the dead,
Thou alone, our strong Defender,
　Liftest up thy people's head.
　　Alleluya,
　Jesu, true and living Bread!

2 Here our humblest homage pay we;
　Here in loving reverence bow;
Here for Faith's discernment pray we,
　Lest we fail to know thee now.
　　Alleluya,
　Thou art here, we ask not how.

3*Though the lowliest form doth veil thee
　As of old in Bethlehem,
Here as there thine Angels hail thee,
　Branch and Flower of Jesse's stem.
　　Alleluya,
　We in worship join with them.

4*Paschal Lamb, thine Offering, finished
　Once for all when thou wast slain,
In its fullness undiminished
　Shall for evermore remain,
　　Alleluya,
　Cleansing souls from every stain.

Unison. 5.*Life-imparting heavenly Manna,
　Stricken Rock with streaming side,
Heaven and earth with loud hosanna
　Worship thee, the Lamb who died,
　　Alleluya,
　Risen, ascended, glorified!

A - men.

SACRAMENTS AND OTHER RITES

SIMEON. (L. M.)
Moderately slow ♩ = 63.

320

S. STANLEY, 1767-1822.

NOTE.—*This hymn may also be sung to* ROCKINGHAM (*Appendix, No. 45, or No.* 107).

P. Doddridge, 1702-51.

MY God, and is thy Table spread,
    And does thy Cup with Love o'erflow?
Thither be all thy children led,
    And let them all thy sweetness know.

2 Hail, sacred Feast, which Jesus makes!
    Rich Banquet of his Flesh and Blood!
Thrice happy he, who here partakes
    That sacred Stream, that heavenly Food.

3. O let thy Table honoured be,
    And furnished well with joyful guests;
And may each soul salvation see,
    That here its sacred Pledges tastes.

A - men.

HOLY COMMUNION
321

IN ALLEN MEINEN THATEN. (7 76. D.)
Slow 𝅗𝅥 = 56.

'Zions Harfe,' 1855 (from Davidisches Harfen- und Psalterspiel, 1744).

At the Communion.

O esca viatorum.

c. 1661. Tr. A. R.

O FOOD of men wayfaring,
　The Bread of Angels sharing,
　O Manna from on high!
We hunger; Lord, supply us,
Nor thy delights deny us,
　Whose hearts to thee draw nigh.

2 O Stream of love past telling,
O purest Fountain, welling
　From out the Saviour's side!
We faint with thirst; revive us,
Of thine abundance give us,
　And all we need provide.

3. O Jesu, by thee bidden,
We here adore thee, hidden
　'Neath forms of bread and wine.
Grant when the veil is riven,
We may behold, in heaven,
　Thy countenance divine.

A - men.

SACRAMENTS AND OTHER RITES

322

LEICESTER (OR BEDFORD). (8 8. 8 8. 8 8.)
Moderately slow ♩ = 63.

JOHN BISHOP (c. 1665–1737), *from A Sett of New Psalm Tunes* (1700).

NOTE —*This hymn may also be sung to* LAMBETH (*No.* 340).

W. E. Gladstone, 1809–98.

O LEAD my blindness by the hand,
   Lead me to thy familiar Feast,
Not here or now to understand,
   Yet even here and now to taste,
How the eternal Word of heaven
On earth in broken bread is given.

2 We, who this holy precinct round
   In one adoring circle kneel,
May we in one intent be bound,
   And one serene devotion feel;
And grow around thy sacred shrine
Like tendrils of the deathless Vine.

3. We, who with one blest Food are fed,
   Into one body may we grow,
And one pure life from thee, the Head,
   Informing all the members flow;
One pulse be felt in every vein,
One law of pleasure and of pain.

A - men.

HOLY COMMUNION
323

SCHÖNSTER HERR JESU. (10 7. 10 7.)

Very slow ♩ = 40 (♩ = 80).

Bishop R. Heber, 1783–1826.
Melody from
'Münster Gesangbuch,' 1677.

O, most mer-ci-ful! O, most boun-ti-ful!
God the Fa-ther Al-migh-ty! By the Re-deem-er's Sweet in-ter-ces-sion
Hear us, help us when we cry. A-men.

NOTE.—*As this hymn consists of one verse only it is suggested that it be sung twice; once by the* CHOIR ALONE *and again by choir and people in unison.*

It may also be used as a short motet for unaccompanied singing by the choir.

SACRAMENTS AND OTHER RITES

324

FFIGYSBREN. (10 10. 10 10. 10 10.)
In moderate time ♩ = 84.

Welsh Hymn Melody.

Col. W. H. Turton, 1856-1938.

1. O THOU, who at thy Eucharist didst pray
That all thy Church might be for ever one,
Grant us at every Eucharist to say
With longing heart and soul, 'Thy will be done.'
Oh, may we all one Bread, one Body be,
One through this Sacrament of unity.

2. For all thy Church, O Lord, we intercede; [cease;
Make thou our sad divisions soon to cease;
Draw us the nearer each to each, we plead, [Peace:
By drawing all to thee, O Prince of Peace:
Thus may we all one Bread, one Body be,
One through this Sacrament of unity.

3. We pray thee too for wanderers from thy Fold;
O bring them back, good Shepherd of the sheep,
Back to the Faith which Saints believed of old,
Back to the Church which still that Faith doth keep:
Soon may we all one Bread, one Body be,
One through this Sacrament of unity.

4. So, Lord, at length when Sacraments shall cease,
We may be one with all thy Church above,
One with thy Saints in one unbroken peace,
One with thy Saints in one unbounded love:
More blessèd still, in peace and love to be
One with the Trinity in Unity.

A - men.

HOLY COMMUNION

325

Ὁ μονογενὴς Υἱός.

SONG 24. (10 10. 10 10.)
Moderately slow ♩ = 69.

Emperor Justinian, 483–565.
Tr. T. A. L.
O. GIBBONS, 1583–1625.

1. O Word immortal of eternal God,
   Only-begotten of the only Source,
   For our salvation stooping to the course
   Of human life, and born of Mary's blood;
   Sprung from the ever-virgin womanhood
   Of her who bare thee, God immutable,
   Incarnate, made as man with man to dwell,
   And condescending to the bitter Rood;

2. Save us, O Christ our God, for thou hast died
   To save thy people to the uttermost,
   And dying tramplest death in victory;
   One of the ever-blessed Trinity,
   In equal honour with the Holy Ghost,
   And with th' eternal Father glorified. Amen.

SACRAMENTS AND OTHER RITES

326

Mode iii.   arr. J. H. A.

HOLY COMMUNION

St. Thomas Aquinas, 1227-74.
Tr. J. M. Neale, E. Caswall, and others

Pange lingua, gloriosi Corporis mysterium.

OF the glorious Body telling,
 O my tongue, its mysteries sing,
And the Blood, all price excelling,
 Which the world's eternal King,
In a noble womb once dwelling,
 Shed for this world's ransoming.

2 Given for us, for us descending,
 Of a Virgin to proceed,
Man with man in converse blending,
 Scattered he the Gospel seed,
Till his sojourn drew to ending,
 Which he closed in wondrous deed.

3 At the last great Supper lying
 Circled by his brethren's band,
Meekly with the law complying,
 First he finished its command,
Then, immortal Food supplying,
 Gave himself with his own hand.

4 Word made Flesh, by word he maketh
 Very bread his Flesh to be;
Man in wine Christ's Blood partaketh:
 And if senses fail to see,
Faith alone the true heart waketh
 To behold the mystery.

At the Communion.

Part 2.

Tantum ergo.

5 Therefore we, before him bending,
 This great Sacrament revere;
Types and shadows have their ending,
 For the newer rite is here;
Faith, our outward sense befriending,
 Makes the inward vision clear.

6. Glory let us give, and blessing
 To the Father, and the Son;
Honour, might, and praise addressing,
 While eternal ages run;
Ever too his love confessing,
 Who, from both, with both is one.
  Amen.

SACRAMENTS AND OTHER RITES

326 (Mechlin Version)

PANGE LINGUA. (87.87.87.)
In free rhythm: to be sung in unison.
Melody from the Mechlin Gradual,
arr. J. H. A.

The following may also be sung for verses 3 and 5 by the CHOIR ALONE, *the people singing the other verses (Nos. 1, 2, and 4) to the tune above. The Doxology to be sung by all to the Mechlin Melody.*

TANTUM ERGO (No. 2). (87.87.87.)
Very slow and solemn ♩ = 60.
Probably by
G. P. da PALESTRINA, *d.* 1594.

HOLY COMMUNION

NOTE.—*This hymn may also be sung to* ORIEL (*No. 507*).

St. Thomas Aquinas, 1227-74.
Tr. J. M. Neale, E. Caswall, and others.

Pange, lingua, gloriosi Corporis mysterium.

OF the glorious Body telling,
   O my tongue, its mysteries sing,
And the Blood, all price excelling,
   Which the world's eternal King,
In a noble womb once dwelling,
   Shed for this world's ransoming.

2 Given for us, for us descending,
   Of a Virgin to proceed.
Man with man in converse blending,
   Scattered he the Gospel seed,
Till his sojourn drew to ending,
   Which he closed in wondrous deed.

3 At the last great Supper lying
   Circled by his brethren's band,
Meekly with the law complying,
   First he finished its command,
Then, immortal Food supplying,
   Gave himself with his own hand.

4 Word made Flesh, by word he maketh
   Very bread his Flesh to be;
Man in wine Christ's Blood partaketh:
   And if senses fail to see,
Faith alone the true heart waketh
   To behold the mystery.

At the Communion.

Part 2.

Tantum ergo.

5 Therefore we, before him bending,
   This great Sacrament revere;
Types and shadows have their ending,
   For the newer rite is here;
Faith, our outward sense befriending,
   Makes the inward vision clear.

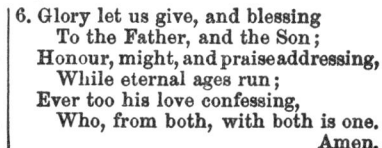

6. Glory let us give, and blessing
   To the Father, and the Son;
Honour, might, and praise addressing,
   While eternal ages run;
Ever too his love confessing,
   Who, from both, with both is one.
                    Amen.

NOTE.—*Either Amen may be used.*

SACRAMENTS AND OTHER RITES

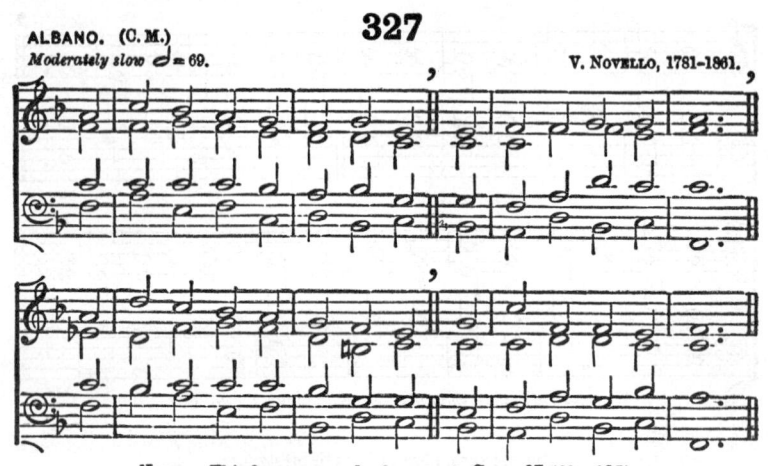

327

ALBANO. (C.M.)
Moderately slow ♩ = 69.
V. Novello, 1781-1861.

NOTE.—*This hymn may also be sung to* Song 67 (*No.* 197).

W. Bright, 1824-1901.

1. ONCE, only once, and once for all,
His precious life he gave;
Before the Cross in faith we fall,
And own it strong to save.

2. 'One offering, single and complete,'
With lips and hearts we say;
But what he never can repeat
He shows forth day by day.

3. For as the priest of Aaron's line
Within the holiest stood,
And sprinkled all the mercy-shrine
With sacrificial blood;

4. So he, who once atonement wrought,
Our Priest of endless power,
Presents himself for those he bought
In that dark noontide hour.

5. His Manhood pleads where now it lives
On heaven's eternal throne,
And where in mystic rite he gives
Its presence to his own.

6. And so we show thy death, O Lord,
Till thou again appear,
And feel, when we approach thy board,
We have an altar here.

A - men.

328

HYMNUS EUCHARISTICUS. (L. M.)
Very slow ♩ = 60.
B. Rogers, 1614-98
(*The Magdalen Tower Hymn*).

HOLY COMMUNION

NOTE.—*This Hymn was originally written for the tune* BEATA NOBIS (*No. 185*), *which is equally suitable to it with the above tune.*

At the Communion.   W. H. H. *Jervois*, 1852–1905.

SEE, Father, thy belovèd Son,
  Whom here we now present to thee;
The all-sufficient Sacrifice,
  The sinner's one and only plea.
2. Through him we pray for all we love,
  For all by pain or sin opprest;
For souls departed in thy fear:
  O grant them thine eternal rest.

A - men.

ACH GOTT UND HERR. (8 7. 8 7.)   **329**   *Melody in Neu-Leipziger-Gesangbuch*, 1682.
Very slow and dignified ♩ = 46.   *Adapted and harmonized by* J. S. BACH.

After Communion.   نبيلا مَنْ اتبوا وَعفيتَ   *Liturgy of Malabar.*
                                                     Tr. C. W. H. *and* P. D.

STRENGTHEN for service, Lord, the
That holy things have taken; [hands
Let ears that now have heard thy songs
  To clamour never waken.

2 Lord, may the tongues which 'Holy'
  Keep free from all deceiving; [sang
The eyes which saw thy love be bright,
  Thy blessèd hope perceiving.

3. The feet that tread thy holy courts
  From light do thou not banish;
The bodies by thy Body fed
  With thy new life replenish.

A - men.

SACRAMENTS AND OTHER RITES

330

Mode viii.   *arr.* J. H. A.

St. Thomas Aquinas, 1227-74.
Tr. J. M. Neale, E. Caswall
and others.

Verbum supernum prodiens, nec Patris.

THE Word of God, proceeding forth
   Yet leaving not his Father's side,
And going to his work on earth,
   Had reached at length life's eventide;

HOLY COMMUNION

330 (Modern Tune)

O SALUTARIS. (L. M.)
In moderate time ♩ = 72.

Abbé Duguet (?)

[*May be sung in unison throughout.*]

Note.—*This hymn may also be sung to the Mechlin Melody at Hymn 2, to* Melcombe *(No. 260) or* Wareham *(No. 475).*

2 By false disciple to be given
  To foemen for his blood athirst,
 Himself, the living Bread from heaven,
  He gave to his disciples first.

3 In twofold form of sacrament
  He gave his Flesh, he gave his Blood,
 That man, of twofold substance blent,
  Might wholly feed on mystic food.

4 In birth man's fellow-man was he,
  His meat while sitting at the board;
 He died, his ransomer to be,
  He reigns to be his great reward.

Part 2.
O salutaris.

5 O saving Victim! opening wide
  The gate of heaven to man below,
 Our foes press hard on every side,—
  Thine aid supply, thy strength bestow.

6. All praise and thanks to thee ascend
  For evermore, blest One in Three;
 O grant us life that shall not end
  In our true native land with thee.
                       Amen.

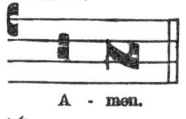

A - men.

Note.—*Another tune for this Part will be found in the Appendix (No. 46).*

A - men.

SACRAMENTS AND OTHER RITES

331

ADORO TE. (10 10. 10 10.)   *Proper Melody (from the Solesmes Version).*
To be sung in unison, freely, but without hurry.   arr. J. H. A.

The quarter-bar pauses are to be observed only if the sense admits.

Adoro te devote.   St. Thomas Aquinas, 1227-74.
Tr. Bishop J. R. Woodford.

THEE we adore, O hidden Saviour, thee,
  Who in thy Sacrament art pleased to be;
Both flesh and spirit in thy presence fail,
Yet here thy Presence we devoutly hail.

2 O blest Memorial of our dying Lord,
  Who living Bread to men doth here afford!
  O may our souls for ever feed on thee,
  And thou, O Christ, for ever precious be.

3* Fountain of goodness, Jesu, Lord and God,
  Cleanse us, unclean, with thy most cleansing Blood;
  Increase our faith and love, that we may know
  The hope and peace which from thy Presence flow.

4*. O Christ, whom now beneath a veil we see,
  May what we thirst for soon our portion be,
  To gaze on thee unveiled, and see thy face,
  The vision of thy glory and thy grace.

HOLY COMMUNION
332

WINDSOR. (C.M.)
Slow ♩ = 56.

Melody from Damon's Psalter, 1591.
rhythm according to the Scottish Psalter, 1633.

NOTE.—*This hymn may also be sung to* WILTSHIRE (*No.* 502).

Suitable also for other occasions.   W. *Cowper*, 1731-1800.

1. THERE is a fountain filled with Blood,
    Drawn from Emmanuel's veins,
  And sinners plunged beneath that flood
    Lose all their guilty stains.

2. The dying thief rejoiced to see
    That fountain in his day;
  And there have I, as vile as he,
    Washed all my sins away.

3. Dear dying Lamb, thy precious Blood
    Shall never lose its power,
  Till all the ransomed Church of God
    Be saved to sin no more.

4. E'er since by faith I saw the stream
    Thy flowing wounds supply,
  Redeeming love has been my theme,
    And shall be till I die.

5. Then in a nobler, sweeter song,
    I'll sing thy power to save,
  When this poor lisping, stammering tongue
    Lies silent in the grave.

6. Lord, I believe thou hast prepared,
    Unworthy though I be,
  For me a blood-bought free reward,
    A golden harp for me.

Unison. 7. 'Tis strung and tuned for endless years,
    And formed by power divine,
  To sound in God the Father's ears
    No other name but thine.

A - men.

SACRAMENTS AND OTHER RITES
333

COLERAINE (VICENZA). (8 8. 8 8. 8 8.)
In moderate time ♩ = 72.
Melody from 'La Scala Santa,' 1681.

NOTE.—*This hymn may also be sung to* SOUTH CERNEY (*No.* 359).

C. Wesley, 1707-88.

VICTIM Divine, thy grace we claim
    While thus thy precious Death we show;
Once offered up, a spotless Lamb,
In thy great temple here below,
Thou didst for all mankind atone,
And standest now before the throne.

2 Thou standest in the holiest place,
    As now for guilty sinners slain;
Thy Blood of sprinkling speaks and prays
All-prevalent for helpless man;
Thy Blood is still our ransom found,
And spreads salvation all around.

3. We need not now go up to heaven
    To bring the long-sought Saviour down;
Thou art to all already given,
Thou dost e'en now thy banquet crown:
To every faithful soul appear,
And show thy real Presence here.

A - men.

HOLY COMMUNION

334

CAERLLEON. (7 6. 7 6. D.)
In moderate time ♩ = 80.   *Welsh Hymn Melody, harmonized by* DAVID EVANS.

A-men.

NOTE.—*This hymn may also be sung to* MEIRIONYDD (*No.* 473).

WE pray thee, heavenly Father,
　To hear us in thy love,
And pour upon thy children
　The unction from above;
That so in love abiding,
　From all defilement free,
We may in pureness offer
　Our Eucharist to thee.

2 All that we have we offer,
　For it is all thine own,
All gifts, by thine appointment,
　In bread and cup are shown;
One thing alone we bring not,
　The wilfulness of sin,
And all we bring is nothing
　Save that which is within.

3 Within the pure oblation,　*V. S. S. G*
　Beneath the outward sign,
By that his operation,—
　The Holy Ghost divine,—
Lies hid the sacred Body,
　Lies hid the precious Blood,
Once slain, now ever glorious,
　Of Christ our Lord and God.

4. Wherefore, though all unworthy
　To offer sacrifice,
We pray that this our duty
　Be pleasing in thine eyes;
For praise, and thanks and worship,
　For mercy and for aid,
The Catholic oblation
　Of Jesus Christ is made.

SACRAMENTS AND OTHER RITES
335

CHRISTE FONS JUGIS. (11 11. 11 5.)
Slow ♩ = 72. To be sung in unison.

Rouen Church Melody.

At the Communion.

W. H. H. Jervois, 1852-1905.

WHEREFORE, O Father, we thy humble servants
   Here bring before thee Christ thy well-belovèd,
All-perfect Offering, Sacrifice immortal,
         Spotless Oblation.

2. See now thy children, making intercession
   Through him our Saviour, Son of God incarnate,
For all thy people, living and departed,
         Pleading before thee.

A... men.

HOLY BAPTISM

336

LIEBSTER JESU. (7 8. 7 8. 8 8.)
Very slow and quiet ♩ = 46.

Melody by J. R. AHLE, 1625–78.

HOLY BAPTISM

B. Schmolck, 1672–1737.
Tr. Catherine Winkworth †.

Liebſter Jeſu, wir ſind hier.

BLESSÈD Jesu! here we stand,
　　Met to do as thou hast spoken:
And this child, at thy command,
　　Now we bring to thee, in token
That to Christ it here is given;
For of such shall be his heaven.

2 * Yes! thy warning voice is plain,
　　And we fain would keep it duly:
He who is not born again,
　　Heart and life renewing truly,
Born of water and the Spirit,
Will God's kingdom ne'er inherit.

8 Make it, Head, thy member now;
　　Shepherd, take thy lamb and feed it:
Prince of Peace, its peace be thou;
　　Way of life, to heaven, O, lead it:
Vine, this branch may nothing sever,
Grafted firm in thee for ever.

4. Now upon thy heart it lies,
　　What our hearts so dearly treasure;
Heavenward lead our burdened sighs,
　　Pour thy blessing without measure;
Write the name we now have given,
Write it in the book of heaven.

SACRAMENTS AND OTHER RITES

337

ST. STEPHEN. (C.M.)
Slow ♩ = 58.
W. Jones, 1726-1800.

H. Alford, 1810-71.

IN token that thou shalt not fear
  Christ crucified to own,
We print the Cross upon thee here.
  And stamp thee his alone.

2 In token that thou shalt not blush
  To glory in his name,
We blazon here upon thy front
  His glory and his shame.

3 In token that thou shalt not flinch
  Christ's quarrel to maintain,
But 'neath his banner manfully
  Firm at thy post remain;

4 In token that thou too shalt tread
  The path he travelled by,
Endure the Cross, despise the shame,
  And sit thee down on high:

5 Thus outwardly and visibly
  We seal thee for his own;
And may the brow that wears his Cross
  Hereafter share his crown.

A - men.

HOLY BAPTISM

338

IN EINEM KRIPPLEIN LAG EIN KIND (8.8.8.8.8.8.)

Melody from H. von Laufenberg's MS., c. 1480.

In moderate time ♩ = 96.

NOTE.—*This hymn may also be sung to* LAMBETH (*No.* 340).

H. von Laufenberg, d. c. 1458.
Tr. C. Winkworth ‡.

Ach lieber Herre, Jesu Christ.

LORD Jesu Christ, our Lord most dear,
As thou wast once an infant here,
So give this child of thine, we pray,
Thy grace and blessing day by day.
    O holy Jesu, Lord Divine,
    We pray thee guard this child of thine.

2 As in thy heavenly kingdom, Lord,
All things obey thy sacred word,
Do thou thy mighty succour give,
And shield this child by morn and eve.

3. Their watch let angels round *him* keep
Where'er *he* be, awake, asleep;
Thy holy Cross now let *him* bear,
That *he* thy crown with Saints may wear.

A - - men.

SACRAMENTS AND OTHER RITES

339

FARRANT. (C. M.)
Slow ♩ = 58.

Adapted from an Anthem of the school of R. FARRANT, c. 1530–85.

J. M. Neale, 1818–66.

WITH Christ we share a mystic grave,
  With Christ we buried lie;
But 'tis not in the darksome cave
  By mournful Calvary.

2 The pure and bright baptismal flood
  Entombs our nature's stain:
New creatures from the cleansing wave
  With Christ we rise again.

3 Thrice blest, if through this world of sin
  And lust and selfish care
Our resurrection mantle white
  And undefiled we wear.

4 Thrice blest, if through the gate of death,
  Glorious at last and free,
We to our joyful rising pass,
  O risen Lord, with thee.

5. And now to thy thrice holy Name,
  The God whom we adore,
To Father, Son, and Holy Ghost,
  Be glory evermore. Amen.

A - men.

The following are also suitable:

93 The God of love my Shepherd is.
389 Fight the good fight with all thy might.
426 Lead us, heavenly Father, lead us.
484 Take up thy cross, the Saviour said.
488 The Church of God a kingdom is.

CONFIRMATION

340

LAMBETH. (8 8. 8 8. 8 8.)
Moderately slow ♩ = 63.

S. AKEROYD in the
'*Divine Companion*,' 1701.

CONFIRMATION

W. Bright, 1824–1901.

BEHOLD us, Lord, before thee met,
　Whom each bright angel serves and fears,
Who on thy throne rememberest yet
　Thy spotless boyhood's quiet years;
Whose feet the hills of Nazareth trod,
Who art true Man and perfect God.

2 * To thee we look, in thee confide,
　　Our help is in thine own dear name;
For who on Jesus e'er relied,
　And found not Jesus still the same?
Thus far thy love our souls hath brought:
O stablish well what thou hast wrought.

3 The seed of our baptismal life,
　O living Word, by thee was sown;
So where thy soldiers wage their strife
　Our post we take, our vows we own,
And ask, in thine appointed way,
Confirm us in thy grace to-day.

4 * We need thee more than tongue can speak, [down;
　'Mid foes that well might cast us
But thousands, once as young and weak, [crown;
　Have fought the fight, and won the
We ask the help that bore them through,
We trust the Faithful and the True.

5. So bless us with the gift complete
　By hands of thy chief pastors given,
That awful Presence kind and sweet
　Which comes in sevenfold might from heaven;
Eternal Christ, to thee we bow,
　Give us thy Spirit here and now.

A - men.

SACRAMENTS AND OTHER RITES

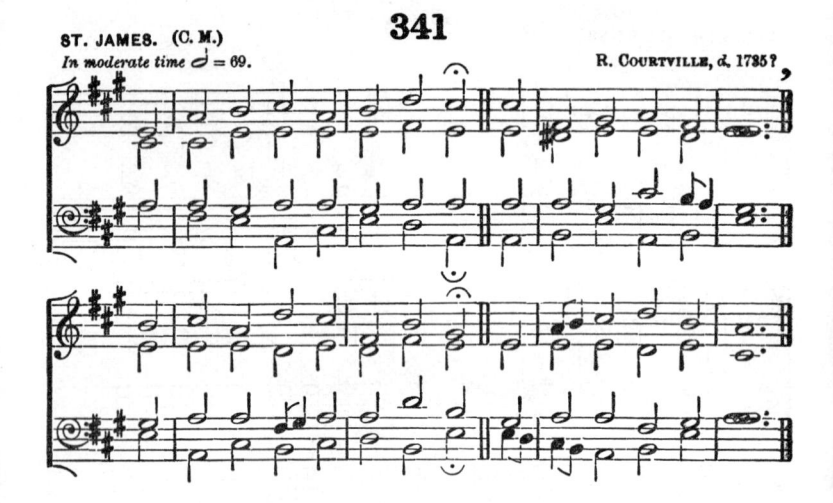

341

ST. JAMES. (C. M.)
In moderate time ♩ = 69.
R. COURTVILLE, d. 1735?

M. Bridges, 1800-94.

MY God, accept my heart this day,
And make it always thine,
That I from thee no more may stray,
No more from thee decline.

2 Before the Cross of him who died,
Behold, I prostrate fall;
Let every sin be crucified,
And Christ be All in all.

3 Anoint me with thy heavenly grace,
And seal me for thine own;
That I may see thy glorious face,
And worship at thy throne.

4 Let every thought, and work, and word
To thee be ever given;
Then life shall be thy service, Lord,
And death the gate of heaven.

5. All glory to the Father be,
All glory to the Son,
All glory, Holy Ghost, to thee,
While endless ages run. Amen.

A - men.

CONFIRMATION

342

ADVENT. (8 8 6. D.)
In moderate time ♩ = 120.

'Western Melody' in
Plymouth Collection (U. S. A.), 1855.

NOTE.— *This hymn may also be sung to* MAGDALEN COLLEGE (*No.* 457).

Anon ‡ (*c.* 1850).

LORD, in thy presence dread and sweet,
Thine own dear Spirit we entreat
  His sevenfold gifts to shed
On us, who fall before thee now,
Bearing the Cross upon our brow
  On which our Master bled.

2 Spirit of Wisdom! turn our eyes
From earth and earthly vanities,
  To heavenly truth and love.
Spirit of Understanding true!
Our souls with holy light endue
  To seek the things above.

3 Spirit of Counsel! be our guide;
Teach us by earthly struggles tried
  Our heavenly crown to win.

Spirit of Fortitude! thy power
Be with us in temptation's hour,
  To keep us pure from sin.

4 Spirit of Knowledge! lead our feet
In thine own paths secure and sweet,
  By angel footsteps trod;
Where thou our Guardian true shalt be,
Spirit of gentle Piety!
  To keep us close to God.

5 But most of all, be ever near,
Spirit of God's most holy Fear,
  In our heart's inmost shrine:
Our souls with loving reverence fill,
To worship his most holy Will
  All-righteous and divine.

6. So, dearest Lord, through peace or strife,
  Lead us to everlasting life,
    Where only rest may be.
  What matter where our lot is cast,
  If only it may end at last
    In Paradise with thee!

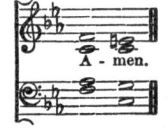

A - men.

SACRAMENTS AND OTHER RITES

343

AFFECTION. (L. M.)
In moderate time ♩ = 76.

'*Greenwood's Psalmody*,' *Halifax, 1888.*

NOTE.—*This hymn may also be sung to* HERR JESU CHRIST (*No.* 173).

C. *Wesley,* 1707-88.

O THOU who camest from above,
  The pure celestial fire to impart,
Kindle a flame of sacred love
  On the mean altar of my heart.

2 There let it for thy glory burn
    With inextinguishable blaze,
  And trembling to its source return
    In humble prayer, and fervent praise.

3 Jesus, confirm my heart's desire
    To work, and speak, and think for thee;
  Still let me guard the holy fire,
    And still stir up thy gift in me.

4 Ready for all thy perfect will,
    My acts of faith and love repeat,
  Till death thy endless mercies seal,
    And make my sacrifice complete.

A - men.

CONFIRMATION

344

HORSHAM. (77.77.)
Slow ♩ = 92 (𝅗𝅥 = 46).

English Traditional Melody.

Mrs. M. F. Maude, 1820–1913.

1 THINE for ever! God of love,
   Hear us from thy throne above;
   Thine for ever may we be
   Here and in eternity.

2 Thine for ever! O, how blest
   They who find in thee their rest!
   Saviour, Guardian, heavenly Friend,
   O defend us to the end.

3 Thine for ever! Lord of life,
   Shield us through our earthly strife;
   Thou the Life, the Truth, the Way,
   Guide us to the realms of day.

4* Thine for ever! Shepherd, keep
   These thy frail and trembling sheep;
   Safe alone beneath thy care,
   Let us all thy goodness share.

5. Thine for ever! thou our Guide,
   All our wants by thee supplied,
   All our sins by thee forgiven,
   Led by thee from earth to heaven.

A - men.

The following are also suitable:

152 Come down, O Love divine.
153 Come, Holy Ghost, our souls inspire.
154 Come, O Creator Spirit, come.
155 Come, thou holy Paraclete
157 Our blest Redeemer, ere he breathed.
384 Eternal Ruler.
389 Fight the good fight with all thy might.

429 'Lift up your hearts!'
438 Love of the Father, love of God the Son.
439 My faith looks up to thee.
479 Soldiers of Christ, arise.
480 Soldiers, who are Christ's below.
518 Ye servants of the Lord.

SACRAMENTS AND OTHER RITES

345

DANK SEI GOTT IN DER HÖHE. (7 6. 7 6. D.)

Very slow and dignified ♩ = 46.

Melody in J. S. BACH'S 'Vierstimmige Choralgesänge' (1769) (*founded on* GESIUS' '*Geduld die soll'n wir haben*').

MARRIAGE
J. Ellerton, 1826-93.

O FATHER all creating,
  Whose wisdom, love, and power
First bound two lives together
  In Eden's primal hour,
To-day to these thy children
  Thine earliest gifts renew,—
A home by thee made happy,
  A love by thee kept true.

2 O Saviour, Guest most bounteous
  Of old in Galilee,
Vouchsafe to-day thy presence
  With these who call on thee;
Their store of earthly gladness
  Transform to heavenly wine,
And teach them, in the tasting,
  To know the gift is thine.

3 O Spirit of the Father,
  Breathe on them from above,
So mighty in thy pureness,
  So tender in thy love;
That guarded by thy presence,
  From sin and strife kept free,
Their lives may own thy guidance,
  Their hearts be ruled by thee.

4. Except thou build it, Father,
  The house is built in vain;
Except thou, Saviour, bless it,
  The joy will turn to pain;
But nought can break the marriage
  Of hearts in thee made one,
And love thy Spirit hallows
  Is endless love begun.

A-men.

MARRIAGE

346

WELWYN. (11 10. 11 10.)
Moderately slow ♩ = 96.

A. SCOTT-GATTY.

Mrs. Dorothy Frances Gurney, 1858-1932.

O PERFECT Love, all human thought transcending,
   Lowly we kneel in prayer before thy throne,
That theirs may be the love which knows no ending
   Whom thou for evermore dost join in one.

2 O perfect Life, be thou their full assurance
   Of tender charity and steadfast faith,
Of patient hope, and quiet brave endurance,
   With childlike trust that fears nor pain nor death.

3. Grant them the joy which brightens earthly sorrow,
   Grant them the peace which calms all earthly strife;
And to life's day the glorious unknown morrow
   That dawns upon eternal love and life.

A - men.

SACRAMENTS AND OTHER RITES

347

KENT. (L.M.)
In moderate time ♩ = 80.
J. F. LAMPE, 1703-51.

NOTE —*This hymn may also be sung to* DAS WALT' GOTT VATER (*No.* 36).

Bishop Mandell Creighton, 1843-1901.

O THOU who gavest power to love
    That we might fix our hearts on thee,
Preparing us for joys above
    By that which here on earth we see:

2 Thy Spirit trains our souls to know
    The growing purpose of thy will,
And gives to love the power to show
    That purpose growing larger still;

3 *Larger, as love to reverent eyes
    Makes manifest another soul,
And shows to life a richer prize,
    A clearer course, a noble goal.

4 Lord, grant thy servants who implore
    Thy blessing on the hearts they blend,
That from that union evermore
    New joys may blossom to the end.

5 Make what is best to each combine
    To purge all earthly dross away,
To strengthen, purify, refine,
    To beautify each coming day.

6 So may they hand in hand advance
    Along life's path from troubles free;
Brave to meet adverse circumstance
    Because their love points up to thee.

A - men.

MARRIAGE

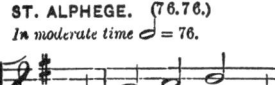

348

ST. ALPHEGE. (76.76.)
In moderate time ♩ = 76.

H. J. GAUNTLETT, 1805–76.

J. Keble, 1792–1866.

THE voice that breathed o'er Eden,
  That earliest wedding day,
The primal marriage blessing,
  It hath not passed away:

2 Still in the pure espousal
  Of Christian man and maid
The Holy Three are with us,
  The threefold grace is said,

3 For dower of blessèd children,
  For love and faith's sweet sake,
For high mysterious union
  Which naught on earth may break.

4* Be present, awful Father,
  To give away this bride,
As Eve thou gav'st to Adam
  Out of his own pierced side;

5* Be present, Son of Mary,
  To join their loving hands,
As thou didst bind two natures
  In thine eternal bands;

6* Be present, holiest Spirit,
  To bless them as they kneel,
As thou for Christ, the Bridegroom,
  The heavenly Spouse dost seal.

7 O spread thy pure wing o'er them,
  Let no ill power find place,
When onward to thine altar
  The hallowed path they trace,

8. To cast their crowns before thee
  In perfect sacrifice,
Till to the home of gladness
  With Christ's own Bride they rise.

A - men.

The following also are suitable:

385 Father, hear the prayer we offer.
387 Father of heaven, whose love profound.
396 Happy are they, they that love God.
426 Lead us, heavenly Father, lead us.
437 Love divine, all loves excelling.

450 O God, our help in ages past.
453 O Holy Spirit, Lord of grace.
454 O King enthroned on high.
502 Through all the changing scenes of life.

SACRAMENTS AND OTHER RITES

349

DOLGELLY. (66.66.88.)
In moderate time ♩ = 72.
Welsh Hymn Melody.

NOTE.—*This hymn may also be sung to* LOVELY (*No.* 303).

THE SICK

Troparia: Greek Office of Anointing. *Tr. J. B.*

Ταχὺς εἰς ἀντίληψιν, μόνος ὑπάρχων Χριστέ.

THOU, Lord, hast power to heal,
And thou wilt quickly aid,
For thou dost deeply feel
The stripes upon us laid:
Thou who wast wounded by the rod
Uplifted in the hand of God.

2 Send speedy help, we pray,
To *him* who ailing lies,
That from *his* couch *he* may
With thankful heart arise;
Through prayers which all availing find
Thine ear, O Lover of mankind.

3. O blinded are our eyes,
And all are held in night;
But like the blind who cries,
We cry to thee for light;
In penitence, O Christ, we pray,
Give us the radiant light of day.

A - men.

THE SICK—THE DEPARTED
350

AD PERENNIS VITAE FONTEM. (8 7. 8 7. 8 7.)
In free rhythm ♩ = 80. To be sung in unison.

Source unknown (said to be 'from the Tours Breviary').

Note.—*This hymn may also be sung to* Bryntirion (*No.* 248).

THE DEPARTED

Verses 2 and 3 at Holy Communion only. 13*th cent. Tr. R. F. Littledale.*
De profundis exclamantes.

CHRIST, enthroned in highest heaven,
  Hear us crying from the deep,
For the faithful ones departed,
  For the souls of all that sleep;
As thy kneeling Church entreateth,
  Hearken, Shepherd of the sheep.

2 * King of Glory, hear our voices,
  Grant thy faithful rest, we pray;
We have sinned, and may not bide it,
  If thou mark our steps astray,
Yet we plead that saving Victim,
  Which for them we bring to-day.

3 * That which thou thyself hast offered
  To thy Father, offer we;
Let it win for them a blessing,
  Bless them, Jesu, set them free:
They are thine, they wait in patience,
  Merciful and gracious be.

4 They are thine, O take them quickly,
  Thou their Hope, O raise them high;
Ever hoping, ever trusting,
  Unto thee they strive and cry;
Day and night, both morn and even,
  Be, O Christ, their Guardian nigh.

5 * Let thy plenteous loving-kindness
  On them, as we pray, be poured;
Let them through thy boundless mercy,
  From all evil be restored;
Hearken to the gentle pleading
  Of thy Mother, gracious Lord.

6 * When, O kind and radiant Jesu,
  Kneels the Queen thy throne before,
Let the court of Saints attending,
  Mercy for the dead implore;
Hearken, loving Friend of sinners,
  Whom the Cross exalted bore.

7. Hear and answer prayers devoutest,
  Break, O Lord, each binding chain,
Dash the gates of death asunder,
  Quell the devil and his train;
Bring the souls which thou hast ransomed
  Evermore in joy to reign.

Harmony.
A . . men.
Org.

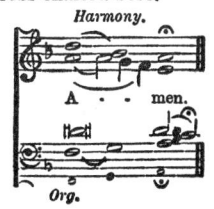

SACRAMENTS AND OTHER RITES

351

Sequence.   Thomas of Celano, 13th cent.
Tr. W. J. Ironst.
Mode i.   Dies irae, dies illa.   arr. J. H. A.

1 Day of wrath and doom impending, David's word with Sibyl's blending!
7 What shall I, frail man, be pleading? Who for me be interceding,
13 Through the sinful woman shriven, Through the dying thief forgiven,

Heaven and earth in ashes ending! 2 O, what fear man's bosom rendeth,
When the just are mercy needing? 8 King of majesty tremendous,
Thou to me a hope hast given. 14 Worthless are my prayers and sighing,

When from heav'n the Judge descendeth, On whose sentence all dependeth!
Who dost free salvation send us, Fount of pity then befriend us!
Yet, good Lord, in grace complying, Rescue me from fires undying.

THE DEPARTED

351 (*continued*)

3 Wondrous sound the trumpet fling-eth, Through earth's sepulchres it ring-eth,
9 Think, kind Je-su!— my sal-va-tion Caused thy wondrous In-car-na-tion;
15 With thy sheep a place pro-vide me, From the goats a-far di-vide me,

All be-fore the throne it bringeth. 4 Death is struck, and na-ture quak-ing,
Leave me not to re-pro-ba-tion. 10 Faint & wea-ry thou hast sought me,
To thy right hand do thou guide me. 16 When the wick-ed are con-found-ed,

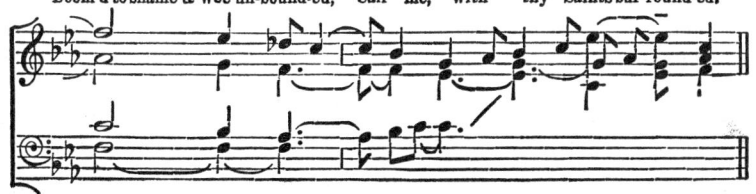

All cre-a-tion is a-wak-ing, To its Judge an an-swer mak-ing.
On the Cross of suff'ring bought me; Shall such grace be vain-ly brought me?
Doom'd to shame & woe un-bound-ed, Call me, with thy Saints sur-round-ed.

SACRAMENTS AND OTHER RITES

351 (continued)

5 Lo! the book exactly worded,
Wherein all hath been recorded;
11 Righteous Judge! for sin's pollution, Grant thy gift of absolution,
17 Low I kneel, with heart submission; See, like ashes my contrition!

Thence shall judgement be awarded.
Ere that day of retribution.
Help me in my last condition! (*to v. 18 opposite*).
6 When the Judge his seat attaineth, 12 Guilty, now I pour my moaning,

And each hidden deed arraigneth, Nothing unaveng'd remaineth.
All my shame with anguish owning; Spare, O God, thy suppliant groaning!

THE DEPARTED

351 (*continued*)

18. Ah! that day of tears and mourning! From the dust of earth re-turn-ing, Man for judge-ment must pre-pare him: Spare, O God, in mer - cy spare him!

SACRAMENTS AND OTHER RITES

351 (continued)

Lord, all-pity-ing, Je-su blest, Grant them thine e-ter-nal rest.

352

OLD 124TH. (10. 10. 10. 10. 10.)
Slow 𝅗𝅥 = 66.

English form of melody in Genevan Psalter, 1551.

THE DEPARTED

352 (*continued*)

NOTE.—*An alternative setting of this tune, with the melody in the tenor will be found at Hymn* 114.

Prudentius, b. 348.　*Tr. P. D*
Deus ignee fons animarum.

FATHER of spirits, whose divine control
　Doth bind the soul and body into one,
　Thou wilt restore this body now undone;
For once it was the mansion of a soul,
　Where dwelt the glowing wisdom of thy Son.

2 Thou, Maker of the body, dost ordain
　　That this thine image, moulded by thy will,
　　Our every hope in glory shall fulfil;
　So, till the body thou dost build again,
　　Thou wilt preserve the spirit freed from ill.

3 In that blest region shall this spirit dwell
　　Where flowers undying bloom on every side:
　　For, lo, we trust thy word, O Crucified,
　When in thy triumph over death and hell,
　　The thief forgiven took thee for his guide.

4. Our *brother* goeth by the shining way,
　　That ever to the faithful open lies:
　　Lord, train thy servant now in Paradise,
　And bless *him* in *his* fatherland, we pray,
　　Till thou shalt bid *his* body to arise.

A - men.

SACRAMENTS AND OTHER RITES

353

JESU MEINES GLAUBENS ZIER. (78. 87. 87. 87.)

Very slow and solemn ♩ = 46.

Melody from FREYLINGHAUSEN'S *Gesangbuch* (1784).
Harmony from J. S. BACH, 1685–1750.

NOTE.—*A lower setting of this tune will be found at Hymn 118.*

THE DEPARTED

Part 1. For a Child. *J. W. Meinhold*, 1797–1851.
Tr. C. Winkworth and others.

Guter Hirt, du haft geftillt.

GENTLE Shepherd, thou hast stilled
   Now thy little lamb's long weeping,
   In thy loving arms 'tis sleeping—
Ah! how peaceful, pure and mild!
Now no sigh of helpless anguish
   Heaves that little bosom more;
Ne'er again in pain to languish,
   He has reached the happy shore.

2. In this world of pain and care,
   Lord, thou wouldst no longer leave *him*;
   Lovingly thou dost receive *him*
To thy meadows bright and fair.
Ah, Lord Jesu, bring us thither
   Where *he* dwells with thee above;
Where thy Saints rejoice together
   Reunite us to our love.

Part 2. For an Adult. *P. D.*

God, we thank thee; not in vain
   Lived our friend on thee believing;
   Not for *him* can we be grieving:
Ours the loss, but *his* the gain.
Ours the vanity of sorrow,
   His the vision from the height;
His to-day, and ours to-morrow,
   Change and awe and love and light.

2. What thou doest, Lord, is good:
   Though *his* body now is sleeping,
   Lives *his* spirit in thy keeping,
Pain and sorrow understood.
Grant *him* rest among the living,
   Bring *him* to thy vision clear,
All *his* sin in love forgiving
   When as Judge thou dost appear.

A - men.

SACRAMENTS AND OTHER RITES

WIGTON. (C.M.)
Moderately slow ♩ = 63

354

Scottish Psalter, 1635.

I. Watts, 1674-1748.

HEAR what the voice from heaven proclaims
　For all the pious dead;
Sweet is the savour of their names,
　And soft their sleeping bed.

2 They die in Jesus and are blest;
　　How kind their slumbers are;
From sufferings and from sins released,
　　And freed from every snare.

3. Far from this world of toil and strife,
　　They're present with the Lord;
The labours of their mortal life
　　End in a large reward.

A - men.

THE DEPARTED

HAMBRIDGE. (7 6. 7 6.)
In moderate time ♩ = 120.

355

English Traditional Melody.

For a young child.

R. F. *Littledale*, 1833–90.

IN Paradise reposing,
  By life's eternal well,
The tender lambs of Jesus
  In greenest pastures dwell.

2 There palms and tiny crownlets
  Aglow with brightest gem,
Bedeck the baby martyrs
  Who died in Bethlehem.

3 With them the rose-wreathed army
  Of children undefiled,
Who passed through mortal torments
  For love of Christ the Child;

4 With them in peace unending,
  With them in joyous mirth,
Are all the stainless infants
  Which since have gone from earth.

5*The Angels, once their guardians,
  Their fellows now in grace,
With them, in love adoring,
  See God the Father's face.

6*The lullaby to hush them
  In that eternal rest,
Is sweet angelic singing,
  Their nurse God's Mother blest.

7. O Jesu, loving Shepherd,
  Who tenderly dost bear
Thy lambs in thine own bosom,
  Bring us to join them there.

A - men.

SACRAMENTS AND OTHER RITES

DUN ALUINN. (6 5. 6 5. D.)
In moderate time ♩ = 88.

356 *Adapted from an Irish Traditional Melody.*
Harmonized by MARTIN SHAW.

A-men.

NOTE.—*This hymn may also be sung to* CORPUS DOMINI (*Appendix, No.* 47).

At Holy Communion.   Yesu Bin Mariamu.   *Written in Swahili, and tr.* E. S. Palmer, 1857–1931.

JESU, Son of Mary,
  Fount of life alone,
Here we hail thee present
  On thine altar-throne.
Humbly we adore thee,
  Lord of endless might,
In the mystic symbols
  Veiled from earthly sight.

2 Think, O Lord, in mercy
  On the souls of those
Who, in faith gone from us,
  Now in death repose.
Here 'mid stress and conflict
  Toils can never cease;
There, the warfare ended,
  Bid them rest in peace.

3 Often were they wounded
  In the deadly strife;
Heal them, Good Physician,
  With the balm of life.
Every taint of evil,
  Frailty and decay,
Good and gracious Saviour,
  Cleanse and purge away.

4. Rest eternal grant them,
  After weary fight;
Shed on them the radiance
  Of thy heavenly light.
Lead them onward, upward,
  To the holy place,
Where thy saints made perfect
  Gaze upon thy face.

THE DEPARTED

SONG 18. (8 8 6. D.)
Slow ♩ = 80.

357

O. GIBBONS, 1583–1625.

NOTE.—*This hymn may also be sung to* ADVENT (*No.* 342).

H. D. Rawnsley, 1850–1920.

LORD Jesu, who at Lazarus' tomb
  To weeping friends from death's dark womb
Didst bring new joy to life,
Grant to the friends who stand forlorn
A vision of that larger morn
  Where peace has conquered strife.

2 May we behold across the bar
The dear immortals as they are,
  Empowered in act and will,
With purer eyes to see their King,
With fuller hearts his praise to sing,
  With strength to help us still;

3 Not fettered now by fleshly bond,
But tireless in the great beyond,
  And growing day by day.
Can we not make their gladness ours,
And share their thoughts, their added powers,
  And follow as we pray?

4. O Holy Ghost, the strength and guide
Of those who to this earth have died,
  But live more near to God,
Give us thy grace to follow on,
Till we with them the crown have won
  Who duty's paths have trod.

A - men.

SACRAMENTS AND OTHER RITES

PRESSBURG (NICHT SO TRAURIG). (7 7. 7 7. 7 7.)
Slow and solemn ♩ = 50.

358

FREYLINGHAUSEN, '*Neues Geistreiches Gesangbuch,*' 1714, simplified form of melody.

NOTE.—*This hymn may also be sung to* REDHEAD *No.* 76 (*No.* 477).

G. Moultrie †, 1829-85.

NOW the labourer's toils are o'er,
    Fought the battle, won the crown:
On life's rough and barren shore
    Thou hast laid thy burden down:
Grant him, Lord, eternal rest,
With the spirits of the blest.

2 Angels bear thee to the land
    Where the towers of Sion rise;
Safely lead thee by the hand
    To the fields of Paradise:

3 White-robed, at the golden gate
    Of the new Jerusalem,
May the host of Martyrs wait;
    Give thee part and lot with them:

4 Friends and dear ones gone before
    To the land of endless peace,
Meet thee on that further shore
    Where all tears and weeping cease:

5 * Rest in peace: the gates of hell
    Touch thee not, till he shall come
For the souls he loves so well,—
    Dear Lord of the heavenly home:

6 *. Earth to earth, and dust to dust,
    Clay we give to kindred clay,
In the sure and certain trust
    Of the Resurrection day:

A - men.

THE DEPARTED

SOUTH CERNEY. (8 8. 8 8. 8 8.) **359**
Moderately slow ♩ = 66.   W. H. HADOW.

NOTE.—*This Hymn may also be sung to* LODSWORTH (*No.* 275).

R. F. Littledale ‡, 1833–90.

O LORD, to whom the spirits live
  Of all the faithful passed away,
Upon their path that brightness give
  Which shineth to the perfect day:
O Light eternal, Jesu blest,
Shine on them all, and grant them rest.

2 In thy green, pleasant pastures feed
    The sheep which thou hast summoned hence;
  And by the still, cool waters lead
    Thy flock in loving providence:

3 * How long, O holy Lord, how long
    Must we and they expectant wait
  To hear the gladsome bridal song,
    To see thee in thy royal state?

4 O hearken, Saviour, to their cry,
    O rend the heavens and come down,
  Make up thy jewels speedily,
    And set them in thy golden crown:

5. Direct us with thine arm of might,
    And bring us perfected with them
  To dwell within thy city bright,
    The heavenly Jerusalem:

499

SACRAMENTS AND OTHER RITES

360

CHRISTUS DER IST MEIN LEBEN. (7 6. 7 6.)

Melody by
MELCHIOR VULPIUS, 1560–1616.

Slow ♩ = 50.

NOTE.—J. S. BACH'S *harmonization of this tune (in a higher key) will be found at Hymn 232.*

St. John Damascene, c. 750. Tr. A. R.

Ποία τοῦ βίου τρυφὴ διαμένει λύπης ἀμέτοχος.

WHAT sweet of life endureth
    Unmixed with bitter pain?
'Midst earthly change and chances
    What glory doth remain?

2 All is a feeble shadow,
    A dream that will not stay;
Death cometh in a moment,
    And taketh all away.

3 O Christ, a light transcendent
    Shines in thy countenance,
And none can tell the sweetness,
    The beauty of thy glance.

4. In this may thy poor servant
    His joy eternal find;
Thou calledst *him*, O rest *him*,
    Thou Lover of mankind!

A - men.

The following are also suitable :

134 Jesus lives ! thy terrors now (*to the first tune*).
251 O heavenly Jerusalem.
371 Brief life is here our portion.
373 Children of the heavenly King.
401 He wants not friends that hath thy love.
428 Let saints on earth in concert sing.
455 O let him whose sorrow.
498 There is a land of pure delight.
500 They whose course on earth is o'er.
744 Give rest, O Christ, to thy servant.

PART V
GENERAL HYMNS
361

LEOMINSTER. (D. S. M.)
In moderate time ♩ = 92.

G. W. MARTIN, 1828–81.

NOTE.—*This hymn may also be sung to* OLD 25TH (*No.* 149).

H. *Bonar* †, 1808–89.

A FEW more years shall roll,
 A few more seasons come,
And we shall be with those that rest
 In peace beyond the tomb.
Then, O my Lord, prepare
 My soul for that great day;
O wash me in thy precious Blood,
 And take my sins away.

2 A few more suns shall set
  O'er these dark hills of time,
And we shall be where suns are not,
 A far serener clime.
Then, O my Lord, prepare
 My soul for that blest day;
O wash me in thy precious Blood,
 And take my sins away.

3 A few more storms shall beat
  On this wild rocky shore,
And we shall be where tempests cease,
 And surges swell no more.
Then, O my Lord, prepare
 My soul for that calm day;
O wash me in thy precious Blood,
 And take my sins away.

4 A few more struggles here,
  A few more partings o'er,
A few more toils, a few more tears,
 And we shall weep no more.
Then, O my Lord, prepare
 My soul for that blest day;
O wash me in thy precious Blood,
 And take my sins away.

5. 'Tis but a little while
  And he shall come again,
Who died that we might live, who lives
 That we with him may reign.
Then, O my Lord, prepare
 My soul for that glad day;
O wash me in thy precious Blood,
 And take my sins away.

GENERAL HYMNS

362

EIN' FESTE BURG. (87. 87. 66. 667.)

Very slow and solemn ♩ = 40.

Present form of melody by
M. LUTHER, 1483-1546.

GENERAL HYMNS

Martin Luther, 1483-1546. Tr. Thomas Carlyle.

Ein' feste Burg.

Unison. A SAFE stronghold our God is still,
A trusty shield and weapon;
He'll help us clear from all the ill
That hath us now o'ertaken.
   The ancient prince of hell
   Hath risen with purpose fell;
   Strong mail of craft and power
   He weareth in this hour;
On earth is not his fellow.

2 With force of arms we nothing can,
   Full soon were we down-ridden;
But for us fights the proper Man,
   Whom God himself hath bidden.
   Ask ye, Who is this same?
   Christ Jesus is his name,
   The Lord Sabaoth's Son;
   He, and no other one,
Shall conquer in the battle.

3 * And were this world all devils o'er
   And watching to devour us,
We lay it not to heart so sore;
   Not they can overpower us.
   And let the prince of ill
   Look grim as e'er he will,
   He harms us not a whit;
   For why?—his doom is writ;
A word shall quickly slay him.

Unison. 4. God's word, for all their craft and force,
   One moment will not linger,
But, spite of hell, shall have its course;
   'Tis written by his finger.
   And though they take our life,
   Goods, honour, children, wife,
   Yet is their profit small;
   These things shall vanish all,
The city of God remaineth.

A - men.

GENERAL HYMNS

363

EVENTIDE. (10 10. 10 10.)
Slow ♩ = 66.

W. H. Monk, 1823–89.

NOTE.—*The tune* OLD 124TH (*No.* 114) *is equally suitable to this hymn, and can be sung to it by repeating the words of the last line of each verse.*

H. F. Lyte, 1793–1847.

ABIDE with me; fast falls the eventide;
    The darkness deepens; Lord, with me abide!
When other helpers fail, and comforts flee,
Help of the helpless, O abide with me.

2 Swift to its close ebbs out life's little day;
Earth's joys grow dim, its glories pass away;
Change and decay in all around I see;
O thou who changest not, abide with me.

3 I need thy presence every passing hour;
What but thy grace can foil the tempter's power?
Who like thyself my guide and stay can be?
Through cloud and sunshine, O abide with me.

4 I fear no foe with thee at hand to bless;
Ills have no weight, and tears no bitterness.
Where is death's sting? where, grave, thy victory?
I triumph still, if thou abide with me.

5 Hold thou thy Cross before my closing eyes;
Shine through the gloom, and point me to the skies;
Heaven's morning breaks, and earth's vain shadows flee;
In life, in death, O Lord, abide with me!

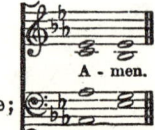

A - men.

GENERAL HYMNS

364

MILES LANE. (C. M.)
In moderate time ♩ = 92.

W. SHRUBSOLE, 1760-1806
(*Modern form of second line*).

In strict time.

crown him, crown him, crown him, crown him Lord of all.

E. Perronet, 1721-92; *and others.*

ALL hail the power of Jesu's name;
Let Angels prostrate fall;
Bring forth the royal diadem
To crown him Lord of all.

2*Crown him, ye morning stars of light,
Who fixed this floating ball;
Now hail the Strength of Israel's might,
And crown him Lord of all.

    3 Crown him, ye Martyrs of your God,
      Who from his altar call;
    Praise him whose way of pain ye trod,
      And crown him Lord of all.

    4 * Ye seed of Israel's chosen race,
      Ye ransomed of the fall,
    Hail him who saves you by his grace,
      And crown him Lord of all.

Unison.   5 * Hail him, ye heirs of David's line,
      Whom David Lord did call;
    The God Incarnate, Man Divine,
      And crown him Lord of all.

    6 Sinners, whose love can ne'er forget
      The wormwood and the gall,
    Go spread your trophies at his feet,
      And crown him Lord of all.

Unison.   7. Let every tribe and every tongue
      To him their hearts enthral,
    Lift high the universal song,
      And crown him Lord of all.

A - men.

GENERAL HYMNS

365

OLD HUNDREDTH. (L. M.)
Slow and dignified ♩ = 66 (𝅗𝅥 = 33).

Melody from Genevan Psalter, 1551
(*English form of final line*).

Ps. 100.

ALL people that on earth do dwell,
   Sing to the Lord with cheerful voice;
Him serve with fear, his praise forth tell,
   Come ye before him, and rejoice.

2 The Lord, ye know, is God indeed,
   Without our aid he did us make;
We are his folk, he doth us feed,
   And for his sheep he doth us take.

Unison.   W. Kethe, *Daye's Psalter* (1560-1).

3 O enter then his gates with praise,
   Approach with joy his courts unto;
Praise, laud, and bless his name always,
   For it is seemly so to do.

4 For why? the Lord our God is good:
   His mercy is for ever sure;
His truth at all times firmly stood,
   And shall from age to age endure.

Unison. 5. To Father, Son, and Holy Ghost,
   The God whom heaven and earth adore,
From men and from the angel-host
   Be praise and glory evermore. Amen.

A - men.

ALTERNATIVE VERSION

PEOPLE'S PART.

CHOIR OR ORGAN.

Harmonized by J. DOWLAND *in*
Ravenscroft's Psalter, 1621.

GENERAL HYMNS

365 (*continued*)

A SIMPLER ALTERNATIVE VERSION

PEOPLE'S PART.

CHOIR OR ORGAN.

Harmony by
J. DOWLAND, 1563–1626.

NOTE.—*These alternative versions may be used in connexion with the first for one or more verses, the people singing the melody as usual.*

GENERAL HYMNS

366

CUTTLE MILLS. (8 5. 8 8.)
In moderate time ♩ = 80.

W. GRIFFITH.

NOTE.—*Another tune for this hymn will be found in the Appendix (No. 18).*

J. M. Neale, 1818-66.

ART thou weary, art thou languid,
　Art thou sore distrest?
'Come to me,' saith One, 'and coming
　　Be at rest!'

2 Hath he marks to lead me to him,
　If he be my Guide?
'In his feet and hands are wound-prints,
　　And his side.'

3 Is there diadem as Monarch
　That his brow adorns?
'Yea, a crown, in very surety,
　　But of thorns.'

4 If I find him, if I follow,
　What his guerdon here?
'Many a sorrow, many a labour,
　　Many a tear.'

Unison. 5 If I still hold closely to him,
　What hath he at last?
'Sorrow vanquished, labour ended,
　　Jordan past.'

6 If I ask him to receive me,
　Will he say me nay?
'Not till earth, and not till heaven
　　Pass away.'

Unison. 7. Finding, following, keeping, struggling,
　Is he sure to bless?
'Angels, Martyrs, Prophets, Virgins,
　　Answer, Yes!'

A - men

GENERAL HYMNS

MARTYRDOM. (C.M.)
Very slow ♩ = 69.

367

Smith's '*Sacred Music*,' 1825.
Possibly an Old Scottish Melody.

Ps. 42.

N. Tate and N. Brady, *New Version* (1696).

AS pants the hart for cooling streams
    When heated in the chase,
So longs my soul, O God, for thee,
    And thy refreshing grace.

2 For thee, my God, the living God,
    My thirsty soul doth pine:
O when shall I behold thy face,
    Thou Majesty Divine!

3 Why restless, why cast down, my soul?
    Hope still, and thou shalt sing
The praise of him who is thy God,
    Thy health's eternal spring.

4. To Father, Son, and Holy Ghost,
    The God whom we adore,
Be glory, as it was, is now,
    And shall be evermore. **Amen.**

A - men.

GENERAL HYMNS

368

KING'S WESTON. (6 5. 6 5. D.)
With vigour ♩ = 80. Unison.

R. VAUGHAN WILLIAMS.

Con 8va.

[*Copyright, 1925, by R. Vaughan Williams.*]
NOTE.—*This hymn may also be sung to* LAUS TIBI CHRISTE (*No. 534*).

v. 5, *l.* 1 Name him, bro - thers, name him, With

l. 7 and 8 Ev - er to be wor - shipped, Trust - ed, and a - dored.
(*The organ part must conform.*)

GENERAL HYMNS

Caroline M. Noel, 1817-77.

AT the name of Jesus
   Every knee shall bow,
Every tongue confess him
   King of glory now;
'Tis the Father's pleasure
   We should call him Lord,
Who from the beginning
   Was the mighty word.

2*At his voice creation
   Sprang at once to sight,
All the Angel faces,
   All the hosts of light,
Thrones and dominations,
   Stars upon their way,
All the heavenly orders,
   In their great array.

3 Humbled for a season,
   To receive a name
From the lips of sinners
   Unto whom he came,
Faithfully he bore it
   Spotless to the last,
Brought it back victorious
   When from death he passed:

4 Bore it up triumphant
   With its human light,
Through all ranks of creatures,
   To the central height,
To the throne of Godhead,
   To the Father's breast;
Filled it with the glory
   Of that perfect rest.

5 Name him, brothers, name him,
   With love as strong as death,
But with awe and wonder,
   And with bated breath;
He is God the Saviour,
   He is Christ the Lord,
Ever to be worshipped,
   Trusted, and adored.

6* In your hearts enthrone him;
   There let him subdue
All that is not holy,
   All that is not true:
Crown him as your captain
   In temptation's hour;
Let his will enfold you
   In its light and power.

7.* Brothers, this Lord Jesus
   Shall return again,
With his Father's glory,
   With his Angel train;
For all wreaths of empire
   Meet upon his brow,
And our hearts confess him
   King of glory now.

A - men.

GENERAL HYMNS

ABRIDGE. (C. M.)
In moderate time ♩ = 96.

369

I. SMITH, *d. c.* 1800.

I. Williams, 1802–65.

BE thou my Guardian and my Guide,
  And hear me when I call;
Let not my slippery footsteps slide,
  And hold me lest I fall.

2 The world, the flesh, and Satan dwell
  Around the path I tread;
O, save me from the snares of hell,
  Thou Quickener of the dead.

3 And if I tempted am to sin,
  And outward things are strong,
Do thou, O Lord, keep watch within,
  And save my soul from wrong.

4. Still let me ever watch and pray,
  And feel that I am frail;
That if the tempter cross my way,
  Yet he may not prevail.

A - men.

GENERAL HYMNS

FRANCONIA. (S. M.)
In moderate time ♩ = 72.

370

W. H. HAVERGAL, 1798–1870
(*founded on a melody by* J. B. KÖNIG).

NOTE.—*This hymn may also be sung to* SELMA (*No.* 290).

J. Keble, 1792–1866.

BLEST are the pure in heart,
   For they shall see our God,
The secret of the Lord is theirs,
   Their soul is Christ's abode.

2   The Lord, who left the heavens
     Our life and peace to bring,
  To dwell in lowliness with men,
     Their Pattern and their King;

3   Still to the lowly soul
     He doth himself impart,
  And for his dwelling and his throne
     Chooseth the pure in heart.

4.   Lord, we thy presence seek;
     May ours this blessing be;
  Give us a pure and lowly heart
     A temple meet for thee.

A - men.

GENERAL HYMNS
371

THULE. (76. 76.)
In moderate time ♩ = 60.

German Volkslied.
Harmonized by G. R. WOODWARD.

NOTE.—*This hymn may also be sung to* DEVONSHIRE (*No.* 294) *or to* ST. ALPHEGE (*No.* 348).

Part of Hora novissima (495).

Hic breve vivitur.

Bernard of Cluny, 12th cent.
Tr. J. M. Neale.

BRIEF life is here our portion,
　Brief sorrow, short-lived care;
The life that knows no ending,
　The tearless life, is there.

2 O happy retribution,
　Short toil, eternal rest,
For mortals and for sinners
　A mansion with the blest!

3 And martyrdom hath roses
　Upon that heavenly ground,
And white and virgin lilies
　For virgin-souls abound.

4 There grief is turned to pleasure,
　Such pleasure as below
No human voice can utter,
　No human heart can know.

Unison.
5 And now we fight the battle,
　But then shall wear the crown
Of full and everlasting
　And passionless renown.

6 And now we watch and struggle,
　And now we live in hope,
And Sion in her anguish
　With Babylon must cope.

7 But he whom now we trust in
　Shall then be seen and known,
And they that know and see him
　Shall have him for their own.

8 The morning shall awaken,
　The shadows shall decay,
And each true-hearted servant
　Shall shine as doth the day.

Unison. 9. Then all the halls of Sion
　For ay shall be complete,
And, in the Land of Beauty,
　All things of beauty meet.

A - men.

GENERAL HYMNS

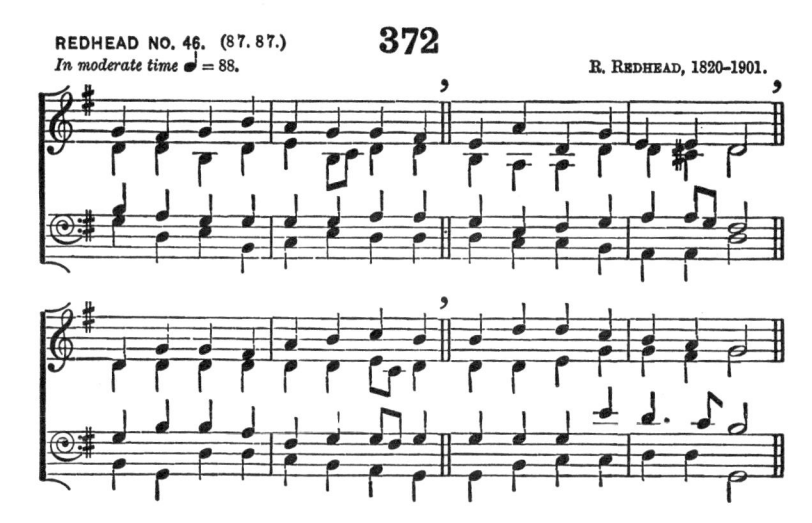

REDHEAD NO. 46. (87. 87.)   **372**
In moderate time ♩ = 88.
R. REDHEAD, 1820-1901.

Bishop R. Mant, 1776-1848.

BRIGHT the vision that delighted
  Once the sight of Judah's seer;
Sweet the countless tongues united
  To entrance the prophet's ear.

2 Round the Lord in glory seated
  Cherubim and Seraphim
Filled his temple, and repeated
  Each to each the alternate hymn:

Unison.   3 'Lord, thy glory fills the heaven;
    Earth is with its fullness stored;
  Unto thee be glory given,
    Holy, Holy, Holy, Lord.'

4 Heaven is still with glory ringing,
  Earth takes up the Angels' cry,
'Holy, Holy, Holy,' singing,
  'Lord of hosts, the Lord most high.'

5 With his seraph train before him,
  With his holy Church below,
Thus conspire we to adore him,
  Bid we thus our anthem flow:

Unison.   6 'Lord, thy glory fills the heaven;
    Earth is with its fullness stored;
  Unto thee be glory given,
    Holy, Holy, Holy, Lord.'

A - men.

GENERAL HYMNS
373

MELLING. (77.77.)
With vigour ♩ = 96.

*From a New Set of Sacred Music
by* JOHN FAWCETT, *c.* 1822.
Harmonized by GEOFFREY SHAW.

NOTE.—*This hymn may also be sung to* GOTT SEI DANK (*No.* 552).

J. *Cennick*, 1718–55.

CHILDREN of the heavenly King,
As ye journey sweetly sing;
Sing your Saviour's worthy praise,
Glorious in his works and ways.

2 We are travelling home to God,
In the way the fathers trod;
They are happy now, and we
Soon their happiness shall see.

Unison. 3 Fear not, brethren; joyful stand
On the borders of your land:
Jesus Christ your Father's Son,
Bids you undismayed go on.

4. Lord, obediently we go,
Gladly leaving all below:
Only thou our Leader be
And we still will follow thee.

A - men.

GENERAL HYMNS

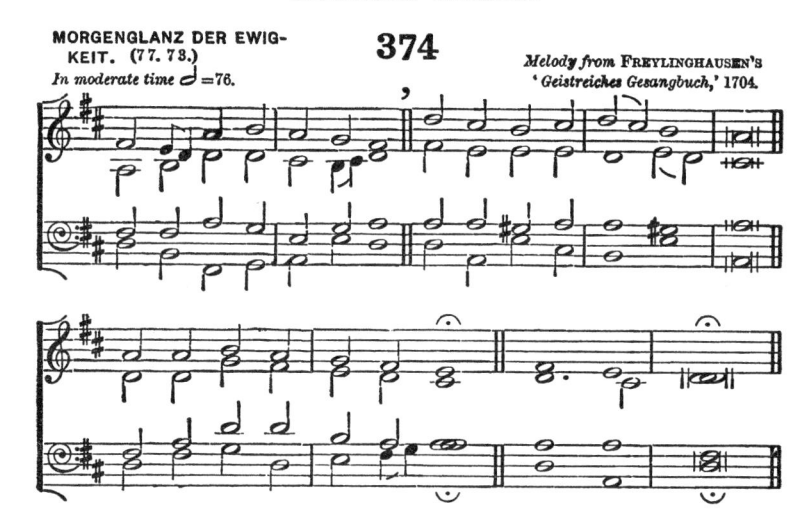

MORGENGLANZ DER EWIG-KEIT. (77. 78.)
In moderate time ♩=76.

374

Melody from FREYLINGHAUSEN'S
'*Geistreiches Gesangbuch*,' 1704.

Charlotte Elliott, 1789–1871.

'CHRISTIAN, seek not yet repose,'
  Hear thy guardian Angel say;
'Thou art in the midst of foes:
       Watch and pray!'

2 Principalities and powers,
  Mustering their unseen array,
Wait for thy unguarded hours:
       Watch and pray!

3 Gird thy heavenly armour on,
  Wear it ever, night and day;
Ambushed lies the evil one:
       Watch and pray!

4 Hear the victors who o'ercame;
  Still they mark each warrior's way;
All with one sweet voice exclaim:
       'Watch and pray!'

5 Hear, above all, hear thy Lord,
  Him thou lovest to obey;
Hide within thy heart his word:
       'Watch and pray!'

6. Watch, as if on that alone
  Hung the issue of the day;
Pray, that help may be sent down:
       Watch and pray!

A - men.

GENERAL HYMNS

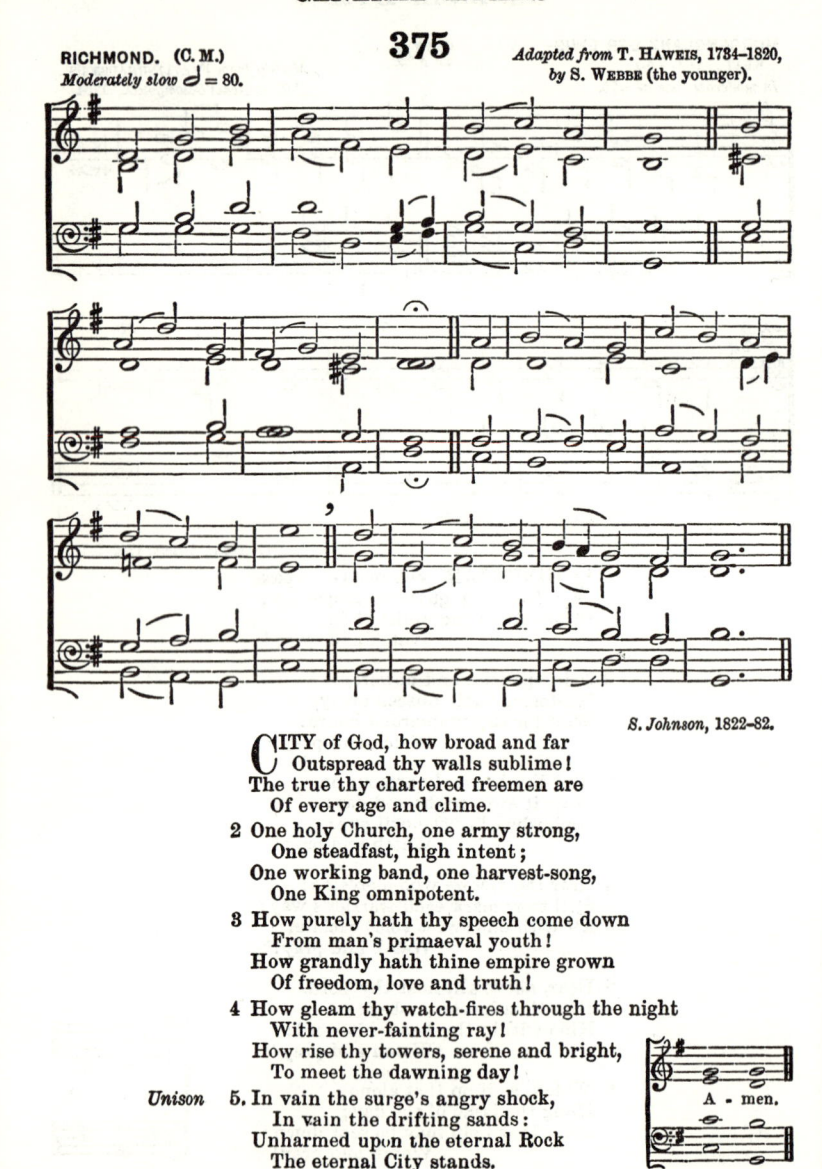

375

RICHMOND. (C.M.)
Moderately slow ♩ = 80.

Adapted from T. HAWEIS, 1734–1820,
by S. WEBBE (the younger).

S. Johnson, 1822–82.

CITY of God, how broad and far
  Outspread thy walls sublime!
The true thy chartered freemen are
  Of every age and clime.

2 One holy Church, one army strong,
  One steadfast, high intent;
One working band, one harvest-song,
  One King omnipotent.

3 How purely hath thy speech come down
  From man's primaeval youth!
How grandly hath thine empire grown
  Of freedom, love and truth!

4 How gleam thy watch-fires through the night
  With never-fainting ray!
How rise thy towers, serene and bright,
  To meet the dawning day!

Unison 5. In vain the surge's angry shock,
  In vain the drifting sands:
Unharmed upon the eternal Rock
  The eternal City stands.

A - men.

GENERAL HYMNS

376

CHEERFUL. (C. M.)
Moderately fast ♩ = 100.

MARTIN SHAW.

[Copyright, 1915, by J. Curwen & Sons, Ltd.]
NOTE.—*This hymn may also be sung to* RICHMOND (*No.* 375) *or to* NATIVITY, *Appendix, No.* 48.

I. Watts, 1674–1748.

COME, let us join our cheerful songs
With Angels round the throne;
Ten thousand thousand are their tongues,
But all their joys are one.

Unison. 2 'Worthy the Lamb that died,' they cry,
'To be exalted thus';
'Worthy the Lamb,' our lips reply,
'For he was slain for us.'

3 Jesus is worthy to receive
Honour and power divine;
And blessings more than we can give
Be, Lord, for ever thine.

Unison. 4. The whole creation join in one
To bless the sacred name
Of him that sits upon the throne,
And to adore the Lamb.

A - men.

GENERAL HYMNS

377

LOUEZ DIEU. (77.77.)
In moderate time ♩ = 100.

Melody of Psalm 136,
Genevan Psalter, 1562.

J. Newton, 1725–1807.

COME, my soul, thy suit prepare,
Jesus loves to answer prayer;
He himself has bid thee pray,
Therefore will not say thee nay.

2 Thou art coming to a King,
Large petitions with thee bring;
For his grace and power are such
None can ever ask too much.

3 With my burden I begin;
Lord, remove this load of sin;
Let thy Blood, for sinners spilt,
Set my conscience free from guilt.

4 Show me what I have to do,
Ev'ry hour my strength renew;
Let me live a life of faith,
Let me die thy people's death.

5. While I am a pilgrim here,
Let thy love my spirit cheer;
Be my Guide, my Guard, my Friend;
Lead me to my journey's end.

A - men.

GENERAL HYMNS

378

DAVID'S HARP. (8 8. 8 8. 8 8.)
Moderately slow ♩ = 63.

ROBERT KING in 'The Divine Companion,' 1709.

C. Wesley †, 1707-88.

COME, O thou Traveller unknown,
  Whom still I hold, but cannot see,
My company before is gone,
  And I am left alone with thee;
With thee all night I mean to stay,
And wrestle till the break of day.

2 I need not tell thee who I am,
  My misery or sin declare;
Thyself hast called me by my name;
  Look on thy hands, and read it there!
But who, I ask thee, who art thou?
Tell me thy name, and tell me now.

3 Yield to me now, for I am weak,
  But confident in self-despair;
Speak to my heart, in blessings speak,
  Be conquered by my instant prayer!
Speak, or thou never hence shalt move,
And tell me if thy name is Love.

4. 'Tis Love! 'tis Love! Thou diedst for me!
  I hear thy whisper in my heart!
The morning breaks, the shadows flee;
  Pure universal Love thou art;
To me, to all, thy mercies move;
Thy nature and thy name is Love.

A - men.

GENERAL HYMNS
379

RUSPER. (7 6. 7 6. D.)
Moderately slow ♩ = 80.

From an English Traditional Melody.

NOTE.—*This hymn may also be sung to* MEIRIONYDD (*No.* 473).

W. Chatterton Dix, 1837-98.

'COME unto me, ye weary,
   And I will give you rest.'
O blessèd voice of Jesus,
   Which comes to hearts opprest;
It tells of benediction,
   Of pardon, grace, and peace,
Of joy that hath no ending,
   Of love which cannot cease.

2 'Come unto me, ye wanderers,
   And I will give you light.'
O loving voice of Jesus,
   Which comes to cheer the night;
Our hearts were filled with sadness,
   And we had lost our way;
But morning brings us gladness,
   And songs the break of day.

3 'Come unto me, ye fainting,
   And I will give you life.'
O cheering voice of Jesus,
   Which comes to aid our strife;
The foe is stern and eager,
   The fight is fierce and long;
But thou hast made us mighty,
   And stronger than the strong.

4. 'And whosoever cometh,
   I will not cast him out.'
O patient love of Jesus,
   Which drives away our doubt;
Which calls us very sinners,
   Unworthy though we be
Of love so free and boundless,
   To come, dear Lord, to thee.

A - men.

GENERAL HYMNS

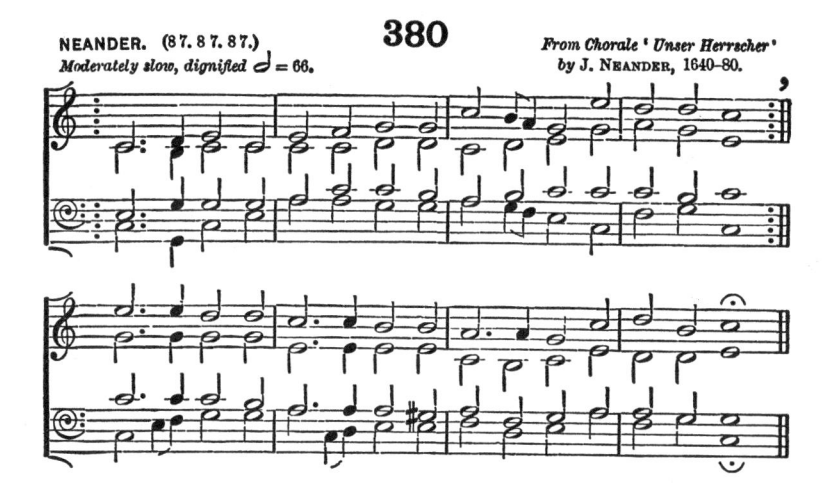

380

NEANDER. (8 7. 8 7. 8 7.)
Moderately slow, dignified 𝅗𝅥 = 66.

From Chorale ' Unser Herrscher '
by J. Neander, 1640-80.

J. Hupton, 1762–1849, and J. M. Neale.

COME, ye faithful, raise the anthem,
  Cleave the skies with shouts of praise;
Sing to him who found the ransom,
  Ancient of eternal days,
God eternal, Word incarnate,
  Whom the heaven of heaven obeys.

2 Ere he raised the lofty mountains,
  Formed the sea, or built the sky,
Love eternal, free, and boundless,
  Forced the Lord of life to die,
Lifted up the Prince of princes
  On the throne of Calvary.

Unison. 3 Now on those eternal mountains
  Stands the sapphire throne, all bright,
With the ceaseless alleluyas
  Which they raise, the sons of light;
Sion's people tell his praises,
  Victor after hard-won fight.

4 Bring your harps, and bring your incense,
  Sweep the string and pour the lay;
Let the earth proclaim his wonders,
  King of that celestial day;
He the Lamb once slain is worthy,
  Who was dead, and lives for ay.

5. Laud and honour to the Father,
  Laud and honour to the Son,
Laud and honour to the Spirit,
  Ever Three and ever One,
Consubstantial, co-eternal,
  While unending ages run. Amen.

A - men.

GENERAL HYMNS

381

MILITES. (D.S.M.)
Moderately fast ♩ = 100. Unison. Adapted from melody in the Foundery Collection, 1742.

NOTE.—*This hymn may also be sung to* ICH HALTE TREULICH STILL (*No.* 644) *or* OLIVA SPECIOSA (*Appendix, No.* 49).

M. Bridges, 1800-94.

1. CROWN him with many crowns,
  The Lamb upon his throne;
Hark! how the heavenly anthem drowns
  All music but its own:
Awake, my soul, and sing
Of him who died for thee,
And hail him as thy matchless King
Through all eternity.

2. Crown him the Virgin's Son,
  The God incarnate born,
Whose arm those crimson trophies won
  Which now his brow adorn:
Fruit of the mystic Rose,
As of that Rose the Stem;
The Root whence mercy ever flows,
The Babe of Bethlehem.

GENERAL HYMNS

3 Crown him the Lord of love!
　Behold his hands and side,
Rich wounds yet visible above
　In beauty glorified:
　No Angel in the sky
　Can fully bear that sight,
But downward bends his burning eye
　At mysteries so bright.

4 Crown him the Lord of peace,
　Whose power a sceptre sways
From pole to pole, that wars may cease,
　Absorbed in prayer and praise:
　His reign shall know no end,
　And round his piercèd feet
Fair flowers of Paradise extend
　Their fragrance ever sweet.

Unison.
5. Crown him the Lord of years,
　The Potentate of time,
Creator of the rolling spheres,
　Ineffably sublime.
　Glassed in a sea of light,
　Where everlasting waves
Reflect his throne—the Infinite!
　Who lives—and loves—and saves.

CORONA. (D. S. M.)　　(ALTERNATIVE TUNE)
Moderately fast ♩ = 116.　　　　　C. HYLTON STEWART, 1884–1932.

[Copyright, 1927, by Oxford University Press.]

GENERAL HYMNS

382

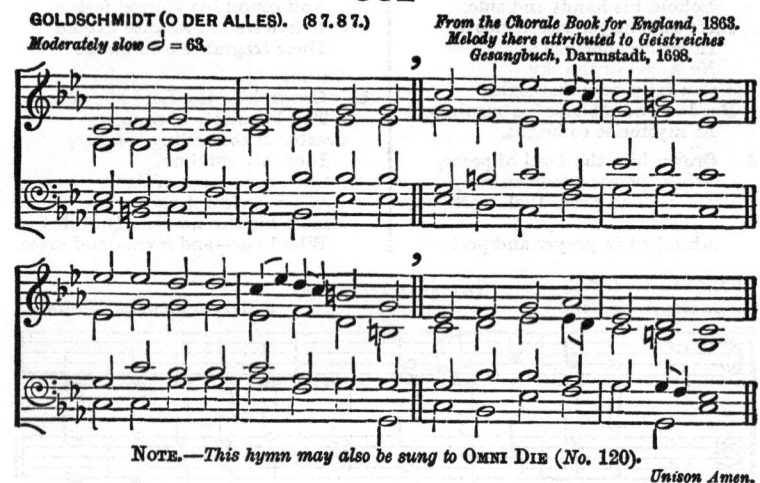

GOLDSCHMIDT (O DER ALLES). (8 7. 8 7.)
Moderately slow ♩ = 63.

*From the Chorale Book for England, 1863.
Melody there attributed to Geistreiches
Gesangbuch, Darmstadt, 1698.*

NOTE.—*This hymn may also be sung to* OMNI DIE (*No.* 120).

Unison Amen.

E. Caswall, 1814–78; *and others.*

DAYS and moments quickly flying
  Blend the living with the dead;
Soon our bodies will be lying
  Each within its narrow bed.

2 Soon our souls to God who gave them
  Will have sped their rapid flight:
Able now by grace to save them,
  O that, while we can, we might!

3 Jesu, infinite Redeemer,
  Maker of this mighty frame,
Teach, O teach us to remember
  What we are, and whence we came.

4 Whence we came and whither wend-
  So that by thy mercy we [ing,
May at last, in life unending,
  Find our perfect rest with thee.

5 Jesu, merciful Redeemer,
  Rouse dead souls to hear thy voice;
Wake, O wake each idle dreamer
  Now to make the eternal choice.

6. Soon before the Judge all glorious
  We with all the dead shall stand:
Saviour, over death victorious,
  Place us then on thy right hand.

383

REPTON. (8 6. 8 8 6.)
In moderate time ♩ = 100.   *Voices in unison.*

C. HUBERT H. PARRY, 1848–1918
(from *Judith*).

GENERAL HYMNS

383 (continued)

[By permission of Novello & Co., Ltd.]
(It is suggested that the melody line be played in the accompaniment for the first verse.)
NOTE.—This hymn may also be sung to HAMMERSMITH (Appendix, No. 50).

J. G. Whittier, 1807-92.

DEAR Lord and Father of mankind,
   Forgive our foolish ways!
Re-clothe us in our rightful mind,
In purer lives thy service find,
   In deeper reverence praise.

2 In simple trust like theirs who heard,
   Beside the Syrian sea,
The gracious calling of the Lord,
Let us, like them, without a word
   Rise up and follow thee.

3 * O Sabbath rest by Galilee!
   O calm of hills above,
Where Jesus knelt to share with thee
The silence of eternity,
   Interpreted by love!

4 Drop thy still dews of quietness,
   Till all our strivings cease;
Take from our souls the strain and stress,
And let our ordered lives confess
   The beauty of thy peace.

5. Breathe through the heats of our desire
   Thy coolness and thy balm;
Let sense be dumb, let flesh retire:
Speak through the earthquake, wind, and fire,
   O still small voice of calm!

A - men.

GENERAL HYMNS

384

SONG 1. (10 10. 10 10. 10 10.)
Moderately slow ♩ = 69.

O. GIBBONS, 1583–1625.

NOTE.—*A higher setting of this tune will be found at Hymn 302.*

J. W. Chadwick, 1840–1904.

ETERNAL Ruler of the ceaseless round
  Of circling planets singing on their way;
Guide of the nations from the night profound
  Into the glory of the perfect day;
Rule in our hearts, that we may ever be
Guided and strengthened and upheld by thee.

GENERAL HYMNS

2 We are of thee, the children of thy love,
    The brothers of thy well-belovèd Son;
Descend, O Holy Spirit, like a dove
    Into our hearts, that we may be as one:
As one with thee, to whom we ever tend;
    As one with him, our Brother and our Friend.

3 We would be one in hatred of all wrong,
    One in our love of all things sweet and fair,
One with the joy that breaketh into song,
    One with the grief that trembleth into prayer,
One in the power that makes thy children free
To follow truth, and thus to follow thee.

4 O clothe us with thy heavenly armour, Lord,
    Thy trusty shield, thy sword of love divine;
Our inspiration be thy constant word;
    We ask no victories that are not thine:
Give or withhold, let pain or pleasure be;
Enough to know that we are serving thee.

A - men.

385

SUSSEX. (87.87.)
In moderate time ♩ = 72.

Adapted from an English Traditional Melody.

Mrs. L. M. Willis (1864).

FATHER, hear the prayer we offer;
    Not for ease that prayer shall be,
But for strength that we may ever
    Live our lives courageously.

2 Not for ever in green pastures
    Do we ask our way to be;
But the steep and rugged pathway
    May we tread rejoicingly.

3 Not for ever by still waters
    Would we idly rest and stay;
But would smite the living fountains
    From the rocks along our way.

Unison. 4. Be our Strength in hours of weakness,
    In our wanderings be our Guide;
Through endeavour, failure, danger,
    Father, be thou at our side.

A - men.

GENERAL HYMNS

386

WARSAW. (6 6. 6 6. 8 8.)
In moderate time ♩ = 108 (𝅗𝅥 = 54).

— CLARK (? THOMAS, 1775–1859),
as given in the Church Hymnary, 1928.

NOTE.—*This hymn may also be sung to* DOLGELLY (*No.* 349).

J. *Julian*, 1839–1913.

FATHER of all, to thee
  With loving hearts we pray
Through him, in mercy given,
  The Life, the Truth, the Way:
From heaven, thy throne, in mercy shed
Thy blessings on each bended head.

2 * Father of all, to thee
  Our contrite hearts we raise,
Unstrung by sin and pain,
  Long voiceless in thy praise:
Breathe thou the silent chords along,
Until they tremble into song.

3 Father of all, to thee
    We breathe unuttered fears,
  Deep hidden in our souls,
    That have no voice but tears:
  Take thou our hand, and through the wild
  Lead gently on each trustful child.

Unison. 4. Father of all, may we
    In praise our tongues employ,
  When gladness fills the soul
    With deep and hallowed joy:
  In storm and calm give us to see
  The path of peace which leads to thee.

A - men.

GENERAL HYMNS

DAS LEIDEN DES HERRN. (L. M.)   **387**   *German Traditional Melody*
Very slow ♩ = 63   *(Harmonized by* E. W. GOLDSMITH*).*

NOTE.—*Another harmonization of this tune will be found at Appendix, No.* 11.
This hymn may also be sung to CANNONS (*No.* 66).

E. Cooper †, 1770–1833.

FATHER of heaven, whose love profound
  A ransom for our souls hath found,
Before thy throne we sinners bend:
To us thy pardoning love extend.

2 Almighty Son, incarnate Word,
  Our Prophet, Priest, Redeemer, Lord,
Before thy throne we sinners bend:
To us thy saving grace extend.

3 Eternal Spirit, by whose breath
  The soul is raised from sin and death,
Before thy throne we sinners bend:
To us thy quickening power extend.

4. Thrice Holy! Father, Spirit, Son,
  Mysterious Godhead, Three in One,
Before thy throne we sinners bend:
Grace, pardon, life to us extend. Amen.

GENERAL HYMNS

388

ST. ISSEY. (6 4. 6 4. D.)
Slow ♩ = 76.

English Traditional Melody.

Anatolius, c. 8th cent. *Tr. J. M. Neale.*

Ζοφερᾶς τρικυμίας.

FIERCE was the wild billow,
　Dark was the night;
Oars laboured heavily,
　Foam glimmered white;
Trembled the mariners,
　Peril was nigh:
Then said the God of God,
　'Peace! it is I.'

2 Ridge of the mountain-wave,
　Lower thy crest!
Wail of Euroclydon
　Be thou at rest!
Sorrow can never be,
　Darkness must fly,
Where saith the Light of light,
　'Peace! it is I.'

3. Jesu, Deliverer,
　Near to us be;
Soothe thou my voyaging
　Over life's sea:
Thou, when the storm of death
　Roars, sweeping by,
Whisper, O Truth of truth,
　'Peace! It is I.'

A - men.

GENERAL HYMNS

389

SHEPTON-BEAUCHAMP. (L. M.)
In moderate time ♩ = 92.

English Traditional Melody.

NOTE.—*This hymn may also be sung to* DUKE STREET (*No.* 167)

J. S. B. Monsell, 1811-75.

FIGHT the good fight with all thy might,
Christ is thy strength, and Christ thy right;
Lay hold on life, and it shall be
Thy joy and crown eternally

Unison. 2 Run the straight race through God's good grace,
Lift up thine eyes, and seek his face;
Life with its way before us lies,
Christ is the path, and Christ the prize.

3 Cast care aside, upon thy Guide
Lean, and his mercy will provide;
Lean, and the trusting soul shall prove
Christ is its life, and Christ its love.

Unison. 4. Faint not nor fear, his arms are near,
He changeth not, and thou art dear;
Only believe, and thou shalt see
That Christ is all in all to thee.

A - men.

GENERAL HYMNS

390

SHIPSTON. (87. 87.)
In moderate time ♩ = 96.
English Traditional Melody.

NOTE.—*This hymn may be also sung to* STUTTGART (*No.* 40).

J. H. Newman, 1801-90.

FIRMLY I believe and truly
   God is Three, and God is One;
And I next acknowledge duly
   Manhood taken by the Son.

2 And I trust and hope most fully
   In that Manhood crucified;

And each thought and deed unruly
   Do to death, as he has died.

3 Simply to his grace and wholly
   Light and life and strength belong,
And I love supremely, solely,
   Him the Holy, him the Strong.

4*And I hold in veneration,
   For the love of him alone,
Holy Church as his creation,
   And her teachings as his own.

5. Adoration ay be given,
   With and through the angelic host,
To the God of earth and heaven,
   Father, Son, and Holy Ghost.
        Amen.

A - men.

391

LLANLLYFNI. (D. S. M.)
Moderately slow ♩ = 63.
Adapted by DAVID JENKINS, 1849-1915.

GENERAL HYMNS

391 (*continued*)

NOTE.—*This hymn may also be sung to* MONTGOMERY (*Appendix, No.* 51).

J. Montgomery, 1771–1854.

1. 'FOR ever with the Lord!'
   Amen; so let it be;
Life from the dead is in that word,
   'Tis immortality,
   Here in the body pent,
   Absent from him I roam,
Yet nightly pitch my moving tent
A day's march nearer home.

2. My Father's house on high,
   Home of my soul, how near
At times to faith's foreseeing eye
   Thy golden gates appear!
   Ah! then my spirit faints
   To reach the land I love,
The bright inheritance of Saints,
   Jerusalem above.

3. 'For ever with the Lord!'—
   Father, if 'tis thy will,
The promise of that faithful word
   E'en here to me fulfil.
   Be thou at my right hand,
   Then can I never fail;
Uphold thou me, and I shall stand;
   Fight, and I must prevail.

4. So when my latest breath
   Shall rend the veil in twain,
   By death I shall escape from death,
   And life eternal gain.
   Knowing as I am known,
   How shall I love that word,
   And oft repeat before the throne,
   'For ever with the Lord!'

A - men.

GENERAL HYMNS

392

MAGDALENA. (7 6. 7 6.)
In moderate time ♩ = 144.

German Mediaeval Melody
(16th cent. ?).

Verse 10, line 3, must be sung:

O prince - ly bowers! O land of flowers.

Part of Hora novissima (495).
O bona patria!

Bernard of Cluny, 12th cent.
Tr. J. M. Neale.

FOR thee, O dear, dear country,
   Mine eyes their vigils keep;
For very love, beholding
   Thy happy name, they weep.

2 The mention of thy glory
   Is unction to the breast,
And medicine in sickness,
   And love and life and rest.

3 With jaspers glow thy bulwarks,
   Thy streets with emeralds blaze;
The sardius and the topaz
   Unite in thee their rays;

4 Thine ageless walls are bonded
   With amethyst unpriced;
Thy saints build up its fabric,
   The corner-stone is Christ.

5 O one, O only mansion!
   O Paradise of joy!
Where tears are ever banished
   And smiles have no alloy;

6 The Cross is all thy splendour,
   The Crucified thy praise:
His laud and benediction
   Thy ransomed people raise.

7 Thou hast no shore, fair ocean!
   Thou hast no time, bright day!
Dear fountain of refreshment
   To pilgrims far away!

8 Upon the Rock of Ages
   They raise thy holy tower;
Thine is the victor's laurel,
   And thine the golden dower.

9 O mine, my golden Sion!
   O lovelier far than gold!
With laurel-girt battalions,
   And safe victorious fold.

10. O fields that see no sorrow!
   O state that fears no strife!
O princely bowers! O land of flowers!
   O realm and home of life!

A - men.

GENERAL HYMNS

393

AUSTRIAN HYMN. (87. 87. D.)
Moderately slow ♩ = 63.

F. J. HAYDN, 1732-1809.

J. Newton, 1725-1807.

GLORIOUS things of thee are spoken,
  Sion, city of our God!
He whose word cannot be broken
  Formed thee for his own abode:
On the Rock of Ages founded,
  What can shake thy sure repose?
With salvation's walls surrounded,
  Thou may'st smile at all thy foes.

2 See, the streams of living waters,
  Springing from eternal love,
Well supply thy sons and daughters,
  And all fear of want remove:
Who can faint while such a river
  Ever flows their thirst to assuage?
Grace, which like the Lord the Giver,
  Never fails from age to age.

3. Saviour, if of Sion's city
  I, through grace, a member am,
Let the world deride or pity,
  I will glory in thy name:
Fading is the worldling's pleasure,
  All his boasted pomp and show;
Solid joys and lasting treasure
  None but Sion's children know.

A - men.

GENERAL HYMNS

394

LONDON NEW. (C.M.)
Slow and dignified ♩ = 60.

Playford's Psalms, 1671. Adapted from NEWTOUN in Scottish Psalter, 1635.

W. Cowper, 1731–1800.

GOD moves in a mysterious way
    His wonders to perform;
He plants his footsteps in the sea,
    And rides upon the storm.

2 Deep in unfathomable mines
    Of never-failing skill
He treasures up his bright designs,
    And works his sovereign will.

3 Ye fearful saints, fresh courage take,
    The clouds ye so much dread
Are big with mercy, and shall break
    In blessings on your head.

4 Judge not the Lord by feeble sense,
    But trust him for his grace;
Behind a frowning providence
    He hides a smiling face.

5 His purposes will ripen fast,
    Unfolding every hour;
The bud may have a bitter taste,
    But sweet will be the flower.

6. Blind unbelief is sure to err,
    And scan his work in vain;
God is his own interpreter,
    And he will make it plain.

A - men.

GENERAL HYMNS

395

HEATHLANDS. (77.77.77.)
In moderate time ♩ = 72.

H. SMART, 1813–79.

H. F. Lyte, 1798–1847.

GOD of mercy, God of grace,
Show the brightness of thy face:
Shine upon us, Saviour, shine,
Fill thy Church with light divine;
And thy saving health extend
Unto earth's remotest end.

2 Let the people praise thee, Lord;
Be by all that live adored:
Let the nations shout and sing,
Glory to their Saviour King;
At thy feet their tributes pay,
And thy holy will obey.

3. Let the people praise thee, Lord;
Earth shall then her fruits afford:
God to man his blessing give,
Man to God devoted live;
All below, and all above,
One in joy, and light, and love.

A - men.

GENERAL HYMNS
396

DIAN. (7 7. 7 5.)
In moderate time ♩ = about 100.

MARTIN SHAW.

[Copyright, 1932, by the English Hymnal Company Ltd.]
NOTE.—*This hymn may also be sung to* CAPETOWN (*No.* 501).

Bp. Chr. Wordsworth, 1807-85.

GRACIOUS Spirit, Holy Ghost,
Taught by thee, we covet most
Of thy gifts at Pentecost,
  Holy, heavenly love.

2 Love is kind, and suffers long,
Love is meek, and thinks no wrong,
Love than death itself more strong;
  Therefore give us love.

3 Prophecy will fade away,
Melting in the light of day;
Love will ever with us stay;
  Therefore give us love.

4 Faith will vanish into sight;
Hope be emptied in delight;
Love in heaven will shine more bright;
  Therefore give us love.

5 Faith and hope and love we see
Joining hand in hand agree;
But the greatest of the three,
  And the best, is love.

6. From the overshadowing
Of thy gold and silver wing
Shed on us, who to thee sing,
  Holy, heavenly love.

A - men.

GENERAL HYMNS

397

CAERSALEM. (87.87.47.)
In moderate time ♩ = 80.

R. EDWARDS, 1797–1862.

Arglwydd arwain trwy'r anialwch.

W. Williams, 1717–91.
Tr. P. and W. Williams †.

GUIDE me, O thou great Redeemer,
  Pilgrim through this barren land;
I am weak, but thou art mighty,
  Hold me with thy powerful hand:
    Bread of heaven,
Feed me till I want no more.

2 Open now the crystal fountain,
  Whence the healing stream doth flow;
Let the fire and cloudy pillar
  Lead me all my journey through:
    Strong Deliverer,
Be thou still my strength and shield.

3. When I tread the verge of Jordan,
  Bid my anxious fears subside;
Death of death, and hell's Destruction,
  Land me safe on Canaan's side:
    Songs of praises
I will ever give to thee.

A - men.

GENERAL HYMNS

BINCHESTER. (C.M.)
In moderate time ♩ = 88.

398

DR. CROFT, 1678-1727.

O quam juvat fratres.   C. *Coffin*, 1676-1749.   Tr. Y. H.

HAPPY are they, they that love God,
  Whose hearts have Christ confest,
Who by his Cross have found their life,
  And 'neath his yoke their rest.

2 Glad is the praise, sweet are the songs,
  When they together sing;
And strong the prayers that bow the ear
  Of heaven's eternal King.

3 Christ to their homes giveth his peace,
  And makes their loves his own:
But ah, what tares the evil one
  Hath in his garden sown.

4 Sad were our lot, evil this earth,
  Did not its sorrows prove
The path whereby the sheep may find
  The fold of Jesu's love.

5. Then shall they know, they that love him,
  How all their pain is good;
And death itself cannot unbind
  Their happy brotherhood.

A - men.

399

PILGRIMS OF THE NIGHT. (11 10. 11 10. 9 11.)

Moderately slow ♩. = 51 (♪ = 153).   *Probably adapted from a Swiss Melody.*

GENERAL HYMNS

399 (*continued*)

F. W. Faber, 1814–63.

HARK! hark, my soul! Angelic songs are swelling
O'er earth's green fields, and ocean's wave-beat shore;
How sweet the truth those blessèd strains are telling
Of that new life when sin shall be no more!
Angels of Jesus, Angels of light,
Singing to welcome the pilgrims of the night!

2 Onward we go, for still we hear them singing,
Come, weary souls, for Jesus bids you come:
And through the dark, its echoes sweetly ringing,
The music of the Gospel leads us home.

3 Far, far away, like bells at evening pealing,
The voice of Jesus sounds o'er land and sea,
And laden souls, by thousands meekly stealing,
Kind Shepherd, turn their weary steps to thee.

4 Rest comes at length; though life be long and dreary,
The day must dawn, and darksome night be past;
All journeys end in welcomes to the weary,
And heaven, the heart's true home, will come at last.

5. Angels! sing on, your faithful watches keeping,
Sing us sweet fragments of the songs above;
While we toil on, and soothe ourselves with weeping,
Till life's long night shall break in endless love.

A - men.

GENERAL HYMNS
400

WHITE LADIES ASTON. (7 7. 7 7.)
Rather slow ♩ = 80. Voices in unison.

IVOR ATKINS.

[Copyright, 1931, by Oxford University Press.]
NOTE.—*This hymn may also be sung to* SAVANNAH (*No.* 135) *or* ST. BEES
(*Appendix, No.* 52).

W. Cowper, 1731–1800.

HARK, my soul! it is the Lord;
'Tis thy Saviour, hear his word;
Jesus speaks, and speaks to thee:
'Say, poor sinner, lov'st thou me?

2 'I delivered thee when bound,
And, when wounded, healed thy wound;
Sought thee wandering, set thee right,
Turned thy darkness into light.

3 'Can a woman's tender care
Cease towards the child she bare?
Yes, she may forgetful be,
Yet will I remember thee.

4 'Mine is an unchanging love,
Higher than the heights above,
Deeper than the depths beneath,
Free and faithful, strong as death.

5 'Thou shalt see my glory soon,
When the work of grace is done;
Partner of my throne shalt be;
Say, poor sinner, lov'st thou me?'

6. Lord, it is my chief complaint
That my love is weak and faint;
Yet I love thee, and adore,
O for grace to love thee more!

A - men.

544

GENERAL HYMNS

401

CAMERONIAN MIDNIGHT HYMN. (L.M.)

In moderate time ♩ = 72.   *Scottish Hymn Melody*

NOTE.—*This hymn may also be sung to* DAS WALT' GOTT VATER (*No. 36*).

R. Baxter, 1615–91.

HE wants not friends that hath thy love,
   And may converse and walk with thee,
And with thy Saints here and above,
   With whom for ever I must be.

2 In the communion of Saints
   Is wisdom, safety and delight;
And when my heart declines and faints,
   It's raisèd by their heat and light!

3 As for my friends, they are not lost;
   The several vessels of thy fleet,
Though parted now, by tempests tost,
   Shall safely in the haven meet.

4 Still we are centred all in thee,
   Members, though distant, of one Head;
In the same family we be,
   By the same faith and spirit led.

5 Before thy throne we daily meet
   As joint-petitioners to thee;
In spirit we each other greet,
   And shall again each other see.

6. The heavenly hosts, world without end,
   Shall be my company above;
And thou, my best and surest Friend,
   Who shall divide me from thy love?

A - men.

GENERAL HYMNS

402

MONKS GATE. (11 11. 12 11.)
Brightly ♩ = 112.

Adapted from an English Traditional Melody.

J. Bunyan, 1628-88, and others.

HE who would valiant be
'Gainst all disaster,
Let him in constancy
    Follow the Master.
There's no discouragement
Shall make him once relent
His first avowed intent
    To be a pilgrim.

2 Who so beset him round
With dismal stories,
Do but themselves confound—
    His strength the more is.
No foes shall stay his might,
Though he with giants fight:
He will make good his right
    To be a pilgrim.

3. Since, Lord, thou dost defend
    Us with thy Spirit,
We know we at the end
    Shall life inherit.
Then fancies flee away!
I'll fear not what men say,
I'll labour night and day
    To be a pilgrim.

A - men

GENERAL HYMNS

MISERERE MEI. (4 8. 8 4.)
Slow ♩ = 69 (𝅗𝅥 = 35).

403

Melody from
'*Seven Sobs of a Sorrowful Soul,*' 1585
(*slightly adapted*).

W. Canton, 1845–1926.

HOLD thou my hands!
In grief and joy, in hope and fear,
Lord, let me feel that thou art near:
    Hold thou my hands!

2 If e'er by doubts
Of thy good Fatherhood depressed,
I cannot find in thee my rest:
    Hold thou my hands!

3 Hold thou my hands!
These passionate hands too quick to smite,
These hands so eager for delight:
    Hold thou my hands!

4. And when at length,
With darkened eyes and fingers cold,
I seek some last loved hand to hold,
    Hold thou my hands!

A - men.

GENERAL HYMNS

404

OLD 137TH. (D.C.M.)
Moderately slow ♩ = 66.
Day's Psalter, 1563.

John Mason, c. 1645–94.

1. HOW shall I sing that Majesty
   Which Angels do admire?
   Let dust in dust and silence lie;
   Sing, sing, ye heavenly choir.
   Thousands of thousands stand around
   Thy throne, O God most high;
   Ten thousand times ten thousand sound
   Thy praise; but who am I?

2. Thy brightness unto them appears,
   Whilst I thy footsteps trace;
   A sound of God comes to my ears,
   But they behold thy face.
   They sing because thou art their Sun;
   Lord, send a beam on me;
   For where heaven is but once begun
   There Alleluyas be.

GENERAL HYMNS

3 Enlighten with faith's light my heart,
   Inflame it with love's fire;
Then shall I sing and bear a part
   With that celestial choir.

I shall, I fear, be dark and cold,
   With all my fire and light;
Yet when thou dost accept their gold,
   Lord, treasure up my mite.

4. How great a being, Lord, is thine,
   Which doth all beings keep!
Thy knowledge is the only line
   To sound so vast a deep.
Thou art a sea without a shore,
   A sun without a sphere;
Thy time is now and evermore,
   Thy place is everywhere.

A - men.

ST. PETER. (C.M.)
In moderate time ♩ = 76.

405

A. R. REINAGLE, 1799–1877.

J. Newton, 1725–1807.

HOW sweet the name of Jesus sounds
   In a believer's ear!
It soothes his sorrows, heals his wounds,
   And drives away his fear.

2 It makes the wounded spirit whole,
   And calms the troubled breast;
'Tis manna to the hungry soul,
   And to the weary rest.

3 Dear name! the rock on which I build,
   My shield and hiding-place,
My never-failing treasury filled
   With boundless stores of grace.

4 Jesus! my Shepherd, Husband, Friend,
   My Prophet, Priest, and King,
My Lord, my Life, my Way, my End,
   Accept the praise I bring.

5 Weak is the effort of my heart,
   And cold my warmest thought;
But when I see thee as thou art,
   I'll praise thee as I ought.

6. Till then I would thy love proclaim
   With every fleeting breath;
And may the music of thy name
   Refresh my soul in death.

A - men.

549

GENERAL HYMNS

406

O JESU. (86.86.88.)
Moderately slow ♩ = 66.

J. B. REIMANN, 1702-1749.

S. *Longfellow*, 1819–92.

I LOOK to thee in every need,
   And never look in vain;
I feel thy strong and tender love,
   And all is well again:
The thought of thee is mightier far
Than sin and pain and sorrow are.

2 Discouraged in the work of life,
   Disheartened by its load,
Shamed by its failures or its fears,
   I sink beside the road;
But let me only think of thee,
And then new heart springs up in me.

3 Thy calmness bends serene above,
   My restlessness to still;
Around me flows thy quickening life,
   To nerve my faltering will:
Thy presence fills my solitude;
Thy providence turns all to good.

4. Embosomed deep in thy dear love,
   Held in thy law, I stand;
Thy hand in all things I behold,
   And all things in thy hand;
Thou leadest me by unsought ways,
And turn'st my mourning into praise.

A - men.

GENERAL HYMNS

407

ST. DENIO. (11 11. 11 11.)
In moderate time ♩ = 92.
Welsh Hymn Melody.

W. Chalmers Smith, 1824–1908.

IMMORTAL, invisible, God only wise,
In light inaccessible hid from our eyes,
Most blessèd, most glorious, the Ancient of Days,
Almighty, victorious, thy great name we praise.

2 Unresting, unhasting, and silent as light,
Nor wanting, nor wasting, thou rulest in might;
Thy justice like mountains high soaring above
Thy clouds which are fountains of goodness and love.

3 To all life thou givest—to both great and small;
In all life thou livest, the true life of all;
We blossom and flourish as leaves on the tree,
And wither and perish—but nought changeth thee.

4. Great Father of Glory, pure Father of Light,
Thine Angels adore thee, all veiling their sight;
All laud we would render: O help us to see
'Tis only the splendour of light hideth thee.

A - men.

GENERAL HYMNS
408

BISHOPTHORPE (OR ST. PAUL'S). (C. M.)

In moderate time ♩ = 92.

J. CLARK, 1670–1707.

J. G. Whittier, 1807-92.

IMMORTAL love for ever full,
   For ever flowing free,
For ever shared, for ever whole,
   A never-ebbing sea!

2 Our outward lips confess the name,
   All other names above;
Love only knoweth whence it came
   And comprehendeth love.

3 We may not climb the heavenly steeps
   To bring the Lord Christ down;

In vain we search the lowest deeps,
   For him no depths can drown;

4 But warm, sweet, tender, even yet
   A present help is he;
And faith has still its Olivet,
   And love its Galilee.

5 The healing of his seamless dress,
   Is by our beds of pain;
We touch him in life's throng and press,
   And we are whole again.

6 Through him the first fond prayers are said
   Our lips of childhood frame;
The last low whispers of our dead
   Are burdened with his name.

7. Alone, O Love ineffable,
   Thy saving name is given
To turn aside from thee is hell,
   To walk with thee is heaven.

A - men.

GENERAL HYMNS

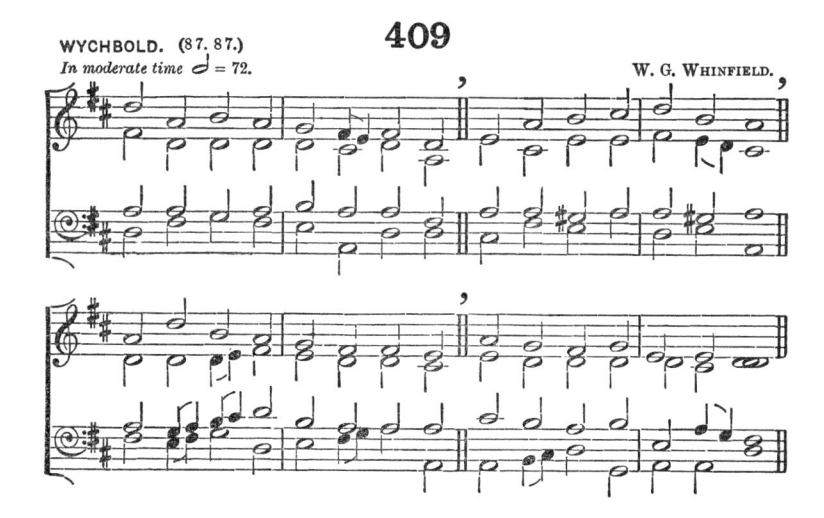

409

WYCHBOLD. (87. 87.)
In moderate time ♩ = 72.

W. G. WHINFIELD.

Sir J. Bowring, 1792–1872.

IN the Cross of Christ I glory,
   Towering o'er the wrecks of time;
All the light of sacred story
   Gathers round its head sublime.

2 When the woes of life o'ertake me,
   Hopes deceive and fears annoy,
Never shall the Cross forsake me,
   Lo! it glows with peace and joy.

3 When the sun of bliss is beaming
   Light and love upon my way,
From the Cross the radiance streaming,
   Adds more lustre to the day.

4. Bane and blessing, pain and pleasure,
   By the Cross are sanctified;
Peace is there that knows no measure,
   Joys that through all time abide.

A - men.

GENERAL HYMNS

410

HOLY COMFORT. (7 7. 7 6.)
Moderately slow ♩ = 66.

R. S. GENGE.

R. Herrick, 1591-1674.

IN the hour of my distress,
   When temptations me oppress,
And when I my sins confess,
        Sweet Spirit, comfort me.

2 When I lie within my bed,
   Sick in heart, and sick in head,
And with doubts discomforted,
        Sweet Spirit, comfort me.

3 When the house doth sigh and weep,
   And the world is drowned in sleep,
Yet mine eyes the watch do keep,
        Sweet Spirit, comfort me.

4 When, God knows, I'm tost about,
   Either with despair or doubt,
Yet, before the glass be out,
        Sweet Spirit, comfort me.

5. When the Judgement is revealed,
   And that opened which was sealed,
When to thee I have appealed,
        Sweet Spirit, comfort me.

A - men.

GENERAL HYMNS

411

CHRISTCHURCH. (66.66.88.)
Moderately fast ♩ = 100.
C. STEGGALL, 1826–1905.

NOTE.—*This hymn may also be sung to* CROFT'S 136TH (*No.* 565).

S. Crossman †, 1624–88.

JERUSALEM on high
  My song and city is,
My home whene'er I die,
  The centre of my bliss:
    O happy place! when shall I be,
    My God, with thee, to see thy face.

2 There dwells my Lord, my King,
  Judged here unfit to live;
There Angels to him sing,
  And lowly homage give:

3 The Patriarchs of old
  There from their travels cease;
The Prophets there behold
  Their longed-for Prince of peace:

4 The Lamb's Apostles there
  I might with joy behold,
The harpers I might hear
  Harping on harps of gold:

5 The bleeding Martyrs, they
  Within those courts are found,
Clothèd in pure array,
  Their scars with glory crowned:

6.*Ah me! ah me! that I
  In Kedar's tents here stay;
No place like that on high;
  Lord, thither guide my way:

A - men.

GENERAL HYMNS

412

EWING. (7 6. 7 6. D.)
In moderate time ♩ = 80.

*Later form of melody
by A. Ewing, 1830–95.*

✱ *In verse 4 ♩ ♩ must be here substituted for ♩*

Part of Hora novissima (495).

Urbs Sion aurea.

*Bernard of Cluny, 12th cent.
Tr. J. M. Neale.*

JERUSALEM the golden,
  With milk and honey blest,
Beneath thy contemplation
  Sink heart and voice opprest.
I know not, O I know not,
  What social joys are there,
What radiancy of glory,
  What light beyond compare.

2 They stand, those halls of Sion,
  Conjubilant with song,
And bright with many an Angel,
  And all the Martyr throng:
The Prince is ever in them,
  The daylight is serene,
The pastures of the blessèd
  Are decked in glorious sheen.

GENERAL HYMNS

3 There is the throne of David,
   And there, from care released,
The song of them that triumph,
   The shout of them that feast;

And they who, with their Leader,
   Have conquered in the fight,
For ever and for ever
   Are clad in robes of white.

4. O sweet and blessèd country,
   Shall I ever see thy face?
O sweet and blessèd country,
   Shall I ever win thy grace?
Exult, O dust and ashes!
   The Lord shall be thy part:
His only, his for ever,
   Thou shalt be, and thou art!

413

SONG 13. (7 7. 7 7.)
Slow and solemn ♩ = 60.

O. GIBBONS, 1583–1625
(*original version of melody and bass*).

17th cent. Tr. Sir H. W. Baker.
Dignare me, O Jesu, rogo te.

JESU, grant me this, I pray,
   Ever in thy heart to stay;
Let me evermore abide
Hidden in thy wounded side.

2 If the evil one prepare,
   Or the world, a tempting snare,
I am safe when I abide
In thy heart and wounded side.

3 If the flesh, more dangerous still,
   Tempt my soul to deeds of ill,
Naught I fear when I abide
In thy heart and wounded side.

4. Death will come one day to me;
   Jesu, cast me not from thee:
Dying let me still abide
In thy heart and wounded side.

GENERAL HYMNS

414

HOLLINGSIDE. (77. 77. D.)
Moderately slow ♩ = 66.
J. B. DYKES, 1823–76.

414 (ALTERNATIVE TUNE)

ABERYSTWYTH. (77. 77. D.)
Slow ♩ = 58.
JOSEPH PARRY, 1841–1903.

A-men.

GENERAL HYMNS

414 (continued)

[By permission of Messrs. Hughes & Son, Wrexham.]

C. Wesley, 1707–88.

JESU, Lover of my soul,
  Let me to thy bosom fly,
While the nearer waters roll,
  While the tempest still is high:
Hide me, O my Saviour, hide,
  Till the storm of life is past;
Safe into the haven guide,
  O receive my soul at last.

2 Other refuge have I none;
  Hangs my helpless soul on thee;
Leave, ah! leave me not alone,
  Still support and comfort me.
All my trust on thee is stayed,
  All my help from thee I bring;
Cover my defenceless head
  With the shadow of thy wing.

3*Thou, O Christ, art all I want;
  More than all in thee I find:
Raise the fallen, cheer the faint,
  Heal the sick, and lead the blind.
Just and holy is thy name;
  I am all unrighteousness;
False and full of sin I am,
  Thou art full of truth and grace.

4. Plenteous grace with thee is found,
  Grace to cover all my sin;
Let the healing streams abound;
  Make and keep me pure within.
Thou of life the fountain art;
  Freely let me take of thee;
Spring thou up within my heart,
  Rise to all eternity.

GENERAL HYMNS

415

BELSIZE. (6 5. 6 5.)
In moderate time ♩ = 96.

MARTIN SHAW.

Last verse.

[*Copyright, 1915, by J. Curwen & Sons, Ltd.*]

NOTE.—*This hymn may also be sung to* CASWALL (*No.* 315) *or to* ST. CONSTANTINE (*Appendix, No.* 53).

G. R. Prynne, 1818–1903.

JESU, meek and gentle,
  Son of God most high,
Pitying, loving Saviour,
  Hear thy children's cry.

2 Pardon our offences,
  Loose our captive chains,
Break down every idol
  Which our soul detains.

3 Give us holy freedom,
  Fill our hearts with love,
Draw us, holy Jesu,
  To the realms above.

4 Lead us on our journey,
  Be thyself the Way
Through terrestrial darkness
  To celestial day.

5. Jesu, meek and gentle,
  Son of God most high,
Pitying, loving Saviour,
  Hear thy children's cry.

A - men.

GENERAL HYMNS

416

ST. MARTIN. (6 6. 6 6.)
Moderately slow ♩ = 63.

C. Ett, 'Cantica Sacra,' 1840.

H. Collins, 1827–1919.

1. JESU, meek and lowly,
Saviour, pure and holy,
On thy love relying
Hear me humbly crying.

2. Prince of life and power,
My salvation's tower,
On the Cross I view thee
Calling sinners to thee.

3. There behold me gazing
At the sight amazing;
Bending low before thee,
Helpless I adore thee.

4.* By thy red wounds streaming,
With thy Life-blood gleaming,
Blood for sinners flowing,
Pardon free bestowing;

5. By that fount of blessing,
Thy dear love expressing,
All my aching sadness
Turn thou into gladness.

6. Lord, in mercy guide me,
Be thou e'er beside me;
In thy ways direct me,
'Neath thy wings protect me.

A - men.

GENERAL HYMNS
417

GESIUS (HEUT' TRIUMPHIRET). (8 8. 8 8. 8 8.)
Moderately slow ♩ = 84.

B. GESIUS, 1555–1614.
Adapted and harmonised by J. S. BACH.

A - men.

NOTE.—*Other tunes to this hymn will be found in the Appendix at Nos. 19 and 54.*

H. *Collins*, 1827–1919.

1. JESU, my Lord, my God, my All,
Hear me, blest Saviour, when I call;
Hear me, and from thy dwelling-place
Pour down the riches of thy grace:
   Jesu, my Lord, I thee adore,
   O make me love thee more and more.

2. Jesu, too late I thee have sought,
How can I love thee as I ought?
And how extol thy matchless fame,
The glorious beauty of thy name?

3. Jesu, what didst thou find in me,
That thou hast dealt so lovingly?
How great the joy that thou hast brought,
So far exceeding hope or thought!

4. Jesu, of thee shall be my song,
To thee my heart and soul belong;
All that I am or have is thine,
And thou, sweet Saviour, thou art mine.

GENERAL HYMNS

WERDE MUNTER. (7 6. 7 6. 8 8. 7 7.) **418**
Slow ♩ = 50.
From a melody by J. Schop, c. 1640.

'Ιησοῦ γλυκύτατε.

Theoctistus, c. 890.
Tr. J. M. Neale.

1 JESU, name all names above;
　Jesu, best and dearest;
Jesu, Fount of perfect love,
　Holiest, tenderest, nearest:
Jesu, Source of grace completest;
Jesu purest, Jesu sweetest;
Jesu, Well of power Divine,
Make me, keep me, seal me thine!

2 Woe that I have turned aside
　After fleshly pleasure!
Woe that I have never tried
　For the heavenly treasure!
Treasure, safe in homes supernal,
Incorruptible, eternal;
Treasure no less price hath won
Than the Passion of the Son!

3 Jesu, crowned with thorns for me,
　Scourged for my transgression!
Witnessing, through agony,
　That thy good confession!
Jesu, clad in purple raiment,
For my evils making payment:
Let not all thy woe and pain,
Let not Calvary be in vain!

4. Jesu, open me the gate
　　That of old he entered
　Who, in that most lost estate,
　　Wholly on thee ventured;
　Thou, whose wounds are ever pleading
　And thy Passion interceding,
　From my misery let me rise
　To a home in Paradise!

A - men.

GENERAL HYMNS

419

ST. BOTOLPH. (C.M.)
In moderate time ♩ = 128.

GORDON SLATER.

[*Copyright, 1929, by Oxford University Press.*]

NOTE.—*This hymn may also be sung to* ST. AGNES (*Appendix, No.* 55).

Jesu, dulcis memoria.

11th cent. Tr. E. Caswall.

JESU, the very thought of thee
   With sweetness fills my breast;
But sweeter far thy face to see,
   And in thy presence rest.

2 Nor voice can sing, nor heart can frame,
   Nor can the memory find,
A sweeter sound than thy blest name,
   O Saviour of mankind!

3 O hope of every contrite heart,
   O joy of all the meek,
To those who fall, how kind thou art!
   How good to those who seek!

4 But what to those who find? Ah! this
   Nor tongue nor pen can show;
The love of Jesus! what it is,
   None but his loved ones know.

5 Jesu, our only joy be thou,
   As thou our prize wilt be;
Jesu, be thou our glory now,
   And through eternity.

PARTS 2 AND 3.

KING'S NORTON. (C.M.)
Very slow ♩ = 63.

J. CLARK, 1670–1707.

GENERAL HYMNS

419 (continued)

NOTE.—*This tune may also be used for Part 1.*

Part 2.

Jesu, Rex admirabilis.

6 O Jesu, King most wonderful,
    Thou Conqueror renowned,
 Thou sweetness most ineffable,
    In whom all joys are found!

7 When once thou visitest the heart,
    Then truth begins to shine;
 Then earthly vanities depart;
    Then kindles love divine.

8 O Jesu! Light of all below!
    Thou Fount of life and fire,
 Surpassing all the joys we know,
    And all we can desire:

9 May every heart confess thy name,
    And ever thee adore;
 And, seeking thee, itself inflame
    To seek thee more and more.

10 Thee may our tongues for ever bless,
    Thee may we love alone;
 And ever in our lives express
    The image of thine own.

A - men.

Part 3.

Jesu, decus angelicum.

11 O Jesu, thou the beauty art
    Of Angel worlds above;
 Thy name is music to the heart,
    Enchanting it with love.

12 Celestial sweetness unalloyed!
    Who eat thee hunger still;
 Who drink of thee still feel a void,
    Which nought but thou can fill.

13 O my sweet Jesu! hear the sighs
    Which unto thee I send;
 To thee mine inmost spirit cries,
    My being's hope and end!

14 Stay with us, Lord, and with thy light
    Illume the soul's abyss;
 Scatter the darkness of our night,
    And fill the world with bliss.

15. O Jesu! spotless virgin-flower!
    Our life and joy! to thee
 Be praise, beatitude, and power
    Through all eternity.

A - men.

GENERAL HYMNS

TRURO. (L. M.)
In moderate time ♩ = 96.

420

Psalmodia Evangelica, 1789.

I. Watts, 1674–1748.

JESUS shall reign where'er the sun
Does his successive journeys run;
His kingdom stretch from shore to shore, [more.
Till moons shall wax and wane no

2 People and realms of every tongue
Dwell on his love with sweetest song,
And infant voices shall proclaim
Their early blessings on his name.

3 Blessings abound where'er he reigns;
The prisoner leaps to lose his chains;
The weary find eternal rest,
And all the sons of want are blest.

Unison. 4. Let every creature rise and bring
Peculiar honours to our King;
Angels descend with songs again,
And earth repeat the long amen.

A - men.

NUN DANKET ALL. (C. M.)
Moderately slow ♩ = 100 (♩ = 50).

421

Praxis Pietatis Melica, 1653.

GENERAL HYMNS

Ray Palmer, 1808–87.

JESUS, these eyes have never seen
  That radiant form of thine;
The veil of sense hangs dark between
  Thy blessèd face and mine.

2 I see thee not, I hear thee not,
  Yet art thou oft with me;
And earth hath ne'er so dear a spot
  As where I met with thee.

3 Yet, though I have not seen, and still
  Must rest in faith alone,
I love thee, dearest Lord, and will,
  Unseen, but not unknown.

4. When death these mortal eyes shall seal,
  And still this throbbing heart,
The rending veil shall thee reveal
  All glorious as thou art.

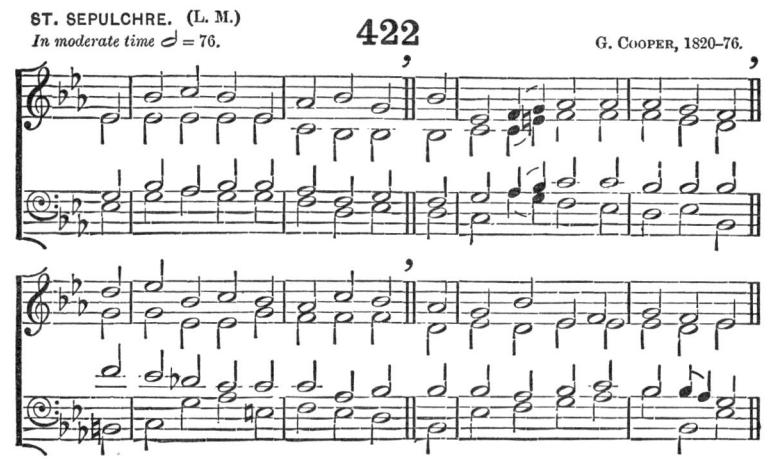

A - men.

ST. SEPULCHRE. (L. M.)
In moderate time ♩ = 76.

422

G. COOPER, 1820–76.

W. Cowper, 1731–1800.

JESUS, where'er thy people meet,
  There they behold thy mercy-seat;
Where'er they seek thee, thou art found,
And every place is hallowed ground.

2 For thou, within no walls confined,
  Inhabitest the humble mind;
Such ever bring thee where they come,
And going, take thee to their home.

3 Dear Shepherd of thy chosen few,
  Thy former mercies here renew;
Here to our waiting hearts proclaim
The sweetness of thy saving name.

4 Here may we prove the power of prayer,
  To strengthen faith and sweeten care;
  To teach our faint desires to rise,
  And bring all heaven before our eyes.

5. Lord, we are few, but thou art near;
  Nor short thine arm, nor deaf thine ear;
  O rend the heavens, come quickly down,
  And make a thousand hearts thine own!

A - men.

GENERAL HYMNS

423

RHUDDLAN. (87. 87. 87.)
Moderately slow ♩ = 88.
Welsh Traditional Melody.

Henry Scott Holland, 1847–1918.

Unison. JUDGE eternal, throned in splendour,
    Lord of lords and King of kings,
With thy living fire of judgement
    Purge this realm of bitter things:
Solace all its wide dominion
    With the healing of thy wings.

2 Still the weary folk are pining
    For the hour that brings release:
And the city's crowded clangour
    Cries aloud for sin to cease;
And the homesteads and the woodlands
    Plead in silence for their peace.

Unison. 3. Crown, O God, thine own endeavour:
    Cleave our darkness with thy sword:
Feed the faint and hungry heathen
    With the richness of thy Word:
Cleanse the body of this empire
    Through the glory of the Lord.

A - men.

GENERAL HYMNS

424

GWALCHMAI. (7 4. 7 4. D.)
In moderate time ♩ = 72.

J. D. JONES, 1827–70.

A-men.

George Herbert, 1593-1632.

KING of glory, King of peace,
    I will love thee,
And that love may never cease,
    I will move thee
Thou hast granted my request,
    Thou hast heard me;
Thou didst note my working breast,
    Thou hast spared me.

2 Wherefore with my utmost art
    I will sing thee,
And the cream of all my heart
    I will bring thee.
Though my sins against me cried,
    Thou didst clear me;
And alone, when they replied,
    Thou didst hear me.

3. Seven whole days, not one in seven,
    I will praise thee;
In my heart, though not in heaven,
    I can raise thee.
Small it is, in this poor sort
    To enrol thee:
E'en eternity's too short
    To extol thee.

GENERAL HYMNS

425

LUX BENIGNA. (10 4. 10 4. 10 10.)
Slow ♩ = 100 (♩ = 50).

J. B. DYKES, 1823-76.

J. H. Newman, 1801-90.

LEAD, kindly Light, amid the encircling gloom,
    Lead thou me on;
The night is dark, and I am far from home,
    Lead thou me on.
Keep thou my feet; I do not ask to see
The distant scene; one step enough for me.

2 I was not ever thus, nor prayed that thou
    Shouldst lead me on;
I loved to choose and see my path; but now
    Lead thou me on.
I loved the garish day, and, spite of fears,
Pride ruled my will: remember not past years.

3. So long thy power hath blest me, sure it still
    Will lead me on
O'er moor and fen, o'er crag and torrent, till
    The night is gone,
And with the morn those Angel faces smile,
Which I have loved long since, and lost awhile.

A - men.

GENERAL HYMNS

426

MANNHEIM. (87. 87. 87.)
Moderately slow ♩ = 66.

*Altered from Chorale
by F. Filitz, 1804-76.*

J. Edmeston, 1791-1867.

Lead us, heavenly Father, lead us
  O'er the world's tempestuous sea;
Guard us, guide us, keep us, feed us,
  For we have no help but thee;
Yet possessing every blessing
  If our God our Father be.

2 Saviour! breathe forgiveness o'er us,
  All our weakness thou dost know,
Thou didst tread this earth before us,
  Thou didst feel its keenest woe;
Lone and dreary, faint and weary,
  Through the desert thou didst go.

3. Spirit of our God, descending,
  Fill our hearts with heavenly joy,
Love with every passion blending,
  Pleasure that can never cloy:
Thus provided, pardoned, guided,
  Nothing can our peace destroy!

A - men.

GENERAL HYMNS

427

HIGH ROAD. (10 4. 6 6. 6 6. 10 4.)
Moderately fast ♩. = 80.

MARTIN SHAW.

[*Copyright*, 1915, *by J. Curwen & Sons, Ltd.*]
(*If desired, the 1st verse can be repeated after the 2nd.*)
NOTE.—*This hymn may also be sung to* UNIVERSAL PRAISE (*Appendix, No.* 56).

George Herbert, 1593–1632.

LET all the world in every corner sing,
   My God and King!
  The heavens are not too high,
  His praise may thither fly;
  The earth is not too low,
  His praises there may grow.
Let all the world in every corner sing,
   My God and King!

2. Let all the world in every corner sing,
   My God and King!
  The Church with psalms must shout,
  No door can keep them out;
  But above all, the heart
  Must bear the longest part.
Let all the world in every corner sing,
   My God and King!

GENERAL HYMNS

428

DUNDEE. (C. M.)
Moderately slow ♩ = 66.

Scottish Psalter, 1615, *as given in Ravenscroft's Psalter*, 1621.

NOTE.—*Another version of this tune, with the melody in the tenor, will be found at Hymn* **48**.

C. Wesley, 1707-88, *and others*.

LET saints on earth in concert sing
   With those whose work is done;
For all the servants of our King
   In earth and heaven are one.

2 One family, we dwell in him,
   One Church, above, beneath;
Though now divided by the stream,
   The narrow stream of death.

3 One army of the living God,
   To his command we bow;
Part of his host hath crossed the flood,
   And part is crossing now.

4 E'en now to their eternal home
   There pass some spirits blest,
While others to the margin come,
   Waiting their call to rest.

5. Jesu, be thou our constant Guide;
   Then, when the word is given,
Bid Jordan's narrow stream divide,
   And bring us safe to heaven.

A - men.

GENERAL HYMNS

BIRMINGHAM. (10 10. 10 10.) **429** From Rev. F. Cunningham's
In moderate time ♩ = 72. 'A Selection of Psalm Tunes', 1834.

Note.—*This hymn may also be sung to* Farley Castle (*No.* 217)
or to All Souls (*Appendix, No.* 57).

H. Montagu Butler, 1833–1918.

'LIFT up your hearts!' We lift them, Lord, to thee;
  Here at thy feet none other may we see:
'Lift up your hearts!' E'en so, with one accord,
We lift them up, we lift them to the Lord.

2 Above the level of the former years,
  The mire of sin, the slough of guilty fears,
  The mist of doubt, the blight of love's decay,
  O Lord of Light, lift all our hearts to-day!

3 Above the swamps of subterfuge and shame,
  The deeds, the thoughts, that honour may not name,
  The halting tongue that dares not tell the whole,
  O Lord of Truth, lift every Christian soul!

4 Lift every gift that thou thyself hast given;
  Low lies the best till lifted up to heaven:
  Low lie the bounding heart, the teeming brain,
  Till, sent from God, they mount to God again.

5. Then, as the trumpet-call, in after years,
  'Lift up your hearts!' rings pealing in our ears,
  Still shall those hearts respond, with full accord
  'We lift them up, we lift them to the Lord!'

A - men.

GENERAL HYMNS

430

ERFYNIAD. (10 10. 10 10.)
In moderate time ♩ = 80.

Welsh Hymn Melody, harmonized by DAVID EVANS.

NOTE.—*This hymn may also be sung to* SONG 24 (*No.* 325) *or to*
ALL SOULS (*Appendix, No.* 57.

Mrs. Frances M. Owen, 1842-83.

LIGHTEN the darkness of our life's long night,
    Through which we blindly stumble to the day.
Shadows mislead us: Father, send thy light
    To set our footsteps in the homeward way.

2 Lighten the darkness of our self-conceit—
    The subtle darkness that we love so well,
Which shrouds the path of wisdom from our feet,
    And lulls our spirits with its baneful spell.

3 Lighten our darkness when we bow the knee
    To all the gods we ignorantly make
And worship, dreaming that we worship thee,
    Till clearer light our slumbering souls awake.

4. Lighten our darkness when we fail at last,
    And in the midnight lay us down to die;
We trust to find thee when the night is past,
    And daylight breaks across the morning sky.

A - men.

GENERAL HYMNS

431

REGENT SQUARE. (8 7. 8 7. 8 7.)
Cheerfully ♩ = 88.

H. SMART, 1813–79.

NOTE.—*This hymn may also be sung to* URBS COELESTIS (*No.* 169).

Jerusalem luminosa.
15*th cent. Tr. J. M. Neale.*

LIGHT'S abode, celestial Salem,
   Vision dear whence peace doth spring,
Brighter than the heart can fancy,
   Mansion of the highest King;
O, how glorious are the praises
   Which of thee the prophets sing!

2 There for ever and for ever
   Alleluya is outpoured;
For unending, for unbroken
   Is the feast-day of the Lord;
All is pure and all is holy
   That within thy walls is stored.

3 There no cloud nor passing vapour
   Dims the brightness of the air;
Endless noon-day, glorious noon-day,
   From the Sun of suns is there;
There no night brings rest from labour,
   There unknown are toil and care.

4 O how glorious and resplendent,
   Fragile body, shalt thou be,
When endued with so much beauty,
   Full of health, and strong, and free,
Full of vigour, full of pleasure
   That shall last eternally!

5 Now with gladness, now with courage,
   Bear the burden on thee laid,
That hereafter these thy labours
   May with endless gifts be paid,
And in everlasting glory
   Thou with joy may'st be arrayed.

6. Laud and honour to the Father,
   Laud and honour to the Son,
Laud and honour to the Spirit,
   Ever Three and ever One,
Consubstantial, co-eternal,
   While unending ages run. Amen.

A - men.

GENERAL HYMNS

432

BATTLE. (10 10. 10 10. 10 10.)
Moderately slow ♩ = 69.

H. LAWES, 1596–1662.

J. Quarles, 1624–65, and H. F. Lyte.

LONG did I toil, and knew no earthly rest,
  Far did I rove, and found no certain home;
At last I sought them in his sheltering breast,
  Who opes his arms, and bids the weary come:
With him I found a home, a rest divine,
And I since then am his, and he is mine.

2 The good I have is from his stores supplied,
  The ill is only what he deems the best;
He for my Friend, I'm rich with nought beside,
  And poor without him, though of all possessed:
Changes may come, I take, or I resign,
Content, while I am his, while he is mine.

3 Whate'er may change, in him no change is seen,
  A glorious Sun that wanes not nor declines,
Above the clouds and storms he walks serene,
  And on his people's inward darkness shines:
All may depart, I fret not, nor repine,
While I my Saviour's am, while he is mine.

4.*While here, alas! I know but half his love,
  But half discern him, and but half adore;
But when I meet him in the realms above
  I hope to love him better, praise him more,
And feel, and tell, amid the choir divine,
How fully I am his, and he is mine.

A - men.

GENERAL HYMNS

433

DIBDIN. (C. M.)
In moderate time ♩ = 72.

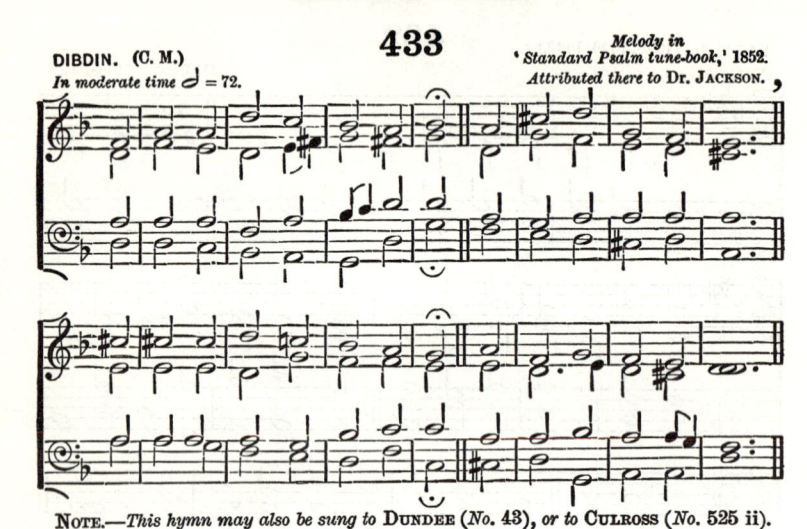

Melody in
'*Standard Psalm tune-book*,' 1852.
Attributed there to Dr. JACKSON.

NOTE.—*This hymn may also be sung to* DUNDEE (*No.* 43), *or to* CULROSS (*No.* 525 ii).

Richard Baxter ‡, 1615-91.

LORD, it belongs not to my care
    Whether I die or live;
To love and serve thee is my share,
    And this thy grace must give.

2 If life be long, I will be glad,
    That I may long obey;
If short, yet why should I be sad
    To end my little day?

3 Christ leads me through no darker rooms
    Than he went through before;
He that into God's kingdom comes
    Must enter by this door.

4 Come, Lord, when grace hath made me meet
    Thy blessèd face to see:
For if thy work on earth be sweet,
    What will thy glory be!

5 Then I shall end my sad complaints
    And weary, sinful days,
And join with the triumphant Saints
    That sing my Saviour's praise.

6. My knowledge of that life is small,
    The eye of faith is dim;
But 'tis enough that Christ knows all,
    And I shall be with him.

A - men.

GENERAL HYMNS

434

UFFINGHAM. (L. M.)
Very slow ♩ = 66.

J. CLARK, 1670–1707.

O. Wendell Holmes, 1809–94.

LORD of all being, throned afar,
Thy glory flames from sun and star;
Centre and soul of every sphere,
Yet to each loving heart how near!

2 Sun of our life, thy quickening ray
Sheds on our path the glow of day;
Star of our hope, thy softened light
Cheers the long watches of the night.

3 Our midnight is thy smile withdrawn,
Our noontide is thy gracious dawn,
Our rainbow arch thy mercy's sign;
All, save the clouds of sin, are thine.

4 Lord of all life, below, above,
Whose light is truth, whose warmth is love,
Before thy ever-blazing throne
We ask no lustre of our own.

5. Grant us thy truth to make us free
And kindling hearts that burn for thee,
Till all thy living altars claim
One holy light, one heavenly flame.

A - men.

GENERAL HYMNS

435

ISTE CONFESSOR (2). (11 11, 11 5.)
In moderate time ♩ = 96.
Rouen Church Melody.

NOTE.—*A unison setting of this tune will be found at Hymn 636. The proper melody for this hymn is* CHRISTE DU BEISTAND (*No.* 160).

P. Pusey ‡, 1799–1855. Based on Christe du Beistand, M. von Löwenstern, 1594–1648.

1. LORD of our life, and God of our salvation,
Star of our night, and Hope of every nation,
Hear and receive thy Church's supplication,
    Lord God Almighty.

2. See round thine ark the hungry billows curling;
See how thy foes their banners are unfurling;
Lord, while their darts envenomed they are hurling,
    Thou canst preserve us.

Unison. 3. Lord, thou canst help when earthly armour faileth,
Lord, thou canst save when deadly sin assaileth;
Christ, o'er thy Rock nor death nor hell prevaileth;
    Grant us thy peace, Lord.

4 * Peace in our hearts, our evil thoughts assuaging;
Peace in thy Church, where brothers are engaging;
Peace, when the world its busy war is waging:
    Calm thy foes' raging.

Unison. 5. Grant us thy help till backward they are driven,
Grant them thy truth, that they may be forgiven;
Grant peace on earth, and, after we have striven,
    Peace in thy heaven.

A - men.

GENERAL HYMNS

436 RAVENSHAW. (6 6. 6 6.)
Moderately slow ♩ = 63.
Melody abridged by W. H. MONK, *from 'Ave Hierarchia'* in M. WEISSE'S *Neu Gesengbuchlen,* 1531.

NOTE.—*This hymn may also be sung to* AVE MARIS STELLA (*No.* 213).

Sir H. W. Baker, 1821-77.

LORD, thy word abideth,
And our footsteps guideth;
Who its truth believeth
Light and joy receiveth.

2 When our foes are near us,
Then thy word doth cheer us,
Word of consolation,
Message of salvation.

3 When the storms are o'er us,
And dark clouds before us,
Then its light directeth,
And our way protecteth.

4 Who can tell the pleasure,
Who recount the treasure
By thy word imparted
To the simple-hearted?

5 Word of mercy, giving
Succour to the living;
Word of life, supplying
Comfort to the dying.

6. O that we discerning
Its most holy learning,
Lord, may love and fear thee,
Evermore be near thee!

A - men.

GENERAL HYMNS

MORIAH. (87. 87. D.)   **437**   *Welsh Hymn Melody.*
Slow ♩ = 80.

NOTE.—*This hymn may also be sung to* LUGANO (*No.* 529).

C. Wesley, 1707–88.

LOVE Divine, all loves excelling,
  Joy of heaven, to earth come down,
Fix in us thy humble dwelling,
  All thy faithful mercies crown.
Jesu, thou art all compassion,
  Pure unbounded love thou art;
Visit us with thy salvation,
  Enter every trembling heart.

2 Come, almighty to deliver,
  Let us all thy life receive;
Suddenly return, and never,
  Never more thy temples leave.
Thee we would be always blessing,
  Serve thee as thy hosts above,
Pray, and praise thee, without ceasing,
  Glory in thy perfect love.

3. Finish then thy new creation,
  Pure and spotless let us be;
Let us see thy great salvation,
  Perfectly restored in thee,
Changed from glory into glory,
  Till in heaven we take our place,
Till we cast our crowns before thee,
  Lost in wonder, love, and praise!

GENERAL HYMNS

438

SONG 22. (10 10. 10 10.)
In moderate time ♩ = 72.
O. GIBBONS, 1583–1625.

Amor Patris et Filii.

12th cent. *Tr.* Y. H.

LOVE of the Father, love of God the Son,
From whom all came, in whom was all begun;
Who formest heavenly beauty out of strife,
Creation's whole desire and breath of life.

2 Thou the all-holy, thou supreme in might,
Thou dost give peace, thy presence maketh right;
Thou with thy favour all things dost enfold,
With thine all-kindness free from harm wilt hold.

3 Hope of all comfort, splendour of all aid,
That dost not fail nor leave the heart afraid:
To all that cry thou dost all help accord,
The Angels' armour, and the Saints' reward.

4 Purest and highest, wisest and most just,
There is no truth save only in thy trust;
Thou dost the mind from earthly dreams recall,
And bring through Christ to him for whom are all.

5. Eternal glory, all men thee adore,
Who art and shalt be worshipped evermore:
Us whom thou madest, comfort with thy might,
And lead us to enjoy the heavenly light.

A - men.

GENERAL HYMNS
439

DENBIGH. (6 6 4. 6 6 6. 4.)
In moderate time ♩ = 80.
Welsh Hymn Melody.

NOTE.—*This hymn may also be sung to* OLIVET (*Appendix, No.* 58).

Ray Palmer, 1808–87.

MY faith looks up to thee,
  Thou Lamb of Calvary,
    Saviour divine!
Now hear me while I pray,
Take all my guilt away,
O let me from this day
    Be wholly thine.

2 May thy rich grace impart
  Strength to my fainting heart,
    My zeal inspire;
As thou hast died for me,
O may my love to thee
Pure, warm, and changeless be,
    A living fire.

3 While life's dark maze I tread,
  And griefs around me spread,
    Be thou my guide;
Bid darkness turn to day,
Wipe sorrow's tears away,
Nor let me ever stray
    From thee aside.

4. When ends life's transient dream,
  When death's cold sullen stream
    Shall o'er me roll,
Blest Saviour, then in love
Fear and distrust remove;
O bear me safe above,
    A ransomed soul.

A - men.

GENERAL HYMNS

440

LAYRIZ (INS FELD GEH). (88.84.)
In moderate time ♩ = 80.

*Melody from Layriz Collection, 1853
(probably based on a German traditional melody).*

NOTE.—*This hymn may also be sung to* TROYTE *No. 1 (Appendix, No. 59).*

Charlotte Elliott, 1789-1871.

MY God and Father, while I stray,
  Far from my home, in life's rough way,
O teach me from my heart to say,
        'Thy will be done!'

2 If but my fainting heart be blest
  With thy sweet Spirit for its guest,
My God, to thee I leave the rest—
        Thy will be done!

3 Renew my will from day to day,
  Blend it with thine, and take away
All that now makes it hard to say,
        'Thy will be done!'

4. Then when on earth I breathe no more
  The prayer oft mixed with tears before,
I'll sing upon a happier shore—
        'Thy will be done!'

A - men.

GENERAL HYMNS

441

WESTMINSTER. (C. M.)
In moderate time ♩ = 76.

J. TURLE, 1802-82.

F. W. Faber, 1814-63.

1. MY God, how wonderful thou art,
    Thy majesty how bright,
  How beautiful thy mercy-seat,
    In depths of burning light!

2. How dread are thine eternal years,
    O everlasting Lord,
  By prostrate spirits day and night
    Incessantly adored!

3. How wonderful, how beautiful,
    The sight of thee must be,
  Thine endless wisdom, boundless power,
    And awful purity!

4. O, how I fear thee, living God,
    With deepest, tenderest fears,
  And worship thee with trembling hope,
    And penitential tears!

5. Yet I may love thee too, O Lord,
    Almighty as thou art,
  For thou hast stooped to ask of me
    The love of my poor heart.

6. No earthly father loves like thee,
    No mother, e'er so mild,
  Bears and forbears as thou hast done
    With me thy sinful child.

7. Father of Jesus, love's reward,
    What rapture will it be
  Prostrate before thy throne to lie,
    And gaze and gaze on thee.

A - men.

GENERAL HYMNS

442

SONG 20. (S. M.)
In moderate time ♩ = 72.

O. GIBBONS, 1583-1625.

Y. H., based on I. Watts.

MY Lord, my Life, my Love,
   To thee, to thee I call;
I cannot live if thou remove:
   Thou art my joy, my all.

2 My only sun to cheer
   The darkness where I dwell;
The best and only true delight
   My song hath found to tell.

3 To thee in very heaven
   The Angels owe their bliss;
To thee the Saints, whom thou hast called
   Where perfect pleasure is.

4 And how shall man, thy child,
   Without thee happy be,
Who hath no comfort nor desire
   In all the world but thee?

5. Return my Love, my Life,
   Thy grace hath won my heart;
If thou forgive, if thou return,
   I will no more depart.

A - men.

GENERAL HYMNS

MARIA JUNG UND ZART. (66.66.)   **443**

In moderate time ♩ = 72.

Melody and harmony from 'Psalteriolum Harmonicum,' 1642.

J. Byrom †, 1692-1763.

MY spirit longs for thee
   Within my troubled breast,
Though I unworthy be
   Of so divine a Guest.

2 Of so divine a Guest
   Unworthy though I be,
Yet has my heart no rest
   Unless it come from thee.

3 Unless it come from thee,
   In vain I look around;
In all that I can see
   No rest is to be found.

4. No rest is to be found
   But in thy blessèd love:
O, let my wish be crowned,
   And send it from above!

A - men.

GENERAL HYMNS

444

HORBURY. (6 4. 6 4. 6 6 4.)
Very slow ♩ = 56.

J. B. DYKES, 1823-76

Sarah F. Adams, 1805-48

NEARER. my God, to thee,
    Nearer to thee!
E'en though it be a cross
    That raiseth me:
Still all my song would be,
'Nearer, my God, to thee,—
    Nearer to thee!'

2 Though, like the wanderer,
    The sun gone down,
Darkness be over me,
    My rest a stone;
Yet in my dreams I'd be
Nearer, my God, to thee,
    Nearer to thee!

3. There let the way appear,
    Steps unto heaven;
All that thou send'st to me
    In mercy given:
Angels to beckon me
Nearer, my God, to thee,
    Nearer to thee!

A - men.

GENERAL HYMNS

445

(FIRST TUNE)

CAITHNESS. (C. M.)
Moderately slow ♩ = 66.
Melody in Scottish Psalter, 1635.

(SECOND TUNE)

STRACATHRO. (C. M.)
In moderate time ♩ = 92.
Melody by CHARLES HUTCHESON, 1792-1860, *from Christian Vespers, Glasgow, 1832.*
Harmonized by GEOFFREY SHAW.

W. Cowper, 1731-1800.

O FOR a closer walk with God,
  A calm and heavenly frame;
A light to shine upon the road
  That leads me to the Lamb!

2 Return, O holy Dove, return,
  Sweet messenger of rest;
I hate the sins that made thee mourn,
  And drove thee from my breast.

3 The dearest idol I have known,
  Whate'er that idol be,
Help me to tear it from thy throne,
  And worship only thee.

4. So shall my walk be close with God,
  Calm and serene my frame;
So purer light shall mark the road
  That leads me to the Lamb.

GENERAL HYMNS

446

O GOD OF LOVE. (C. M.)
Moderately slow ♩ = 80.

'B. R.' in 'The Divine Companion,' 1709.

NOTE.—*This hymn may also be sung to* RICHMOND (*No.* 375).

C. Wesley, 1707-88.

O FOR a thousand tongues to sing
   My dear Redeemer's praise,
The glories of my God and King,
   The triumphs of his grace!

2 Jesus—the name that charms our fears,
   That bids our sorrows cease;
'Tis music in the sinner's ears,
   'Tis life, and health, and peace.

3*He breaks the power of cancelled sin,
   He sets the prisoner free;
His Blood can make the foulest clean;
   His Blood availed for me.

4 He speaks;—and, listening to his voice,
   New life the dead receive,
The mournful broken hearts rejoice,
   The humble poor believe.

5 Hear him, ye deaf; his praise, ye dumb,
   Your loosened tongues employ;
Ye blind, behold your Saviour come;
   And leap, ye lame, for joy!

6. My gracious Master and my God,
   Assist me to proclaim
And spread through all the earth abroad
   The honours of thy name.

A- men.

GENERAL HYMNS

447

BURFORD. (C.M.)
Slow ♩ = 72.

From Chetham's Psalmody, 1718.

P. Doddridge, 1702-51, and J. Logan.

O GOD of Bethel, by whose hand
   Thy people still are fed,
Who through this weary pilgrimage
   Hast all our fathers led:

2 Our vows, our prayers, we now present
    Before thy throne of grace;
  God of our fathers, be the God
    Of their succeeding race.

3 Through each perplexing path of life
    Our wandering footsteps guide;
  Give us each day our daily bread,
    And raiment fit provide.

4. O spread thy covering wings around,
    Till all our wanderings cease,
  And at our Father's loved abode
    Our souls arrive in peace.

A - men.

GENERAL HYMNS

FITZWILLIAM. (88. 86.) **448**
Moderately slow ♩ = 66.
From an English Traditional Melody.

G. Thring, 1823-1903.

O GOD of mercy, God of might,
　In love and pity infinite,
Teach us, as ever in thy sight,
　To live our life to thee.

2 And thou, who cam'st on earth to die
That fallen man might live thereby,
O hear us, for to thee we cry,
　In hope, O Lord, to thee.

3 Teach us the lesson thou hast taught,
To feel for those thy Blood hath bought,
That every word, and deed, and thought
　May work a work for thee.

4 For all are brethren, far and wide,
Since thou, O Lord, for all hast died:
Then teach us, whatsoe'er betide,
　To love them all in thee.

5 In sickness, sorrow, want, or care,
Whate'er it be, 'tis ours to share;
May we, where help is needed, there
　Give help as unto thee.

6. And may thy Holy Spirit move
All those who live to live in love,
Till thou shalt greet in heaven above
　All those who give to thee.

A - men.

GENERAL HYMNS

MARTYRS. (C.M.)
Slow and solemn ♩ = 56.
To be sung in unison

449

Scottish Psalter, 1635 (original form of the melody).

NOTE.—*This hymn may also be sung to* YORK (*No. 472*).

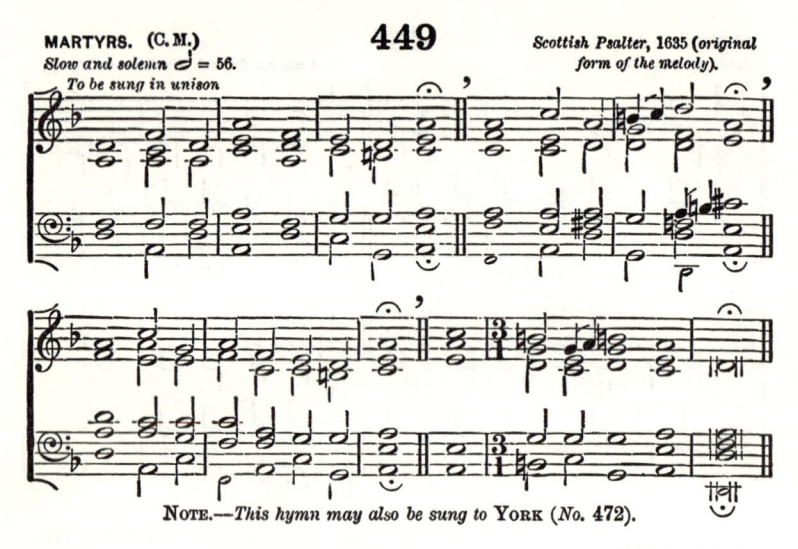

T. Hughes, 1823-96.

O GOD of truth, whose living word
   Upholds whate'er hath breath,
Look down on thy creation, Lord,
   Enslaved by sin and death.

2 Set up thy standard, Lord, that we
   Who claim a heavenly birth
May march with thee to smite the lies
   That vex thy groaning earth.

3 Ah! would we join that blest array,
   And follow in the might
Of him, the Faithful and the True,
   In raiment clean and white!

4 We fight for truth! we fight for God!
   Poor slaves of lies and sin;
He who would fight for thee on earth
   Must first be true within.

5 Then, God of truth, for whom we long—
   Thou who wilt hear our prayer—
Do thine own battle in our hearts,
   And slay the falsehood there.

6. Yea, come! then, tried as in the fire.
   From every lie set free,
Thy perfect truth shall dwell in us,
   And we shall live in thee.

Harmony.

A - men.

GENERAL HYMNS

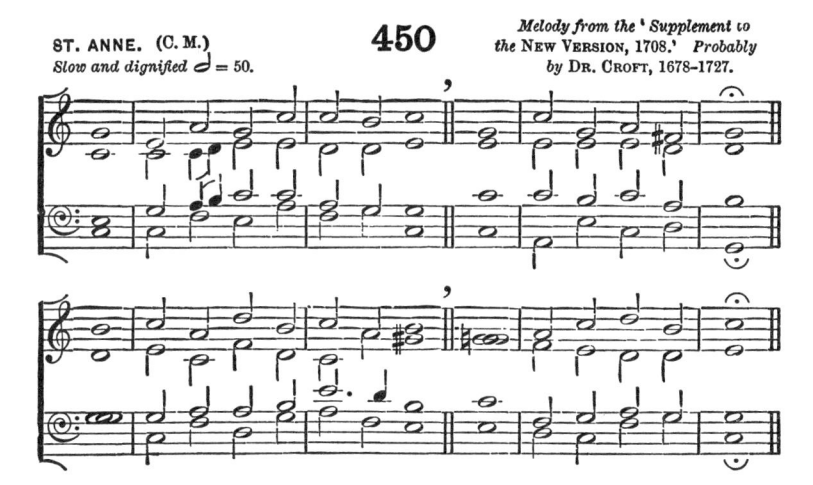

ST. ANNE. (C.M.) **450** Melody from the 'Supplement to the NEW VERSION, 1708.' Probably by DR. CROFT, 1678-1727.
Slow and dignified ♩ = 50.

Ps. 90.   *I. Watts* †, 1674–1748.

O GOD, our help in ages past,
   Our hope for years to come,
Our shelter from the stormy blast,
   And our eternal home;

2 Under the shadow of thy throne
   Thy Saints have dwelt secure;
Sufficient is thine arm alone,
   And our defence is sure.

Unison. 3 Before the hills in order stood,
   Or earth received her frame.
From everlasting thou art God,
   To endless years the same.

4 A thousand ages in thy sight
   Are like an evening gone,
Short as the watch that ends the night
   Before the rising sun.

5 Time, like an ever-rolling stream,
   Bears all its sons away;
They fly forgotten, as a dream
   Dies at the opening day.

Unison. 6. O God, our help in ages past,
   Our hope for years to come,
Be thou our guard while troubles last,
   And our eternal home.

A - men.

GENERAL HYMNS

451

MELROSE. (C.M.)
Moderately slow ♩ = 66.
Scottish Psalter, 1635.

NOTE.—*This hymn may also be sung to* PRAETORIUS (*No.* 549).

F. W. Faber, 1814–63

O GOD, thy power is wonderful,
    Thy glory passing bright;
Thy wisdom, with its deep on deep,
    A rapture to the sight.

2 Thy justice is the gladdest thing
    Creation can behold;
Thy tenderness so meek, it wins
    The guilty to be bold.

3 Yet more than all, and ever more,
    Should we thy creatures bless,
Most worshipful of attributes,
    Thine awful holiness.

4 There's not a craving in the mind
    Thou dost not meet and still;
There's not a wish the heart can have
    Which thou dost not fulfil.

5. O little heart of mine, shall pain
    Or sorrow make thee moan,
When all this God is all for thee,
    A Father all thine own?

A - men.

GENERAL HYMNS

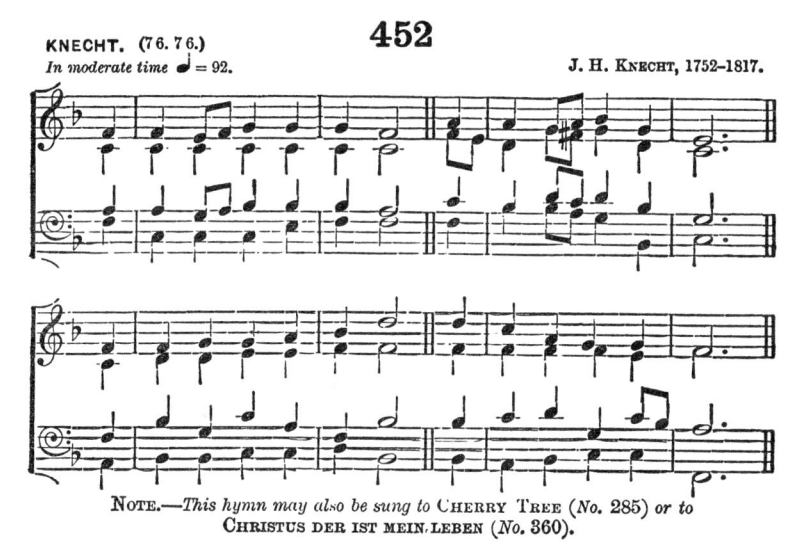

452

KNECHT. (76. 76.)
In moderate time ♩ = 92.

J. H. KNECHT, 1752–1817.

NOTE.—*This hymn may also be sung to* CHERRY TREE (*No.* 285) *or to* CHRISTUS DER IST MEIN LEBEN (*No.* 360).

J. M. Neale, 1818–66.

O HAPPY band of pilgrims,
   If onward ye will tread
With Jesus as your fellow
   To Jesus as your Head!

2 O happy if ye labour
   As Jesus did for men;
O happy if ye hunger
   As Jesus hungered then!

3*The Cross that Jesus carried
   He carried as your due;
The Crown that Jesus weareth,
   He weareth it for you.

4*The faith by which ye see him,
   The hope in which ye yearn,
The love that through all troubles
   To him alone will turn,

5*What are they but forerunners
   To lead you to his sight?
What are they save the effluence
   Of uncreated Light?

6 The trials that beset you,
   The sorrows ye endure,
The manifold temptations
   That death alone can cure,

7 What are they but his jewels
   Of right celestial worth?
What are they but the ladder
   Set up to heaven on earth?

8. O happy band of pilgrims,
   Look upward to the skies,
Where such a light affliction
   Shall win you such a prize!

A - men.

GENERAL HYMNS

TALLIS' ORDINAL ('9TH TUNE'). (C.M.) 453
Moderately slow ♩=66. T. TALLIS, c. 1515–85

C. *Coffin*, 1676–1749.   Tr. J. Chandler.
O fons amoris, Spiritus.

O HOLY Spirit, Lord of grace,
  Eternal source of love,
Inflame, we pray, our inmost hearts
  With fire from heaven above.

2 As thou dost join with holiest bonds
  The Father and the Son.
So fill thy saints with mutual love
  And link their hearts in one.

3. To God the Father, God the Son,
  And God the Holy Ghost,
Eternal glory be from man,
  And from the Angel-host. Amen.

A - men.

TEMPLE. (66.84.) 454
Stately ♩=80. H. WALFORD DAVIES.

NOTE.—*The barring of this tune is necessarily irregular, but it will be found easy of performance if the time-value of a minim be kept in mind.*

GENERAL HYMNS

Pentecostarion, c. 8th cent. Tr. J. B.

Βασιλεῦ οὐράνιε, Παράκλητε.

O KING enthroned on high,
   Thou Comforter divine,
Blest Spirit of all truth, be nigh
   And make us thine.

2 Thou art the Source of life,
   Thou art our treasure-store;
Give us thy peace, and end our strife
   For evermore.

3. Descend, O heavenly Dove,
   Abide with us alway;
And in the fullness of thy love
   Cleanse us, we pray.

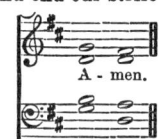

A - men.

CLEWER. (65.65.)   **455**   ANON.
Moderately slow ♩ = 63.

NOTE.—*This hymn may also be sung to* CASWALL *(No. 315), which is proper to it.*

H. S. Oswald, 1751–1834.
Wem in Leidenstagen.   *Tr. F. E. Cox ‡.*

O LET him whose sorrow
   No relief can find,
Trust in God, and borrow
   Ease for heart and mind.

2 Where the mourner weeping
   Sheds the secret tear,
God his watch is keeping,
   Though none else be near.

3 God will never leave thee,
   All thy wants he knows,
Feels the pains that grieve thee,
   Sees thy cares and woes.

4 Raise thine eyes to heaven
   When thy spirits quail,
When, by tempests driven,
   Heart and courage fail.

5 When in grief we languish,
   He will dry the tear,
Who his children's anguish
   Soothes with succour near.

6 All our woe and sadness
   In this world below
Balance not the gladness
   We in heaven shall know.

7. Jesu, gracious Saviour,
   In the realms above
Crown with us thy favour,
   Fill us with thy love.

A - men.

GENERAL HYMNS

456

BLACKBOURNE. (C. M.)
In moderate time ♩ = 92.

Harrison's Sacred Harmony, 1784.

NOTE.—*This hymn may also be sung to* WALSALL (*No. 13*).

J. G. Whittier, 1807-92.

O LORD, and Master of us all,
   Whate'er our name or sign,
We own thy sway, we hear thy call,
   We test our lives by thine.

2 Thou judgest us; thy purity
   Doth all our lusts condemn;
The love that draws us nearer thee
   Is hot with wrath to them;

3 Our thoughts lie open to thy sight;
   And naked to thy glance

Our secret sins are in the light
   Of thy pure countenance.

4 Yet weak and blinded though we be
   Thou dost our service own;
We bring our varying gifts to thee,
   And thou rejectest none.

5 To thee our full humanity,
   Its joys and pains belong;
The wrong of man to man on thee
   Inflicts a deeper wrong.

6 Who hates, hates thee; who loves, becomes
   Therein to thee allied:
All sweet accords of hearts and homes
   In thee are multiplied.

7. Apart from thee all gain is loss,
   All labour vainly done;
The solemn shadow of the Cross
   Is better than the sun.

A - men.

GENERAL HYMNS

457

MAGDALEN COLLEGE. (886. D.)
In moderate time ♩ = 92.

W. HAYES, 1706–77.

J. Anstice, 1808–36.

O LORD, how happy should we be
  If we could cast our care on thee,
    If we from self could rest;
  And feel at heart that One above,
  In perfect wisdom, perfect love,
    Is working for the best.

2 Could we but kneel, and cast our load,
  E'en while we pray, upon our God,
    Then rise with lightened cheer;
  Sure that the Father, who is nigh
  To still the famished raven's cry,
    Will hear in that we fear.

3. Lord, make these faithless hearts of ours
  Such lessons learn from birds and flowers—
    Make them from self to cease;
  Leave all things to a Father's will,
  And taste, before him lying still,
    E'en in affliction, peace.

A - men.

458

NEUMARK. (98.98.88.)
Slow 𝅗𝅥 = 72.

Original version of melody by
G. NEUMARK, 1621–81.

E. H. Plumptre, 1821–91.

O LORD of hosts, all heaven possessing,
  Behold us from thy sapphire throne,
In doubt and darkness dimly guessing,
  We might thy glory half have known;
But thou in Christ hast made us thine,
And on us all thy beauties shine.

2 Illumine all, disciples, teachers,
  Thy law's deep wonders to unfold;
With reverent hand let wisdom's preachers
  Bring forth their treasures, new and old;
Let oldest, youngest, find in thee
Of truth and love the boundless sea.

3 Let faith still light the lamp of science,
  And knowledge pass from truth to truth,
And wisdom, in its full reliance,
  Renew the primal awe of youth;
So holier, wiser, may we grow,
As time's swift currents onward flow.

GENERAL HYMNS

4.*Bind thou our life in fullest union
  With all thy Saints from sin set free;
Uphold us in that blest communion
  Of all thy Saints on earth with thee;
Keep thou our souls, or there, or here,
In mightiest love, that casts out fear.

EISENACH. (L. M.)
Very slow and solemn ♩ = 46.

459

Adapted from a melody by
J. H. SCHEIN, 1586-1630.
Harmony from J. S. BACH.

NOTE.—*This melody is an adaptation of the first tune at Hymn* 138. *It may, therefore, be thought advisable to sing this hymn to another tune.* ILLSLEY (*No.* 61) *is suggested as being suitable.*

O Amor, quam ecstaticus.   15th cent.   *Tr.* B. Webb.

O LOVE, how deep, how broad, how high!
How passing thought and fantasy
That God, the Son of God, should take
Our mortal form for mortals' sake.

2 He sent no Angel to our race
Of higher or of lower place,
But wore the robe of human frame,
And he himself to this world came.

3 For us baptized, for us he bore
His holy fast, and hungered sore;
For us temptations sharp he knew;
For us the tempter overthrew.

4 For us to wicked men betrayed,
Scourged, mocked, in crown of thorns arrayed;
For us he bore the Cross's death;
For us at length gave up his breath.

Unison.
5 For us he rose from death again,
For us he went on high to reign,
For us he sent his Spirit here
To guide, to strengthen, and to cheer.

6. All honour, laud, and glory be,
O Jesu, Virgin-born, to thee,
All glory, as is ever meet,
To Father and to Paraclete. Amen.

GENERAL HYMNS

460

CHRISTCHURCH. (88.88.88.)
In moderate time ♩= 72.

F. A. GORE OUSELEY, 1825-89.

NOTE.—*This hymn may also be sung to* SOUTH CERNEY (*No.* 359).

J. Scheffler, 1624-77. Tr. C. Winkworth.

Liebe die du mich zum Bilde.

1. O LOVE, who formedst me to wear
The image of thy Godhead here;
Who soughtest me with tender care
Through all my wanderings wild and drear:
    O Love, I give myself to thee,
    Thine ever, only thine to be.

2. O Love, who once in time was slain,
Pierced through and through with bitter woe;
O Love, who wrestling thus didst gain
That we eternal joy might know:

3. O Love, of whom is truth and light,
The Word and Spirit, life and power,
Whose heart was bared to them that smite,
To shield us in our trial hour:

4.*O Love, who lovest me for ay,
Who for my soul dost ever plead;
O Love, who didst my ransom pay,
Whose power sufficeth in my stead:

5.*O Love, who once shalt bid me rise
From out this dying life of ours;
O Love, who once above yon skies
Shalt set me in the fadeless bowers:

A - men.

GENERAL HYMNS

461

OLD 81ST (OLD 77TH). (D. C. M.)
Slow and dignified ♩ = 76.

Este's Psalter, 1592.
Original version appeared in Day's Psalter, 1562.

Unison.

Harriet Auber, 1773–1862.

O PRAISE our great and gracious Lord
And call upon his name;
To strains of joy tune every chord,
His mighty acts proclaim;
Tell how he led his chosen race
To Canaan's promised land;
Tell how his covenant of grace
Unchanged shall ever stand.

2 * He gave the shadowing cloud by day,
The moving fire by night;
To guide his Israel on their way,
He made their darkness light;
And have not we a sure retreat,
A Saviour ever nigh,
The same clear light to guide our feet,
The Dayspring from on high?

3 We too have Manna from above,
The Bread that came from heaven;
To us the same kind hand of love
Hath living waters given.
A Rock we have, from whence the spring
In rich abundance flows;
That Rock is Christ, our Priest, our King,
Who life and health bestows.

Unison. 4. O let us prize this blessèd food,
And trust our heavenly Guide;
So shall we find death's fearful flood
Serene as Jordan's tide,
And safely reach that happy shore,
The land of peace and rest,
Where Angels worship and adore,
In God's own presence blest.

A - men.

GENERAL HYMNS

VATER UNSER. (8 8. 8 8. 8 8.)
Very slow and solemn ♩ = 48.

462

Melody from Schumann's Gesangbuch, 1539.
Harmony from J. S. BACH.

L. Tuttiett, 1825–99.

1 O QUICKLY come, dread Judge of all;
   For, awful though thine advent be,
All shadows from the truth will fall,
   And falsehood die, in sight of thee:
O quickly come; for doubt and fear
Like clouds dissolve when thou art near.

Unison.
2 O quickly come, great King of all;
   Reign all around us, and within;
Let sin no more our souls enthral,
   Let pain and sorrow die with sin:
O quickly come; for thou alone
Canst make thy scattered people one.

3 O quickly come, true Life of all,
   For death is mighty all around;
On every home his shadows fall,
   On every heart his mark is found:
O quickly come; for grief and pain
Can never cloud thy glorious reign.

GENERAL HYMNS

4. O quickly come, sure Light of all,
   For gloomy night broods o'er our way,
And weakly souls begin to fall
   With weary watching for the day:
O quickly come; for round thy throne
No eye is blind, no night is known.

A - men.

CROWLE. (C.M.)   **463**   *Melody from 'A Book of Psalmody'*
Slow ♩ = 72.   *by* JAMES GREEN, 1724.

F. L. Hosmer, 1840-1929.

O THOU in all thy might so far,
   In all thy love so near,
Beyond the range of sun and star,
   And yet beside us here:

2 What heart can comprehend thy name,
   Or searching find thee out,
Who art within, a quickening flame,
   A presence round about?

3 Yet though I know thee but in part,
   I ask not, Lord, for more;
Enough for me to know thou art,
   To love thee, and adore.

4. And dearer than all things I know
   Is childlike faith to me,
That makes the darkest way I go
   An open path to thee.

A - men.

607

GENERAL HYMNS

OLD 120TH. (66.66.66.)
Moderately slow ♩ = 66.

464

Melody from Damon's Psalter, 1579, and Este's Psalter, 1592, rhythm slightly adapted.

F. T. Palgrave, 1824–97.

O THOU not made with hands,
   Not throned above the skies,
Nor walled with shining walls,
   Nor framed with stones of price,
More bright than gold or gem,
God's own Jerusalem!

2 Where'er the gentle heart
   Finds courage from above;
Where'er the heart forsook
   Warms with the breath of love;
Where faith bids fear depart,
City of God, thou art.

3 Thou art where'er the proud
   In humbleness melts down;
Where self itself yields up;
   Where Martyrs win their crown;
Where faithful souls possess
Themselves in perfect peace;

4 Where in life's common ways
   With cheerful feet we go;
Where in his steps we tread,
   Who trod the way of woe;
Where he is in the heart,
City of God, thou art.

5. Not throned above the skies,
    Nor golden-walled afar,
But where Christ's two or three
    In his name gathered are,
Be in the midst of them,
God's own Jerusalem.

A - men.

608

GENERAL HYMNS

REGNATOR ORBIS. (10 10. 10 10.) **465** *Adapted from a melody in* LA FEILLÉE,
In moderate time ♩ = 96. '*Méthode du plain-chant,*' 1808.

To be sung in unison.

O quanta qualia sunt illa Sabbata.

P. Abelard, 1079–1142.
Tr. J. M. *Neale.*

O WHAT their joy and their glory must be,
   Those endless Sabbaths the blessèd ones see!
Crown for the valiant; to weary ones rest;
   God shall be all, and in all ever blest.

2*What are the Monarch, his court, and his throne?
   What are the peace and the joy that they own?
Tell us, ye blest ones, that in it have share,
   If what ye feel ye can fully declare.

3 Truly Jerusalem name we that shore,
   'Vision of peace,' that brings joy evermore!
Wish and fulfilment can severed be ne'er,
   Nor the thing prayed for come short of the prayer.

4 We, where no trouble distraction can bring,
   Safely the anthems of Sion shall sing;
While for thy grace, Lord, their voices of praise
   Thy blessèd people shall evermore raise.

5*There dawns no Sabbath, no Sabbath is o'er,
   Those Sabbath-keepers have one and no more;
One and unending is that triumph-song
   Which to the Angels and us shall belong.

6*Now in the meanwhile, with hearts raised on high,
   We for that country must yearn and must sigh,
Seeking Jerusalem, dear native land,
   Through our long exile on Babylon's strand.

7. Low before him with our praises we fall,
   Of whom, and in whom, and through whom are all;
Of whom, the Father; and through whom, the Son;
   In whom, the Spirit, with these ever One.   Amen.

Harmony.

A - men.

GENERAL HYMNS

466

HANOVER. (55. 55. 65. 65.)
Slow ♩ = 72.

Probably by Dr. Croft, 1678-1727.

Ps. 104.

Sir R. Grant: 1779-1838.

O WORSHIP the King
  All glorious above;
O gratefully sing
  His power and his love:
Our Shield and Defender,
  The Ancient of days,
Pavilioned in splendour,
  And girded with praise.

GENERAL HYMNS

Unison. 2 O tell of his might,
  O sing of his grace,
 Whose robe is the light,
  Whose canopy space.
 His chariots of wrath
  The deep thunder-clouds form.
 And dark is his path
  On the wings of the storm.

3 This earth, with its store
  Of wonders untold,
 Almighty, thy power
  Hath founded of old;
 Hath stablished it fast
  By a changeless decree,
 And round it hath cast,
  Like a mantle, the sea.

4* Thy bountiful care
  What tongue can recite?
 It breathes in the air,
  It shines in the light;
 It streams from the hills,
  It descends to the plain,
 And sweetly distils
  In the dew and the rain.

5* Frail children of dust,
  And feeble as frail,
 In thee do we trust,
  Nor find thee to fail:
 Thy mercies how tender!
  How firm to the end!
 Our Maker, Defender,
  Redeemer, and Friend.

Unison. 6. O measureless Might,
  Ineffable Love,
 While Angels delight
  To hymn thee above,
 Thy humbler creation,
  Though feeble their lays,
 With true adoration
  Shall sing to thy praise.

A - men.

GENERAL HYMNS

467

UNIVERSITY COLLEGE. (77.77.)
Moderately quick ♩ = 108.

H. J. GAUNTLETT, 1805–76.

H. Kirke White (1785–1806),
Frances S. Fuller-Maitland and others (1827).

OFT in danger, oft in woe,
  Onward, Christians, onward go;
Bear the toil, maintain the strife,
Strengthened with the Bread of Life.

2 Onward, Christians, onward go,
  Join the war, and face the foe;
Will ye flee in danger's hour?
Know ye not your Captain's power?

Unison.   3 Let your drooping hearts be glad;
  March in heavenly armour clad;
Fight, nor think the battle long,
Victory soon shall tune your song.

4 Let not sorrow dim your eye,
  Soon shall every tear be dry;
Let not fears your course impede,
Great your strength, if great your need.

Unison.   5. Onward then in battle move;
  More than conquerors ye shall prove;
Though opposed by many a foe,
Christian soldiers, onward go.

A - men.

GENERAL HYMNS

468

SONG 46. (10. 10.)
Slow ♩ = 60.

First strain of Song 46.
O. GIBBONS, 1583-1625.

Bishop E. H. Bickersteth, 1825-1906.

PEACE perfect peace, in this dark world of sin?
The Blood of Jesus whispers peace within.

2 Peace, perfect peace, by thronging duties pressed?
To do the will of Jesus, this is rest.

3 Peace, perfect peace, with sorrows surging round?
On Jesus' bosom nought but calm is found.

4 Peace, perfect peace, with loved ones far away?
In Jesus' keeping we are safe and they.

5 Peace, perfect peace, our future all unknown?
Jesus we know, and he is on the throne.

6 Peace, perfect peace, death shadowing us and ours?
Jesus has vanquished death and all its powers.

7. It is enough: earth's struggles soon shall cease,
And Jesus call us to heaven's perfect peace.

A - men.

GENERAL HYMNS

469

BENEVENTO. (77.77. D.)
Moderately slow, dignified ♩ = 69.

Adapted from S. WEBBE'S
'Motetts or Antiphons,' 1792.

NOTE.—*Another tune for this hymn will be found in the Appendix* (No. 20).

Ps. 84. H. F. Lyte, 1793–1847.

PLEASANT are thy courts above
In the land of light and love;
Pleasant are thy courts below
In this land of sin and woe:
O, my spirit longs and faints
For the converse of thy Saints,
For the brightness of thy face,
For thy fullness, God of grace.

2 Happy birds that sing and fly
Round thy altars, O most High;
Happier souls that find a rest
In a heavenly Father's breast;
Like the wandering dove that found
No repose on earth around,
They can to their ark repair,
And enjoy it ever there.

3 Happy souls, their praises flow
Even in this vale of woe;
Waters in the desert rise,
Manna feeds them from the skies;
On they go from strength to strength,
Till they reach thy throne at length,
At thy feet adoring fall,
Who hast led them safe through all.

4. Lord, be mine this prize to win,
Guide me through a world of sin,
Keep me by thy saving grace,
Give me at thy side a place;
Sun and shield alike thou art,
Guide and guard my erring heart.
Grace and glory flow from thee;
Shower, O shower them, Lord, on me.

A - men.

GENERAL HYMNS

Ps. 103.
PRAISE MY SOUL.* (87. 87. 87.)   **470**   H. F. Lyte, 1793–1847

In moderate time ♩ = 80.   J. Goss, 1800–80.

Unison.

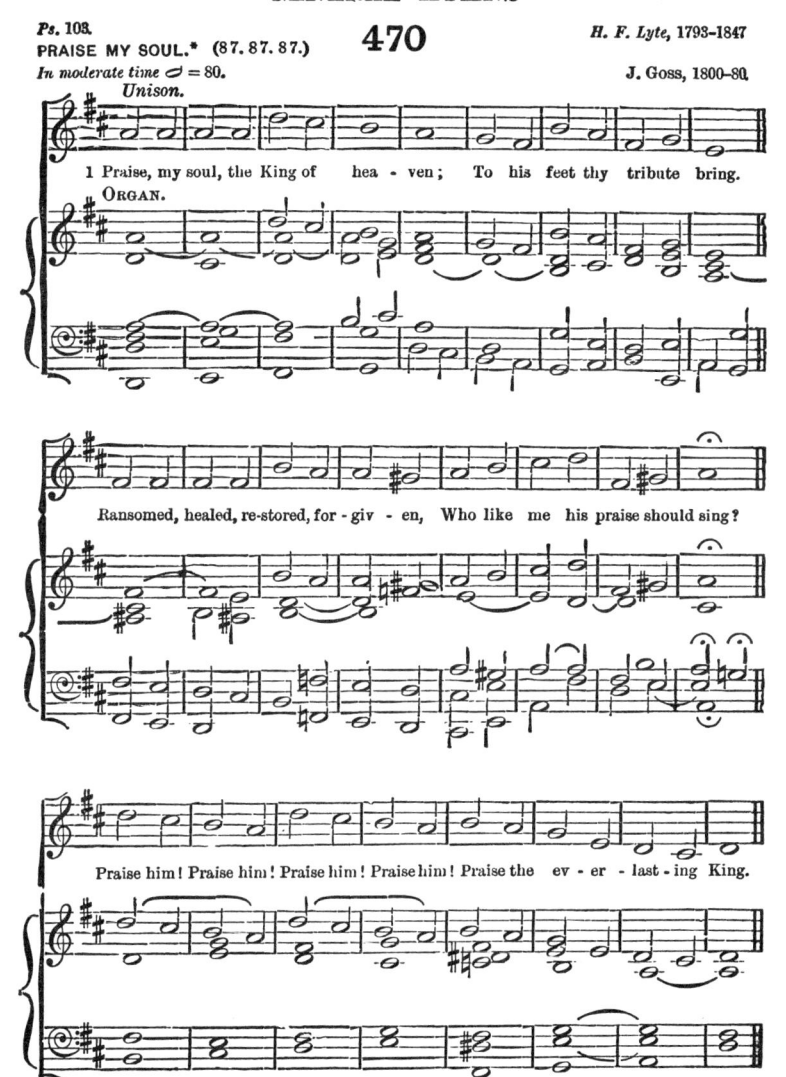

1 Praise, my soul, the King of hea-ven; To his feet thy tribute bring.

ORGAN.

Ransomed, healed, re-stored, for-giv-en, Who like me his praise should sing?

Praise him! Praise him! Praise him! Praise him! Praise the ev-er-last-ing King.

NOTE.—*This hymn may also be sung to* TANTUM ERGO (*No. 63).*

* *If desired, the music of verse 2 may be used for the hymn throughout.*

GENERAL HYMNS

470 (*continued*)

Harmony.

2 Praise him for his grace and fa - vour   To our fa - thers in dis - tress;
  Praise him still the same for ev - er, Slow to chide, and swift to bless.
  Praise him! Praise him! Praise him! Praise him! Glo - rious in his faith - ful - ness.

3 Fa - ther - like, he tends and spares us; Well our fee - ble frame he knows;
  In his hands he gen - tly bears us, Res - cues us from all our foes.
  Praise him! Praise him! Praise him! Praise him! Wide - ly as his mer - cy flows.

GENERAL HYMNS

470 (continued)

4. Angels, help us to adore him; Ye behold him face to face;
Sun and moon, bow down before him; Dwellers all in time and space.
Praise him! Praise him! Praise him! Praise him! Praise with us the God of grace.

A-men.

GENERAL HYMNS

471

RICHMOND. (C. M.)
Moderately slow ♩ = 80.

Adapted from T. HAWEIS, 1734-1820,
by S. WEBBE (the younger)

J. H. Newman, 1801-90.

PRAISE to the Holiest in the height,
    And in the depth be praise,
In all his words most wonderful,
    Most sure in all his ways.

2 O loving wisdom of our God!
    When all was sin and shame,
A second Adam to the fight
    And to the rescue came.

3*O wisest love! that flesh and blood
    Which did in Adam fail,
Should strive afresh against their foe,
    Should strive and should prevail;

4*And that a higher gift than grace
    Should flesh and blood refine,
God's presence and his very Self,
    And Essence all-divine.

5 O generous love! that he who smote
    In Man for man the foe,
The double agony in Man
    For man should undergo;

6 And in the garden secretly,
    And on the Cross on high,
Should teach his brethren, and inspire
    To suffer and to die.

7. Praise to the Holiest in the height,
    And in the depth be praise,
In all his words most wonderful,
    Most sure in all his ways.

A - men.

472

YORK. (C. M.)
Moderately slow ♩ = 66.

Melody from Scottish Psalter, 1615.
Harmony from J. MILTON, d. 1647.

GENERAL HYMNS

472 (continued)

Ps 122. *Scottish Psalter* (1650).

PRAY that Jerusalem may have
　Peace and felicity:
Let them that love thee and thy peace
　Have still prosperity.

2 Therefore I wish that peace may still
　Within thy walls remain,
And ever may thy palaces
　Prosperity retain.

　　3. Now, for my friends' and brethren's sake,
　　　Peace be in thee, I'll say;
　　And for the house of God our Lord
　　　I'll seek thy good alway.

A - men.

ALTERNATIVE VERSION

PEOPLE'S PART.

Harmonized by S. STUBBS *in Ravenscroft's Psalter,* 1621

CHOIR OR ORGAN.

NOTE.—*This version may be used, in connexion with the other, for verse* 2,
the people singing the melody as usual.

GENERAL HYMNS

473

MEIRIONYDD. (7 6. 7 6. D.)
In moderate time ♩ = 80.

Later form of melody by
W. Lloyd, 1785–1852.

Mrs. J. C Simpson, 1811–86, and others.

PRAY when the morn is breaking,
　Pray when the noon is bright,
Pray with the eve's declining,
　Pray in the hush of night:
With mind made pure of passion,
　All meaner thoughts away,
Low in thy chamber kneeling
　Do thou in secret pray.

2 Remember all who love thee,
　All who are loved by thee,
And next for those that hate thee
　Pray thou, if such there be:
Last for thyself in meekness
　A blessing humbly claim,
And link with each petition
　Thy great Redeemer's name.

GENERAL HYMNS

8. But if 'tis e'er denied thee
In solitude to pray,
Should holy thoughts come o'er thee
Upon life's crowded way,
E'en then the silent breathing
That lifts thy soul above
Shall reach the thronèd Presence
Of Mercy, Truth and Love.

474

WIGTON. (C.M.)
Moderately slow ♩ = 63.

Scottish Psalter, 1635.

J. Montgomery, 1771-1854.

PRAYER is the soul's sincere desire,
Uttered or unexpressed;
The motion of a hidden fire
That trembles in the breast.

2 Prayer is the burden of a sigh,
The falling of a tear,
The upward glancing of an eye
When none but God is near.

3 Prayer is the simplest form of speech
That infant lips can try;
Prayer the sublimest strains that reach
The Majesty on high.

4 Prayer is the contrite sinner's voice,
Returning from his ways,
While Angels in their songs rejoice,
And cry, 'Behold, he prays!'

5 Prayer is the Christian's vital breath,
The Christian's native air,
His watchword at the gates of death:
He enters heaven with prayer.

6 The saints in prayer appear as one
In word, and deed, and mind,
While with the Father and the Son
Sweet fellowship they find.

7. O thou by whom we come to God,
The Life, the Truth, the Way,
The path of prayer thyself hast trod:
Lord, teach us how to pray

A - men.

GENERAL HYMNS

475

WAREHAM. (L. M.)
Very slow and dignified ♩ = 63.

Later version of melody by
W. KNAPP, 1698(?)-1768.

NOTE.—*A lower setting of this tune will be found at Hymn 52.*

Y. H.

REJOICE, O land, in God thy might,
His will obey, him serve aright;
For thee the Saints uplift their voice:
Fear not, O land, in God rejoice.

2 Glad shalt thou be, with blessing crowned,
With joy and peace thou shalt abound;
Yea, love with thee shall make his home
Until thou see God's kingdom come.

3. He shall forgive thy sins untold:
Remember thou his love of old;
Walk in his way, his word adore,
And keep his truth for evermore.

A - men.

GENERAL HYMNS

476

GOPSAL. (6 6. 6 6. 8 8.)
In moderate time ♩ = 80.

G. F. HANDEL, 1685-1759.

C. Wesley, 1707-88.

REJOICE, the Lord is King,
   Your Lord and King adore;
Mortals, give thanks and sing,
   And triumph evermore:
     Lift up your heart, lift up your voice;
     Rejoice, again I say, rejoice.

2 Jesus, the Saviour, reigns,
   The God of truth and love;
When he had purged our stains,
   He took his seat above:

3 His kingdom cannot fail;
   He rules o'er earth and heaven;
The keys of death and hell
   Are to our Jesus given:

4. He sits at God's right hand
   Till all his foes submit,
And bow to his command,
   And fall beneath his feet·

A - men.

GENERAL HYMNS

REDHEAD No. 76. (77. 77. 77.) **477**
Moderately slow ♩ = 66.
R. REDHEAD, 1820–1901.

NOTE.—*This hymn may also be sung to* PRESSBURG (*No.* 358).

A. M. Toplady †, 1740–78.

ROCK of ages, cleft for me,
  Let me hide myself in thee;
Let the Water and the Blood,
From thy riven side which flowed,
Be of sin the double cure,
Cleanse me from its guilt and power.

2*Not the labours of my hands
  Can fulfil thy law's demands;
Could my zeal no respite know,
Could my tears for ever flow,
All for sin could not atone;
Thou must save, and thou alone.

3 Nothing in my hand I bring,
  Simply to thy Cross I cling;
Naked, come to thee for dress;
Helpless, look to thee for grace;
Foul, I to the Fountain fly;
Wash me, Saviour, or I die.

4. While I draw this fleeting breath,
  When mine eyes are closed in death,
When I soar through tracts unknown,
See thee on thy judgement throne;
Rock of ages, cleft for me,
Let me hide myself in thee.

A - men.

GENERAL HYMNS

478

WITTENBERG (ES IST DAS HEIL).
(8 7. 8 7. 8 8 7.)

Melody from Christliche Lieder, Wittenberg, 1524.
Adapted and harmonized by J. S. BACH.

Slow 𝅗𝅥 = 50.

NOTE.—*This hymn may also be sung to* NUN FREUT EUCH (*No.* 148).

Sei Lob und Ehr' dem höchsten Gut.

J. J. *Schütz*, 1640-90.
Tr. F. E. Cox.

SING praise to God who reigns above,
 The God of all creation,
The God of power, the God of love,
 The God of our salvation;
With healing balm my soul he fills,
And every faithless murmur stills:
 To God all praise and glory!

2 The Angel-host, O King of kings,
 Thy praise for ever telling,
In earth and sky all living things
 Beneath thy shadow dwelling,
Adore the wisdom which could span
And power which formed creation's plan:

3 What God's almighty power hath made
 His gracious mercy keepeth;
By morning glow or evening shade
 His watchful eye ne'er sleepeth:
Within the kingdom of his might
Lo! all is just, and all is right:

4 *Then all my gladsome way along
 I sing aloud thy praises,
That men may hear the grateful song
 My voice unwearied raises:
Be joyful in the Lord, my heart!
Both soul and body bear your part!

5. O ye who name Christ's holy name,
 Give God all praise and glory:
All ye who own his power, proclaim
 Aloud the wondrous story!
Cast each false idol from his throne,
The Lord is God, and he alone:

A - men.

GENERAL HYMNS

479

ST. ETHELWALD. (S. M.)
In moderate time ♩ = 92.

W. H. MONK, 1823–89.

C. Wesley, 1707–85.

SOLDIERS of Christ, arise,
  And put your armour on;
Strong in the strength which God supplies,
  Through his eternal Son;

2 Strong in the Lord of Hosts,
    And in his mighty power;
  Who in the strength of Jesus trusts
    Is more than conqueror.

3 Stand then in his great might,
    With all his strength endued;
  And take, to arm you for the fight,
    The panoply of God.

4 From strength to strength go on,
    Wrestle, and fight, and pray;
  Tread all the powers of darkness down,
    And win the well-fought day.

5. That having all things done,
    And all your conflicts past,
  Ye may o'ercome, through Christ alone,
    And stand entire at last.

A - men.

GENERAL HYMNS

ORIENTIS PARTIBUS. (77. 77.) **480**
In moderate time ♩ = 144. To be sung in unison.

Mediaeval French Melody.
Harmonized by R. V. W.

18th cent. Tr. J. H. Clark.

Pugnate, Christi milites.

SOLDIERS, who are Christ's below,
Strong in faith resist the foe;
Boundless is the pledged reward
Unto them who serve the Lord.

2 'Tis no palm of fading leaves
That the conqueror's hand receives;
Joys are his, serene and pure,
Light that ever shall endure.

3 For the souls that overcome
Waits the beauteous heavenly home,
Where the blessèd evermore
Tread on high the starry floor.

4 Passing soon and little worth
Are the things that tempt on earth;
Heavenward lift thy soul's regard;
God himself is thy reward;

5. Father who the crown dost give,
Saviour by whose death we live,
Spirit who our hearts dost raise,
Three in One, thy name we praise. Amen.

Harmony.

A - men.

GENERAL HYMNS

481

RILEY. (7 7. 7 7. D.)
Brightly ♩ = 100.
MARTIN SHAW.

[*Copyright*, 1915, *by J. Curwen & Sons, Ltd.*]
NOTE.—*This hymn may also be sung to* CULBACH (*No.* 286).

J. Montgomery†, 1771–1854.

SONGS of praise the Angels sang,
Heaven with Alleluyas rang,
When creation was begun,
When God spake and it was done.

2 Songs of praise awoke the morn
When the Prince of peace was born;
Songs of praise arose when he
Captive led captivity.

3 Heaven and earth must pass away,
Songs of praise shall crown that day;
God will make new heavens and earth,
Songs of praise shall hail their birth,

4 And will man alone be dumb
Till that glorious kingdom come?
No, the Church delights to raise
Psalms and hymns and songs of praise

5 Saints below, with heart and voice,
Still in songs of praise rejoice;
Learning here, by faith and love,
Songs of praise to sing above.

6. Hymns of glory, songs of praise,
Father, unto thee we raise;
Jesu, glory unto thee,
Ever with the Spirit be. Amen.

GENERAL HYMNS

STANSTEAD. (11 10. 11 6.)
In moderate time ♩ = 120. *Unison.*

482

S. L. RUSSELL.

[*Copyright*, 1931, *by Oxford University Press.*]

NOTE.—*This hymn may also be sung to* LANGA (*Appendix, No.* 60).

W. H. Burleigh, 1812–71.

STILL will we trust, though earth seem dark and dreary,
    And the heart faint beneath his chastening rod,
Though rough and steep our pathway, worn and weary,
    Still will we trust in God!

2 Our eyes see dimly till by faith anointed,
    And our blind choosing brings us grief and pain;
Through him alone, who hath our way appointed,
    We find our peace again.

3 Choose for us, God, nor let our weak preferring
    Cheat our poor souls of good thou hast designed:
Choose for us, God; thy wisdom is unerring,
    And we are fools and blind.

4 *So from our sky the night shall furl her shadows,
    And day pour gladness through his golden gates,
Our rough path lead to flower-enamelled meadows,
    Where joy our coming waits.

5. Let us press on: in patient self-denial,
    Accept the hardship, shrink not from the loss;
Our guerdon lies beyond the hour of trial,
    Our crown beyond the cross.

A - men.

GENERAL HYMNS

483

SONG 5. (L. M.)
Slow and dignified ♩ = 69.

O. GIBBONS, 1583–1625,
rhythm slightly adapted.

NOTE.—*This hymn may also be sung to* WAREHAM (*No.* 475).

Alfred, Lord Tennyson, 1809–92.

STRONG Son of God, immortal Love,
  Whom we, that have not seen thy face,
  By faith, and faith alone, embrace,
Believing where we cannot prove:

2 Thou wilt not leave us in the dust;
  Thou madest man, he knows not why;
  He thinks he was not made to die:
And thou hast made him, thou art just.

3 Thou seemest human and divine,
  The highest, holiest manhood thou:
  Our wills are ours, we know not how;
Our wills are ours, to make them thine.

4. Our little systems have their day;
  They have their day and cease to be:
  They are but broken lights of thee,
And thou, O Lord, art more than they.

A - men.

GENERAL HYMNS

BRESLAU. (L.M.)   **484**   Melody in 'As hymnodus sacer,' Leipzig, 1625. *Adapted and harmonized by* F. MENDELSSOHN-BARTHOLDY.
Very slow ♩ = 48.

C. W. Everest ‡, 1814–77.

TAKE up thy cross, the Saviour said,
  If thou wouldst my disciple be;
Deny thyself, the world forsake,
  And humbly follow after me.

2 Take up thy cross; let not its weight
  Fill thy weak spirit with alarm;
His strength shall bear thy spirit up,
  And brace thy heart, and nerve thine arm.

3*Take up thy cross, nor heed the shame,
  Nor let thy foolish pride rebel;
The Lord for thee the Cross endured,
  To save thy soul from death and hell.

4 Take up thy cross then in his strength,
  And calmly every danger brave;
'Twill guide thee to a better home,
  And lead to victory o'er the grave.

5 Take up thy cross, and follow Christ,
  Nor think till death to lay it down;
For only he who bears the cross
  May hope to wear the glorious crown.

6. To thee, great Lord, the One in Three,
  All praise for evermore ascend;
O grant us in our Home to see
  The heavenly life that knows no end.

A - men.

GENERAL HYMNS

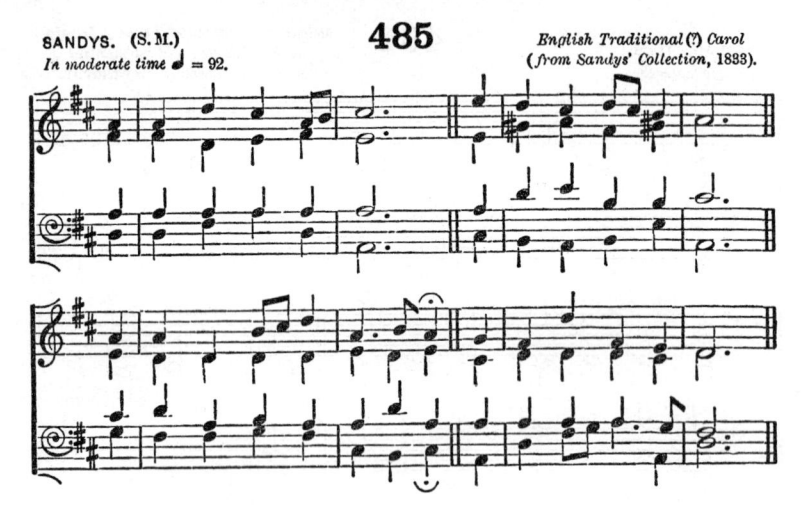

485

SANDYS. (S.M.)
In moderate time ♩ = 92.

*English Traditional (?) Carol
(from Sandys' Collection, 1833).*

G. Herbert, 1593-1682.

TEACH me, my God and King,
    In all things thee to see;
And what I do in anything
    To do it as for thee!

2 A man that looks on glass,
    On it may stay his eye;
Or if he pleaseth, through it pass,
    And then the heaven espy.

3 All may of thee partake;
    Nothing can be so mean,
Which with this tincture, 'for thy sake,'
    Will not grow bright and clean.

4 A servant with this clause
    Makes drudgery divine;
Who sweeps a room, as for thy laws,
    Makes that and the action fine.

5. This is the famous stone
    That turneth all to gold;
For that which God doth touch and own
    Cannot for less be told.

A - men.

GENERAL HYMNS

KOMM, SEELE. (7 6. 8 6. D.) **486**
Brightly ♩ = 100.
Melody by J. W. FRANCK, c. 1681.

H. Alford, 1810–71.

TEN thousand times ten thousand,
　In sparkling raiment bright,
The armies of the ransomed Saints
　Throng up the steeps of light;
'Tis finished! all is finished,
　Their fight with death and sin;
Fling open wide the golden gates,
　And let the victors in.
Unison.
2 What rush of Alleluyas
　Fills all the earth and sky!
What ringing of a thousand harps
　Bespeaks the triumph nigh!
O day, for which creation
　And all its tribes were made!
O joy, for all its former woes
　A thousandfold repaid!

3 O, then what raptured greetings
　On Canaan's happy shore,
What knitting severed friendships up,
　Where partings are no more!
Then eyes with joy shall sparkle
　That brimmed with tears of late;
Orphans no longer fatherless,
　Nor widows desolate.

Unison. 4. Bring near thy great salvation,
　Thou Lamb for sinners slain,
Fill up the roll of thine elect,
　Then take thy power and reign:
Appear, Desire of nations;
　Thine exiles long for home;
Show in the heaven thy promised sign;
　Thou Prince and Saviour, come.

A - men.

GENERAL HYMNS

BABYLON'S STREAMS. (L. M.) **487**
Moderately slow, solemn ♩ = 69.
T. CAMPION, 1575-1619.

Sir Walter Scott, 1771-1832. *Based on* Dies irae

THAT day of wrath, that dreadful day,
When heaven and earth shall pass away,
What power shall be the sinner's stay?
How shall he meet that dreadful day?

Unison. 2 When, shrivelling like a parchèd scroll,
The flaming heavens together roll;
When louder yet, and yet more dread,
Swells the high trump that wakes the dead:

3. O, on that day, that wrathful day,
When man to judgement wakes from clay,
Be thou the trembling sinner's stay,
Though heaven and earth shall pass away!

A - men.

GENERAL HYMNS

488

CAPEL. (C. M.)
In moderate time ♩ = 92.

English Traditional Carol Melody.

NOTE.—*This hymn may also be sung to* UNIVERSITY (*No. 93*).

L. B. C. L. Muirhead. 1845–1925

1. THE Church of God a kingdom is,
    Where Christ in power doth reign,
   Where spirits yearn till seen in bliss
    Their Lord shall come again.

2. Glad companies of saints possess
    This Church below, above;
   And God's perpetual calm doth bless
    Their paradise of love.

3. An altar stands within the shrine
    Whereon, once sacrificed,
   Is set, immaculate, divine,
    The Lamb of God, the Christ.

4. There rich and poor, from countless lands,
    Praise Christ on mystic Rood;
   There nations reach forth holy hands
    To take God's holy Food.

5. There pure life-giving streams o'erflow
    The sower's garden-ground;
   And faith and hope fair blossoms show,
    And fruits of love abound.

Unison. 6. O King, O Christ, this endless grace
    To us and all men bring,
   To see the vision of thy face
    In joy, O Christ, our King.

A - men.

GENERAL HYMNS

489

AURELIA. (76. 76. D.)
In moderate time ♩ = 70.

S. S. WESLEY, 1810–76.

S. J. Stone, 1839–1900.

THE Church's one foundation
  Is Jesus Christ, her Lord;
She is his new creation
  By water and the Word:
From heaven he came and sought her
  To be his holy Bride,
With his own Blood he bought her,
  And for her life he died.

Unison. 2 Elect from every nation,
  Yet one o'er all the earth,
 Her charter of salvation
  One Lord, one Faith, one Birth;
 One holy name she blesses,
  Partakes one holy Food,
 And to one hope she presses
  With every grace endued.

 3*Though with a scornful wonder
  Men see her sore opprest,
 By schisms rent asunder,
  By heresies distrest,
 Yet Saints their watch are keeping,
  Their cry goes up, 'How long?'
 And soon the night of weeping
  Shall be the morn of song.

 4 'Mid toil, and tribulation,
  And tumult of her war,
 She waits the consummation
  Of peace for evermore;
 Till with the vision glorious
  Her longing eyes are blest,
 And the great Church victorious
  Shall be the Church at rest.

 5. Yet she on earth hath union
  With God the Three in One,
 And mystic sweet communion
  With those whose rest is won:
 O happy ones and holy!
  Lord, give us grace that we
 Like them, the meek and lowly,
  On high may dwell with thee.

A - men.

GENERAL HYMNS

490

ST. COLUMBA. (87.87.)
In moderate time ♩ = 108.

Ancient Irish Hymn Melody
(Original form).

Ps. 23.

Sir H. W. Baker, 1821-77.

1. THE King of love my Shepherd is,
    Whose goodness faileth never;
  I nothing lack if I am his
    And he is mine for ever.

2. Where streams of living water flow
    My ransomed soul he leadeth,
  And where the verdant pastures grow
    With food celestial feedeth.

3. Perverse and foolish oft I strayed,
    But yet in love he sought me,
  And on his shoulder gently laid,
    And home, rejoicing, brought me.

4. In death's dark vale I fear no ill
    With thee, dear Lord, beside me;
  Thy rod and staff my comfort still,
    Thy Cross before to guide me.

5. Thou spread'st a table in my sight;
    Thy unction grace bestoweth·
  And O what transport of delight
    From thy pure chalice floweth!

6. And so through all the length of days
    Thy goodness faileth never;
  Good Shepherd, may I sing thy praise
    Within thy house for ever.

A - men.

638

GENERAL HYMNS

491

SURREY. (88.88.88.)
Moderately slow ♩ = 84.

H. CAREY, c. 1690-1743.

Ps. 23.   J. Addison, 1672-1719.

THE Lord my pasture shall prepare,
  And feed me with a shepherd's
    care;
His presence shall my wants supply,
And guard me with a watchful eye;
My noonday walks he shall attend,
And all my midnight hours defend.

2 When in the sultry glebe I faint,
  Or on the thirsty mountain pant,
  To fertile vales and dewy meads
  My weary wandering steps he leads,
  Where peaceful rivers, soft and slow,
  Amid the verdant landscape flow.

3 Though in a bare and rugged way
  Through devious lonely wilds I stray,
  Thy bounty shall my pains beguile;
  The barren wilderness shall smile
  With sudden greens and herbage
    crowned,
  And streams shall murmur all around.

4. Though in the paths of death I tread,
  With gloomy horrors overspread,
  My steadfast heart shall fear no ill,
  For thou, O Lord, art with me still:
  Thy friendly crook shall give me aid,
  And guide me through the dreadful
    shade.

GENERAL HYMNS

492

COLESHILL. (C. M.)
Slow ♩ = 58.
Barton's Psalms, 1706 *(later version of melody)*.

NOTE.—*This hymn may also be sung to* ST. STEPHEN (*No*. 337).

Ps. 85-6.   *J. Milton (cento)*, 1608-74.

THE Lord will come and not be slow,
　His footsteps cannot err;
Before him righteousness shall go,
　His royal harbinger.

2 Truth from the earth, like to a flower,
　Shall bud and blossom then;
And justice, from her heavenly bower,
　Look down on mortal men.

Unison.
3 Rise, God, judge thou the earth in might,
　This wicked earth redress;
For thou art he who shalt by right
　The nations all possess.

4 The nations all whom thou hast made
　Shall come, and all shall frame
To bow them low before thee, Lord,
　And glorify thy name.

Unison. 5. For great thou art, and wonders great
　By thy strong hand are done:
Thou in thy everlasting seat
　Remainest God alone.

A - men.

493

OLD 107TH. (D. C. M.)
Slow ♩ = 96 (♩ = 48).
Scottish Psalter, 1635,
based on the *Genevan Psalter*.

GENERAL HYMNS

493 (continued)

[*It is suggested that the first part of this tune be sung by the* CHOIR ALONE *and the refrain by choir and people together. The last verse should be sung full throughout.*]

NOTE.—*This hymn may also be sung to* SOLL'S SEIN (*No.* 288).

Mrs. C. F. Alexander, 1818-95.

THE roseate hues of early dawn,
   The brightness of the day,
The crimson of the sunset sky,
   How fast they fade away!
Unison.
O for the pearly gates of heaven,
   O for the golden floor;
O for the Sun of righteousness
   That setteth nevermore!

2 The highest hopes we cherish here,
   How fast they tire and faint;
How many a spot defiles the robe
   That wraps an earthly saint!
Unison.
O for a heart that never sins,
   O for a soul washed white;
O for a voice to praise our King,
   Nor weary day or night!

3. Here faith is ours, and heavenly hope,
   And grace to lead us higher;
But there are perfectness and peace,
   Beyond our best desire.
Unison. O by thy love and anguish, Lord,
   O by thy life laid down,
O that we fall not from thy grace,
   Nor cast away our crown!

A - men.

GENERAL HYMNS
494

The Alleluyatic Sequence.
TROYTE No. 2. (Irreg.)
In moderate time ♩ = 80.

Cantemus cuncti melodum.

B. *Notker*, 840–912. *Tr. J. M. Neale.*

A. H. DYKE TROYTE, 1811–57.

THE strain upraise of joy and praise, Alle-	-lu - - - ya!	To the glory of their King Shall the ransomed	peo - ple sing
And the choirs that ...	dwell on high	Shall re-echo	through the sky,
2 They, through the fields of *Unison.* Paradise that roam,	The blessèd ones, repeat through	that bright home
The planets glittering on their *Harmony.*	heaven - ly way,	The shining constellations,	join and say
3 Ye clouds that onward sweep, Ye winds on	pin - ions light,	Ye thunders, echoing loud and deep, Ye lightnings,	wild - ly bright,
4 Ye floods and ocean billows, Ye storms and	win - ter snow,	Ye days of cloudless beauty, Hoar frost and	sum - mer glow,
5 First let the birds, with painted	plum - age gay,	Exalt their great Creator's	praise, and say
Then let the beasts of earth, with *Unison.*	vary - ing strain,	Join in creation's hymn, and	cry a - gain
6 Here let the mountains thunder forth so-	-nor - - ous	Alle - - - -lu - - ya!
Thou jubilant abyss of . *Harmony.*	o - cean, cry	Alle - - - -lu - - ya!
7 To God, who all cre - -	-a - tion made,	The frequent hymn be	du - ly paid,
This is the strain, the eternal strain, the Lord of	all things loves,	Alle - - - -lu - - ya!
Wherefore we sing, both heart and voice a- *Unison.*	-wak - - ing,	Alle - - - -lu - - ya!
8. Now from all men ... *Harmony.*	be out-poured	Alleluya	to the Lord;
Praise be done to the ..	Three in One.	Alle - - - -lu - - ya!

GENERAL HYMNS

494 (*continued*)

Alle - - - - -	-lu - - ya!	Alle - - - -	- lu - ya!
Alle - - - - -	-lu - - ya!	Alle - - - -	- lu - ya!
(2) Alle - - - -	-lu - - ya!	Alle - - - -	- lu - ya!
Alle - - - - -	-lu - - ya!	Alle - - - -	- lu - ya!
(3) In sweet con- - -	-sent u - nite	your Alle - -	- lu - ya!
(4) Ye groves that wave in spring, And glorious	fo - rests, sing		
(5) Alle - - - - -	-lu - - ya!	Alle - - - -	- lu - ya!
Alle - - - - -	-lu - - ya!	Alle - - - -	- lu - ya!
(6) There let the valleys sing in gentler	cho - - rus	Alle - - - -	- lu - ya!
Ye tracts of earth and conti-	-nents, re - ply	Alle - - - -	- lu - ya!
(7) Alle - - - - -	-lu - - ya!	Alle - - - -	- lu - ya!
This is the song, the heavenly song, that Christ him-	-self ap - proves,	Alle - - - -	- lu - ya!
Trebles only. And children's voices echo, answer	mak - - ing,	Alle - - - -	- lu - ya!
(8) With Alleluya . . .	e - ver - more	The Son and Spirit	we adore.
Alle - - - - -	-lu - - ya!	Alle - - - -	- lu - ya!

A - men.

GENERAL HYMNS

495

PEARSALL. (7 6. 7 6. D.)
In moderate time ♩ = 80.

R. L. de Pearsall,
1795–1856.

(Nos. 371, 392, 412 are from the same source.)
Bernard of Cluny, 12th cent. Tr. J. M. Neale.

Hora novissima.

THE world is very evil;
   The times are waxing late;
Be sober and keep vigil,
   The Judge is at the gate:
The Judge that comes in mercy,
   The Judge that comes with might,
To terminate the evil,
   To diadem the right.

GENERAL HYMNS

2 Arise, arise, good Christian,
    Let right to wrong succeed;
Let penitential sorrow
    To heavenly gladness lead.
Then glory yet unheard of
    Shall shed abroad its ray,
Resolving all enigmas,
    An endless Sabbath-day.

3 The home of fadeless splendour,
    Of flowers that fear no thorn,
Where they shall dwell as children
    Who here as exiles mourn;
The peace of all the faithful,
    The calm of all the blest,
Inviolate, unvaried,
    Divinest, sweetest, best;

4 The peace that is for heaven,
    And shall be too for earth;
The palace that re-echoes
    With festal song and mirth;
The garden breathing spices,
    The paradise on high;
Grace beautified to glory,
    Unceasing minstrelsy.

5 O happy, holy portion,
    Refection for the blest;
True vision of true beauty,
    Sweet cure of all distrest!
Strive, man, to win that glory;
    Toil, man, to gain that light;
Send hope before to grasp it,
    Till hope be lost in sight;

6. And through the sacred lilies
    And flowers on every side,
The happy dear-bought people
    Go wandering far and wide;
Their one and only anthem,
    The fullness of his love,
Who gives, instead of torment
    Eternal joys above.

A - men.

GENERAL HYMNS

496

7TH MODE MELODY. (6 6. 6 6. D.)
In moderate time ♩ = 92.

T. TALLIS, *c.* 1515–1585.

NOTE.—*An alternative tune to this hymn is given below.*

ALTERNATIVE TUNE

HAWARDEN. (6 6. 6 6. D.)
In moderate time ♩ = 96.

S. S. WESLEY, 1810–76.

GENERAL HYMNS

496 *(continued)*

NOTE.—*This hymn may also be sung to* ANNUE CHRISTE (No. 174).

Sir H. W. Baker, 1821–77.

THERE is a blessèd home
  Beyond this land of woe,
Where trials never come,
  Nor tears of sorrow flow;
Where faith is lost in sight,
  And patient hope is crowned,
And everlasting light
  Its glory throws around.

2 There is a land of peace,
  Good Angels know it well,
Glad songs that never cease
  Within its portals swell;
Around its glorious throne
  Ten thousand Saints adore
Christ, with the Father One
  And Spirit, evermore.

3*O joy all joys beyond,
  To see the Lamb who died,
And count each sacred wound
  In hands, and feet, and side;
To give to him the praise
  Of every triumph won,
And sing through endless days
  The great things he hath done.

Unison.   4. Look up, ye saints of God,
  Nor fear to tread below
The path your Saviour trod
  Of daily toil and woe;
Wait but a little while
  In uncomplaining love,
His own most gracious smile
  Shall welcome you above.

A - men.   A - men.

GENERAL HYMNS
497

RELIEF. (C. M.)
Moderately slow ♩ = 63.

From A New Set of Sacred Music by
JOHN FAWCETT, c. 1822. Harmonized
by GEOFFREY SHAW.

NOTE —*This hymn may also be sung to* ST. FLAVIAN (*No.* 161).

J. Keble, 1792–1866

THERE is a book who runs may read,
   Which heavenly truth imparts,
And all the lore its scholars need,
   Pure eyes and Christian hearts.

2 The works of God above, below,
   Within us and around,
Are pages in that book, to show
   How God himself is found.

3 The glorious sky, embracing all,
   Is like the Maker's love, [small
Wherewith encompassed, great and
   In peace and order move.

4 The moon above, the Church below,
   A wondrous race they run;
But all their radiance, all their glow,
   Each borrows of its sun.

5 * The Saviour lends the light and heat
   That crowns his holy hill;
The Saints, like stars, around his seat
   Perform their courses still.

6 * The Saints above are stars in heaven—
   What are the saints on earth?
Like trees they stand whom God has
   Our Eden's happy birth. [given,

7 * Faith is their fixed unswerving root,
   Hope their unfading flower,
Fair deeds of charity their fruit,
   The glory of their bower.

8 * The dew of heaven is like thy grace,
   It steals in silence down;
But where it lights, the favoured place
   By richest fruits is known.

9 * One name, above all glorious names,
   With its ten thousand tongues
The everlasting sea proclaims,
   Echoing angelic songs.

10 The raging fire, the roaring wind,
   Thy boundless power display;
But in the gentler breeze we find
   Thy Spirit's viewless way.

11 Two worlds are ours: 'tis only sin
   Forbids us to descry
The mystic heaven and earth within,
   Plain as the sea and sky.

12. Thou, who hast given me eyes to see
   And love this sight so fair,
Give me a heart to find out thee,
   And read thee everywhere.

A - men.

GENERAL HYMNS

MENDIP. (C.M.)
In moderate time ♩ = 92.

498

English Traditional Melody.

I. Watts, 1674-1748.

THERE is a land of pure delight,
   Where Saints immortal reign;
Infinite day excludes the night,
   And pleasures banish pain.

2 There everlasting spring abides,
   And never-withering flowers;
Death, like a narrow sea, divides
   This heavenly land from ours.

3 Sweet fields beyond the swelling flood
   Stand dressed in living green;
So to the Jews old Canaan stood,
   While Jordan rolled between.

4 But timorous mortals start and shrink
   To cross this narrow sea,
And linger shivering on the brink,
   And fear to launch away.

5 O could we make our doubts remove,
   These gloomy doubts that rise,
And see the Canaan that we love
   With unbeclouded eyes!

6. Could we but climb where Moses stood,
   And view the landscape o'er,
Not Jordan's stream, nor death's cold flood,
   Should fright us from the shore!

A - men.

GENERAL HYMNS

ZUM FRIEDEN. (87. 87. D.) **499**
Very slow and dignified ♩ = 48.

J. S. BACH, 1685–1750.

[May be sung in unison or as a solo.]

NOTE.—*This hymn, when used at Mission Services, may be sung to* DAILY, DAILY
(*No.* 568).

F. W. Faber, 1814–63.

1. THERE'S a wideness in God's mercy,
Like the wideness of the sea;
There's a kindness in his justice,
Which is more than liberty.

2. There is no place where earth's sorrows
Are more felt than up in heaven;
There is no place where earth's failings
Have such kindly judgement given.

3. There is grace enough for thousands
Of new worlds as great as this;
There is room for fresh creations
In that upper home of bliss.

4. For the love of God is broader
Than the measures of man's mind;
And the heart of the Eternal
Is most wonderfully kind.

5. But we make his love too narrow
By false limits of our own;
And we magnify his strictness
With a zeal he will not own.

6.*There is plentiful redemption
In the Blood that has been shed,
There is joy for all the members
In the sorrows of the Head.

7.*'Tis not all we owe to Jesus;
It is something more than all;
Greater good because of evil,
Larger mercy through the fall.

8. If our love were but more simple,
We should take him at his word;
And our lives would be all sunshine
In the sweetness of our Lord.

A - men.

650

GENERAL HYMNS

VIENNA. (77. 77.)
In moderate time ♩ = 72.

500

Melody from J. H. KNECHT, 1752–1817.

J. M. Neale, 1818–66, and others.

THEY whose course on earth is o'er,
Think they of their brethren more?
They before the throne who bow,
Feel they for their brethren now?

2 We, by enemies distrest—
They in Paradise at rest;
We the captives—they the freed—
We and they are one indeed;

3 One in all we seek or shun,
One—because our Lord is one;
One in home and one in love—
We below, and they above.

4 Those whom space on earth divides,
Mountains, rivers, ocean-tides;
Have they with each other part?
Have they fellowship in heart?

5 Each to each may be unknown,
Wide apart their lots be thrown;
Differing tongues their lips may speak,
One be strong, and one be weak;

6 Yet in Sacrament and prayer
Each with other hath a share;
Hath a share in tear and sigh,
Watch, and fast and litany.

7 Saints departed even thus
Hold communion still with us;
Still with us, beyond the veil,
Praising, pleading without fail.

Unison. 8. So with them our hearts we raise,
Share their work and join their praise,
Rendering worship, thanks, and love
To the Trinity above.

A - men.

GENERAL HYMNS

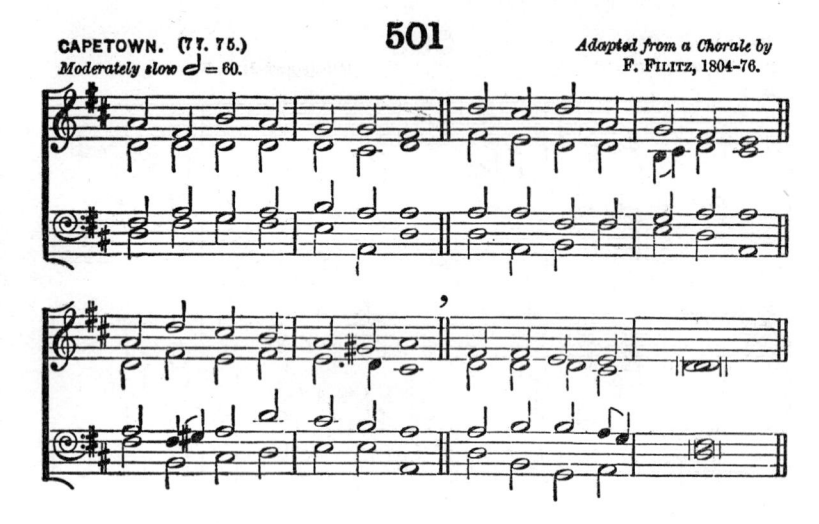

501

CAPETOWN. (7 7. 7 5.)
Moderately slow ♩ = 60.

Adapted from a Chorale by
F. FILITZ, 1804-76.

G. Rorison, 1821-69.

THREE in One, and One in Three,
Ruler of the earth and sea,
Hear us, while we lift to thee
    Holy chant and psalm.

2 Light of lights! with morning-shine
Lift on us thy Light Divine;
And let charity benign
    Breathe on us her balm.

3 Light of lights! when falls the even,
Let it sink on sin forgiven;
Fold us in the peace of heaven;
    Shed a vesper calm.

Unison. 4. Three in One, and One in Three,
Darkling here we worship thee;
With the Saints hereafter we
    Hope to bear the palm.

A - men.

GENERAL HYMNS

502

WILTSHIRE. (C.M.)
In moderate time ♩ = 92.

G. SMART, 1776-1867.

NOTE.—*This hymn may also be sung to* YORK (*No.* 472).

Ps. 34.

N. Tate and N. Brady, *New Version* (1696).

1 THROUGH all the changing scenes of life,
In trouble and in joy,
The praises of my God shall still
My heart and tongue employ.

2 O magnify the Lord with me,
With me exalt his name;
When in distress to him I called,
He to my rescue came.

3 The hosts of God encamped around
The dwellings of the just;
Deliverance he affords to all
Who on his succour trust.

4 O make but trial of his love,
Experience will decide
How blest they are, and only they,
Who in his truth confide.

5 Fear him, ye saints, and you will then
Have nothing else to fear;
Make you his service your delight,
Your wants shall be his care.

6. To Father, Son, and Holy Ghost,
The God whom we adore,
Be glory, as it was, is now,
And shall be evermore. Amen.

A - men.

GENERAL HYMNS

503

MARCHING. (8 7. 8 7.)
With vigour ♩ = 100.

MARTIN SHAW.

[Copyright, 1915, by J. Curwen & Sons, Ltd.]
NOTE.—*This hymn may also be sung to* SUSSEX (*No.* 385) *or to* ST. OSWALD (*App. No.* 61).

B. S. Ingemann, 1789–1862.
Tr. S. Baring-Gould.

Igjennem Nat og Trængsel.

THROUGH the night of doubt and sorrow
Onward goes the pilgrim band,
Singing songs of expectation,
Marching to the Promised Land.

2 Clear before us through the darkness
Gleams and burns the guiding light;
Brother clasps the hand of brother,
Stepping fearless through the night.

3 One the light of God's own presence
O'er his ransomed people shed,
Chasing far the gloom and terror,
Brightening all the path we tread;

4 One the object of our journey,
One the faith which never tires,
One the earnest looking forward,
One the hope our God inspires:

5*One the strain that lips of thousands
Lift as from the heart of one;
One the conflict, one the peril,
One the march in God begun;

6*One the gladness of rejoicing
On the far eternal shore,
Where the One Almighty Father
Reigns in love for evermore.

Part 2.

7*Onward, therefore, pilgrim brothers,
Onward with the Cross our aid;
Bear its shame, and fight its battle,
Till we rest beneath its shade.

Unison. 8.*Soon shall come the great awaking,
Soon the rending of the tomb;
Then the scattering of all shadows,
And the end of toil and gloom.

A - men.

GENERAL HYMNS

504

IRISH. (C. M.)
In moderate time 𝅗𝅥 = 92.

Melody from 'A Collection of Hymns and Sacred Poems,' Dublin, 1749.

NOTE.—*This hymn may also be sung to* ST. STEPHEN (*No.* 337).

F. L. Hosmer, 1840–1929.

1 THY kingdom come! on bended knee
　The passing ages pray;
And faithful souls have yearned to see
　On earth that kingdom's day.

2 But the slow watches of the night
　Not less to God belong;
And for the everlasting right
　The silent stars are strong.

3 And lo, already on the hills
　　The flags of dawn appear;
　Gird up your loins, ye prophet souls,
　　Proclaim the day is near:

4 The day in whose clear-shining light
　　All wrong shall stand revealed,
　When justice shall be throned in might,
　　And every hurt be healed;

5 When knowledge, hand in hand with peace,
　　Shall walk the earth abroad;—
　The day of perfect righteousness,
　　The promised day of God.

A - men.

GENERAL HYMNS

505

PSALM 32. (6 6. 6 6.)
In moderate time ♩ = 72.

H. LAWES, 1596–1662.

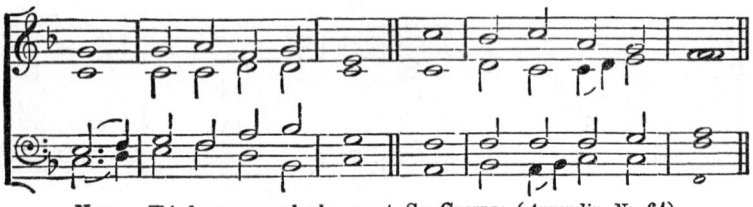

NOTE.—*This hymn may also be sung to* ST. CECILIA (*Appendix, No.* 64).

H. Bonar, 1808–89.

THY way, not mine, O Lord,
　However dark it be;
Lead me by thine own hand,
　Choose out the path for me.

2 Smooth let it be or rough,
　　It will be still the best;
　Winding or straight, it leads
　　Right onward to thy rest.

3 I dare not choose my lot;
　　I would not if I might;
　Choose thou for me, my God,
　　So shall I walk aright.

4 The kingdom that I seek
　　Is thine, so let the way
　That leads to it be thine,
　　Else I must surely stray.

5 Take thou my cup, and it
　　With joy or sorrow fill,
　As best to thee may seem;
　　Choose thou my good and ill.

6 Choose thou for me my friends,
　　My sickness or my health;
　Choose thou my cares for me,
　　My poverty or wealth.

7. Not mine, not mine, the choice
　　In things or great or small;
　Be thou my Guide, my Strength,
　　My Wisdom, and my All.

A - men.

GENERAL HYMNS

EPSOM. (C.M.)
In moderate time ♩ = 112.

506

*Melody in Arnold's
'Complete Psalmodist,' 1756.*

William Blake, 1757-1827.

TO Mercy, Pity, Peace, and Love,
　All pray in their distress,
And to these virtues of delight
　Return their thankfulness.

2 For Mercy, Pity, Peace, and Love,
　Is God our Father dear;
And Mercy, Pity, Peace, and Love,
　Is Man, his child and care.

3 For Mercy has a human heart,
　Pity, a human face;
And Love, the human form divine,
　And Peace, the human dress.

4 Then every man, of every clime,
　That prays in his distress,
Prays to the human form divine:
　Love, Mercy, Pity, Peace.

5.*And all must love the human form,
　In heathen, Turk, or Jew;
Where Mercy, Love, and Pity dwell,
　There God is dwelling too.

A - men.

GENERAL HYMNS

507

ORIEL. (87. 87. 87.)
Moderately slow ♩ = 66.

C. Ett, 'Cantica Sacra,' 1840.

GENERAL HYMNS

Gloriosi Salvatoris. *c. 15th cent. Tr. J. M. Neale*

TO the name that brings salvation
  Honour, worship, laud we pay:
That for many a generation
  Hid in God's foreknowledge lay,
But to every tongue and nation
  Holy Church proclaims to-day.

2 * Name of gladness, name of pleasure,
  By the tongue ineffable,
Name of sweetness passing measure,
  To the ear delectable;
'Tis our safeguard and our treasure,
  'Tis our help 'gainst sin and hell.

3 * 'Tis the name for adoration,
  'Tis the name of victory;
'Tis the name for meditation
  In the vale of misery:
'Tis the name for veneration
  By the citizens on high.

4 'Tis the name that whoso preaches
  Finds it music in his ear;
'Tis the name that whoso teaches
  Finds more sweet than honey's cheer:
Who its perfect wisdom reaches
  Makes his ghostly vision clear.

5 'Tis the name by right exalted
  Over every other name:
That when we are sore assaulted
  Puts our enemies to shame:
Strength to them that else had halted,
  Eyes to blind, and feet to lame.

6. Jesu, we thy name adoring,
  Long to see thee as thou art:
Of thy clemency imploring
  So to write it in our heart,
That hereafter, upward soaring,
  We with Angels may have part.

A - men.

GENERAL HYMNS

508

QUAM DILECTA. (6 6. 6 6.)
In moderate time ♩ = 76.

BISHOP JENNER, 1820-98.

W. Bullock, 1798-1874, and Sir H. W. Baker.

WE love the place, O God,
   Wherein thine honour dwells;
The joy of thine abode
   All earthly joy excels.

2 We love the house of prayer,
   Wherein thy servants meet;
And thou, O Lord, art there
   Thy chosen flock to greet.

3 We love the sacred font,
   For there the holy Dove
To pour is ever wont
   His blessing from above.

4 We love thine altar, Lord;
   O, what on earth so dear!
For there, in faith adored,
   We find thy presence near.

5 We love the word of life,
   The word that tells of peace,
Of comfort in the strife,
   And joys that never cease.

6 We love to sing below
   For mercies freely given;
But O, we long to know
   The triumph-song of heaven!

7. Lord Jesus, give us grace
   On earth to love thee more,
In heaven to see thy face.
   And with thy Saints adore.

A - men.

GENERAL HYMNS

509

FARMBOROUGH. (88.88.88.)
In moderate time ♩ = 72.
ARTHUR S. WARRELL.

[Copyright, 1931, by Oxford University Press.]
NOTE.—*This hymn may also be sung to* DAVID'S HARP (*No.* 378).

Mrs. A. Richter (1834), *J. H. Gurney* (1851), *and others.*

1. WE saw thee not when thou didst come
To this poor world of sin and death,
Nor e'er beheld thy cottage-home
In that despisèd Nazareth;
But we believe thy footsteps trod
Its streets and plains, thou Son of God.

2. We did not see thee lifted high
Amid that wild and savage crew,
Nor heard thy meek, imploring cry,
'Forgive, they know not what they do';
Yet we believe the deed was done
Which shook the earth and veiled the sun.

3. We stood not by the empty tomb
Where late thy sacred Body lay,
Nor sat within that upper room,
Nor met thee in the open way;
But we believe that Angels said,
'Why seek the living with the dead?'

4. We did not mark the chosen few,
When thou didst in the cloud ascend,
First lift to heaven their wondering view,
Then to the earth all prostrate bend;
Yet we believe that mortal eyes
From that far mountain saw thee rise.

5. And now that thou dost reign on high,
And thence thy waiting people bless,
No ray of glory from the sky
Doth shine upon our wilderness;
But we believe thy faithful word,
And trust in our redeeming Lord.

A - men.

GENERAL HYMNS
510

CALVISIUS (ACH BLEIB BEI UNS). (L. M.)
Slow ♩ = 50.

Founded on a melody by
S. CALVISIUS (1594). *Harmonized by* J. S. BACH.

NOTE.—*This hymn may also be sung to* BRESLAU (*No.* 484).

T. *Kelly*, 1769-1854.

1. WE sing the praise of him who died,
Of him who died upon the Cross;
The sinner's hope let men deride,
For this we count the world but loss.

2. Inscribed upon the Cross we see
In shining letters, 'God is love';
He bears our sins upon the Tree;
He brings us mercy from above.

3. The Cross! it takes our guilt away;
It holds the fainting spirit up;
It cheers with hope the gloomy day,
And sweetens ev'ry bitter cup.

4. It makes the coward spirit brave,
And nerves the feeble arm for fight;
It takes its terror from the grave,
And gilds the bed of death with light;

5. The balm of life, the cure of woe,
The measure and the pledge of love,
The sinners' refuge here below,
The Angels' theme in heaven above.

A - men.

GENERAL HYMNS

511

BELGRAVE. (C.M.)
In moderate time ♩ = 92.

W. HORSLEY, 1774–1858.

J. Addison, 1672–1719.

WHEN all thy mercies, O my God,
My rising soul surveys,
Transported with the view, I'm lost
In wonder, love, and praise.

2 Unnumbered comforts to my soul
Thy tender care bestowed,
Before my infant heart conceived
From whom those comforts flowed.

3 When in the slippery paths of youth
With heedless steps I ran,
Thine arm unseen conveyed me safe,
And led me up to man.

4 When worn with sickness oft hast thou
With health renewed my face;
And when in sins and sorrows sunk,
Revived my soul with grace.

5 Through every period of my life
Thy goodness I'll pursue,
And after death in distant worlds
The glorious theme renew.

6. Through all eternity to thee
A joyful song I'll raise;
For O! eternity's too short
To utter all thy praise.

A - men.

663

GENERAL HYMNS

512

O SEIGNEUR. (667.667.D.)
With vigour ♩ = 80.

Psalm 3 in Genevan Psalter, 1551.

May Jesus Christ be prais - ed.

May Jesus Christ be prais - ed.

Org. Ped.

May Jesus Christ be prais - ed.

GENERAL HYMNS

512 (continued)

May Jesus Christ be praised.

Beim frühen Morgenlicht.

19th cent. Tr. E. Caswall.

1. WHEN morning gilds the skies,
My heart awaking cries,
 May Jesus Christ be praisèd:
Alike at work and prayer
To Jesus I repair;
 May Jesus Christ be praisèd.

2. The sacred minster bell
It peals o'er hill and dell,
 May Jesus Christ be praisèd:
O hark to what it sings,
As joyously it rings,
 May Jesus Christ be praisèd.

3 * My tongue shall never tire
Of chanting in the choir,
 May Jesus Christ be praisèd.
The fairest graces spring
In hearts that ever sing,
 May Jesus Christ be praisèd.

4 * When sleep her balm denies,
My silent spirit sighs,
 May Jesus Christ be praisèd:
When evil thoughts molest,
With this I shield my breast,
 May Jesus Christ be praisèd.

5 * Does sadness fill my mind?
A solace here I find,
 May Jesus Christ be praisèd:
Or fades my earthly bliss?
My comfort still is this,
 May Jesus Christ be praisèd.

6 * The night becomes as day,
When from the heart we say,
 May Jesus Christ be praisèd:
The powers of darkness fear,
When this sweet chant they hear,
 May Jesus Christ be praisèd.

Unison. 7. In heaven's eternal bliss
The loveliest strain is this,
 May Jesus Christ be praisèd:
Let air, and sea, and sky
From depth to height reply,
 May Jesus Christ be praisèd.

Unison. 8. Be this, while life is mine,
My canticle divine,
 May Jesus Christ be praisèd:
Be this the eternal song
Through all the ages on,
 May Jesus Christ be praisèd.

A - men.

GENERAL HYMNS
513

REDHEAD NO. 47. (77. 77.)
Moderately slow ♩ = 66.
R. REDHEAD, 1820–1901.

NOTE.—*This hymn may also be sung to* NUN KOMM (*No.* 110).

H. H. Milman, 1791–1868.

WHEN our heads are bowed with woe,
When our bitter tears o'erflow,
When we mourn the lost, the dear,
Gracious Son of Mary, hear.

2 Thou our throbbing flesh hast worn,
Thou our mortal griefs hast borne,
Thou hast shed the human tear;
Gracious Son of Mary, hear.

3 When the sullen death-bell tolls
For our own departed souls,
When our final doom is near,
Gracious Son of Mary, hear.

4 Thou hast bowed the dying head,
Thou the blood of life hast shed,
Thou hast filled a mortal bier;
Gracious Son of Mary, hear.

5 When the heart is sad within
With the thought of all its sin,
When the spirit shrinks with fear,
Gracious Son of Mary, hear.

6. Thou the shame, the grief, hast known,
Though the sins were not thine own;
Thou hast deigned their load to bear;
Gracious Son of Mary, hear.

A - men.

666

GENERAL HYMNS

514

LLANSANNAN. (8 7. 8 7. D.)
In moderate time, dignified ♩ = 80.

Welsh Hymn Melody.

Bishop W. W. How, 1823-97.

WHO is this so weak and helpless,
  Child of lowly Hebrew maid,
Rudely in a stable sheltered,
  Coldly in a manger laid?
'Tis the Lord of all creation,
  Who this wondrous path hath trod;
He is God from everlasting,
  And to everlasting God.

2 Who is this—a Man of Sorrows,
  Walking sadly life's hard way,
Homeless, weary, sighing, weeping
  Over sin and Satan's sway?

'Tis our God, our glorious Saviour,
  Who above the starry sky
Now for us a place prepareth
  Where no tear can dim the eye.

3 Who is this—behold Him raining
  Drops of blood upon the ground?
Who is this—despised, rejected,
  Mocked, insulted, beaten, bound?
'Tis our God, who gifts and graces
  On his Church now poureth down;
Who shall smite in holy vengeance
  All his foes beneath his throne.

4. Who is this that hangeth dying,
  With the thieves on either side?
Nails his hands and feet are tearing,
  And the spear hath pierced his side.
'Tis the God who ever liveth
  'Mid the shining ones on high,
In the glorious golden city
  Reigning everlastingly.

A - men.

GENERAL HYMNS

SO GIEBST DU (DRESDEN).
(10 10. 10 10. 8 4.)

515

Melody from a Dresden song book (1694)
(second line slightly adapted).
Harmony from J. S. Bach, 1685–1750.

Moderately slow ♩ = 66.

[*May also be sung as a solo.*]

John Donne †, 1573–1631.

WILT thou forgive that sin, by man begun,
    Which was my sin though it were done before?
Wilt thou forgive that sin, through which I run,
    And do run still, though still I do deplore?
When thou hast done, thou hast not done,
        For I have more.

GENERAL HYMNS

2 Wilt thou forgive that sin which I have won
  Others to sin, and made my sin their door?
  Wilt thou forgive that sin which I did shun
  A year or two, but wallowed in a score?
  When thou hast done, thou hast not done,
          For I have more.

3. I have a sin of fear, that when I've spun
   My last thread, I shall perish on the shore,
   But swear by thyself, that at my death thy Son
   Shall shine, as he shines now and heretofore:
   And, having done that, thou hast done:
           I fear no more.

A - men.

516

VOLLER WUNDER. (77. 77. 77.)
In moderate time ♩ = 120.

J. G. EBELING, 1620–76.

NOTE.—*This hymn may also be sung to* MINISTRES DE L'ÉTERNEL (*No.* 258).

G. *Thring*, 1823–1903.

WORK is sweet, for God has blest
  Honest work with quiet rest;
Rest below, and rest above,
In the mansions of his love,
When the work of life is done,
When the battle's fought and won.

2 Work ye, then, while yet 'tis day,
  Work, ye Christians, while ye may;
  Work for all that's great and good,
  Working for your daily food,
  Working whilst the golden hours,
  Health, and strength, and youth, are yours.

3 Working not alone for gold,
  Not for work that's bought and sold;
  Not the work that worketh strife,
  But the working of a life;
  Careless both of good or ill,
  If ye can but do his will.

4. Working ere the day is gone,
   Working till your work is done;
   Not as traffickers at marts,
   But as fitteth honest hearts;
   Working till your spirits rest
   With the spirits of the blest.

A - men.

GENERAL HYMNS

517

DARWALL'S 148TH. (6 6. 6 6. 4 4. 4 4.)
In moderate time ♩ = 96.

J. DARWALL, 1731–89.

R. Baxter, 1681; and J. H. Gurney, 1838 and 1851.

YE holy Angels bright,
  Who wait at God's right hand,
Or through the realms of light
  Fly at your Lord's command,
    Assist our song,
      For else the theme
      Too high doth seem
    For mortal tongue.

2 Ye blessèd souls at rest,
  Who ran this earthly race,
And now, from sin released,
  Behold the Saviour's face,
    God's praises sound,
      As in his sight
      With sweet delight
    Ye do abound.

3 Ye saints, who toil below,
  Adore your heavenly King,
And onward as ye go
  Some joyful anthem sing;
    Take what he gives
      And praise him still,
      Through good or ill,
    Who ever lives!

4. My soul, bear thou thy part,
  Triumph in God above:
And with a well-tuned heart
  Sing thou the songs of love!
    Let all thy days
      Till life shall end,
      Whate'er he send,
    Be filled with praise.

A - men.

GENERAL HYMNS

518

NARENZA. (S.M.)
In moderate time ♩ = 72.

W. H. HAVERGAL, 1793–1870, *founded on*
'Ave, Maria klare' (Cöln Gesangbuch, 1619).

A higher setting of this tune will be found at Hymn 627.
NOTE.—*This hymn may also be sung to* SELMA (*No.* 290).

P. Doddridge†, 1702-51.

YE servants of the Lord,
  Each in his office wait,
Observant of his heavenly word,
  And watchful at his gate.

2 Let all your lamps be bright,
  And trim the golden flame;
Gird up your loins as in his sight,
  For awful is his name.

3 Watch! 'tis your Lord's command,
  And while we speak, he's near;
Mark the first signal of his hand,
  And ready all appear.

4 O, happy servant he,
  In such a posture found!
He shall his Lord with rapture see,
  And be with honour crowned.

5. Christ shall the banquet spread
  With his own royal hand,
And raise that faithful servant's head
  Amidst the angelic band.

A - men.

GENERAL HYMNS

LASST UNS ERFREUEN. (88. 44. 88. and Alleluyas.) **519**

In moderate time, dignified ♩ = 100.

Melody from 'Geistliche Kirchengesäng'
(Cöln, 1623).

Al - le - lu - ya, Al - le - lu - ya, Al - le - lu - ya, Al - le - lu - ya, Al - le - lu - ya!

GENERAL HYMNS

A. R.

YE watchers and ye holy ones,
  Bright Seraphs, Cherubim and Thrones,
    Raise the glad strain, Alleluya!
Cry out Dominions, Princedoms, Powers',
Virtues, Archangels, Angels' choirs,
    Alleluya, Alleluya, Alleluya, Alleluya, Alleluya!

2 O higher than the Cherubim,
  More glorious than the Seraphim,
    Lead their praises, Alleluya!
Thou Bearer of the eternal Word,
Most gracious, magnify the Lord,
    Alleluya, Alleluya, Alleluya, Alleluya, Alleluya!

3 Respond, ye souls in endless rest,
  Ye Patriarchs and Prophets blest,
    Alleluya, Alleluya!
Ye holy Twelve, ye Martyrs strong,
All Saints triumphant, raise the song
    Alleluya, Alleluya, Alleluya, Alleluya, Alleluya!

4. O friends, in gladness let us sing,
  Supernal anthems echoing,
    Alleluya, Alleluya!
To God the Father, God the Son,
And God the Spirit, Three in One,
    Alleluya, Alleluya, Alleluya, Alleluya, Alleluya!

Part VI
SPECIAL OCCASIONS

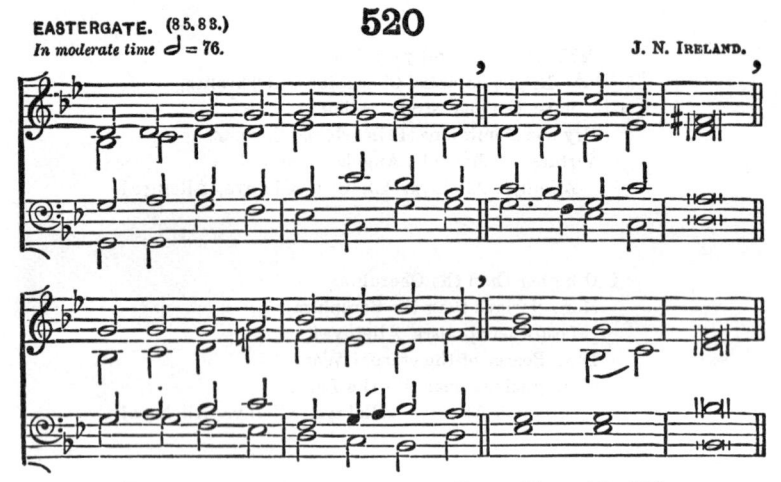

EASTERGATE. (8 5. 8 8.)
In moderate time ♩ = 76.

520

J. N. IRELAND.

NOTE.—*This hymn may also be sung to* CUTTLE MILLS (*No.* 366).

FOR ABSENT FRIENDS
Isabella S. Stevenson, 1843-90.

HOLY Father, in thy mercy,
   Hear our anxious prayer,
Keep our loved ones, now far distant,
   'Neath thy care.

2 Jesus, Saviour, let thy presence
   Be their light and guide;
Keep, O, keep them, in their weakness,
   At thy side.

3 When in sorrow, when in danger,
   When in loneliness,
In thy love look down and comfort
   Their distress.

4 May the joy of thy salvation
   Be their strength and stay;
May they love and may they praise thee
   Day by day.

5 Holy Spirit, let thy teaching
   Sanctify their life;
Send thy grace, that they may conquer
   In the strife.

6. Father, Son, and Holy Spirit,
   God the One in Three,
Bless them, guide them, save them, keep
   them   Near to thee.

A - men.

ALMSGIVING

521

ES IST KEIN TAG. (8 8. 8 4.)
Moderately slow ♩ = 63.

Melody in
J. MEYER's '*Seelenfreud*,' 1692.

ALMSGIVING — *Bishop Chr. Wordsworth*, 1807-85.

1. O LORD of heaven, and earth, and sea,
   To thee all praise and glory be;
   How shall we show our love to thee,
   Giver of all?

2. The golden sunshine, vernal air,
   Sweet flowers and fruits, thy love declare;
   Where harvests ripen, thou art there,
   Giver of all!

3. For peaceful homes, and healthful days,
   For all the blessings earth displays,
   We owe thee thankfulness and praise,
   Giver of all!

4. Thou didst not spare thine only Son,
   But gav'st him for a world undone,
   And freely with that Blessèd One
   Thou givest all.

5. Thou giv'st the Spirit's blessèd dower,
   Spirit of life, and love, and power,
   And dost his sevenfold graces shower
   Upon us all.

6. For souls redeemed, for sins forgiven,
   For means of grace and hopes of heaven,
   Father, what can to thee be given,
   Who givest all?

7. We lose what on ourselves we spend,
   We have as treasure without end
   Whatever, Lord, to thee we lend,
   Who givest all;

Unison. 8. To thee, from whom we all derive
   Our life, our gifts, our power to give:
   O may we ever with thee live,
   Giver of all!

A-men.

SPECIAL OCCASIONS

522

WINDERMERE. (S. M.)
In moderate time ♩ = 84.

A. SOMERVELL.

Bishop W. W. How, 1823-97.

WE give thee but thine own,
　Whate'er the gift may be:
All that we have is thine alone
　A trust, O Lord, from thee.

2　May we thy bounties thus
　　As stewards true receive,
　And gladly, as thou blessest us,
　　To thee our first-fruits give.

3　O hearts are bruised and dead;
　　And homes are bare and cold;
　And lambs, for whom the Shepherd bled,
　　Are straying from the fold.

4　To comfort and to bless,
　　To find a balm for woe,
　To tend the lone and fatherless,
　　Is Angels' work below.

5　The captive to release,
　　To God the lost to bring,
　To teach the way of life and peace,—
　　It is a Christlike thing.

6.　And we believe thy word,
　　Though dim our faith may be;
　Whate'er for thine we do, O Lord,
　　We do it unto thee.

A - men.

The following are also suitable:

309　For the beauty of the earth.
529　Son of God, eternal Saviour.

BEGINNING AND END OF TERM

DISMISSAL. (8 7. 8 7. 8 7.) **523**
In moderate time ♩ = 96.

W. L. Viner, c. 1856.

Small notes for Organ.

Note.—*This hymn may also be sung to* Tantum Ergo (*No. 63*).

BEGINNING AND END OF TERM

H. J. Buckoll, 1803-71.

LORD, behold us with thy blessing,
  Once again assembled here;
Onward be our footsteps pressing,
  In thy love and faith and fear:
    Still protect us
  By thy presence ever near.

Unison.
2 For thy mercy we adore thee,
    For this rest upon our way;
  Lord, again we bow before thee,
    Speed our labours day by day:
      Mind and spirit
    With thy choicest gifts array.

Part 2.
3 Lord, dismiss us with thy blessing;
    Thanks for mercies past receive;
  Pardon all, their faults confessing;
    Time that's lost may all retrieve:
      May thy children
    Ne'er again thy Spirit grieve.

Unison.
4. Let thy Father-hand be shielding
    All who here shall meet no more;
  May their seed-time past be yielding
    Year by year a richer store:
      Those returning
    Make more faithful than before.

A - men.

SPECIAL OCCASIONS

524

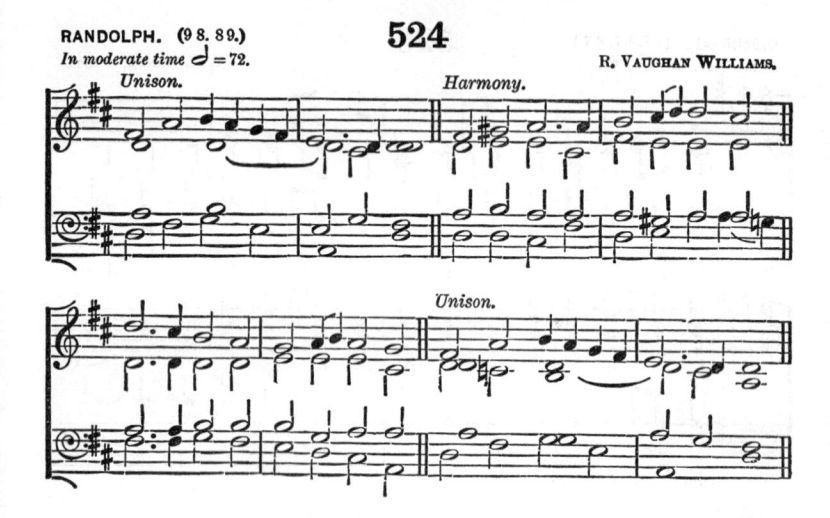

RANDOLPH. (9 8. 8 9.)
In moderate time ♩ = 72.

R. VAUGHAN WILLIAMS.

AT A FAREWELL

J. E. Rankin, 1828-1904.

GOD be with you till we meet again;
By his counsels guide, uphold you,
With his sheep securely fold you:
God be with you till we meet again.

2 God be with you till we meet again;
'Neath his wings protecting hide you,
Daily manna still provide you:
God be with you till we meet again.

3 God be with you till we meet again;
When life's perils thick confound you,
Put his arm unfailing round you:
God be with you till we meet again.

4. God be with you till we meet again;
Keep love's banner floating o'er you,
Smite death's threatening wave before you:
God be with you till we meet again.

A - men.

HOSPITALS
525
(First Tune)

FARNHAM. (C. M.)
In moderate time ♩ = 88.
From an English Traditional Melody.

A-men.

CULROSS. (C. M.)   525 (Second Tune)
Moderately slow ♩ = 66.
Scottish Psalter, 1634.

A-men.

Note.—*This hymn may also be sung to* Stockton (*No.* 82).

HOSPITALS
Charles Kingsley, 1819–75.

FROM thee all skill and science flow,
  All pity, care, and love,
All calm and courage, faith and hope—
  O, pour them from above!

2 And part them, Lord, to each and all,
  As each and all shall need
To rise, like incense, each to thee,
  In noble thought and deed.

3 And hasten, Lord, that perfect day
  When pain and death shall cease,
And thy just rule shall fill the earth
  With health, and light, and peace;

4. When ever blue the sky shall gleam,
  And ever green the sod,
And man's rude work deface no more
  The Paradise of God.

SPECIAL OCCASIONS

526

ST. MATTHEW. (D.C.M.)
In moderate time ♩ = 92.

DR. CROFT, 1678–1727
(modern form of tune).

HOSPITALS

526 (*continued*)

E. H. Plumptre, 1821-91.

THINE arm, O Lord, in days of old
  Was strong to heal and save;
It triumphed o'er disease and death,
  O'er darkness and the grave;
To thee they went, the blind, the dumb,
  The palsied and the lame,
The leper with his tainted life,
  The sick with fevered frame.

2 And lo! thy touch brought life and health,
  Gave speech, and strength, and sight;
And youth renewed and frenzy calmed
  Owned thee the Lord of light;
And now, O Lord, be near to bless,
  Almighty as of yore,
In crowded street, by restless couch,
  As by Gennesareth's shore.

Unison. 3. Be thou our great deliverer still,
  Thou Lord of life and death;
Restore and quicken, soothe and bless
  With thine almighty breath;
To hands that work, and eyes that see,
  Give wisdom's heavenly lore,
That whole and sick, and weak and strong,
  May praise thee evermore.

A - men.

SPECIAL OCCASIONS

527

ST. LEONARD. (8 7. 8 7. 7 7.)
In moderate time ♩ = 72.

Melody by
J. Christoph Bach, 1642-1703.

Note.—*Another tune for this hymn will be found in the Appendix (No. 21).*

G. Thring, 1823-1903.

1 THOU to whom the sick and dying
    Ever came, nor came in vain,
Still with healing words replying
    To the wearied cry of pain,
      Hear us, Jesu, as we meet
      Suppliants at thy mercy-seat.

2 Still the weary, sick, and dying
    Need a brother's, sister's care;
On thy higher help relying
    May we now their burden share,
      Bringing all our offerings meet,
      Suppliants at thy mercy-seat.

3 May each child of thine be willing,
    Willing both in hand and heart,
All the law of love fulfilling,
    Ever comfort to impart;
      Ever bringing offerings meet,
      Suppliant to thy mercy-seat.

4. So may sickness, sin, and sadness
    To thy healing power yield,
Till the sick and sad, in gladness,
    Rescued, ransomed, cleansèd, healed,
      One in thee together meet,
      Pardoned at thy judgement-seat.

A - men.

The following are also suitable:

266 At even when the sun was set.
349 Thou, Lord, hast power to heal.
529 Son of God, eternal Saviour.

SOCIETIES: FRIENDLY

528

EXETER. (888.888.)
In moderate time ♩ = 88.

W. JACKSON (of Exeter), 1730–1803.

SOCIETIES: FRIENDLY

H. C. Shuttleworth, 1850–1900.

FATHER of men, in whom are one
   All humankind beneath thy sun,
Stablish our work in thee begun.
Except the house be built of thee,
In vain the builder's toil must be:
O strengthen our infirmity!

2 Man lives not for himself alone,
In others' good he finds his own,
Life's worth in fellowship is known.
We, friends and comrades on life's way,
Gather within these walls to pray:
Bless thou our fellowship to-day.

3 O Christ, our Elder Brother, who
By serving man God's will didst do,
Help us to serve our brethren too.
Guide us to seek the things above,
The base to shun, the pure approve,
To live by thy free law of love.

Unison. 4. In all our work, in all our play,
Be with us, Lord, our Friend. our Stay;
Lead onward to the perfect day:
Then may we know, earth's lesson o'er,
With comrades missed or gone before,
Heaven's fellowship for evermore.

A - men.

SPECIAL OCCASIONS

529

LUGANO. (87. 87. D.)
Moderately slow ♩ = 72.

Adapted from a melody in
'Catholic Hymn Tunes,' 1849.

NOTE.—*This hymn may also be sung to* IN BABILONE (*No.* 145).

SOCIETIES: GENERAL

S. C. Lowry, 1855–1932.

SON of God, eternal Saviour,
  Source of life and truth and grace,
Son of Man, whose birth amongst us
  Hallows all our human race,
Thou, our Head, who, throned in glory,
  For thine own dost ever plead,
Fill us with thy love and pity,
  Heal our wrongs, and help our need

SOCIETIES: GENERAL

2 As thou, Lord, hast lived for others
So may we for others live;
Freely have thy gifts been granted,
Freely may thy servants give.
Thine the gold and thine the silver,
Thine the wealth of land and sea,
We but stewards of thy bounty,
Held in solemn trust for thee.

3 Come, O Christ, and reign among us,
King of love, and Prince of peace,
Hush the storm of strife and passion,
Bid its cruel discords cease;
By thy patient years of toiling,
By thy silent hours of pain,
Quench our fevered thirst of pleasure,
Shame our selfish greed of gain.

4 Dark the path that lies behind us,
Strewn with wrecks and stained with blood;
But before us gleams the vision
Of the coming brotherhood.
See the Christlike host advancing,
High and lowly, great and small,
Linked in bonds of common service
For the common Lord of all.

Unison. 5. Son of God, eternal Saviour,
Source of life and truth and grace,
Son of Man, whose birth amongst us
Hallows all our human race,
Thou who prayedst, thou who willest
That thy people should be one,
Grant, O grant our hope's fruition:
Here on earth thy will be done.

A - men.

The following are suitable for any gatherings of Unions and Societies:

  45 Hail to the Lord's Anointed.
 365 All people that on earth do dwell.
 412 Jerusalem the golden.
 423 Judge eternal, throned in splendour.
 426 Lead us, heavenly Father, lead us.
 448 O God of mercy, God of might.
 458 O Lord of hosts, all heaven possessing.
 475 Rejoice, O land, in God thy might.
 483 Strong Son of God, immortal Love.
 492 The Lord will come and not be slow.
 516 Work is sweet, for God has blest.
 531 Father, who on man dost shower.
 544, 545 (The Church).
 557-566 (National).

The following are suitable for Guilds, G.F.S. meetings, &c., in addition to Nos. 448 and 516 above:

370 Blest are the pure in heart.
398 Happy are they, they that love God.
452 O happy band of pilgrims.
453 O Holy Spirit, Lord of grace.

485 Teach me, my God and King.
544, 545 (The Church).
555 Dismiss me not thy service, Lord.

SPECIAL OCCASIONS

CALVARY. (87. 87. 87.) **530**
In moderate time ♩ = 80.

S. STANLEY, 1767–1822.

NOTE.—*This hymn may also be sung to* LEWES (*No.* 250) *or* COLLAUDEMUS (*No.* 229).

SOCIETIES: MOTHERS'

Christian Burke, 1857–1944.

1. LORD of life and King of glory,
Who didst deign a child to be,
Cradled on a mother's bosom,
Throned upon a mother's knee:
For the children thou hast given
We must answer unto thee!

2. Since the day the blessèd Mother
Thee, the world's Redeemer, bore,
Thou hast crowned us with an honour
Women never knew before;
And that we may bear it meetly
We must seek thine aid the more.

3. Grant us, then, pure hearts and patient,
That in all we do or say
Little souls our deeds may copy,
And be never led astray;
Little feet our steps may follow
In a safe and narrow way.

4. When our growing sons and daughters
Look on life with eager eyes,
Grant us then a deeper insight
And new powers of sacrifice:
Hope to trust them, faith to guide them,
Love that nothing good denies.

5. May we keep our holy calling
Stainless in its fair renown,
That when all the work is over
And we lay the burden down,
Then the children thou hast given
Still may be our joy and crown!

A - men.

TEMPERANCE SOCIETIES

531

CHARING. (8 8. 8 7.)
Not too slow ♩ = 100. Unison.
S. L. RUSSELL.

[*Copyright*, 1931, *by Oxford University Press.*]

NOTE.—*This hymn may also be sung to* QUEM PASTORES LAUDAVERE (*No.* 598).

SOCIETIES: FRIENDLY AND TEMPERANCE
P. D.

1. FATHER, who on man dost shower
Gifts of plenty from thy dower,
To thy people give the power
All thy gifts to use aright.

2. Give pure happiness in leisure,
Temperance in every pleasure,
Wholesome use of earthly treasure,
Bodies clear and spirits bright.

3. Lift from this and every nation
All that brings us degradation;
Quell the forces of temptation;
Put thine enemies to flight.

4. Be with us, thy strength supplying,
That with energy undying,
Every foe of man defying,
We may rally to the fight.

5. Thou who art our Captain ever
Lead us on to great endeavour;
May thy Church the world deliver,
Give us wisdom, courage, might.

6. Father, who hast sought and found us,
Son of God, whose love has bound us,
Holy Spirit, in us, round us,
Hear us, Godhead infinite. Amen.

A - men.

The following are also suitable for Temperance Societies:

369 Be thou my Guardian and my Guide.
402 He who would valiant be.
423 Judge eternal, throned in splendour.
426 Lead us, heavenly Father, lead us.

447 O God of Bethel, by whose hand.
479 Soldiers of Christ, arise.
480 Soldiers, who are Christ's below.
529 Son of God, eternal Saviour.

SPECIAL OCCASIONS

MONKLAND. (77. 77.)
In moderate time ♩ = 76.

532

Melody from 'Hymn Tunes of the United Brethren' (1824), arranged by J. Wilkes (1861).

THANKSGIVING

Ps. 136. *J. Milton ‡, 1608-74.*

LET us, with a gladsome mind,
Praise the Lord, for he is kind:
For his mercies ay endure,
Ever faithful, ever sure.

Unison.

2 Let us blaze his name abroad,
For of gods he is the God:

3 He with all-commanding might
Filled the new-made world with light:

4 He the golden-tressèd sun
Caused all day his course to run:

5 The hornèd moon to shine by night,
'Mid her spangled sisters bright:

6*He his chosen race did bless
In the wasteful wilderness:

7*He hath, with a piteous eye,
Looked upon our misery:

8 All things living he doth feed,
His full hand supplies their need:

Unison. 9. Let us, with a gladsome mind,
Praise the Lord, for he is kind:

A - men.

NUN DANKET. (67. 67. 66. 66.)
Very slow and majestic ♩ = 42.

533

Present form of melody by
J. Crüger, 1598-1662.

Org.

688

THANKSGIVING

533 (*continued*)

M. Rinkart, 1586–1649. Tr. C. Winkworth.

Nun danket alle Gott.

Unison.

NOW thank we all our God,
　With heart and hands and voices,
Who wondrous things hath done,
In whom his world rejoices;
　Who from our mother's arms
　　Hath blessed us on our way
With countless gifts of love,
　And still is ours to-day.

2　O may this bounteous God
　Through all our life be near us,
With ever joyful hearts
And blessèd peace to cheer us;
　And keep us in his grace,
　　And guide us when perplexed,
And free us from all ills
　In this world and the next.

Unison.　3.　All praise and thanks to God
　The Father now be given,
　The Son, and him who reigns
　With them in highest heaven,
　　The One eternal God,
　　　Whom earth and heaven adore;
　For thus it was, is now,
　　And shall be evermore. Amen.

A - men.

SPECIAL OCCASIONS

LAUS TIBI CHRISTE. (6 5. 6 5. D.)
Moderately slow, dignified ♩ = 69.

534

From a 14th century German Processional Melody.

Ps. 148

Thomas Browne Browne, 1805–74.

Laudate Dominum.

PRAISE the Lord of heaven; praise him in the height;
  Praise him, all ye Angels; praise him, stars and light;
Praise him, skies and waters, which above the skies,
When his word commanded, stablished did arise.

2 Praise the Lord, ye fountains of the deeps and seas,
Rocks and hills and mountains, cedars and all trees;
Praise him, clouds and vapours, snow and hail and fire,
Unison. Stormy wind fulfilling only his desire.

3. Praise him, fowls and cattle, princes and all kings;
Praise him, men and maidens, all created things;
For the name of God is excellent alone;
On the earth his footstool, over heaven his throne.

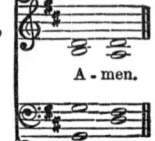

A - men.

THANKSGIVING

535

PRAISE. (87.87.D.)
With spirit ♩. = 60.
GEOFFREY SHAW.

[Copyright, 1915, by J. Curwen & Sons, Ltd.]
NOTE.—*This hymn may also be sung to* AUSTRIAN HYMN (*No.* 393).

Ps. 148. *Foundling Hospital Coll.* (1796).

PRAISE the Lord! ye heavens,
   adore him;
  Praise him, Angels, in the height;
Sun and moon, rejoice before him,
  Praise him, all ye stars and light:
Praise the Lord! for he hath spoken,
  Worlds his mighty voice obeyed;
Laws, which never shall be broken,
  For their guidance hath he made.

2 Praise the Lord! for he is glorious;
  Never shall his promise fail;
God hath made his Saints victorious,
  Sin and death shall not prevail.
Praise the God of our salvation;
  Hosts on high, his power proclaim;
Heaven and earth, and all creation,
  Laud and magnify his name!

Unison.   Part 2.   E. *Osler,* 1798–1863.

3. Worship, honour, glory, blessing,
  Lord, we offer to thy name;
Young and old, thy praise expressing,
  Join their Saviour to proclaim.
As the Saints in heaven adore thee,
  We would bow before thy throne,
As thine Angels serve before thee,
  So on earth thy will be done.

SPECIAL OCCASIONS

HAST DU DENN, JESU. (14 14. 4. 7. 8.) **536**

Moderately slow ♩ = 80.

Melody from
Stralsund Gesangbuch, 1665 (as given in
'the Chorale Book for England,' 1863).

J. Neander, 1650–80.
Tr. C. Winkworth and others.

Lobe den Herren.

PRAISE to the Lord, the Almighty, the King of creation;
O my soul, praise him, for he is thy health and salvation:
 Come ye who hear,
 Brothers and sisters draw near,
 Praise him in glad adoration.

THANKSGIVING

2 Praise to the Lord, who o'er all things so wondrously reigneth,
Shelters thee under his wings, yea, so gently sustaineth:
      Hast thou not seen
      All that is needful hath been
      Granted in what he ordaineth?

3 Praise to the Lord, who doth prosper thy work, and defend thee;
Surely his goodness and mercy here daily attend thee:
      Ponder anew
      All the Almighty can do.
      He who with love doth befriend thee.

Part 2.

4 * Praise to the Lord, who, when tempests their warfare are waging,
Who, when the elements madly around thee are raging,
      Biddeth them cease,
      Turneth their fury to peace,
      Whirlwinds and waters assuaging.

5 * Praise to the Lord, who when sickness with terror uniting,
Deaf to entreaties of mortals, its victims is smiting,
      Pestilence quells,
      Sickness and fever dispels,
      Grateful thanksgiving inviting.

6 * Praise to the Lord, who when darkness of sin is abounding,
Who, when the godless do triumph, all virtue confounding,
      Sheddeth his light,
      Chaseth the horrors of night,
      Saints with his mercy surrounding.

Unison.   *Conclusion.*
7. Praise to the Lord! O let all that is in me adore him!
All that hath life and breath come now with praises before him!
      Let the amen
      Sound from his people again:
      Gladly for ay we adore him.

A - men.

SPECIAL OCCASIONS

EIN' FESTE BURG. (87.87.66.667.) **537**

Very slow and solemn ♩ = 40.

Present form of melody by
M. LUTHER, 1483–1546.

THANKSGIVING

Sir H. W. Baker, 1821-77

Unison.

REJOICE to-day with one accord
  Sing out with exultation;
Rejoice and praise our mighty Lord,
  Whose arm hath brought salvation.
    His works of love proclaim
    The greatness of his name;
    For he is God alone,
    Who hath his mercy shown:
  Let all his Saints adore him!

2. When in distress to him we cried
  He heard our sad complaining;
O trust in him, whate'er betide,
  His love is all-sustaining
    Triumphant songs of praise
    To him our hearts shall raise;
    Now every voice shall say,
    O praise our God alway,
  Let all his Saints adore him

The first verse may be repeated.

A - men.

The following are sometimes suitable:

257 (11) Praise God, from whom all blessings flow.
309 For the beauty of the earth.
380 Come, ye faithful, raise the anthem.
461 O praise our great and gracious Lord.
475 Rejoice, O land, in God thy might.
478 Sing praise to God who reigns above.
494 The strain upraise of joy and praise.
517 Ye holy Angels bright.
519 Ye watchers and ye holy ones.
559 God of our fathers, unto thee.
564 The King, O God, his heart to thee upraiseth.

SPECIAL OCCASIONS

538

L'OMNIPOTENT. (11 10. 11 10.)
Moderately slow ♩ = 72.

Melody composed or adapted by
L. BOURGEOIS *for the Genevan Psalter*, 1551.

NOTE.—*This hymn may also be sung to* ZU MEINEM HERREN (*No.* 119) *or* WELWYN (*No.* 346).

IN TIME OF TROUBLE

F. L. Hosmer, 1840–1929.

FATHER, to thee we look in all our sorrow,
  Thou art the fountain whence our healing flows;
Dark though the night, joy cometh with the morrow;
  Safely they rest who on thy love repose.

2 When fond hopes fail and skies are dark before us,
  When the vain cares that vex our life increase,
Comes with its calm the thought that thou art o'er us,
  And we grow quiet, folded in thy peace.

3 Nought shall affright us, on thy goodness leaning;
  Low in the heart faith singeth still her song;
Chastened by pain we learn life's deeper meaning,
  And in our weakness thou dost make us strong.

4. Patient, O heart, though heavy be thy sorrows;
  Be not cast down, disquieted in vain;
Yet shalt thou praise him, when these darkened furrows,
  Where now he ploughteth, wave with golden grain.

A - men.

The following are also suitable:

394 God moves in a mysterious way.
435 Lord of our life, and God of our salvation.
455 O let him whose sorrow.

482 Still will we trust.
513 When our heads are bowed with woe.
557 From foes that would the land devour.

IN TIME OF WAR

539

LLANGOEDMOR. (888. D.)
In moderate time ♩ = 80.
Welsh Hymn Melody. Harmonized by DAVID EVANS.

NOTE.—*This hymn may also be sung to* VATER UNSER (*No.* 462).

A. C. Benson, 1862-1925.

O LORD of hosts, who didst upraise
   Strong captains to defend the right,
In darker years and sterner days,
   And armedst Israel for the fight;
Thou madest Joshua true and strong,
And David framed the battle-song.

2 And must we battle yet? Must we,
   Who bear the tender name Divine,
Still barter life for victory,
   Still glory in the crimson sign?
The Crucified between us stands,
And lifts on high his wounded hands.

3 Lord, we are weak and wilful yet,
   The fault is in our clouded eyes;
But thou, through anguish and regret,
   Dost make thy faithless children wise: [dost approve
Through wrong, through hate, thou
The far-off victories of love.

4*And so, from out the heart of strife,
   Diviner echoes peal and thrill;
The scorned delights, the lavished life,
   The pain that serves a nation's will:
Thy comfort stills the mourner's cries,
And love is crowned by sacrifice.

5. As rains that weep the clouds away,
   As winds that leave a calm in heaven,
So let the slayer cease to slay;—
   The passion healed, the wrath forgiven,
Draw nearer, bid the tumult cease,
Redeemer, Saviour, Prince of Peace!

A - men.

SPECIAL OCCASIONS

540

MELITA. (8 8. 8 8. 8 8.)
Moderately slow ♩ = 66.

J. B. DYKES, 1828-76.

NOTE.—*This hymn may also be sung to* VATER UNSER (*No. 462*).

IN TIME OF ROUGH WEATHER

W. Whiting, 1825-78.

ETERNAL Father, strong to save,
 Whose arm doth bind the restless wave,
Who bidd'st the mighty ocean deep
Its own appointed limits keep :
 O hear us when we cry to thee
 For those in peril on the sea.

2 O Saviour, whose almighty word
 The winds and waves submissive heard,
Who walkedst on the foaming deep,
And calm amid its rage didst sleep :
 O hear us when we cry to thee
 For those in peril on the sea.

3 O sacred Spirit, who didst brood
 Upon the chaos dark and rude,
Who bad'st its angry tumult cease,
And gavest light and life and peace :
 O hear us when we cry to thee
 For those in peril on the sea.

Unison. 4. O Trinity of love and power,
 Our brethren shield in danger's hour;
 From rock and tempest, fire and foe,
 Protect them wheresoe'er they go :
  And ever let there rise to thee
  Glad hymns of praise from land and sea.

A - men.

IN TIME OF ROUGH WEATHER

541

WHITE GATES. (8 8. 8 3.)
In moderate time ♩ = 86.
R. VAUGHAN WILLIAMS.

[Copyright, 1931, by R. Vaughan Williams.]
NOTE.—*This hymn may also be sung to* ST. AËLRED (*Appendix, No.* 62).

G. Thring, 1823-1903.

FIERCE raged the tempest o'er the deep,
Watch did thine anxious servants keep,
But thou wast wrapped in guileless sleep,
  Calm and still.

2 'Save, Lord, we perish!' was their cry,
'O save us in our agony!'
Thy word above the storm rose high,
  'Peace, be still.'

3 The wild winds hushed; the angry deep
Sank, like a little child, to sleep;
The sullen billows ceased to leap,
  At thy will.

4. So, when our life is clouded o'er,
And storm-winds drift us from the shore,
Say, lest we sink to rise no more,
  'Peace, be still.'

A - men.

SPECIAL OCCASIONS

542

KILMARNOCK. (C. M.)
In moderate time ♩ = 72.

NEIL DOUGALL, 1776–1862.

NOTE.—*This hymn may also be sung to* LONDON NEW (*No. 394*).

FOR USE AT SEA

J. Addison ‡, 1672–1719.

HOW are thy servants blest, O Lord!
　How sure is their defence!
Eternal Wisdom is their guide,
　Their help Omnipotence.

2 In foreign realms and lands remote,
　　Supported by thy care,
　Through burning climes they pass unhurt,
　　And breathe in tainted air.

Unison. 3 And though in dreadful whirls they hang
　　High on the broken wave,
　They know thou art not slow to hear,
　　Nor impotent to save.

4 The storm is laid, the winds retire,
　　Obedient to thy will;
　The sea, that roars at thy command,
　　At thy command is still.

Unison. 5 In midst of dangers, fears, and death,
　　Thy goodness we'll adore;
　And praise thee for thy mercies past,
　　And humbly hope for more.

6. Our life, while thou preserv'st that life,
　　Thy sacrifice shall be;
　And death, when death shall be our lot,
　　Shall join our souls to thee.

A - men.

FOR USE AT SEA

543

QUEM PASTORES LAUDAVERE. (8 8. 8 7.)
In moderate time ♩ = 144.

Melody from a 14th cent. German MS.

P. D.

1 LORD, the wind and sea obey thee,
　Moon and stars their homage pay
Listen to us, as we pray thee, [thee;
　Who on thee for all depend.

2 Bless all travellers and strangers,
　Safely keep the ocean rangers,
Guide them in the midst of dangers:
　All to thee we now commend.

3 Bless the friends we've left behind us;
　Closer may our parting bind us:
May they dearer, better, find us,
　When we reach our journey's end.

4 On our way, dear Lord, direct us;
　Where we err do thou correct us;
From the powers of ill protect us,
　From all perils us defend.

5 May we know thy presence o'er us,
　See thy guiding hand before us,
Till thou safely dost restore us,
　Love to love and friend to friend.

6. Holy God, in mercy bending,
　Human souls with love befriending,
Fit us all for joy unending
　When this earthly course doth end.

A - men.

The following are also suitable:

388 Fierce was the wild billow.
394 God moves in a mysterious way.
501 Three in One, and One in Three.

520 Holy Father, in thy mercy.
536 Praise to the Lord, the Almighty, the King of Creation. (*After a storm.*)

Also many of the Morning and Evening Hymns, and those in the List of Simple Hymns.

Part VII

CHURCH AND PEOPLE

THE CHURCH

544

PSALM 68. (8 8 7. 8 8 7 D.)
In moderate time, very dignified ♩ = 65.

T. A. Lacey, 1853–1931.
Composed or adapted by M. Greiter, *c.* 1525
(melody as given in the Genevan Psalter).

1. O Faith of England, taught of old By faithful shepherds of the fold, The hallowing of our nation;
   Thou wast through many a wealthy year, Through many a darkened day of fear The rock of our salvation.
2. Our fathers heard the trumpet call Through many a lowly cot and kingly hall From o'er-sea resounding;
   They bowed their stubborn wills to learn The truths that live, the thoughts that burn, With new resolve abounding.

Arise, arise, good Christian men, Your glorious
Arise, arise, good Christian men, Your glorious

Note.—*Verses 3 and 4 must always be sung in unison, but the organ accompaniment of verses 1 and 2 may, if preferred, be used throughout.*

THE CHURCH

544 (*continued*)

stan-dard raise a-gain, The Cross of Christ who calls you; . .
stan-dard raise a-gain, The Cross of Christ who guides you; . .

Who bids you live and bids you die, For his great
Whose arm is bared to join the fray, Who mar-shals

cause, and stands on high To wit-ness what be-falls you.
you in stern ar-ray, Fear-less, what-e'er be-tides you.

CHOIR AND PEOPLE IN UNISON.

3. { Our fa-thers held the faith re-ceived, By Saints de-
   { Through pain of doubt and bit-ter-ness, Through pain of
4. { Though fre-quent be the loud a-larms, Though still we
   { With Christ for Chief we fear no foe, Nor force nor

(*Small notes 2nd time only.*)

CHURCH AND PEOPLE

544 (*continued*)

-clared, by Saints be-lieved, By Saints in death de-fend-ed;
trea-son and dis-tress, They for the right con-tend-ed.
march by am-bushed arms Of death and hell sur-round-ed,
craft can o-ver-throw The Church that he has found-ed.

A-rise, a-rise, good Chris-tian men, Your glo-rious
A-rise, a-rise, good Chris-tian men, Your glo-rious

stan-dard raise a-gain, The Cross of Christ who
stan-dard raise a-gain, The Cross where-with he

THE CHURCH

544 (*continued*)

bought you, ... Who leads you forth in
signed you; . . . . The King him-self shall

Very broad.

this new age, With long-en-dur-ing hearts to
lead you on, Shall watch you till the strife be

wage, The war-fare he has taught you
done, Then near his throne shall find you

A-men.

CHURCH AND PEOPLE

545

THORNBURY. (7 6. 7 6. D.)
Moderately slow ♩ = 66. *Unison.*

BASIL HARWOOD.

NOTE.—*This hymn may also be sung to* CRÜGER (*No.* 45), *or to* ST. THEODULPH (VALET WILL ICH DIR GEBEN) (*No.* 622).

THE CHURCH

E. H. Plumptre, 1821-91.

THY hand, O God, has guided
  Thy flock, from age to age;
The wondrous tale is written,
  Full clear, on every page;
Our fathers owned thy goodness,
  And we their deeds record;
And both of this bear witness,
  One Church, one Faith, one Lord.

2 Thy heralds brought glad tidings
  To greatest, as to least;
They bade men rise, and hasten
  To share the great King's feast;
And this was all their teaching,
  In every deed and word,
To all alike proclaiming
  One Church, one Faith, one Lord.

3 Through many a day of darkness,
  Through many a scene of strife,
The faithful few fought bravely
  To guard the nation's life.
Their Gospel of redemption,
  Sin pardoned, man restored,
Was all in this enfolded,
  One Church, one Faith, one Lord.

4* And we, shall we be faithless?
  Shall hearts fail, hands hang down?
Shall we evade the conflict,
  And cast away our crown?
Not so: in God's deep counsels
  Some better thing is stored;
We will maintain, unflinching,
  One Church, one Faith, one Lord.

5. Thy mercy will not fail us,
  Nor leave thy work undone;
With thy right hand to help us,
  The victory shall be won;
And then, by men and angels,
  Thy name shall be adored,
And this shall be their anthem,
  One Church, one Faith, one Lord.

The following are also suitable:

362 A safe stronghold our God is still.
375 City of God, how broad and far.
384 Eternal Ruler of the ceaseless round.
393 Glorious things of thee are spoken.
435 Lord of our life, and God of our salvation.
450 O God, our help in ages past.
458 O Lord of hosts, all heaven possessing.
464 O thou not made with hands.
472 Pray that Jerusalem may have.
488 The Church of God a kingdom is.

CHURCH AND PEOPLE

546

CATHCART. (L. M.)
In moderate time ♩ = 100.

W. H. BELL.

NOTE.—*This hymn may also be sung to* DUKE STREET (*No.* 167).

HOME AND FOREIGN MISSIONS

Foreign.

1. FLING out the banner! let it float
Skyward and seaward, high and wide,—
The sun that lights its shining folds,
The Cross on which the Saviour died.

2. Fling out the banner! angels bend
In anxious silence o'er the sign,
And vainly seek to comprehend
The wonders of the love divine.

Unison. Bishop G. W. Doane, 1799–1859.

3. Fling out the banner! heathen lands
Shall see from far the glorious sight,
And nations, crowding to be born,
Baptize their spirits in its light.

4. Fling out the banner! sin-sick souls
That sink and perish in the strife,
Shall touch in faith its radiant hem,
And spring immortal into life.

5. Fling out the banner! let it float
Skyward and seaward, high and wide,
Our glory only in the Cross,
Our only hope the Crucified.

Unison.
6. Fling out the banner! wide and high,
Seaward and skyward let it shine;
Nor skill, nor might, nor merit ours:
We conquer only in that sign.

A - men.

HOME AND FOREIGN MISSIONS

CALCUTTA. (76.76. D.) **547**
In moderate time ♩ = 92.
Melody by BISHOP HEBER, 1783–1826.

NOTE.—*This hymn may also be sung to* AURELIA (*No.* 489).

Foreign.　　　　　　　　　　　　　　　　　　　　　　　　*Bishop R. Heber,* 1783–1826.

FROM Greenland's icy mountains,
　From India's coral strand,
Where Afric's sunny fountains
　Roll down their golden sand;
From many an ancient river,
　From many a palmy plain,
They call us to deliver
　Their land from error's chain.

2 What though the spicy breezes
　Blow soft o'er Java's isle,
Though every prospect pleases
　And only man is vile:

In vain with lavish kindness
　The gifts of God are strown,
The heathen in his blindness
　Bows down to wood and stone!

3 Can we, whose souls are lighted
　With wisdom from on high,
Can we to men benighted
　The lamp of life deny?
Salvation! O salvation!
　The joyful sound proclaim,
Till each remotest nation
　Has learned Messiah's name.

　Unison. 4. Waft, waft, ye winds, his story,
　　　　And you, ye waters, roll,
　　　　Till, like a sea of glory,
　　　　　It spreads from pole to pole;
　　　　Till o'er our ransomed nature
　　　　　The Lamb for sinners slain,
　　　　Redeemer, King, Creator,
　　　　　In bliss returns to reign.

A - men.

CHURCH AND PEOPLE

548

PURPOSE. (Irreg.)
With breadth ♩ = 104.
MARTIN SHAW.

1. God is work-ing his pur-pose out as year suc-ceeds to year; God is work-ing his pur-pose out and the time is draw-ing near; Near-er and near-er
2.* From ut-most east to ut-most west where-'er man's foot hath trod, By the mouth of man-y mes-sen-gers goes forth the voice of God, 'Give ear to me, ye
3. What can we do to work God's work, to pros-per and in-crease The bro-ther-hood of all man-kind, the reign of the Prince of Peace? What can we do to
4. March we forth in the strength of God with the banner of Christ un-furled, That the light of the glo-rious gos-pel of truth may shine through-out the world; Fight we the fight with
5.* All we can do is noth-ing worth un-less God blesses the deed; Vain-ly we hope for the har-vest-tide till God gives life to the seed; Yet near-er and near-er

HOME AND FOREIGN MISSIONS
548 (continued)

draws the time, the time that shall sure-ly be,
con-ti-nents, ye isles, give ear to me,
hasten the time, the time that shall sure-ly be,
sorrow and sin, to set their cap-tives free,
draws the time, the time that shall sure-ly be,

When the earth shall be filled with the glo-ry of God as the
That the earth may be filled with the glo-ry of God as the
When the earth shall be filled with the glo-ry of God as the
That the earth may be filled with the glo-ry of God as the
When the earth shall be filled with the glo-ry of God as the

1, &c. | **Last verse.**

wa-ters co-ver the sea.
wa-ters co-ver the sea.'
wa-ters co-ver the sea?
wa-ters co-ver the sea.
wa-ters co-ver the sea.

Unison Amen.

[Copyright, 1931, by Martin Shaw.]   A. C. Ainger, 1841-1919.

NOTE.—*This hymn may also be sung to* BENSON (*Appendix, No. 63*).

CHURCH AND PEOPLE

PRAETORIUS (FÜR DEIN EMPFANGEN SPEIS UND TRANK). (C. M.) **549**

Melody from the Görlitz Gesangbuch, 1599.

NOTE.—*This hymn may also be sung to* ST. DAVID (*No.* 166).

Foreign.

J. Montgomery, 1771-1854.

LIFT up your heads, ye gates of brass;
  Ye bars of iron, yield,
And let the King of glory pass:
  The Cross is in the field.

2 That banner, brighter than the star
    That leads the train of night,
  Shines on their march, and guides from far
    His servants to the fight.

3 A holy war those servants wage;
    Mysteriously at strife,
  The powers of heaven and hell engage
    For more than death or life.

Unison. 4 Ye armies of the living God,
    His sacramental host!
  Where hallowed footsteps never trod,
    Take your appointed post.

5 Though few and small and weak your bands,
    Strong in your Captain's strength,
  Go to the conquest of all lands,
    All must be his at length.

Unison. 6. Uplifted are the gates of brass,
    The bars of iron yield;
  Behold the King of glory pass:
    The Cross hath won the field.

A - men.

HOME AND FOREIGN MISSIONS

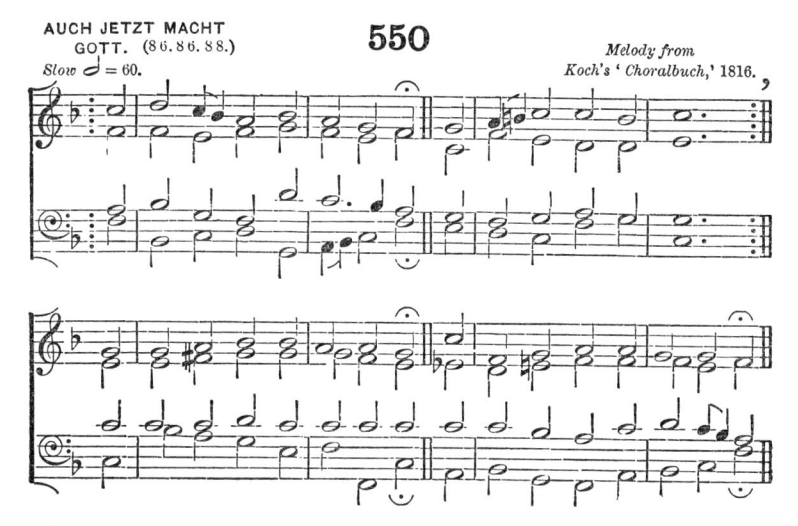

AUCH JETZT MACHT GOTT. (86.86.88.)

550

Melody from Koch's 'Choralbuch,' 1816.

Slow ♩ = 60.

Foreign.   *W. Cullen Bryant*, 1794–1878.

O NORTH, with all thy vales of green!
   O South, with all thy palms!
From peopled towns and fields between
   Uplift the voice of psalms.
Raise, ancient East, the anthem high,
And let the youthful West reply.

2 Lo! in the clouds of heaven appears
   God's well-belovèd Son;
He brings a train of brighter years,
   His kingdom is begun:
He comes a guilty world to bless
With mercy, truth and righteousness.

Unison. 3 O Father, haste the promised hour
   When at his feet shall lie
All rule, authority, and power
   Beneath the ample sky:
When he shall reign from pole to pole,
The Lord of every human soul;

4. When all shall heed the words he said,
   Amid their daily cares,
And by the loving life he led
   Shall strive to pattern theirs;
And he, who conquered death, shall win
The mightier conquest over sin.

A - men.

CHURCH AND PEOPLE

551

HOPE. (8 7. 8 7. D.)
In moderate time ♩ = 72.
R. DAVIES [?].

NOTE.—*This hymn may also be sung to* IN BABILONE (*No.* 145).

Foreign.
Bishop A. Cleveland Coxe, 1818-96.

SAVIOUR, sprinkle many nations,
  Fruitful let thy sorrows be;
By thy pains and consolations
  Draw the Gentiles unto thee:
Of thy Cross the wondrous story,
  Be it to the nations told;
Let them see thee in thy glory
  And thy mercy manifold.

2 Far and wide, though all unknowing,
  Pants for thee each mortal breast;
Human tears for thee are flowing,
  Human hearts in thee would rest;
Thirsting, as for dews of even,
  As the new-mown grass for rain,
Thee they seek, as God of heaven,
  Thee, as Man, for sinners slain.

3. Saviour, lo! the isles are waiting,
    Stretched the hand, and strained the sight,
  For thy Spirit new creating,
    Love's pure flame and wisdom's light;
  Give the word, and of the preacher
    Speed the foot and touch the tongue,
  Till on earth by every creature,
    Glory to the Lamb be sung.

A - men.

714

HOME AND FOREIGN MISSIONS

GOTT SEI DANK. (7 7. 7 7.)
Moderately slow ♩ = 60.

552

FREYLINGHAUSEN'S
'*Geistreiches Gesangbuch*,' 1704.

Home or Foreign.

J. F. Bahnmaier, 1774–1841.
Tr. C. Winkworth.

Walte fürder, nah und fern.

SPREAD, O spread, thou mighty word,
Spread the kingdom of the Lord,
Wheresoe'er his breath has given
Life to beings meant for heaven.

2 Tell them how the Father's will
Made the world, and keeps it still,
How he sent his Son to save
All who help and comfort crave.

3 Tell of our Redeemer's love,
Who for ever doth remove
By his holy sacrifice
All the guilt that on us lies.

4 Tell them of the Spirit given
Now to guide us up to heaven,
Strong and holy, just and true,
Working both to will and do.

Unison. 5 Word of life, most pure and strong,
Lo! for thee the nations long;
Spread, till from its dreary night
All the world awakes to light.

6 Up! the ripening fields ye see,
Mighty shall the harvest be;
But the reapers still are few,
Great the work they have to do.

Unison. 7. Lord of harvest, let there be
Joy and strength to work for thee,
Till the nations, far and near,
See thy light, and learn thy fear.

A - men.

CHURCH AND PEOPLE

553

MOSCOW (664. 666. 4.)
Moderately slow ♩ = 84.

Adapted from
F. DE GIARDINI, 1716-96.

Home or Foreign.

J. Marriott †, 1780-1825.

THOU whose almighty Word
　Chaos and darkness heard,
　And took their flight;
Hear us, we humbly pray,
And where the Gospel-day
Sheds not its glorious ray
　Let there be light!

2 Thou who didst come to bring
　On thy redeeming wing
　　Healing and sight,
Health to the sick in mind,
Sight to the inly blind,
Ah! now to all mankind
　Let there be light!

3 Spirit of truth and love,
Life-giving, holy Dove,
　Speed forth thy flight!
Move on the waters' face,
Bearing the lamp of grace,
And in earth's darkest place
　Let there be light!

4. Blessèd and holy Three
Glorious Trinity,
　Wisdom, Love, Might;
Boundless as ocean tide
Rolling in fullest pride,
Through the world far and wide
　Let there be light!

A - men.

HOME AND FOREIGN MISSIONS

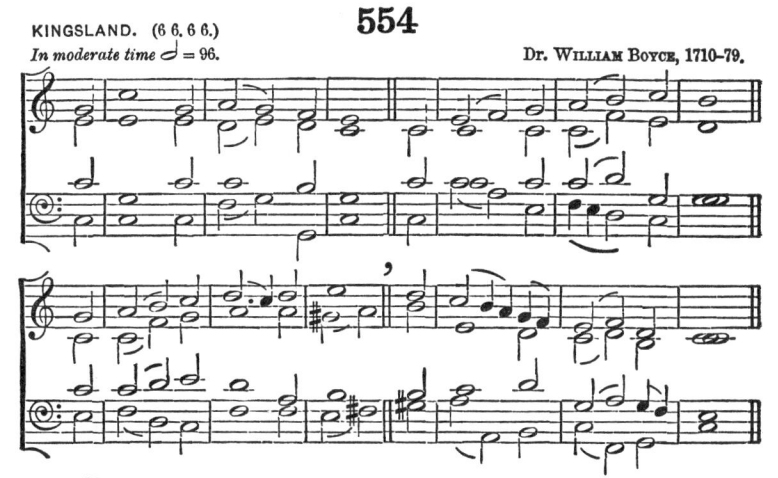

554

KINGSLAND. (6 6, 6 6.)
In moderate time ♩ = 96.
Dr. WILLIAM BOYCE, 1710-79.

NOTE.—*This hymn may also be sung to* ST. CECILIA (*Appendix, No.* 64).

Home or Foreign.   L. Hensley, 1827-1905.

THY kingdom come, O God,
  Thy rule, O Christ, begin;
Break with thine iron rod
  The tyrannies of sin.

2 Where is thy reign of peace,
  And purity, and love?
When shall all hatred cease,
  As in the realms above?

3 When comes the promised time
  That war shall be no more,—
Oppression, lust, and crime
  Shall flee thy face before?

4 We pray thee, Lord, arise,
  And come in thy great might;
Revive our longing eyes,
  Which languish for thy sight.

5*Men scorn thy sacred name,
  And wolves devour thy fold;
By many deeds of shame
  We learn that love grows cold.

6. O'er heathen lands afar
  Thick darkness broodeth yet ·
Arise, O morning Star,
  Arise, and never set!

A - men.

The following are also suitable:

Foreign Missions.
43 The race that long in darkness pined.
45 Hail to the Lord's Anointed.
420 Jesus shall reign where'er the sun.

Home Missions.
423 Judge eternal, throned in splendour.
448 O God of mercy, God of might.

Home or Foreign Missions.
126 A brighter dawn is breaking.
384 Eternal Ruler of the ceaseless round.
395 God of mercy, God of grace.
492 The Lord will come, and not be slow.
504 Thy kingdom come! on bended knee.
544, 545 (The Church).

CHURCH AND PEOPLE

555

BRUNSWICK. (8 6. 8 6. 8 6.)
In moderate time ♩ = 96.

Adapted from
G. F. HANDEL, 1685–1759.

CHURCH WORK

T. T. *Lynch*, 1818–71.

DISMISS me not thy service, Lord,
   But train me for thy will;
For even I, in fields so broad,
   Some duties may fulfil;
And I will ask for no reward,
   Except to serve thee still.

2 All works are good, and each is best
   As most it pleases thee;
Each worker pleases, when the rest
   He serves in charity;
And neither man nor work unblest
   Wilt thou permit to be.

3. Our Master all the work hath done
   He asks of us to-day;
Sharing his service, every one
   Share too his Sonship may:
Lord, I would serve and be a son;
   Dismiss me not, I pray.

A - men.

CHURCH WORK

LLANGOLLEN (LLEDROD). (L. M.) **556**
With vigour ♩ = 80. *May be sung in unison.*
Welsh Hymn Melody.

NOTE.—*This hymn may also be sung to* ANGEL'S SONG (SONG 34), *No.* 259.

H. Bonar, 1808–89.

GO, labour on; spend, and be spent,
Thy joy to do the Father's will;
It is the way the Master went;
Should not the servant tread it still?

2 Go, labour on; 'tis not for nought;
Thy earthly loss is heavenly gain;
Men heed thee, love thee, praise thee not:
The Master praises; what are men?

3 Toil on, faint not, keep watch and pray;
Be wise the erring soul to win;
Go forth into the world's highway,
Compel the wanderer to come in.

4. Toil on, and in thy toil rejoice;
For toil comes rest, for exile home;
Soon shalt thou hear the Bridegroom's voice,
The midnight peal, 'Behold, I come!'

A-men.

The following are also suitable:

448 O God of mercy, God of might.
467 Oft in danger, oft in woe.
472 Pray that Jerusalem may have.
479 Soldiers of Christ, arise.
516 Work is sweet, for God has blest.
518 Ye servants of the Lord.

CHURCH AND PEOPLE

557
ISLEWORTH. (88.86.)
Moderately slow ♩ = 66.
Melody by S. HOWARD, 1710–82.

NOTE.—*This hymn may also be sung to* FITZWILLIAM (*No.* 448).

NATIONAL
Bishop R. Heber, 1783–1826.

FROM foes that would the land devour;
From guilty pride and lust of power;
From wild sedition's lawless hour;
From yoke of slavery:

2 From blinded zeal by faction led;
From giddy change by fancy bred;
From poisonous error's serpent head
Good Lord, preserve us free!

Unison. 3. Defend, O God! with guardian hand,
The laws and ruler of our land,
And grant our Church thy grace to stand
In faith and unity!

A - men.

558
FOLKINGHAM. (88.88.88.)
Moderately slow, dignified ♩ = 66.
From the 'Supplement to the NEW VERSION,' 1708.

NATIONAL

558 *continued*.

Verses 2 and 5 should commence

Unison. *Rudyard Kipling.*

GOD of our fathers, known of old,
   Lord of our far-flung battle-line,
Beneath whose awful hand we hold
   Dominion over palm and pine—
Lord God of Hosts, be with us yet,
Lest we forget—lest we forget!

2* The tumult and the shouting dies;
   The captains and the kings depart:
Still stands thine ancient sacrifice,
   An humble and a contrite heart.
Lord God of Hosts, be with us yet,
Lest we forget—lest we forget!

Line 5 of verse 5 should run

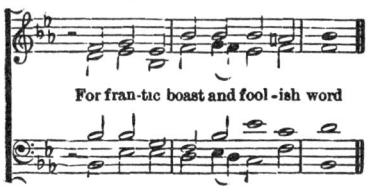

For fran-tic boast and fool-ish word

3* Far-called, our navies melt away;
   On dune and headland sinks the fire:
Lo, all our pomp of yesterday
   Is one with Nineveh and Tyre!
Judge of the Nations, spare us yet,
Lest we forget—lest we forget!

4 If, drunk with sight of power, we loose
   Wild tongues that have not thee in awe,
Such boastings as the Gentiles use,
   Or lesser breeds without the Law—
Lord God of Hosts, be with us yet
Lest we forget—lest we forget!

Unison. 5. For heathen heart that puts her trust
   In reeking tube and iron shard,
All valiant dust that builds on dust,
   And guarding, calls not thee to guard,
For frantic boast and foolish word—
Thy mercy on thy people, Lord!

A - men.

CHURCH AND PEOPLE

559

ETONA. (88.88.88.88.88.)
In moderate time ♩ = 80.
Unison. (𝄐 1st verse only.)

A. M. GOODHART.

(*Only small notes to be played in lower stave.*)

𝄐 Harmony.

𝄐 Unison.

NATIONAL

559 (*continued*)

[*By permission of Novello & Co., Ltd.*]

Suitable for National Thanksgivings and other occasions.   A. C. Ainger, 1841-1919.

GOD of our fathers, unto thee
   Our fathers cried in danger's hour,
And then thou gavest them to see
   The acts of thine almighty power.
They cried to thee, and thou didst hear;
   They called on thee, and thou didst save;
And we their sons to-day draw near
   Thy name to praise, thy help to crave.

> *Lord God of Hosts, uplift thine hand,*
> *Protect and bless our Fatherland.*

2 Thine is the majesty, O Lord,
   And thine dominion over all;
When thou commandest, at thy word,
   Great kings and nations rise or fall.
For eastern realms, for western coasts,
   For islands washed by every sea,
The praise be given, O God of Hosts,
   Not unto us but unto thee.

3. If in thy grace thou should'st allow
   Our fame to wax through coming days,
Still grant us humbly, then as now,
   Thy help to crave, thy name to praise.
Not all alike in speech or birth
   Alike we bow before thy throne;
One fatherland throughout the earth
   Our Father's noble acts we own.

A - men.

CHURCH AND PEOPLE

NATIONAL ANTHEM. (664.6664.) **560**

Very slow ♩ = 56. *Source unknown.*

National Anthem. 17th or 18th cent.

1. GOD save our gracious King,
   Long live our noble King,
     God save the King!
   Send him victorious,
   Happy and glorious,
   Long to reign over us;
     God save the King!

2. *Thy choicest gifts in store
   On him be pleased to pour,
     Long may he reign;
   May he defend our laws,
   And ever give us cause
   To say with heart and voice
     God save the King!

The whole or part of this hymn may be added.

Part 2.

W. E. Hickson, 1803-70.

3. God bless our native land,
   May heaven's protecting hand
     Still guard our shore;
   May peace her power extend,
   Foe be transformed to friend,
   And Britain's rights depend
     On war no more.

4. May just and righteous laws
   Uphold the public cause,
     And bless our isle.
   Home of the brave and free,
   The land of liberty,
   We pray that still on thee
     Kind heaven may smile.

NATIONAL

5. Nor on this land alone—
   But be God's mercies known
      From shore to shore.
   Lord, make the nations see
   That men should brothers be,
   And form one family
      The wide world o'er.

A - men.

561

ABERDEEN. (C.M.)
In moderate time ♩ = 72.

Melody in BREMNER'S *Collection*, 1763.

J. R. Wreford, 1800-81.

LORD, while for all mankind we pray
   Of every clime and coast,
O hear us for our native land,
   The land we love the most.

2 O guard our shores from every foe;
   With peace our borders bless;
   With prosperous times our cities crown,
   Our fields with plenteousness.

3 Unite us in the sacred love
   Of knowledge, truth, and thee;
   And let our hills and valleys shout
   The songs of liberty.

4. Lord of the nations, thus to thee
   Our country we commend;
   Be thou her Refuge and her Trust,
   Her everlasting Friend.

A - men.

CHURCH AND PEOPLE

562

KINGS LYNN. (76.76.D.)
In moderate time, dignified ♩ = 76.
To be sung in unison.

English Traditional Melody.

NATIONAL

G. K. Chesterton

O GOD of earth and altar,
   Bow down and hear our cry,
Our earthly rulers falter,
   Our people drift and die;
The walls of gold entomb us,
   The swords of scorn divide,
Take not thy thunder from us,
   But take away our pride.

2 From all that terror teaches,
   From lies of tongue and pen,
From all the easy speeches
   That comfort cruel men,
From sale and profanation
   Of honour and the sword,
From sleep and from damnation,
   Deliver us, good Lord!

3. Tie in a living tether
   The prince and priest and thrall,
Bind all our lives together,
   Smite us and save us all;
In ire and exultation
   Aflame with faith, and free,
Lift up a living nation,
   A single sword to thee.

CHURCH AND PEOPLE

563

YN Y GLYN. (8 7. 8 7. D.)

Moderately slow ♩ = 63.

DAVID EVANS.

[*Copyright*, 1927, *by David Evans.*]

NOTE.—*This hymn may also be sung to* HYFRYDOL (*No.* 301).

NATIONAL

J. Russell Lowell ‡, 1819-91

ONCE to every man and nation
  Comes the moment to decide,
In the strife of truth with falsehood,
  For the good or evil side;
Some great cause, God's new Messiah,
  Offering each the bloom or blight—
And the choice goes by for ever
  'Twixt that darkness and that light.

2 Then to side with truth is noble,
    When we share her wretched crust,
  Ere her cause bring fame and profit,
    And 'tis prosperous to be just;
  Then it is the brave man chooses,
    While the coward stands aside,
  Till the multitude make virtue
    Of the faith they had denied.

3 * By the light of burning martyrs,
    Christ, thy bleeding feet we track,
  Toiling up new Calvaries ever
    With the Cross that turns not back.
  New occasions teach new duties;
    Time makes ancient good uncouth;
  They must upward still and onward
    Who would keep abreast of truth.

4. Though the cause of evil prosper,
    Yet 'tis truth alone is strong;
  Though her portion be the scaffold,
    And upon the throne be wrong—
  Yet that scaffold sways the future,
    And, behind the dim unknown,
  Standeth God within the shadow,
    Keeping watch above his own.

A - men.

CHURCH AND PEOPLE

564

DONNE SECOURS. (11 10. 11 10.)
Moderately slow ♩ = 88.
To be sung in unison.

Psalm 12 in the Genevan Psalter, 1551.

NOTE.—*This hymn may also be sung to* WELWYN (*No.* 346).

NATIONAL

Y. H. based on F. R. Tailour (1615).

THE King, O God, his heart to thee upraiseth;
  With him the nation bows before thy face;
With high thanksgiving thee thy glad Church praiseth,
Our strength thy spirit, our trust and hope thy grace.

2 Unto great honour, glory undeservèd,
  Hast thou exalted us, and drawn thee nigh;
Nor, from thy judgements when our feet had swervèd,
  Didst thou forsake, nor leave us, Lord most high.

Part 2.

3 In thee our fathers trusted and were savèd,
  In thee destroyèd thrones of tyrants proud;
From ancient bondage freed the poor enslavèd:
  To sow thy truth poured out their saintly blood.

4*Us now, we pray, O God, in anger scorn not,
  Nor to vainglorying leave, nor brutish sense;
In time of trouble thy face from us turn not,
  Who art our Rock, our stately sure defence.

5 Unto our minds give freedom and uprightness;
  Let strength and courage lead o'er land and wave;
To our souls' armour grant celestial brightness,
  Joy to our hearts, and faith beyond the grave.

6. Our plenteous nation still in power extending,
  Increase our joy uphold us by thy Word;
Beauty and wisdom all our ways attending,
  Goodwill to man and peace through Christ our Lord.

CHURCH AND PEOPLE

565

CROFT'S 136TH. (66.66.88.)
In moderate time ♩ = 76.

Dr. Croft, 1678–1727.

Note.—*This hymn may also be sung to* Darwall's 148th (*No.* 517).

Bishop W. W. How, 1823–97.

To thee our God we fly
　For mercy and for grace;
O hear our lowly cry,
　And hide not thou thy face.
O Lord, stretch forth thy mighty hand,
And guard and bless our fatherland.

Unison.　2 Arise, O Lord of hosts!
　　Be jealous for thy name,
　And drive from out our coasts
　　The sins that put to shame.

NATIONAL

3 Thy best gifts from on high
    In rich abundance pour,
That we may magnify
    And praise thee more and more.

4 The powers ordained by thee
    With heavenly wisdom bless:
May they thy servants be,
    And rule in righteousness.

5 The Church of thy dear Son
    Inflame with love's pure fire,
Bind her once more in one,
    And life and truth inspire.

6*The pastors of thy fold
    With grace and power endue,
That faithful, pure, and bold,
    They may be pastors true.

7*O let us love thy house,
    And sanctify thy day,
Bring unto thee our vows,
    And loyal homage pay.

8*Give peace, Lord, in our time;
    O let no foe draw nigh,
Nor lawless deed of crime
    Insult thy majesty.

9.*Though vile and worthless, still
    Thy people, Lord, are we;
And for our God we will
    None other have but thee.

A - men.

CHURCH AND PEOPLE

KENDAL. (7 6. 7 6. 8 8. 8 5.)   **566**   *Ebenezer Elliott †, 1781-1849.*
Moderately slow ♩ = 69.
                                                                                              A. SOMERVELL.

1 When wilt thou save the peo - ple? O God of mer - cy, when? The peo - ple, Lord, the peo - ple, Not thrones and crowns, but men! Flowers of thy heart, O God, are they;

2 Shall crime bring crime for ev - er, Strength aid - ing still the strong? Is it thy will, O Fa - ther, That man shall toil for wrong? 'No,' say thy mountains; 'No,' thy skies;

3 When wilt thou save the peo - ple? O God of mer - cy, when? The peo - ple, Lord, the peo - ple, Not thrones and crowns, but men! God save the peo - ple; thine they are,

784

NATIONAL

566 (continued)

Let them not pass, like weeds, a-way— Their he-ri-tage a sun-less day. God save the peo-ple!
Man's cloud-ed sun shall bright-ly rise, And songs be heard in-stead of sighs. God save the peo-ple!
Thy chil-dren, as thy An-gels fair; From vice, op-pres-sion, and des-pair, God save the peo-ple!

Harmony.

A - men.

The following are also suitable:

423 Judge eternal, throned in splendour.
450 O God, our help in ages past.
458 O Lord of hosts, all heaven possessing.
475 Rejoice, O land, in God thy might.
492 The Lord will come, and not be slow.
529 Son of God, eternal Saviour.

Part VIII

FOR MISSION SERVICES

Not for ordinary use.

567

GLORIA. (76. 86. 86. 86.)
In moderate time ♩ = 96

R. L. De Pearsall, 1795–1856.

Note.—*Another tune for this hymn will be found in the Appendix (No. 22).*

Elizabeth C. Clephane, 1830-69.

BENEATH the Cross of Jesus
  I fain would take my stand—
The shadow of a mighty Rock
  Within a weary land;
A home within a wilderness,
  A rest upon the way,
From the burning of the noontide heat
  And the burden of the day.

2 O safe and happy shelter!
  O refuge tried and sweet!
O trysting-place where heaven's love
  And heaven's justice meet!
As to the exiled patriarch
  That wondrous dream was given,
So seems my Saviour's Cross to me
  A ladder up to heaven.

3 There lies beneath its shadow,
  But on the further side,
The darkness of an open grave
  That gapes both deep and wide:
And there between us stands the Cross,
  Two arms outstretched to save,
Like a watchman set to guard the way
  From that eternal grave.

4 Upon that Cross of Jesus
  Mine eye at times can see
The very dying form of One,
  Who suffered there for me.
And from my stricken heart, with tears,
  Two wonders I confess,—
The wonders of redeeming love,
  And my own worthlessness

5. I take, O Cross, thy shadow
  For my abiding-place;
I ask no other sunshine than
  The sunshine of his face:
Content to let the world go by,
  To know no gain nor loss,—
My sinful self my only shame
  My glory all—the Cross.

A - men.

MISSION SERVICES

568

DAILY, DAILY. (87.87.D.)
With vigour ♩ = 80.

Melody from a French Paroissien.

MISSION SERVICES

S Baring Gould 1884 1924

DAILY, daily sing the praises
  Of the City God hath made;
In the beauteous fields of Eden
  Its foundation stones are laid:

O, that I had wings of Angels
  Here to spread and heavenward fly;
I would seek the gates of Sion,
  Far beyond the starry sky!

2 All the walls of that dear City
  Are of bright and burnished gold;
It is matchless in its beauty,
  And its treasures are untold:

3 In the midst of that dear City
  Christ is reigning on his seat,
And the Angels swing their censers
  In a ring about his feet:

4 From the throne a river issues,
  Clear as crystal, passing bright,
And it traverses the City
  Like a beam of living light:

5 There the meadows green and dewy
  Shine with lilies wondrous fair;
Thousand, thousand are the colours
  Of the waving flowers there:

6 There the forests ever blossom,
  Like our orchards here in May;
There the gardens never wither,
  But eternally are gay:

7 There the wind is sweetly fragrant,
  And is laden with the song
Of the Seraphs, and the Elders,
  And the great redeemèd throng

8. O I would my ears were open
  Here to catch that happy strain!
  O I would my eyes some vision
  Of that Eden could attain!

MISSION SERVICES

EVENING HYMN. (87.87.87.87.87.106.) **569**

In moderate time ♩ = 92.

CAROLINE MAUDE.
(Viscountess Hawarden)

MISSION SERVICES

569 (*continued*)

J. Purchas †, 1823-72.

EVENSONG is hushed in silence,
And the hour of rest is nigh;
Strengthen us for work to-morrow,
Son of Mary—God most high!
Thou who in the village workshop,
Fashioning the yoke and plough,
Didst eat bread by daily labour,
Succour them that labour now.

We are weary of life-long toil,
Of sorrow, and pain, and sin;
But there is a City with streets of gold,
And all is peace within.

2 How are we to reach that City,
Whose delights no tongue may tell?
By the faith that looks to Jesus,
By a life of doing well.
Sinful men and sinful women,
He will wash our sins away;
He will take us to the sheepfold
Whence no sheep can ever stray.

3. There the dear ones who have left us
We shall some day meet again;
There will be no bitter partings,
No more sorrow, death, or pain.
Evensong has closed in silence,
And the hour of rest is nigh;
Lighten thou our darkness, Jesu,
Son of Mary—God most high!

A - men.

MISSION SERVICES

HOLD THE FORT. (8 5. 8 5. D.) **570**
Brightly ♩ = 108.
P. P. Bliss, 1838-76.

P. P. Bliss, 1838-76.

HO! my comrades, see the signal
  Waving in the sky!
Reinforcements now appearing,
  Victory is nigh!
  'Hold the fort, for I am coming,'
    Jesus signals still;
  Wave the answer back to heaven,
    'By thy grace we will.'

2 See the mighty host advancing,
  Satan leading on;
  Mighty men around us falling,
  Courage almost gone!

3 See the glorious banner waving!
  Hear the trumpet blow!
  In our Leader's name we'll triumph
  Over every foe.

4. Fierce and long the battle rages,
  But our help is near;
  Onward comes our great Commander,
  Cheer, my comrades, cheer!

A - men.

BOSSINEY. (10 7. 9 7. 9 7. 9 7. and refrain.) **571**
In moderate time ♩ = 92.
G. Holst.

MISSION SERVICES

571 (*continued*)

F. W. Faber, 1814-63.

1 HOLY Ghost, come down upon thy children,
Give us grace and make us thine;
Thy tender fires within us kindle,
Blessèd Spirit, Dove divine.

2 For all within us good and holy
Is from thee, thy precious gift;
In all our joys, in all our sorrows,
Wistful hearts to thee we lift.
Holy Ghost, come down, &c.

3 For thou to us art more than father,
More than sister, in thy love;
So gentle, patient, and forbearing,
Holy Spirit, heavenly Dove.
Holy Ghost, come down, &c.

4 O we have grieved thee, gracious Spirit!
Wayward, wanton, cold are we;
And still our sins, new every morning,
Never yet have wearied thee.
Holy Ghost, come down, &c.

5 Ah! sweet Consoler, though we cannot
Love thee as thou lovest us,
Yet if thou deign'st our hearts to kindle
They will not be always thus.
Holy Ghost, come down, &c.

6. With hearts so vile how dare we venture,
King of kings, to love thee so?
And how canst thou, with such compassion,
Bear so long with things so low?
Holy Ghost, come down, &c.

A - men.

MISSION SERVICES

572

GOSTERWOOD. (76. 76. D.)
In moderate time ♩ = 100.

English Traditional Melody.

Frances R. Havergal, 1836–79.

I COULD not do without thee,
  O Saviour of the lost,
Whose precious Blood redeemed me
  At such tremendous cost;
Thy righteousness, thy pardon,
  Thy precious Blood must be
My only hope and comfort,
  My glory and my plea.

2 I could not do without thee,
  I cannot stand alone,
I have no strength or goodness,
  No wisdom of my own;
But thou, belovèd Saviour,
  Art all in all to me,
And weakness will be power
  If leaning hard on thee.

3 I could not do without thee,
  O Jesus, Saviour dear;
E'en when my eyes are holden
  I know that thou art near;
How dreary and how lonely
  This changeful life would be
Without the sweet communion,
  The secret rest with thee.

4. I could not do without thee,
  For years are fleeting fast,
And soon in solemn loneliness
  The river must be passed;
But thou wilt never leave me,
  And though the waves roll high,
I know thou wilt be near me,
  And whisper, 'It is I.'

A - men.

MISSION SERVICES

I HEAR THY WELCOME VOICE. (66. 86. 55. 76.)

573

Moderately slow ♩ = 80.

L. HARTSOUGH, 1828–1919.

L. Hartsough, 1828–1919.

1. I HEAR thy welcome voice,
   That calls me, Lord, to thee,
   For cleansing in thy precious Blood
   That flowed on Calvary.

   I am coming, Lord!
   Coming now to thee!
   Wash me, cleanse me, in the Blood
   That flowed on Calvary.

2. Though coming weak and vile,
   Thou dost my strength assure;
   Thou dost my vileness fully cleanse,
   Till spotless all and pure.

3. 'Tis Jesus calls me on
   To perfect faith and love,
   To perfect hope, and peace, and trust
   For earth and heaven above.

4. 'Tis Jesus who confirms
   The blessèd work within,
   By adding grace to welcomed grace,
   Where reigned the power of sin.

5. All hail, atoning Blood!
   All hail, redeeming grace!
   All hail, the gift of Christ our Lord,
   Our Strength and Righteousness!

A - men.

MISSION SERVICES

574

KINGSFOLD. (D.C.M.)
In moderate time ♩ = 80.

From an English Traditional Melody.

MISSION SERVICES

Other occasions also. *H. Bonar,* 1808-89.

I HEARD the voice of Jesus say,
    'Come unto me and rest;
Lay down, thou weary one, lay down
    Thy head upon my breast':
I came to Jesus as I was,
    Weary, and worn, and sad;
I found in him a resting-place,
    And he has made me glad.

2 I heard the voice of Jesus say,
    'Behold, I freely give
The living water, thirsty one;
    Stoop down, and drink, and live':
I came to Jesus, and I drank
    Of that life-giving stream;
My thirst was quenched, my soul revived,
    And now I live in him.

3. I heard the voice of Jesus say,
    'I am this dark world's Light;
Look unto me, thy morn shall rise.
    And all thy day be bright':
I looked to Jesus. and I found
    In him my Star, my Sun;
And in that light of life I'll walk
    Till travelling days are done.

A - men.

In verses 2 and 3 lines 5 and 6 run thus

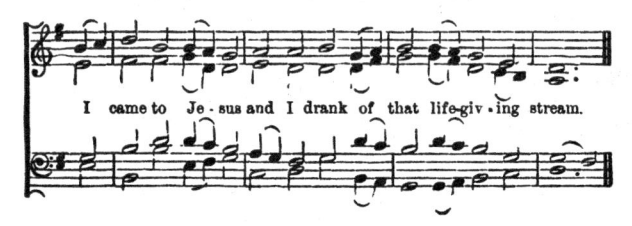

I came to Je-sus and I drank of that life-giv-ing stream.

MISSION SERVICES

575, 576

PRYSGOL. (7 6. 7 6. D.)
In moderate time ♩ = 96.

W. OWEN, 1814–93.

NOTE.—*These hymns may also be sung to* GOSTERWOOD (*No.* 572) *or* MISSIONARY HYMN (*No.* 577).

575

H. Bonar, 1808–89.

I LAY my sins on Jesus,
  The spotless Lamb of God;
He bears them all, and frees us
  From the accursèd load.
I bring my guilt to Jesus,
  To wash my crimson stains
White in his Blood most precious,
  Till not a spot remains.

2 I lay my wants on Jesus—
  All fullness dwells in him;
He heals all my diseases,
  He doth my soul redeem.

I lay my griefs on Jesus,
  My burdens and my cares;
He from them all releases,
  He all my sorrows shares.

3 I rest my soul on Jesus,
  This weary soul of mine;
His right hand me embraces,
  I on his breast recline.
I love the name of Jesus—
  Immanuel, Christ, the Lord;
Like fragrance on the breezes
  His name abroad is poured.

4. I long to be like Jesus,
    Meek, loving, lowly, mild;
  I long to be like Jesus,
    The Father's holy Child.
  I long to be with Jesus,
    Amid the heavenly throng,
  To sing with Saints his praises,
    To learn the Angels' song.

A - men.

576

F. Whitfield †, 1827–1904.

I NEED thee, precious Jesu,
  For I am full of sin;
My soul is dark and guilty,
  My heart is dead within.
I need the cleansing fountain
  Where I can always flee,
The Blood of Christ most precious,
  The sinner's perfect plea.

2 I need thee, precious Jesu,
  For I am very poor;
A stranger and a pilgrim,
  I have no earthly store.

I need the love of Jesus
  To cheer me on my way,
To guide my doubting footsteps,
  To be my strength and stay.

3 I need thee, precious Jesu:
  I need a friend like thee,
A friend to soothe and pity,
  A friend to care for me.
I need the heart of Jesus
  To feel each anxious care,
To tell my every trouble,
  And all my sorrow share.

4. I need thee, precious Jesu,
    And hope to see thee soon,
  Encircled with the rainbow,
    And seated on thy throne;
  There, with thy blood-bought children,
    My joy shall ever be,
  To sing thy praises, Jesu,
    To gaze, my Lord, on thee.

A - men.

MISSION SERVICES

577

MISSIONARY HYMN. (7 6. 7 6. D.)
In moderate time ♩ = 96.

Melody by LOWELL MASON, 1792–1872.

NOTE.—*This hymn may also be sung to* MEIRIONYDD (*No.* 473).

J. E. Bode, 1816–74.

O JESUS, I have promised
　To serve thee to the end;
Be thou for ever near me,
　My Master and my Friend;
I shall not fear the battle
　If thou art by my side,
Nor wander from the pathway
　If thou wilt be my Guide.

2 O let me feel thee near me:
　The world is ever near;
I see the sights that dazzle,
　The tempting sounds I hear;
My foes are ever near me,
　Around me and within;
But, Jesus, draw thou nearer,
　And shield my soul from sin.

3 O let me hear thee speaking
　In accents clear and still,
Above the storms of passion,
　The murmurs of self-will;
O speak to reassure me,
　To hasten or control;
O speak, and make me listen,
　Thou Guardian of my soul.

4 O Jesus, thou hast promised
　To all who follow thee,
That where thou art in glory
　There shall thy servant be;
And, Jesus, I have promised
　To serve thee to the end;
O give me grace to follow,
　My Master and my Friend.

5. O let me see thy footmarks,
　And in them plant mine own;
My hope to follow duly
　Is in thy strength alone:
O guide me, call me, draw me,
　Uphold me to the end;
And then in heaven receive me,
　My Saviour and my Friend.

MISSION SERVICES
578

IN DER WIEGEN. (7 6. 7 6. D.)
In moderate time ♩ = 132.

Melody from Corner's *Geistliche Nachtigall*, 1649.
Harmonized by Martin Shaw.

Note.— *This hymn may also be sung to* Llangloffan (*No* 207) *or* St. Catherine (*Appendix, No.* 65).

Bishop W. W. How, 1823–97.

O JESU, thou art standing
  Outside the fast-closed door,
In lowly patience waiting
  To pass the threshold o'er:
Shame on us, Christian brothers,
  His name and sign who bear,
O shame, thrice shame upon us
  To keep him standing there!

2 O Jesu, thou art knocking:
  And lo! that hand is scarred,
And thorns thy brow encircle,
  And tears thy face have marred:
O love that passeth knowledge
  So patiently to wait!
O sin that hath no equal
  So fast to bar the gate!

3. O Jesu, thou art pleading
  In accents meek and low,
'I died for you, my children,
  And will ye treat me so?'
O Lord, with shame and sorrow
  We open now the door:
Dear Saviour, enter, enter,
  And leave us nevermore.

A - men.

MISSION SERVICES

579

FORTUNATUS. (5 4. 5 4. D.)
Slow ♩ = 63 (♪ = 126).

Old English Melody.

J. S. B. Monsell, 1811-75.

REST of the weary,
　Joy of the sad,
Hope of the dreary,
　Light of the glad;
Home of the stranger,
　Strength to the end,
Refuge from danger,
　Saviour and Friend.

2 Pillow where, lying,
　　Love rests its head;
Peace of the dying,
　　Life of the dead;
Path of the lowly,
　　Prize at the end;
Breath of the holy,
　　Saviour and Friend.

3 When my feet stumble,
　　I'll to thee cry;
Crown of the humble,
　　Cross of the high.
When my steps wander,
　　Over me bend,
Truer and fonder,
　　Saviour and Friend.

4. Ever confessing
　　Thee, I will raise
Unto thee blessing,
　　Glory and praise;
All my endeavour,
　　World without end,
Thine to be ever,
　　Saviour and Friend.

A - men.

580

ARMS OF JESUS. (7 6. 7 6. D. and Refrain.)
In moderate time ♩ = 100.

W. H. Doane, 1832-1916.

MISSION SERVICES

580 (*continued*)

Frances J. Van Alstyne ‡, 1823–1915.

SAFE in the arms of Jesus,
  Safe on his gentle breast,
There, by his love o'ershadowed,
  Sweetly my soul shall rest.
Hark! 'tis the voice of Angels
  Borne in a song to me,
Over the fields of glory,
  Over the jasper sea,
    Safe in the arms, &c.

2 Safe in the arms of Jesus,
  Safe from corroding care,
Safe from the world's temptations
  Sin shall not harm me there.
Free from the blight of sorrow,
  Free from my doubts and fears,
Free from my daily trials,
  Free from my frequent tears.
    Safe in the arms, &c.

3. Jesus, my heart's dear Refuge,
  Jesus has died for me;
Firm on the Rock of ages
  Ever my trust shall be.
Here let me wait with patience,
  Wait till the night is o'er;
Then may I see the morning
  Break on the golden shore.
    Safe in the arms, &c.

A - men.

MISSION SERVICES

581

MORNING LIGHT. (7 6. 7 6. D.)
Brightly ♩ = 108.

G. J. WEBB, 1803–87.

A-men.

G. Duffield, 1818-88.

STAND up!—stand up for Jesus!
  Ye soldiers of the Cross;
Lift high his royal banner,
  It must not suffer loss.
From victory unto victory
  His army he shall lead,
Till every foe is vanquished,
  And Christ is Lord indeed.

2 Stand up!—stand up for Jesus!
  The solemn watchword hear,
If while ye sleep he suffers,
  Away with shame and fear;
Where'er ye meet with evil,
  Within you or without,
Charge for the God of battles,
  And put the foe to rout.

3 Stand up!—stand up for Jesus!
  The trumpet call obey,
Forth to the mighty conflict
  In this his glorious day.
Ye that are men now serve him
  Against unnumbered foes;
Let courage rise with danger,
  And strength to strength oppose.

4 Stand up!—stand up for Jesus!
  Stand in his strength alone;
The arm of flesh will fail you,
  Ye dare not trust your own.
Put on the Gospel armour,
  Each piece put on with prayer;
Where duty calls or danger,
  Be never wanting there!

5. Stand up!—stand up for Jesus!
  The strife will not be long;
This day the noise of battle,
  The next the victor's song.
To him that overcometh
  A crown of life shall be;
He with the King of Glory
  Shall reign eternally.

MISSION SERVICES

582

IVES. (7 7. 7 7. D.)
Brightly ♩ = 100.

Melody from
'*Plymouth Collection*' (*U.S.A.*), 1855.

Frances R. Havergal, 1836-79.

TAKE my life, and let it be
  Consecrated, Lord, to thee;
Take my moments and my days,
Let them flow in ceaseless praise.
Take my hands, and let them move
At the impulse of thy love.
Take my feet, and let them be
Swift and beautiful for thee.

2 Take my voice, and let me sing
Always, only, for my King;
Take my lips, and let them be
Filled with messages from thee.
Take my silver and my gold;
Not a mite would I withhold.
Take my intellect, and use
Every power as thou shalt choose.

3. Take my will, and make it thine ·
It shall be no longer mine.
Take my heart; it is thine own:
It shall be thy royal throne.
Take my love; my Lord, I pour
At thy feet its treasure-store.
Take myself, and I will be
Ever, only, all for thee.

MISSION SERVICES

TELL ME THE OLD, OLD STORY.   **583**
(7 6. 7 6. D. and Refrain.)

In moderate time ♩ = 96.

W. H. DOANE, 1832–1916.

REFRAIN.

Tell me the old, old sto - ry,   Tell me the old, old sto - ry,

MISSION SERVICES

583 (*continued*)

Tell me the old, old sto - ry, Of Je - sus and his love.

A. C. *Hankey*, 1834–1911.

TELL me the old, old story,
  Of unseen things above,
Of Jesus and his glory,
  Of Jesus and his love.
Tell me the story simply,
  As to a little child,
For I am weak and weary,
  And helpless and defiled.
    Tell me the old, old story,
    Of Jesus and his love.

2 Tell me the story slowly,
  That I may take it in—
That wonderful redemption,
  God's remedy for sin.
Tell me the story often,
  For I forget so soon;
The early dew of morning
  Has passed away at noon.

3 Tell me the story softly,
  With earnest tones and grave;
Remember, I'm the sinner
  Whom Jesus came to save.
Tell me that story always,
  If you would really be,
In any time of trouble,
  A comforter to me.

4. Tell me the same old story,
  When you have cause to fear
That this world's empty glory
  Is costing me too dear.
Yes, and when that world's glory
  Shall dawn upon my soul,
Tell me the old, old story,
  'Christ Jesus makes thee whole.'

A - men.

MISSION SERVICES

THE NINETY AND NINE. (9 7. 9 7. 9 9.) **584**
Moderately fast ♩ = 176 (♩. = 59).

I. D. Sankey, 1840-1908.

MISSION SERVICES

Elisabeth C. Clephane, 1830–69.

THERE were ninety and nine that safely lay
  In the shelter of the fold,
And one was out on the hills away,
  Far off from the gates of gold;
Away on the mountains wild and bare,
Away from the tender Shepherd's care.

2 'Lord, thou hast here thy ninety and nine;
  Are they not enough for thee?'
But the Shepherd made answer: 'This of mine
  Has wandered away from me;
And although the road be rough and steep,
I go to the desert to find my sheep.'

3 But none of the ransomed ever knew
  How deep were the waters crossed;
Nor how dark the night that the Lord passed through
  Ere he found his sheep that was lost.
Out in the desert he heard its cry—
Sick and hopeless, and ready to die.

4 'Lord, whence are those blood-drops all the way,
  That mark out the mountain's track?'
'They were shed for one that had gone astray
  Ere the Shepherd could bring him back.'
'Lord, whence are thy hands so rent and torn?'
'They are pierced to-night by many a thorn.'

5. And all through the mountains, thunder-riven,
  And up from the rocky steep,
There rose a cry to the gates of heaven,
  'Rejoice! I have found my sheep!'
And the Angels echoed around the throne,
'Rejoice, for the Lord brings back his own!'

A - men.

MISSION SERVICES

585

MARGARET. (Irreg.)
In moderate time ♩ = 80.

T. R. Matthews, 1826-1910.

[By permission of Novello & Co. Ltd.]

MISSION SERVICES

Emily E. S. Elliott, 1835-97.

THOU didst leave thy throne and thy kingly crown
  When thou camest to earth for me;
But in Bethlehem's home was there found no room
  For thy holy nativity.
> *O come to my heart, Lord Jesus;*
> *There is room in my heart for thee.*

2 Heaven's arches rang when the Angels sang,
  Proclaiming thy royal degree;
But in lowly birth didst thou come to earth,
  And in great humility.

3 The foxes found rest, and the birds had their nest
  In the shade of the cedar tree;
But thy couch was the sod, O thou Son of God,
  In the deserts of Galilee.

4 Thou camest, O Lord, with the living word
  That should set thy people free;
But with mocking scorn, and with crown of thorn
  They bore thee to Calvary.

5. When heaven's arches shall ring, and her choirs shall sing
  At thy coming to victory,
Let thy voice call me home, saying, Yet there is room,
  There is room at my side for thee.

In the edition 'For Young and Old' the simpler hymns are marked with an asterisk.

PART IX
AT CATECHISM
586

KEINE SCHÖNHEIT HAT DIE WELT. (77.77.)
In moderate time ♩ = 144.

SCHEFFLER'S '*Seelenlust*', 1657.

A-men.

A. C. Hankey, 1834–1911.

ADVENT tells us, Christ is near :
Christmas tells us Christ is here!
In Epiphany we trace
All the glory of his grace.

2 Those three Sundays before Lent
Will prepare us to repent ;
That in Lent we may begin
Earnestly to mourn for sin.

3 Holy Week and Easter, then,
Tell who died and rose again :
O that happy Easter Day !
'Christ is risen indeed,' we say.

4 Yes, and Christ ascended, too,
To prepare a place for you ;
So we give him special praise,
After those great Forty Days.

5 Then, he sent the Holy Ghost,
On the Day of Pentecost,
With us ever to abide :
Well may we keep Whitsuntide !

6. Last of all, we humbly sing
Glory to our God and King,
Glory to the One in Three,
On the Feast of Trinity.

587

Mrs. C. F. Alexander‡, 1818–95.
Adapted from an English Traditional Melody
by MARTIN SHAW.

ROYAL OAK. (76.76, and refrain.)
Fast ♩ = 84.   Voices in unison.

1. All things bright and beau-ti-ful, All crea-tures great and small,

AT CATECHISM

587 (*continued*)

All things wise and won-der-ful, The Lord God made them all.

2 Each lit-tle flower that o-pens, Each lit-tle bird that sings, He made their glow-ing col-ours, He made their ti-ny wings.
3 The pur-ple-head-ed moun-tain, The ri-ver run-ning by, The sun-set and the morn-ing, That bright-ens up the sky;
4 The cold wind in the win-ter, The plea-sant sum-mer sun, The ripe fruits in the gar-den,—He made them ev-ery one;
5*The tall trees in the green-wood, The mea-dows for our play, The rush-es by the wa-ter, To ga-ther ev-ery day:—
6. He gave us eyes to see them, And lips that we may tell How great is God Al-migh-ty, Who has made all things well.

A-men.

[*Copyright*, 1915, *by J. Curwen & Sons, Ltd.*]

NOTE.—*The pause* (⌢) *is for the last time only.*

NOTE.—*Another tune for this hymn is given in the Appendix* (No. 66).

AT CATECHISM

588

WESLEY. (6 6. 6 6. 8 8.)
Quietly ♩ = 116.

Source unknown.

Bishop W. W. How, 1823-97.

BEHOLD a little Child,
   Laid in a manger bed;
The wintry blasts blow wild
   Around his infant head.
But who is this so lowly laid?
'Tis he by whom the worlds were made.

2 Alas! in what poor state
   The Son of God is seen;
Why doth the Lord so great
   Choose out a home so mean?
That we may learn from pride to flee,
And follow his humility.

3 Where Joseph plies his trade,
   Lo! Jesus labours too;
The hands that all things made
   An earthly craft pursue,
That weary men in him may rest,
And faithful toil through him be blest.

4 Among the doctors see
   The Boy so full of grace;
Say, wherefore taketh he
   The scholar's lowly place?
That Christian boys, with reverence meet,
May sit and learn at Jesus' feet.

5. Christ! once thyself a boy,
   Our boyhood guard and guide;
Be thou its light and joy,
   And still with us abide,
That thy dear love, so great and free,
May draw us evermore to thee.

A - men.

AT CATECHISM

589

NEWLAND. (6 5. 6 5.)
Brightly ♩ = 100.

JAMES ARMSTRONG, 1840-1928.

Mrs. C. F. Alexander, 1818–95.

DO no sinful action,
   Speak no angry word;
Ye belong to Jesus,
   Children of the Lord.

2 Christ is kind and gentle,
   Christ is pure and true;
And his little children
   Must be holy too.

3*There's a wicked spirit
   Watching round you still,
And he tries to tempt you
   To all harm and ill.

4*But ye must not hear him,
   Though 'tis hard for you
To resist the evil,
   And the good to do.

5*For ye promised truly,
   In your infant days,
To renounce him wholly,
   And forsake his ways.

6 Ye are new-born Christians,
   Ye must learn to fight
With the bad within you,
   And to do the right.

7. Christ is your own Master,
   He is good and true,
And his little children
   Must be holy too.

A - men.

AT CATECHISM

590

LANGDALE. (7 5. 7 5. 7 7.)
In moderate time ♩ = 92.

A. SOMERVELL.

Suitable also for Adults. *Mrs. C. F. Alexander, 1818–95.*

EVERY morning the red sun
  Rises warm and bright;
But the evening cometh on,
  And the dark, cold night.
There's a bright land far away,
Where 'tis never-ending day.

2 Every spring the sweet young flowers
  Open bright and gay,
Till the chilly autumn hours
  Wither them away.
There's a land we have not seen,
Where the trees are always green.

3 Little birds sing songs of praise
  All the summer long,
But in colder, shorter days
  They forget their song.
There's a place where Angels sing
Ceaseless praises to their King.

4 Christ our Lord is ever near
  Those who follow him;
But we cannot see him here,
  For our eyes are dim;
There is a most happy place,
Where men always see his face.

5. Who shall go to that bright land?
  All who do the right:
Holy children there shall stand
  In their robes of white;
For that heaven, so bright and blest,
Is our everlasting rest.

A - men.

591

FARNABY. (7 7. 7 7.)
Moderately fast ♩ = 152.
To be sung in unison.

PART 1.

Adapted from an English Traditional Melody.

AT CATECHISM

591 (continued)

PARTS 2 AND 3.

LEW TRENCHARD. (7 7. 7 7.)
In moderate time ♩ = 72.

From an English Traditional Melody.

NOTE.—*This tune may be used for all the parts of this hymn.
The hymn may be sung also to* GENTLE JESUS (*No.* 602).

C. Wesley, 1707–88.

GENTLE Jesus, meek and mild,
Look upon a little child;
Pity my simplicity,
Suffer me to come to thee.

2 Fain I would to thee be brought,
Dearest God, forbid it not;
Give me, dearest God, a place
In the kingdom of thy grace.

Part 2.

3 Lamb of God, I look to thee;
Thou shalt my example be:
Thou art gentle, meek and mild,
Thou wast once a little child.

4 Fain I would be as thou art;
Give me thy obedient heart.
**Thou art pitiful and kind,
Let me have thy loving mind.**

5 Let me, above all, fulfil
God my heavenly Father's will,
Never his good Spirit grieve,
Only to his glory live.

Part 3.

6 Thou didst live to God alone;
Thou didst never seek thine own;
Thou thyself didst never please:
God was all thy happiness.

7 Loving Jesus, gentle Lamb,
In thy gracious hands I am:
Make me, Saviour, what thou art;
Live thyself within my heart.

8. I shall then show forth thy praise,
Serve thee all my happy days;
Then the world shall always see
Christ, the holy Child, in me.

AT CATECHISM

592

GROOMBRIDGE. (8 5. 8 5. 8 8. 8 5.)
In moderate time ♩ = 92.

W. J. WHITWELL.

REFRAIN.

Suitable also for Adults.   S. Baring-Gould, 1834-1924.

HAIL the Sign, the Sign of Jesus,
   Bright and royal Tree!
Standard of the Monarch, planted
   First on Calvary!

Hail the Sign all signs excelling,
Hail the Sign all ills dispelling,
Hail the Sign hell's power quelling,
Cross of Christ, all hail!

2 Sign the Martyrs' strength and refuge,
   Sign to Saints so dear!
Sign of evil men abhorrèd,
   Sign which devils fear:

3 Sign which, when the Lord returneth,
   In the heavens shall be; [rapture
Sinners quail, while Saints with
   Shall the vision see:

4 Lo, I sign the Cross of Jesus
   Meekly on my breast;
May it guard my heart when living,
   Dying be its rest:

5. In the name of God the Father,
   Name of God the Son,
Name of God the blessèd Spirit,
   Ever Three in One:

A - men.

AT CATECHISM

PLEADING SAVIOUR. (8 7. 8 7. D.) **593**
In moderate time ♩ = 96.

Plymouth Collection (U.S.A.), 1855.

Bishop Chr. Wordsworth, 1807–85.

HEAVENLY Father, send thy blessing
  On thy children gathered here,
May they all, thy name confessing,
  Be to thee for ever dear;
May they be, like Joseph, loving,
  Dutiful, and chaste, and pure;
And their faith, like David proving,
  Steadfast unto death endure.

2 Holy Saviour, who in meekness
    Didst vouchsafe a Child to be,
  Guide their steps, and help their weakness,
    Bless, and make them like to thee;
  Bear thy lambs when they are weary,
    In thine arms, and at thy breast;
  Through life's desert, dry and dreary,
    Bring them to thy heavenly rest.

3. Spread thy golden pinions o'er them,
      Holy Spirit, heavenly Dove,
    Guide them, lead them, go before them,
      Give them peace, and joy, and love;
    Temples of the Holy Spirit,
      May they with thy glory shine,
    And immortal bliss inherit,
      And for evermore be thine!

A - men.

AT CATECHISM

594

GOSTERWOOD. (7 6. 7 6. D.)
In moderate time ♩ = 100.

English Traditional Melody.

Emily Miller, 1833–1915.

I LOVE to hear the story
  Which Angel voices tell,
How once the King of glory
  Came down on earth to dwell.
I am both weak and sinful,
  But this I surely know,
The Lord came down to save me,
  Because he loved me so.

2 I'm glad my blessèd Saviour
  Was once a Child like me,
To show how pure and holy
  His little ones might be;
And if I try to follow
  His footsteps here below,
He never will forsake me,
  Because he loves me so.

3. To tell his love and mercy
  My sweetest songs I'll raise;
And though I cannot see him,
  I know he hears my praise;
For he himself has promised
  That even I may go
To sing among his Angels,
  Because he loves me so.

A - men.

AT CATECHISM

595

EAST HORNDON. (Irreg.)
Moderately fast ♩ = 160 (𝅗𝅥. = 54).
To be sung in unison.

English Traditional Melody.

Mrs. J. Luke, 1818–1906.

I THINK, when I read that sweet story of old,
    When Jesus was here among men,
How he called little children as lambs to his fold,
    I should like to have been with him then.
I wish that his hands had been placed on my head,
    That his arm had been thrown around me,
And that I might have seen his kind look when he said,
    'Let the little ones come unto me.'

2 Yet still to his footstool in prayer I may go,
    And ask for a share in his love;
And if I now earnestly seek him below,
    I shall see him and hear him above :
In that beautiful place he has gone to prepare
    For all that are washed and forgiven.
And many dear children are gathering there,
    'For of such is the kingdom of heaven.'

3. But thousands and thousands who wander and fall
    Never heard of that heavenly home;
I should like them to know there is room for them all,
    And that Jesus has bid them to come.
I long for the joy of that glorious time,
    The sweetest, and brightest, and best,
When the dear little children of every clime
    Shall crowd to his arms and be blest.

A - men.

AT CATECHISM

596

LYNE. (77.77.)
In moderate time ♩ = 120.

'*Magdalen Hymns*,' 1760 (?)

W. Chatterton Dix, 1837-98.

IN our work, and in our play,
   Jesus, be thou ever near;
Guarding, guiding all the day,
   Keeping in thy holy fear.

2 Thou didst toil, O royal Child,
   In the far-off Holy Land,
Blessing labour undefiled,
   Pure and honest, of the hand.

3 Thou wilt bless our play-hour too,
   If we ask thy succour strong;
Watch o'er all we say or do,
   Hold us back from guilt and wrong.

4. O! how happy thus to spend
   Work and playtime in his sight,
Who that day which shall not end
   Gives to those who do the right.

A - men.

AT CATECHISM

597

HERONGATE. (L. M.)
In moderate time ♩ = 144.

English Traditional Melody.

Bishop W. W. How, 1823-97.

IT is a thing most wonderful,
  Almost too wonderful to be,
That God's own Son should come from heaven,
  And die to save a child like me.

2 And yet I know that it is true:
  He chose a poor and humble lot,
And wept, and toiled, and mourned, and died,
  For love of those who loved him not.

3*I cannot tell how he could love
  A child so weak and full of sin;
His love must be most wonderful,
  If he could die my love to win.

4*I sometimes think about the Cross,
  And shut my eyes, and try to see
The cruel nails and crown of thorns,
  And Jesus crucified for me.

5 But even could I see him die,
  I could but see a little part
Of that great love, which, like a fire,
  Is always burning in his heart.

6 It is most wonderful to know
  His love for me so free and sure;
But 'tis more wonderful to see
  My love for him so faint and poor.

7. And yet I want to love thee, Lord;
  O light the flame within my heart,
And I will love thee more and more,
  Until I see thee as thou art.

A - men.

AT CATECHISM

598

QUEM PASTORES LAUDAVERE. (8 8. 8 7.)
In moderate time ♩ = 144.

Melody from a 14th century German MS.

Suitable also for Adults. P. D.

JESUS, good above all other,
  Gentle Child of gentle Mother,
In a stable born our Brother,
  Give us grace to persevere.

2 Jesus, cradled in a manger,
  For us facing every danger,
  Living as a homeless stranger, [dear.
    Make we thee our King most

3 Jesus, for thy people dying,
  Risen Master, death defying,
  Lord in heaven, thy grace supplying,
    Keep us to thy presence near.

4 Jesus, who our sorrows bearest,
  All our thoughts and hopes thou sharest,
  Thou to man the truth declarest;
    Help us all thy truth to hear.

5. Lord, in all our doings guide us;
  Pride and hate shall ne'er divide us;
  We'll go on with thee beside us,
    And with joy we'll persevere!

A - men.

AT CATECHISM

599

SHIPSTON. (87.87.)
In moderate time ♩ = 96.
English Traditional Melody.

Evening.   *Mary L. Duncan,* 1814–40.

JESU, tender Shepherd, hear me,
  Bless thy little lamb to-night;
Through the darkness be thou near me,
  Watch my sleep till morning light.

2 All this day thy hand has led me,
  And I thank thee for thy care;
Thou hast clothed me, warmed and fed me,
  Listen to my evening prayer.

3. Let my sins be all forgiven,
  Bless the friends I love so well;
Take me, when I die, to heaven,
  Happy there with thee to dwell.

A - men.

AT CATECHISM

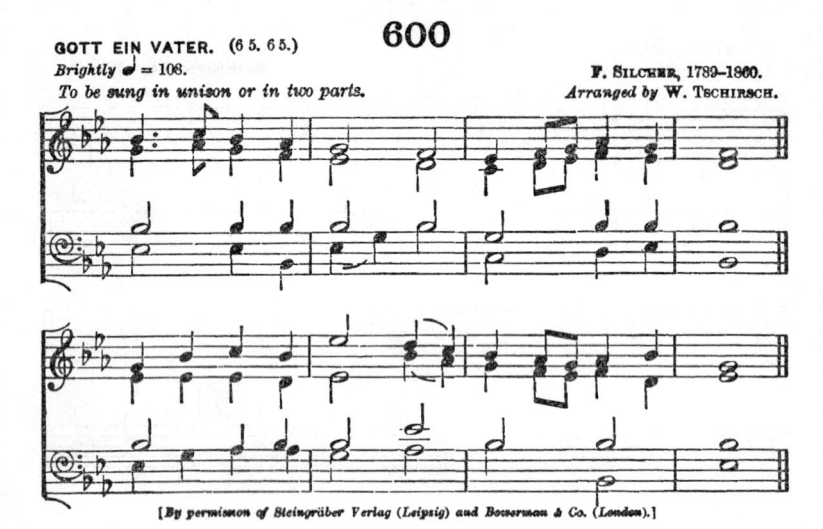

600

GOTT EIN VATER. (6 5. 6 5.)
Brightly ♩ = 108.
To be sung in unison or in two parts.

F. SILCHER, 1789–1860.
Arranged by W. TSCHIRSCH.

[By permission of Steingrüber Verlag (Leipzig) and Bowerman & Co. (London).]

Mrs. J. A. Carney (1845).

LITTLE drops of water,
    Little grains of sand,
Make the mighty ocean
    And the beauteous land.

2 And the little moments,
    Humble though they be,
Make the mighty ages
    Of eternity.

3*Little deeds of kindness,
    Little words of love,
Make our earth an Eden,
    Like the heaven above.

4*So our little errors
    Lead the soul away,
From the paths of virtue
    Into sin to stray.

5 Little seeds of mercy
    Sown by youthful hands,
Grow to bless the nations
    Far in heathen lands.

6. Glory then for ever
    Be to God on high,
Beautiful and loving,
    To eternity. Amen.

A - men.

AT CATECHISM

601

EARDISLEY. (C.M.)
In moderate time ♩ = 92.

English Traditional Melody.

Jane Taylor, 1788–1824.

LORD, I would own thy tender care,
  And all thy love to me;
The food I eat, the clothes I wear,
  Are all bestowed by thee.

2 'Tis thou preservest me from death
  And dangers every hour;
I cannot draw another breath
  Unless thou give me power.

3 Kind Angels guard me every night,
  As round my bed they stay;
Nor am I absent from thy sight
  In darkness or by day.

4 My health and friends and parents dear
  To me by God are given;
I have not any blessing here
  But what is sent from heaven.

5. Such goodness, Lord, and constant care,
  A child can ne'er repay;
But may it be my daily prayer
  To love thee and obey.

A - men.

AT CATECHISM

602

GENTLE JESUS. (7 7. 7 7.)
In moderate time ♩ = 63.

MARTIN SHAW.

[Copyright, 1915, by J. Curwen & Sons, Ltd.]

NOTE.—*This hymn may also be sung to* BUCKLAND (*Appendix, No.* 67).

Jane E. Lesson, 1807–82.

LOVING Shepherd of thy sheep,
Keep thy lamb, in safety keep;
Nothing can thy power withstand,
None can pluck me from thy hand.

2*Loving Saviour, thou didst give
Thine own life that we might live;
And the hands outstretched to bless
Bear the cruel nails' impress.

3 I would bless thee every day,
Gladly all thy will obey,
Like thy blessèd ones above,
Happy in thy precious love.

4 Loving Shepherd, ever near,
Teach thy lamb thy voice to hear;
Suffer not my steps to stray
From the straight and narrow way.

5. Where thou leadest I would go,
Walking in thy steps below,
Till before my Father's throne
I shall know as I am known.

A - men.

AT CATECHISM

603

EUDOXIA. (6 5, 6 5.)
Moderately slow ♩ = 68.

S. BARING-GOULD, 1834–1924.

Suitable also for Adults.　　　　　　　　　　　　　　　　S. *Baring-Gould*, 1834–1924.

NOW the day is over,
　Night is drawing nigh,
Shadows of the evening
　Steal across the sky.

2 Now the darkness gathers,
　　Stars begin to peep,
　Birds and beasts and flowers
　　Soon will be asleep.

3 Jesu, give the weary
　　Calm and sweet repose;
　With thy tenderest blessing
　　May our eyelids close.

4 Grant to little children
　　Visions bright of thee;
　Guard the sailors tossing
　　On the deep blue sea.

5 Comfort every sufferer
　　Watching late in pain;
　Those who plan some evil
　　From their sin restrain.

6*Through the long night watches
　　May thine Angels spread
　Their white wings above me,
　　Watching round my bed.

7*When the morning wakens,
　　Then may I arise
　Pure, and fresh, and sinless
　　In thy holy eyes.

8. Glory to the Father,
　　Glory to the Son,
　And to thee, blest Spirit,
　　Whilst all ages run. Amen.

A - men.

AT CATECHISM

604

For the Close of a Festival.
MIT FREUDEN ZART. (87.87.887.)
In moderate time ♩ = 100 (𝅗𝅥 = 50).

M. F. Bell, 1862–1947
*Hymn Melody
of the Bohemian Brethren.*

VOICES IN UNISON.

ORGAN.

{ O dear-est Lord, by all a-dored, Our tres-pas-ses con-
{ To thee this day thy children pray, The ho-ly Faith pro-

-fess - ing }
-fess - ing ! } Ac-cept, O King, the gifts we bring, Our songs of praise, the

prayers we raise; And grant us, Lord, thy bless - ing.

Harmony.

A-men.

The following is also suitable:
535 *Pt.* 2. Worship, honour, glory, blessing.

AT CATECHISM

605

IRBY. (8 7. 8 7. 7 7.)
In moderate time ♩ = 92.

H. J. GAUNTLETT, 1805–76.

Suitable also for Adults.

Mrs. C. F. Alexander, 1823–95.

ONCE in royal David's city
  Stood a lowly cattle shed,
Where a Mother laid her Baby
  In a manger for his bed:
Mary was that Mother mild,
Jesus Christ her little Child.

2 He came down to earth from heaven,
  Who is God and Lord of all,
And his shelter was a stable,
  And his cradle was a stall;
With the poor, and mean, and lowly,
Lived on earth our Saviour holy.

3* And through all his wondrous child-
  He would honour and obey, [hood
Love, and watch the lowly Maiden,
  In whose gentle arms he lay;
Christian children all must be
Mild, obedient, good as he.

4* For he is our childhood's pattern,
  Day by day like us he grew,
He was little, weak, and helpless,
  Tears and smiles like us he knew;
And he feeleth for our sadness,
And he shareth in our gladness.

5 And our eyes at last shall see him,
  Through his own redeeming love,
For that Child so dear and gentle
  Is our Lord in heaven above;
And he leads his children on
To the place where he is gone.

6. Not in that poor lowly stable,
  With the oxen standing by,
We shall see him; but in heaven,
  Set at God's right hand on high;
When like stars his children crowned
All in white shall wait around.

A - men.

AT CATECHISM

606

ST. HUGH. (C.M.)
Brightly ♩ = 100.

English Traditional Melody.

R. S. Hawker, 1804-75.

SING to the Lord the children's
  His gentle love declare, [hymn,
Who bends amid the Seraphim
  To hear the children's prayer.

2 He at a mother's breast was fed,
  Though God's own Son was he;
He learnt the first small words he said
  At a meek mother's knee.

3 He held us to his mighty breast,
  The children of the earth;
He lifted up his hands and blessed
  The babes of human birth.

4 Lo! from the stars his face will turn
  On us with glances mild;
The Angels of his presence yearn
  To bless the little child.

5.*Keep us, O Jesus, Lord, for thee,
  That so, by thy dear grace,
We, children of the font, may see
  Our heavenly Father's face.

A-men.

607

INGRAVE. (8 6. 7 6. 7 6. 7 6.)
Brightly ♩ = 100.

English Traditional Melody.

AT CATECHISM

607 (*continued*)

A. Midlane, 1825–1909.

THERE'S a Friend for little children
  Above the bright blue sky,
A Friend who never changes,
  Whose love will never die;
Our earthly friends may fail us,
  And change with changing years,
This Friend is always worthy
  Of that dear name he bears.

2 There's a rest for little children
  Above the bright blue sky,
Who love the blessèd Saviour,
  And to the Father cry;
A rest from every trouble,
  From sin and danger free,
Where every little pilgrim
  Shall rest eternally.

3 There's a home for little children
  Above the bright blue sky,
Where Jesus reigns in glory,
  A home of peace and joy;
No home on earth is like it,
  Nor can with it compare;
And every one is happy,
  Nor could be happier there.

4 There's a crown for little children
  About the bright blue sky,
And all who look to Jesus
  Shall wear it by and by;
A crown of brightest glory,
  Which he will then bestow
On those who found his favour
  And loved his name below.

5 There's a song for little children
  Above the bright blue sky,
A song that will not weary,
  Though sung continually;
A song which even Angels
  Can never, never sing;
They know not Christ as Saviour,
  But worship him as King.

6. There's a robe for little children
  Above the bright blue sky,
And a harp of sweetest music,
  And palms of victory.
All, all above is treasured,
  And found in Christ alone;
O come, dear little children,
  That all may be your own.

AT CATECHISM

608

HAPPY LAND. (6 4. 6 4. 6 7. 6 4.)
In moderate time ♩ = 100 (𝅗𝅥 = 50).

'Indian Air.'

Suitable also for Adults.

A. Young, 1807–89.

1. THERE is a happy land,
   Far, far away,
   Where Saints in glory stand,
   Bright, bright as day.
   O, how they sweetly sing,
   Worthy is our Saviour King!
   Loud let his praises ring,
   Praise, praise for ay.

2. Come to this happy land,
   Come, come away;
   Why will ye doubting stand?
   Why still delay?
   O. we shall happy be,
   When, from sin and sorrow free,
   Lord, we shall live with thee,
   Blest, blest for ay.

AT CATECHISM

3. Bright in that happy land
    Beams every eye;
  Kept by a Father's hand
    Love cannot die.
  On then to glory run,
  Be a crown and kingdom won,
  And bright above the sun
    Reign, reign for ay!

A - men.

609

PEACEFIELD. (7 7. 7 7.)
Slow ♩ = 80.

Ancient Irish Lullaby.
Harmonized by DAVID F. R. WILSON.

NOTE.—*This hymn may also be sung to* HORSHAM (*No.* 344).

Morning.
W. Canton, 1845-1926.

THROUGH the night thy Angels kept
  Watch beside me while I slept;
Now the dark has passed away,
Thank thee, Lord, for this new day.

2 North and south and east and west
May thy holy name be blest;
Everywhere beneath the sun,
As in heaven, thy will be done.

3. Give me food that I may live;
Every naughtiness forgive;
Keep all evil things away
From thy little child this day.

A - men.

AT CATECHISM

PUER NOBIS NASCITUR. (L. M.)
In moderate time ♩ = 144.

610

Melody adapted by
M. PRAETORIUS, 1571–1621.
Harmonised by G. R. WOODWARD.

[*May be sung in unison throughout.*]

Mrs. C. F. Alexander, 1818–95.

WE are but little children poor,
And born in very low estate;
What can we do for Jesu's sake,
Who is so high and good and great?

2 * We know the Holy Innocents
Laid down for him their infant life,
And Martyrs brave and patient Saints
Have stood for him in fire and strife.

3 * We wear the Cross they wore of old,
Our lips have learned like vows to make;
We need not die, we cannot fight,—
What may we do for Jesu's sake?

4 O, day by day, each Christian child,
Has much to do, without, within,—
A death to die for Jesu's sake,
A weary war to wage with sin.

5 When deep within our swelling hearts
The thoughts of pride and anger rise,
When bitter words are on our tongues,
And tears of passion in our eyes,—

6 Then we may stay the angry blow,
Then we may check the hasty word,
Give gentle answers back again,
And fight a battle for our Lord.

7. There's not a child so small and weak
But has his little cross to take,
His little work of love and praise
That he may do for Jesu's sake!

A . men.

786

AT CATECHISM

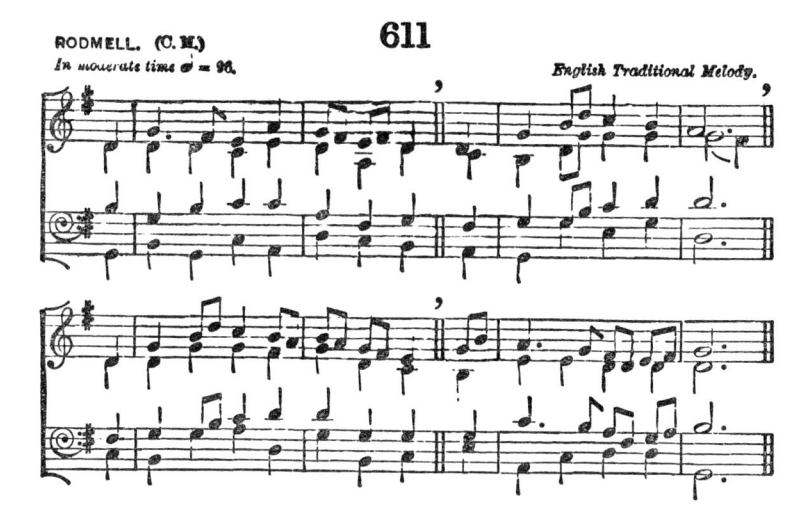

611

RODMELL. (C.M.)
In moderate time ♩ = 96.

English Traditional Melody.

Laurence Housman, 1865-1959.

WHEN Christ was born in Bethlehem,
　Fair peace on earth to bring,
In lowly state of love he came
　To be the children's King.

2 A mother's heart was there his throne,
　His orb a maiden's breast,
Whereby he made through love alone
　His kingdom manifest.

3 And round him, then, a holy band
　Of children blest was born,
Fair guardians of his throne to stand
　Attendant night and morn.

4 And unto them this grace was given
　A Saviour's name to own,
And die for him who out of heaven
　Had found on earth a throne.

5 O blessèd babes of Bethlehem,
　Who died to save our King,
Ye share the Martyrs' diadem,
　And in their anthem sing!

6*Your lips, on earth that never spake,
　Now sound the eternal word;
And in the courts of love ye make
　Your children's voices heard.

7*Lord Jesus Christ, eternal Child,
　Make thou our childhood thine;
That we with these the meek and mild
　May share the love divine.

A - men.

AT CATECHISM

RESONET IN LAUDIBUS. (7 7. 8 8. and Refrain.)

612

B. R. Hanby, 1833—67.
German Carol Melody, 14th century.

Moderately fast ♩ = 72.
VOICES IN UNISON.

Who is he, in yon-der stall, At whose feet the shep-herds fall? 'Tis the Lord! O won-drous sto-ry! 'Tis the Lord, the King of Glo-ry At his feet we hum-bly fall; Crown him, crown him Lord of all!

ORGAN.

AT CATECHISM

612 (continued)

At his feet we humbly fall—the Lord of all: Crown him, crown him, crown him, crown him, crown him Lord of all!

NOTE.—*The first part of each verse may be sung as a solo.*

2*Who is he, in yonder cot,
  Bending to his toilsome lot?

3*Who is he, in deep distress,
  Fasting in the wilderness?

4*Who is he that stands and weeps
  At the grave where Lazarus sleeps?

5*Lo! at midnight, who is he,
  Prays in dark Gethsemane?

6 Who is he, in Calvary's throes,
  Asks for blessings on his foes?

7 Who is he that from the grave
  Comes to heal and help and save?

8. Who is he that on yon throne
  Rules the world of light alone?

A - men.

The simpler Hymns in other parts of the book are also suitable for use at Catechism, and should be freely used in addition to the Hymns in this part. Such hymns are marked with an asterisk in the edition 'For Young and Old' of the English Hymnal.

Part X

PROCESSIONAL

The following Hymns need not always be sung in the order given: those in the first section (613–640) which are not taken from the English processionals are arranged on similar principles, but are suitable also for use as separate hymns on other occasions.

DIVINUM MYSTERIUM. (87.87.87.7.) **613**

Moderately fast ♩ = 152.
To be sung in unison.

Melody from 'Piae Cantiones Theoderici Petri Nylandensis,' 1582.

CHRISTMAS PROCESSION

A CHRISTMAS PROCESSION

Prudentius, b. 348.   Tr. R. F. D.

Corde natus ex parentis.

OF the Father's heart begotten,
   Ere the world from chaos rose,
He is Alpha: from that Fountain
   All that is and hath been flows;
He is Omega, of all things
   Yet to come the mystic Close,
    Evermore and evermore.

2 By his word was all created;
   He commanded and 'twas done;
Earth and sky and boundless ocean,
   Universe of three in one,
All that sees the moon's soft radiance,
All that breathes beneath the sun,

3*He assumed this mortal body,
   Frail and feeble, doomed to die,
That the race from dust created
   Might not perish utterly,
Which the dreadful Law had sentenced
In the depths of hell to lie,

4 O how blest that wondrous birthday,
   When the Maid the curse retrieved,
Brought to birth mankind's salvation,
   By the Holy Ghost conceived;
And the Babe, the world's Redeemer,
   In her loving arms received,

5 This is he, whom seer and sybil
   Sang in ages long gone by;
This is he of old revealèd
   In the page of prophecy;
Lo! he comes, the promised Saviour;
   Let the world his praises cry!

6 Sing, ye heights of heaven, his praises;
   Angels and Archangels, sing!
Wheresoe'er ye be, ye faithful,
   Let your joyous anthems ring,
Every tongue his name confessing,
   Countless voices answering,

7*Hail! thou Judge of souls departed;
   Hail! of all the living King!
On the Father's right hand thronèd,
   Through his courts thy praises ring,
Till at last for all offences   [bring.
   Righteous judgement thou shalt

At the entrance into the Choir.

8 Now let old and young uniting
   Chant to thee harmonious lays,
Maid and matron hymn thy glory,
   Infant lips their anthem raise,
Boys and girls together singing
   With pure heart their song of praise,

9.*Let the storm and summer sunshine,
   Gliding stream and sounding shore,
Sea and forest, frost and zephyr,
   Day and night their Lord adore;
Let creation join to laud thee
   Through the ages evermore,

A - men.

At the Sanctuary step.

℣. Blessed is he that cometh in the name of the Lord.
℟. God is the Lord who hath showed us light.

Collect for Christmas Day.

PROCESSIONAL

614

ADESTE FIDELES. (Irreg.)
Very slow ♩ = 72.

Composer unknown. Probably 18th cent.

Without pedals.

Pedals.

A SECOND CHRISTMAS PROCESSION

Adeste, fideles.

18th cent. Tr. F. Oakeley,
W. T. Brooke, and others.

O COME, all ye faithful,
Joyful and triumphant,
O come ye, O come ye to Bethlehem;
Come and behold him
Born the King of Angels:

O come, let us adore him,
O come, let us adore him,
O come, let us adore him, Christ the Lord!

PROCESSIONAL

2   God of God,
Light of Light,
Lo! he abhors not the Virgin's womb;
Very God,
Begotten, not created:

3   See how the Shepherds,
Summoned to his cradle,
Leaving their flocks, draw nigh with lowly fear;
We too will thither
Bend our joyful footsteps:

4*   Lo! star-led chieftains,
Magi, Christ adoring,
Offer him incense, gold, and myrrh;
We to the Christ Child
Bring our hearts' oblations:

5   Child, for us sinners
Poor and in the manger,
Fain we embrace thee, with awe and love;
Who would not love thee,
Loving us so dearly?

6   Sing, choirs of Angels,
Sing in exultation,
Sing, all ye citizens of heaven above;
Glory to God
In the Highest:

At the entrance into the Choir.

Unison. 7.   Yea, Lord, we greet thee,
Born this happy morning,
Jesu, to thee be glory given;
Word of the Father,
Now in flesh appearing:

A - men.

At the Sanctuary step.
℣. Blessed is he that cometh in the name of the Lord.
℟. God is the Lord, who hath showed us light.
Collect for Lady Day.

PROCESSIONAL

615

SUTTON VALENCE. (6 5 6 5. D.)
In moderate time ♩ = 84.

S. L. RUSSELL.

Has - ting from a - far,

Org.

[*Copyright, 1931, by Oxford University Press.*]

NOTE.—*This hymn may also be sung to* KING'S WESTON (*No.* 368) *or* ZUNDEL (*Appendix, No.* 68).

EPIPHANY PROCESSION

G. Thring, 1823–1903.

FROM the eastern mountains
　Pressing on they come,
Wise men in their wisdom,
　To his humble home;

EPIPHANY PROCESSION

    Stirred by deep devotion,
      Hasting from afar,
    Ever journeying onward,
      Guided by a star.

2 There their Lord and Saviour
    Meek and lowly lay,
  Wondrous light that led them
    Onward on their way,
  Ever now to lighten
    Nations from afar,
  As they journey homeward
    By that guiding star.

3 Thou who in a manger
    Once hast lowly lain,
  Who dost now in glory
    O'er all kingdoms reign,
  Gather in the heathen,
    Who in lands afar
  Ne'er have seen the brightness
    Of thy guiding star.

4 Gather in the outcasts,
    All who've gone astray,
  Throw thy radiance o'er them,
    Guide them on their way;
  Those who never knew thee,
    Those who've wandered far,
  Guide them by the brightness
    Of thy guiding star.

Unison.   5 Onward through the darkness
    Of the lonely night,
  Shining still before them
    With thy kindly light.
  Guide them, Jew and Gentile,
    Homeward from afar,
  Young and old together,
    By thy guiding star.

6*. Until every nation,
    Whether bond or free,
  'Neath thy star-lit banner,
    Jesu, follows thee,
  O'er the distant mountains
    To that heavenly home
  Where nor sin nor sorrow
    Evermore shall come.

A - men.

PROCESSIONAL

616

REX GLORIAE. (8 7. 8 7. D.)
In moderate time ♩ = 72.

H. SMART, 1813–79.

NOTE—*This hymn may also be sung to* REDHEAD No. 46 (*No.* 372).

At the entrance into the Choir.

Basil Woodd, 1760-1831.

HAIL, thou Source of every blessing,
  Sovereign Father of mankind!
Gentiles now, thy grace possessing,
  In thy courts admission find.

2 * Once far off, but now invited,
  We approach thy sacred throne;
In thy covenant united,
  Reconciled, redeemed, made one.

3 * Now revealed to eastern sages,
  See the Star of mercy shine,
Mystery hid in former ages,
  Mystery great of love divine.

4. Hail, thou universal Saviour!
  Gentiles now their offerings bring,
In thy temple seek thy favour,
  Jesus Christ, our Lord and King.

At the Sanctuary step.

℣. The voice of the Lord is upon the waters.
℟. The Lord is upon many waters.

Collect for the Epiphany.

PALM SUNDAY PROCESSION

617

PALM SUNDAY
During the Distribution of Palms.

Anthem. Mode i.　　　　　　　　　　　　　　　　arr. J. H. A.

The chil-dren of the He-brews,* car-ry-ing palms and o-live branch-es, went forth to meet the Lord, cry-ing out and say-ing, Ho-san-na in the high-est!
(*Ps.* cxxii, I. 2).

PROCESSIONAL

617 (continued)

Anthem.

The chil-dren of the He-brews spread in the way their clothes and gar-ments,

and cri-ed, say-ing, Ho-san-na to the Son of Da-vid;

Bles-sed is he that com-eth in the name of the Lord.
(*Ps.* cxxv, l. 2).

[1] *Formerly* EF G E.

PALM SUNDAY PROCESSION

618
The Prophetic Anthem

Tone i. (Introit form)   *arr.* J. H. A.

O Jerusalem, look toward the East, and behold: lift up thine eyes, O Jerusalem, and behold the power of thy King!

PROCESSIONAL

COME FAITHFUL PEOPLE. (88.87.) **619**

Moderately fast ♩ = 152.

Melody by C. BICKNELL, 1842-1918.

If required, the following Carol may also be sung.

G. Moultrie, 1829-85.

COME, faithful people, come away,
Your homage to your Monarch pay;
It is the feast of palms to-day:
Hosanna in the highest!

2 When Christ, the Lord of all, drew nigh
On Sunday morn to Bethany,
He called two loved ones standing by:

3 'To yonder village go,' said he,
'An ass and foal tied shall ye see,
Loose them and bring them unto me':

4* 'If any man dispute your word,
Say, "They are needed by the Lord,"
And he permission will accord':

5 The two upon their errand sped,
And found the ass as he had said,
And on the colt their clothes they spread:

6 They set him on his throne so rude;
Before him went the multitude,
And in their way their garments strewed:

7* Go, Saviour, thus to triumph borne,
Thy crown shall be the wreath of thorn,
Thy royal garb the robe of scorn:

8* They thronged before, behind, around,
They cast palm-branches on the ground,
And still rose up the joyful sound:

9* 'Blessèd is Israel's King,' they cry;
'Blessèd is he that cometh nigh
In name of God the Lord most high'.

10. Thus, Saviour, to thy Passion go,
Arrayed in royalty of woe,
Assumed for sinners here below:

A - men.

800

PALM SUNDAY PROCESSION

WINCHESTER NEW. (L. M.)   **620**   *Adapted from Chorale in the 'Musikalisches Hand-Buch,' Hamburg, 1690.*
Slow and dignified ♩ = 56.

And this Hymn.   *H. H. Milman, 1791-1868.*

RIDE on! ride on in majesty!
Hark, all the tribes hosanna cry;
Thine humble beast pursues his road
With palms and scattered garments strowed.

2 Ride on! ride on in majesty!
In lowly pomp ride on to die:
O Christ, thy triumphs now begin
O'er captive death and conquered sin.

3 Ride on! ride on in majesty!
The wingèd squadrons of the sky
Look down with sad and wondering eyes
To see the approaching sacrifice.

4 Ride on! ride on in majesty!
Thy last and fiercest strife is nigh;
The Father, on his sapphire throne,
Expects his own anointed Son.

Unison. 5. Ride on! ride on in majesty!
In lowly pomp ride on to die;
Bow thy meek head to mortal pain,
Then take, O God, thy power, and reign.

A - men.

The Gospel. St. Matthew xxi. 1-9.

PROCESSIONAL

621

At the Procession.

Gloria, laus et honor.

Theodulph of Orleans, d. 821.
(Sarum Processional.)
Tr. W. J. B., and others.

Mode i.

arr. J. H. A.

Chorus. (*First time, 'seven boys': Chorus repeat.*)

Glo - ry and praise and do - mi - nion be thine,

King Christ the Re - deem - er: Chil - dren in

sweet - ness and grace raised their ho - san - nas to thee.

PROCESSIONAL

621 (*continued*)

'*Seven*' *boys (or less).*

2. Is-ra-el's King art thou, King Da-vid's glo-ri-ous off-spring, Thou that ap-proach-est, a King, blest in the name of the Lord.
3. Thee in the height ex-tol, King thine An-gels, throng-ing a-round thee, Man with na-ture on earth join-ing, in act to a-dore,
4. Palm leaves bear-ing on high came He-brew crowds to thy wel-come; We with our prayers and our hymns now to thy pre-sence draw near.

CHORUS. *Glory, &c.*

At the Chancel step.

Hail, our Monarch, Son of David, &c. (*For melody, see Appendix, No. 3, p. 902*).

PROCESSIONAL

ST. THEODULPH (VALET WILL ICH DIR GEBEN). (7 6. 7 6. D.)   **622**

Very slow and solemn ♩ = 46.

Melody by M. Teschner, c. 1613. *Adapted and harmonized by* J. S. Bach.

Or this Version of the above.   Tr. J. M. Neale ‡.

All glory, laud, and honour
  To thee, Redeemer, King,
To whom the lips of children
  Made sweet hosannas ring.

2 Thou art the King of Israel,
  Thou David's royal Son,
Who in the Lord's name comest,
  The King and blessèd One.

3 The company of Angels
  Are praising thee on high,
And mortal men and all things
  Created make reply.

4 The people of the Hebrews
  With palms before thee went;
Our praise and prayer and anthems
  Before thee we present.

5 To thee before thy passion
  They sang their hymns of praise;
To thee now high exalted
  Our melody we raise.

6. Thou didst accept their praises,
  Accept the prayers we bring,
Who in all good delightest,
  Thou good and gracious King.

A - men.

At the Chancel step.

O Saviour of the world, who by thy Cross and precious Blood hast redeemed us, save us and help us, we humbly beseech thee, O Lord (*or* Hail, our Monarch, *p.* 902).

PALM SUNDAY PROCESSION

ST. THOMAS. (87. 87. 87.)　　**623**　　Melody from S. WEBBE'S 'Motetts or Antiphons,' 1792, and An Essay on the Church Plain Chant, 1782.
Moderately slow, dignified ♩ = 66.

At the entrance into the Choir.

*Claude de Santeüil, 1628–84.
Tr. J. Chandler, and Sir H. W. Baker.*

Prome vocem, mens, canoram.

NOW my soul, thy voice upraising,
　Tell in sweet and mournful strain
How the Crucified, enduring
　Grief and wounds, and dying pain,
Freely of his love was offered,
　Sinless was for sinners slain.

2 * See, his hands and feet are fastened!
　So he makes his people free;
Not a wound whence Blood is flowing
　But a fount of grace shall be;
Yea, the very nails which nail him
　Nail us also to the Tree.

3. Jesu, may those precious fountains
　Drink to thirsting souls afford;
Let them be our cup and healing,
　And at length our full reward:
So a ransomed world shall ever
　Praise thee, its redeeming Lord.

A . men.

At the Sanctuary step.

℣. Deliver me from mine enemies, O God.
℟. Defend me from them that rise up against me.

Collect for Palm Sunday.

# PROCESSIONAL

624

iv. *Chorus (First time, Chanters : chorus repeat)*   *arr.* J. H. A.

Hail thee, Fes - ti - val Day! blest day that art hal - low'd for ev - er;

Day where - in Christ a - rose, break-ing the king-dom of death.

Chanters ('Three clerks')

[*Copyright*, 1931, *by Oxford University Press*.]
* This note is omitted in verses 6 and 11.

EASTER-DAY: MORNING PROCESSION

Bishop Venantius Fortunatus, 530–609.
(Sarum Processional.) *Tr. M. F. B.*†

Salve, festa dies.

*H*AIL thee, Festival Day! blest day that art hallowed for ever;
Day wherein Christ arose, breaking the kingdom of death.

2 Lo, the fair beauty of earth, from the death of the winter arising,
Every good gift of the year now with its Master returns.

3 He who was nailed to the Cross is God and the Ruler of all things;
All things created on earth worship the Maker of all.

4 God of all pity and power, let thy word be assured to the doubting;
Light on the third day returns: rise, Son of God, from the tomb!

5 Ill doth it seem that thy limbs should linger in lowly dishonour,
Ransom and price of the world, veiled from the vision of men.

6* Ill it beseemeth that thou, by whose hand all things are encompassed,
Captive and bound should remain, deep in the gloom of the rock.

7* Rise now, O Lord, from the grave and cast off the shroud that enwrapped
Thou art sufficient for us: nothing without thee exists.   [thee;

8 Mourning they laid thee to rest, who art Author of life and creation;
Treading the pathway of death, life thou bestowedst on man.

9 Show us thy face once more, that the ages may joy in thy brightness;
Give us the light of day, darkened on earth at thy death.

10* Out of the prison of death thou art rescuing numberless captives;
Freely they tread in the way whither their Maker has gone.

11*. Jesus has harrowed hell; he has led captivity captive:
Darkness and chaos and death flee from the face of the light.

Alternative accompaniment for Chanters' verses.

(The Chanters may sing an occasional verse unaccompanied)

PROCESSIONAL

SALVE FESTA DIES. (Irreg.) **624** (MODERN TUNE)

With vigour ♩ = 112. To be sung in unison.

R. VAUGHAN WILLIAMS.

Clerks.

1 Hail thee, Fes - ti - val Day! blest day that art hal - lowed for ev - er; Day where - in Christ a - rose, break-ing the king - dom of death. death.

(Small notes optional.)

1st time. *2nd time.*

Repeat in Chorus.

Verses 2, 4, 6, 8, and 10.

Clerks only.

2 Lo, the fair beau - ty of earth, from the death of the
4 God of all pity and power, let thy word be as
6* Ill it be - seem - eth that thou, by whose hand all . .
8 Mourn-ing they laid thee to rest, who art Au - thor of
10* Out of the pri - son of death thou art res - cu - ing

EASTER-DAY: MORNING PROCESSION

624 (*continued*)

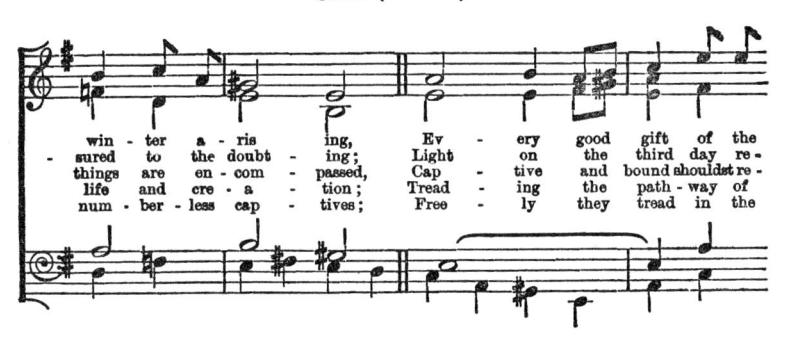

win-	ter	a- ris	ing,	Ev-	ery	good	gift of the
-sured	to	the doubt-	ing;	Light	on	the	third day re-
things	are	en- com-	passed,	Cap-	tive	and	bound shouldst re-
life	and	cre- a-	tion;	Tread-	ing	the	path-way of
num-	ber-	less cap-	tives;	Free-	ly	they	tread in the

Repeat 'Hail thee' in chorus after each verse.

year	now	with its	Mas- ter	re-	turns.
-turns:	rise,	Son of	God, from	the	tomb!
-main,	deep	in the	gloom of	the	rock.
death,	life	thou be-	stow-edst	on	man.
way	whi-	ther their	Ma- ker	has	gone.

Verses 3, 5, 7, 9, and 11.
Clerks only.

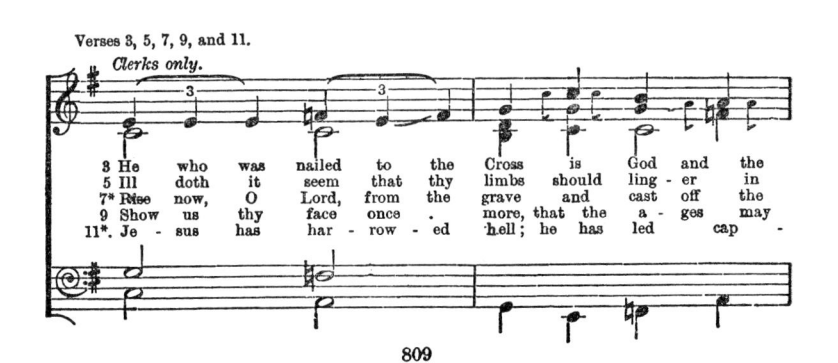

3 He who was nailed to the Cross is God and the
5 Ill doth it seem that thy limbs should ling- er in
7* Rise now, O Lord, from the grave and cast off the
9 Show us thy face once more, that the a- ges may
11* Je- sus has har- row- ed hell; he has led cap-

PROCESSIONAL

624 *(continued)*

Ru - ler of all things; All things cre - a - ted on earth, wor - ship the Ma - ker of all.
low - ly dis - hon - our, Ran - som and price of the world, veiled from the vi - sion of men.
shroud that en - wrapped thee; Thou art suf - fi - cient for us: noth - ing with - out thee ex - ists.
joy in thy bright - ness; Give us the light of day, dark - ened on earth at thy death.
- ti - vi - ty cap - tive: Dark - ness and cha - os and death flee from the face of the light.

REFRAIN AFTER EACH VERSE.

Hail thee, Fes - ti - val Day! blest day that art hal - lowed for ev - er;

Harmony.

Day where - in Christ a - rose, break - ing the king - dom of death. A - men.

(Small notes optional.)

810

EASTER-DAY: MORNING PROCESSION

VICTORY. (8 8. 8 4.)
Slow and dignified ♩ = 80.

625

First three lines adapted from a 'Gloria Patri,' by G. P. DA PALESTRINA, d. 1594. *Alleluya by* W. H. MONK.

At the entrance into the Choir. *Ascribed to 18th cent.* Tr. F. P.
Finita jam sunt praelia.

THE strife is o'er, the battle done;
Now is the Victor's triumph won;
O let the song of praise be sung :
    Alleluya!

2 Death's mightiest powers have done their worst,
And Jesus hath his foes dispersed;
Let shouts of praise and joy outburst :

Unison. 3 * On the third morn he rose again
Glorious in majesty to reign;
O let us swell the joyful strain :

4 * He brake the age-bound chains of hell;
The bars from heaven's high portals fell;
Let hymns of praise his triumph tell :

Unison. 5. Lord, by the stripes which wounded thee
From death's dread sting thy servants free,
That we may live, and sing to thee :

A - men.

At the Sanctuary step.

℣. The Lord is risen from the tomb.
℟. Who for our sakes hung upon the Tree. Alleluya.
Collect for Easter-Day.

811

PROCESSIONAL

O FILII ET FILIAE (1). (8 8 8. and Alleluyas).
In free rhythm ♩ = 112.
To be sung in unison.

626

*Proper melody (Solesmes version)
harmonized by* E. W. GOLDSMITH.
Mode ii.

Al - le - lu - ya! Al - le - lu - ya! Al - le - lu - ya!

Al - le - lu - ya!

O FILII ET FILIAE (2). (8 8 8. and Alleluyas.)

ALTERNATIVE VERSION

In moderate time ♩ = 112.
To be sung in unison.

*Proper melody (modern version)
as given in* WEBBE'S '*Motetts
or Antiphons*,' 1792.

Al - le - lu - ya! Al - le - lu - ya! Al -

- - - le - lu - ya!

EASTER-DAY: EVENING PROCESSION

626 (*continued*)

EASTER-DAY: EVENING PROCESSION
O filii et filiae.

Ascribed to 17th cent.   *Tr. J. M. Neale.*

ALLELUYA! Alleluya! Alleluya!
  Ye sons and daughters of the King,
Whom heavenly hosts in glory sing,
To-day the grave hath lost its sting.
                       Alleluya!

2 On that first morning of the week,
  Before the day began to break,
  The Marys went their Lord to seek.

3 An Angel bade their sorrow flee,
  For thus he spake unto the three:
  'Your Lord is gone to Galilee.'

4 That night the Apostles met in fear,
  Amidst them came their Lord most dear,
  And said: 'Peace be unto you here!'

5 When Thomas afterwards had heard
  That Jesus had fulfilled his word,
  He doubted if it were the Lord.

6 'Thomas, behold my side,' saith he,
  'My hands, my feet, my body see;
  'And doubt not, but believe in me.'

7 No longer Thomas then denied;
  He saw the feet, the hands, the side;
  'Thou art my Lord and God,' he cried.

8* Blessèd are they that have not seen,
  And yet whose faith have constant been,
  In life eternal they shall reign.

9* On this most holy day of days,
  To God your hearts and voices raise
  In laud, and jubilee, and praise.

10*. And we with Holy Church unite,
  As evermore is just and right,
  In glory to the King of Light.

At the Font.

℣. The Lord is risen from the tomb.
℟. Who for our sakes hung upon the Tree. Alleluya.

Collect for Easter Even.

PROCESSIONAL

626 *(continued)*

In returning up the Nave, Ps. 115, Non nobis, Domine, may be sung by Chanters and People in alternate verses, with Alleluya at the end of each verse.

Ps. 115.　　　　　　　　　Non nobis Domine.　　　　　　　　*arr.* J. H. A.

Al - le - lu - ya. 1 Not un - to us, O Lord, not unto us, but unto thy Name give the praise: for thy

loving mercy and for thy truth's sake. Al - le - lu - ya. 2 Wherefore shall the heathen say:

Where is now their God? Al - le - lu - ya. § Glo - ry be to the Fa-ther, and

to the Son: and to the Ho-ly Ghost. Al - le - lu - ya. As it was ... now and

§ *If further verses are needed, see Appendix, No. 4, p. 904.*

EASTER-DAY: EVENING PROCESSION

ev - er shall be: world with - out end. A - men. Al - le - lu - ya.

At the Chancel step all may stand until Gloria Patri *is sung, followed by:*
℣. Tell it out among the heathen.
℟. That the Lord hath reigned from the Tree.   Alleluya.
Collect for Palm Sunday.

NARENZA. (S. M.)   **627**   W. H. HAVERGAL, 1793–1870, founded on 'Ave, Maria klare' (Cöln Gesangbuch, 1619).
In moderate time ♩ = 72.

NOTE.—*This hymn may also be sung to* ST. THOMAS (*No. 11*).
A lower setting of this tune will be found at Hymn 518.

At the entrance into the Choir.   *T. Kelly* ‡, 1769–1854.

THE Lord is risen indeed!
   Now is his work performed;
Now is the mighty Captive freed,
   And death's strong castle stormed.

2 The Lord is risen indeed!
   Then hell has lost his prey;
With him is risen the ransomed seed
   To reign in endless day.

3. The Lord is risen indeed!
   He lives, to die no more;
He lives, the sinner's cause to plead,
   Whose curse and shame he bore.

A - men.

At the Sanctuary step.

℣. O Lord, hear our prayer,
℟. And let our cry come unto thee.
Collect for Lady Day.

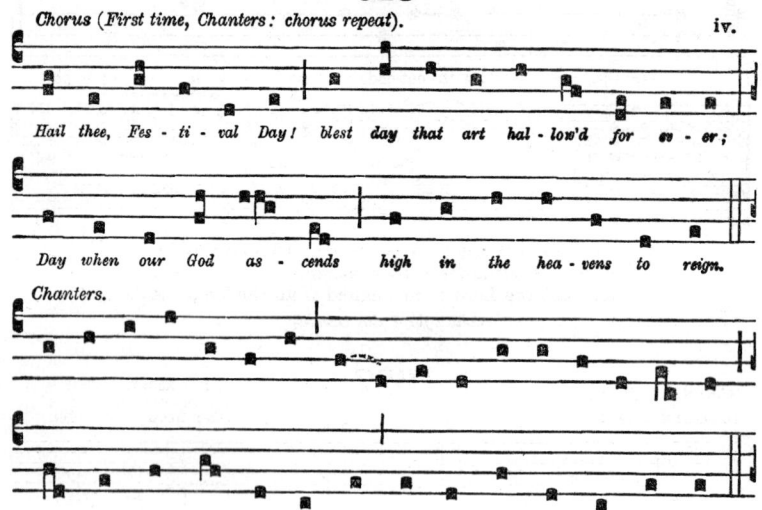

PROCESSIONAL
628

Chorus (First time, Chanters: chorus repeat).   iv.

Hail thee, Fes - ti - val Day! blest day that art hal - low'd for ev - er;

Day when our God as - cends high in the hea - vens to reign.

Chanters.

[*For Accompaniment and modern tune see Hymn 624.*]

ASCENSION-DAY PROCESSION

Bishop Venantius Fortunatus (530–609).
Salve, festa dies.   (*Sarum Processional.*)   *Tr. P. D.*

HAIL thee, Festival Day! blest day that art hallowed for ever;
   Day when our God ascends high in the heavens to reign.

2 Lo, the fair beauty of earth, from the death of the winter arising,
   Every good gift of the year now with its Master returns.

3 Daily the loveliness grows, adorned with the glory of blossom;
   Heav-en her gates ünbars, flinging her increase of light.

4 Christ in his triumph ascends, who hath vanquished the devil's dominion;
   Gay is the woodland with leaves, bright are the meadows with flowers.

5 Christ overwhelms the domain of Hades and rises to heaven;
   Fitly the light gives him praise—meadows and ocean and sky.

6 Loosen, O Lord, the enchained, the spirits imprisoned in darkness;
   Rescue, recall into life those who are rushing to death.

7* So shalt thou bear in thine arms an immaculate people to heaven,
   Bearing them pure unto God, pledge of thy victory here.

8* Jesus the Health of the world, enlighten our minds, thou Redeemer,
   Son of the Father supreme, only-begotten of God!

9* Equal art thou, co-eternal, in fellowship ay with the Father;
   In the beginning by thee all was created and made.

10*.And it was thou, blessèd Lord, who discerning humanity's sorrow,
   Humbledst thyself for our race, taking our flesh for thine own.

ASCENSION-DAY: PROCESSION

629

PARSIFAL. (8 7. 8 7.)
Moderately slow ♩ = 88.
R. WAGNER, 1813–83.
Slightly adapted.

Where-by to heav'n thou lead - est, Where-by to heav'n thou lead - est.
Where-by to heav'n thou lead - est, Where-by to heav'n thou lead - est.
Where-by to heav'n thou lead - est, Where-by to heav'n thou lead - est.
Where-by to heav'n thou lead - est, Where-by to heav'n thou lead - est.

NOTE.—*This hymn may also be sung to* ACH GOTT UND HERR (*No.* 329).

At the entrance into the choir.   17th cent.   Tr. W. J. Blew.
Supreme Rector caelitum.

O KING most high of earth and sky
On prostrate death thou treadest,
And with thy Blood dost mark the road
Whereby to heaven thou leadest.

2*O Christ, behold thine orphaned fold,
Which thou hast borne with anguish,
Steeped in the tide from thy rent side:
O leave us not to languish!

3. The glorious gain of all thy pain
Henceforth dost thou inherit;
Now comes the hour—then gently shower
On us thy promised Spirit!

A - men.

At the Sanctuary step.

℣. God is gone up with a merry noise.
℟. And the Lord with the sound of the trump. Alleluya.

Collect for Ascension-Day.

PROCESSIONAL

630

iv. *Chorus (First time, Chanters: chorus repeat)*   arr. J. H. A.

Hail thee, Fes - ti - val Day! blest day that art hal - low'd for ev - er;

Day where-in God from heav'n shone on the world with his grace.

Chanters ('Three clerks')

* *This note is omitted in verses 4 and 6.*

[*For modern tune see Hymn* 624.]

WHIT-SUNDAY PROCESSION

630 (*continued*)

Salve, festa dies.
c. 14th cent. (York Processional.) Tr. G. G.

HAIL thee, Festival Day! blest day that art hallowed for ever;
Day wherein God from heaven shone on the world with his grace.

2 Lo! in the likeness of fire, on them that await his appearing,
He whom the Lord foretold, suddenly, swiftly, descends.

3 Forth from the Father he comes with his sevenfold mystical dowry,
Pouring on human souls infinite riches of God.

4 Hark! in a hundrĕd tongues Christ's own, his chosen Apostles,
Preach to a hundred tribes Christ and his wonderful works.

5 Praise to the Spirit of life, all praise to the Fount of our being,
Light that dost lighten all, Life that in all dost abide.

6 God, who art Giver of all good gifts and Lover of concord,
Pour thy̆ balm on our souls, order our ways in thy peace.

7* God Ālmighty, who fillest the heaven, the earth and the ocean,
Guard us from harm without, cleanse us from evil within.

8*. Kindle our lips with the live bright coal from the hands of the Seraph;
Shine in our minds with thy light; burn in our hearts with thy love.

MELCOMBE. (L. M.) **631** S. WEBBE (the elder), 1740–1816.
Moderately slow ♩ = 69.

NOTE.—*This hymn may also be sung to* WARRINGTON (*No.* 263).

At the entrance into the Choir. *Foundling Hospital Collection* (1774).

SPIRIT of mercy, truth, and love,
Shed thy blest influence from above,
And still from age to age convey
The wonders of this sacred day.

2* In every clime, in every tongue,
Be God's eternal praises sung; [taught
Through all the listening earth be
The acts our great Redeemer wrought.

3. Unfailing Comfort, heavenly Guide,
Over thy favoured Church preside;
Still may mankind thy blessings prove,
At the Sanctuary step. Spirit of mercy, truth, and love.

A - men.

℣. The Apostles did speak with other tongues.
℟. The wonderful works of God. Alleluya.

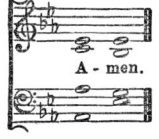

Collect for Whit-Sunday.

PROCESSIONAL

632

MONTGOMERY. (L. M.)
Moderately slow ♩ = 92.

Attributed to W. CHAMPNESS
in CHAPMAN'S 'Musical Companion,' 1772.

NOTE.—*This hymn may also be sung to the Grenoble Melody at Hymn* 181.

TRINITY SUNDAY PROCESSION

Aeterna Lux, Divinitas.   18*th cent.*   *Tr. R. F. Littledale*‡.

ETERNAL Light, Divinity,
O Unity in Trinity,
Thy holy name thy servants bless.
To thee we pray, and thee confess.

2 We praise the Father, mighty One;
We praise the sole-begotten Son;
We praise the Holy Ghost above,
Who joins them in one bond of love.

3 For of the Father infinite
Begotten is the Light of light,
And from his love eternally
Proceeds the Spirit, God most high.

4 None can more high or holy be,
Co-equal is their Deity,
The substance of the Three is One,
And equal laud to them is done.

5 The Three are One Immensity,
The Three One highest Verity,
The Three One perfect Charity,
And they are man's Felicity.

6 O Verity! O Charity!
O Ending and Felicity!
In thee we hope, in thee believe,
Thyself we love, to thee we cleave.

7 Thou First and Last, from whom there springs
The Fount of all created things,
Thou art the Life which moves the whole,
Sure Hope of each believing soul.

8 *Thou who alone the world hast made,
Art still its one sufficing aid,
The only Light for gazing eyes,
And, unto them that hope, the Prize.

9. O Father, Source of God the Word,
O Word with him co-equal Lord,
O Spirit of like majesty,
O Triune God, all praise to thee.
Amen.

TRINITY SUNDAY PROCESSION

633

MONT RICHARD. (L. M.)
In moderate time ♩ = 92. *Unison.*
P. C. BUCK.

NOTE.—*This hymn may also be sung to* ILLSLEY (*No.* 61).

At the entrance into the Choir.
Ave, colenda Trinitas.
Before 11th cent.
Tr. J. D. Chambers.‡

ALL hail, adorèd Trinity;
All hail, eternal Unity;
O God the Father, God the Son,
And God the Spirit, ever One:

2*To thee, upon this holy day,
We offer up our thankful lay;
Thou hearest in thy love's great wealth,
And praising thee is all our health.

3 Three Persons praise we evermore,
One only God our hearts adore;
In thy sweet mercy ever kind
May we our sure protection find.

4. O Trinity! O Unity!
Be present as we worship thee;
And with the songs that Angels sing
Unite the hymns of praise we bring.

A - men.

At the Sanctuary step.

℣. Blessed be the name of the Lord.
℟. From this time forth for evermore.

Collect for Trinity Sunday.

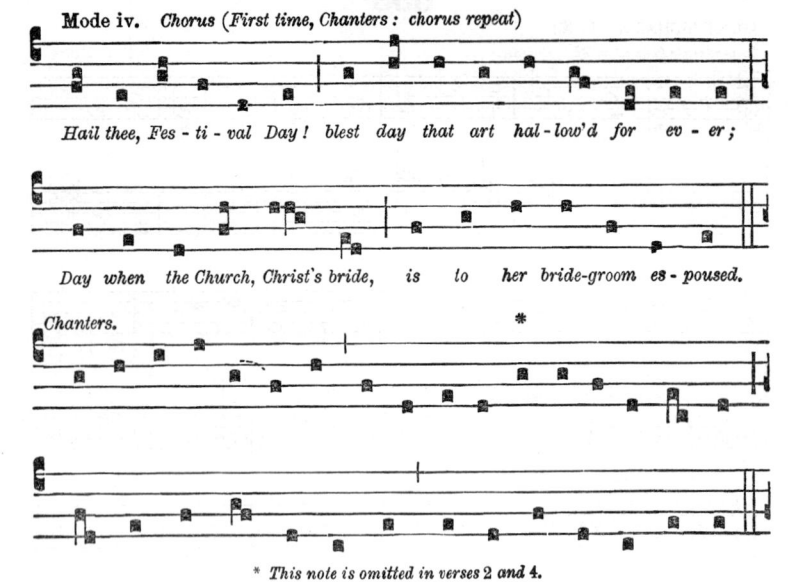

PROCESSIONAL
634

Mode iv. *Chorus (First time, Chanters: chorus repeat)*

Hail thee, Fes-ti-val Day! blest day that art hal-low'd for ev-er;

Day when the Church, Christ's bride, is to her bride-groom es-poused.

Chanters.   *

* *This note is omitted in verses* 2 *and* 4.

[*For accompaniment and modern tune see Hymn* 624.]

DEDICATION FESTIVAL PROCESSION

Salve, festa dies. *c.* 13*th cent.* (*York Processional.*)
Tr. M. F. B.

HAIL thee, Festival Day! blest day that art hallowed for ever;
Day when the Church, Christ's bride, is to her bridegroom espoused.

2 This is the house of God, ä place of peace and refreshing;
Solomon here to the poor offers a treasure untold.

3 Scion of David is he who has called us to share in his glory;
Here in his Fathĕr's house God we shall find him and man.

4 Ye who have put on Christ are indeed his mystical body,
If ye have kept thĕ faith, longed to become as your Lord.

5 Mystical also the new and the heavenly city of Sion,
Fitly adorned for her spouse, clad with the light from on high.

6*Here, at his holy font, does the heavenly King and the righteous
Grace for their cleansing and growth grant to his people on earth.

7*Tower of David is this; here are pledges of life and salvation,
If with unwavering feet swift to this stronghold we run.

8*Here is the ark of God, ä refuge of grace to the faithful;
Safe to the haven it bears mariners tossed by the waves.

9. Ladder of Jacob, by none but by thee we can mount to the heavens;
Grant that thy people, O Lord, thither ascending may reign.

DEDICATION FESTIVAL PROCESSION

635

O JESU MI DULCISSIME. (L. M.)
Moderately slow ♩ = 66.

Melody from the Clausener Gesangbuch, 1653.

NOTE.—*This hymn may also be sung to* PLAISTOW (*No.* 69), TUGWOOD (*No.* 146), *or* WAREHAM (*No.* 475).

At the entrance into the Choir.   I. Watts, 1674–1748, *and* J. Wesley.

ETERNAL Power, whose high abode
Becomes the grandeur of a God,
Infinite lengths beyond the bounds
Where stars revolve their little rounds:

2 Thee while the first Archangel sings,
He hides his face behind his wings;
And ranks of shining thrones around
Fall worshipping and spread the ground.

3. Lord, what shall earth and ashes do?
We would adore our Maker too!
From sin and dust to thee we cry,
The Great, the Holy, and the High!

A - men.

At the Sanctuary step.

℣. Blessèd are they that dwell in thy house.
℟. They will be alway praising thee.
    Collect for St. Simon and St. Jude.

PROCESSIONAL

636

ISTE CONFESSOR (2). (11 11. 11 5.)
In moderate time ♩ = 96. To be sung in unison.
Rouen Church Melody.

A SECOND DEDICATION FESTIVAL PROCESSION

c. 9th cent. Tr. M. J. Blacker.
Christe cunctorum Dominator alme.

1. ONLY-BEGOTTEN, Word of God eternal,
Lord of Creation, merciful and mighty,
List to thy servants, when their tuneful voices
  Rise to thy presence.

2. Thus in our solemn Feast of Dedication, [devotion,
Graced with returning rites of due
Ever thy children, year by year rejoicing,
  Chant in thy temple.

3. This is thy palace; here thy presence-chamber;
Here may thy servants, at the mystic banquet,
Daily adoring, take thy Body broken,
  Drink of thy Chalice.

4. Here for thy children stands the holy laver, [nature,
Fountain of pardon for the guilt of
Cleansed by whose water springs a race anointed,
  Liegemen of Jesus.

5. Here in our sickness, healing grace aboundeth, [freshment;
Light in our blindness, in our toil re-
Sin is forgiven, hope o'er fear prevaileth,
  Joy over sorrow.

6. Hallowed this dwelling where the Lord abideth, [Heaven;
This is none other than the gate of
Strangers and pilgrims, seeking homes eternal,
  Pass through its portals.

7. Lord, we beseech thee, as we throng thy temple,
By thy past blessings, by thy present bounty,
Smile on thy children, and with tender mercy
  Hear our petition.

8. God in Three Persons, Father everlasting,
Son co-eternal, ever-blessèd Spirit,
Thine be the glory, praise, and adoration,
  Now and for ever. Amen.

A - - - men.

DEDICATION FESTIVAL PROCESSION

637

OLD 117TH. (88.88.88.)
Moderately slow, dignified ♩ = 69.

*Melody in the Genevan Psalter, 1551
(as given in the Scottish Psalter, 1635).*

[*May be sung throughout in unison.*]

NOTE.—*This hymn may also be sung to* SOUTH CERNEY (*No.* 359).

At the entrance into the Choir.   G. Tersteegen, 1697–1769. Tr. J. Wesley.

Gott ist gegenwärtig.

1. LO! God is here! let us adore
  And own how dreadful is this place!
  Let all within us feel his power,
   And silent bow before his face,
  Who know his power, his grace who prove,
  Serve him with awe, with reverence love.

Unison. 2. Lo! God is here! Him day and night
  The united choirs of Angels sing;
  To him, enthroned above all height,
   Heaven's hosts their noblest praises bring;
  To thee may all our thoughts arise
  Ceaseless, accepted Sacrifice.

A - men.

At the Sanctuary step.

℣. Let thy priests be clothed with righteousness.
℟. And let thy saints sing with joyfulness.

Collect for St. Simon and St. Jude.

PROCESSIONAL
638 (PART 1)

ST. AUSTIN. (C.M.)
In moderate time ♩ = 144.

English Traditional Melody.

NOTE.—*This tune may also be used for Parts 2 and 3.*

PROCESSION FOR ANY SAINT'S DAY

F. B. P. ‡(c. 1580). Based on St. Augustine.

JERUSALEM, my happy home,
　When shall I come to thee?
When shall my sorrows have an end?
　Thy joys when shall I see?

2 O happy harbour of the Saints!
　O sweet and pleasant soil!
In thee no sorrow may be found,
　No grief, no care, no toil.

3 In thee no sickness may be seen,
　No hurt, no ache, no sore;
In thee there is no dread of death,
　But life for evermore.

4 No dampish mist is seen in thee,
　No cold nor darksome night;
There every soul shines as the sun;
　There God himself gives light.

5 There lust and lucre cannot dwell;
　There envy bears no sway;
There is no hunger, heat, nor cold,
　But pleasure every way.

6 Jerusalem, Jerusalem,
　God grant I once may see
Thy endless joys, and of the same
　Partaker ay may be!

7 Thy walls are made of precious stones,
　Thy bulwarks diamonds square;
Thy gates are of right orient pearl;
　Exceeding rich and rare;

8*Thy turrets and thy pinnacles
　With carbuncles do shine;
Thy very streets are paved with gold,
　Surpassing clear and fine;

9*Thy houses are of ivory,
　Thy windows crystal clear;
Thy tiles are made of beaten gold—
　O God that I were there!

10*Within thy gates no thing doth come
　That is not passing clean,
No spider's web, no dirt, no dust,
　No filth may there be seen.

11 Ah, my sweet home, Jerusalem,
　Would God I were in thee!
Would God my woes were at an end,
　Thy joys that I might see!

A - men.

SAINT'S DAY PROCESSION

638 (Part 2)

SOUTHILL. (C. M.)
In moderate time ♩ = 80.

English Traditional Melody.

Note.—*This tune may also be used for Parts 1 and 3.*

Part 2.

(*If sung separately, may begin with verse 1.*)

12 Thy Saints are crowned with glory great;
　They see God face to face;
　They triumph still, they still rejoice:
　　Most happy is their case.

13 We that are here in banishment,
　Continually do mourn;
　We sigh and sob, we weep and wail,
　　Perpetually we groan.

14 Our sweet is mixed with bitter gall,
　Our pleasure is but pain,
　Our joys scarce last the looking on,
　　Our sorrows still remain.

15 But there they live in such delight,
　Such pleasure and such play,
　As that to them a thousand years
　　Doth seem as yesterday.

16*Thy vineyards and thy orchards are
　　Most beautiful and fair,
　Full furnishèd with trees and fruits,
　　Most wonderful and rare;

17*Thy gardens and thy gallant walks
　　Continually are green;
　There grow such sweet and pleasant flowers
　　As nowhere else are seen.

18*There's nectar and ambrosia made,
　　There's musk and civet sweet;
　There many a fair and dainty drug
　　Is trodden under feet.

19*There cinnamon, there sugar grows,
　　There nard and balm abound;
　What tongue can tell, or heart conceive,
　　The joys that there are found!

A - men.

(*This Part may conclude with verse 26.*)

PROCESSIONAL

638 (Part 3)

STALHAM. (C.M.)
In moderate time ♩ = 80.
English Traditional Melody.

DUNSTAN. (C.M.) (ALTERNATIVE TUNE)
Moderately slow ♩ = 108.
From an English Traditional Melody.

NOTE.—*This hymn may also be sung to* ST. NICHOLAS (*No.* 265) *or to* JERUSALEM (*Appendix, No.* 69).

Part 3.
(If sung separately, may begin with verse 1.)

20 Quite through the streets with silver sound
　The flood of life doth flow,
　Upon whose banks on every side
　The wood of life doth grow.

21 There trees for evermore bear fruit,
　And evermore do spring;
　There evermore the Angels sit,
　And evermore do sing;

22 There David stands with harp in hand
　As master of the choir:
　Ten thousand times that man were blest
　That might this music hear.

23 Our Lady sings Magnificat
　With tune surpassing sweet;
　And all the Virgins bear their parts,
　Sitting about her feet.

SAINT'S DAY PROCESSION

24 Te Deum doth Saint Ambrose sing,
Saint Austin doth the like;
Old Simeon and Zachary
Have not their songs to seek.

25 There Magdalene hath left her moan,
And cheerfully doth sing
With blessèd Saints, whose harmony
In every street doth ring.

26 Jerusalem, my happy home,
Would God I were in thee!
Would God my woes were at an end
Thy joys that I might see!

A-men.

If the starred verses are omitted, Parts 1 and 2 together will form a Procession of average length; or any Part separately will form a short Hymn suitable for general use.

The following are also suitable for Saints' Days:

172 Sion's daughters.
200 Joy and triumph everlasting.
218 Ye who own (B.V.M.).
245 Stars of the morning (Michaelmas).
252 Our Father's home.

412 Jerusalem the golden.
519 Ye watchers.
641 For all the Saints.
642 Forward! be our watchword.
643 Onward, Christian soldiers.

644 Rejoice, ye pure in heart.

639

EATINGTON. (C. M.)
In moderate time ♩ = 72.

DR. CROFT, 1678-1727.

At the entrance into the Choir.

C. Wesley, 1707-88.

THE Church triumphant in thy love,
Their mighty joys we know;
They sing the Lamb in hymns above,
And we in hymns below.

2 Thee in thy glorious realm they praise,
And bow before thy throne;
We in the kingdom of thy grace:
The kingdoms are but one.

3. The holy to the holiest leads,
From hence our spirits rise,
And he that in thy statutes treads
Shall meet thee in the skies.

A - men.

The following are also suitable for Saints' Days, at the entrance into the choir.

196 For all thy Saints, O Lord.
249 (5, 6) Let all who served.

372 (1, 2, 3, or 4, 5, 6) Bright the vision.
535 (2) Praise the Lord.

PROCESSIONAL
640

Or this, on the festivals of St. Mary the Virgin.
MON DIEU, PRÊTE-MOI L'OREILLE. (8 8. 7 7. D.)
In moderate time, very dignified ♩ = 80.

Bishop R. Heber, 1783–1826.

Composed or adapted by
L. BOURGEOIS *for the 86th Psalm in the Genevan Psalter,* 1543.

1. Vir-gin-born, we bow before thee: Bless-èd was the womb that bore thee; Mary, Mother meek and mild, Bless-èd was she in her Child. Bless-èd was the breast that
2. Bless-èd she by all creation, Who brought forth the world's salvation, And bless-èd they—for ever blest, Who love thee most and serve thee best. Virgin-born, we bow be-

SUITABLE FOR USE IN PROCESSION

640 (*continued*)

fed thee; Bless-èd was the hand that led thee; Bless-èd
-fore thee: Bless-èd was the womb that bore thee; Ma-ry,

was the par-ent's eye That watched thy slumbering in-fan-cy.
Mo-ther meek and mild, Bless-èd was she in her Child. *Harmony.*

A-men.

At the Sanctuary step.

℣. Be glad, O ye righteous, and rejoice in the Lord.
℟. And be joyful, all ye that are true of heart.

Collect for All Saints' Day.

NOTE.—*The following tune may also be used.*

URQUELL ALLER SELIGKEITEN. (8 8. 7 7.)

Quietly ♩ = 92.

Melody by C. KOCHER, 1786–1872.

A-men.

PROCESSIONAL

641

SINE NOMINE. (10 10. 10 4.)
In moderate time ♩ = 112.
Verses 1, 2, 3 in unison.

R. VAUGHAN WILLIAMS.

(crotchets v. 2.)

Bishop W. W. How, 1823-97.

FOR all the Saints who from their labours rest,
Who thee by faith before the world confest,
Thy name, O Jesu, be for ever blest.

Alleluya!

2 Thou wast their Rock, their Fortress, and their Might;
Thou, Lord, their Captain in the well-fought fight;
Thou in the darkness drear their one true Light.

3 O may thy soldiers, faithful, true, and bold,
Fight as the Saints who nobly fought of old,
And win, with them, the victor's crown of gold.

SUITABLE FOR USE IN PROCESSION

641 (continued)

Harmony. Verses 4, 5, and 6.

(small notes v. 6.)

NOTE.—*Verses 4 and 6 may be sung by the Choir alone.*

4* O blest communion! fellowship divine!
   We feebly struggle, they in glory shine;
   Yet all are one in thee, for all are thine.

5 And when the strife is fierce, the warfare long,
   Steals on the ear the distant triumph-song,
   And hearts are brave again, and arms are strong.

6 The golden evening brightens in the west;
   Soon, soon to faithful warriors cometh rest:
   Sweet is the calm of Paradise the blest.

[OVER

PROCESSIONAL

641 (*continued*)

Verses 7 and 8 in unison.

(crotchets v. 8.)

Harmony.

A-men.

7* But lo! there breaks a yet more glorious day;
   The Saints triumphant rise in bright array:
   The King of glory passes on his way.

8.* From earth's wide bounds, from ocean's farthest coast,
   Through gates of pearl streams in the countless host,
   Singing to Father, Son, and Holy Ghost.

A Simpler ALTERNATIVE TUNE *to this Hymn is added on the opposite page.*

SUITABLE FOR USE IN PROCESSION

641 (continued)

LUCCOMBE. (10 10. 10 4.)
Moderately slow ♩ = 84.

J. A. FULLER-MAITLAND.

NOTE.—*Another tune to this hymn will be found in the Appendix* (No. 23).

Bishop W. W. How, 1823–97.

FOR all the Saints who from their labours rest,
   Who thee by faith before the world confest,
Thy name, O Jesu, be for ever blest.
                      Alleluya!

2 Thou wast their Rock, their Fortress, and their Might;
   Thou Lord, their Captain in the well-fought fight;
   Thou in the darkness drear their one true Light.

3 O may thy soldiers, faithful, true, and bold,
   Fight as the Saints who nobly fought of old,
   And win, with them, the victor's crown of gold.

4*O blest communion! fellowship divine!
   We feebly struggle, they in glory shine;
   Yet all are one in thee, for all are thine.

5 And when the strife is fierce, the warfare long,
   Steals on the ear the distant triumph-song,
   And hearts are brave again, and arms are strong.

6 The golden evening brightens in the west;
   Soon, soon to faithful warriors cometh rest:
   Sweet is the calm of Paradise the blest.

7* But lo! there breaks a yet more glorious day;
   The Saints triumphant rise in bright array:
   The King of glory passes on his way.

8.*From earth's wide bounds, from ocean's farthest coast,
   Through gates of pearl streams in the countless host,
   Singing to Father, Son, and Holy Ghost.

A - men.

835

PROCESSIONAL

642

UPWICK. (6 5. 6 5. *Ter.*)
Brightly ♩ = 108.

W. G. WHINFIELD.

SUITABLE FOR USE IN PROCESSION

H. Alford †, 1810-71.

FORWARD! be our watchword,
  Steps and voices joined;
Seek the things before us,
  Not a look behind;
Burns the fiery pillar
  At our army's head;
Who shall dream of shrinking,
  By our Captain led?
    Forward through the desert,
      Through the toil and fight;
    Jordan flows before us,
      Sion beams with light.

2 Forward, when in childhood
  Buds the infant mind;
All through youth and manhood,
  Not a thought behind;
Speed through realms of nature,
  Climb the steps of grace;
Faint not, till around us
  Gleams the Father's face.
    Forward, all the life-time,
      Climb from height to height;
    Till the head be hoary,
      Till the eve be light.

3 Forward, flock of Jesus,
  Salt of all the earth,
Till each yearning purpose
  Spring to glorious birth;
Sick, they ask for healing,
  Blind, they grope for day;
Pour upon the nations
  Wisdom's loving ray.
    Forward, out of error,
      Leave behind the night;
    Forward through the darkness,
      Forward into light.

Unison.
4 Glories upon glories
  Hath our God prepared,
By the souls that love him
  One day to be shared;
Eye hath not beheld them,
  Ear hath never heard;
Nor of these hath uttered
  Thought or speech a word;
    Forward, marching eastward,
      Where the heaven is bright,
    Till the veil be lifted,
      Till our faith be sight.

5 * Far o'er yon horizon
    Rise the city towers,
  Where our God abideth;
    That fair home is ours:
  Flash the streets with jasper,
    Shine the gates with gold;
  Flows the gladdening river,
    Shedding joys untold.
      Thither, onward thither,
        In the Spirit's might;
      Pilgrims to your country,
        Forward into light.

6 * Into God's high temple
    Onward as we press,
  Beauty spreads around us,
    Born of holiness;
  Arch, and vault, and carving,
    Lights of varied tone,
  Softened words and holy,
    Prayer and praise alone:
      Every thought upraising
        To our city bright,
      Where the tribes assemble
        Round the throne of light.

7 * Nought that city needeth
    Of these aisles of stone;
  Where the Godhead dwelleth
    Temple there is none;
  All the saints that ever
    In these courts have stood
  Are but babes, and feeding
    On the children's food.
      On through sign and token,
        Stars amidst the night,
      Forward through the darkness,
        Forward into light.

Unison.
8. To the Father's glory
    Loudest anthems raise;
  To the Son and Spirit
    Echo songs of praise;
  To the Lord Almighty,
    Blessèd Three in One,
  Be by men and Angels
    Endless honour done.
      Weak are earthly praises,
        Dull the songs of night;
      Forward into triumph,
        Forward into light!

PROCESSIONAL

643

HAYDN. (6 5. 6 5. *Ter.*)
Brightly ♩ = 108.

Adapted from F. J. HAYDN, 1732-1809.

Fine.

D.C.

NOTE.—*The following tune may also be used.*

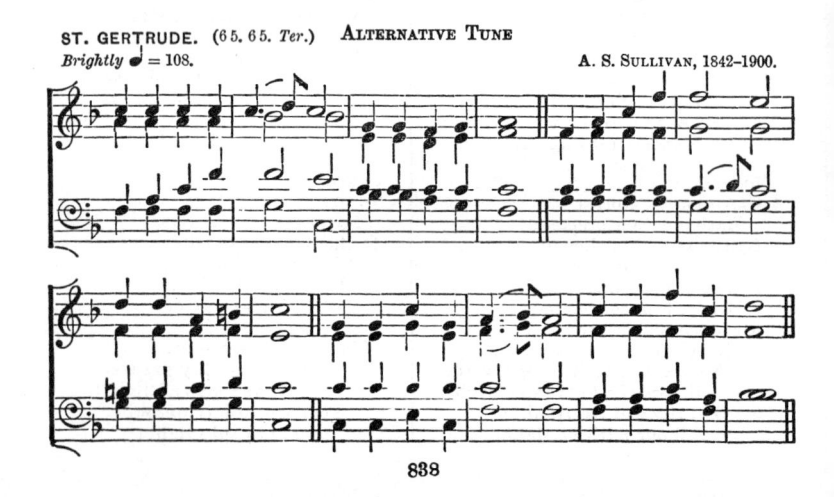

ST. GERTRUDE. (6 5. 6 5. *Ter.*) ALTERNATIVE TUNE
Brightly ♩ = 108.

A. S. SULLIVAN, 1842-1900.

SUITABLE FOR USE IN PROCESSION

643 (*continued*)

[By permission of Novello & Co. Ltd.]

O NWARD, Christian soldiers,
    Marching as to war,
With the Cross of Jesus
    Going on before.
Christ the royal Master
    Leads against the foe;
Forward into battle,
    See, his banners go!
    Onward, Christian soldiers,
      Marching as to war,
    With the Cross of Jesus
      Going on before.

2 At the sign of triumph
    Satan's legions flee;
On then, Christian soldiers,
    On to victory.
Hell's foundations quiver
    At the shout of praise;
Brothers, lift your voices,
    Loud your anthems raise.

S. Baring-Gould, 1834–1924.

3 Like a mighty army
    Moves the Church of God;
Brothers, we are treading
    Where the Saints have trod;
We are not divided,
    All one body we,
One in hope and doctrine
    One in charity.

Unison.

4 Crowns and thrones may perish,
    Kingdoms rise and wane,
But the Church of Jesus
    Constant will remain;
Gates of hell can never
    'Gainst that Church prevail;
We have Christ's own promise,
    And that cannot fail.

5. Onward, then, ye people,
    Join our happy throng,
Blend with ours your voices
    In the triumph song;
Glory, laud, and honour
    Unto Christ the King;
This through countless ages
    Men and Angels sing.

A - men.

PROCESSIONAL

644

ICH HALTE TREULICH STILL. (D. S. M.)

Brightly ♩ = 100.

Attributed to J. S. BACH, 1685–1750.

E. H. Plumptre, 1821–91.

REJOICE, ye pure in heart,
  Rejoice, give thanks, and sing;
Your orient banner wave on high,
  The Cross of Christ your King.

2 Bright youth and snow-crowned age,
  Strong men and maidens meek,
Raise high your free exulting song,
  God's wondrous praises speak.

3 With all the Angel choirs,
  With all the saints on earth,
Pour out the strains of joy and bliss,
  True rapture, noblest mirth.

4 Your clear hosannas raise,
  And alleluyas loud;
Whilst answering echoes upward float,
  Like wreaths of incense cloud.

Unison.
5 With voice as full and strong
  As ocean's surging praise,
Send forth the hymns our fathers loved,
  The psalms of ancient days.

6 Yes on, through life's long path,
  Still chanting as ye go,
From youth to age, by night and day,
  In gladness and in woe.

7 Still lift your standard high,
  Still march in firm array,
As warriors through the darkness toil
  Till dawns the golden day.

8 At last the march shall end,
  The wearied ones shall rest,
The pilgrims find their Father's home,
  Jerusalem the blest.

Unison.
9 Then on, ye pure in heart,
  Rejoice, give thanks, and sing;
Your orient banner wave on high,
  The Cross of Christ your King.

Unison.
10. Praise him who reigns on high,
  The Lord whom we adore,
The Father, Son, and Holy Ghost,
  One God for evermore. Amen.

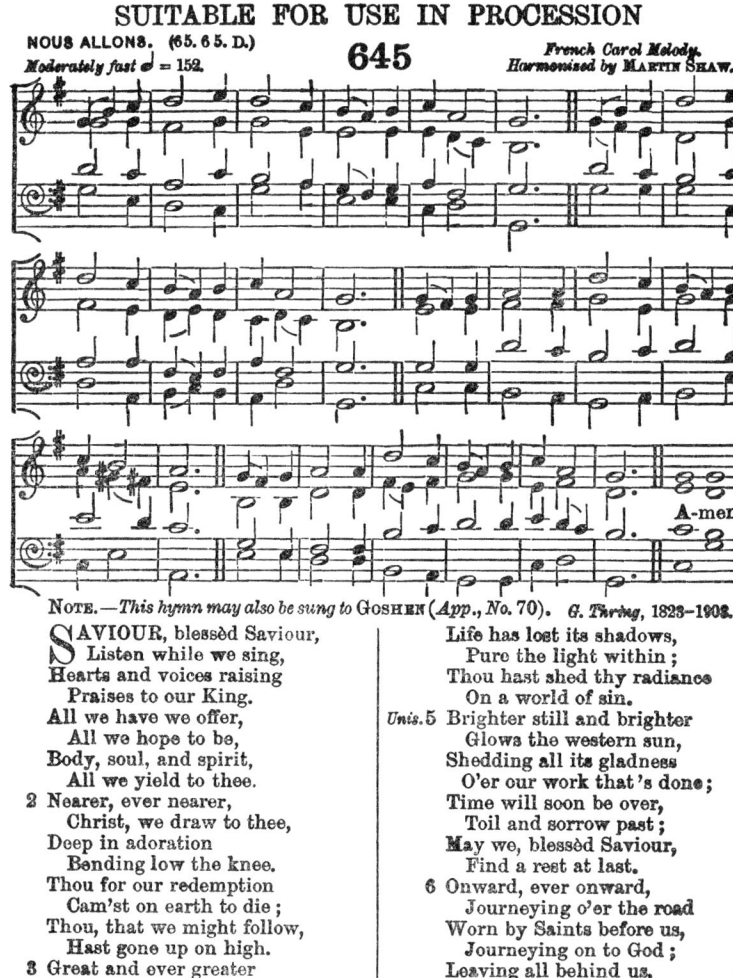

SUITABLE FOR USE IN PROCESSION

NOUS ALLONS. (6 5. 6 5. D.)
Moderately fast ♩ = 152.

645

French Carol Melody.
Harmonised by MARTIN SHAW.

NOTE.—*This hymn may also be sung to* GOSHEN (*App.*, No. 70). G. Thring, 1823-1903.

SAVIOUR, blessèd Saviour,
  Listen while we sing,
Hearts and voices raising
  Praises to our King.
All we have we offer,
  All we hope to be,
Body, soul, and spirit,
  All we yield to thee.

2 Nearer, ever nearer,
  Christ, we draw to thee,
Deep in adoration
  Bending low the knee.
Thou for our redemption
  Cam'st on earth to die;
Thou, that we might follow,
  Hast gone up on high.

3 Great and ever greater
  Are thy mercies here;
True and everlasting
  Are the glories there;
Where no pain, nor sorrow,
  Toil, nor care, is known,
Where the Angel-legions
  Circle round thy throne.

4 Clearer still and clearer
  Dawns the light from heaven,
In our sadness bringing
  News of sins forgiven;
Life has lost its shadows,
  Pure the light within;
Thou hast shed thy radiance
  On a world of sin.

Unis. 5 Brighter still and brighter
  Glows the western sun,
Shedding all its gladness
  O'er our work that's done;
Time will soon be over,
  Toil and sorrow past;
May we, blessèd Saviour,
  Find a rest at last.

6 Onward, ever onward,
  Journeying o'er the road
Worn by Saints before us,
  Journeying on to God;
Leaving all behind us,
  May we hasten on,
Backward never looking
  Till the prize is won.

Unis. 7. Higher then and higher
  Bear the ransomed soul,
Earthly toils forgotten,
  Saviour, to its goal;
Where in joys unthought of
  Saints with Angels sing,
Never weary raising
  Praises to their King.

PROCESSIONAL

646

LEONI. (66. 84. D.)
With vigour ♩ = 84.

Adapted from a Hebrew melody.

T. Olivers ‡, 1725–99. *Based on the Yigdal.*

THE God of Abraham praise
  Who reigns enthroned above,
Ancient of everlasting days,
  And God of love:
To him uplift your voice,
  At whose supreme command
From earth we rise, and seek the joys
  At his right hand.

SUITABLE FOR USE IN PROCESSION

2* Though nature's strength decay,
    And earth and hell withstand,
To Canaan's bounds we urge our way
    At his command.
The watery deep we pass,
    With Jesus in our view;
And through the howling wilderness
    Our way pursue.

3 The goodly land we see,
    With peace and plenty blest;
A land of sacred liberty
    And endless rest;
There milk and honey flow,
    And oil and wine abound,
And trees of life for ever grow,
    With mercy crowned.

Unison.
4 There dwells the Lord our King,
    The Lord our Righteousness,
Triumphant o'er the world and sin,
    The Prince of Peace;
On Sion's sacred height
    His kingdom he maintains,
And glorious with his Saints in light
    For ever reigns.

5 Before the great Three-One
    They all exulting stand,
And tell the wonders he hath done
    Through all their land:
The listening spheres attend,
    And swell the growing fame,
And sing, in songs which never end,
    The wondrous name.

Unison.
6 The God who reigns on high
    The great Archangels sing,
And 'Holy, Holy, Holy,' cry,
    'Almighty King!
Who was, and is, the same,
    And evermore shall be:
Eternal Father, great I AM,
    We worship thee.'

7* Before the Saviour's face
    The ransomed nations bow,
O'erwhelmed at his almighty grace
    For ever new;
He shows his prints of love,—
    They kindle to a flame,   [above
And sound through all the worlds
    The slaughtered Lamb.

8.* The whole triumphant host
    Give thanks to God on high;
'Hail! Father, Son, and Holy Ghost,'
    They ever cry:
Hail! Abraham's God, and mine!
    (I join the heavenly lays)
All might and majesty are thine,
    And endless praise. Amen.

A - men.

The following are also suitable:

172 Sion's daughters! Sons of Jerusalem.
196 Hark! the sound of holy voices.
212 I bind unto myself to-day.
368 At the name of Jesus.
380 Come, ye faithful, raise the anthem.
392 For thee, O dear, dear country.
412 Jerusalem the golden.
494 The strain upraise.
503 Through the night of doubt and sorrow.
519 Ye watchers and ye holy ones.
544 O Faith of England.
735 The Advent Prose.
736 The Lent Prose.

See also Table of Hymns Arranged, p. 946.

Part XI

LITANIES, ETC.

647

TRES MAGI DE GENTIBUS. (7 7. 7 7. and 7 7. 7 6.)

In moderate time ♩ = 144.

Melody in the Andernach Gesangbuch, 1608, slightly adapted.

Spare us, Holy Trinity.
Hear us, Holy Jesu.

NOTE.—*Most of the tunes in 7 7. 7 7. metre can be adapted to the litanies Nos. 647, 648, 649, 651, and 654.*

LITANY OF THE ADVENT

R. F. Littledale, 1833–90; and T. B. Pollock.

GOD the Father, God the Son,
God the Spirit, Three in One,
Hear us from thy heavenly throne:
      Spare us, Holy Trinity.

2 Jesu, King of boundless might,
Jesu, everlasting Light
Jesu, Wisdom infinite:
      Hear us, Holy Jesu.

3 Thou whose wisdom all things planned;
Held by whose almighty hand
All things in their order stand:

LITANY OF THE ADVENT

4 Jesu, sole-begotten Son,
   Jesu, high and holy One,
   Jesu, chiefest Corner-stone:

5 God with us, Emmanuel,
   Coming down as Man to dwell,
   Vanquisher of death and hell:

6 Jesu, Sun of Righteousness,
   Jesu, Mercy fathomless,
   Jesu, ever near to bless:

7 Saviour, full of truth and grace,
   Leaving thine eternal place,
   To restore our fallen race:

8 Jesu, Father of the poor,
   Jesu, Guard and Refuge sure,
   Jesu, Holiness most pure:

9 Word by whom the worlds were made,
   In a lowly manger laid,
   Taught on earth a lowly trade:

10 Jesu, Healer of complaints,
   Jesu, Strength of him that faints,
   Jesu, Teacher of the Saints:

11 Good Physician, come to cure
   All the ills that men endure,
   And to make our nature pure:

12 Jesu, Fount with blessings rife,
   Jesu, Bulwark in the strife,
   Jesu, Way and Truth and Life:

13. Only Hope of those who pray,
   Only Help while here we stay,
   Life of those who pass away:

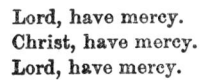

>   Lord, have mercy.
>   Christ, have mercy.
>   Lord, have mercy.
>
>   Our Father.

℣. Thou art fairer than the children of men.
℟. Thou hast loved righteousness and hated iniquity.

Collect for Advent Sunday.

LITANIES

648

HELFER MEINER ARMEN SEELE.
(7 7. 7 7. and 7 7. 7 6.)
In moderate time ♩ = 100.

Melody from
SCHEFFLER'S '*Heilige Seelenlust,*' 1657
(*slightly adapted*).

Spare us, Ho - ly Tri - ni - ty.
We be - seech thee, hear us.

LITANY OF PENITENCE

T. B. Pollock ‡, 1836–96.

GOD the Father, God the Son,
God the Spirit, Three in One,
Hear us from thy heavenly throne :
    Spare us, Holy Trinity.

2 Father, hear thy children's call;
Humbly at thy feet we fall,
Prodigals, confessing all:
    We beseech thee, hear us.

3 Christ, beneath thy Cross we blame
All our life of sin and shame;
Penitent we breathe thy name:

4 Holy Spirit, grieved and tried,
Oft forgotten and defied,
Now we mourn our stubborn pride:

5 Love, that caused us first to be,
Love, that bled upon the Tree,
Love that draws us lovingly:

6 We thy call have disobeyed,
Into paths of sin have strayed,
Have neglected and delayed:

7 Sick, we come to thee for cure,
Guilty, seek thy mercy sure,
Evil, long to be made pure:

8 Blind, we pray that we may see,
Bound, we pray to be made free,
Stained, we pray for sanctity:

LITANY OF PENITENCE

9 Thou who hear'st each contrite sigh,
   Bidding sinful souls draw nigh,
   Willing not that one should die:

10 By the gracious saving call
   Spoken tenderly to all
   Who have shared man's guilt and [fall:

11 By the nature Jesus wore,
   By the stripes and death he bore,
   By his life for evermore:

12 By the love that longs to bless,
   Pitying our sore distress,
   Leading us to holiness:

13 By the love so calm and strong,
   Patient still to suffer wrong
   And our day of grace prolong:

14 By the love that speaks within,
   Calling us to flee from sin
   And the joy of goodness win:

15 By the love that bids thee spare,
   By the heaven thou dost prepare,
   By thy promises to prayer:

16 Teach us what thy love has borne,
   That with loving sorrow torn
   Truly contrite we may mourn:

17 Gifts of light and grace bestow,
   Help us to resist the foe,
   Fearing what indeed is woe:

18 Let not sin within us reign,
   May we gladly suffer pain,
   If it purge away our stain:

19 May we to all evil die,
   Fleshly longings crucify,
   Fix our hearts and thoughts on high:

20 Grant us faith to know thee near,
   Hail thy grace, thy judgement fear,
   And through trial persevere:

21 Grant us hope from earth to rise,
   And to strain with eager eyes
   Towards the promised heavenly prize:

22 Grant us love thy love to own,
   Love to live for thee alone,
   And the power of grace make known:

23 All our weak endeavours bless,
   As we ever onward press,
   Till we perfect holiness:

24 Lead us daily nearer thee,
   Till at last thy face we see,
   Crowned with thine own purity:

A - men.

Lord, have mercy.
Christ, have mercy.
Lord, have mercy.

Our Father.

℣. Wash me throughly from my wickedness.
℟. And cleanse me from my sin.

Collect from the Commination.

LITANIES

649

GALLIARD. (7 7. 7 7.)
In moderate time ♩. = 48.
From a melody by J. DOWLAND, 1562-1626.
Adapted by MARTIN SHAW.

[Copyright, 1925, by Martin Shaw.]
NOTE.—*This hymn may also be sung to* ST. MARK (*Appendix, No.* 71).

LITANY OF THE PASSION

Anon. 1867.

GOD the Father, seen of none,
God the sole-begotten Son,
God the Spirit, with them One:
  Spare us, Holy Trinity.

2 Jesu, who for us didst bear
Scorn and sorrow, toil and care,
Hearken to our lowly prayer:
  Hear us, Holy Jesu.

3 By that hour of agony
Spent while thine Apostles three
Slumbered in Gethsemane:

4 By the prayer thou thrice didst pray
That the cup might pass away,
So thou mightest still obey:

5 By the kiss of treachery
To thy foes betraying thee,
By thy harsh captivity:

6 By thy being bound in thrall,
When they led thee, one and all,
Unto Pilate's judgement-hall:

7 By the scourging thou hast borne,
By the purple robe of scorn,
By the reed, and crown of thorn:

8 By the folly of the Jews
When Barabbas they would choose,
And would Christ their King refuse:

9 By thy going forth to die
When they raised their wicked cry,
'Crucify him, crucify!'

10 By the Cross which thou didst bear,
By the cup they bade thee share,
Mingled gall and vinegar:

11 By thy nailing to the Tree,
By the title over thee,
On the hill of Calvary:

12 By thy seven words then said,
By the bowing of thy head,
By thy numbering with the dead:

13 By the piercing of thy side,
By the stream of double tide,
Blood and Water, thence supplied:

14 When temptation sore is rife,
When we faint amidst the strife,
Thou, whose death hath been our life:
  Save us, Holy Jesu.

15 While on stormy seas we toss,
Let us count all things as loss,
But thee only on thy Cross:

16 So, with hope in thee made fast,
When death's bitterness is past,
We may see thy face at last:

LITANY FOR ROGATIONTIDE

Lord, have mercy.
Christ, have mercy.
Lord, have mercy
Our Father.
℣. The chastisement of our peace was upon him.
℟. And with his stripes we are healed.
First Good Friday Collect.

BEATUS. (8 8. 8 7.)
In moderate time ♩ = 88.

650

T. F. DUNHILL.

NOTE.—*The tune* ACH GOTT UND HERR (*No. 329*) *can also be adapted to this Hymn.*

SUITABLE FOR ROGATIONTIDE

The Great Collect. Ὑπὲρ τῆς ἄνωθεν εἰρήνης. *Tr. J. B.*

LORD, to our humble prayers attend,
Let thou thy peace from heaven descend,
And to our souls salvation send:
Have mercy, Lord, upon us.

2 Rule in our hearts, thou Prince of Peace,
The welfare of thy Church increase,
And bid all strife and discord cease:

3 To all who meet for worship here
Do thou in faithfulness draw near;
Inspire with faith and godly fear:

4 O let thy priests be clothed with might,
To rule within thy Church aright,
That they may serve as in thy sight:

5 The sovereign ruler of our land
Protect by thine almighty hand,
And all around the throne who stand:

6 Let clouds and sunshine bless the earth,
Give flowers and fruit a timely birth,
Our harvests crown with peaceful mirth:

7 Let voyagers by land and sea
In danger's hour in safety be;
The suffering and the captive free:

8. Around us let thine arm be cast,
Till wrath and danger are o'erpast
And tribulation's bitter blast:

Lord, have mercy.
Christ, have mercy.
Lord, have mercy.
Our Father.
℣. Lord, thou hast been our refuge.
℟. From one generation to another.
Collect for Trinity xii.

LITANIES

651

LITANY. (7 7. 7 7. and 7 7. 7 6.)
In moderate time ♩ = 92.

A. H. Brown, 1830-1926.

Spare us, Ho-ly Tri - ni - ty.
We be - seech thee, hear us.

LITANY OF THE CHURCH
T. B. Pollock, 1836–96.

GOD the Father, God the Son,
God the Spirit, Three in One,
Hear us from thy heavenly throne:
    Spare us, Holy Trinity.

2 Jesu, with thy Church abide,
Be her Saviour, Lord, and Guide,
While on earth her faith is tried:
    We beseech thee, hear us.

3 Keep her life and doctrine pure,
Help her patient to endure,
Trusting in thy promise sure:

4 Be thou with her all the days;
May she, safe from error's ways,
Toil for thine eternal praise:

5 May her voice be ever clear,
Warning of a judgement near,
Telling of a Saviour dear:

6 All her ruined works repair,
Build again thy temple fair,
Manifest thy presence there:

7 All her fettered powers release,
Bid our strife and envy cease,
Grant the heavenly gift of peace:

8 May she one in doctrine be,
One in truth and charity,
Winning all to faith in thee:

9 May she guide the poor and blind,
Seek the lost until she find,
And the broken-hearted bind:

10 Save her love from growing cold,
Make her watchmen strong and bold,
Fence her round, thy peaceful fold:

11 May her priests thy people feed,
Shepherds of the flock indeed,
Ready, where they call, to lead:

12 Judge her not for work undone,
Judge her not for fields unwon,
Bless her works in thee begun:

13 For the past give deeper shame,
Make her jealous for thy name,
Kindle zeal's most holy flame:

14 Raise her to her calling high,
Let the nations far and nigh
Hear thy heralds' warning cry:

15 May her lamp of truth be bright,
Bid her bear aloft its light
Through the realms of heathen night:

16 May her scattered children be
From reproach of evil free,
Blameless witnesses for thee:

17 Arm her soldiers with the Cross:
Brave to suffer toil or loss,
Counting earthly gain but dross:

18. May she holy triumphs win,
Overthrow the hosts of sin,
Gather all the nations in:

EVENING LITANY

Lord, have mercy. Christ, have mercy. Lord, have mercy.
Our Father.
℣. Let thy priests be clothed with righteousness;
℟. And let thy saints sing with joyfulness.
Second Good Friday Collect.

652

MICHAEL. (88. 84.)
Moderately slow ♩ = 92. *May be sung in unison.*
Melody by M. WEISSE, c. 1480-1594 (*slightly adapted*).

NOTE.—*This hymn may also be sung to* OLDBRIDGE (*Appendix, No. 72*).

The Litany of the Deacon. **SUITABLE FOR THE EVENING** *Tr. J. B.*
'Ἀντιλαβοῦ, σῶσον, ἐλέησον.

GOD of all grace, thy mercy send;
   Let thy protecting arm defend;
Save us and keep us to the end:
       Have mercy, Lord.

2 And through the coming hours of night,
   Fill us, we pray, with holy light;
Keep us all sinless in thy sight:
       Grant this, O Lord.

3 May some bright messenger abide
For ever by thy servants' side,
A faithful guardian and our guide:

4 From every sin in mercy free,
Let heart and conscience stainless be,
That we may live henceforth for thee:

5 We would not be by care opprest,
But in thy love and wisdom rest;
Give what thou seest to be best:

6 While we of every sin repent,
Let our remaining years be spent
In holiness and sweet content:

7. And when the end of life is near,
May we, unshamed and void of fear,
Wait for the Judgement to appear:

Lord, have mercy. Christ, have mercy. Lord, have mercy.
Our Father.
℣. Except the Lord keep the city.
℟. The watchman waketh but in vain.
Collect for Trinity xxi.

LITANIES

PROMPTO GENTES ANIMO. (7 7 6. D.) **653**

In moderate time ♩ = 146.
To be sung in unison.

Rouen Church Melody.
Harmonized by R. V. W.

Spare us, Ho-ly Tri - ni - ty.
Hear us, Ho-ly Je - su.

LITANY OF THE BLESSED SACRAMENT

Anon. ‡ 1867.

GOD the Father, God the Word,
God the Holy Ghost adored:
    Spare us, Holy Trinity.

2 Spotless Lamb of God most high,
Manna coming from the sky:
    Hear us, Holy Jesu.

3 Very Man and Word Divine,
Hidden under Bread and Wine:

LITANY OF THE BLESSED SACRAMENT

4 Purest Victim, stainless Priest,
Thou the Host, and thou the Feast:

5 Bread of life, the Angels' food,
Cup of blessing, precious Blood:

6 Offering of most perfect might,
Bond, thy faithful to unite:

7 From the tempting lures of sin,
From all pride and lusts within:
Keep us, Holy Jesu.

8 From all unbelief in thee
Veiled in this great Mystery:

9 By thy sitting down to meat,
That last Passover to eat:

10 Through the dread and holy rite,
Founded on that awful night:

11 Through thy presence with us here,
When we draw thine altar near:

12 Help us, guide us, make us pure,
Give us blessings which endure:
Save us, Holy Jesu.

13 Lead thy pilgrims on their way,
Shine on us, unending Day:

14. When we draw our latest breath,
Feed us at the time of death:

A - - - - - men.

Lord, have mercy.
Christ, have mercy.
Lord, have mercy.

Our Father.

℣. Blessèd are they which do hunger and thirst after righteousness;
℟. For they shall be filled.

Collect for Easter ii.

LITANIES

654

FARNABY. (77. 77. and 77.76.)
In moderate time ♩ = 144.
To be sung in unison.

*Adapted from an
English Traditional Melody.*

Spare us, Ho-ly Tri-ni-ty.
Hear us, Ho-ly Je-su.

Note.—*Parts 2 and 3 of this hymn may also be sung to* Tres Magi de Gentibus (*No. 647*).

CHILDREN'S LITANY

Cento.

GOD the Father, God the Son,
God the Spirit, Three in One,
Hear us from thy heavenly throne:
      Spare us, Holy Trinity.

2 Jesu, Saviour ever mild,
Born for us a little Child
Of the Virgin undefiled:
      Hear us, Holy Jesu.

3 Jesu, by the Mother-Maid
In thy swaddling-clothes arrayed,
And within a manger laid:

4 Jesu, at whose infant feet
Shepherds, coming thee to greet,
Knelt to pay their worship meet:

5 Jesu, unto whom of yore
Wise men, hastening to adore,
Gold and myrrh and incense bore:

6 Jesu, to thy temple brought,
Whom, by thy good Spirit taught,
Simeon and Anna sought:

CHILDREN'S LITANY

7 Jesu, who didst deign to flee
  From King Herod's cruelty
  In thy earliest infancy:

8 Jesu, whom thy Mother found
  'Midst the doctors sitting round,
  Marvelling at thy words profound:

Part 2.

9 From all pride and vain conceit,
  From all spite and angry heat,
  From all lying and deceit:
         Save us, Holy Jesu.

10 From all sloth and idleness,
   From not caring for distress,
   From all lust and greediness:

11 From refusing to obey,
   From the love of our own way,
   From forgetfulness to pray:

Part 3.

12 By thy birth and early years,
   By thine infant wants and fears,
   By thy sorrows and thy tears,
         Save us, Holy Jesu.

13 By thy pattern bright and pure,
   By the pains thou didst endure
   Our salvation to procure:

14 By thy wounds and thorn-crowned head,
   By thy Blood for sinners shed,
   By thy rising from the dead:

15 By the name we bow before,
   Human name, which evermore
   All the hosts of heaven adore:

16. By thine own unconquered might,
    By thy glory in the height,
    By thy mercies infinite:

      Lord, have mercy.
      Christ, have mercy.
      Lord, have mercy.

       Our Father.
℣. Lord, hear our prayer;
℟. And let our cry come unto thee.

Collect for Trinity ix.

LITANIES

JESU, JESU DU MEIN HIRT. (7 7. 7 7. 7 7.) **655**
In moderate time ♩ = 72.
Melody by P. HEINLEIN, 1626-80.

NOTE.—*This hymn may also be sung to* REDHEAD *No.* 76 (*No.* 477).

COMMENDATORY LITANY

R. F. Littledale, 1833-90.

GOD the Father, God the Son,
Holy Ghost, the Comforter,
Ever blessèd Three in One,
  Hearken to our humble prayer:
    Hear us when we call to thee,
    Spare us, Holy Trinity.

2 Hear us, Son of God, O hear!
  We approach thee for our dead;
  Lead *them*, in the vale of fear,
    Be thy wings around *them* spread:
      Lord of life and love, we pray,
      Grant them *mercy in that day.*

3 Child of Mary, who didst bear
  Mortal flesh, for man to die;
  Child of sorrow, toil, and care,
    Grant *them* rest eternally:

4 Dweller in the vale of death,
  Second Adam, Source of Life,
  Wearer of the thorny wreath,
    Victor in the deadly strife:

5 Thou who didst let fall the tear
   On the grave of Bethany;
Who at Nain didst stay the bier
   That lone mother's tear to dry:

6 Thou whose voice could wake the dead,
   'Maid! I say to thee, arise!'
Who didst bow thy dying head
   On the day of sacrifice:

7 Thou who passedst through the gloom
   Which enshrouds the vale of death,
Guide *their* footsteps through the tomb,
   Shelter *them* thine arms beneath:

8*By thy flesh with scourges torn,
   By thy suffering human soul,
By the crown of woven thorn,
   By the mocking title-scroll:

9*By the quiet rock-hewn cave,
   Where thy body slept so well,
When thy Spirit, through the grave,
   Entered to the realms of hell:

10*By thy preaching of the Christ
   To the souls in prison bound,
When was rolled away the mist
   Which had hung their vision round:

11*By the eternal Sacrifice
   Which thou pleadest at the throne,
Only gift which can suffice,
   For that gift is all thine own:

12*By the Offering which we plead,
   One with thine in heaven above,
By the Lamb whose five wounds bleed,
   To fill full our Cup of Love:

13*In the fell and fearful day,
   Day of fury and of ire,
When the earth shall melt away
   In the thunder-blast of fire:

14*When to hear the doom are met
   Saints and sinners, quick and dead,
And the great white throne is set,
   And the books are open spread:

     Lord, have mercy.
     Christ, have mercy.
     Lord, have mercy.

      Our Father.

℣. I heard a voice from heaven, saying unto me,
℟. Blessèd are the dead which die in the Lord.

Collect from the Burial Service.

THE STORY OF THE CROSS
656

BRIDGWATER. (6 4. 6 3. D.)   PARTS 1, 2, and 5   *Adapted from an English Traditional Melody.*
In moderate time ♩ = 100.

LANGPORT. (6 4. 6 3. D.)   PARTS 3 and 4   *Adapted from an English Traditional Melody.*
In moderate time ♩ = 100.

THE STORY OF THE CROSS

E. Monro and M. D.

THE QUESTION

SEE him in raiment rent,
  With his blood dyed:
Women walk sorrowing
  By his side.

2 Heavy that Cross to him,
  Weary the weight:
One who will help him stands
  At the gate.

3 Multitudes hurrying
  Pass on the road:
Simon is sharing with
  Him the load.

4 Who is this travelling
  With the curst tree—
This weary prisoner—
  Who is he?

THE STORY OF THE CROSS

THE ANSWER

5 Follow to Calvary,
   Tread where he trod:
   This is the Lord of life—
          Son of God.

6 Is there no loveliness—
   You who pass by—
   In that lone Figure which
          Marks the sky?

7 You who would love him, stand,
   Gaze at his face;
   Tarry awhile in your
          Worldly race.

8 As the swift moments fly
   Through the blest week,
   Jesus, in penitence,
          Let us seek.

THE STORY OF THE CROSS

9 On the Cross lifted up,
   Thy face I scan,
   Scarred by that agony—
          Son of Man.

10 Thorns form thy diadem,
    Rough wood thy throne,
    To thee thy outstretched arms
           Draw thine own.

11 Nails hold thy hands and feet,
    While on thy breast
    Sinketh thy bleeding head
           Sore opprest.

12 Loud is thy bitter cry,
    Rending the night,
    As to thy darkened eyes
           Fails the light.

13 Shadows of midnight fall,
    Though it is day;
    Friends and disciples stand
           Far away.

14 Loud scoffs the dying thief,
    Mocking thy woe;
    Can this my Saviour be
           Brought so low?

15 Yes, see the title clear,
    Written above,—
    'Jesus of Nazareth'—
           Name of love!

16 What, O my Saviour dear,
    What didst thou see,
    That made thee suffer and
           Die for me?

THE MESSAGE OF THE CROSS

17 Child of my grief and pain!
    From realms above,
    I came to lead thee to
           Life and love.

18 For thee my Blood I shed,
    For thee I died:
    Safe in thy faithfulness
           Now abide.

19 I saw thee wandering,
    Weak and at strife;
    I am the Way for thee,
           Truth and Life.

20 Follow my path of pain,
    Tread where I trod:
    This is the way of peace
           Up to God.

THE RESOLVE

21 O I will follow thee,
    Star of my soul!
    Through the great dark I press
           To the goal.

22 Yea, let me know thy grief,
    Carry thy Cross,
    Share in thy sacrifice,
           Gain thy loss.

23 Daily I'll prove my love
    Through joy and woe;
    Where thy hands point the way,
           There I go.

24. Lead me on year by year,
    Safe to the end,
    Jesus, my Lord, my Life,
           King and Friend.

    Lord, have mercy.
    Christ, have mercy.
    Lord, have mercy.
    Our Father.

℣. I will declare thy name unto my brethren.
℟. In the midst of the congregation will I praise thee.

The three Good Friday Collects.

A - men.

(For 656A see page 943)

Part XII

INTROITS AND OTHER ANTHEMS

THE INTROITS, ETC.

NOTE ON NOS. 657 to 733. *For each day the Introit is given first in one paragraph, the Gloria Patri being for convenience omitted. In the second paragraph are given in their order—the Grail or Gradual* (G), *Alleluya* (A), *Tract (for the days between Septuagesima and Easter)* (T), *Offertory* (O), *and Communion* (C). *Sequences are included among the hymns.*

[*The proper melodies of the Introits, and a selection of Grails, Alleluyas, and Tracts may be obtained from St. Mary's Press, The Convent, Wantage, Berkshire. Simple melodies for all the Propers given in Nos. 657 to 733 will be found in* The English Gradual, *Part II, to be obtained from the Plainchant Publications Committee, 6 Hyde Park Gate, London, S.W. 7. A selection of Communions is published by the Plainsong and Mediaeval Music Society, c/o The Faith Press, 7 Tufton Street, S.W. 1.*]

657 ADVENT SUNDAY. *Ad te levavi.* Unto thee, O Lord, lift I up my soul : O my God, in thee have I trusted, let me not be confounded; neither let mine enemies triumph over me; for all they that look for thee shall not be ashamed. *Ps.* Show me thy ways, O Lord : and teach me thy paths.

G. For all they that look for thee shall not be ashamed, O Lord. ℣. Make known to me thy ways, O Lord : and teach me thy paths. A. Alleluya. ℣. Show us thy mercy, O Lord : and grant us thy salvation. O. Unto thee ... ashamed (*as Introit*). C. The Lord shall show loving-kindness : and our land shall give her increase.

658 ADVENT ii. *Populus Sion.* O people of Sion, behold, the Lord is nigh at hand to redeem the nations : and in the gladness of your heart the Lord shall cause his glorious voice to be heard. *Ps.* Hear, O thou Shepherd of Israel : thou that leadest Joseph like a sheep.

G. Out of Sion hath God appeared : in perfect beauty. ℣. Gather my saints together unto me : those that have made a covenant with me with sacrifice. A. Alleluya. ℣. For the powers of heaven shall be shaken : and then shall they see the Son of Man coming in a cloud with power and great glory. O. Wilt not thou turn again, O God, and quicken us; that thy people may rejoice in thee : show us thy mercy, O Lord; and grant us thy salvation. C. Jerusalem, haste thee, and stand on high : and behold the joy and gladness, which cometh unto thee from God thy Saviour.

659 ADVENT iii. *Gaudete.* Rejoice ye in the Lord alway : and again I say, rejoice ye; let your moderation be known unto all men; the Lord is at hand. Be careful for nothing, nor troubled; but in all things, by prayer and supplication, with thanksgiving, let your requests be made known unto God. *Ps.* And the peace of God, which passeth all understanding : shall keep your hearts and minds.

G. Show thyself, O Lord, thou that sittest upon the Cherubim : stir up thy strength and come. ℣. Hear, O thou Shepherd of Israel : thou that leadest Joseph like a sheep. A. Alleluya. ℣. Stir up thy strength, O Lord : and come

ADVENT—CHRISTMAS-DAY

and help us. **O.** Lord, thou art become gracious unto thy land : thou hast turned away the captivity of Jacob ; thou hast forgiven the offence of thy people. **C.** Say to them that are of a fearful heart : Be strong, fear not ; behold, your God will come and save you.

660 ADVENT iv. *Memento nostri.* Remember us, O Lord, with the favour that thou bearest unto thy people : O visit us with thy salvation ; that we, beholding the felicity of thy chosen, may rejoice in the gladness of thy people, and may glory with thine inheritance. *Ps.* We have sinned with our fathers : we have done amiss, and dealt wickedly.

G. The Lord is nigh unto all them that call upon him : yea, all such as call upon him faithfully. **℣.** My mouth shall speak the praise of the Lord : and let all flesh give thanks unto his holy name. **A.** Alleluya. **℣.** Come, O Lord, and tarry not : forgive the misdeeds of thy people. **O.** Be strong, fear not ; behold, our God will come with a recompense : he will come and save us. **C.** Behold, a Virgin shall conceive and bear a Son : and his name shall be called Emmanuel.

661 CHRISTMAS EVE (FALLING ON SUNDAY). *Hodie scietis.* To-day shall ye know that the Lord will come to deliver you : and at sunrise shall ye behold his glory. *Ps.* The earth is the Lord's, and all that is therein : the compass of the world, and they that dwell therein.

G. To-day shall ye know that the Lord will come to deliver you ; and at sunrise shall ye behold his glory. **℣.** Hear, O thou Shepherd of Israel, thou that leadest Joseph like a sheep : show thyself also, thou that sittest upon the Cherubim, before Ephraim, Benjamin, and Manasses. **A.** Alleluya. **℣.** On the morrow the iniquity of the earth shall be blotted out : and the Saviour of the world shall reign over us. **O.** Lift up your heads, O ye gates, and be ye lift up, ye everlasting doors : and the King of Glory shall come in. **C.** The glory of the Lord shall be revealed : and all flesh shall see the salvation of our God.

662 CHRISTMAS-DAY (FIRST SERVICE). *Dominus dixit.* The Lord spake, and said unto me : Thou art my Son, this day have I begotten thee. *Ps.* Why do the heathen so furiously rage together : and why do the people imagine a vain thing?

G. In the day of thy power shall the people offer thee free-will offerings with an holy worship : the dew of thy birth is of the womb of the morning. **℣.** The Lord said unto my Lord : Sit thou on my right hand, until I make thine enemies thy footstool. **A.** Alleluya. **℣.** The Lord said unto me : Thou art my Son, this day have I begotten thee. **O.** Let the heavens rejoice, and let the earth be glad : before the Lord, for he is come. **C.** The dew of thy birth is of the womb of the morning.

663 CHRISTMAS-DAY (LAST SERVICE). *Puer natus est.* Unto us a Child is born, unto us a Son is given : and the government shall be upon his shoulder ; and his name shall be called, Angel of mighty Counsel. *Ps.* O sing unto the Lord a new song : for he hath done marvellous things.

INTROITS AND ANTHEMS

G. All the ends of the earth have seen the salvation of our God : O be joyful in God, all ye lands. ℣. The Lord hath declared his salvation : in the sight of the heathen hath he openly showed his righteousness. **A.** Alleluya. ℣. A hallowed day hath dawned upon us : come, ye nations, and worship the Lord ; for on this day a great light hath descended upon the earth. **O.** The heavens are thine, the earth also is thine ; thou hast laid the foundations of the round world, and all that therein is : righteousness and equity are the habitation of thy seat. **C.** Be joyful, O daughter of Sion ; sing praises, O daughter of Jerusalem : behold, thy King cometh ; he is righteous and having salvation.

664 ST. STEPHEN. *Etenim sederunt.* Princes moreover did sit, and did witness falsely against me ; and the ungodly pressed sore upon me : O Lord, my God, stand up to help me, for thy servant is occupied continually in thy commandments. *Ps.* Blessed are those that are undefiled in the way : and walk in the law of the Lord.

G. Princes also did sit and speak against me : wicked men have persecuted me. ℣. Help me, O Lord my God : save me for thy mercies' sake. **A.** Alleluya. ℣. I see the heavens opened : and Jesus standing on the right hand of God. **O.** The Apostles chose Stephen, a man full of faith and of the Holy Ghost : whom the Jews stoned, calling upon God, and saying, Lord Jesus, receive my spirit, alleluya. **C.** Lo, I see the heavens opened, and Jesus standing on the right hand of the power of God : O Lord Jesus, receive my spirit, and lay not this sin to their charge, for they know not what they do.

665 ST. JOHN THE EVANGELIST. *In medio ecclesiae.* In the midst of the congregation he opened his mouth ; and the Lord filled him with the spirit of wisdom and understanding : in a robe of glory he arrayed him. (*In Eastertide,* alleluya, alleluya.) *Ps.* A treasure of joy and gladness : hath he given him for an inheritance.

G. This saying went abroad among the brethren, that that disciple should not die. ℣. But, If I will that he tarry till I come : follow thou me. **A.** Alleluya. ℣. This is the disciple which testifieth of these things : and we know that his testimony is true. **O.** The righteous shall flourish like a palm tree : and shall spread abroad like a cedar in Libanus. **C.** Then went abroad this saying among the brethren, that that disciple should not die : yet Jesus said not, He shall not die : but, If I will that he tarry till I come.

666 HOLY INNOCENTS. *Ex ore infantium.* Out of the mouth of very babes, O God, and of sucklings, hast thou perfected praise : because of thine adversaries. *Ps.* O Lord, our Governor : how excellent is thy name in all the world.

G. Our soul is escaped even as a bird : out of the snare of the fowler. ℣. The snare is broken, and we are delivered : our help standeth in the name of the Lord, who hath made heaven and earth. **A.** Alleluya. ℣. The noble army of martyrs : praise thee, O Lord. **O.** Our soul is escaped, even as a bird out of the snare of the fowler : the snare is broken, and we are delivered. **C.** In Rama a voice was heard, lamentation, and great mourning : Rachel weeping for her children, and would not be comforted, because they are not.

CHRISTMAS-DAY — EPIPHANY

667 Sunday after Christmas-Day. *Dum medium silentium.* Whenas all the world was in profoundest quietness, and night was in the midst of her swift course : thine almighty Word, O Lord, leaped down from heaven out of thy royal throne. *Ps.* The Lord is King, and hath put on glorious apparel : the Lord hath put on his apparel, and girded himself with strength.

G. Thou art fairer than the children of men : full of grace are thy lips. ℣. My heart is inditing of a good matter, I speak of the things which I have made unto the King : my tongue is the pen of a ready writer. A. Alleluya. ℣. The Lord is King, and hath put on glorious apparel; the Lord hath put on his apparel and girded himself with strength. O. God hath made the round world so sure, that it cannot be moved : ever since the world began hath thy seat, O God, been prepared; thou art from everlasting. C. Take the young Child and his Mother, and go into the land of Israel : for they are dead which sought the young Child's life.

Circumcision of our Lord. *Puer natus est*, 663.

G., O., *and* C., 663. A. Alleluya. ℣. God, who at sundry times and in divers manners spake in time past unto the fathers by the Prophets, hath in these last days spoken unto us by his Son.

668 The Epiphany. *Ecce advenit.* Behold, he appeareth, the Lord and Ruler : and in his hand the kingdom, and power, and dominion. *Ps.* Give the King thy judgements, O God : and thy righteousness unto the King's Son.

G. All they from Saba shall come, bringing gold and incense, and shall show forth the praises of the Lord. ℣. Arise and shine, O Jerusalem : for the glory of the Lord is risen upon thee. A. Alleluya. ℣. We have seen his Star in the East, and are come with offerings to worship the Lord. O. The kings of Tharsis and of the isles shall give presents; the kings of Arabia and Saba shall bring gifts : all kings shall fall down before him; all nations shall do him service. C. We have seen his Star in the East, and are come with our offerings to worship the Lord.

669 Epiphany i. *In excelso throno.* On a throne exalted I beheld, and lo, a Man sitting, whom a legion of Angels worship, singing together : behold, his rule and governance endureth to all ages. *Ps.* O be joyful in God, all ye lands : serve the Lord with gladness.

G. Blessed be the Lord God, even the God of Israel : which only doeth wondrous things. ℣. The mountains also shall bring peace : and the little hills righteousness unto the people. A. Alleluya. ℣. O be joyful in the Lord, all ye lands : serve the Lord with gladness. O. O be joyful in the Lord, all ye lands : serve the Lord with gladness, and come before his presence with a song. Be ye sure that the Lord he is God. C. Son, why hast thou thus dealt with us? Behold, thy father and I have sought thee sorrowing. And he said unto them, How is it that ye sought me? wist ye not that I must be about my Father's business?

INTROITS AND ANTHEMS

670 EPIPHANY ii. *Omnis terra.* All the earth shall worship thee, O God, and sing of thee : they shall sing praise to thy name, O Most Highest. *Ps.* O be joyful in God, all ye lands : sing praises unto the honour of his name : make his praise to be glorious.

G. The Lord sent his Word and healed them : and they were saved from their destruction. ℣. O that men would therefore praise the Lord for his goodness : and declare the wonders that he doeth for the children of men. **A.** Alleluya. ℣. Praise the Lord, all ye angels of his : praise him, all his host. **O.** O be joyful in God, all ye lands : sing praises unto the honour of his name. O come hither, and hearken, all ye that fear God : and I will tell you what the Lord hath done for my soul, alleluya. **C.** The Lord saith unto them : Fill the waterpots with water, and bear unto the governor of the feast. When the ruler of the feast had tasted the water that was made wine, he saith unto the bridegroom : Thou hast kept the good wine until now. This beginning of miracles did Jesus before his disciples.

671 EPIPHANY iii TO vi. *Adorate Deum.* All ye Angels of God, fall down, and worship before him : Sion heard, and was exceeding joyful, and the daughters of Juda were glad. *Ps.* The Lord is King, the earth may be glad thereof : yea, the multitude of the isles may be glad thereof.

G. The heathen shall fear thy name, O Lord : and all the kings of the earth thy majesty. ℣. When the Lord shall build up Sion : and when his glory shall appear. **A.** Alleluya. ℣. The Lord is King, the earth may be glad thereof : yea, the multitude of the isles may be glad thereof. **O.** The right hand of the Lord hath the pre-eminence ; the right hand of the Lord bringeth mighty things to pass : I shall not die, but live, and declare the works of the Lord. **C.** All wondered at the gracious words which proceeded out of his mouth.

672 SEPTUAGESIMA SUNDAY. *Circumdederunt me.* The sorrows of death came about me, the pains of hell gat hold upon me : and in my tribulation I made my prayer unto the Lord, and he regarded my supplication out of his holy temple. *Ps.* I will love thee, O Lord my strength : the Lord is my stony rock, my fortress, and my Saviour.

G. The Lord will be a refuge in the time of trouble ; and they that know thy name will put their trust in thee : for thou, Lord, hast never failed them that seek thee. ℣. For the poor shall not alway be forgotten ; the patient abiding of the meek shall not perish for ever : up, Lord, and let not man have the upper hand. **T.** Out of the deep have I called unto thee, O Lord : Lord, hear my voice. ℣. O let thine ears consider well : the voice of my complaint. ℣. If thou, Lord, wilt be extreme to mark what is done amiss : O Lord, who may abide it ? ℣. For there is mercy with thee : therefore shalt thou be feared. **O.** It is a good thing to give thanks unto the Lord : and to sing praises unto thy name, O Most Highest. **C.** Show thy servant the light of thy countenance, and save me for thy mercies' sake : let me not be confounded, O Lord, for I have called upon thee.

EPIPHANY — ASH-WEDNESDAY

673 SEXAGESIMA SUNDAY. *Exsurge, quare.* Arise, O Lord, wherefore sleepest thou? awaken, and cast us not away for ever : wherefore hidest thou thy countenance, and forgettest our adversity and misery? our belly cleaveth unto the ground; arise, and save us, O Lord, our helper, and our deliverer. *Ps.* O God, we have heard with our ears : our fathers have told us.

G. Let the nations know that thou, whose name is Jehovah : art only the Most Highest over all the earth. ℣. O my God, make them like unto a wheel : and as the stubble before the wind. T. Thou hast moved the land, O Lord, and divided it : heal the sores thereof, for it shaketh. ℣. That they may triumph because of the truth. ℣. That thy Beloved may be delivered. O. O hold thou up my goings in thy paths, that my footsteps slip not : incline thine ear to me, and hearken unto my words : show thy marvellous loving-kindness, O Lord; thou that art the Saviour of them which put their trust in thee. C. I will go to the altar of God : even unto the God of my joy and gladness

674 QUINQUAGESIMA SUNDAY. *Esto mihi.* Be thou my God and defender, and a place of refuge, that thou mayest save me : for thou art my upholder, my refuge, and my Saviour; and for thy holy name's sake be thou my leader, and my sustainer. *Ps.* In thee, O Lord, have I put my trust, let me never be put to confusion : but rid me, and deliver me in thy righteousness.

G. Thou art the God that doeth wonders : and hast declared thy power among the people. ℣. Thou hast mightily delivered thy people : even the sons of Jacob and Joseph. T. O be joyful in the Lord, all ye lands : serve the Lord with gladness. ℣. Come before his presence with a song. ℣. Be ye sure that the Lord he is God. ℣. It is he that hath made us, and not we ourselves : we are his people, and the sheep of his pasture. O. Blessed art thou, O Lord ; O teach me thy statutes : with my lips have I been telling of all the judgements of thy mouth. C. They did eat, and were well filled, for the Lord gave them their own desire : they were not disappointed of their lust.

675 ASH-WEDNESDAY. *Misereris omnium.* Thou hast mercy on all things, O Lord, and hatest nothing which thou hast created : and winkest at man's iniquities, because they should amend, and sparest all men; for they are thine, O Lord, thou lover of souls. *Ps.* Be merciful unto me, O God, be merciful unto me : for my soul trusteth in thee.

G. Be merciful unto me, O God, be merciful unto me : for my soul trusteth in thee. ℣. He shall send from heaven ; and save me from the reproof of him that would eat me up. T. O Lord, deal not with us after our sins : nor reward us according to our wickednesses. ℣. Lord, remember not our old sins, but have mercy upon us, and that soon : for we are come to great misery. ℣. Help us, O God of our salvation, for the glory of thy name, O Lord : O deliver us and be merciful unto our sins, for thy name's sake. O. I will magnify thee, O Lord, for thou hast set me up, and not made my foes to triumph over me : O Lord, my God, I cried unto thee, and thou hast healed me. C. He who doth meditate on the law of the Lord day and night, will bring forth his fruit in due season.

INTROITS AND ANTHEMS

676 Lent i. *Invocabit me.* He shall call on me, and I will hearken unto him: I will deliver him, and will bring him to honour; with length of days will I satisfy him. *Ps.* Whoso dwelleth under the defence of the Most High : shall abide under the shadow of the Almighty.

G. He shall give his Angels charge over thee : to keep thee in all thy ways. ℣. They shall bear thee in their hands : that thou hurt not thy foot against a stone. T. Whoso dwelleth under the defence of the Most High : shall abide under the shadow of the Almighty. ℣. I will say unto the Lord, Thou art my hope and my stronghold : my God, in him will I trust. ℣. For he shall deliver thee from the snare of the hunter : and from the noisome pestilence. ℣. He shall defend thee under his wings : and thou shalt be safe under his feathers. ℣. His faithfulness and truth shall be thy shield and buckler : thou shalt not be afraid for any terror by night. ℣. Nor for the arrow that flieth by day : for the pestilence that walketh in darkness : nor for the sickness that destroyeth in the noonday. ℣. A thousand shall fall beside thee, and ten thousand at thy right hand : but it shall not come nigh thee. ℣. For he shall give his Angels charge over thee : to keep thee in all thy ways. ℣. They shall bear thee in their hands : that thou hurt not thy foot against a stone. ℣. Thou shalt go upon the lion and adder : the young lion and the dragon shalt thou tread under thy feet. ℣. Because he hath set his love upon me, therefore will I deliver him : I will set him up, because he hath known my name. ℣. He shall call upon me, and I will hear him : yea, I am with him in trouble. ℣. I will deliver him and bring him to honour : with long life will I satisfy him, and show him my salvation. O. He shall defend thee under his wings, and thou shalt be safe under his feathers : his faithfulness and truth shall be thy shield and buckler. C. Whoso drinketh of the water that I shall give him, saith the Lord, it shall be in him a well of water springing up unto life eternal.

677 Lent ii. *Reminiscere.* Call to remembrance thy tender compassion and mercy, O Lord, and thy loving-kindnesses towards us, which have been ever of old : neither suffer our enemies to triumph against us ; deliver us, O God of Israel, out of all our misery and trouble. *Ps.* Unto thee, O Lord, do I lift up my soul : my God, in thee have I trusted, let me not be confounded.

G. The sorrows of my heart are enlarged : O bring thou me out of my troubles, O Lord. ℣. Look upon my adversity and misery : and forgive me all my sin. T. The Lord said unto the woman of Canaan, It is not meet to take the children's bread : and to cast it to dogs. ℣. And she said, Truth, Lord : yet the dogs eat of the crumbs which fall from their master's table. ℣. Jesus said unto her, O woman, great is thy faith : be it unto thee even as thou wilt. O. My delight shall be in thy commandments, which I have loved ; my hands also will I lift up unto thy commandments, which I have loved. C. Consider my meditation : O hearken thou unto the voice of my calling, my King and my God : for unto thee will I make my prayer, O Lord.

678 Lent iii. *Oculi mei.* Mine eyes are ever towards the Lord, for he shall pluck my feet out of the net : look thou upon me, and have mercy upon me, for I am desolate, afflicted, and in

LENT—PASSION SUNDAY

misery. *Ps.* Unto thee, O Lord, do I lift up my soul: my God, in thee have I trusted, let me not be confounded.

G. Up, Lord and let not man have the upper hand: let the heathen be judged in thy sight. ℣. While mine enemies are driven back: they shall fall and perish at thy presence. **T.** Unto thee lift I up mine eyes: O thou that dwellest in the heavens. ℣. Behold, even as the eyes of servants: look unto the hand of their masters. ℣. And as the eyes of a maiden: unto the hand of her mistress. ℣. Even so our eyes wait upon the Lord our God: until he have mercy upon us. ℣. Have mercy upon us, O Lord: have mercy upon us. **O.** The statutes of the Lord are right, and rejoice the heart; sweeter also than honey and the honeycomb: moreover by them is thy servant taught. **C.** The sparrow hath found her an house, and the swallow a nest, where she may lay her young: even thy altars, O Lord of hosts, my King and my God; blessed are they that dwell in thy house: they will be alway praising thee.

679 LENT iv. *Laetare.* Rejoice ye with Jerusalem; and be ye glad for her, all ye that delight in her: exult and sing for joy with her, all ye that in sadness mourn for her; that ye may suck, and be satisfied with the breasts of her consolations. *Ps.* I was glad when they said unto me: We will go into the house of the Lord.

G. I was glad when they said unto me: We will go into the house of the Lord. ℣. Peace be within thy walls, and plenteousness within thy palaces. **T.** They that put their trust in the Lord shall be even as the Mount Sion: which may not be removed, but standeth fast for ever. ℣. The hills stand about Jerusalem: even so standeth the Lord round about his people, from this time forth for evermore. **O.** O praise the Lord, for the Lord is gracious: O sing praises unto his name, for it is lovely. **C.** Jerusalem is built as a city that is at unity in itself: for thither the tribes go up, even the tribes of the Lord, to give thanks unto the name of the Lord.

680 PASSION SUNDAY. *Judica me.* Give sentence with me, O Lord, and defend the cause of my soul against the ungodly people: deliver me, and rid me from the deceitful and wicked man; for thou, O Lord, art my God, and my strong salvation. *Ps.* O send out thy light and thy truth, that they may lead me: and bring me unto thy holy hill, and to thy dwelling. *The* Gloria *is omitted during Passiontide.*

G. Deliver me, O Lord, from mine enemies: teach me to do the thing that pleaseth thee. ℣. It is the Lord that delivereth me from my cruel enemies, and setteth me up above mine adversaries: thou shalt rid me from the wicked man. **T.** Many a time have they fought against me from my youth up. ℣. May Israel now say: yea, many a time have they vexed me from my youth up. ℣. But they have not prevailed against me: the plowers plowed upon my back. ℣. And made long furrows: but the righteous Lord hath hewn the snares of the ungodly in pieces. **O.** I will give thanks unto the Lord with my whole heart; O do well unto thy servant, that I may live, and keep thy word: quicken thou me, according to thy word, O Lord. **C.** This is my Body, which is given for you; this cup is the new Testament in my Blood, saith the Lord: this do ye, as oft as

INTROITS AND ANTHEMS

ye drink it, in remembrance of me. *Or this, during Passiontide.* **C.** Deliver me not, O Lord, unto the will of mine adversaries : forasmuch as false witnesses have risen up against me, and against me have they breathed out cruelty.

681 PALM SUNDAY. *Domine, ne longe.* O Lord, remove not thy succour afar from me, have respect to my defence, and hear me : deliver me from the mouth of the lion; yea, from the horns of the unicorns hast thou regarded my cry. *Ps.* My God, my God, look upon me, why hast thou forsaken me : and art so far from my health, and from the words of my complaint?

G. Thou hast holden me by my right hand; thou shalt guide me with thy counsel, and after that receive me with glory. ℣. Truly God is loving unto Israel, even unto such as are of a clean heart. Nevertheless, my feet were almost gone, my treadings had well nigh slipt : and why? I was grieved at the wicked, I do also see the ungodly in such prosperity. **T.** My God, my God, look upon me : why hast thou forsaken me? ℣. And art so far from my health; and from the words of my complaint? ℣. O my God, I cry in the daytime, but thou hearest not : and in the night season also I take no rest. ℣. And thou continuest holy : O thou worship of Israel. Our fathers hoped in thee : they trusted in thee, and thou didst deliver them. ℣. They called upon thee, and were holpen : they put their trust in thee, and were not confounded. ℣. But as for me, I am a worm, and no man : a very scorn of men, and the outcast of the people. ℣. All they that see me laugh me to scorn : they shoot out their lips, and shake their heads saying : ℣. He trusted in God, that he would deliver him : let him deliver him, if he will have him. ℣. They stand staring and looking upon me : they part my garments among them, and cast lots upon my vesture. ℣. Save me from the lion's mouth : thou hast heard me also from among the horns of the unicorns. ℣. O praise the Lord, ye that fear him : magnify him, all ye of the seed of Jacob. ℣. They shall be counted unto the Lord for a generation; they shall come, and the heavens shall declare his righteousness : unto a people that shall be born, whom the Lord hath made. **O.** Thy rebuke hath broken my heart; I am full of heaviness : I looked for some to have pity on me, but there was no man, neither found I any to comfort me. They gave me gall to eat : and when I was thirsty they gave me vinegar to drink. **C.** O my Father, if this cup may not pass away from me, except I drink it : thy will be done.

682 MAUNDY THURSDAY, &c. *Nos autem.* But as for us, it behoveth us to glory in the Cross of our Lord Jesus Christ : in whom is our salvation, our life, and resurrection; by whom we were saved, and obtained our freedom. *Ps.* God be merciful unto us, and bless us : and show us the light of his countenance and be merciful unto us.

(*Also with* Gloria *added, for the Invention of the Cross, and for Holy Cross Day. Good Friday and Easter Even have no Introit.*)

G. (*Maundy Thursday and Holy Cross Day.*) Christ became obedient for our sakes unto death, even the death of the Cross. ℣. Wherefore God also hath highly exalted him : and given him the name which is above every name. **T.** (*Good Friday only.*) Deliver me, O Lord, from the evil man : and preserve me from the wicked man. ℣. Who imagine mischief in their hearts : and stir up

PALM SUNDAY—EASTER ii

strife all the day long. ℣. They have sharpened their tongues like a serpent: adders' poison is under their lips. ℣. Keep me, O Lord, from the hands of the ungodly: and preserve me from the wicked men. ℣. Who are purposed to overthrow my goings: the proud have laid a snare for me. ℣. And spread a net abroad with cords: yea, and set traps in my way. ℣. I said unto the Lord, Thou art my God: hear the voice of my prayers, O Lord. ℣. O Lord God, thou strength of my health: thou hast covered my head in the day of battle. ℣. Let not the ungodly have his desire, O Lord: let not his mischievous imagination prosper, lest they be too proud. ℣. Let the mischief of their own lips fall upon the head of them: that compass me about. ℣. The righteous also shall give thanks unto thy name: and the just shall continue in thy sight. **A.** (*Holy Cross Day only.*) Alleluya. ℣. Sweetest wood, sweetest iron, that bare so sweet a burden: which only was counted worthy to sustain the King of heaven and its Lord. **A.** (*Invention of the Cross only.*) Alleluya. ℣. Tell it out among the heathen: that the Lord hath reigned from the Tree. **O.** (*Maundy Thursday only.*) The right hand of the Lord hath the pre-eminence, the right hand of the Lord bringeth mighty things to pass: I shall not die, but live; and declare the works of the Lord. **C.** (*Maundy Thursday only.*) The Lord Jesus, after he had supped with his disciples, and had washed their feet, said unto them: Know ye what I your Lord and Master have done to you? I have given you an example, that ye should do as I have done to you.

683 EASTER-DAY. *Resurrexi.* I am risen, and am still with thee, alleluya: thou hast laid thine hand upon me, alleluya; thy knowledge is too wonderful and excellent for me, alleluya, alleluya. *Ps.* O Lord, thou hast searched me out, and known me: thou knowest my down-sitting, and mine up-rising.

G. This is the day which the Lord hath made: we will be joyful and glad in it. ℣. O give thanks unto the Lord, for he is gracious: and his mercy endureth for ever. **A.** Alleluya. ℣. Christ our Passover is sacrificed for us. **O.** The earth trembled and was still: when God arose to judgement, alleluya. **C.** Christ our Passover is sacrificed for us, alleluya: therefore let us keep the feast with the unleavened bread of sincerity and truth, alleluya, alleluya, alleluya.

684 LOW SUNDAY. *Quasi modo.* As new-born babes, alleluya, desire ye the guileless milk of the word: alleluya, alleluya, alleluya. *Ps.* Sing we merrily unto God, our helper: make a cheerful noise unto the God of Jacob.

A. Alleluya. ℣. And after eight days, when the doors were shut, stood Jesus in the midst of his disciples, and said: Peace be unto you. **A.** Alleluya. ℣. The Angel of the Lord descended from heaven, and came and rolled away the stone, and sat upon it. **O.** 683. **C.** Christ being raised from the dead, dieth no more, alleluya: death hath no more dominion over him, alleluya, alleluya.

685 EASTER ii. *Misericordia Domini.* The loving-kindness of the Lord filleth the whole world, alleluya: by the Word of God the heavens were stablished, alleluya, alleluya. *Ps.* Rejoice in the Lord, O ye righteous: for it becometh well the just to be thankful.

INTROITS AND ANTHEMS

A. Alleluya. ℣. I am the Good Shepherd : and know my sheep, and am known of mine. **A.** Alleluya. ℣. The Good Shepherd hath risen : who hath given his life for his sheep. **O.** O God, thou art my God, early will I seek thee : and lift up my hands in thy name, alleluya. **C.** I am the Good Shepherd, alleluya : and know my sheep, and am known of mine, alleluya, alleluya.

686 Easter iii. *Jubilate Deo.* O be joyful in God, all ye lands, alleluya : sing ye praises to the honour of his name, alleluya; make his praise to be exceeding glorious, alleluya, alleluya, alleluya. *Ps.* Say unto God, O how wonderful art thou in thy works, O Lord : through the greatness of thy power.

A. Alleluya. ℣. A little while, and ye shall not see me, saith the Lord Jesus : and again, a little while and ye shall see me, because I go to the Father. **A.** Alleluya. ℣. But I will see you again, and your heart shall rejoice : and your joy no man taketh from you. **O.** Praise the Lord, O my soul ; while I live will I praise the Lord : yea, as long as I have any being, I will sing praises unto my God, alleluya. **C.** A little while, and ye shall not see me, alleluya : and again, a little while and ye shall see me, because I go to the Father, alleluya, alleluya.

687 Easter iv. *Cantate Domino.* O sing unto the Lord a new song, alleluya : for the Lord hath done marvellous things, alleluya; in the sight of the nations hath he showed his righteous judgements, alleluya, alleluya. *Ps.* With his own right hand, and with his holy arm : hath he gotten himself the victory.

A. Alleluya. ℣. I go to him that sent me : but because I have said these things unto you, sorrow hath filled your hearts. **A.** Alleluya. ℣. I tell you the truth : it is expedient for you that I go away. **O.** O be joyful in God, all ye lands, sing praises unto the honour of his name : O come hither, and hearken, all ye that fear God, and I will tell you what the Lord hath done for my soul, alleluya. **C.** When the Comforter, the Spirit of Truth, is come : he will reprove the world of sin, and of righteousness, and of judgement, alleluya, alleluya.

688 Easter v. *Vocem jocunditatis.* With a voice of singing declare ye this, and let it be heard, alleluya : utter it even unto the ends of the earth ; the Lord hath delivered his people, alleluya, alleluya. *Ps.* O be joyful in God, all ye lands : sing praises to the honour of his name, make his praise to be glorious.

A. Alleluya. ℣. Hitherto have ye asked nothing in my name : ask, and ye shall receive. **A.** Alleluya. ℣. Christ being raised from the dead, dieth no more : death hath no more dominion over him. **O.** O praise our God, ye people, and make the voice of his praise to be heard ; who holdeth our soul in life, and suffereth not our feet to slip. Praised be God, who hath not cast out my prayer : nor turned his mercy from me, alleluya. **C.** O sing unto the Lord, alleluya, sing unto the Lord, and praise his name : be telling of his salvation from day to day, alleluya, alleluya.

689 Ascension-Day. *Viri Galilaei.* Ye men of Galilee, why stand ye gazing up into heaven? alleluya : in like manner as ye have seen him going up into heaven, so shall he come again,

EASTER iii—TRINITY SUNDAY

alleluya, alleluya, alleluya. *Ps.* And while they looked steadfastly toward heaven, as he went up : behold, two men stood by them in white apparel: which said unto them.

A. Alleluya. ℣. God is gone up with a merry noise : and the Lord with the sound of the trumpet. A. Alleluya. ℣. Christ to highest heaven ascending, led captivity captive, and gave gifts unto men. O. God is gone up with a merry noise ; and the Lord with the sound of the trumpet, alleluya. C. Sing ye to the Lord, who ascended to the heaven of heavens, to the sunrising, alleluya.

690 Sunday after Ascension-Day. *Exaudi, Domine.* Consider, O Lord, and hear me, when I cry unto thee, alleluya : unto thee my heart hath said, Thy face, Lord, have I sought; thy face, Lord, will I seek ; O hide not thou thy face from thy servant, alleluya, alleluya. *Ps.* The Lord is my light, and my salvation : whom then shall I fear ?

A. Alleluya. ℣. God reigneth over the heathen : God sitteth upon his holy seat. A. Alleluya. ℣. I will not leave you comfortless : I go away and come again unto you, and your heart shall rejoice. O. Praise the Lord, O my soul ; while I live will I praise the Lord : as long as I have any being I will sing praises unto my God, alleluya. C. Father, while I was with them in the world, I kept those that thou gavest me, alleluya : and now I come to thee ; I pray not that thou shouldest take them out of the world : but that thou shouldest keep them from the evil, alleluya, alleluya.

691 Whit-Sunday. *Spiritus Domini.* The Spirit of the Lord hath filled the whole world, alleluya : and that which containeth all things hath knowledge of the voice, alleluya, alleluya, alleluya. *Ps.* Let God arise, and let his enemies be scattered : let them also that hate him flee before him.

A. Alleluya. ℣. O send forth thy Spirit, and they shall be made : and thou shalt renew the face of the earth. A. Alleluya. ℣. The Holy Spirit, proceeding from the throne, came down in unseen majesty, as on this day, upon the Twelve, purifying their inmost hearts. O. Stablish the thing, O God, that thou hast wrought in us : for thy temple's sake at Jerusalem, shall kings bring presents unto thee, alleluya. C. I will not leave you comfortless : I will come to you yet again, alleluya : and your heart shall be joyful, alleluya, alleluya.

692 Trinity Sunday. *Benedicta sit.* Blessed be the holy Trinity, and the undivided Unity : we will praise and glorify him, because he hath showed his mercy upon us. *Ps.* Let us bless the Father and the Son : with the Holy Spirit.

G. Blessed art thou, O Lord, which beholdest the great deep, and sittest upon the Cherubim. ℣. O bless the God of heaven, for he hath showed his mercy upon us. A. Alleluya. ℣. Blessed art thou, O Lord God of our fathers, and worthy to be praised for evermore. O. Blessed be God, the Father, and the only-begotten Son of God, and blessed be the Holy Spirit : for the mercy he hath done unto us. C. Let us bless the God of heaven, and in the sight of all living will we give thanks unto him : because he hath done to us-ward after his loving-kindness.

INTROITS AND ANTHEMS

693 Trinity i. *Domine, in tua misericordia.* O Lord my God, in thy loving-kindness and mercy have I trusted, and my heart is joyful in thy salvation : I will sing unto the Lord, for he hath dealt lovingly with me. *Ps.* How long wilt thou forget me, O Lord, for ever : how long wilt thou hide thy face from me?

G. I said, Lord, be merciful unto me : heal my soul, for I have sinned against thee. ℣. Blessed is he that considereth the poor and needy : the Lord shall deliver him in the time of trouble. **A.** Alleluya. ℣. Ponder my words, O Lord : consider my meditation. **O.** O hearken thou unto the voice of my calling, my King and my God : for unto thee, O Lord, will I make my prayer. **C.** I will speak of all thy marvellous works ; I will be glad, and rejoice in thee : yea, my songs will I make of thy name, O thou Most Highest.

694 Trinity ii. *Factus est.* The Lord was my refuge and upholder, and he brought me forth into a place of liberty : he delivered me, because he delighted in me. *Ps.* I will love thee, O Lord my strength : the Lord is my rock, my fortress, and my Saviour.

G. When I was in trouble I called upon the Lord : and he heard me. ℣. Deliver my soul, O Lord : from lying lips : and from a deceitful tongue. **A.** Alleluya. ℣. God is a righteous Judge, strong, and patient : and God is provoked every day. **O.** Turn thee, O Lord, and deliver my soul : O save me for thy mercies' sake. **C.** I will sing of the Lord, because he hath dealt so lovingly with me : yea, I will praise the name of the Lord Most Highest.

695 Trinity iii. *Respice in me.* Turn thee unto me, and have mercy upon me, O Lord : for I am desolate, and in tribulation; look thou on mine affliction, and my travail; and forgive me all mine iniquities, O my God. *Ps.* Unto thee, O Lord, do I lift up my soul : my God, in thee have I trusted, let me never be confounded.

G. O cast thy burden upon the Lord : and he shall nourish thee. ℣. When I cried unto the Lord, he heard my voice : from the battle that was against me. **A.** Alleluya. ℣. I will love thee, O Lord, my strength : the Lord is my stony rock, my fortress, and my Saviour. **O.** They that know thy name will put their trust in thee : for thou, Lord, hast never failed them that seek thee ; O praise the Lord which dwelleth in Sion : for he forgetteth not the complaint of the poor. **C.** I have called upon thee, O God, for thou shalt hear me : incline thine ear unto me, and hearken unto my words.

696 Trinity iv. *Dominus illuminatio mea.* The Lord is my light, and my salvation, whom then shall I fear : the Lord is the stronghold of my life, of whom shall I be afraid? when mine enemies pressed sore upon me, they stumbled and fell. *Ps.* Though an host of men were laid against me : yet shall not my heart be afraid.

G. Be merciful, O Lord, unto our sins : wherefore do the heathen say, Where is now their God? ℣. Help us, O God of our salvation : and for the honour of

SUNDAYS AFTER TRINITY

thy name, deliver us, O Lord. **A.** Alleluya. ℣. The King shall rejoice in thy strength, O Lord : exceeding glad shall he be of thy salvation. **O.** Lighten mine eyes, that I sleep not in death : lest mine enemy say, I have prevailed against him. **C.** The Lord is my strong rock, and my defence : my Saviour, my God, and my might.

697 TRINITY v. *Exaudi, Domine.* Consider, O Lord, and hear me, when I cry unto thee : be thou my succour, O cast me not away, neither forsake me utterly, O God of my salvation. *Ps.* The Lord is my light, and my salvation : whom then shall I fear?

G. Behold, O God, our defender : and look upon thy servants. ℣. O Lord God of hosts : hear the prayer of thy servants. **A.** Alleluya. ℣. In thee, O Lord, have I put my trust, let me never be put to confusion : rid me and deliver me in thy righteousness, bow down thine ear to me, make haste to help me. **O.** I will bless the Lord, who hath given me counsel : I have set God always before me; for he is on my right hand, therefore I shall not fall. **C.** One thing have I desired of the Lord, which I will require : even that I may dwell in the house of the Lord all the days of my life.

698 TRINITY vi. *Dominus fortitudo.* The Lord is the strength of his people, and a stronghold of salvation to his Anointed One : O Lord, save thine own people, and give thy blessing unto thine inheritance ; O feed them also, and set them up for ever. *Ps.* Unto thee will I cry, O Lord ; my God, be not silent unto me : lest, if thou make as though thou hearest not, I become like them that go down into the pit.

G. Turn thee again, O Lord, at the last : and be gracious unto thy servants. ℣. Lord, thou hast been our refuge : from one generation to another. **A.** Alleluya. ℣. O deliver me from mine enemies, O my God : defend me from them that rise up against me. **O.** O hold thou my goings in thy paths, that my footsteps slip not ; incline thine ear to me, and hearken unto my words, show thy marvellous loving-kindness : thou that art the Saviour of them which put their trust in thee, O Lord. **C.** I will offer in his dwelling an oblation with great gladness : I will sing, and speak praises unto the Lord.

699 TRINITY vii. *Omnes gentes.* O clap your hands, all ye people : O sing to God with the voice of joy and triumph. *Ps.* He shall subdue the people under us : and the nations under our feet.

G. Come, ye children, and hearken unto me : I will teach you the fear of the Lord. ℣. Come unto me and be enlightened : and your faces shall not be ashamed. **A.** Alleluya. ℣. Thou, O God, art praised in Sion : and unto thee shall the vow be performed in Jerusalem. **O.** Like as in the burnt offerings of rams and bullocks ; and like as in ten thousands of fat lambs ; so let our sacrifice be in thy sight this day, that it may please thee : for they shall not be confounded that put their trust in thee, O Lord. **C.** Bow down thine ear to me : make haste to deliver me.

INTROITS AND ANTHEMS

700 Trinity viii. *Suscepimus.* We have waited, O God, for thy loving-kindness in the midst of thy temple : according to thy name, O God, so is thy praise also unto the world's end; thy right hand is full of righteousness. *Ps.* Great is the Lord, and highly to be praised : in the city of our God, even upon his holy hill.

G. Be thou my strong rock and house of defence, that thou mayest save me. ℣. In thee, O Lord, have I put my trust : let me never be put to confusion. **A.** Alleluya. ℣. Hear my law : O my people. **O.** Thou shalt save the people that are in adversity, O Lord : and shalt bring down the high looks of the proud, for who is God, but the Lord? **C.** O taste and see how gracious the Lord is : blessed is he that putteth his trust in him.

701 Trinity ix. *Ecce Deus.* Behold, God is my helper, the Lord is he that upholdeth my soul : reward thou evil unto mine enemies; destroy them in thine anger, for thy righteousness' sake, O Lord my strength, and my defender. *Ps.* Save me, O God, for thy name's sake : and avenge me in thy strength.

G. O Lord our Governor : how excellent is thy name in all the world. ℣. Thou hast set thy glory : above the heavens. **A.** Alleluya. ℣. Sing we merrily unto God our strength : make a cheerful noise unto the God of Jacob, take the psalm, the merry harp with the lute. **O.** The statutes of the Lord are right, and rejoice the heart : sweeter also than honey, and the honeycomb; moreover by them is thy servant taught. **C.** Seek ye first of all the kingdom of God : and all these things shall be added unto you, saith the Lord.

702 Trinity x. *Dum clamarem.* When I called upon the Lord, he regarded my petition, yea, from the battle that was against me : and he hath brought them down, even he that is of old, and endureth for ever ; O cast thy burden upon the Lord, and he shall nourish thee. *Ps.* Hear my prayer, O Lord, and hide not thyself from my petition : take heed unto me, and hear me.

G. Keep me, O Lord, as the apple of an eye : hide me under the shadow of thy wings. ℣. Let my sentence come forth from thy presence : and let thine eyes look upon the thing that is equal. **A.** Alleluya. ℣. O Lord God of my salvation : I have cried day and night before thee. **O.** Unto thee, O Lord, lift I up my soul : O my God, in thee have I trusted, let me not be confounded : neither let mine enemies triumph over me : for all they that look for thee shall not be ashamed. **C.** Thou shalt be pleased with the sacrifice of righteousness, with the burnt offerings and oblations : upon thine altar, O Lord.

703 Trinity xi. *Deus in loco sancto.* God in his holy habitation, it is he that maketh brethren to be of one mind in an house : he will give the dominion and pre-eminence unto his people. *Ps.* Let God arise, and let his enemies be scattered : let them also that hate him flee before him.

G. My heart hath trusted in God and I am helped : therefore my heart danceth for joy, and in my song will I praise him. ℣. Unto thee will I cry, O Lord : be not silent, O my God, nor depart from me. **A.** Alleluya. ℣. Lord,

SUNDAYS AFTER TRINITY

thou hast been our refuge : from one generation to another. **O.** I will magnify thee, O Lord, for thou hast set me up : and not made my foes to triumph over me ; O Lord, my God, I cried unto thee : and thou hast healed me. **C.** Honour the Lord with thy substance, and with the firstfruits of all thine increase : so shall thy barns be filled with plenty, and thy presses shall burst out with new wine.

704 TRINITY xii. *Deus in adjutorium.* Haste thee, O God, unto my rescue, and save me : O Lord, make haste to my deliverance : let mine enemies be ashamed and confounded, that seek after my soul. *Ps.* Let them be turned backward, and put to confusion : that wish me evil.

G. I will alway give thanks unto the Lord : his praise shall ever be in my mouth. ℣. My soul shall make her boast in the Lord . the humble shall hear thereof, and be glad. **A.** Alleluya ! ℣. O come, let us sing unto the Lord : let us heartily rejoice in the strength of our salvation. **O.** Moses besought the Lord his God, and said : Why, O Lord, doth thy wrath wax hot against thy people ? turn from thy fierce wrath ; remember Abraham, Isaac, and Jacob, to whom thou swarest to give a land flowing with milk and honey : and the Lord repented of the evil which he thought to do unto his people. **C.** The earth, O Lord, is filled with the fruit of thy works : that thou mayest bring food out of the earth, and wine that maketh glad the heart of man ; and oil to make him a cheerful countenance : and bread to strengthen man's heart.

705 TRINITY xiii. *Respice, Domine.* Look, O Lord, graciously upon thy covenant, and forsake not the congregation of thy poor for ever : arise, O Lord, maintain thine own cause ; and be not unmindful of the voices of them that seek thee. *Ps.* O God, wherefore art thou absent from us so long : why is thy wrath so hot against the sheep of thy pasture ?

G. Look upon thy covenant, O Lord : and forget not the congregation of the poor for ever. ℣. Arise, O Lord, maintain thine own cause : remember how the foolish man blasphemeth thee daily. **A.** Alleluya. ℣. For the Lord is a great God : and a great King over all the earth. **O.** My hope hath been in thee, O Lord : I have said, Thou art my God, my time is in thy hand. **C.** Thou hast given us Bread from heaven, O Lord : having every delight, and every taste of sweetness.

706 TRINITY xiv. *Protector noster.* Behold, O God, our defender, and look upon the face of thine Anointed : for one day in thy courts is better than a thousand. *Ps.* O how amiable are thy dwellings, thou Lord of hosts : my soul hath a desire and longing to enter into the courts of the Lord.

G. It is a good thing to give thanks unto the Lord : and to sing praises unto thy name, O Most Highest. ℣. To tell of thy loving-kindness early in the morning : and of thy truth in the night-season. **A.** Alleluya. ℣. O give thanks unto the Lord, and call upon his name : tell the people what things he hath done. **O.** The Angel of the Lord tarrieth round about them that fear him, and delivereth them : O taste and see how gracious the Lord is. **C.** The Bread that I will give is my Flesh : which I will give for the life of the world.

INTROITS AND ANTHEMS

707 Trinity xv. *Inclina, Domine.* Bow down, O Lord, thine ear to me, and hear me : O my God, save thy servant, that trusteth in thee : have mercy upon me, O Lord, for I have called daily upon thee. *Ps.* Comfort the soul of thy servant : for unto thee, O Lord, do I lift up my soul.

G. It is better to trust in the Lord : than to put any confidence in man. **℣.** It is better to trust in the Lord : than to put any confidence in princes. **A.** Alleluya. ℣ My heart is ready, O God, my heart is ready : I will sing, yea, I will praise thee, with the best member that I have. **O.** I waited patiently for the Lord, and he inclined unto me : he heard my calling, and hath put a new song in my mouth, even a thanksgiving unto our God. **C.** Whoso eateth my Flesh, and drinketh my Blood, dwelleth in me, and I in him, saith the Lord.

708 Trinity xvi. *Miserere mihi.* Have mercy upon me, O Lord, for I have called daily upon thee : for thou, O Lord, art gracious and merciful, and plenteous in thy loving-kindnesses toward all them that call upon thee. *Ps.* Bow down thine ear, O Lord, and hear me : for I am poor and in misery.

G. The heathen shall fear thy name, O Lord : and all the kings of the earth thy majesty. ℣. When the Lord shall build up Sion : and when his glory shall appear. **A.** Alleluya. ℣. Ye that fear the Lord, put your trust in the Lord : he is their helper and defender. **O.** Look down, O Lord, to help me : let them be ashamed, and confounded together, that seek after my soul to destroy it; look down, O Lord, to help me. **C.** O Lord, I will make mention of thy righteousness only : thou, O God, hast taught me from my youth up until now; forsake me not, O God, in mine old age, when I am gray-headed.

709 Trinity xvii. *Justus es, Domine.* Righteous art thou, O Lord, and true is thy judgement : deal with thy servant according unto thy merciful kindness. *Ps.* Blessed are those that are undefiled in the way : and walk in the law of the Lord.

G. Blessed is the people whose God is the Lord : and blessed are the folk that he hath chosen to him to be his inheritance. ℣. By the Word of the Lord were the heavens made : and all the hosts of them by the breath of his mouth. **A.** Alleluya. ℣. The right hand of the Lord bringeth mighty things to pass : the right hand of the Lord hath the pre-eminence. **O.** I, Daniel, prayed unto the Lord my God, and said, Hear, O our God, the prayer of thy servant : cause thy face to shine upon thy sanctuary ; and behold, O God, this thy people, who are called by thy name. **C.** Promise unto the Lord your God, and keep it; all ye that are round about him bring presents unto him that ought to be feared : he shall refrain the spirit of princes ; and is wonderful among the kings of the ea th.

710 Trinity xviii. *Da pacem.* Give peace, O Lord, to them that wait for thee, and let thy Prophets be found faithful : regard the prayers of thy servant, and of thy people Israel. *Ps.* I was glad when they said unto me : We will go into the house of the Lord.

SUNDAYS AFTER TRINITY

G. I was glad when they said unto me : We will go into the house of the Lord. ℣. Peace be within thy walls : and plenteousness within thy palaces. A. Alleluya. ℣. I was glad when they said unto me : We will go into the house of the Lord. O. Moses consecrated an altar unto the Lord, offering burnt offerings upon it, and sacrificing peace offerings : and he made an evening sacrifice for a sweet-smelling savour unto the Lord God, in the sight of the children of Israel. C. Bring offerings and come into his courts : O worship the Lord in the beauty of holiness.

711 TRINITY xix. *Salus populi.* I am the saving health of my people, saith the Lord God : out of whatsoever tribulation they shall pray to me, I will surely hear them ; and I will be their God for ever and ever. *Ps.* Hear my law, O my people : incline your ears unto the words of my mouth.

G. Let my prayer be set forth in thy sight : O Lord, as the incense. ℣. And let the lifting up of my hands be an evening sacrifice. A. Alleluya. ℣. They that put their trust in the Lord shall be even as the Mount Sion : he who dwelleth in Jerusalem may not be removed, but standeth fast for ever. O. Though I walk in the midst of trouble, yet shalt thou refresh me, O Lord : thou shalt stretch forth thy right hand upon the furiousness of mine enemies, and thy right hand shall save me. C. Thou hast charged that we shall diligently keep thy commandments : O that my ways were made so direct, that I might keep thy statutes.

712 TRINITY xx. *Omnia quae fecisti.* Everything that thou hast brought upon us, O Lord God, thou hast done in righteousness and judgement : for we have trespassed against thee, and have not obeyed thy commandments, but give glory and honour to thy name, and deal with us according to the multitude of thy tender mercies. *Ps.* Great is the Lord, and highly to be praised : in the city of our God, even upon his holy hill.

G. The eyes of all wait upon thee, O Lord : and thou givest them their meat in due season. ℣. Thou openest thine hand : and fillest all things living with plenteousness. A. Alleluya. ℣. Out of the deep have I called unto thee, O Lord : Lord, hear my voice. O. By the waters of Babylon we sat down and wept : when we remembered thee, O Sion. C. Remember thy word unto thy servant, O Lord, wherein thou hast caused me to put my trust : the same is my comfort in my affliction.

713 TRINITY xxi. *In voluntate tua.* O Lord Almighty, everything is in subjection unto thee : and there is no man that is able to resist thy power : for thou hast created everything, heaven and earth, and all the wonders which beneath the vault of heaven are contained ; thou art the Lord and King of all things. *Ps.* Blessed are those that are undefiled in the way : and walk in the law of the Lord.

G. Lord, thou hast been our refuge : from one generation to another. ℣. Before the mountains were brought forth, or ever the earth and the world were made : thou art God from everlasting, and world without end. A. Alleluya. ℣. Praise

INTROITS AND ANTHEMS

the Lord, O my soul; while I live will I praise the Lord : yea, as long as I have any being, I will sing praises unto my God. **O.** There was a man in the land of Uz, whose name was Job, perfect and upright, and one that feared God : and Satan sought to tempt him; and power was given him by the Lord over his possessions and over his flesh : and he destroyed all his substance and his sons, and he smote his flesh with sore boils. **C.** My soul hath longed for thy salvation : and I have a good hope in thy word; when wilt thou be avenged of them that persecute me? they persecute me falsely : O be thou my help, O Lord my God.

714 TRINITY xxii. *Si iniquitates.* If thou, O Lord, wilt be extreme to mark iniquities: Lord, who may abide it? for unto thee belongeth mercy, O God of Israel. *Ps.* Out of the deep have I called unto thee, O Lord : Lord, hear my voice.

G. Behold, how good and joyful a thing it is : brethren, to dwell together in unity. ℣. It is like the precious ointment upon the head : that ran down unto the beard, even unto Aaron's beard. **A.** Alleluya. ℣. He healeth those that are broken in heart : and bindeth up their wounds. **O.** Remember me, O Lord, King of all power : and put a well-ordered speech in my mouth, that my words may be pleasing in thy sight. **C.** I say unto you, there is joy among the Angels of God over one sinner that repenteth.

715 TRINITY xxiii, AND ALL FOLLOWING SUNDAYS UNTIL ADVENT. *Dicit Dominus.* Thus saith the Lord, I know the thoughts that I think towards you, thoughts of peace, and not of affliction : ye shall call upon me, and I will hearken unto you, and will bring again your captivity from every nation. *Ps.* Lord, thou art become gracious unto thy land : thou hast turned away the captivity of Jacob.

G. It is thou, O Lord, that savest us from our enemies : and puttest them to confusion that hate us. ℣. We make our boast of God all day long : and will praise thy name for ever. **A.** Alleluya. ℣. He maketh peace in thy borders : and filleth thee with the flour of wheat. **O.** Out of the deep have I called unto thee, O Lord : Lord, hear my voice. **C.** Verily I say unto you, what things soever ye desire, when ye pray : believe that ye receive them, and it shall be done unto you.

716 DEDICATION OF A CHURCH. *Terribilis est.* O how dreadful is this place! this is the house of God, and gate of heaven : and men shall call it the Palace of God. (*In Eastertide*, alleluya.) *Ps.* The Lord is King, and hath put on glorious apparel : the Lord hath put on his apparel, and girded himself with strength.

G. This dwelling is God's handywork; it is a mystery beyond all price, that cannot be spoken against. ℣. O God, in whose presence the choirs of Angels are standing, graciously hear the prayers of thy servants. **A.** Alleluya. ℣. I will worship toward thy holy temple : and will sing praises unto thy name. *Or*, **T.** *Ps.* 84. 1-5. **O.** O Lord God, in the uprightness of mine heart I have willingly offered all the things; and now I have seen with joy thy people, which are present here ; O Lord God of Israel : keep for ever this imagination of the heart of thy people. (*In Eastertide*, alleluya.) **C.** My house shall be called of all

SAINTS' DAYS

nations the house of prayer, saith the Lord : in it every one that asketh receiveth : and he that seeketh findeth, and to him that knocketh it shall be opened.

717 AN APOSTLE OR EVANGELIST. *Mihi autem.* Right dear, O God, are thy friends unto me, and held in highest honour : their rule and governance is exceeding steadfast. *Ps.* O Lord, thou hast searched me out, and known me : thou knowest my down-sitting, and mine up-rising.

G. Their sound is gone out into all lands : and their words unto the ends of the world. ℣. The heavens declare the glory of God : and the firmament showeth his handywork. **A.** Alleluya. I first will say to Sion, Behold, behold them; and I will give to Jerusalem one that bringeth good tidings. *Or,* **T.** Blessed is the man that feareth the Lord : he hath great delight in his commandments. ℣. His seed shall be mighty upon earth : the generation of the faithful shall be blessed. ℣. Riches and plenteousness shall be in his house : and his righteousness endureth for ever. **O.** Thou shalt make them princes in all lands : they shall remember thy name, O Lord, from one generation to another. **C.** Ye which have followed me shall sit upon twelve thrones judging the twelve tribes of Israel, saith the Lord.

718 A MARTYR. *Gloria et honore.* With glory and worship hast thou crowned him : thou madest him to have dominion over the works of thy fingers. *Ps.* O Lord our Governor : how excellent is thy name in all the world.

G. Thou hast set, O Lord : a crown of pure gold upon his head. ℣. Thou hast given him his heart's desire : and hast not denied him the request of his lips. **A.** Alleluya. ℣. Thou hast (*as above*). **O.** With glory (*as Introit*). **C.** He that will come after me, let him deny himself : and take up his cross and follow me.

719 AN APOSTLE OR MARTYR IN EASTERTIDE. *Protexisti.* Thou hast hidden me, O God, from the gathering together of the froward, alleluya : from the insurrection of the workers of iniquity, alleluya, alleluya. *Ps.* Hear my voice, O God, in my prayer : preserve my life from fear of the enemy.

A. Alleluya. ℣. Thou hast set, *as* 718. **A.** Alleluya. ℣. The righteous shall be joyful in the Lord, and shall put his trust in him : and all the upright of heart shall be thankful. **O.** The righteous (*as above*). **C.** *As* 718.

720 A BISHOP. *Statuit ei.* The Lord hath established a covenant of peace with him, and made him a chief of his people : that he should have the priestly dignity for ever and ever. (*In Eastertide,* alleluya, alleluya.) *Ps.* My song shall be alway : of the loving-kindness of the Lord.

G. Behold a mighty prelate, who in his lifetime was pleasing unto God. ℣. There was none found like unto him, that observed the law of the Most High. **A.** Alleluya. ℣. The righteous shall blossom as the lily : and shall flourish for ever before the Lord. **O.** My truth also and my mercy shall be with him : and in my name shall his horn be exalted. **C.** *As* 718.

INTROITS AND ANTHEMS

721 A BISHOP. *Sacerdotes Dei.* O ye priests of God, bless ye the Lord : O ye holy and humble men of heart, exalt him for ever. (*In Eastertide*, alleluya, alleluya.) *Ps.* O all ye works of the Lord, bless ye the Lord : praise him, and magnify him for ever.

A. Alleluya. ℣. The Lord loved him, and adorned him, and clothed him with a robe of glory. **G., O., C.** *As* 720.

722 A CONFESSOR. *Os justi.* The mouth of the righteous is exercised in wisdom, and his tongue will be talking of equity : the law of his God is in his heart. *Ps.* Fret not thyself because of the ungodly : neither be thou envious against the evil doers.

G. I have found David my servant, with my holy oil have I anointed him : my hand shall hold him fast, and my arm shall strengthen him. ℣. The enemy shall not be able to do him violence : the son of wickedness shall not hurt him. **A.** Alleluya. ℣. I have laid help upon one that is mighty : I have exalted one chosen out of the people. *Or*, **T.** 717. **O.** My truth also and my mercy shall be with him : and in my name shall his horn be exalted. **C.** Lord, thou deliveredst unto me five talents; behold, I have gained beside them five talents more : Well done, thou good and faithful servant, thou hast been faithful over a few things ; I will make thee ruler over many things, enter thou into the joy of thy Lord.

723 A VIRGIN. *Loquebar.* I have spoken of thy testimonies in the sight of princes, and was not confounded : and my delight hath been in thy commandments, which I have loved greatly. *Ps.* Blessed are those that are undefiled in the way : and walk in the law of the Lord.

G. Thou hast loved righteousness and hated iniquity. ℣. Wherefore God, even thy God : hath anointed thee with the oil of gladness. **A.** Alleluya. ℣. Full of grace are thy lips : because God hath blessed thee for ever. *Or*, **T.** Full of (*as above*). **O.** The virgins that be her fellows shall bear her company : and shall be brought unto thee. **C.** The Kingdom of heaven is likened unto a man that is a merchant, seeking goodly pearls : who, when he had found one pearl of great price, went and sold all that he had and bought it.

724 CONVERSION OF ST. PAUL. *Laetemur.* Rejoice we all, and praise the Lord, devoutly keeping this festival with due solemnity : wherein Paul, the blessed Apostle, by his wonderful conversion, did greatly illumine this present world. *Ps.* For the light of his holy preaching : and for the conversion of blessed Paul.

G. He that wrought effectually in Peter to the apostleship, was also mighty in me toward the Gentiles : and they perceived the grace that was given unto me. ℣. The grace of God which was bestowed upon me was not in vain : but his grace ever abideth in me. **A.** Alleluya. ℣. The Apostle Paul, the chosen vessel : is very worthy to be extolled. **O.** How dear are thy friends unto me, O God : O how great is the pre-eminence of them. **C.** Amen, I say unto you, that ye which have forsaken all and followed me, shall receive an hundredfold, and shall inherit everlasting life.

SAINTS' DAYS

725 Feasts of the Blessed Virgin.

The Purification. *Suscepimus* (700).

G. We have waited, O God, for thy loving-kindness in the midst of thy temple : according to thy name, O Lord, so is thy praise unto the world's end. ℣. Like as we have heard, so have we seen, in the city of our God, even upon his holy hill. A. Alleluya. ℣. I will worship toward thy holy temple : and will sing praises unto thy name. *Or*, T. *Nunc dimittis*. O. Full of grace are thy lips : because God hath blessed thee for ever. C. It was revealed unto Simeon by the Holy Spirit, that he should not see death, before he had seen the Lord's Anointed.

The Annunciation. *Rorate, caeli*. Drop down, ye heavens, from above, and let the skies pour down righteousness : let the earth open, and let her bring forth salvation. (*In Eastertide*, alleluya, alleluya.) *Ps.* And let righteousness spring up together : I the Lord have created it.

G. (*Before Easter*.) Lift up your heads, O ye gates; and be ye lift up, ye everlasting doors : and the King of Glory shall come in. ℣. Who shall ascend unto the hill of the Lord : or who shall stand in his holy place? even he that hath clean hands and a pure heart. *And* T. And the Angel came in unto her, and said, Hail, Mary, full of grace : the Lord is with thee. ℣. Blessed art thou among women : and blessed is the fruit of thy womb. ℣. The Holy Ghost shall come upon thee : and the power of the Highest shall overshadow thee. ℣. Therefore also that holy thing which shall be born of thee : shall be called the Son of God. A. (*In Eastertide*.) Alleluya. ℣. And the Angel came in unto her, and said, Hail, Mary, full of grace, the Lord is with thee : blessed art thou among women. A. Alleluya. ℣. (*One of those of the Resurrection*.) O. Hail, Mary, full of grace, the Lord is with thee : blessed art thou among women, and blessed is the fruit of thy womb. C. Behold, a Virgin shall conceive, and bear a Son : and his name shall be called Emmanuel.

726 St. Philip and St. James. *Exclamaverunt*. They cried unto thee, O Lord, in the time of their misery and trouble : and thou didst hear them from thy holy heaven, alleluya, alleluya. *Ps.* Rejoice in the Lord, O ye righteous : for it becometh well the just to be thankful.

A. Alleluya. ℣. The righteous man shall stand in great boldness : before the face of such as have afflicted him. A. Alleluya. ℣. Did not our heart burn within us : while he talked with us by the way concerning Jesus? O. O Lord, the very heavens shall praise thy wondrous works : and thy truth in the congregation of the saints, alleluya, alleluya. C. Have I been so long time with you, and yet hast thou not known me, Philip? he that hath seen me hath seen the Father, alleluya : Believest thou not that I am in the Father, and the Father in me? Alleluya, alleluya.

727 St. John Baptist. *De ventre*. From the womb of my mother the Lord hath called me by my name : and hath made my mouth as it were a sharp sword, beneath the shadow of his hand hath he hidden me, and hath made me like to a polished

INTROITS AND ANTHEMS

arrow. *Ps.* It is a good thing to give thanks unto the Lord : and to sing praises unto thy name, O Most Highest.

G. Before I formed thee in the belly, I knew thee : and before thou camest forth out of the womb I sanctified thee. ℣. The Lord put forth his hand and touched my mouth : and said unto me. A. Alleluya. ℣. Among them that are born of women, a greater hath not risen than John the Baptist. O. The righteous shall flourish like a palm-tree : and shall spread abroad like a cedar in Libanus. C. And thou, child, shalt be called the Prophet of the Highest : for thou shalt go before the face of the Lord to prepare his ways.

728 St. Peter. *Nunc scio.* Now I know of a surety that the Lord hath sent his Angel : and hath delivered me from the hand of Herod, and from all the expectation of the people of the Jews. *Ps.* And when Peter was come to himself, he said :

G. Thou shalt make them princes over all the earth : they shall have thy name in remembrance, O Lord. ℣. Instead of thy fathers thou shalt have children : therefore shall the people give thanks unto thee. A. Alleluya. ℣. Thou art Simon Bar-Jona, and to thee hath been revealed the word of the Father; not by flesh and blood, but by my Father which is in heaven. O. *As* 717. C. Thou art Peter, and upon this rock I will build my Church.

729 The Name of Jesus. *In nomine Jesu.* In the name of Jesus let every knee be bowed, of things above, and things in earth, and things beneath : and let every tongue confess and acknowledge that Jesus Christ is Lord, to the glory of God the Father. *Ps.* O praise the Lord, for the Lord is gracious : sing praises unto his name, for it is lovely.

G. God the Father hath set Jesus Christ at his own right hand in the heavenly places, far above all principality, and power, and might, and dominion : and every name that is named, not only in this world, but also in that which is to come, and hath put all things under his feet. ℣. Help us, O God of our salvation : and for the glory of thy name, O Lord, deliver us, and be merciful unto our sins, for thy name's sake. A. Alleluya. ℣. Sweet to the heart is the name of Jesus Christ : music to the ear, honey to the taste, which turns the heart to joy and praise, and puts to flight the despite of the world. O. In my name shall they cast out devils, they shall speak with new tongues; they shall take up serpents : and if they drink any deadly thing, it shall not hurt them ; they shall lay hands on the sick and they shall recover, alleluya. C. To him that overcometh will I give to eat of the hidden manna : and will give him a white stone, and in the stone a new name written, which no man knoweth, saving he that receiveth it, alleluya.

730 St. Michael and all Angels. *Benedicite Dominum.* O praise the Lord, all ye his Angels: ye mighty in power, that execute his commandment, and hearken unto the voice of his words. *Ps.* Praise the Lord, O my soul : and all that is within me, praise his holy name.

G. (*As Introit.*) A. Alleluya. ℣. In the presence of the Angels will I praise thee, O Lord my God. O. An Angel stood by the altar of the temple, having a

SAINTS' DAYS

golden censer in his hand : and there was given unto him much incense, and the smoke of the incense ascended up before God, alleluya. **C.** O ye Angels of the Lord, bless ye the Lord : sing ye praises and magnify him above all for ever.

731 ALL SAINTS. *Gaudeamus.* Rejoice we all, and praise the Lord, celebrating a holy day in honour of *All Hallows* : *in whose solemnity* the Angels are joyful, and glorify the Son of God. *Ps.* Rejoice in the Lord, O ye righteous : for it becometh well the just to be thankful.

On St. Mary Magdalene's Day, and other Saints' Days, the name of the Saint may be substituted; and on the lesser days of the Blessed Virgin may be substituted the Virgin Mary : for whose Conception (*or* Visitation, *or* Nativity).

G. O fear the Lord, all ye saints of his : for they that fear him lack nothing. ℣. But they that seek the Lord : shall want no manner of thing that is good. **A.** Alleluya. ℣. The saints shall judge the nations, and have dominion over the people : and their Lord shall reign for ever. **O.** O God, wonderful art thou in thy holy places : even the God of Israel, he will give strength and power unto his people ; blessed be God, alleluya. **C.** The souls of the righteous are in the hand of God, and there shall no torment touch them : in the sight of the unwise they seemed to die ; but they are in peace.

732 FOR THE BLESSED SACRAMENT. *Cibavit eos.* He fed them also with the finest wheat flour, alleluya : and with honey from the rock hath he satisfied them, alleluya, alleluya, alleluya. *Ps.* Sing we merrily unto God our helper : make a cheerful noise unto the God of Jacob.

G. The eyes of all wait upon thee, O Lord : and thou givest them their meat in due season. ℣. Thou openest thine hand : and fillest all things living with plenteousness. **A.** Alleluya. ℣. My Flesh is meat indeed, and my Blood is drink indeed : he that eateth my Flesh and drinketh my Blood, dwelleth in me, and I in him. **O.** The priests of the Lord do offer the offerings of the Lord made by fire and the bread of their God : therefore they shall be holy unto their God, and not profane the name of their God, alleluya. **C.** As often as ye do eat of this Bread, and drink of this Cup, ye do show the Lord's death till he come : wherefore, whosoever shall eat of this Bread, and drink of this Cup of the Lord, unworthily, shall be guilty of the Body and Blood of the Lord, alleluya.

733 IN COMMEMORATION OF THE DEPARTED. *Requiem eternam.* Rest eternal grant unto them, O Lord : and may light perpetual shine upon them. *Ps.* Thou, O God, art praised in Sion : and unto thee shall the vow be performed in Jerusalem; thou that hearest the prayer, unto thee shall all flesh come. (*The* Gloria *is omitted.*)

G. Rest eternal grant to them, O Lord, and may light perpetual shine upon them. ℣. Let their souls dwell at ease : and their seed inherit the land. *Or this* **G.** Yea, though I walk through the valley of the shadow of death, I will fear no evil : for thou, O Lord, art with me. ℣. Thy rod and thy staff, they have been my comfort. **T.** (*Day of Burial.*) Like as the hart desireth the water brooks : so longeth my soul for thee, my God. ℣. My soul is athirst for God, yea, even for the living God : when shall I come to appear before the

INTROITS AND ANTHEMS

presence of God ? ℣. My tears have been my meat day and night : while they daily say unto me, Where is now thy God? T. (*Other occasions.*) Out of the deep have I called unto thee, O Lord : Lord, hearken unto my voice. ℣. O let thine ears consider well the supplication of thy servant. ℣. If thou, O Lord, wilt be extreme to mark what is done amiss : Lord, who may abide it. ℣. For to thee belongeth mercy and compassion, and for thy Name's sake have I waited for thee, O Lord. O. (*General.*) O Lord Jesu Christ, King of Majesty, deliver the souls of all the faithful departed from the hand of hell, and from the pit of destruction : deliver them from the lion's mouth, that the grave devour them not; that they go not down to the realms of darkness : but let Michael, the holy standard-bearer, make speed to restore them to the brightness of glory : which thou promisedst in ages past to Abraham and his seed. ℣. Sacrifice and prayer do we offer to thee, O Lord : do thou accept them for the souls departed in whose memory we make this oblation : and grant them, Lord, to pass from death unto life : which thou promisedst in ages past to Abraham and his seed. O. (*All Souls.*) O kind Creator, who hast recalled the first man to eternal glory : O Good Shepherd, who on thy loving shoulder hast brought again the lost sheep to the sheepfold : O just Judge, when thou shalt come for judgement, deliver from death the souls of them whom thou hast redeemed : nor give to the beasts the souls of them that confess thee, nor forsake them utterly for ever. C. (*Day of Burial, Anniversaries, All Souls.*) To them in whose memory the Body of Christ is received, grant, O Lord, rest everlasting. ℣. And may light perpetual shine upon them. To them in whose memory the Blood of Christ is received, grant, O Lord, rest everlasting. C. (*Other occasions.*) May light eternal shine, O Lord, upon them, for endless ages with thy blessed ones, for thou art gracious. ℣. Rest eternal grant to them, O Lord, and may light perpetual shine upon them : for endless ages with thy blessed ones, for thou art gracious.

THE GREAT ADVENT ANTIPHONS.

734 Dec. 16. *O Sapientia.* O Wisdom, which camest out of the mouth of the Most High, and reachest from one end to another, mightily and sweetly ordering all things : Come and teach us the way of prudence.

Dec. 17. *O Adonai.* O Adonai, and Leader of the house of Israel, who appearedst in the bush to Moses in a flame of fire, and gavest him the Law in Sinai : Come and deliver us with an outstretched arm.

Dec. 18. *O Radix Jesse.* O Root of Jesse, which standest for an ensign of the people, at whom kings shall shut their mouths, to whom the Gentiles shall seek : Come and deliver us, and tarry not.

Dec. 19. *O Clavis David.* O Key of David, and Sceptre of the house of Israel; that openest, and no man shutteth, and shuttest, and no man openeth : Come and bring the prisoner out of the prison-house, and him that sitteth in darkness and the shadow of death.

Dec. 20. *O Oriens.* O Day-spring, Brightness of Light Everlasting, and Sun of Righteousness : Come and enlighten him that sitteth in darkness and the shadow of death.

THE ADVENT ANTIPHONS

Dec. 21. *O Rex gentium.* O King of the Nations, and their desire; the Corner-stone, who makest both one : Come and save mankind, whom thou formedst of clay.

Dec. 22. *O Emmanuel.* O Emmanuel, our King and Lawgiver, the Desire of all nations, and their Salvation : Come and save us, O Lord our God.

Dec. 23. *O Virgo virginum.* O Virgin of virgins, how shall this be? For neither before thee was any like thee, nor shall there be after. Daughters of Jerusalem, why marvel ye at me? The thing which ye behold is a divine mystery.

(*The melodies of the Advent Antiphons are obtainable from St. Mary's Convent, Wantage.*)

735

A PROSE FOR ADVENT OR OTHER TIMES

Suitable also for use in procession.

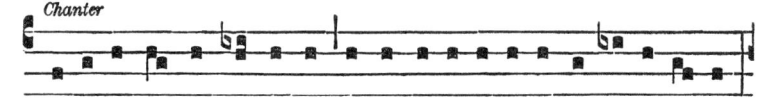

Mode i.   Rorate, caeli.   arr. J. H. A.

Chanter   *Chorus*

Drop down, ye hea-vens, from a - bove,* and let the skies pour down right-eous-ness.

Chanter

1 Be not wroth ve - ry sore, O Lord, nei - ther re-mem-ber in - i - qui - ty for ev - er:

INTROITS AND ANTHEMS

thy ho-ly ci-ties are a wil-der-ness, Si-on is a wil-der-ness, Je-ru-sa-lem a de-so-la-tion: our ho-ly and our beauti-ful house, where our fa-thers praised thee.

Chorus

℞. Drop down, ye hea-vens, from a-bove, and let the skies pour down right-eous-ness.

Chanter

2 We have sin-ned, and are as an un-clean thing, and we all do fade as a leaf:

ADVENT PROSE

and our in-i-qui-ties, like the wind, have ta-ken us a-way; thou hast hid thy face from us: and hast con-sum-ed us, be-cause of our in-i-qui-ties.

Chorus

R. Drop down, ye hea-vens, from a-bove, and let the skies pour down right-eous-ness.

Chanter

3 Ye are my wit-ness-es, saith the Lord, and my ser-vant whom I have cho-sen;

INTROITS AND ANTHEMS

that ye may know me and be-lieve me: I, e-ven I, am the Lord, and be-side me there is no Sa-viour: and there is none that can de-liv-er out of my hand.

Chorus

℟. *Drop down, ye hea-vens, from a-bove, and let the skies pour down right-eous-ness.*

Chanter

4. Com-fort ye, com-fort ye my peo-ple, my sal-va-tion shall not tar-ry:

888

ADVENT PROSE

I have blot-ted out as a thick cloud thy trans-gres-sions: Fear not, for I will save thee: for I am the Lord thy God, the Ho-ly One of Is-ra-el, thy Re-deem-er.

Chorus

℞. Drop down, ye hea-vens from a-bove, and let the skies pour down right-eous-ness.

(*The Chanter may sing an occasional verse unaccompanied.*)

FAUX-BOURDON *for optional use*
In free speech-rhythm (as plainsong), unaccompanied

Drop down, ye hea-vens from a-bove, and let the skies pour down right-eous-ness.

C.F.

INTROITS AND ANTHEMS
736
LENT PROSE Attende.

arr. J. H. A.

Hear us, O Lord, * *have mer-cy up-on us: for we have sin-ned a-gainst thee.*

1. *To thee, Re-deem-er, on thy throne of glo-ry: lift we our weep-ing eyes in ho-ly plead-ings: lis-ten O Je-su, to our sup-pli-ca-tions.* ℟. *Hear*

(Quarter bar pauses to be observed only if the sense admits.)

2. O thou chief Corner-stone, Right Hand of the Father : Way of Salvation, Gate of Life Celestial : cleanse thou our sinful souls from all defilement. ℟. *Hear us, O Lord,*

3. God, we implore thee, in thy glory seated : bow down and hearken to thy weeping children : pity and pardon all our grievous trespasses. ℟. *Hear us, O Lord,*

4. Sins oft committed now we lay before thee : with true contrition, now no more we veil them : grant us, Redeemer, loving absolution. ℟. *Hear us, O Lord,*

5. Innocent, captive, taken unresisting : falsely accused, and for us sinners sentenced, save us, we pray thee, Jesu our Redeemer. ℟. *Hear us, O Lord,*

GOOD FRIDAY

737

GOOD FRIDAY : THE REPROACHES

℣. *Two chanters*   Mode i.

1 O my peo - ple, what have I done un - to thee,

or where - in have I wea-ri - ed thee? Tes-ti - fy a-gainst me.

Be - cause I brought thee forth from the land of E - gypt,

thou pre - par - edst a Cross for thy Sa - viour.

Two clerks

Ho - ly God, Ho - ly, Migh - ty, Ho - ly and

Im - mor - tal, have mer - cy up - on us.

The Choir repeat
Holy God, &c.

℣. *Chanters*

2 Be-cause I led thee through the de - sert for - ty years,

INTROITS AND ANTHEMS

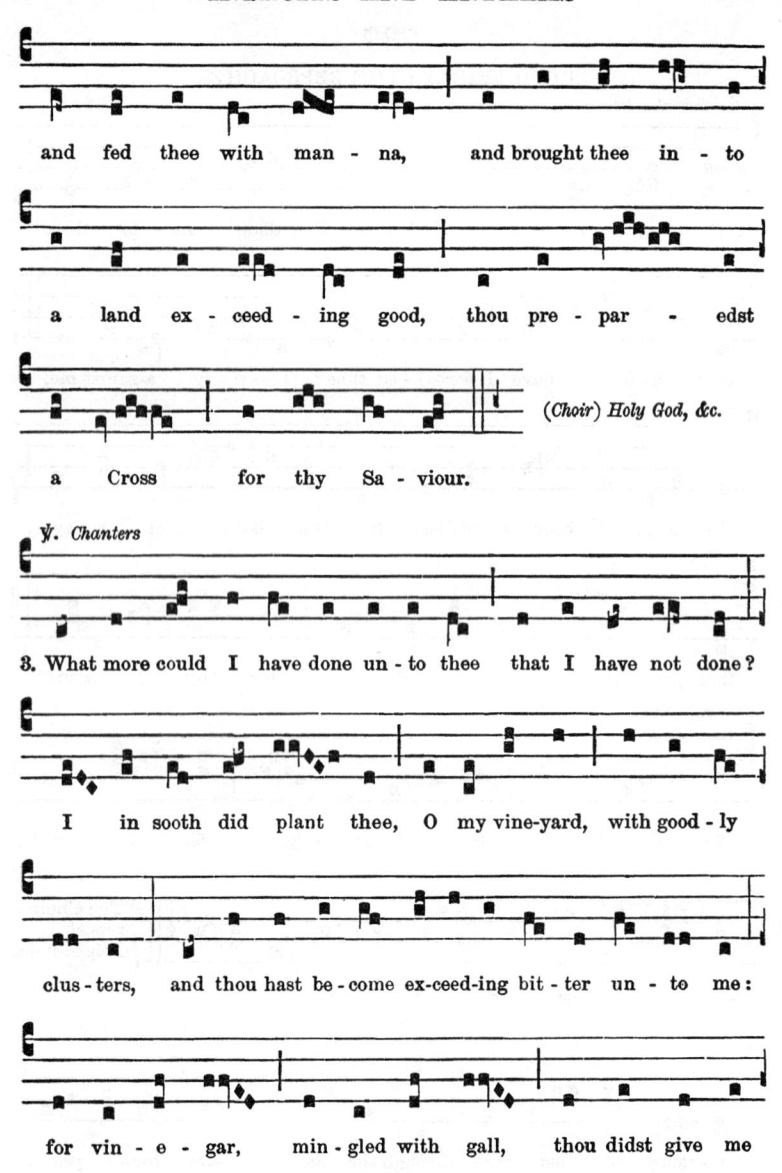

and fed thee with man - na, and brought thee in - to

a land ex - ceed - ing good, thou pre - par - edst

(*Choir*) Holy God, &c.

a Cross for thy Sa - viour.

℣. *Chanters*

3. What more could I have done un - to thee that I have not done?

I in sooth did plant thee, O my vine-yard, with good - ly

clus - ters, and thou hast be - come ex - ceed - ing bit - ter un - to me:

for vin - e - gar, min - gled with gall, thou didst give me

GOOD FRIDAY

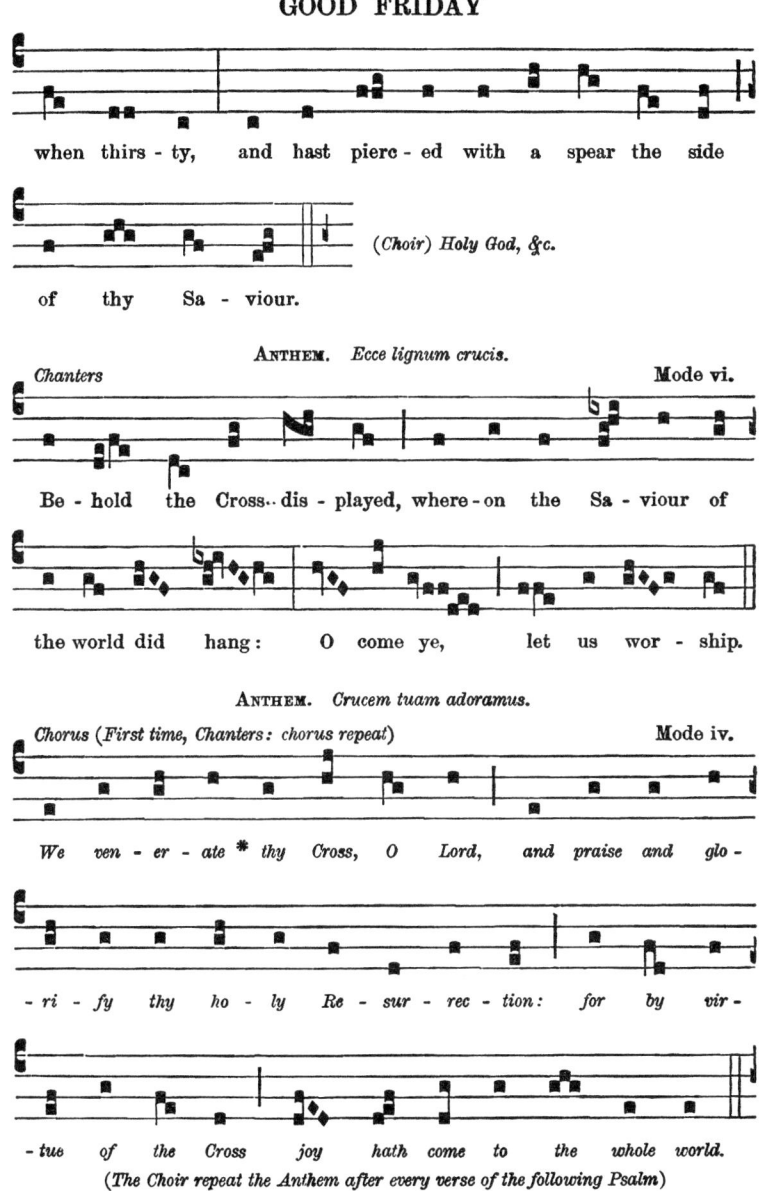

when thirs - ty, and hast pierc - ed with a spear the side of thy Sa - viour.

(Choir) Holy God, &c.

ANTHEM. *Ecce lignum crucis.*

Chanters   Mode vi.

Be - hold the Cross dis - played, where - on the Sa - viour of the world did hang: O come ye, let us wor - ship.

ANTHEM. *Crucem tuam adoramus.*

Chorus (First time, Chanters: chorus repeat)   Mode iv.

We ven - er - ate * thy Cross, O Lord, and praise and glo - ri - fy thy ho - ly Re - sur - rec - tion: for by vir - tue of the Cross joy hath come to the whole world.

(The Choir repeat the Anthem after every verse of the following Psalm)

INTROITS AND ANTHEMS

PSALM 67. *Deus misereatur.*

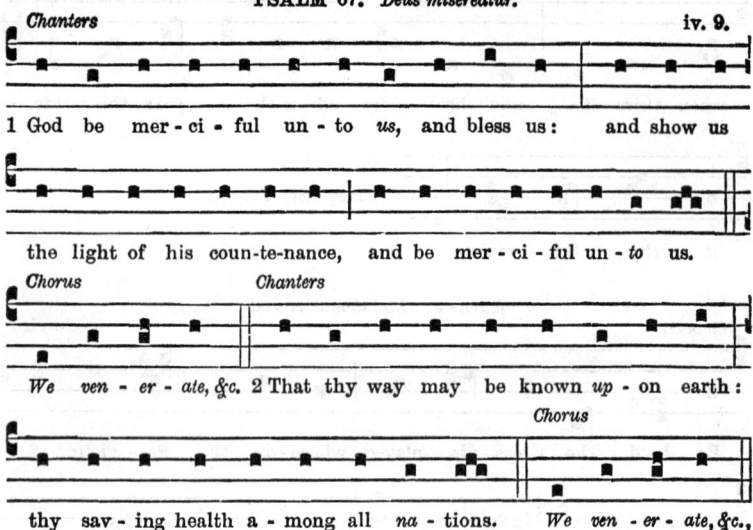

Chanters   iv. 9.

1 God be mer-ci-ful un-to *us,* and bless us : and show us the light of his coun-te-nance, and be mer-ci-ful un-*to* us.

Chorus   *Chanters*

We ven-er-ate, &c. 2 That thy way may be known *up*-on earth : thy sav-ing health a-mong all *na*-tions. *We ven-er-ate, &c.,*

and the rest of the Psalm in the same way, thus :—

3 Let the people praise *thee,* O God : yea let all the people *praise* thee.
   We venerate, &c.

4 O let the nations rejoice *and* be glad : for thou shalt judge the folk **righteously** | and govern the nations up-*on* earth.
   We venerate, &c.

5 Let the people praise *thee,* O God : let all the people *praise* thee.
   We venerate, &c.

ending thus (without Gloria) :—

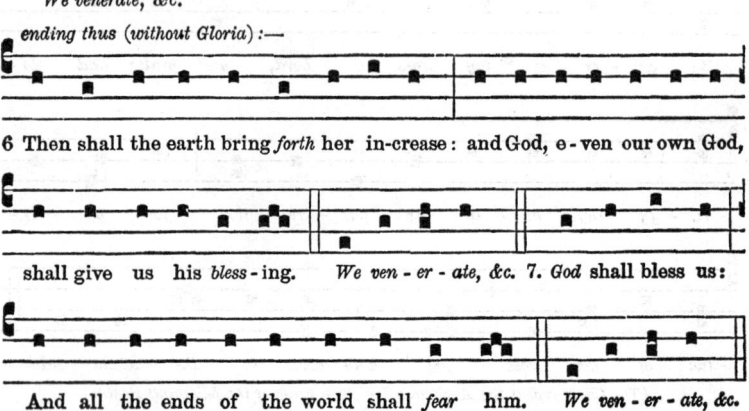

6 Then shall the earth bring *forth* her in-crease : and God, e-ven our own God, shall give us his *bless*-ing. *We ven-er-ate, &c.* 7. God shall bless us : And all the ends of the world shall *fear* him. *We ven-er-ate, &c.*

GOOD FRIDAY

737 (*continued*)

Hymns 95 and 96 (Part 1), opening with the following verse (which is repeated after each verse as chorus), and ending with the Doxology and chorus.

Crux fidelis

CRUX FIDELIS.
Chorus (First time, Chanters : chorus repeat)　　　　　　　　　　　arr. J. H. A.

Faith-ful Cross! a-bove all o-ther, One and on-ly no-ble Tree!

None in fo-liage, none in blos-som, None in fruit thy peer may be;

Sweet-est wood, and sweet-est i-ron! Sweet-est weight is hung on thee.

738

At Evensong.　　　EASTER GRAIL AND ALLELUYA

Grail: This is the day which the Lord hath made : we will be joyful and glad in it. ℣. O give thanks unto the Lord, for he is gracious : and his mercy endureth for ever. *Alleluya* : Christ our Passover is sacrificed for us. Alleluya.

For Plainsong melody see Grails, Alleluyas, and Tracts (*S. Mary's Convent, Wantage*).

INTROITS AND ANTHEMS
739
AN EVENING RESPOND
(Suitable after a late Evening Service)

Mode vi. In manus tuas arr. J. H. A.

℟. In-to thy hands, O Lord,* I com-mend my spi-rit.

℣. Thou hast re-deem-ed me, O Lord, thou God of truth.

℟. I com-mend my spi-rit. ℣. Glo-ry be to the Fa-ther,

and to the Son, and to the Ho-ly Ghost. ℟. Into thy hands, &c.

EASTERTIDE—EVENING RESPOND

740

Mode vi.   THE SAME, IN EASTERTIDE   *arr.* J. H. A.

℟. In - to thy hands, O Lord, I com-mend my spi-rit.* Al - le - lu - ya, al - le - lu - ya. ℣. Thou hast re-deem-ed me, O Lord, thou God of truth. ℟. Al - le - lu - ya, al - le - lu - ya.

℣. Glo - ry be to the Fa-ther, and to the Son, and to the Ho-ly Ghost.
℟. Into, &c.

INTROITS AND ANTHEMS

AT THE HOLY COMMUNION

741

Benedictus.

Blessed is he that cometh in the name of the Lord. Hosanna in the highest.

742

Agnus Dei.

O Lamb of God, that takest away the sins of the world, have mercy upon us.

O Lamb of God, that takest away the sins of the world, have mercy upon us.

O Lamb of God, that takest away the sins of the world, grant us thy peace.

743

Agnus Dei.

O Lamb of God, that takest away the sins of the world, grant them rest.

O Lamb of God, that takest away the sins of the world, grant them rest.

O Lamb of God, that takest away the sins of the world, grant them rest everlasting.

744

RUSSIAN CONTAKION OF THE DEPARTED (KIEFF MELODY)

Со святыми упокой, Хрісте

(Μετὰ τῶν ἁγίων ἀνάπαυσον, Χριστέ)

The words translated by W. J. BIRKBECK; *the music edited by* SIR WALTER PARRATT.

Give .. rest, O . Christ, to thy .. ser-vant with thy Saints:

RUSSIAN CONTAKION OF THE DEPARTED

744 (continued)

where sorrow and pain are no more; neither sighing, but life everlasting. Thou only art immortal, the Creator and Maker of man: and we are mortal, formed of the earth, and unto earth shall we return:

INTROITS AND ANTHEMS

744 (*continued*)

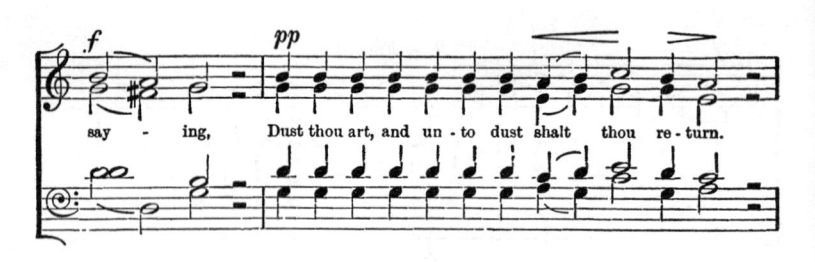

[*Copyright, 1902, by Novello & Co., Ltd.*]

This Contakion should, if possible, be sung by the Choir unaccompanied. It can be sung by men's voices only, if transposed a fifth lower.

APPENDIX

PART I

Additional plainsong melodies

1

PLAINSONG MELODY TO HYMN 81

Mode ii.   *arr.* J. H. A.

A - men.

APPENDIX

2

PLAINSONG MELODY TO HYMN 104

Mode viii. *arr. J. H. A.*

A - men.

3

PALM SUNDAY PROCESSION

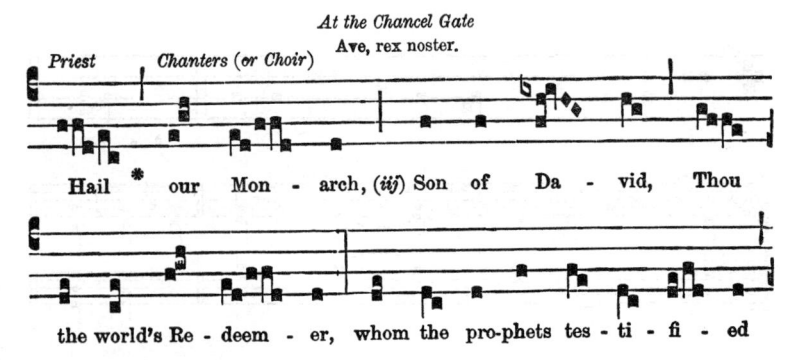

At the Chancel Gate
Ave, rex noster.

Priest — *Chanters (or Choir)*

Hail * our Mon - arch, (*iij*) Son of Da - vid, Thou the world's Re - deem - er, whom the pro - phets tes - ti - fi - ed

APPENDIX

should come un-to the house of Is - ra - el, to be their Sa - viour.

For Thou in truth wast sent from the Fa - ther un - to us

to be our sa - viour vic - tim, for whom the right - eous in

all a - ges from the be - gin - - ning have been wait - ing.

And now Ho - san - na to the Son of Da - vid:

Bles-sed is he that com - eth in the Name of the Lord:

Ho - san - na in the high - est.

APPENDIX

4

FURTHER VERSES OF ALLELUIATIC PSALM 115. SEE No. 626

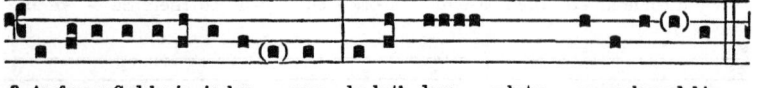

3 As for our God, he is in hea - ven: he hath done whatso - ev - er pleas-ed him.
4 Their i-dols are sil - ver and gold: e - ven the work of men's hands.
15 Ye are the bless-ed of the Lord: who made hea-ven and earth.
16 All the whole hea-vens are the Lord's: the earth hath he given to the chil-dren of men.
17 The dead praise not thee, O Lord: nei-ther all they that go down in - to si - lence.
18 But we will praise the Lord: from this time forth for ev - er - more.

For Gloria see p. 814.

5

EXAMPLES OF VERSICLES AND RESPONSES FOR THE PROCESSION

Ending with a monosyllable.

℣. Blessed is he that cometh in the name of the Lord:
℞. God is the Lord who hath shewed us light.
℣. O Saviour of the world . . . redeem - ed us:
℞. Save us and help us, we humbly beseech thee, O Lord.
℣. O Lord, hear our prayer:
℞. And let our cry come un - to thee.

Ending otherwise.

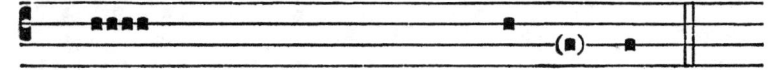

℣. The voice of the Lord is up - on the wa - ters:
℣. Tell it out among the hea - then:
℞. That the Lord hath reigned from the tree, Alle - lu - ya.
℣. Let thy priests be clothed with right - eous - ness:
℞. And let thy saints sing with joy - ful - ness.

APPENDIX

6

ALTERNATIVE MELODY FOR NOS. 255, 261, 262

Mode viii. *arr.* J. H. A.

A - men.

7

ALTERNATIVE TUNE TO HYMN 172

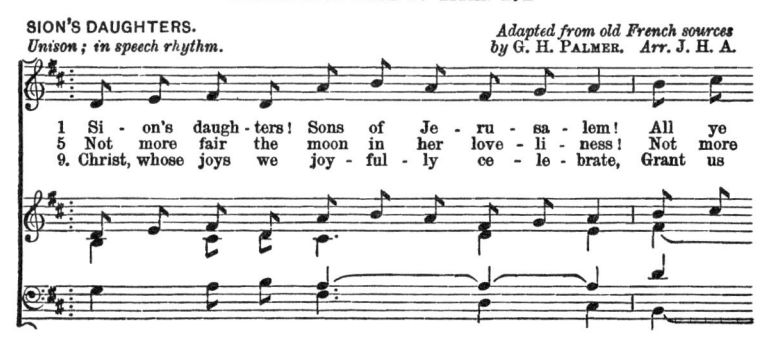

SION'S DAUGHTERS.
Unison; in speech rhythm.

Adapted from old French sources by G. H. PALMER. *Arr.* J. H. A.

1 Si - on's daugh - ters! Sons of Je - ru - sa - lem! All ye
5 Not more fair the moon in her love - li - ness! Not more
9. Christ, whose joys we joy - ful - ly ce - le - brate, Grant us

APPENDIX
7 (continued)

hosts of heaven-ly chi-val-ry! Lift your voi-ces, sing-ing right mer-ri-ly Al-le-lu-ya!
bright the sun in his ma-jes-ty! Like an ar-my splen-did and ter-ri-ble, Ranged for bat-tle—
all a place with thy cho-sen ones, True de-lights, in-ef-fa-ble hap-pi-ness, Rest e-ter-nal.

Fine.

2 Christ our Sa-viour weds on this fes-ti-val Ho-ly Church, the Pat-tern of Right-eous-ness, Whom from
6 So the Church shines forth on her pil-grim-age, Signed with Jor-dan's wa-ters of pen-i-tence. Drawn to

906

APPENDIX

7 (*continued*)

depths of ut - ter - most mi - se - ry He hath res - cued.
hear the wis - dom of So - lo - mon, From the world's end.

3 Now the Bride re - ceiv - eth his be - ni - son, Tas - teth
7 So, fore - told by fi - gures and pro - phe - cies, Clothed in

now the joys of the Pa - ra - clete; Kings and
nup - tial ves - ture of cha - ri - ty, Joined with

queens with ju - bi - lant me - lo - dy Call her bless - ed.
Christ, o'er hea - ven's glad ci - ti - zens Now she reign - eth.

APPENDIX

7 (*continued*)

4 Mo-ther meet for sin - ful hu - man - i - ty, Life's sure ha-
8 Wel-come! feast of light and fe - li - ci - ty, Bride to Bride-

-ven, rest for the sor - row - ful, Strong pro - tec - tress,
-groom join - ing in u - ni - ty; In her mys - tic

born in a mys - te - ry Ev - er won - drous.
mar - riage is ty - pi - fied Our sal - va - tion.

APPENDIX

PART II

Additional tunes which do not enter into the general scheme of the book

Copyright note. Acknowledgements of copyright in such words as are printed in this Part of the Appendix are listed in the General Acknowledgements on pp. xxii–xxiii, but the references there given are to the numbers of the hymns as they appear in the body of the book.

8

ALTERNATIVE TUNE TO HYMN 30

NORTHROP. (C.M.)
Cheerfully ♩ = 126.

A. NORTHROP (?)
(*Tune often sung in Cornwall*).

Nahum Tate, 1652–1715.

WHILE shepherds watched their flocks by night,
All seated on the ground,
The Angel of the Lord came down,
And glory shone around.

2 'Fear not,' said he (for mighty dread
Had seized their troubled mind);
'Glad tidings of great joy I bring
To you and all mankind.

3 'To you in David's town this day
Is born of David's line
A Saviour, who is Christ the Lord;
And this shall be the sign:

4 'The heavenly Babe you there shall find
To human view displayed,
All meanly wrapped in swathing bands,
And in a manger laid.'

5 Thus spake the Seraph; and forthwith
Appeared a shining throng
Of Angels praising God, who thus
Addressed their joyful song:

6. 'All glory be to God on high,
And on the earth be peace;
Good-will henceforth from heaven to men
Begin and never cease.'

APPENDIX

9

Alternative Tune to Hymn 41

EPIPHANY. (11 10. 11 10.)
Cheerfully ♩ = 76 (♪ = 152).

F. J. Thrupp, 1827-67.

Bishop R. Heber, 1783–1826.

BRIGHTEST and best of the sons of the morning,
Dawn on our darkness and lend us thine aid
Star of the East, the horizon adorning,
    Guide where our infant Redeemer is laid.

2 Cold on his cradle the dew-drops are shining,
    Low lies his head with the beasts of the stall:
Angels adore him in slumber reclining,
    Maker and Monarch and Saviour of all.

3 Say, shall we yield him, in costly devotion,
    Odours of Edom and offerings divine ?
Gems of the mountain and pearls of the ocean,
    Myrrh from the forest or gold from the mine ?

4 Vainly we offer each ample oblation,
    Vainly with gifts would his favour secure;
Richer by far is the heart's adoration,
    Dearer to God are the prayers of the poor.

Unison. 5. Brightest and best of the sons of the morning,
    Dawn on our darkness and lend us thine aid;
Star of the East, the horizon adorning,
    Guide where our infant Redeemer is laid.

APPENDIX

10

ALTERNATIVE TUNE TO HYMN 76

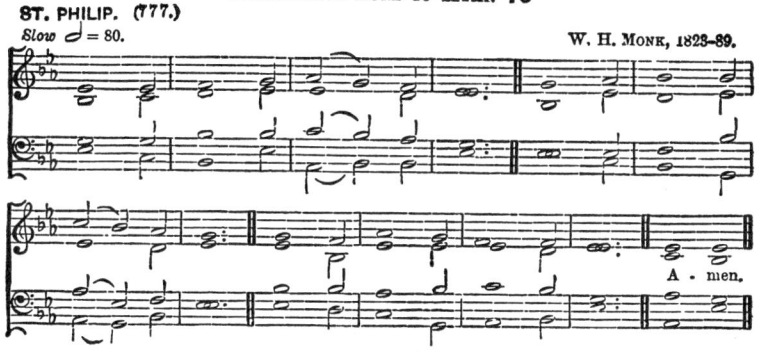

ST. PHILIP. (777.)
Slow ♩ = 80.
W. H. MONK, 1823–89.

Isaac Williams‡, 1802–65.

LORD, in this thy mercy's day,
Ere it pass for ay away,
On our knees we fall and pray.

2 Holy Jesu, grant us tears,
Fill us with heart-searching fears,
Ere that awful doom appears.

3 Lord, on us thy Spirit pour,
Kneeling lowly at the door,
Ere it close for evermore.

4 By thy night of agony,
By thy supplicating cry,
By thy willingness to die;

5 By thy tears of bitter woe
For Jerusalem below,
Let us not thy love forgo.

6. Grant us 'neath thy wings a place,
Lest we lose this day of grace,
Ere we shall behold thy face.

APPENDIX

11

ALTERNATIVE TUNE TO HYMN 111

DAS LEIDEN DES HERRN. (L. M.)

Very slow ♩ = 63.

German Traditional Melody.

Another harmonization of this tune will be found at No. 387.

F. W. Faber, 1814–63.

1. O COME and mourn with me awhile;
   See Mary calls us to her side;
   O come and let us mourn with her:
   Jesus, our Love, is crucified.

2. Have we no tears to shed for him,
   While soldiers scoff and Jews deride?
   Ah, look how patiently he hangs:
   Jesus, our Love, is crucified.

3.* How fast his hands and feet are nailed;
   His blessèd tongue with thirst is tied;
   His failing eyes are blind with blood:
   Jesus, our Love is crucified.

4.* His Mother cannot reach his face;
   She stands in helplessness beside;
   Her heart is martyred with her Son's:
   Jesus, our Love, is crucified.

5. Seven times he spoke, seven words of love;
   And all three hours his silence cried
   For mercy on the souls of men:
   Jesus, our Love, is crucified.

6.* O break, O break, hard heart of mine;
   Thy weak self-love and guilty pride
   His Pilate and his Judas were:
   Jesus, our Love, is crucified.

7.* A broken heart, a fount of tears,
   Ask, and they will not be denied;
   A broken heart love's cradle is:
   Jesus, our Love, is crucified.

8. O Love of God! O sin of Man!
   In this dread act your strength is tried;
   And victory remains with Love:
   For he, our Love, is crucified.

APPENDIX

12

ALTERNATIVE TUNE TO HYMN 129

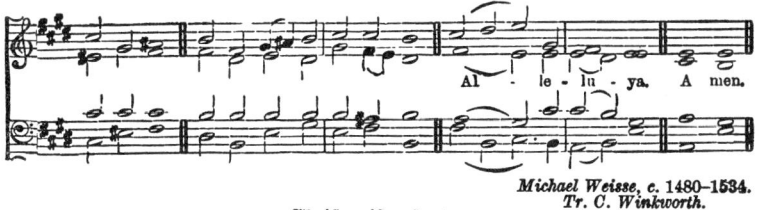

WIRTEMBURG. (7 7. 7 7. 4.)
In moderate time ♩ = 72.

W. H. MONK, 1823–89 (*founded on* '*Straf mich nicht,*' *Dresden,* 1694).

Christus ist erstanden.

Michael Weisse, c. 1480–1534.
Tr. C. Winkworth.

CHRIST the Lord is risen again!
Christ hath broken every chain!
Hark, the angels shout for joy,
Singing evermore on high,
    Alleluya!

2 He who gave for us his life,
Who for us endured the strife,
Is our Paschal Lamb to-day!
We too sing for joy, and say
    Alleluya!

3 He who bore all pain and loss
Comfortless upon the Cross,
Lives in glory now on high,
Pleads for us, and hears our cry.
    Alleluya!

4 He whose path no records tell,
Who descended into hell;
Who the strong man armed hath bound,
Now in highest heaven is crowned.
    Alleluya!

5 Now he bids us tell abroad
How the lost may be restored,
How the penitent forgiven,
How we too may enter heaven.
    Alleluya!

6. Thou, our Paschal Lamb indeed,
Christ, to-day thy people feed;
Take our sins and guilt away,
That we all may sing for ay,
    Alleluya!

APPENDIX

13
A Higher Setting of the Tune to Hymn 133

EASTER HYMN. (7 4. 7 4. D.)

Slow ♩ = 58.

Altered from a melody in Lyra Davidica, 1708.

Lyra Davidica (1708), and the *Supplement* (1816).
Based partly on Surrexit Christus hodie.
c. 14th cent.

JESUS Christ is risen to-day,   Alleluya!
  Our triumphant holy day,   Alleluya!
Who did once, upon the Cross,   Alleluya!
Suffer to redeem our loss.   Alleluya!

2 Hymns of praise then let us sing,   Alleluya!
Unto Christ, our heavenly King,   Alleluya!
Who endured the Cross and grave,   Alleluya!
Sinners to redeem and save.   Alleluya!

3. But the pains that he endured   Alleluya!
Our salvation have procured;   Alleluya!
Now above the sky he's King,   Alleluya!
Where the angels ever sing.   Alleluya!

APPENDIX

14

A Higher Setting of the Tune to Hymn 162

NICAEA. (11 12 12 10.)

Moderately slow ♩ = 63.

J. B. Dykes, 1823–76.

Bishop R. Heber, 1783–1826.

HOLY, Holy, Holy! Lord God Almighty!
Early in the morning our song shall rise to thee;
Holy, Holy, Holy! Merciful and mighty!
God in three Persons, blessèd Trinity!

2 Holy, Holy, Holy! all the Saints adore thee,
Casting down their golden crowns around the glassy sea,
Cherubim and Seraphim falling down before thee,
Which wert, and art, and evermore shalt be.

3 Holy, Holy, Holy! though the darkness hide thee,
Though the eye of sinful man thy glory may not see,
Only thou art holy, there is none beside thee
Perfect in power, in love, and purity.

Unison. 4. Holy, Holy, Holy! Lord God Almighty!
All thy works shall praise thy name, in earth, and sky, and sea;
Holy Holy, Holy! Merciful and mighty!
God in three Persons, blessèd Trinity! Amen.

APPENDIX

15

ALTERNATIVE TUNE TO HYMN 268

NUTFIELD. (84.84.88.84.)
In moderate time ♩ = 72.
W. H. MONK, 1823–89.

1. *Bishop Heber* (1827).   2. *Archbishop Whately* (1855).

GOD, that madest earth and heaven,
 Darkness and light;
Who the day for toil hast given,
 For rest the night;
May thine Angel-guards defend us,
Slumber sweet thy mercy send us,
Holy dreams and hopes attend us,
 This livelong night.

2. Guard us waking, guard us sleeping;
 And, when we die,
May we in thy mighty keeping
 All peaceful lie:
When the last dread call shall wake us,
Do not thou our God forsake us,
But to reign in glory take us
 With thee on high.

APPENDIX

16

ALTERNATIVE TUNE TO HYMN 277

ST. CLEMENT. (98.98)
In moderate time ♩ = 112.

C. C. SCHOLEFIELD, 1839–1905.

A-men.

J. Ellerton, 1826–93.

THE day thou gavest Lord, is ended,
　The darkness falls at thy behest;
To thee our morning hymns ascended,
　Thy praise shall sanctify our rest.

2 We thank thee that thy Church unsleeping,
　　While earth rolls onward into light,
　Through all the world her watch is keeping,
　　And rests not now by day or night.

3 As o'er each continent and island
　　The dawn leads on another day,
　The voice of prayer is never silent,
　　Nor dies the strain of praise away.

4 The sun that bids us rest is waking
　　Our brethren 'neath the western sky,
　And hour by hour fresh lips are making
　　Thy wondrous doings heard on high.

5. So be it, Lord; thy throne shall never,
　　Like earth's proud empires, pass away;
　Thy kingdom stands, and grows for ever,
　　Till all thy creatures own thy sway.

APPENDIX

17

ALTERNATIVE TUNE TO HYMN 292

GOLDEN SHEAVES. (87 87. D.)
Brightly ♩ = 100.

A. S. SULLIVAN, 1842–1900.

A - men.

[*By permission of Novello & Co. Ltd.*]

W. *Chatterton Dix*, 1837–98.

TO thee, O Lord, our hearts we raise
  In hymns of adoration;
To thee bring sacrifice of praise
  With shouts of exultation.
Bright robes of gold the fields adorn,
  The hills with joy are ringing,
The valleys stand so thick with corn
  That even they are singing.

2 And now, on this our festal day,
  Thy bounteous hand confessing,
Upon thine altar, Lord, we lay
  The first-fruits of thy blessing;
By thee the souls of men are fed
  With gifts of grace supernal;
Thou who dost give us daily bread,
  Give us the Bread eternal.

3 We bear the burden of the day,
  And often toil seems dreary;
But labour ends with sunset ray,
  And rest is for the weary;
May we, the Angel-reaping o'er,
  Stand at the last accepted,
Christ's golden sheaves for evermore
  To garners bright elected.

Unison. 4. O, blessèd is that land of God,
    Where Saints abide for ever;
  Where golden fields spread fair and broad,
    Where flows the crystal river:
  The strains of all its holy throng
    With ours to-day are blending;
  Thrice blessèd is that harvest-song
    Which never hath an ending.

APPENDIX

18

ALTERNATIVE TUNE TO HYMN 366

BULLINGER. (8 5 8 3.)
In moderate time ♩ = 92.

E W. BULLINGER, 1837-1913.

A . men.

J. M. Neale, 1818–66.

ART thou weary, art thou languid,
    Art thou sore distrest ?
'Come to me,' saith One, 'and coming
      Be at rest!'

2 Hath he marks to lead me to him,
    If he be my Guide ?
'In his feet and hands are wound-prints,
      And his side.'

3 Is there diadem as Monarch
    That his brow adorns ?
'Yea, a crown, in very surety,
      But of thorns.'

4 If I find him, if I follow,
    What his guerdon here ?
'Many a sorrow, many a labour,
      Many a tear.'

Unison. 5 If I still hold closely to him,
    What hath he at last ?
'Sorrow vanquished, labour ended,
      Jordan past.'

6 If I ask him to receive me,
    Will he say me nay ?
'Not till earth, and not till heaven
      Pass away.'

Unison. 7. Finding, following, keeping, **struggling,**
    Is he sure to bless ?
'Angels, Martyrs, Prophets, Virgins,
      Answer, Yes!'

APPENDIX

19

ALTERNATIVE TUNE TO HYMN 417

ST. CHRYSOSTOM. (8 8. 8 8. 8 8.)   J. BARNBY, 1838-96.

In moderate time ♩ = 92.

Slower.

[By permission of Novello & Co. Ltd.]

H. Collins, 1827-1919.

JESU, my Lord, my God, my All,
Hear me, blest Saviour, when I call;
Hear me, and from thy dwelling-place
Pour down the riches of thy grace:

Jesu, my Lord, I thee adore,
O make me love thee more and more.

2 Jesu, too late I thee have sought,
How can I love thee as I ought?
And how extol thy matchless fame,
The glorious beauty of thy name?

3 Jesu, what didst thou find in me,
That thou hast dealt so lovingly?
How great the joy that thou hast brought,
So far exceeding hope or thought!

4. Jesu, of thee shall be my song,
To thee my heart and soul belong;
All that I am or have is thine,
And thou, sweet Saviour, thou art mine.

APPENDIX

20

ALTERNATIVE TUNE TO HYMN 469

MAIDSTONE (7 7. 7 7. D.)
In moderate time ♩ = 100.

W. B. GILBERT, 1829–1910.

[By permission of Novello & Co., Ltd.]

H. F. Lyte, 1793–1847.

PLEASANT are thy courts above
In the land of light and love;
Pleasant are thy courts below
In this land of sin and woe:
O, my spirit longs and faints
For the converse of thy Saints,
For the brightness of thy face,
For thy fullness, God of grace.

2 Happy birds that sing and fly
Round thy altars, O most High;
Happier souls that find a rest
In a heavenly Father's breast;
Like the wandering dove that found
No repose on earth around,
They can to their ark repair
And enjoy it ever there.

3 Happy souls, their praises flow
Even in this vale of woe;
Waters in the desert rise,
Manna feeds them from the skies;
On they go from strength to strength,
Till they reach thy throne at length,
At thy feet adoring fall,
Who hast led them safe through all.

4. Lord, be mine this prize to win,
Guide me through a world of sin,
Keep me by thy saving grace,
Give me at thy side a place;
Sun and shield alike thou art,
Guide and guard my erring heart.
Grace and glory flow from thee;
Shower, O shower them, Lord, on me.

APPENDIX

21

ALTERNATIVE TUNE TO HYMN 527

REQUIEM. (87.87.77.)
In moderate time ♩ = 72.

W. SCHULTHES, 1816–79.

G. Thring, 1823–1903.

THOU to whom the sick and dying
  Ever came, nor came in vain,
Still with healing words replying
  To the wearied cry of pain,
    Hear us, Jesu, as we meet
    Suppliants at thy mercy-seat.

APPENDIX

2 Still the weary, sick, and dying
 Need a brother's, sister's care;
On thy higher help relying
 May we now their burden share,
  Bringing all our offerings meet,
  Suppliants at thy mercy-seat.

3 May each child of thine be willing,
 Willing both in hand and heart,
All the law of love fulfilling,
 Ever comfort to impart;
  Ever bringing offerings meet.
  Suppliant to thy mercy-seat.

4. So may sickness, sin, and sadness
 To thy healing power yield,
Till the sick and sad, in gladness,
 Rescued, ransomed, cleansèd, healed,
  One in thee together meet,
  Pardoned at thy judgement-seat.

APPENDIX

22

ALTERNATIVE TUNE TO HYMN 567

BENEATH THE CROSS. (76.86.86 86.)

In moderate time ♩ = 80.

D. SANKEY, 1840–1908

[*From 'Sacred Songs and Solos,' by permission of Messrs. Marshall, Morgan & Scott, Ltd.*]

Elizabeth C. Clephane, 1830–69.

BENEATH the Cross of Jesus
  I fain would take my stand—
The shadow of a mighty Rock
  Within a weary land;
A home within a wilderness,
  A rest upon the way,
From the burning of the noontide heat
  And the burden of the day.

APPENDIX

2 O safe and happy shelter!
   O refuge tried and sweet!
O trysting-place where heaven's love
   And heaven's justice meet!
As to the exiled patriarch
   That wondrous dream was given,
So seems my Saviour's Cross to me
   A ladder up to heaven.

3 There lies beneath its shadow,
   But on the further side,
The darkness of an open grave
   That gapes both deep and wide;
And there between us stands the Cross,
   Two arms outstretched to save,
Like a watchman set to guard the way
   From that eternal grave.

4 Upon that Cross of Jesus
   Mine eye at times can see
The very dying form of One,
   Who suffered there for me.
And from my stricken heart, with tears,
   Two wonders I confess,—
The wonders of redeeming love,
   And my own worthlessness.

5. I take, O Cross, thy shadow,
   For my abiding-place;
I ask no other sunshine than
   The sunshine of his face:
Content to let the world go by,
   To know no gain nor loss,—
My sinful self my only shame,
   My glory all—the Cross.

APPENDIX

23

ALTERNATIVE TUNE TO HYMN 641

FOR ALL THE SAINTS. (10 10. 10 4.)

In moderate time ♩ = 100.

J. BARNBY, 1838–96.

Bishop W. W. How, 1823–97.

FOR all the Saints who from their labours rest,
  Who thee by faith before the world confest,
Thy name, O Jesu, be for ever blest.

Alleluya!

2 Thou wast their Rock, their Fortress, and their Might;
  Thou, Lord, their Captain in the well-fought fight;
  Thou in the darkness drear their one true Light.

APPENDIX

3 O may thy soldiers, faithful, true, and bold,
Fight as the Saints who nobly fought of old,
And win, with them, the victor's crown of gold.

4*O blest communion! fellowship divine!
We feebly struggle, they in glory shine;
Yet all are one in thee, for all are thine.

5 And when the strife is fierce, the warfare long,
Steals on the ear the distant triumph-song,
And hearts are brave again, and arms are strong.

6 The golden evening brightens in the west;
Soon, soon to faithful warriors cometh rest:
Sweet is the calm of Paradise the blest.

7*But lo! there breaks a yet more glorious day;
The Saints triumphant rise in bright array:
The King of glory passes on his way.

8.*From earth's wide bounds, from ocean's farthest coast,
Through gates of pearl streams in the countless host,
Singing to Father, Son, and Holy Ghost.

APPENDIX

PART III

Tunes and settings transferred from the body of the book in 1933

24

ALTERNATIVE ACCOMPANIMENT TO HYMN 8.

VENI EMMANUEL. (88. 88. 88.)
In free rhythm ♩ = 80. Unison.

Adapted by T. HELMORE
'*from a French Missal.*'

APPENDIX

Veni, veni, Emmanuel. 18*th cent.* *Tr. T. A. L.*

O COME, O come, Emmanuel!
Redeem thy captive Israel,
That into exile drear is gone
Far from the face of God's dear Son.
Rejoice! Rejoice! Emmanuel
Shall come to thee, O Israel.

2 O come, thou Branch of Jesse! draw
The quarry from the lion's claw;
From the dread caverns of the grave,
From nether hell, thy people save.

3 O come, O come, thou Dayspring bright!
Pour on our souls thy healing light;
Dispel the long night's lingering gloom,
And pierce the shadows of the tomb.

4 O come, thou Lord of David's Key!
The royal door fling wide and free;
Safeguard for us the heavenward road,
And bar the way to death's abode.

5. O come, O come, Adonaï,
Who in thy glorious majesty
From that high mountain clothed with awe
Gavest thy folk the elder law.

APPENDIX

25

Alternative Tune to Hymn 91

DALKEITH. (10 10. 10 10.)
In moderate time ♩ = 80.

T. Hewlett, 1845-74.

S. J. Stone, 1839-1900.

WEARY of earth and laden with my sin,
　　I look at heaven and long to enter in;
But there no evil thing may find a home,
And yet I hear a voice that bids me 'Come.'

2 So vile I am, how dare I hope to stand
　　In the pure glory of that holy land?
Before the whiteness of that throne appear?
Yet there are hands stretched out to draw me near.

APPENDIX

3 The while I fain would tread the heavenly way,
  Evil is ever with me day by day;
  Yet on mine ears the gracious tidings fall,
  'Repent, confess, thou shalt be loosed from all.'

4 It is the voice of Jesus that I hear,
  His are the hands stretched out to draw me near,
  And his the Blood that can for all atone,
  And set me faultless there before the throne.

Part 2.

5 O great Absolver, grant my soul may wear
  The lowliest garb of penitence and prayer,
  That in the Father's courts my glorious dress
  May be the garment of thy righteousness.

6 Yea, thou wilt answer for me, righteous Lord;
  Thine all the merits, mine the great reward;
  Thine the sharp thorns, and mine the golden crown;
  Mine the life won, and thine the life laid down.

7. Naught can I bring, dear Lord, for all I owe,
  Yet let my full heart what it can bestow;
  Like Mary's gift, let my devotion prove,
  Forgiven greatly, how I greatly love.

APPENDIX

26

ADDITIONAL MODERN TUNE TO HYMN 125

JESU REDEMPTOR SAECULI. (L. M.) *Adapted from a melody in* LA FEILLÉE, 'Méthode du plain-chant,' 1782.
In free rhythm ♩ = 76.
To be sung in unison.

OFFICE HYMN. *Low Sunday till Ascension*, E.   Ad cenam Agni providi.   *7th cent.* Tr. J. M. Neale.

THE Lamb's high banquet we await
In snow-white robes of royal state;
And now, the Red Sea's channel past,
To Christ, our Prince, we sing at last.

2 Upon the altar of the Cross
His Body hath redeemed our loss;
And tasting of his roseate Blood
Our life is hid with him in God.

3 That Paschal eve God's arm was bared;
The devastating Angel spared:
By strength of hand our hosts went free
From Pharaoh's ruthless tyranny.

4 Now Christ our Paschal Lamb is slain,
The Lamb of God that knows no stain;
The true Oblation offered here,
Our own unleavened Bread sincere.

5 O thou from whom hell's monarch flies,
O great, O very Sacrifice,
Thy captive people are set free,
And endless life restored in thee.

6 For Christ, arising from the dead,
From conquered hell victorious sped;
He thrusts the tyrant down to chains,
And Paradise for man regains.

7 Maker of all, to thee we pray,
Fulfil in us thy joy to-day;
When death assails, grant, Lord, that we
May share thy Paschal victory.

8. To thee who, dead, again dost live,
All glory, Lord, thy people give;
All glory, as is ever meet,
To Father and to Paraclete. **Amen.**

APPENDIX

27

ALTERNATIVE TUNE TO HYMN 127

EVERTON. (8 7. 8 7. D.)
In moderate time ♩ = 96.

H. SMART, 1813-79.

Bishop Chr. Wordsworth, 1807-85.

ALLELUYA! Alleluya!
  Hearts to heaven and voices raise;
Sing to God a hymn of gladness,
  Sing to God a hymn of praise;
He who on the Cross a victim
  For the world's salvation bled,
Jesus Christ, the King of glory,
  Now is risen from the dead.

2 Christ is risen, Christ the first-fruits
    Of the holy harvest field,
  Which will all its full abundance
    At his second coming yield;
  Then the golden ears of harvest
    Will their heads before him wave,
  Ripened by his glorious sunshine
    From the furrows of the grave.

3 Christ is risen, we are risen;
    Shed upon us heavenly grace,
  Rain, and dew, and gleams of glory
    From the brightness of thy face;
  That we, Lord, with hearts in heaven
    Here on earth may fruitful be,
  And by angel-hands be gathered,
    And be ever safe with thee.

4. Alleluya! Alleluya!
     Glory be to God on high;
   To the Father, and the Saviour,
     Who has gained the victory;
   Glory to the Holy Spirit,
     Fount of love and sanctity;
   Alleluya! Alleluya!
     To the Triune Majesty. Amen.

APPENDIX

28

Alternative Tune to Hymn 136

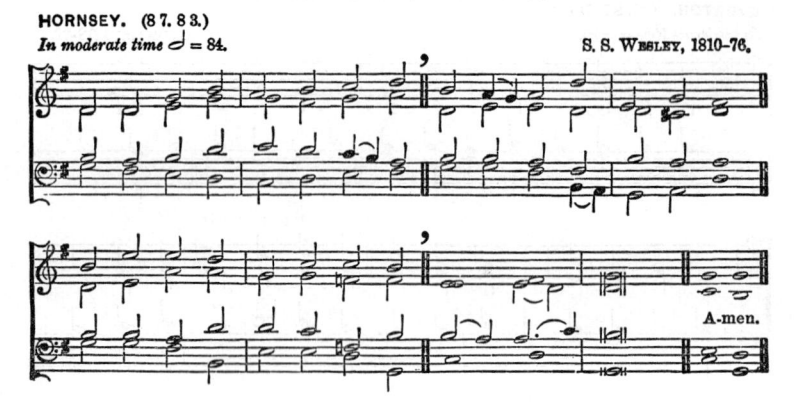

HORNSEY. (8 7. 8 3.)
In moderate time ♩ = 84.

S. S. WESLEY, 1810–76.

A-men.

S. Baring-Gould, 1834–1924.

ON the Resurrection morning
  Soul and body meet again;
No more sorrow, no more weeping,
  No more pain!

2*Here awhile they must be parted,
  And the flesh its Sabbath keep,
Waiting in a holy stillness,
  Wrapt in sleep.

3*For a while the wearied body
  Lies with feet toward the morn;
Till the last and brightest Easter
  Day be born.

4*But the soul in contemplation
  Utters earnest prayer and strong,
Bursting at the Resurrection
  Into song.

5 Soul and body reunited
  Thenceforth nothing shall divide,
Waking up in Christ's own likeness.
  Satisfied.

6 O the beauty, O the gladness
  Of that Resurrection day,
Which shall not through endless ages
  Pass away!

7 On that happy Easter morning
  All the graves their dead restore;
Father, sister, child, and mother
  Meet once more.

8. To that brightest of all meetings
  Bring us, Jesu Christ, at last,
  By thy Cross, through death and judgement,
    Holding fast.

APPENDIX

29

ALTERNATIVE TUNE TO HYMN 144

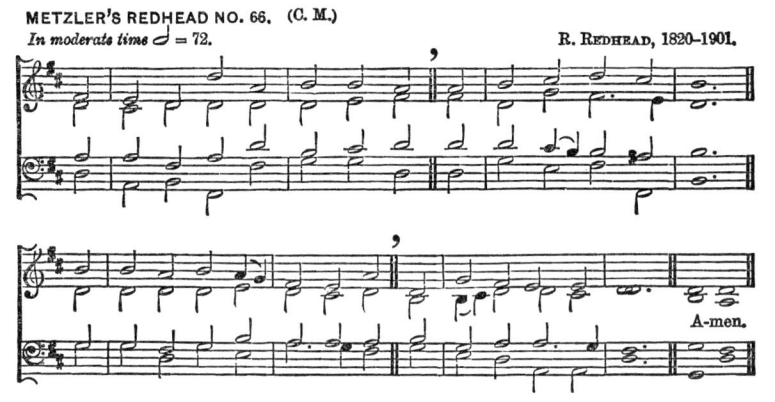

METZLER'S REDHEAD NO. 66. (C. M.)
In moderate time ♩ = 72.

R. REDHEAD, 1820-1901.

A-men.

Compline.   Jesu nostra redemptio.   *c. 8th cent.*   *Tr. J. Chandler†.*

O CHRIST, our hope, our hearts' desire,
    Redemption's only spring;
Creator of the world art thou,
    Its Saviour and its King.

2 How vast the mercy and the love
    Which laid our sins on thee,
And led thee to a cruel death
    To set thy people free.

3 But now the bonds of death are burst,
    The ransom has been paid;
And thou art on thy Father's throne
    In glorious robes arrayed.

4 O may thy mighty love prevail
    Our sinful souls to spare;
O may we come before thy throne,
    And find acceptance there!

5 O Christ, be thou our present joy,
    Our future great reward;
Our only glory may it be
    To glory in the Lord.

6. All praise to thee, ascended Lord;
    All glory ever be
To Father, Son, and Holy Ghost,
    Through all eternity. Amen.

APPENDIX

30

ALTERNATIVE ACCOMPANIMENT TO HYMN 154 (MECHLIN VERSION)

VENI CREATOR. (L. M.)
In free rhythm. To be sung in unison.

Melody from 'Vesperale Romanum'
(Mechlin) Mode viii.

Terce. *Before 10th cent. Tr. and rev. Y. H.*

Veni, Creator Spiritus.

COME, O Creator Spirit, come,
And make within our hearts thy home;
To us thy grace celestial give,
Who of thy breathing move and live.

2 O Comforter, that name is thine,
Of God most high the gift divine;
The well of life, the fire of love,
Our souls' anointing from above.

3 Thou dost appear in sevenfold dower
The sign of God's almighty power;
The Father's promise, making rich
With saving truth our earthly speech.

4 Our senses with thy light inflame,
Our hearts to heavenly love reclaim;
Our bodies' poor infirmity
With strength perpetual fortify.

5 Our mortal foe afar repel,
Grant us henceforth in peace to dwell;
And so to us, with thee for guide,
No ill shall come, no harm betide.

6 May we by thee the Father learn,
And know the Son, and thee discern,
Who art of both; and thus adore
In perfect faith for evermore. Amen.

APPENDIX

31

Alternative Tune to Hymn 157

ST. CUTHBERT. (8 6. 3 4.)
Slow ♩ = 58.

J. B. Dykes, 1823–76.

Harriet Auber, 1773–1862.

OUR blest Redeemer, ere he breathed
    His tender last farewell,
A Guide, a Comforter, bequeathed
    With us to dwell.

2 He came in tongues of living flame,
    To teach, convince, subdue;
All-powerful as the wind he came,
    As viewless too.

3 He came sweet influence to impart,
    A gracious, willing Guest,
While he can find one humble heart
    Wherein to rest.

4 And his that gentle voice we hear,
    Soft as the breath of even,
That checks each fault, that calms each fear,
    And speaks of heaven.

5 And every virtue we possess,
    And every victory won,
And every thought of holiness,
    Are his alone.

6. Spirit of purity and grace,
    Our weakness, pitying, see:
O make our hearts thy dwelling-place,
    And worthier thee.

APPENDIX

32

ALTERNATIVE TUNE TO HYMN 198

DEERHURST. (8 7. 8 7. D.)
In moderate time ♩ = 80.

J. LANGRAN, 1835–1909.

[By permission of Novello & Co., Ltd.]

Bishop Chr. Wordsworth, 1807–85.

HARK! the sound of holy voices,
  Chanting at the crystal sea,
Alleluya, Alleluya,
  Alleluya, Lord, to thee:
Multitude, which none can number,
  Like the stars in glory stands,
Clothed in white apparel, holding
  Palms of victory in their hands.

APPENDIX

2 Patriarch, and holy Prophet,
    Who prepared the way of Christ,
King, Apostle, Saint, Confessor,
    Martyr, and Evangelist,
Saintly Maiden, godly Matron,
    Widows who have watched to prayer,
Joined in holy concert, singing
    To the Lord of all, are there.

3 They have come from tribulation,
    And have washed their robes in blood,
Washed them in the Blood of Jesus;
    Tried they were, and firm they stood;
Mocked, imprisoned, stoned, tormented,
    Sawn asunder, slain with sword,
They have conquered death and Satan
    By the might of Christ the Lord.

4 Marching with thy Cross their banner,
    They have triumphed following
Thee, the Captain of salvation,
    Thee, their Saviour and their King;
Gladly, Lord, with thee they suffered;
    Gladly, Lord, with thee they died,
And by death to life immortal
    They were born, and glorified.

5 Now they reign in heavenly glory,
    Now they walk in golden light,
Now they drink, as from a river,
    Holy bliss and infinite,
Love and peace they taste for ever,
    And all truth and knowledge see
In the beatific vision
    Of the blessèd Trinity.

6. God of God, the One-begotten,
    Light of light, Emmanuel.
In whose Body joined together
    All the Saints for ever dwell;
Pour upon us of thy fullness,
    That we may for evermore
God the Father, God the Son, and
    God the Holy Ghost adore. Amen.

APPENDIX

33

ALTERNATIVE TUNE TO HYMN 201

PALMS OF GLORY. (7 7. 7 7.)

Moderately fast ♩ = 100.

ARCHBISHOP MACLAGAN, 1826–1910.

J. Montgomery, 1771–1854.

PALMS of glory, raiment bright,
    Crowns that never fade away,
Gird and deck the Saints in light,
    Priests, and kings, and conquerors they.

2 Yet the conquerors bring their palms
    To the Lamb amidst the throne,
And proclaim in joyful psalms
    Victory through his Cross alone.

3 Kings for harps their crowns resign,
    Crying, as they strike the chords,
'Take the kingdom, it is thine,
    King of kings, and Lord of lords.'

4 Round the altar priests confess,
    If their robes are white as snow,
'Twas the Saviour's righteousness,
    And his Blood, that made them so.

5. They were mortal too like us;
    Ah! when we like them must die,
May our souls translated thus
    Triumph, reign, and shine on high.

APPENDIX

34

ALTERNATIVE TUNE TO HYMN 227

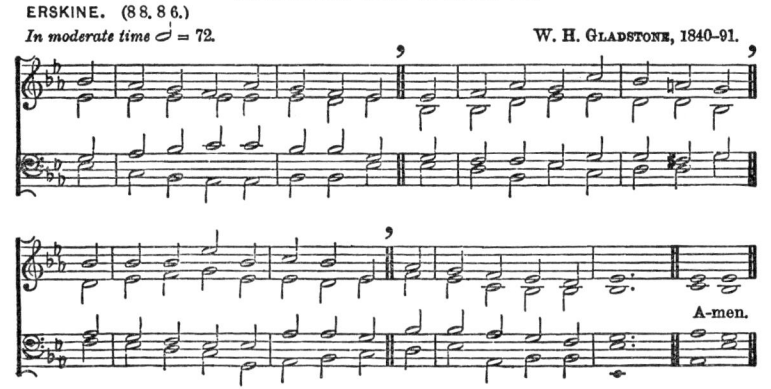

ERSKINE. (8 8. 8 6.)
In moderate time ♩ = 72.

W. H. GLADSTONE, 1840-91.

Mrs. C. F. Alexander, 1823-95.

FORSAKEN once, and thrice denied,
　The risen Lord gave pardon free,
Stood once again at Peter's side,
　　And asked him, 'Lov'st thou me?'

2 How many times with faithless word
　Have we denied his holy name,
How oft forsaken our dear Lord,
　　And shrunk when trial came!

3 Saint Peter, when the cock crew clear,
　Went out, and wept his broken faith;
Strong as a rock through strife and fear,
　　He served his Lord till death.

4 How oft his cowardice of heart
　We have without his love sincere,
The sin without the sorrow's smart,
　　The shame without the tear!

5 O oft forsaken, oft denied,
　Forgive our shame, wash out our sin;
Look on us from thy Father's side
　　And let that sweet look win.

6. Hear when we call thee from the deep,
　Still walk beside us on the shore,
Give hands to work, and eyes to weep,
　　And hearts to love thee more.

APPENDIX

35

ALTERNATIVE MODERN TUNE TO HYMN 233

VOM HIMMEL HOCH. (L. M.)
Very slow and dignified ♩ = 46.   *Melody from* MARTIN LUTHER, 1483-1546.

NOTE.—*Another harmonization of this tune, in a lower key, will be found at Hymn* 17.

OFFICE HYMN. E.   Caelestis formam gloriae.   15th cent. *Tr.* R. E. R.

1. AN image of that heavenly light,
The goal the Church keeps ay in sight,
Christ on the holy mount displays
Where he outshines the sun's bright rays.

2. Let every age proclaimer be
How, on this day, the chosen three
With Moses and Elias heard
The Lord speak many a gracious word.

3. As witnesses to grace are nigh
Those twain, the Law and Prophecy;
And to the Son, from out the cloud,
The Father's record thunders loud.

4. With garments whiter than the snows,
And shining face, Lord Jesus shows
What glory for those saints shall be
Who joy in God with piety.

5. The vision and the mystery
Make faithful hearts beat quick and high,
So on this solemn day of days
The cry goes up of prayer and praise.

6. O God the Father, God the Son,
And Holy Spirit, Three in One,
Vouchsafe to bring us, by thy grace,
To see thy glory face to face. Amen.

APPENDIX

36

ALTERNATIVE TUNE TO HYMNS 101 AND 246

ST. CRISPIN. (L. M.)
In moderate time ♩ = 92.

G. J. ELVEY, 1816–93.

HYMN 246

R. Campbell, 1814–68, and others.

THEY come, God's messengers of love,
They come from realms of peace above,
From homes of never-fading light,
From blissful mansions ever bright.

2 They come to watch around us here,
To soothe our sorrow, calm our fear:
Ye heavenly guides, speed not away,
God willeth you with us to stay

3 But chiefly at its journey's end
'Tis yours the spirit to befriend,
And whisper to the willing heart,
'O Christian soul, in peace depart.'

4 Blest Jesu, thou whose groans and tears
Have sanctified frail nature's fears,
To earth in bitter sorrow weighed,
Thou didst not scorn thine Angel's aid.

5 To us the zeal of Angels give,
With love to serve thee while we live;
To us an Angel-guard supply,
When on the bed of death we lie.

6. To God the Father, God the Son,
And God the Spirit, Three in One,
From all above and all below
Let joyful praise unceasing flow. Amen.

APPENDIX

37

Alternative Tune to Hymn 270

HUDDERSFIELD. (7 7. 7 5.)
In moderate time ♩ = 76.

W. Parratt, 1841-1924.

R. H. Robinson, 1842-92.

HOLY Father, cheer our way
With thy love's perpetual ray;
Grant us every closing day
Light at evening time.

2 Holy Saviour, calm our fears
When earth's brightness disappears;
Grant us in our latter years
Light at evening time.

3 Holy Spirit, be thou nigh
When in mortal pains we lie;
Grant us, as we come to die,
Light at evening time.

4. Holy, blessèd Trinity,
Darkness is not dark with thee;
Those thou keepest always see
Light at evening time.

APPENDIX

38

ALTERNATIVE TUNE TO HYMN 273

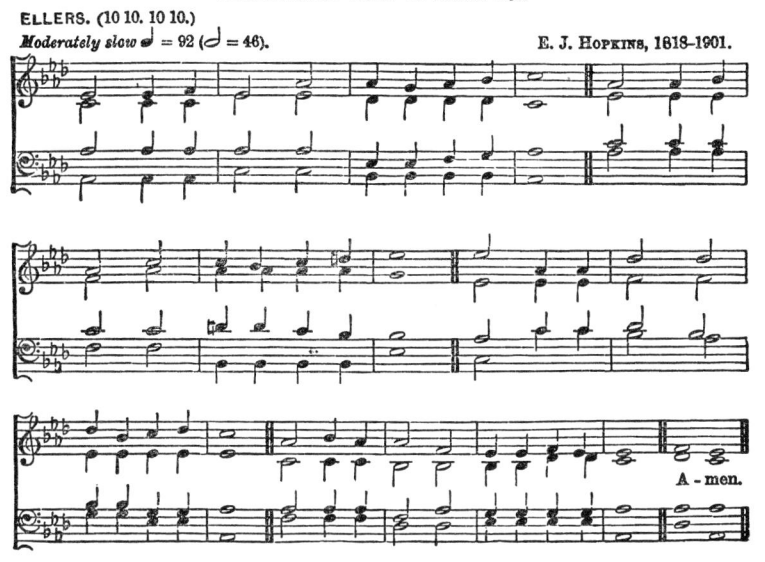

ELLERS. (10 10. 10 10.)
Moderately slow ♩ = 92 (𝅗𝅥 = 46).

E. J. HOPKINS, 1818-1901.

J. Ellerton, 1826-93

SAVIOUR, again to thy dear name we raise
With one accord our parting hymn of praise.
Guard thou the lips from sin, the hearts from shame,
That in this house have called upon thy name.

2 Grant us thy peace, Lord, through the coming night;
Turn thou for us its darkness into light;
From harm and danger keep thy children free,
For dark and light are both alike to thee.

3 Grant us thy peace throughout our earthly life;
Peace to thy Church from error and from strife;
Peace to our land, the fruit of truth and love;
Peace in each heart, thy Spirit from above:

4. Thy peace in life, the balm of every pain;
Thy peace in death, the hope to rise again;
Then, when thy voice shall bid our conflict cease,
Call us, O Lord, to thine eternal peace.

APPENDIX

39

ALTERNATIVE TUNE TO HYMN 274

HURSLEY. (L.M.)
Slow ♩ = 80.

Abridged from melody in
'*Katholisches Gesangbuch,*' Vienna, c. 1774.

J. Keble, 1792–1866

SUN of my soul, thou Saviour dear,
It is not night if thou be near:
O may no earth-born cloud arise
To hide thee from thy servant's eyes.

2 When the soft dews of kindly sleep
My wearied eyelids gently steep,
Be my last thought, how sweet to rest
For ever on my Saviour's breast.

3 Abide with me from morn till eve,
For without thee I cannot live;
Abide with me when night is nigh,
For without thee I dare not die.

4 If some poor wand'ring child of thine
Have spurned to-day the voice divine,
Now, Lord, the gracious work begin;
Let him no more lie down in sin.

5 Watch by the sick; enrich the poor
With blessings from thy boundless store;
Be every mourner's sleep to-night
Like infant's slumbers, pure and light.

6. Come near and bless us when we wake,
Ere through the world our way we take;
Till in the ocean of thy love
We lose ourselves in heaven above.

APPENDIX

40

ALTERNATIVE TUNE TO HYMN 276

ST. ANATOLIUS. (7 6. 7 6. 8 8.)

In moderate time ♩ = 76.

A. H. BROWN, 1830–1926.

Ascribed to 6th cent. Tr. J. M. Neale.

Τὴν ἡμέραν διελθών

THE day is past and over;
　All thanks, O Lord, to thee;
I pray thee that offenceless
　The hours of dark may be:
O Jesu, keep me in thy sight,
And guard me through the coming
　　　　　　　　　　　　[night.

2　The joys of day are over;
　I lift my heart to thee,
And call on thee that sinless
　The hours of dark may be:
O Jesu, make their darkness light,
And guard me through the coming
　　　　　　　　　　　　[night.

3　The toils of day are over;
　I raise the hymn to thee,
And ask that free from peril
　The hours of dark may be:
O Jesu, keep me in thy sight,
And guard me through the coming night.

4.　Be thou my soul's preserver,
　O God! for thou dost know
How many are the perils
　Through which I have to go:
Lover of men! O hear my call,
And guard and save me from them all.

APPENDIX

41

ALTERNATIVE TUNE TO HYMN 279

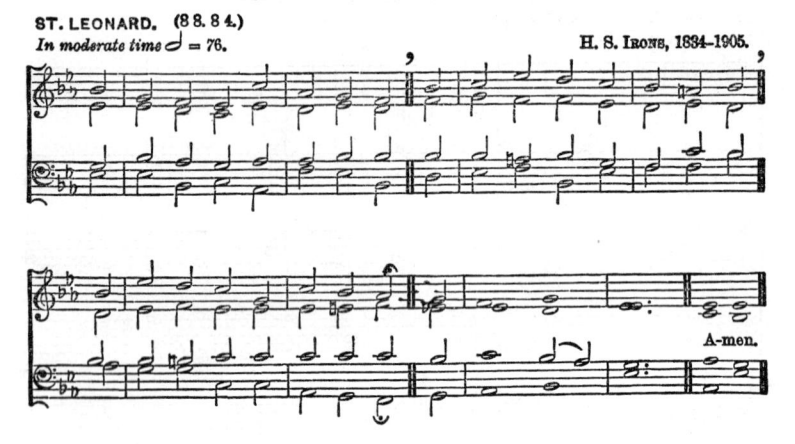

ST. LEONARD. (8 8. 8 4.)
In moderate time ♩ = 76.

H. S. Irons, 1834-1905.

A-men.

G. Thring, 1823-1908.

THE radiant morn hath passed away,
And spent too soon her golden store;
The shadows of departing day
           Creep on once more.

2 Our life is but an autumn sun,
Its glorious noon how quickly past;
Lead us, O Christ, our life-work done,
           Safe home at last.

3 O by thy soul-inspiring grace
Uplift our hearts to realms on high;
Help us to look to that bright place
           Beyond the sky;—

4 Where light, and life, and joy, and peace
In undivided empire reign,
And thronging Angels never cease
           Their deathless strain;—

5. Where Saints are clothed in spotless white,
And evening shadows never fall,
Where thou, eternal Light of light,
           Art Lord of all.

APPENDIX

42

ALTERNATIVE TUNE TO HYMN 280

ST. COLUMBA. (6 4. 6 6.)
In moderate time ♩ = 72.

H. S. IRONS, 1834–1905.

A-men.

Sol praeceps rapitur.

c. 18th cent. Tr. E. Caswall.

1 THE sun is sinking fast,
   The daylight dies;
Let love awake, and pay
   Her evening sacrifice.

2 As Christ upon the Cross
   In death reclined,
Into his Father's hands
   His parting soul resigned,

3 So now herself my soul
   Would wholly give
Into his sacred charge,
   In whom all spirits live;

4 So now beneath his eye
   Would calmly rest,
Without a wish or thought
   Abiding in the breast,

5 Save that his will be done,
   Whate'er betide,
Dead to herself, and dead
   In him to all beside.

6 Thus would I live; yet now
   Not I, but he
In all his power and love
   Henceforth alive in me—

7. One sacred Trinity,
   One Lord Divine,
Myself for ever his,
   And he for ever mine!

APPENDIX

43

ALTERNATIVE TUNE TO HYMN 304

BREAD OF HEAVEN. (7 7. 7 7. 7 7.)

Moderately slow ♩ = 69.

ARCHBISHOP MACLAGAN, 1826–1910.

A-men.

At the Communion. *J. Conder ‡. 1789–1855.*

BREAD of heaven, on thee we feed,
For thy Flesh is meat indeed;
Ever may our souls be fed
With this true and living Bread,
Day by day with strength supplied
Through the life of him who died.

2. Vine of heaven, thy Blood supplies
This blest cup of sacrifice;
'Tis thy wounds our healing give;
To thy Cross we look and live:
Thou our life! O let us be
Rooted, grafted, built on thee.

APPENDIX

44

ALTERNATIVE TUNE TO HYMN 307

THE SACRED HEART. (10 10. 10 10.)

Moderately slow ♩ = 96 (𝅗𝅥 = 48).

J. ST. O. DYKES.

A-men.

7th cent. Tr. J. M. Neale.

Sancti, venite, Christi Corpus sumite.

DRAW nigh, and take the Body of the Lord,
And drink the holy Blood for you outpoured,
Saved by that Body, hallowed by that Blood,
Whereby refreshed we render thanks to God.

2 Salvation's giver, Christ the only Son,
By that his Cross and Blood the victory won.
Offered was he for greatest and for least:
Himself the Victim, and himself the Priest.

3*Victims were offered by the law of old,
That, in a type, celestial mysteries told.
He, Ransomer from death and Light from shade,
Giveth his holy grace his saints to aid.

4 Approach ye then with faithful hearts sincere,
And take the safeguard of salvation here.
He that in this world rules his saints and shields,
To all believers life eternal yields:

5.*With heavenly Bread makes them that hunger whole,
Gives living waters to the thirsty soul.
Alpha and Omega, to whom shall bow
All nations at the Doom, is with us now.

APPENDIX

45

ALTERNATIVE TUNE TO HYMN 320

ROCKINGHAM. (L.M.)
Very slow ♩ = 60.
Adapted by E. MILLER, 1731-1807.

NOTE.—*This tune may also be used as an alternative setting to No. 107.*

P. Doddridge. 1702-51.

MY God, and is thy Table spread,
And does thy Cup with Love o'erflow?
Thither be all thy children led,
And let them all thy sweetness know.

2 Hail, sacred Feast, which Jesus makes!
Rich Banquet of his Flesh and Blood!
Thrice happy he, who here partakes
That sacred Stream, that heavenly Food.

3. O let thy Table honoured be,
And furnished well with joyful guests;
And may each soul salvation see,
That here its sacred Pledges tastes.

APPENDIX

46

ADDITIONAL MODERN TUNE TO HYMN 330 (PT. 2)

O JESU CHRIST. (L. M.)
Slow 𝅗𝅥 = 50.

Melody from
'Haus Kirchen Cantorei,' 1587
(*rhythm slightly simplified*).

A-men.

Part 2.

O salutaris.

5 O saving Victim! opening wide
    The gate of heaven to man below,
  Our foes press hard on every side,—
    Thine aid supply, thy strength bestow.

6. All praise and thanks to thee ascend
    For evermore, blest One in Three;
  O grant us life that shall not end
    In our true native land with thee.
                      Amen.

APPENDIX

47

ALTERNATIVE TUNE TO HYMN 356

CORPUS DOMINI. (6 5. 6 5. D.)

Slow ♩ = 92.

G. E. W. MALET, 1839–1918.

At Holy Communion.   Yesu Bin Mariamu.   *Written in Swahili, and tr. E. S. Palmer,* 1857–1931.

JESU, Son of Mary,
  Fount of life alone,
Here we hail thee present
  On thine altar-throne.
Humbly we adore thee,
  Lord of endless might,
In the mystic symbols
  Veiled from earthly sight.

2 Think, O Lord, in mercy
  On the souls of those
Who, in faith gone from us,
  Now in death repose.
Here 'mid stress and conflict
  Toils can never cease;
There, the warfare ended,
  Bid them rest in peace.

3 Often were they wounded
  In the deadly strife,
Heal them, Good Physician,
  With the balm of life.
Every taint of evil,
  Frailty and decay,
Good and gracious Saviour,
  Cleanse and purge away.

4. Rest eternal grant them,
  After weary fight:
Shed on them the radiance
  Of thy heavenly light.
Lead them onward, upward,
  To the holy place,
Where thy saints made perfect
  Gaze upon thy face.

APPENDIX

48

NATIVITY. (C. M.)   ALTERNATIVE TUNE TO HYMN 276

Moderately fast ♩ = 100.

H. LAHEE, 1826–1912.

A-men.

I. Watts, 1674–1748.

COME, let us join our cheerful songs
   With Angels round the throne;
Ten thousand thousand are their tongues,
   But all their joys are one.

Unison.   2 'Worthy the Lamb that died,' they cry,
     'To be exalted thus';
   'Worthy the Lamb,' our lips reply,
     'For he was slain for us.'

  3 Jesus is worthy to receive
     Honour and power divine;
   And blessings more than we can give
     Be, Lord, for ever thine.

Unison.   4. The whole creation join in one
     To bless the sacred name
   Of him that sits upon the throne,
     And to adore the Lamb.

APPENDIX

49

ALTERNATIVE TUNE TO HYMN 381

OLIVA SPECIOSA. (D. S. M.)

Moderately fast ♩ = 100.

Italian Melody (18th cent.).

A-men.

M. Bridges, 1800–94.

CROWN him with many crowns,
 The Lamb upon his throne;
Hark! how the heavenly anthem drowns
 All music but its own:
 Awake, my soul, and sing
 Of him who died for thee,
And hail him as thy matchless King
 Through all eternity.

APPENDIX

    2 Crown him the Virgin's Son,
        The God incarnate born,
    Whose arm those crimson trophies won
        Which now his brow adorn:
    Fruit of the mystic Rose,
        As of that Rose the Stem;
    The Root whence mercy ever flows,
        The Babe of Bethlehem.

    3 Crown him the Lord of love!
        Behold his hands and side,
    Rich wounds yet visible above
        In beauty glorified:
    No Angel in the sky
        Can fully bear that sight,
    But downward bends his burning eye
        At mysteries so bright.

    4 Crown him the Lord of peace,
        Whose power a sceptre sways
    From pole to pole, that wars may cease,
        Absorbed in prayer and praise:
    His reign shall know no end,
        And round his piercèd feet
    Fair flowers of Paradise extend
        Their fragrance ever sweet.

Unison. 5. Crown him the Lord of years,
        The Potentate of time,
    Creator of the rolling spheres,
        Ineffably sublime.
    Glassed in a sea of light,
        Where everlasting waves
    Reflect his throne—the Infinite!
        Who lives—and loves—and saves.

APPENDIX

50

ALTERNATIVE TUNE TO HYMN 383

HAMMERSMITH. (8 6. 8 8 6.)
In moderate time ♩ = 76.

W. H. GLADSTONE, 1840-91.

J. G. Whittier, 1807-92.

DEAR Lord and Father of mankind,
 Forgive our foolish ways!
Re-clothe us in our rightful mind,
In purer lives thy service find,
 In deeper reverence praise.

2 In simple trust like theirs who heard,
 Beside the Syrian sea,
The gracious calling of the Lord,
Let us, like them, without a word
 Rise up and follow thee.

3*O Sabbath rest by Galilee!
 O calm of hills above,
Where Jesus knelt to share with thee
The silence of eternity,
 Interpreted by love!

4 Drop thy still dews of quietness,
 Till all our strivings cease;
Take from our souls the strain and stress,
And let our ordered lives confess
 The beauty of thy peace.

5. Breathe through the heats of our desire
 Thy coolness and thy balm;
Let sense be dumb, let flesh retire;
Speak through the earthquake, wind, and fire,
 O still small voice of calm!

APPENDIX

51

ALTERNATIVE TUNE TO HYMN 391

MONTGOMERY. (D. S. M.)
In moderate time ♩ = 92.

I. WOODBURY, 1819–58.

J. Montgomery, 1771–1854.

1. 'For ever with the Lord!'
   Amen; so let it be;
   Life from the dead is in that word,
   'Tis immortality,
   Here in the body pent,
   Absent from him I roam,
   Yet nightly pitch my moving tent
   A day's march nearer home.

2. My Father's house on high,
   Home of my soul, how near
   At times to faith's foreseeing eye
   Thy golden gates appear!
   Ah! then my spirit faints
   To reach the land I love,
   The bright inheritance of Saints,
   Jerusalem above.

3. 'For ever with the Lord!'—
   Father, if 'tis thy will,
   The promise of that faithful word
   E'en here to me fulfil.
   Be thou at my right hand,
   Then can I never fail;
   Uphold thou me, and I shall stand;
   Fight, and I must prevail.

4. So when my latest breath
   Shall rend the veil in twain,
   By death I shall escape from death,
   And life eternal gain.
   Knowing as I am known,
   How shall I love that word,
   And oft repeat before the throne,
   'For ever with the Lord!'

APPENDIX

52

ALTERNATIVE TUNE TO HYMN 400

ST. BEES. (7 7. 7 7.)
Moderately slow ♩ = 66.
J. B. DYKES, 1823-76.

W. Cowper, 1731-1800.

HARK, my soul! it is the Lord;
'Tis thy Saviour, hear his word;
Jesus speaks, and speaks to thee:
'Say, poor sinner, lov'st thou me?

2 'I delivered thee when bound,
And, when wounded, healed thy wound;
Sought thee wandering, set thee right,
Turned thy darkness into light.

3 'Can a woman's tender care
Cease towards the child she bare?
Yes, she may forgetful be,
Yet will I remember thee.

4 'Mine is an unchanging love,
Higher than the heights above,
Deeper than the depths beneath,
Free and faithful, strong as death.

5 'Thou shalt see my glory soon,
When the work of grace is done;
Partner of my throne shalt be;
Say, poor sinner, lov'st thou me?'

6. Lord, it is my chief complaint
That my love is weak and faint;
Yet I love thee, and adore;
O for grace to love thee more!

APPENDIX

53

ALTERNATIVE TUNE TO HYMN 415

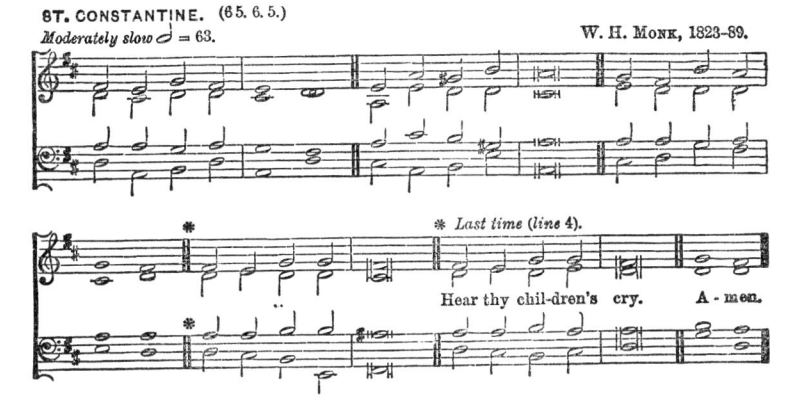

ST. CONSTANTINE. (6 5. 6. 5.)
Moderately slow ♩ = 63.

W. H. MONK, 1823–89.

Hear thy chil-dren's cry. A - men.

G. R. Prynne, 1818–1903.

JESU, meek and gentle,
Son of God most high,
Pitying, loving Saviour,
  Hear thy children's cry.

2 Pardon our offences,
   Loose our captive chains,
Break down every idol
   Which our soul detains.

3 Give us holy freedom,
   Fill our hearts with love,
Draw us, holy Jesu,
   To the realms above.

4 Lead us on our journey,
   Be thyself the Way
Through terrestrial darkness
   To celestial day.

5. Jesu, meek and gentle,
   Son of God most high,
Pitying, loving Saviour,
   Hear thy children's cry.

APPENDIX

54

ALTERNATIVE TUNE TO HYMN 417

STELLA. (88. 88. 88.)
In moderate time ♩ = 112.

Founded on an English Traditional Melody.

H. Collins, 1827–1919.

JESU, my Lord, my God, my All,
Hear me, blest Saviour, when I call;
Hear me, and from thy dwelling-place
Pour down the riches of thy grace:
Jesu, my Lord, I thee adore,
O make me love thee more and more.

2 Jesu, too late I thee have sought,
How can I love thee as I ought?
And how extol thy matchless fame,
The glorious beauty of thy name?

3 Jesu, what didst thou find in me,
That thou hast dealt so lovingly?
How great the joy that thou hast brought,
So far exceeding hope or thought!

4. Jesu, of thee shall be my song,
To thee my heart and soul belong;
All that I am or have is thine,
And thou, sweet Saviour, thou art mine.

APPENDIX

55

ALTERNATIVE TUNE TO HYMN 419

ST. AGNES. (C. M.)
Moderately slow ♩ = 84.
J. B. DYKES, 1823–76.

A-men.

Jesu, dulcis memoria.

11*th. cent. Tr. E. Caswall.*

JESU, the very thought of thee
 With sweetness fills my breast;
But sweeter far thy face to see,
 And in thy presence rest.

2 Nor voice can sing, nor heart can frame,
 Now can the memory find,
A sweeter sound than thy blest name,
 O Saviour of mankind!

3 O hope of every contrite heart,
 O joy of all the meek,
To those who fall, how kind thou art!
 How good to those who seek!

4 But what to those who find? Ah! this
 Nor tongue nor pen can show;
The love of Jesus! what it is,
 None but his loved ones know.

5 Jesu, our only joy be thou,
 As thou our prize wilt be;
Jesu, be thou our glory now,
 And through eternity.

APPENDIX

56

ALTERNATIVE TUNE TO HYMN 427

UNIVERSAL PRAISE. (10 4. 6 6. 6 6. 10 4.)

Brightly ♩ = 100.

W. G. WHINFIELD.

A-men.

APPENDIX

George Herbert, 1593-1632

LET all the world in every corner sing,
  My God and King!
 The heavens are not too high,
 His praise may thither fly;
 The earth is not too low,
 His praises there may grow.
Let all the world in every corner sing,
  My God and King!

2. Let all the world in every corner sing,
  My God and King!
 The Church with psalms must shout,
 No door can keep them out;
 But above all, the heart
 Must bear the longest part.
Let all the world in every corner sing,
  My God and King!

APPENDIX

57

ALTERNATIVE TUNE TO HYMNS 113, 312 429, AND 430

ALL SOULS. (10 10. 10 10.)
In moderate time ♩ = 96 (♩ = 48).

J. YOAKLEY.

HYMN 429

H. Montagu Butler, 1833–1918.

'LIFT up your hearts!' We lift them, Lord, to thee;
Here at thy feet none other may we see:
'Lift up your hearts!' E'en so, with one accord,
We lift them up, we lift them to the Lord.

2 Above the level of the former years,
The mire of sin, the slough of guilty fears,
The mist of doubt, the blight of love's decay,
O Lord of Light, lift all our hearts to-day!

3 Above the swamps of subterfuge and shame,
The deeds, the thoughts, that honour may not name,
The halting tongue that dares not tell the whole,
O Lord of Truth, lift every Christian soul!

4 Lift every gift that thou thyself hast given;
Low lies the best till lifted up to heaven:
Low lie the bounding heart, the teeming brain,
Till, sent from God, they mount to God again.

5. Then, as the trumpet-call, in after years,
'Lift up your hearts!' rings pealing in our ears,
Still shall those hearts respond, with full accord
'We lift them up, we lift them to the Lord!'

APPENDIX

58

ALTERNATIVE TUNE TO HYMN 439

OLIVET. (6 6 4. 6 6. 6 4.)
In moderate time ♩ = 80.

LOWELL MASON, 1792–1872.

A-men.

Ray Palmer, 1808–87.

MY faith looks up to thee,
  Thou Lamb of Calvary,
    Saviour divine!
Now hear me while I pray,
Take all my guilt away,
O let me from this day
  Be wholly thine.

2 May thy rich grace impart
  Strength to my fainting heart,
    My zeal inspire;
As thou hast died for me,
O may my love to thee
Pure, warm, and changeless be,
  A living fire.

3 While life's dark maze I tread,
  And griefs around me spread,
    Be thou my guide;
Bid darkness turn to day,
Wipe sorrow's tears away,
Nor let me ever stray
  From thee aside.

4. When ends life's transient dream,
  When death's cold sullen stream
    Shall o'er me roll,
Blest Saviour, then in love
Fear and distrust remove;
O bear me safe above,
  A ransomed soul.

APPENDIX

59

ALTERNATIVE TUNE TO HYMN 440

TROYTE NO. 1. (88. 84.)
In moderate time ♩ = 80.

A. H. DYKE TROYTE, 1811-57.

Charlotte *Elliott*, 1789-1871.

MY God and Father, while I stray,
Far from my home, in life's rough way,
O teach me from my heart to say,
        'Thy will be done!'

2 If but my fainting heart be blest
With thy sweet Spirit for its guest,
My God, to thee I leave the rest—
        Thy will be done!

3 Renew my will from day to day,
Blend it with thine, and take away
All that now makes it hard to say,
        'Thy will be done!'

4. Then when on earth I breathe no more
The prayer oft mixed with tears before,
I'll sing upon a happier shore—
        'Thy will be done!'

APPENDIX

60

ALTERNATIVE TUNE TO HYMN 482

LANGA. (11 10. 11 6.)
Moderately slow ♩ = 88 (𝅗𝅥 = 44).

Melody by F. Soto, 1534–1619.

A-men.

W. H. Burleigh, 1812–71.

STILL will we trust, though earth seem dark and dreary,
    And the heart faint beneath his chastening rod,
Though rough and steep our pathway, worn and weary,
    Still will we trust in God!

2 Our eyes see dimly till by faith anointed,
    And our blind choosing brings us grief and pain;
Through him alone, who hath our way appointed,
    We find our peace again.

3 Choose for us, God, nor let our weak preferring
    Cheat our poor souls of good thou hast designed:
Choose for us, God; thy wisdom is unerring,
    And we are fools and blind.

4*So from our sky the night shall furl her shadows,
    And day pour gladness through his golden gates,
Our rough path lead to flower-enamelled meadows,
    Where joy our coming waits.

5. Let us press on: in patient self-denial,
    Accept the hardship, shrink not from the loss;
Our guerdon lies beyond the hour of trial,
    Our crown beyond the cross.

APPENDIX

61

Alternative Tune to Hymn 503

ST. OSWALD. (8 7. 8 7.)
Brightly ♩ = 96.
J. B. Dykes, 1823–76.

B. S. Ingemann, 1789–1862.
Tr. S. Baring-Gould.

Igjennem Nat og Trængsel.

1. THROUGH the night of doubt and sorrow
Onward goes the pilgrim band,
Singing songs of expectation,
Marching to the Promised Land.

2. Clear before us through the darkness
Gleams and burns the guiding light;
Brother clasps the hand of brother,
Stepping fearless through the night.

3. One the light of God's own presence
O'er his ransomed people shed,
Chasing far the gloom and terror,
Brightening all the path we tread;

4. One the object of our journey,
One the faith which never tires,
One the earnest looking forward,
One the hope our God inspires:

5.*One the strain that lips of thousands
Lift as from the heart of one;
One the conflict, one the peril,
One the march in God begun;

6.*One the gladness of rejoicing
On the far eternal shore,
Where the One Almighty Father
Reigns in love for evermore.

Part 2

7.*Onward, therefore, pilgrim brothers,
Onward with the Cross our aid;
Bear its shame, and fight its battle,
Till we rest beneath its shade.

Unison. 8.*Soon shall come the great awaking,
Soon the rending of the tomb;
Then the scattering of all shadows,
And the end of toil and gloom.

APPENDIX

62

ALTERNATIVE TUNE TO HYMN 541

ST. AËLRED. (8 8. 8 3.)
Very slow ♩ = 66.

J. B. DYKES, 1823–76 (*original version*).

Slower.

The following version of the last line (as altered by the composer) may also be used:

A - men.

G. *Thring*, 1823–1903.

FIERCE raged the tempest o'er the deep,
   Watch did thine anxious servants keep,
But thou wast wrapped in guileless sleep,
        Calm and still.

2 'Save, Lord, we perish!' was their cry,
  'O save us in our agony!'
Thy word above the storm rose high,
        'Peace, be still.'

3 The wild winds hushed; the angry deep
Sank, like a little child, to sleep;
The sullen billows ceased to leap,
        At thy will.

4. So, when our life is clouded o'er,
And storm-winds drift us from the shore,
Say, lest we sink to rise no more,
        'Peace, be still.'

APPENDIX

63

ALTERNATIVE TUNE TO HYMN 548

BENSON. (Irreg.)
In moderate time ♩ = 84.

M. D. KINGHAM.

vv. 1, 5. ‖ vv. 2, 3, 4.

When the

A-men.

* *For verses 2 and 5.*

APPENDIX

A. C. Ainger, 1841–1919.

GOD is working his purpose out as year succeeds to year;
God is working his purpose out and the time is drawing near;
Nearer and nearer draws the time, the time that shall surely be,
When the earth shall be filled with the glory of God as the waters
cover the sea.

2*From utmost east to utmost west where'er man's foot hath trod,
By the mouth of many messengers goes forth the voice of God,
'Give ear to me, ye continents, ye isles, give ear to me,
That the earth may be filled with the glory of God as the waters
cover the sea.'

3 What can we do to work God's work, to prosper and increase
The brotherhood of all mankind, the reign of the Prince of Peace ?
What can we do to hasten the time, the time that shall surely be,
When the earth shall be filled with the glory of God as the waters
cover the sea ?

4 March we forth in the strength of God with the banner of Christ
unfurled,
That the light of the glorious gospel of truth may shine throughout
the world;
Fight we the fight with sorrow and sin, to set their captives free,
That the earth may be filled with the glory of God as the waters
cover the sea.

5.*All we can do is nothing worth unless God blesses the deed;
Vainly we hope for the harvest-tide till God gives life to the seed;
Yet nearer and nearer draws the time, the time that shall surely be,
When the earth shall be filled with the glory of God as the waters
cover the sea.

APPENDIX

64

ALTERNATIVE TUNE TO HYMNS 505 AND 554

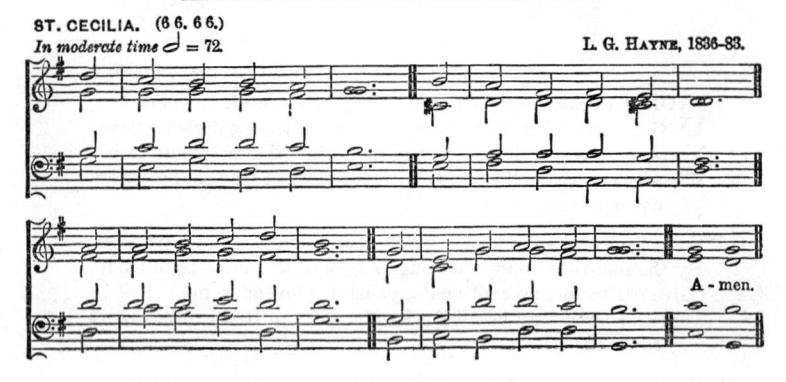

ST. CECILIA. (6 6. 6 6.)
In moderate time ♩ = 72.

L. G. HAYNE, 1836-83.

HYMN 554

Home or Foreign.

L. Hensley, 1827-1905.

THY kingdom come, O God,
    Thy rule, O Christ, begin;
Break with thine iron rod
    The tyrannies of sin.

2 Where is thy reign of peace,
    And purity, and love?
When shall all hatred cease,
    As in the realms above?

3 When comes the promised time
    That war shall be no more,—
Oppression, lust, and crime
    Shall flee thy face before?

4 We pray thee, Lord, arise,
    And come in thy great might;
Revive our longing eyes,
    Which languish for thy sight.

5*Men scorn thy sacred name,
    And wolves devour thy fold;
By many deeds of shame
    We learn that love grows cold.

6. O'er heathen lands afar
    Thick darkness broodeth yet:
Arise, O morning Star,
    Arise, and never set!

APPENDIX

65

ALTERNATIVE TUNE TO HYMN 578

ST. CATHERINE. (7 6. 7 6. D.)
In moderate time ♩ = 92.

R. F. DALE, 1845–1919.

Bishop W. W. How, 1823–97.

O JESU, thou art standing
Outside the fast-closed door,
In lowly patience waiting
To pass the threshold o'er:
Shame on us, Christian brothers,
His name and sign who bear,
O shame, thrice shame upon us
To keep him standing there!

2 O Jesu, thou art knocking:
And lo! that hand is scarred,
And thorns thy brow encircle,
And tears thy face have marred:
O love that passeth knowledge
So patiently to wait!
O sin that hath no equal
So fast to bar the gate!

3. O Jesu, thou art pleading
In accents meek and low,
'I died for you, my children,
And will ye treat me so?'
O Lord, with shame and sorrow
We open now the door:
Dear Saviour, enter, enter,
And leave us nevermore.

APPENDIX

66

ALTERNATIVE TUNE TO HYMN 587

GREYSTONE. (7 6. 7 6, D. and Refrain.)

Brightly ♩ = 104.

W. R. WAGHORNE.

Mrs. C. F. Alexander‡, 1823–95.

1. *All things bright and beautiful,*
   All creatures great and small,
   All things wise and wonderful,
   The Lord God made them all.

2. Each little flower that opens,
   Each little bird that sings,
   He made their glowing colours,
   He made their tiny wings.

3. The purple-headed mountain,
   The river running by,
   The sunset and the morning,
   That brightens up the sky;

4. The cold wind in the winter,
   The pleasant summer sun,
   The ripe fruits in the garden,—
   He made them every one;

5.*The tall trees in the greenwood,
   The meadows for our play,
   The rushes by the water,
   To gather every day;—

6. He gave us eyes to see them,
   And lips that we may tell
   How great is God Almighty,
   Who has made all things well.

APPENDIX

67

Alternative Tune to Hymn 602

BUCKLAND. (77.77.)
In moderate time ♩ = 76.

L. G. Hayne, 1836–83.

Jane E. Leeson, 1807–82.

LOVING Shepherd of thy sheep,
Keep thy lamb, in safety keep;
Nothing can thy power withstand,
None can pluck me from thy hand.

2*Loving Saviour, thou didst give
Thine own life that we might live;
And the hands outstretched to bless
Bear the cruel nails' impress.

3 I would bless thee every day,
Gladly all thy will obey,
Like thy blessèd ones above,
Happy in thy precious love.

4 Loving Shepherd, ever near,
Teach thy lamb thy voice to hear;
Suffer not my steps to stray
From the straight and narrow way.

5. Where thou leadest I would go,
Walking in thy steps below,
Till before my Father's throne
I shall know as I am known.

APPENDIX

68

ALTERNATIVE TUNE TO HYMN 615

ZUNDEL. (6 5. 6 5. D.)
Brightly ♩ = 100.

J. ZUNDEL, *c.* 1855.

A-men.

G. Thring, 1823–1903.

FROM the eastern mountains
　Pressing on they come,
Wise men in their wisdom,
　To his humble home;
Stirred by deep devotion,
　Hasting from afar,
Ever journeying onward,
　Guided by a star.

APPENDIX

2 There their Lord and Saviour
   Meek and lowly lay,
Wondrous light that led them
   Onward on their way,
Ever now to lighten
   Nations from afar,
As they journey homeward
   By that guiding star.

3 Thou who in a manger
   Once hast lowly lain,
Who dost now in glory
   O'er all kingdoms reign,
Gather in the heathen,
   Who in lands afar
Ne'er have seen the brightness
   Of thy guiding star.

4 Gather in the outcasts,
   All who've gone astray,
Throw thy radiance o'er them,
   Guide them on their way;
Those who never knew thee,
   Those who've wandered far,
Guide them by the brightness
   Of thy guiding star.

Unison. 5 Onward through the darkness
   Of the lonely night,
Shining still before them
   With thy kindly light,
Guide them, Jew and Gentile,
   Homeward from afar,
Young and old together,
   By thy guiding star.

6*. Until every nation,
   Whether bond or free,
'Neath thy star-lit banner,
   Jesu, follows thee,
O'er the distant mountains
   To that heavenly home
Where nor sin nor sorrow
   Evermore shall come.

APPENDIX

69

ALTERNATIVE TUNE TO HYMN 638

JERUSALEM. (C.M.)
In moderate time ♩ = 80.

T. WORSLEY STANIFORTH, 1845–1909.

[By permission of Novello & Co., Ltd.]

(*Part* 3.)

JERUSALEM, my happy home,
   When shall I come to thee?
When shall my sorrows have an end?
   Thy joys when shall I see?

20 Quite through the streets with silver sound
   The flood of life doth flow,
Upon whose banks on every side
   The wood of life doth grow.

21 There trees for evermore bear fruit,
   And evermore do spring;
There evermore the Angels sit,
   And evermore do sing;

22 There David stands with harp in hand
   As master of the choir:
Ten thousand times that man were blest
   That might this music hear.

23 Our Lady sings Magnificat
   With tune surpassing sweet;
And all the Virgins bear their parts,
   Sitting about her feet.

24 Te Deum doth Saint Ambrose sing,
   Saint Austin doth the like;
Old Simeon and Zachary
   Have not their songs to seek.

25 There Magdalene hath left her moan,
   And cheerfully doth sing
With blessèd Saints, whose harmony
   In every street doth ring.

26 Jerusalem, my happy home,
   Would God I were in thee!
Would God my woes were at an end
   Thy joys that I might see!

APPENDIX
70
ALTERNATIVE TUNE TO HYMN 645

GOSHEN. (6 5, 6 5, D.)
Brightly ♩ = 108.

The Bible Class Magazine, 1860.

A - men.

G. Thring, 1823–1903.

SAVIOUR, blessèd Saviour,
   Listen while we sing,
Hearts and voices raising
   Praises to our King.
All we have we offer,
   All we hope to be,
Body, soul, and spirit,
   All we yield to thee.

2 Nearer, ever nearer,
   Christ, we draw to thee,
Deep in adoration
   Bending low the knee.
Thou for our redemption
   Cam'st on earth to die;
Thou, that we might follow,
   Hast gone up on high.

3 Great and ever greater
   Are thy mercies here;
True and everlasting
   Are the glories there;
Where no pain, nor sorrow,
   Toil, nor care, is known,
Where the Angel-legions
   Circle round thy throne.

4 Clearer still and clearer
   Dawns the light from heaven,
In our sadness bringing
   News of sins forgiven;
Life has lost its shadows,
   Pure the light within;
Thou hast shed thy radiance
   On a world of sin.

Unis. 5 Brighter still and brighter
   Glows the western sun,
Shedding all its gladness
   O'er our work that's done;
Time will soon be over,
   Toil and sorrow past;
May we, blessèd Saviour,
   Find a rest at last.

6 Onward, ever onward,
   Journeying o'er the road
Worn by Saints before us,
   Journeying on to God;
Leaving all behind us,
   May we hasten on,
Backward never looking
   Till the prize is won.

Unis. 7. Higher then and higher
   Bear the ransomed soul,
Earthly toils forgotten,
   Saviour, to its goal;
Where in joys unthought of
   Saints with Angels sing.
Never weary raising
   Praises to their King.

APPENDIX

71

Alternative Tune to Hymn 649

ST. MARK. (7 7. 7 7. and 7 7. 7 6.)
Quietly ♩ = 72. To be sung in unison.
M. F. BELL.

Spare us, Ho - ly Tri - ni - ty.
Hear us, Ho - ly Je - su.

A - men.

LITANY OF THE PASSION

Anon. 1867.

GOD the Father, seen of none,
God the sole-begotten Son,
God the Spirit, with them One:
  Spare us, Holy Trinity.

2 Jesu, who for us didst bear
Scorn and sorrow, toil and care,
Hearken to our lowly prayer:
  Hear us, Holy Jesu.

3 By that hour of agony
Spent while thine Apostles three
Slumbered in Gethsemane:

4 By the prayer thou thrice didst pray
That the cup might pass away,
So thou mightest still obey:

5 By the kiss of treachery
To thy foes betraying thee,
By thy harsh captivity:

6 By thy being bound in thrall,
When they led thee, one and all,
Unto Pilate's judgement-hall:

7 By the scourging thou hast borne,
By the purple robe of scorn,
By the reed, and crown of thorn:

8 By the folly of the Jews
When Barabbas they would choose,
And would Christ their King refuse:

9 By thy going forth to die
When they raised their wicked cry,
'Crucify him, crucify!'

10 By the Cross which thou didst bear,
By the cup they bade thee share,
Mingled gall and vinegar:

11 By thy nailing to the Tree,
By the title over thee,
On the hill of Calvary:

12 By thy seven words then said,
By the bowing of thy head,
By thy numbering with the dead:

13 By the piercing of thy side,
By the stream of double tide,
Blood and Water, thence supplied:

14 When temptation sore is rife,
When we faint amidst the strife,
Thou, whose death hath been our
  life: *Save us, Holy Jesu.*

15 While on stormy seas we toss,
Let us count all things as loss,
But thee only on thy Cross:

16 So, with hope in thee made fast,
When death's bitterness is past,
We may see thy face at last:

APPENDIX

Lord, have mercy.
Christ, have mercy.
Lord, have mercy.
Our Father.
℣. The chastisement of our peace was upon him.
℟. And with his stripes we are healed.
First Good Friday Collect.

72

ALTERNATIVE TUNE TO HYMN 652

OLDBRIDGE. (8 8, 8 4.)
In moderate time ♩ = 100.
R. N. QUAILE.

SUITABLE FOR THE EVENING

The Litany of the Deacon.
'Ἀντιλαβοῦ, σῶσον, ἐλέησον.
Tr. J. B.

GOD of all grace, thy mercy send;
Let thy protecting arm defend;
Save us and keep us to the end:
    Have mercy, Lord.

2 And through the coming hours of night,
Fill us, we pray, with holy light;
Keep us all sinless in thy sight:
    Grant this, O Lord.

3 May some bright messenger abide
For ever by thy servants' side,
A faithful guardian and our guide:

4 From every sin in mercy free,
Let heart and conscience stainless be,
That we may live henceforth for thee:

5 We would not be by care opprest,
But in thy love and wisdom rest;
Give what thou seest to be best:

6 While we of every sin repent,
Let our remaining years be spent
In holiness and sweet content:

7. And when the end of life is near,
May we, unshamed and void of fear,
Wait for the Judgement to appear:

Lord, have mercy. Christ, have mercy. Lord, have mercy.
Our Father.
℣. Except the Lord keep the city.
℟. The watchman waketh but in vain.
Collect for Trinity xxi.

APPENDIX

656 A

JERUSALEM

William Blake, 1757-1827.

AND did those feet in ancient time
  Walk upon England's mountains green?
And was the holy Lamb of God
  On England's pleasant pastures seen?
And did the countenance divine
  Shine forth upon our clouded hills?
And was Jerusalem builded here
  Among those dark satanic mills?

2. Bring me my bow of burning gold!
    Bring me my arrows of desire!
  Bring me my spear! O clouds, unfold!
    Bring me my chariot of fire!
  I will not cease from mental fight,
    Nor shall my sword sleep in my hand,
  Till we have built Jerusalem
    In England's green and pleasant land.

TABLE OF OFFICE HYMNS FOR SAINTS' DAYS

NOVEMBER
30 *St. Andrew, Ap.*, 174, 175, 176.

DECEMBER
6 St. Nicolas, Bp. & C., 188, 189.
8 Conception of V. Mary, 213, 214, 215.
13 St. Lucy, V. & M., 191. 192.
21 *St. Thomas, Ap.*, 174, 175, 176.
26 *St. Stephen, M.*, (M.) 180; (M. E.) 31.
27 *St. John, Ev.*, (M.) 174 or 175, (M. E.) 176.
28 *Innocents*, (M.) 182 (1, 4, 5); (M. E.) 183.
31 St. Silvester, Bp. & C., 188, 189.

JANUARY
8 St. Lucian, P. & M., 180, 181.
13 St Hilary, Bp. & C., 188, 189.
18 St. Prisca, V. & M., 191, 192.
20 St. Fabian, Bp. & M., 182, 183.
21 St. Agnes, V. & M., 191, 192.
22 St. Vincent, D. & M., 180.
25 *Conversion of St. Paul*, 174, 175, 176.

FEBRUARY
2 *Purification of V. Mary*, (E.) 208; (M.) 214 or 215; (E.) 22.
3 St. Blasius, Bp. & M., 180, 181.
5 St. Agatha, V. & M., 191, 192.
14 St. Valentine, Bp. & M., 180, 181.
24 *St. Matthias, Ap.*, 174, 175, 176.

MARCH
1 St. David. Abp. & C., 188, 189.
2 St. Chad. Bp. & C., 188, 189.
7 St Perpetua, M., 192, 183.
12 St. Gregory, Bp. & C., 188, 189.
18 St. Edward, K. & M., 180, 181.
21 St. Benedict, Ab. & C., 188, 189.
25 *Annunciation of V. Mary*, (E.) **213**; (M.) **214** or **215**.

APRIL
3 Richard, Bp. & C., 188, 189.
4 St. Ambrose, Bp. & C., 188, 189.
19 St. Alphege, Abp. & M., 180, 181.
23 St. George, M., 180, 181.
25 *St. Mark, Ev.*, (E.) 123 (Pt. 2); (M. E.) 124 (Pt. 2), being in Eastertide.

MAY
1 St. *Philip & St. James, App.*, (E.) **123** (Pt. 2); (M. E.) 124 (Pt. 2).
3 Invention of Cross, (E.) **94** (Pt. 2); (M.) 95; (E.) 96 (Pt. 2).
6 St. John, Ev., a Port Lat., (M. E.) 124 (Pt. 2).
19 St. Dunstan, Abp. & C., 188, 189.
26 St. Augustin, Abp. & C., 188, 189.
27 Ven. Bede, P. & C., 188, 189.

JUNE
1 St. Nicomede, P. & M., 180, 181.
5 St. Boniface, Bp. & M., 182, 183.
11 *St. Barnabas, Ap.*, 174, 175, 176 (or as on May 1 if before Whitsunday).
17 St. Alban, M., 180, 181.
20 Trans. of St. Edward, K. & M., 180, 181.
24 *St. John Baptist*, (E.) 223; (M.) 224.
29 *St. Peter, Ap.*, (E.) 226; (M.) 226, 175 or 176.

JULY
2 Visitation of V. Mary, 228, 229.
4 Trans. of St. Martin, Bp. & C., 188, 189.
15 St. Swithun, Bp. & C., 182 (1, 2. 5), 183.
20 St. Margaret, V. & M., 191, 192.
22 St. Mary Magd., 230, 231.
25 *St. James, Ap.*, 174, 175, 176.
26 St. Anne, 189 (Pt. 2), **191** (Pt. **2**).

TABLE OF OFFICE HYMNS FOR SAINTS' DAYS

AUGUST
- 1 **Lammas Day**, 174, 175, 176.
- 6 Transfiguration, 233, 234.
- 7 Name of Jesus, 237, 238.
- 10 St. Laurence, D. & M., 180, 181.
- 24 *St. Bartholomew, Ap.*, 174, 175, 176.
- 28 St. Augustin, Bp. & C., 188, 189.
- 29 Beheading of St. John Baptist, 180, 181.

SEPTEMBER
- 1 St. Giles, Abbot & C., 188, 189.
- 7 St. Evurtius, Bp. & C., 188, 189.
- 8 Nat. of V. Mary, 213, 214, 215, 22.
- 14 Holy Cross Day, (E.) 94 (Pt. 2); (M.) 95; (E.) 96 (Pt. 2).
- 17 St. Lambert, Bp. & M., 180, 181.
- 21 *St. Matthew, Ap.*, 174, 175, 176.
- 26 St. Cyprian, Abp. & M., 180, 181.
- 29 *St. Michael & All Angels*, 241, 242.
- 30 St. Jerome, P. & C., 188, 189.

OCTOBER
- 1 St. Remigius, Bp. & C., 182 (1, 2, 5), 183.
- 6 St. Faith, V. & M., 191, 192.
- 9 St. Denys, Bp. & M., 182, 183.
- 13 Trans. K. Edw. Conf., 188, 189
- 17 St. Etheldreda, V., 191 (1, 4, 5), 192.
- 18 *St. Luke, Ev.*, 174, 175, 176.
- 25 St. Crispin, M., 182, 183.
- 28 *St. Simon & St. Jude, App.*, 174, 175, 176.

NOVEMBER
- 1 *All Saints' Day*, 249.
- 6 St. Leonard, C., 188, 189.
- 11 St. Martin, Bp. & C., 188, 189.
- 13 St. Britius, Bp. & C., 188, 189.
- 15 St. Machutus, Bp. & C., 188, 189.
- 17 St. Hugh, Bp. & C., 188, 189.
- 20 St. Edmund, K. & M., 180, 181.
- 22 St. Cecilia, V. & M., 191, 192.
- 23 St. Clement, Bp. & M., 180, 181.
- 25 St. Catherine, V. & M., 191, 192.

	1ST E.	M.	2ND E.
APOSTLE or EVANGELIST	174	174, 175, or 176	176
ONE MARTYR	180	180 or 181	181
MANY MARTYRS	182	182 or 183	183
CONFESSOR	188	188 or 189	189
VIRGIN	191	191 or 192	192

HYMNS SELECTED AND ARRANGED FOR SUNDAYS AND HOLY DAYS

M. = *Mattins*, the Office Hymn being first. **G.** = *General*, i.e. hymns which may be added when more hymns are required for Mattins, or which may be used in the place of any of the hymns that are suggested for Morning or Evening. **P.** = *Procession.* **H.C.** = *Holy Communion*, the hymns being in the following order; (1) Before the Gospel; (2) At the Offertory; (3) At the Communion; (4) After the Blessing. **E.** = *Evensong*, the hymns being in the following order: (1) Office Hymn; (2) Instead of the Anthem; (3) Before the Sermon; (4) After the Sermon. **L.** = *Litany*.

ADVENT SUNDAY

M. 2 *Verbum supernum prodiens.*
    553 Thou whose almighty (*or* 3).
G.   6 Hark the glad sound (*or* 518).
    504 Thy kingdom come!
H.C. 10 Saviour eternal (*or* 492).
    12 Wake, O wake (*or* 495).
    420 Jesus shall reign.
    11 The advent of our God.
E.   1 *Conditor alme siderum.*
    450 O God, our help.
    5 Hark! a herald voice
    7 Lo! he comes (*or* 365).
(L.   *If any*, 735, *Advent Prose*.)

ADVENT II

M.   2 *Verbum supernum prodiens.*
    408 Immortal love.
G.   549 Lift up your heads (*or* 548).
    436 Lord, thy word abideth.
H.C. 10 Saviour eternal (*or* 492)
    3 Behold the Bridegroom (*or* 464).
    310 From glory to glory.
    13 When came in flesh.
E.   1 *Conditor alme siderum.*
    6 Hark the glad sound.
    462 O quickly come (*or* 43).
    495 The world is very evil.
(L.   *If any*, 735).

ADVENT III

M.   2 *Verbum supernum prodiens.*
    9 On Jordan's bank.
G.   7 Lo! he comes (*or* 467).
    5 Hark! a herald voice.
H.C. 10 Saviour eternal.

    8 O come, O come.
    325 O Word immortal (*or* 420).
    562 O God of earth.
E.   1 *Conditor alme siderum.*
    13 When came in flesh.
    492 The Lord will come.
    374 Christian seek not (*or* 8).
(L.   *If any*, 735).

ADVENT IV

M.   2 *Verbum supernum prodiens.*
    6 Hark the glad sound.
G.   9 On Jordan's bank (*or* 558).
    13 When came in flesh.
H.C. 10 Saviour, eternal.
    12 Wake, O wake (*or* 8).
    323 O most merciful.
    11 The advent of our God.
E.   1 *Conditor alme siderum.*
    404 How shall I sing (*or* 7).
    518 Ye servants of the Lord.
    8 O come, O come.
(L.   *If any*, 735).

CHRISTMAS EVE

E.   14 *Veni, Redemptor gentium.*
    16 The Maker of the sun.
    30 While shepherds watched.
    15 O little town.
P.   613 Of the Father's heart.

CHRISTMAS-DAY

M.   17 *Christe Redemptor* (*or* 18).
    21 Christians, awake.
G.   30 While shepherds watched.
    24 Hark! the herald (*or* 20).

TABLE OF HYMNS FOR

P.   614 O come, all ye faithful.
H.C. 22 Come rejoicing (*or* 30).
      24 Hark! the herald Angels.
    613 Of the Father's heart.
      19 A great and mighty (*or* 30).
E.   18 *A solis ortus cardine*.
      24 Hark! the herald (*or* 23).
      25 In the bleak mid-winter.
      26 It came upon the midnight.
P.   613 Of the Father's heart.

CHRISTMAS I

M.   17 *Christe Redemptor omnium*.
      15 O little town.
G.   26 It came upon the midnight.
      24 Hark! the herald (*or* 25).
P.   613 Of the Father's heart.
H.C. 22 Come rejoicing (*or* 611).
      28 O come all ye (*or* 24).
    310 From glory (*or* 28).
      20 Behold the great Creator.
E.   18 *A solis ortus cardine*.
      30 While shepherds watched.
      24 Hark! the herald (*or* 20).
      25 In the bleak mid-winter.
P.   614 O come all ye faithful.

THE EPIPHANY

M.   38 *Hostis Herodes impie*.
      43 The race that long.
P.   615 From the eastern mountains.
    616 Hail, thou Source.
H.C. 19 A great and mighty (*or* 373).
      42 O worship the Lord (*or* 40).
    325 O Word immortal.
      44 What star is this (*or* 39).
E.   38 *Hostis Herodes impie*.
      40 Bethlehem, of noblest.
      41 Brightest and best.
      39 As with gladness.
P.   615 From the eastern (*or* 45).
    616 Hail, thou Source.

EPIPHANY I

M.   38 *Hostis Herodes impie*.
      44 What star is this.
G.   41 Brightest and best.
      29 The great God of heaven.
P.   615 From the eastern mountains.
    616 Hail, thou Source.
H.C. 19 A great and mighty.
      39 As with gladness.
    306 (Pt. 2) Sun, who all my life.
      40 Bethlehem, of noblest.

E.   38 *Hostis Herodes impie*.
      43 The race that long.
      26 It came upon the midnight.
      42 O worship the Lord.
P.   615 From the eastern (*or* 45).
    616 Hail, thou Source.

EPIPHANY II

(If not the last Sunday)

M.   50 *Primo dierum omnium*.
      48 The Lord is come.
G.   375 City of God.
      43 The race that long.
H.C. 20 Behold the great Creator.
    364 All hail the power.
    306 (Pt. 2) Sun, who (*or* 397).
      45 Hail to the Lord's (*or* 364).
E.   51 *Lucis Creator optime*.
    407 Immortal, invisible.
    295 'Tis winter now (*or* 427).
      47 Songs of thankfulness.

EPIPHANY III

(If not the last Sunday)

M.   50 *Primo dierum omnium*.
    536 Praise to the Lord.
G.   459 O Love, how deep.
      26 It came upon the midnight.
H.C. 420 Jesus shall reign.
      47 Songs of thankfulness.
    312 Here, O my Lord.
    365 All people (*or* 43).
E.   51 *Lucis Creator optime*.
    503 Through the night (*or* 381).
    470 Praise, my soul.
    364 All hail the power (*or* 45).

EPIPHANY IV

(If not the last Sunday)

M.   50 *Primo dierum omnium*.
    481 Songs of praise.
G.   388 Fierce was the wild billow.
    514 Who is this so weak (*or* 393).
H.C. 419 Jesu, the very thought (*or* 464).
    380 Come, ye faithful . . .
    309 For the beauty (*or* 310).
    373 Children of the heavenly.
E.   51 *Lucis Creator optime*.
      48 The Lord is come.
    423 Judge eternal, throned.
    274 Sun of my soul.

EPIPHANY V

(If not the last Sunday)

M.   50 *Primo dierum omnium*.

SUNDAYS AND HOLY DAYS

	420 Jesus shall reign.
G.	47 Songs of thankfulness.
	48 The Lord is come.
H.C.	376 Come, let us join.
	42 O worship the Lord (*or* 407).
	303 Author of life divine.
	43 The race that long.
E.	51 *Lucis Creator optime.*
	598 Jesus, good above.
	45 Hail to the Lord's Anointed.
	266 At even when the sun.

LAST SUNDAY AFTER THE EPIPHANY

M.	50 *Primo dierum omnium.*
	395 God of mercy.
G.	420 Jesus shall reign.
	45 Hail to the Lord's Anointed.
H.C.	238 (Pts. 1 and 3) Jesu!—the very.
	364 All hail the power (*or* 63).
	303 Author of life divine.
	384 Eternal Ruler.
E.	51 *Lucis Creator optime.*
	427 Let all the world.
	365 All people.
	404 How shall I sing.

SEPTUAGESIMA

M.	50 *Primo dierum omnium.*
	299 When spring unlocks (*or* 284).
G.	258 Christ, whose glory fills.
	407 Immortal, invisible.
H.C.	64 Maker of earth, to thee.
	297 The spacious firmament.
	384 Eternal Ruler.
	412 Jerusalem the golden (*or* 298).
E.	51 *Lucis Creator optime.*
	497 There is a book.
	466 O worship the King.
	587 All things bright.

SEXAGESIMA

M.	50 *Primo dierum omnium*
	257 (Pt. 1) Awake, my soul.
G.	464 O thou not made.
	448 O God of mercy.
H.C.	434 Lord of all being.
	470 Praise, my soul.
	326 (Pt. 2) Therefore we.
	471 Praise to the Holiest (*or* 298).
E.	51 *Lucis Creator optime*
	402 He who would valiant be.
	281 Through the day (*or* 296).
	267 Glory to thee, my God.

QUINQUAGESIMA

M.	50 *Primo dierum omnium.*
	257 (Pt. 2) Glory to thee.
G.	283 Most glorious Lord.
	408 Immortal love for ever.
H.C.	64 Maker of earth, to thee.
	438 Love of the Father.
	437 Love Divine, all loves.
	506 To Mercy, Pity.
E.	51 *Lucis Creator optime.*
	396 Gracious Spirit.
	460 O Love, who formest me.
	392 For thee, O dear, dear.

ASH WEDNESDAY

M.	66 *Audi benigne Conditor.*
	442 My Lord, my Life (*or* 87).
H.C.	74 Have mercy, Lord, on me.
	107 When I survey (*or* 86).
	331 Thee we adore.
	327 Once, only once (*or* 76).
E.	65 *Ex more docti mystico.*
	84 O Lord, turn not away (*or* 449).
	73 Forty days and forty.
	529 Son of God, eternal.
L.	Psalm 51 (1-18).

LENT I

M.	66 *Audi benigne Conditor.*
	85 O thou from whom (*or* 889).
G.	80 My God, I love thee.
	562 O God of earth (*or* 445)
H.C.	92 When, rising from (*or* 78).
	70 Ah, holy Jesu (*or* 168).
	331 Thee we adore.
	167 Pour out thy Spirit.
E.	65 *Ex more docti mystico.*
	167 Pour out thy Spirit.
	90 To my humble.
	411 Jerusalem on high (*or* 72).
(L.	*If any,* 736, *or* 652.)

LENT II

M.	66 *Audi benigne Conditor.*
	515 Wilt thou forgive (*or* 83).
G.	400 Hark, my soul (*or* 82).
	84 O Lord, turn not away.
H.C.	442 My Lord, my Life.
	450 O God, our help (*or* 92).
	320 My God, and is thy Table.
	423 Judge eternal.
E.	65 *Ex more docti mystico.*
	477 Rock of ages, cleft for me.
	77 Lord Jesus, think (*or* 479).

TABLE OF HYMNS FOR

    498 There is a land (*or* 408).
(L.   *If any*, 736, *or* 652).

LENT III

M.   **68** *Clarum decus jejunii* (*or* 69).
    397 Guide me, O thou.
G.   **456** O Lord, and Master.
    418 Jesu, name all names above.
H.C. 430 Lighten the darkness.
    484 Take up thy cross (*or* 72).
    405 How sweet the name.
    385 Father, hear the prayer.
E.   **67** *Ecce tempus idoneum*.
    79 Lord, when we bend (*or* 448).
    83 O help us, Lord.
    267 Glory to thee, my God.
(L.   *If any*, 736, *or* 652.)

MOTHERING SUNDAY or REFRESHMENT SUNDAY

M.   **68** *Clarum decus jejunii* (*or* 69).
    529 Son of God (*or* 82).
G.   **510** We sing the praise (*or* 447).
    422 Jesus, where'er (*or* 406).
H.C. 367 As pants the hart (*or* 90).
    528 Father of men (*or* 316).
    490 The King of love.
    475 Rejoice, O land (*or* 93, *or* 531).
E.   **67** *Ecce tempus idoneum*.
    93 The God of love (*or* 490).
    531 Father, who (*or* 272).
    383 Dear Lord and Father (*or* 491).
(L.   *If any*, 652, *or* 736.)

PASSION SUNDAY

M.   **95** *Pange lingua gloriosi* (*or* 96).
    106 There is a green hill.
G.   **96** Thirty years among us.
    107 When I survey (*or* 409).
H.C. **98** Drop, drop, slow tears.
    97 Dost thou truly seek.
    305 Bread of the world.
    102 O sacred head.
E.   **94** *Vexilla Regis prodeunt*.
    105 Sweet the moments.
    103 O sinner, raise the eye.
    418 Jesu, name (*or* 97).
(L.   *If any*, Psalm 51 (1-18).)

PALM SUNDAY

M.   **95** *Pange lingua gloriosi* (*or* 96).
    109 O thou who through.
G.   **96** Thirty years among us.
    102 O sacred head (*or* 622).
P.   **617** to 623.

H.C. **98** Drop, drop, slow tears.
    107 When I survey.
    305 Bread of the world.
    100 Go to dark Gethsemane.
E.   **94** *Vexilla Regis prodeunt*.
    106 There is a green hill.
    620 Ride on! ride on (*or* 97).
    477 Rock of ages (*or* 108).
(L.   *If any*, Psalm 51 (1-18).)

EASTER EVEN

E.   **339** With Christ we share.
    121 By Jesus' grave.
    118 It is finished.
(P.   *If any*, 652, *or* 461.)

EASTER-DAY

M. (**139** Ye choirs of new Jerusalem).
    133 Jesus Christ is risen.
G. **137** The Day of (*or* 124).
    132 He is risen, he is risen.
P. **624** Hail thee, Festival Day.
    625 The strife is o'er.
H.C. 130 Christians, to the (*or* 124).
    128 At the Lamb's high.
    303 Father, see thy children.
    133 Jesus Christ is risen.
E.   (*If any*, **738** *Haec dies*.)
    133 Jesus Christ is risen.
    129 Christ the Lord is risen.
    131 Come, ye faithful, raise.
P. **626** Alleluya! (Ye sons).
    627 The Lord is risen.

EASTER I

M. **123** *Aurora lucis rutilat* (*or* 124).
    127 Alleluya! Alleluya!
G. **124** His cheering (*or* 135).
    126 A brighter dawn.
P. **624** Hail thee, Festival Day.
    625 The strife is o'er.
H.C 130 Christians, to the (*or* 122).
    131 Come, ye faithful, raise.
    133 Jesus Christ is risen (*or* 310).
    134 Jesus lives!
E. **125** *Ad cenam Agni providi*.
    133 Jesus Christ is risen.
    135 Love's redeeming work.
    137 The Day of Resurrection.
P. **626** Alleluya! (Ye sons).
    627 The Lord is risen.

EASTER II (SHEPHERD SUNDAY)

M. **123** *Aurora lucis rutilat* (*or* 124).
    93 The God of love.

SUNDAYS AND HOLY DAYS

- G. 461 O praise our great (*or* 124).
- 139 Ye choirs of new Jerusalem.
- H.C. 130 Christians, to the Paschal.
- 491 The Lord my pasture.
- 319 Lord, enthroned (*or* 238, Pt. 2).
- 135 Love's redeeming work.
- E. 125 *Ad cenam Agni providi.*
- 490 The King of love.
- 138 Thou hallowed chosen.
- 491 The Lord my pasture.

EASTER III

- M. 123 *Aurora lucis rutilat* (*or* 124).
- 283 Most glorious Lord.
- G. 131 Come, ye faithful (*or* 124).
- 134 Jesus lives!
- H.C. 130 Christians, to the (*or* 555).
- 587 All things bright (*or* 534).
- 319 Lord, enthroned.
- 126 A brighter dawn.
- E. 125 *Ad cenam Agni providi.*
- 287 Kindly spring again.
- 132 He is risen, he is risen.
- 535 Praise the Lord! ye.

EASTER IV

- M. 123 *Aurora lucis rutilat* (*or* 124).
- 137 The Day of Resurrection.
- G. 138 Thou hallowed (*or* 124).
- 135 Love's redeeming work.
- H.C. 130 Christians, to the (*or* 504).
- 519 Ye watchers and ye holy.
- 463 O thou in all thy might (*or* 318).
- 534 Praise the Lord of heaven.
- E. 125 *Ad cenam Agni providi.*
- 380 Come, ye faithful ...
- 126 A brighter dawn.
- 512 When morning gilds (*or* 536)

ROGATION SUNDAY

- M. 123 *Aurora lucis rutilat* (*or* 124).
- 423 Judge eternal, throned.
- G. 377 Come, my soul (*or* 565).
- 447 O God of Bethel (*or* 375).
- H.C. 475 Rejoice, O land.
- 474 Prayer is the soul's (*or* 559).
- 140 Lord, in thy name.
- 449 O God of truth (*or* 557).
- E. 125 *Ad cenam Agni providi.*
- 561 Lord, while for all (*or* 384).
- 504 Thy kingdom come.
- 528 Father of men.

- P.L. 558 God of our fathers.
- 565 To thee, our God (*also* 564, 650).

ASCENSION DAY

- M. 142 *Tu Christe nostrum gaudium.*
- 149 Thou art gone up on high.
- P. 628 Hail thee, Festival Day.
- 629 O King most high.
- H.C. 148 The Lord ascendeth up (*or* 380).
- 143 Hail the day.
- 424 King of glory (*or* 301).
- 145 See the Conqueror.
- E. 141 *Aeterne Rex altissime.*
- 147 The head that once.
- 144 O Christ, our hope.
- 146 Sing we triumphant (*or* 476).
- P. 143 Hail the day.
- 629 O King most high.

ASCENSION I

- M. 142 *Tu Christe nostrum gaudium.*
- 143 Hail the day.
- G. 148 The Lord ascendeth up.
- 146 Sing we triumphant.
- P. 628 Hail thee, Festival Day.
- 629 O King most high.
- H.C. 149 Thou art gone up on high.
- 470 Praise, my soul, the King.
- 304 Bread of heaven.
- 147 The head that once.
- E. 141 *Aeterne Rex altissime.*
- 476 Rejoice, the Lord is King.
- 364 All hail the power (*or* 368).
- 145 See the Conqueror.
- P. 143 Hail, the day.
- 629 O King most high.

WHITSUNDAY

- M. 150 *Jam Christus astra ascenderat.*
- 153 Come, Holy Ghost.
- G. 154 Come, O Creator Spirit.
- 384 Eternal Ruler (*or* 158).
- P. 630 Hail thee, Festival Day.
- 631 Spirit of mercy, truth.
- H.C. 155 Come, thou holy Paraclete.
- 152 Come down, O Love.
- 309 For the beauty.
- 157 Our blest Redeemer.
- E. 151 *Beata nobis gaudia.*
- 156 Creator Spirit, by whose aid
- 145 (Pt. 2) Holy Ghost (*or* 152).
- 438 Love of the Father.
- P. 155 Come, thou holy (*or* 212).
- 631 Spirit of mercy, truth.

TABLE OF HYMNS FOR

TRINITY SUNDAY
- **M.** 160 *O Pater sancte (or* 159).
  161, 2–8, Most ancient of *(or* 212).
- **G.** 387 Father of heaven *(or* 434).
  404 How shall I sing.
- **P.** 632 Eternal Light *(or* 384).
  633 All hail, adored *(or* 533).
- **H.C.** 163 O Unity of threefold.
  407 Immortal, invisible.
  384 Eternal Ruler.
  162 Holy, Holy, Holy!
- **E.** 159 *Adesto, sancta Trinitas.*
  463 O thou in all *(or* 501).
  372 Bright the vision.
  466 O worship the King *(or* 162).
- **P.** 212 I bind unto myself *(or* 646).
  212 (9) *(or* 533) Now thank.

TRINITY I
- **M.** 165 *Nocte surgentes.*
  259 Forth in thy name.
- **G.** 562 O God of earth and altar.
  394 God moves in a mysterious.
- **H.C.** 312 Here, O my Lord.
  488 The Church of God.
  313 Holy God, we show forth.
  456 O Lord, and Master.
- **E.** 51 *Lucis Creator optime.*
  467 Oft in danger, oft in woe.
  369 Be thou my Guardian.
  587 All things bright.

TRINITY II
- **M.** 165 *Nocte surgentes.*
  502 Through all the changing.
- **G.** 506 To Mercy, Pity, Peace.
  445 O for a closer walk.
- **H.C.** 312 Here, O my Lord *(or* 475).
  507 To the name that brings.
  329 Strengthen for service.
  398 Happy are they.
- **E.** 51 *Lucis Creator optime.*
  448 O God of mercy.
  473 Pray when the morn.
  407 Immortal, invisible.

TRINITY III
- **M.** 165 *Nocte surgentes.*
  365 All people that on earth.
- **G.** 470 Praise, my soul, the King.
  405 How sweet the name *or* (504).
- **H.C.** 463 O thou in all thy might.
  464 O thou not made with hands.
  300 According to.

480 Soldiers, who are Christ's.
- **E.** 51 *Lucis Creator optime.*
  491 The Lord my pasture.
  492 The Lord will come.
  299 When spring unlocks.

TRINITY IV
- **M.** 165 *Nocte surgentes.*
  424 King of glory.
- **G.** 450 O God, our help in ages.
  414 Jesu, Lover of my soul.
- **H.C.** 472 Pray that Jerusalem.
  449 O God of truth.
  321 O Food of men wayfaring.
  371 Brief life is here our portion.
- **E.** 51 *Lucis Creator optime.*
  269 O gladsome light.
  439 My faith looks up to thee.
  452 O happy band *(or* 587).

TRINITY V
- **M.** 165 *Nocte surgentes.*
  288 The summer days.
- **G.** 496 There is a blessèd home.
  503 Through the night.
- **H.C.** 428 Let saints on earth.
  383 Dear Lord and Father.
  329 Strengthen for service.
  506 To Mercy, Pity, Peace.
- **E.** 51 *Lucis Creator optime.*
  435 Lord of our life.
  409 In the Cross *(or* 555).
  278 The duteous day.

TRINITY VI
- **M.** 165 *Nocte surgentes.*
  256 At thy feet, O Christ.
- **G.** 411 Jerusalem on high.
  587 All things bright.
- **H.C.** 472 Pray that Jerusalem.
  432 Long did I toil.
  421 Jesus, these eyes.
  446 O for a thousand tongues.
- **E.** 51 *Lucis Creator optime.*
  296 Hark, my soul, how *(or* 574).
  430 Lighten the darkness.
  465 O what their joy *(or* 274).

TRINITY VII
- **M.** 165 *Nocte surgentes.*
  258 Christ, whose glory fills.
- **G.** 474 Prayer is the soul's.
  406 I look to thee in every need.
- **H.C.** 443 My spirit longs for thee.

SUNDAYS AND HOLY DAYS

    408 Immortal love for ever.
    307 Draw nigh, and take.
    434 Lord of all being.
E.   51 *Lucis Creator optime.*
    485 Teach me, my God.
    376 Come, let us join our.
    498 There is a land of pure.

TRINITY VIII

M. 165 *Nocte surgentes.*
    442 My Lord, my Life.
G. 479 Soldiers of Christ, arise.
    516 Work is sweet.
H.C. 448 My spirit longs for thee.
    362 A safe stronghold (*or* 403).
    305 Bread of the world.
    449 O God of truth.
E.   51 *Lucis Creator optime.*
    425 Lead, kindly Light.
    389 Fight the good fight.
    544 O Faith of England (*or* 529).

TRINITY IX

M. 165 *Nocte surgentes.*
    451 O God, thy power.
G. 504 Thy kingdom come.
    365 All people.
H.C. 598 Jesus, good above all other.
    298 Thou art, O God, the life.
    414 Jesu, lover of my soul.
    397 Guide me, O thou great.
E.   51 *Lucis Creator optime.*
    373 Children of the heavenly.
    398 Happy are they.
    279 The radiant morn (*or* 278).

TRINITY X

M. 165 *Nocte surgentes.*
    257 (Pt. 2) Glory to thee.
G. 412 Jerusalem the golden (*or* 497)
    518 Ye servants of the Lord.
H.C. 375 City of God.
    458 O Lord of hosts, all heaven.
    302 And now, O Father.
    427 Let all the world.
E.   51 *Lucis Creator optime.*
    407 Immortal, invisible.
    385 Father, hear the prayer.
    431 Light's abode (*or* 503).

TRINITY XI

M. 165 *Nocte surgentes.*
    394 God moves in a mysterious.

G. 456 O Lord, and Master of us all.
    509 We saw thee not.
H.C. 472 Pray that Jerusalem.
    464 O thou not made.
    406 I look to thee.
    510 We sing the praise.
E.   51 *Lucis Creator optime.*
    402 He who would valiant be.
    272 Round me falls the night.
    411 Jesusalem on high.

TRINITY XII

M. 165 *Nocte surgentes.*
    423 Judge eternal.
G. 421 Jesus, these eyes.
    473 Pray when the morn.
H.C. 453 O Holy Spirit, Lord.
    393 Glorious things of thee.
    309 For the beauty.
    310 From glory to glory.
E.   51 *Lucis Creator optime.*
    574 I heard the voice (*or* 268).
    401 He wants not friends.
    363 Abide with me.

TRINITY XIII

M. 165 *Nocte surgentes.*
    375 City of God.
G. 446 O for a thousand tongues.
    492 The Lord will come.
H.C. 333 Victim Divine.
    499 There's a wideness.
    314 Holy Jesus! (*or* 313).
    506 To Mercy, Pity, Peace.
E.   51 *Lucis Creator optime.*
    297 The spacious firmament.
    405 How sweet the name.
    529 Son of God, eternal.

TRINITY XIV

M. 165 *Nocte surgentes.*
    429 Lift up your hearts.
G. 365 All people that on earth.
    480 Soldiers, who are Christ's.
H.C. 422 Jesus, where'er (*or* 238, Pts.
             1, 3).
    461 O praise our great.
    307 Draw nigh, and take.
    511 When all thy mercies.
E.   51 *Lucis Creator optime.*
    267 Glory to thee, my God.
    517 Ye holy angels bright.
    470 Praise, my soul, the King.

TABLE OF HYMNS FOR

TRINITY XV

M.	165	*Nocte surgentes.*
	406	I look to thee in every need.
G.	485	Teach me, my God.
	463	O thou in all thy might.
H.C.	457	O Lord, how happy.
	309	For the beauty of the earth.
	322	O lead my blindness.
	409	In the Cross of Christ.
E.	51	*Lucis Creator optime.*
	402	He who would valiant be.
	270	Holy Father, cheer our way.
	466	O worship the King (*or* 516).

TRINITY XVI

M.	165	*Nocte surgentes.*
	260	New every morning.
G.	383	Dear Lord and Father.
	467	Oft in danger, oft in woe.
H.C.	300	According to thy gracious.
	438	Love of the Father (*or* 489).
	464	O thou not made (*or* 405).
	437	Love Divine, all loves.
E.	51	*Lucis Creator optime.*
	375	City of God.
	433	Lord, it belongs not.
	414	Jesu, Lover of my soul.

TRINITY XVII

M.	165	*Nocte surgentes.*
	422	Jesus, where'er thy people.
G.	489	The Church's one (*or* 544).
	483	Strong Son of God.
H.C.	472	Pray that Jerusalem.
	334	Eternal Ruler (*or* 464).
	458	O Lord of hosts.
	488	The Church of God.
E.	51	*Lucis Creator optime.*
	503	Through the night.
	278	The duteous day (*or* 294, *cf. Trin.* xx).
	435	Lord of our life (*or* 277).

TRINITY XVIII

M.	165	*Nocte surgentes.*
	441	My God, how wonderful.
G.	458	O Lord of hosts, all heaven.
	391	For ever with the Lord.
H.C.	463	O thou in all thy might.
	404	How shall I sing.
	406	I look to thee.
	434	Lord of all being, throned.
E.	51	*Lucis Creator optime.*
	408	Immortal love for ever.

	389	Fight the good fight.
	273	Saviour, again (*or* 464).

TRINITY XIX

M.	165	*Nocte surgentes.*
	421	Jesus, these eyes.
G.	383	Dear Lord and Father.
	377	Come, my soul.
H.C.	320	My God, and is thy Table.
	512	When morning gilds (*or* 404).
	329	Strengthen for service.
	449	O God of truth.
E.	51	*Lucis Creator optime.*
	267	Glory to thee, my God.
	499	There's a wideness.
	486	Ten thousand times (*or* 274).

TRINITY XX

M.	165	*Nocte surgentes.*
	410	In the hour of my distress (*or* 463).
G.	376	Come, let us join our.
	412	Jerusalem the golden.
H.C.	475	Rejoice, O land.
	478	Sing praise to God.
	424	King of glory.
	491	The Lord my pasture.
E.	51	*Lucis Creator optime.*
	294	The year is swiftly (*or* 278, *cf. Trin.* xvii).
	274	Sun of my soul.
	498	There is a land of pure.

TRINITY XXI

M.	165	*Nocte surgentes.*
	367	As pants the hart (*or* 503).
G.	362	A safe stronghold (*or* 456).
	485	Teach me, my God.
H.C.	454	O King enthroned.
	474	Prayer is the soul's.
	427	Let all the world.
	385	Father, hear the prayer.
E.	51	*Lucis Creator optime.*
	479	Soldiers of Christ, arise.
	268	God, that madest earth.
	500	They whose course.

TRINITY XXII

M.	165	*Nocte surgentes.*
	257	Awake, my soul.
G.	439	My faith looks up to thee.
	365	All people that on earth.
H.C.	472	Pray that Jerusalem.
	507	To the name that brings.
	458	O Lord of hosts.
	373	Children of the heavenly.

SUNDAYS AND HOLY DAYS

E. 51 *Lucis Creator optime.*
    464 O thou not made with hands.
    450 O God, our help.
    407 Immortal, invisible.

TRINITY XXIII

M. 165 *Nocte surgentes.*
    375 City of God.
G. 444 Nearer, my God, to thee.
    376 Come, let us join.
H.C. 238 (Pts. 1, 3) Jesu!—the very.
    393 Glorious things of thee.
    324 O thou who at (*or* 419, Pt. 2).
    395 God of mercy, God of grace.
E. 51 *Lucis Creator optime.*
    397 Guide me, O thou great.
    445 O for a closer walk.
    363 Abide with me (*or* 392).

TRINITY XXIV

M. 165 *Nocte surgentes.*
    400 Hark, my soul! it is the Lord.
G. 379 Come unto me, ye weary.
    378 Come, O thou (*or* 504).
H.C. 498 There is a land.
    455 O let him whose sorrow.
    318 Let all mortal flesh.
    398 Happy are they.
E. 51 *Lucis Creator optime.*
    272 Round me falls the night.
    428 Let saints on earth.
    470 Praise, my soul, the King.

LAST SUNDAY AFTER TRINITY

M. 165 *Nocte surgentes.*
    426 Lead us, heavenly Father.
G. 536 Praise to the Lord, the.
    371 Brief life is here our portion.
H.C. 447 O God of Bethel.
    502 Through all the changing.
    318 Let all mortal flesh.
    365 All people that on earth.
E. 51 *Lucis Creator optime.*
    450 O God, our help.
    271 O Strength and Stay.
    533 Now thank we all our God.

DEDICATION FESTIVAL AND OCTAVE

M. 169 *Urbs beata Jerusalem* (*or* 170).
    171 O Word of God above (*or* 464).
G. 469 Pleasant are thy courts (*or* 401).
    500 They whose course.
    393 Glorious things (*or* 508).

    489 The Church's one foundation.
P. 634 Hail thee, Festival (*or* 503).
    635 Eternal Power.
H.C. 172 Sion's daughters!
    544 O Faith of England.
    322 O lead my blindness.
    533 Now thank we all our God.
E. 170 *Angularis fundamentum.*
    450 O God, our help.
    472 Pray that Jerusalem.
    545 Thy hand, O God.
P. 636 Only-Begotten (*or* 172, 544, 643, 644, 645).
    637 Lo! God (*or* 533, 526, v. 3).

PATRONAL FESTIVAL

M. (Proper Office Hymn of the Saint.)
    195 Another year completed.
    (See Apostles, &c., 177–179; Martyrs, 184–187; Bishops, 190; Matrons, 193).
P. 643 Onward, Christian (*or* 641).
    639 The Church triumphant.
H.C. (Proper Hymn of the Saint.)
    200 Joy and triumph (*or* 411).
    329 Strengthen for service.
    199 How bright these glorious.
E. (Proper Office Hymn of the Saint.)
    393 Glorious things.
    196 For all thy Saints.
    198 Hark! the sound of holy.
P. 641 For all the Saints (*or* 638).
    535 (Pt. 2) Worship, honour.

A SAINT'S DAY; APOSTLE OR EVANGELIST [174).

M. 175 *Aeterna Christi munera* (*or* 176, (Proper Hymn of the Saint.)
    239 Saints of God.
G. 401 He wants not friends.
    412 Jerusalem the golden.
P. 200 Joy and triumph (*or* 204, 641).
    639 The Church (*or* 535, Pt. 1).
H.C. 177 Captains of the (*Ap.*).
    or 179 Come sing (*Ev.*).
    203 What are these that glow.
    313 Holy God, we show (*or* 310).
    198 Hark! the sound of holy.
E. 176 *Exultet caelum laudibus.*
    197 Give me the wings.
    199 How bright these glorious.
    178 Disposer supreme.
P. 641 For all (*or* 198, 412, 638).
    536, v. 1, Praise to (*or* 196, 639).

HYMNS FOR SUNDAYS AND HOLY DAYS

A SAINT'S DAY. MARTYR

M. Proper Office Hymns, 180–183.
185 Blest Martyr, let thy triumph.
G. 480 Soldiers, who are Christ's.
P. 202 The Son (or 203, 641, 645).
639 The Church (or 536, v. 1).
H.C. 184 Blessèd Feasts of blessèd.
186 Come, let us join the Church.
458 O Lord of hosts.
187 Let our choir new anthems.
E. Proper Office Hymns, 180–183.
203 What are these (or 198, 519).
204 Who are these, like stars.
201 Palms of glory.
202 The Son of God goes forth.
P. 641 For all (or 202, 412, 638, 642).
196 For all thy Saints (or 639).

ST. MARY THE VIRGIN

M. 214 *Quem terra* (or 215).
217 Her Virgin eyes saw God.
G. 370 Blest are the pure (or 218).
215 O glorious (*Mod. tune*, 14).
P. 644 Rejoice, ye pure in heart.
640 Virgin-born, we bow.
H.C. 22 Come rejoicing.
252 Our Father's home.
19 A great and mighty.
519 Ye watchers.
F. 213 *Ave, maris Stella*.
605 Once in royal (or 216).
217 Her Virgin eyes (or 215).
200 Joy and triumph.
P. 638 Jerusalem (or 371, 645).
640 Virgin-born, we bow.

MICHAELMAS

M. 242 *Christe, sanctorum* (or **241**).
243 Around the throne.
G. 517 Ye holy Angels bright.
376 Come, let us join our.
P. 245 Stars of the (or 519).
372 (1, 2, 3) Bright the vision.
H.C. 246 They come, God's.
244 O God the Son eternal.
317 (Pt. 2) Lo! the (or 318).
404 How shall I sing.
E. 241 *Tibi, Christe*.
26 It came upon the midnight.
243 Around the throne.
535 Praise the Lord.
P. 203 What are these (or 245).
372 (4, 5, 6) Heaven is still.

ALL SAINTS

M. 249 *Jesu, Salvator saeculi*.
204 Who are these, like stars.
G. 197 Give me the wings.
202 The Son of God goes.
P. 641 For all (or 200, 203, 464).
639 The Church triumphant.
H.C. 253 Spouse of Christ (or 431).
250 If there be that skills.
500 They whose course.
251 O heavenly Jerusalem.
E. 249 *Jesu, Salvator saeculi*.
199 How bright these glorious.
401 He wants not friends.
486 Ten thousand (or 252).
P. 641 For all the (or 638, or 643).
519 Ye watchers (or 535, v. 2, or Pt. 2, 536, v. 1, 6, or 7).

In the old books Saturday evenings had the same Office Hymn as Sunday evenings, except the eves of the Sunday after Christmas (14), of the Sundays from the Octave of the Epiphany till Lent (49), of the Sundays after Easter (122), of Whit-Sunday (150), and of the Sundays after Trinity (164). But the Office Hymns for the first Evensong of most Saints' Days were the same as those for Mattins, as is shown in the table on p. 945. The Epiphany and Ascension Day (with their Octaves) had the same Office Hymns for first and second Evensong; but no hymns were provided for Easter Even.

Modern hymns that are specially fine in words and music are in many cases suggested for use four or five times in this Table, and are sometimes noted as alternatives also; but some other hymns, reluctantly included in the book in 1906, are omitted in the Table.

The Mission hymns are not intended for ordinary use, nor are metrical litanies: in the latter case only a very reserved use of the better forms for occasions such as Lent is noted in this Table. The singing of a hymn after the Blessing at Evensong is to be deprecated, except on special occasions of thanksgiving.

METRICAL INDEX OF TUNES

Short Metre (S. M.).
Carlisle, 190, 236.
Franconia, 370.
Mount Ephraim, 196.
Narenza, 518, 627.
St. Bride, 74.
St. Edmund, 171.
St. Ethelwald, 479.
St. Michael (Old 134th), 27.
St. Thomas, 11.
Sandys, 485.
Selma, 290.
Song 20, 442.
Southwell, 77.
Windermere, 522.

Double Short Metre (D. S. M.).
Corona, 381.
Ich halte treulich still, 644.
Leominster, 361.
Llanllyfni, 391.
Milites, 281.
Montgomery, *App.* 51.
Old 25th, 149.
Oliva Speciosa, *App.* 49.

Common Metre (C. M.).
Aberdeen, 561.
Abridge, 369.
Albano, 327.
Balfour, 186.
Ballerma, 199.
Bangor, 300.
Bedford, 83.
Belgrave, 511.
Binchester, 398.
Bishopthorpe (or St. Paul's), 408.
Blackbourne, 456.
Bromsgrove, 144.
Bristol, 6.
Burford, 447.
Caithness, 445.
Capel, 488.
Cheerful, 376.
Cheshire, 109.
Coleshill, 492.
Cornhill, 46.
Crediton, 206.
Crowle, 463.
Culross, 525.
Dibdin, 433.
Dundee, 43, 428.
Dunfermline, 64.
Dunstan, 638.
Eardisley, 601.
Eatington, 639.
Epsom, 506.
Farnham, 525.
Farrant, 339.
Harington (Retirement), 85.
Horsley, 106.
Hunnys, 79.
Irish, 504.
Jackson, 210.
Jerusalem, *App.* 69.
Kilmarnock, 542.
King's Langley (Irreg.), 221.
King's Norton, 419.
Lincoln, 140.
London New, 394.
Manchester, 168.
Martyrdom, 367.
Martyrs, 449.
Melrose, 451.
Mendip, 498.
Metzler's Redhead No. 66, *App.* 29.
Miles Lane, 364.
Nativity, *App.* 48.
Newbury, 16.
Northrop, *App.* 8.
Nun danket all, 421.
O God of Love, 446.
Praetorius (Für dein empfangen Speis und Trank), 549.
Relief, 497.
Richmond, 375, 471.
Rodmell, 611.
St. Agnes, *App.* 55.
St. Anne, 450.
St. Austin, 638.
St. Bernard, 71.
St. Botolph, 419.
St. David, 166.
St. Flavian, 161.
St. Fulbert, 139.
St. Hugh, 606.
St. James, 341.
St. Magnus (Nottingham), 147.
St. Mary, 84.
St. Nicholas, 265.
St. Peter, 405.
St. Stephen, 337.
Solomon, 80.
Song 67, 197.
Southill, 639.
Stalham, 638.
Stockton, 82.
Stracathro, 445.
Stroudwater, 158.
Tallis' Ordinal ('9th Tune'), 453.
This Endris Nyght, 20.
University, 93.
Walsall, 13.
Westminster, 441.
Wigton, 354, 474.
Wiltshire, 502.
Winchester Old, 30.
Windsor, 332.
York, 472.

Double Common Metre (D. C. M.).
First Mode Melody, 78.
Forest Green, 15.
Kingsfold, 574.
Noel, 26.
Old 22nd, 163.
Old 44th, 211.
Old 81st (Old 77th), 461.
Old 107th, 493.
Old 137th, 404.
St. Matthew, 526.
Second Mode Melody, 3.
Soll's sein, 288.
Stettin (Nun seht), 202.
Third Mode Melody, 92.

Long Metre (L. M.).
Adesto Sancta Trinitas, 159.
Aeterna Christi Munera, 175.

METRICAL INDEX

Aeterna Christi Munera (Rouen), 151.
Affection, 343.
Alfreton, 240.
Andernach, 50.
Angel's Song (Song 34), 259.
Angelus (Du meiner Seelen), 266.
Auctoritate Saeculi, 176.
Babylon's Streams, 487.
Beata Nobis Gaudia, 185.
Birling, 274.
Breslau, 484.
Brockham, 220.
Calvisius (Ach bleib bei uns), 510.
Cameronian Midnight Hymn, 401.
Cannons, 66.
Cathcart, 546.
Caton (Rockingham), 107, *App.* 45.
Cromer, 237.
Danby, 295.
Daniel, 246.
Das Leiden des Herrn, 387, *App.* 11.
Das walt' Gott Vater, 36.
Deo Gracias, 249.
Der Tag bricht an, 101.
Deus Tuorum Militum, 181.
Duke Street, 167.
Ein Kind gebor'n, 44.
Eisenach, 459.
Erhalt' uns, Herr, 68.
Gaude, regina gloriae, 54, 56.
Gonfalon Royal, 141, 142.
Herongate, 597.
Herr Gott Vater, 274.
Herr Jesu Christ, 173.
Hilariter (Die ganze Welt), 164.
Hursley, *App.* 39.
Hymnus Eucharisticus, 328.
Illsley, 61, 62.
Jena (Das neugeborne Kindelein), 67.
Jesu Corona, 65.
Jesu Dulcis Memoria, 238.

Jesu Redemptor Saeculi, *App.* 26.
Kent, 347.
Leighton, 180.
Llangollen (Lledrod), 556.
Lledrod, *see* Llangollen.
Lucis Creator, 51.
Melcombe, 260, 631.
Monte Cassino, 150.
Montgomery, 632.
Montesano, 122.
Mont Richard, 633.
Morning Hymn, 257.
O amor quam ecstaticus, 214, 215.
O invidenda martyrum, 58, 59, 60.
O Jesu Christ, *App.* 46.
O Jesu mi Dulcissime, 635.
O Salutaris, 330.
Old Hundredth, 365.
Plaistow, 69.
Puer Nobis Nascitur, 14, 610.
Rex Gloriose (French), 125.
Rex Gloriose (Andernach), 183.
Richard, 56, 57.
Rockingham (*see* Caton).
Rouen, 18.
St. Ambrose, 193, 194.
St. Bartholomew, 81.
St. Crispin, *App.* 36.
St. Cross, 111.
St. Gregory (Zeuch meinen Geist), 49.
St. Sepulchre, 422.
St. Venantius, 38.
Sarratt, 34.
Shepton-Beauchamp, 389.
Simeon, 320.
Solemnis Haec Festivitas, 123, 124.
Solothurn, 243.
Song 5, 483.
Tallis' Canon, 267.
Te Lucis Ante Terminum, 264.
The Rosy Sequence, 238.
Truro, 420.

Tugwood, 146.
Uffingham, 434.
Veni Creator (Mechlin version), 154, *App.* 30.
Veni Creator (Tallis), 153.
Verbum Supernum, 2.
Vom Himmel hoch, 17, *App.* 35.
Wareham, 52, 53, 475.
Warrington, 263.
Whitehall, 234.
Winchester New, 9, 620.

PLAINSONG.

1, 2, 14, 17, 18, 38, 49, 50, 51, 52, 53, 54, 55, 56, 57, 58, 59, 60, 61, 62, 65, 66, 67, 68, 69, 94, 122, 123, 124, 125, 141, 142, 150, 151, 154, 159, 164, 175, 176, 180, 181, 183, 189, 192, 214, 215, 233, 234, 237, 238, 249, 254, 255, 261, 262, 264, 330, *App.* 1–6.

Double Long Metre (D. L. M.).

Cantate Domino, 48.
London (Addison's), 297.
Nostre Dieu, 233.
St. Patrick, 212.
Tallis' Lamentation, 235.
Wer da wonet, 35.

48. 84.

Miserere Mei, 403.

54. 54. D.

Fortunatus, 579.

55. 55. 65. 65.

Hanover, 466.
Old 104th, 178.

55. 88. 55.

Seelenbräutigam, 272.

64. 63. D.

Bridgwater, 656.
Langport, 656.

64. 64. D.

St. Issey, 388.

METRICAL INDEX

6 4. 6 4. 6 6 4.
Horbury, 444.

6 4. 6 4. 6 7. 6 4.
Happy Land, 608.

6 4. 6 6.
St. Columba, *App.* 42.
Speer (Sag was hilft), 280.

6 5. 6 5.
Belsize, 415.
Boundary, 99.
Caswall (Wem in Leidenstagen), 315.
Clewer, 455.
Eudoxia, 315, 603.
Gott ein Vater, 600.
Newland, 589.
St. Constantine, *App.* 53.

6 5. 6 5. D.
Adoro Te (No. 2), 308.
Corpus Domini, *App.* 47.
Dun Aluinn, 356.
Goshen, *App.* 70.
Gute Bäume bringen, 72.
King's Weston, 368.
Laus Tibi Christe, 534.
Nous allons, 645.
Sutton Valence, 615.
Zundel, *App.* 68.

6 5. 6 5 *Ter.*
Haydn, 643.
St. Gertrude, 643.
Upwick, 642.

6 6 4. 6 6 6. 4.
Denbigh, 439.
Moscow, 553.
National Anthem, 560.
Olivet, *App.* 58.

6 6. 6 6.
Ave Maris Stella, 213 (Trochaic).
Kingsland, 554 (Iambic).
Maria jung und zart, 443 (Iambic).
Psalm 32, 505 (Iambic).
Quam Dilecta, 508 (Iambic).
Ravenshaw, 436 (Trochaic).
St. Cecilia, *App.* 64 (Iambic).
St. Martin, 416 (Trochaic).
PLAINSONG, 213 (Trochaic).

6 6. 6 6. 4 4. 4 4.
Darwall's 148th, 517.

6 6. 6 6. 6 6.
Old 120th, 209, 464.

6 6. 6 6. D.
Hawarden, 496.
Seventh Mode Melody, 496.

6 6. 6 6. 6 6 8.
Das herrlich hohe Fest, 182.
PLAINSONG, 182.

6 6. 6 6. 8 8.
Christchurch, 411.
Croft's 136th, 565.
Dolgelly, 349.
Gopsal, 476.
Lovely, 303.
Warsaw, 386.
Wesley, 588.

6 6 7. 6 6 7.
Nunc dimittis, 269.

6 6 7. 6 6 7. D.
O Seigneur, 512.

6 6. 8 4.
Temple, 454.

6 6. 8 4. D.
Leoni, 646.

6 6. 8 6. 5 5. 7 6.
I Hear Thy Welcome Voice, 573.

6 6. 10. D.
Hail Harbinger of Morn, 225.

6 6. 11. D.
Down Ampney, 152.

6 7. 6 7. 6 6. 6 6.
Nun danket, 533.

7 4. 7 4. D.
Easter Hymn, 133, *App.* 13.
Gwalchmai, 424.
Llanfair, 143.

7 5. 7 5. 7 7.
Langdale, 590.

7 6. 7 6.
Cherry Tree, 285.
Christus der ist mein Leben, 232, 360.
Devonshire, 294.
Hambridge, 355.
Knecht, 452.
Magdalena, 392.
Paderborn, 251.
St. Alphege, 348.
St. Mary Magdalene, 112.
Thule, 371.

7 6. 7 6. 6 7 6.
Es ist ein' Ros' entsprungen, 19 (Iambic).

7 6. 7 6. D.
Ach Gott von Himmelreiche, 179.
Au fond de ma pensée, *see* Au fort de ma détresse.
Au fort de ma détresse, 252.
Aurelia, 489.
Ave Virgo Virginum, 131 (Trochaic).
Bremen, 195.
Caerlleon, 334.
Calcutta, 547.
Crüger, 45.
Dank sei Gott in der Höhe, 345.
Ellacombe, 137.
Ewing, 412.
Gosterwood, 572, 594, (*See also* 13 13. 14 14.)

METRICAL INDEX

Herzlich thut mich erfreuen, 284.
In der Wiegen, 578.
Kings Lynn, 562.
Llangloffan, 207.
Meirionydd, 473.
Missionary Hymn, 577.
Morning Light, 581.
Passion Chorale, 102.
Pearsall, 495.
Prysgol, 575, 576.
Rhyddid, 222.
Rusper, 379.
St. Catherine, *App.* 65.
St. Theodulph (Valet will ich dir geben), 622.
Thornbury, 545.
Weimar, 187 (Trochaic).
Wohlauf, thut nicht verzagen, 32.

7 6. 7 6. D. and Refrain.

Arms of Jesus, 580.
Greystone, *App.* 66 (Trochaic, Iambic).
Royal Oak, 587 (Trochaic, Iambic).
Tell Me the Old, Old Story, 583.

7 6. 7 6. 7 6. 7 6. 6 6. 8 4.

Wir pflügen, 293.

7 6. 7 6. 7 7 6.

Das ist meine Freude, 97 (Trochaic).

7 6. 7 6. 8 8.

Hominum Amator, 276.
St. Anatolius, *App.* 40.

7 6. 7 6. 8 8. 7 7.

Werde Munter, 418.

7 6. 7 6. 8 8. 8 5.

Kendal, 566.

7 6. 8 6. D.

Komm, Seele, 486.

7 6. 8 6. 8 6. 8 6.

Beneath the Cross, *App.* 22.
Gloria, 567.

7 7 6. D.

In allen meinen Thaten, 321 (Iambic).
Prompto Gentes Animo, 653 (Trochaic).

7 7 6. 7 7 8.

Innsbruck, 86, 278.

7. 7. 7.

Heiliger Geist (Berlin), 76.
St. Philip, *App.* 10.

7 7. 7 3.

Morgenglanz der Ewigkeit, 374.

7 7. 7 5.

Capetown, 501.
Dian, 396.
Huddersfield, *App.* 37.
Ton-Mân, 270.

7 7. 7 6.

Holy comfort, 410 (Trochaic, Iambic).

7 7. 7 7.

Aus der Tiefe, 73.
Boyce, 201.
Buckland, *App.* 67.
Culbach, 286.
Da Christus geboren war, 287.
Dent Dale, 23.
Farnaby, 591. (*See also* 7 7. 7 7 and 7 7. 7 6.)
Freuen wir uns, 314.
Galliard, 649.
Gentle Jesus, 602.
Gott sei Dank, 552.
Harts, 177.
Horsham, 344.
Innocents, 37.
Keine Schönheit hat die Welt, 586.
Lew Trenchard, 591.
Louez Dieu, 377.
Lyne, 296, 596.
Melling, 373.
Monkland, 532.
Nun komm, der Heiden Heiland, 110.

Nun lasst uns geh'n, 104 (Iambic).
Nun lasst uns Gott dem Herren, 126 (Iambic).
Orientis Partibus, 480. (*See also* 7 7. 7 7. 4.)
Palms of Glory, *App.* 33.
Peacefield, 609.
Redhead No. 47, 513.
St. Bees, *App.* 52.
Savannah (Herrnhut), 135.
Song 13, 413.
Tunbridge, 88.
University College, 467.
Vienna, 500.
White Ladies Aston, 400.

PLAINSONG, *App.* 2 (Iambic).

7 7. 7 7. and 7 7. 7 6.

Farnaby, 654. (*See also* 7 7. 7 7.)
Helfer meiner armen Seele, 648.
Litany, 651.
St. Mark, *App.* 71.
Tres Magi de Gentibus, 647.

7 7. 7 7. 4.

Orientis Partibus, 129. (*See also* 7 7. 7 7.)
Wirtemburg, *App.* 12.

7 7 7. D.

Veni Sancte Spiritus, 155.

PLAINSONG, 155.

7 7. 7 7. 7 7.

Arfon, 116.
Bread of Heaven, *App.* 43.
Christopher (Ihr Gestirn'), 304.
Dix, 39.
England's Lane, 309.
Heathlands, 395.
Jesu, Jesu du mein Hirt, 655.
Jesu, meine Zuversicht (*see* Ratisbon).

1000

METRICAL INDEX

Ministres de l'Éternel, 258.
Nicht so traurig, 100.
Pressburg (Nicht so traurig), 358.
Ratisbon (Jesu, meine Zuversicht), 282.
Redhead No. 76, 477.
Voller Wunder, 256, 516.

7 7. 7 7. 7 7. 4 4. 5 5.

Da zu dir der Heiland kam, 313.

7 7. 7 7. D.

Aberystwyth, 87.
Anima Christi, 89.
Benevento, 469.
Hollingside, 414.
Ives, 582.
Maidstone, *App.* 20.
Riley, 481.
Salzburg, 128.
St. Edmund, 47.
St. George, 289.

7 7 7 7. 7 7 7 7. 7 7.

Mendelssohn, 24.

7 7. 8 8. and Refrain.

Resonet in Laudibus, 612.

7 8. 7 8 4.

Christ ist erstanden, 134.
St. Albinus, 134.

7 8. 7 8. 7 8. 8 8.

Jesus ist das schönste Licht (Meine Liebe lebet noch), 247.

7 8. 7 8. 8 8.

Liebster Jesu, 336.

7 8. 8 7. 8 7. 8 7.

Jesu meines Glaubens Zier, 118, 353.

8 4. 8 4. 8 8. 8 4.

Ar Hyd y Nos, 268.
Nutfield, *App.* 15.

8 5. 8 3.

Bullinger, *App.* 18.

Cuttle Mills, 366.
Eastergate, 520.

8 5. 8 5. D.

Hold the Fort, 570.

8 5. 8 5. 8 8. 8 5.

Groombridge, 592.

8 6. 7 6. 7 6. 7 6.

Ingrave, 607.

8 6. 8 4.

St. Cuthbert, *App.* 31.
Wicklow, 157.

8 6. 8 6. 8 6.

Brunswick, 555.

8 6. 8 6. 8 8.

Auch jetzt macht Gott, 550.
O Jesu, 406.

8 6. 8 8 6.

Hammersmith, *App.* 50.
Repton, 383.

8 7. 8 3.

Hornsey, *App.* 28.
Resurrection Morning, 136.

8 7. 8 7.

Ach Gott und Herr, 329 (Iambic).
Batty, 105.
Goldschmidt (O der Alles), 382.
Gott will's machen, 253.
Herald, 205.
Marching, 503.
Merton, 5.
Omni Die, 120.
Parsifal, 629 (Iambic).
Redhead No. 46, 372.
St. Columba, 490 (Iambic).
St. Oswald, *App.* 61.
Shipston, 390, 599.
Stuttgart, 40.
Sussex, 239, 385.
Wychbold, 409.
PLAINSONG, 253.

8 7. 8 7. 4 7.

Bryn Calfaria, 319.
Caersalem, 397.
Helmsley, 7.
Llanilar, 75.
St. Raphael, 75.

8 7. 8 7. 6 6. 6 6 7.

Ein' feste Burg, 362, 537.

8 7. 8 7. 7 7.

All Saints, 204.
Dretzel, 281.
Gott des Himmels, 132.
Irby, 605.
Requiem, *App.* 21.
St. Leonard, 527.

8 7. 8 7. 7 7. 8 8.

Psalm 42, 200.

8 7. 8 7. 8 7.

Ad Perennis Vitae Fontem, 350.
Bryntirion, 248.
Calvary, 530.
Collaudemus, 229, 230.
Dismissal, 523.
Grafton, 33.
Lewes, 250.
Mannheim, 426.
Munster Square, *see* Grafton.
Neander, 241, 380.
Oriel, 228, 507.
Pange Lingua, 326.
Picardy, 318.
Praise my Soul, 470.
Regent Square, 431.
Rhuddlan, 423.
St. Thomas, 31, 623.
Tantum Ergo, 63.
Tantum Ergo (No. 2), 326.
Urbs Coelestis, 169, 170.

PLAINSONG.
31, 95, 96, 169, 170, 228, 229, 230, 231, 241, 326, 737 (p. 895).

8 7. 8 7. 8 7. 6.

Den des Vaters Sinn geboren, 218.

1001

METRICAL INDEX

87. 87. 87. 7.
Divinum Mysterium, 613.

87. 87. D.
Alta Trinita Beata, 184.
Austrian Hymn, 393.
Daily, Daily, 568.
Deerhurst, *App.* 32.
Ebenezer (Ton-y-Botel), 108.
Everton, *App.* 27.
Golden Sheaves, *App.* 17 (Iambic).
Hope, 551.
Hyfrydol, 301.
In Babilone, 145.
Llansannan, 514.
Lugano, 529.
Moriah, 437.
Pleading Saviour, 593.
Praise, 535.
Rex Gloriae, 616.
St. Gall, 292 (Iambic).
Vision, 198.
Würzburg, 127.
Yn y Glyn, 563.
Zum Frieden, 499.

87. 87. 87. 87. 87. 10 6.
Evening Hymn, 569.

87. 87. 88.
Dies ist der Tag, 138.
Mach's mit mir Gott, 138.

87. 87. 887.
Allein Gott in der Höh sei Ehr, 103.
Mit Freuden zart, 604.
Nun freut euch, 148.
Luther's Hymn (Nun freut euch), 4.
Wittenberg (Es ist das Heil), 478.

88. 44. 88. and Alleluyas.
Lasst uns erfreuen, 519.

88 6. D.
Advent, 342.
Magdalen College, 457.
St. Alban, 216.
Song 18, 357.

88. 77.
De Profundis, 90.
Urquell aller Seligkeiten, 640.

88. 77. D.
Mon Dieu, prête-moi l'oreille, 640.

887. D.
Christi Mutter stund vor Schmerzen, 115.
Stabat Mater, 115.
Stabat Mater Dolorosa, 115.

887. 887. D.
Psalm 68, 544.
En moy le secret, *see* Psalm 68.

888.
O Mensch sieh, 121.

888. and Alleluyas.
O Filii et Filiae (1), 626.
O Filii et Filiae (2), 626.

88. 83.
St. Aëlred, *App.* 62.
White Gates, 541.

88. 84.
Es ist kein Tag, 521.
Gaza, 279.
Layriz (Ins Feld geh), 440.
Michael, 652.
Oldbridge, *App.* 72.
St. Leonard, *App.* 41.
Troyte No. 1, *App.* 59.
Victory, 625.

88. 86.
Childhood, 227.
Erskine, *App.* 34.
Fitzwilliam, 448.
Isleworth, 557.
Saffron Walden, 117, 316.

88. 87.
Beatus, 650.
Charing, 531.

Come Faithful People, 619.
Quem Pastores laudavere, 543, 598 (Trochaic).

88. 88 (Trochaic).
Deirdre, 212.

88. 88. 88.
Christchurch, 460.
Coleraine (Vicenza), 333.
David's Harp, 378.
Falkland, 219.
Farmborough, 509.
Folkingham, 558.
Gesius (Heut' triumphiret), 417.
In einem Kripplein lag ein Kind, 338.
Lambeth, 340.
Leicester (or Bedford), 322.
Lodsworth, 275.
Melita, 540.
New 113th, 298.
Old 117th, 637.
St. Chrysostom, *App.* 19.
South Cerney, 359.
Stella, *App.* 54.
Surrey, 491.
Vater unser, 462.
Veni Creator (Attwood), 156.
Veni Emmanuel, 8, *App.* 24.

888. 888.
Exeter, 528.
Llangoedmor, 539.

88. 88. D. (Trochaic).
Schmücke dich, 306.

88. 88. 88. 88. 88.
Etona, 559.

898. 898. 664. 88.
Wachet auf! 12.

97. 97. 99.
The Ninety and Nine, 584.

METRICAL INDEX

9 8. 8 9.
Randolph, 524.

9 8. 9 8.
Les commandemens de Dieu, 277.
St. Clement, *App.* **16.**

9 8. 9 8. 8 8.
Neumark, 458.

9 8. 9 8. D.
Rendez à Dieu, 305.

10 4. 6 6. 6 6. 10 4.
High Road, 427.
Universal Praise, *App.* 56.

10 4. 10 4. 10 10.
Lux Benigna, 425.

10 7. 9 7. 9 7. 9 7. and Refrain.
Bossiney, 571.

10 7. 10 7.
Schönster Herr Jesu, 323.

10 10.
Song 46, 98, 468.

10 10. 6 6. 10.
St. Michael New, 244.

10 10. 10 4.
For all the Saints, *App.* 23.
Luccombe, 641.
Sine Nomine, 641.
Sion's Daughters, *App.* 7 (Trochaic-Dactylic).
PLAINSONG, 172, *App.* 7 (Trochaic-Dactylic).

10 10. 10 10.
Adoro Te, 331.
All Souls, *App.* 57.
Birmingham, 429.
Congleton, 312.
Dalkeith, *App.* 25.
Draw Nigh, 307.
Ellers, *App.* 38.
Erfyniad, 430.
Eventide, 363.

Farley Castle, 217, 283.
Magda, 273.
Psalm 67, 291 (Amphibrachic).
Quedlinburg, 245 (Dactylic).
Regnator Orbis, 465 (Dactylic).
Song 4, 113.
Song 22, 438.
Song 24, 325.
The Sacred Heart, *App.* 44.
Valor, 91.

10 10. 10 10. 8 4.
So giebst du, 515.

10. 10. 10. 10. 10.
Old 124th, 114, 352.

10 10. 10 10. 10 10.
Battle, 432.
Ffigysbren, 324.
Song 1, 302, 384.
Yorkshire (Stockport), 21.

11 10. 11 6.
Langa, *App.* 60.
Stanstead, 482.

11 10. 11 10.
Donne Secours, 564.
Epiphany, *App.* 9 (Dactylic).
Liebster Immanuel, 41 (Dactylic).
L'Omnipotent, 538.
School House, 271.
Welwyn, 346.
Zu meinem Herrn, 119.

11 10. 11 10. 9 11.
Pilgrims of the Night, 399.

11 11. 11 5.
Christe du Beistand, 160.
Christe Fons Jugis, 335.
Christe Sanctorum, 165.
Coelites Plaudant, 242.
Diva Servatrix, 208.
Herr, deinen Zorn, 223, 224.
Herzliebster Jesu, 70.

Iste Confessor, 188.
Iste Confessor (2), **435,** 636.
Ut Queant Laxis, 191.
PLAINSONG.
160, 165, 188, 191, 208, 223, 224, 242.

11 11. 11 11.
St. Denio, 407.

11 11. 11 11. and Refrain.
A Virgin Unspotted, 29.

11 11. 12 11.
Monks Gate, 402.

11 12. 12 10.
Nicaea, 162, *App.* 14.

12 12. 12 12.
Annue Christe, 174.
PLAINSONG, 174, 226.

13 10. 13 10.
Was lebet, was schwebet, 42.

13 13. 14 14.
Gosterwood, 299. (*See also* 7 6. 7 6. D.)

14 14. 4. 7. 8.
Hast du denn, Jesu, 536.

14 14. 14 15.
Sheen, 310.

Irregular.
Adeste Fideles, 28, **614.**
Ave Verum, 311.
Benson, *App.* 63.
Cranham, 25.
East Horndon, 595.
Laetabundus, 22.
Margaret, 585.
Purpose, 548.
Salve Festa Dies, 624.
Troyte No. 2, 494.
Ymdaith Mwngc, 203.
PLAINSONG.
10, 22, 130, 317, 351, 617, 618, 621, 624, 634, *App.* 3.

ALPHABETICAL INDEX OF TUNES

A Virgin Unspotted, 29.
Aberdeen, 561.
Aberystwyth, 87.
Abridge, 369.
Ach bleib bei uns, *see* Calvisius.
Ach, dass ich die letzte Stunde, *see* Zum Frieden.
Ach Gott und Herr, 329.
Ach Gott von Himmelreiche, 179.
Ad Perennis Vitae Fontem, 350.
Addison's, *see* London.
Adeste Fideles, 28, 614.
Adesto Sancta Trinitas, 159.
Adoro Te, 331.
Adoro Te (No. 2), 308.
Advent, 342.
Aeterna Christi Munera, 175.
Aeterna Christi Munera, (Rouen), 151.
Affection, 343.
Agincourt, *see* Deo Gracias.
Albano, 327.
Alfreton, 240.
All Saints, 204.
All Souls, *App.* 57.
Allein Gott in der Höh sei Ehr, 103.
Alle Menschen müssen sterben, *see* Salzburg.
Alta Trinita Beata, 184.
Andernach, 50.
Angel's Song (Song 34), 259.
Angelus (Du meiner Seelen), 266.
Anima Christi, 89.
Annue Christe, 174.
Ar Hyd y Nos, 268.
Arfon, 116.
Arms of Jesus, 580.
Arnstadt, *see* Seelenbräutigam.
Attwood, *see* Veni Creator.

Au fond de ma pensée, *see* Au fort de ma détresse.
Au fort de ma détresse, 252.
Auch jetzt macht Gott, 550.
Auctoritate Saeculi, 176.
Aurelia, 489.
Aus der Tiefe, 73.
Austrian Hymn, 393.
Ave Maris Stella, 213.
Ave Verum, 311.
Ave Virgo Virginum, 131.

Babylon's Streams, 487.
Balfour, 186.
Ballerma, 199.
Bangor, 300.
Battle, 432.
Batty, 105.
Beata Nobis Gaudia, 185.
Beatus, 650.
Bedford (Bishop), *see* Leicester.
Bedford (Weale), 83.
Belgrave, 511.
Belsize, 415.
Beneath the Cross, *App.* 22.
Benevento, 469.
Benson, *App.* 63.
Berlin, *see* Heiliger Geist.
Binchester, 398.
Birling, 274.
Birmingham, 429.
Bishopthorpe (or St. Paul's), 408.
Blackbourne, 456.
Bohemian, *see* O Mensch sieh.
Bossiney, 571.
Boundary, 99.
Boyce, 201.
Bread of Heaven, *App.* 43.
Bremen, 195.
Breslau, 484.
Bridgwater, 656.
Bristol, 6.

Brockham, 220.
Bromsgrove, 144.
Brunswick, 555.
Bryn Calfaria, 319.
Bryntirion, 248.
Buckland, *App.* 67.
Bullinger, *App.* 18.
Burford, 447.

Caerlleon, 334.
Caersalem, 397.
Caithness, 445.
Calcutta, 547.
Calvary, 530.
Calvisius (Ach bleib bei uns), 510.
Cameronian Midnight Hymn, 401.
Cannons, 66.
Cantate Domino, 48.
Capel, 488.
Capetown, 501.
Carlisle, 190, 236.
Caswall (Wem in Leidenstagen), 315.
Cathcart, 546.
Caton (Rockingham), 107, *App.* 45.
Charing, 531.
Cheerful, 376.
Cherry Tree, 285.
Cheshire, 109.
Childhood, 227.
Christ ist erstanden, 134.
Christchurch, 8 8. 8 8. 8 8 (Ouseley), 460.
Christchurch, 6 6. 6 6. 8 8 (Steggall), 411.
Christe du Beistand, 160.
Christe Fons Jugis, 335.
Christe Sanctorum, 165.
Christi Mutter stund vor Schmerzen, 115.
Christopher (Ihr Gestirn'), 304.
Christus der ist mein Leben, 232, 360.
Clewer, 455.
Coelites Plaudant, 242.

1004

ALPHABETICAL INDEX OF TUNES

Coleraine (Vicenza), 333.
Coleshill, 492.
Collaudemus, 229, 230.
Come Faithful People, 619.
Congleton, 312.
Corner, *see* Christi Mutter stund vor Schmerzen.
Cornhill, 46.
Corona, 381.
Corpus Domini, *App.* 47.
Cranham, 25.
Crediton, 206.
Croft's 136th, 565.
Cromer, 237.
Crowle, 463.
Crüger, 45.
Crux fidelis, 737 (p. 895).
Culbach, 286.
Culross, 525.
Cuttle Mills, 366.

Da Christus geboren war, 287.
Daily, Daily, 568.
Dalkeith, *App.* 25.
Danby, 295.
Daniel, 246.
Dank sei Gott in der Höhe, 345.
Darwell's 148th, 517.
Das herrlich hohe Fest, 182.
Das ist meine Freude, 97.
Das Leiden des Herrn, 387, *App.* 11.
Das neugeborne Kindelein, *see* Jena.
Das walt' Gott Vater, 36.
David's Harp, 378.
Da zu dir der Heiland kam, 313.
Deerhurst, *App.* 32.
Deirdre, 212.
Denbigh, 439.
Den des Vaters Sinn geboren, 218.
Dent Dale, 23.
Deo Gracias, 249.
De Profundis, 90.
Der Tag bricht an, 101.
Dessau, *see* Liebster Jesu.
Deus Tuorum Militum, 181.

Devonshire, 294.
Dibdin, 433.
Dian, 396.
Die ganze Welt, *see* Hilariter.
Dies ist der Tag, 138.
Dismissal, 523.
Diva Servatrix, 208.
Divinum Mysterium, 613.
Dix, 39.
Dolgelly, 349.
Donne Secours, 564.
Down Ampney, 152.
Draw Nigh, 307.
Dresden, *see* So giebst du.
Dretzel, 281.
Du meiner Seelen, *see* Angelus.
Duke Street, 167.
Dun Aluinn, 356.
Dundee, 43, 428.
Dunfermline, 64.
Dunstan, 638.

Eardisley, 601.
East Horndon, 595.
Easter Alleluya, *see* Lasst uns erfreuen.
Easter Hymn, 133, *App.* 13.
Eastergate, 520.
Eatington, 639.
Ebenezer (Ton-y-Botel), 108.
Ein' feste Burg, 362, 537.
Ein Kind gebor'n, 44.
Eisenach, 459.
Ellacombe, 137.
Ellers, *App.* 38.
England's Lane, 309.
En moy le secret, *see* Psalm 68.
Epiphany, *App.* 9.
Epsom, 506.
Erfyniad, 430.
Erhalt' uns, Herr, 68.
Erskine, *App.* 34.
Es ist das Heil, *see* Wittenberg.
Es ist ein' Ros' entsprungen, 19.
Es ist kein Tag, 521.
Etona, 559.
Eudoxia, 315, 603.

Evening Hymn, 569.
Eventide, 363.
Everton, *App.* 27.
Ewing, 412.
Exeter, 528.

Falkland, 219.
Farley Castle, 217, 283.
Farmborough, 509.
Farnaby, 591, 654.
Farnham, 525.
Farrant, 339.
Ffigysbren, 324.
First Mode Melody, 78.
Fitzwilliam, 448.
Folkingham, 558.
For all the Saints, *App.* 23.
Forest Green, 15.
Fortunatus, 579.
Franconia, 370.
French, *see* Dundee.
Freu dich, du werthe Christenheit, *see* Wittenberg.
Freuen wir uns, 314.
Für dein empfangen Speis und Trank, *see* Praetorius.

Galliard, 649.
Gaude, regina gloria, 54, 55.
Gaza, 279.
Geduld die soll'n wir haben, *see* Dank sei Gott.
Gentle Jesus, 602.
Gesius (Heut' triumphiret), 417.
Ghent, *see* Adoro Te No. 2.
Gloria, 567.
Golden Sheaves, *App.* 17.
Goldschmidt (O der Alles), 382.
Gonfalon Royal, 141, 142.
Gopsal, 476.
Görlitz, *see* Ach Gott von Himmelreiche.
Goshen, *App.* 70.
Gosterwood, 299, 572, 594.
Gott des Himmels, 132.
Gott ein Vater, 600.
Gott sei Dank, 552.

ALPHABETICAL INDEX OF TUNES

Gott will's machen, 253.
Gräfenberg, *see* Nun danket all.
Grafton, 33.
Greystone, *App.* 66.
Groombridge, 592.
Gute Bäume bringen, 72.
Gwalchmai, 424.

Hail Harbinger of Morn, 225.
Hambridge, 355.
Hammersmith, *App.* 50.
Hanover, 466.
Happy Land, 608.
Harington (Retirement), [85.
Harts, 177.
Hast du denn, Jesu, 536.
Hawarden, 496.
Haydn, 643.
Heathlands, 395.
Heiliger Geist (Berlin), 76.
Heinlein, *see* Aus der Tiefe.
Helder, *see* Wohlauf.
Helfer meiner armen Seele, 648.
Helmsley, 7.
Herald, 205.
Herongate, 597.
Herr, deinen Zorn, 223, 224.
Herr Gott Vater, 274.
Herr Jesu Christ, 173.
Herrnhut, *see* Savannah.
Herzlich thut mich erfreuen, 284.
Herzlich thut mich verlangen, *see* Passion Chorale.
Herzliebster Jesu, 70.
Heut' triumphiret, *see* Gesius.
High Road, 427.
Hilariter (Die ganze Welt), 164.
Hold the Fort, 570.
Hollingside, 414.
Holy Comfort, 410.
Hominum Amator, 276.
Hope, 551.
Horbury, 444.
Hornsey, *App.* 28.
Horsham, 344.

Horsley, 106.
Huddersfield, *App.* 37.
Hunnys, 79.
Hursley, *App.* 39.
Hyfrydol, 301.
Hymnus Eucharisticus, 328.

Ich halte treulich still, 644.
I Hear Thy Welcome Voice, 573.
Ihr Gestirn', *see* Christopher.
Illsley, 61, 62.
In allen meinen Thaten, 321.
In Babilone, 145.
In der Wiegen, 578.
In einem Kripplein lag ein Kind, 338.
Ingrave, 607.
Innocents, 37.
Innsbruck, 86, 278.
Ins Feld geh, *see* Layriz.
Irby, 605.
Irish, 504.
Isleworth, 557.
Iste Confessor, 188.
Iste Confessor (2), 435, 636.
Ives, 582.

Jackson, 210.
Jena (Das neugeborne Kindelein), 67.
Jerusalem, *App.* 69.
Jesu Corona, 65.
Jesu Dulcis Memoria, 238.
Jesu, Jesu du mein Hirt, 655.
Jesu Leiden, Pein und Tod, *see* Weimar.
Jesu, meine Zuversicht, *see* Ratisbon.
Jesu meines Glaubens Zier, 118, 353.
Jesu Redemptor Saeculi, *App.* 26.
Jesus ist das schönste Licht, 247.

Keine Schönheit hat die Welt, 586.

Kendal, 566.
Kent, 347.
Kilmarnock, 542.
Kingsland, 554.
King's Langley, 221.
Kings Lynn, 562.
King's Norton, 419.
King's Weston, 368.
Kingsfold, 574.
Knecht, 452.
Komm, Seele, 486.

Laetabundus, 22.
Lambeth, 340.
Langa, *App.* 60.
Langdale, 590.
Langport, 656.
Lasst uns erfreuen, 519.
Laus Deo, *see* Redhead No. 46.
Laus Tibi Christe, 534.
Layriz (Ins Feld geh), 440.
Leicester (or Bedford), Leighton, 180. [322.
Leominster, 361.
Leoni, 646.
Les commandemens de Dieu, 277.
Lew Trenchard, 591.
Lewes, 250.
Liebster Immanuel, 41.
Liebster Jesu, 336.
Lincoln, 140.
Litany, 651.
Llanfair, 143.
Llangloffan, 207.
Llangoedmor, 539.
Llangollen, 556.
Llanilar, 75.
Llanllyfni, 391.
Llansannan, 514.
Lledrod, *see* Llangollen.
Lobe den Herren, *see* Hast du denn, Jesu.
Lodsworth, 275.
L'Omnipotent, 538.
London (Addison's), 297.
London New, 394.
Louez Dieu, 377.
Lovely, 303.
Luccombe, 641.
Lucis Creator, 51.
Lugano, 529.

ALPHABETICAL INDEX OF TUNES

Luther's Hymn (Nun freut euch), 4.
Lux Benigna, 425.
Lyne, 296, 596.

Mach's mit mir Gott, 138.
Magda, 273.
Magdalen College, 457.
Magdalen Tower Hymn, *see* Hymnus Eucharisticus.
Magdalena, 392.
Maidstone, *App.* 20.
Mainz, *see* Maria jung und zart.
Manchester, 168.
Mannheim, 426.
Marching, 503.
Margaret, 585.
Maria jung und zart, 443.
Martyrdom, 367.
Martyrs, 449.
Meine Liebe lebet noch, *see* Jesus ist das schönste Licht.
Meirionydd, 473.
Melcombe, 260, 631.
Melita, 540.
Melling, 373.
Melrose, 451.
Mendelssohn, 24.
Mendip, 498.
Merton, 5.
Metzler's Redhead No. 66, *App.* 29.
Meyer, *see* Es ist kein Tag.
Michael, 652.
Miles Lane, 364.
Milites, 381.
Ministres de l'Éternel, 258.
Miserere Mei, 403.
Missionary Hymn, 577.
Mit Freuden zart, 604.
Mon Dieu prête-moi l'oreille, 640.
Monkland, 532.
Monks Gate, 402.
Monk's March, *see* Ymdaith Mwngc.
Monte Cassino, 150.
Montesano, 122.
Montgomery (Champness), 632.

Montgomery (Woodbury), *App.* 51.
Mont Richard, 633.
Morgenglanz der Ewigkeit, 374.
Moriah, 437.
Morning Hymn, 257.
Morning Light, 581.
Moscow, 553.
Mount Ephraim, 196.
Munster Square, *see* Grafton.

Narenza, 518, 627.
National Anthem, 560.
Nativity, *App.* 48.
Neander, 241, 380.
Neumark, 458.
New 113th, 298.
Newbury, 16.
Newland, 589.
Newtown, *see* London New.
Nicaea, 162, *App.* 14.
Nicht so traurig, 100.
Nicht so traurig (Pressburg), 358.
Ninth Tune, *see* Tallis' Ordinal.
Noel, 26.
Northrop, *App.* 8.
Nostre Dieu, 233.
Nottingham, *see* St. Magnus.
Nous allons, 645.
Nun danket, 533.
Nun danket all, 421.
Nun freut euch, 148.
Nun freuteuch('Luther's Hymn'), 4.
Nun komm, der Heiden Heiland, 110.
Nun lasst uns geh'n, 104.
Nun lasst uns Gott dem Herren, 126.
Nun seht, *see* Stettin.
Nunc dimittis, 269.
Nutfield, *App.* 15.

O Amor Quam Ecstaticus, 214, 215.
O der Alles, *see* Goldschmidt.
O Filii et Filiae, 626.

O God of Love, 446.
O invidenda martyrum, 58, 59, 60.
O Jesu, 406.
O Jesu Christ, *App.* 46.
O Jesu mi Dulcissime, 635.
O Mensch sieh, 121.
O Salutaris, 330.
O Seigneur, 512.
O Welt, ich muss dich lassen, *see* Innsbruck.
Old 22nd, 163.
Old 25th, 149.
Old 44th, 211.
Old 81st (Old 77th), 461.
Old 100th, 365.
Old 104th, 178.
Old 107th, 493.
Old 117th, 637.
Old 120th, 209, 464.
Old 124th, 114, 352.
Old 134th, *see* St. Michael.
Old 137th, 404.
Oldbridge, *App.* 72.
Oliva Speciosa, *App.* 49.
Olivet, *App.* 58.
Omni Die, 120.
Oriel, 228, 507.
Orientis Partibus, 129, 480.

Paderborn, 251.
Palms of Glory, *App.* 33.
Pange lingua, 326.
Parsifal, 629.
Passion Chorale, 102.
Peacefield, 609.
Pearsall, 495.
Picardy, 318.
Pilgrims of the Night, 399.
Plainsong, *see* p. 968.
Plaistow, 69.
Pleading Saviour, 593.
Praetorius (Für dein empfangen Speis und Trank), 549.
Praise, 535.
Praise my Soul, 470.
Pressburg (Nicht so traurig), 358.
Prompto Gentes Animo, 653.

ALPHABETICAL INDEX OF TUNES

Prysgol, 575, 576.
Psalm 32, 505.
Psalm 42, 200.
Psalm 67, 291.
Psalm 68, 544.
Puer Nobis Nascitur, 14, 610.
Purpose, 548.

Quam Dilecta, 508.
Quedlinburg, 245.
Quem Pastores laudavere, 543, 598.

Randolph, 524.
Ratisbon (Jesu, meine Zuversicht), 282.
Ravenshaw, 436.
Redhead No. 46, 372.
Redhead No. 47, 513.
Redhead No. 76, 477.
Regent Square, 431.
Regnator Orbis, 465.
Relief, 497.
Rendez à Dieu, 305.
Repton, 383.
Requiem, *App.* 21.
Resonet in Laudibus, 612.
Resurrection Morning, 136.
Retirement, *see* Harington.
Rex Gloriae, 616.
Rex Gloriose (French), 125.
Rex Gloriose (Andernach), 183.
Rhosymedre, *see* Lovely.
Rhuddlan, 423.
Rhyddid, 222.
Richard, 56, 57.
Richmond, 375, 471.
Riley, 481.
Rockingham, *see* Caton.
Rodmell, 611.
Rouen, 18.
Royal Oak, 587.
Rusper, 379.

Saffron Walden, 117, 316.
Sag was hilft, *see* Speer.
St. Aëlred, *App.* 62.
St. Agnes, *App.* 55.
St. Alban, 216.
St. Albinus, 134.
St. Alphege, 348.
St. Ambrose, 193, 194.
St. Anatolius, *App.* 40.
St. Anne, 450.
St. Austin, 638.
St. Bartholomew, 81.
St. Bees, *App.* 52.
St. Bernard, 71.
St. Botolph, 419.
St. Bride, 74.
St. Catherine, *App.* 65.
St. Cecilia, *App.* 64.
St. Chrysostom, *App.* 19.
St. Clement, *App.* 16.
St. Columba (Irons), *App.* 42.
St. Columba (Irish melody), 490.
St. Constantine, *App.* 53.
St. Crispin, *App.* 36.
St. Cross, 111.
St. Cuthbert, *App.* 31.
St. David, 166.
St. Denio, 407.
St. Edmund (Gilding), 171.
St. Edmund (Steggall), 47.
St. Ethelwald, 479.
St. Flavian, 161.
St. Fulbert, 139.
St. Gall, 292.
St. George, 289.
St. Gertrude, 643.
St. Gregory (Zeuch meinen Geist), 49.
St. Hugh, 606.
St. Issey, 388.
St. James, 341.
St. Leonard (J. C. Bach), 527.
St. Leonard (Irons), *App.* 41.
St. Magnus (Nottingham), 147.
St. Mark, *App.* 71.
St. Martin, 416.
St. Mary, 84.
St. Mary Magdalene, 112.
St. Matthew, 526.
St. Michael (Old 134th), 27.
St. Michael New, 244.
St. Nicholas, 265.
St. Oswald, *App.* 61.
St. Patrick, 212.
St. Paul's, *see* Bishopthorpe.
St. Peter, 405.
St. Philip, *App.* 10.
St. Raphael, 75.
St. Sepulchre, 422.
St. Stephen, 337.
St. Theodulph (Valet will ich der geben), 622.
St. Thomas (S. M.), 11.
St. Thomas (8 7. 8 7. 8 7), 31, 623.
St. Venantius, 38.
Salve Festa Dies, 624.
Salzburg, 128.
Sandys, 485.
Sarratt, 34.
Savannah (Herrnhut), 135.
Schmücke dich, 306.
Schönster Herr Jesu, 323.
School House, 271.
Sebastian, *see* Jesu meines Glaubens zier.
Second Mode Melody, 3.
Seelenbräutigam, 272.
Selma, 290.
Selnecher, *see* Nun lasst uns Gott dem Herren.
Seventh Mode Melody, 496.
Sheen, 310.
Shepton - Beauchamp, 389.
Shipston, 390, 599.
Simeon, 320.
Sine Nomine, 641.
Sion's Daughters, *App.* 7.
So giebst du, 515.
Solemnis Haec Festivitas, 123, 124.
Soll's sein, 288.
Solomon, 80.
Solothurn, 243.
Song 1, 302, 384.
Song 4, 113.
Song 5, 483.
Song 13, 413.
Song 18, 357.
Song 20, 442.

ALPHABETICAL INDEX OF TUNES

Song 22, 433.
Song 24, 325.
Song 34, see Angel's Song.
Song 46, 98, 468.
Song 67, 197.
South Cerney, 359.
Southill, 638.
Southwell, 77.
Speer (Sagwashilft), 280.
Stabat Mater, 115.
Stabat Mater Dolorosa, 115.
Stalham, 638.
Stanstead, 482.
Stella, App. 54.
Stettin (Nun seht), 202.
Stockport, see Yorkshire.
Stockton, 82.
Stracathro, 445.
Stroudwater, 158.
Stuttgart, 40.
Surrey, 491.
Sussex, 239, 385.
Sutton Valence, 615.

Tallis' Canon, 267.
Tallis' Lamentation, 235.
Tallis' Ordinal ('9th Tune'), 453.
Tantum Ergo, 63.
Tantum Ergo (No. 2), 326.
Te Lucis Ante Terminum, 264.
Tell Me the Old, Old Story, 583.
Temple, 454.
The Ninety and Nine, 584.
The Rosy Sequence, 238.
The Sacred Heart, App. 44.
Third Mode Melody, 92.
This Endris Nyght, 20.
Thornbury, 545.
Thule, 371.
Ton-Mân, 270.
Ton-y-Botel, see Ebenezer.
Tres Magi de Gentibus, 647.
Treuer Heiland, wir sind hier, see Dix.

Troyte No. 1, App. 59.
Troyte No. 2, 494.
Truro, 420.
Tugwood, 146.
Tunbridge, 88.

Uffingham, 434.
Universal Praise, App. 56.
University, 93.
University College, 467.
Upwick, 642.
Urbs Coelestis, 169, 170.
Urquell aller Seligkeiten, 640.
Ut Queant Laxis, 191.

Valet will ich dir geben, see St. Theodulph.
Valor, 91.
Vater unser, 462.
Veni Creator (Attwood), 156.
Veni Creator (Tallis), 153.
Veni Creator (Mechlin version), 154, App. 30.
Veni Emmanuel, 8.
Veni Sancte Spiritus, 155.
Verbum Supernum, 2.
Vicenza, see Coleraine.
Victory, 625.
Vienna, 500.
Vision, 198.
Voller Wunder, 256, 516.
Vom Himmel hoch, 17, App. 35.

Wachet auf! 12.
Walsall, 13.
Wareham, 52, 53, 475.
Warrington, 263.
Warsaw, 386.
Was lebet, was schwebet, 42.
Weimar, 187.
Welwyn, 346.
Wem in Leidenstagen, see Caswall.
Wer da wonst, 35.
Werde Munter, 418.
Wesley, 588.
Westminster, 441.
White Gates, 541.

White Ladies Aston, 400.
Whitehall, 234.
Wicklow, 157.
Wigton, 354, 474.
Wiltshire, 502.
Winchester New, 9, 620.
Winchester Old, 30.
Windermere, 522.
Windsor, 332.
Wir pflügen, 293.
Wirtemburg, App. 12.
Wittenberg (Es ist das Heil), 478.
Wohlauf, thut nicht verzagen, 32.
Würzburg, 127.
Wychbold, 409.

Ymdaith Mwngc, 203.
Yn y Glyn, 563.
York, 472.
Yorkshire (Stockport), 21.

Zeuch meinen Geist, see St. Gregory.
Zu meinem Herrn, 119.
Zum Frieden, 499.
Zundel, App. 68.

Plainsong, 1, 2, 10, 14, 17, 18, 22, 31, 38, 49, 50, 51, 52, 53, 54, 55, 56, 57, 58, 59, 60, 61, 62, 65, 66, 67, 68, 69, 94, 95, 96, 122, 123, 124, 125, 130, 141, 142, 150, 151, 154, 155, 159, 160, 164, 165, 169, 170, 172, 174, 175, 176, 180, 181, 182, 183, 188, 189, 191, 192, 208, 213, 214, 215, 223, 224, 226, 228, 229, 230, 231, 233, 234, 237, 238, 241, 242, 249, 253, 254, 255, 261, 262, 264, 317, 326, 330, 351 617, 618, 621, 624, 626, 628, 630, 634, 735, 736, 737, 739, 740, App. 1, App. 2, App. 3, App. 4, App. 5, App. 6.
See also 2 ii, 8, 115 iii, 154 ii, 238 iii, 311, 326 ii, 331, App. 7.

INDEX OF COMPOSERS AND SOURCES

Ahle, J. R., 336.
Akeroyd, S., 340.
Albert, H., 132.
A new set of Sacred Music, 373, 497.
Ancient Irish Lullaby, 609.
Anchors, W., 13.
Andächtige und auserlesene Gesänger, 127.
Andernach *Gesangbuch*, 50, 183, 264, 647.
Angers Church Melody, 51, 123, 124, 176, 188.
Anglo-Genevan Psalter, 211.
Anonymous, 28, 455, 560, 588, 614.
Antiphonale Romanum, 237.
Armstrong, J. (?), 589.
Arnold, *Complete Psalmodist*, 506.
As hymnodus sacer, 484.
A Selection of Psalm Tunes, 429.
A Sett of New Psalm Tunes, 322.
Atkins, I., 400.
Attwood, T., 156.

B. R., 446.
Bach, J. Christoph, 527.
Bach, J. S., 100, 499, 644.
Bach, J. S. (*harmony*), 12, 36, 68, 70, 86, 102, 110, 118, 128, 138, 148, 232, 278, 329, 353, 417, 459, 462, 478, 510, 515, 622.
Baring-Gould, S., 315, 603.
Barking Hymnal, 229.
Barnby, J., 48, *App.* 19, *App.* 23.
Barthélémon, F. H., 199, 257.
Barton's *Psalms*, 492.

Bayeux Church Melody, 208.
Bell, M. F., *App.* 71.
Bell, W. H., 225, 546.
Besler, S., 274.
Bible Class Magazine, 293, *App.* 70.
Bicknell, C., 619.
Bishop, J., 61, 62, 322.
Bliss, P. P., 570.
Bohemian Brethren *Gesangbuch*, 54, 55, 121, 202, 604.
Book of Psalmody (Green), 463.
Bourgeois, L., 27, 200, 269, 277, 305, 538, 640.
Boyce, W., 201, 554.
Bremner's *Collection*, 561.
Brown, A. H., 117, 316, 651, *App.* 40.
Buck, P. C., 136, 141, 142, 307, 633.
Bullinger, E. W., *App.* 18.

Calvin's *Psalter*, 233.
Calvisius, S., 510.
Campion, T., 487.
Cantica Spiritualia, 266.
Carey, H., 491.
Catholic Hymn Tunes, 529.
Champness, W., 632.
Chapman's *Musical Companion*, 632.
Chartres Church Melody, 159.
Cheetham's Psalmody, 447.
Choice Collection of Psalm Tunes, 13.
Chorale Book for England, 382, 536.
Christian Vespers, 445.
Christliche Lieder, 148, 478.
Clark, J., 88, 147, 220, 408, 419, 434.

Clark, T., 206, 386.
Clausener *Gesangbuch*, 635.
Collection of Hymns and Sacred Poems, 504.
Cologne (Cöln) *Gesangbuch*, 164, 238, 518, 519, 627.
Cooper, G., 422.
Corner's *Gesangbuch*, 115, 120.
Corner's *Geistliche Nachtigall*, 288, 578.
Courtville, R., 341.
Croft, W., 398, 450, 466, 526, 565, 639.
Crüger, J., 45, 70, 76, 223, 224, 282, 306, 533.

Dale, R. F., *App.* 65.
Damon's *Psalter*, 77, 209, 332, 464.
Darke, H. E., 46.
Darmstadt *Gesangbuch*, 204.
Darwall, J., 517.
Davies, H. Walford, 454.
Davies, R. (?), 551.
Day's *Psalter*, 114, 149, 161, 163, 235, 404, 461.
Dijon Church Melody, 58, 59, 60.
Divine Companion, 340, 378, 446.
Doane, W. H., 580, 583.
Doles, J. F., 287.
Dougall, N., 542.
Dowland, J., 365, 649.
Drei schöne neue geistliche Lieder, 288.
Dresden Song-book, 515.
Drese, A., 272.
Dretzel, C. H., 281.
Duguet, Abbé (?), 330.
Duncalf, H., 81.
Dunhill, T. F., 650.
Dutch Traditional Melody, 145.

1010

INDEX OF COMPOSERS

Dykes, J. B., 111, 162, 414, 425, 444, 540, *App.* 14, *App.* 31, *App.* 52, *App.* 55, *App.* 61, *App.* 62.
Dykes, J. St. O., *App.* 44.

Ebeling, J. G., 256, 516.
Edwards, J. D., 303.
Edwards, R., 397.
Elvey, G. J., 289, *App.* 36.
English Melody, 274, 309.
English Traditional Carol, 20, 29, 285, 485, 488.
English Traditional May-Day Carol, 221.
English Traditional Melody, 7, 15, 16, 23, 89, 90, 213, 239, 249, 275, 294, 295, 299, 344, 355, 379, 385, 388, 389, 390, 402, 448, 498, 525, 562, 572, 574, 579, 587, 591 (Parts 1 and 2), 594, 595, 597, 599, 601, 606, 607, 611, 638, 654, 656, *App.* 54.
Erbaulicher musikalischen Christenschatz, 105.
Essay on the Church Plain Chant, 31, 623.
Este's Psalter, 27, 30, 109, 163, 209, 211, 461, 464.
Ett, C., *Cantica Sacra*, 228, 416, 507.
Evans, D., 270, 563.
Ewing, A., 412.

Farrant, R., 339.
Fawcett, J., 373, 497.
Ferguson, W. H., 276.
Filitz, F., 315, 426, 501.
Foundery Collection, 135, 381.
Franck, J. W., 486.
French Carol, 229, 230, 318, 645.
French Church Melody, 33, 115, 125, 214, 736, 737, *see also* Angers, Dijon, &c.
French Mediaeval Melody, 129, 480.

French Paroissien Melody, 568.
Freylinghausen, J. A., 97, 218, 247.
Freylinghausen's *Neues Geistreiches Gesangbuch*, 118, 353, 358, 374, 552.
Fuller-Maitland, J. A., 641.

Gatty, N., 22, 146.
Gauntlett, H. J., 134, 139, 348, 467, 605.
Geistliche Kirchengesäng, 519.
Geistliche Lieder (Wittenberg), 4.
Genevan Psalter, 27, 114, 200, 252, 258, 269, 277, 305, 352, 365, 377, 493, 512, 538, 564, 637, 640, *see also* Calvin's *Psalter*.
Genge, R. S., 410.
German Carol Melody, 44, 612.
German Mediaeval Melody, 392.
German Melody, 19, 134, 543, 598.
German Processional Melody, 534.
German 16th century Melody, 478.
German Traditional Melody, 86, 278, 284, 387, *App.* 11.
German Volkslied, 371.
Gesius, B., 345, 417.
Giardini, F. de, 624.
Gibbons, O., 98, 113, 197, 259, 302, 325, 357, 384, 413, 438, 442, 468, 483.
Gilbert, W. B., *App.* 20.
Gilding, E., 171.
Gisburn Hymnal, see Guisborough.
Gladstone, W. H., *App.* 34, *App.* 50.
Gloria in Excelsis (Easter Plainsong), 103.
Goodhart, A. M., 559.
Görlitz *Gesangbuch*, 549.
Goss, J., 470.

Green, J., 463.
Greenwood's *Psalmody*, 343.
Greiter, M., 544.
Grenoble Church Melody, 181.
Griffith, W., 366.
Guidetti's *Directorium Chori*, 175. [57.
Guisborough Hymnal, 56,

Hadow, W. H., 359.
Handel, G. F., 66, 80, 476, 555.
Harington, H., 85.
Harrison, R., 263.
Harrison, W., 140.
Harrison's *Sacred Harmony*, 456.
Hartsough, L., 573.
Harwood, B., 545.
Hassler, H. L., 102.
Hatton, J., 167.
Haus Kirchen Cantorei, *App.* 46.
Havergal, W. H., 370, 518, 627.
Hawarden, Viscountess (Caroline Maude), 569.
Haweis, T., 375, 471.
Haydn, F. J., 393, 643.
Hayes, W., 298, 457.
Hayne, L. G., *App.* 64, *App.* 67.
Heber, Bishop, 547.
Hebrew Melody, 646.
Heinlein, P., 655.
Helder, B., 32.
Helmore, T., 8.
Herbst, Martin, 73.
Hereford Hymnal, 180.
Hewlett, T., *App.* 25.
Himmels-Lust, 41.
Hintze, J., 128.
Hodson, H. E., 169, 170.
Holdroyd's *Spiritual Man's Companion*, 265.
Holst, G., 25, 310, 571.
Hopkins, E. J., 75, *App.* 38.
Horsley, W., 106, 511.
Howard, S., 74, 557.
Hutcheson, C., 445.

1011

INDEX OF COMPOSERS

Hylton Stewart, C., 381.
Hymn Tunes of the United Brethren, 532.

'Indian Air,' 608.
Ireland, J. N., 520.
Irish Hymn Melody, Ancient, 212, 490.
Irish Traditional Melody, 157, 246, 356.
Irons, H. S., *App.* 41, *App.* 42.
Isle of Arran Traditional Melody, 290.
Italian Hymn Melody, 150, *App.* 49.

Jackson, Dr., 433.
Jackson, T., 210.
Jackson, W. (of Exeter), 528.
Jeboult, H. A., 112.
Jenkins, D., 391.
Jenner, Bishop, 508.
Jewish Melody, 279.
Jones, J. D., 424.
Jones, W., 337.
Joseph, G., 266.

Katholische Kirchengesänge, 251.
Katholisches Gesangbuch, *App.* 39.
King, Robert, 378.
Kingham, M. D., *App.* 63.
Kirchen- und Haus-Buch, 104.
Kittel, J. C., 245.
Klug, *Geistliche Lieder*, 68.
Knapp, W., 52, 53, 475.
Knecht, J. H., 452, 500.
Knowles, G. J., 186.
Koch's *Choralbuch*, 550.
Kocher, C., 39, 640.
Köln, *see* Cologne.
König's *Choralbuch*, 49.

La Feillée, *Méthode du plain-chant*, 165, 174, 193, 194, 465, *App.* 26.
Lampe, J. F., 347.
La Scala Santa, 333.
Lahee, H., *App.* 48.
Langran, J., *App.* 32.

Laudi Spirituali, 184.
Laufenberg, H. von, 338.
Law, J., 122.
Lawes, H., 217, 219, 234, 283, 432, 505.
Layriz Collection, 440.
Leighton, W., 180.
Leisentritt's *Gesangbuch*, 131, 436.
Lloyd, J. A., 237.
Lloyd, W., 473.
Lockhart, C., 190, 236.
Löwenstern, M. A. von, 160.
Luther, Martin, 362, 537, *App.* 35.
Lyra Davidica, 133, *App.* 13.

Maclagan, Archbishop, *App.* 33, *App.* 43.
Magdalen Hymns, 69, 296, 596.
Mainz *Gesangbuch*, 137.
Malet, G. E. W., *App.* 47.
Martin, G. W., 361.
Mason, L., 577, *App.* 58.
Mason, S., 198.
Matthews, T. R., 585.
Mechlin *Antiphonarium Romanum*, 2.
Mechlin *Gradual*, 115, 326.
Mechlin *Vesperale Romanum*, 154.
Mendelssohn-Bartholdy, F., 24, 484.
Meyer, J., *Seelenfreud*, 521.
Milgrove, B., 177, 196.
Miller, E., 107, *App.* 45.
Milton, J., 472.
Monk, W. H., 5, 45, 281, 363, 479, 625, *App.* 10, *App.* 12, *App.* 15, *App.* 53.
Münster *Gesangbuch*, 323.
Musikalisches Hand-Buch, 9, 620.
Neander, J., 241, 380.
Neu Gesengbuchlen (Weisse), 436.
Neu-Leipziger Gesangbuch, 529.

Neumark, G., 458.
Nicolai, Philip, 12.
Northrop, A., *App.* 8.
Novello, V., 327.

Ouseley, F. A. Gore, 460.
Owen, M., 56, 57.
Owen, W., 319, 575, 576.

Palestrina, G. P. da, 326, 625.
Parratt, W., *App.* 37.
Parry, C. H. H., 383.
Parry, J., 87.
Parsons, W., 114.
Pearsall, R. L. de, 495, 567.
Pensum Sacrum, 173.
Peter, C., 182, 304, 329.
Piae Cantiones Theoderici Petri Nylandensis, 613.
Plainsong, *see* p. 968.
Playford's *Psalms*, 84, 394.
Plymouth Collection (U.S.A.), 342, 582, 593.
Praetorius, M., 14, 19, 179, 610.
Praxis Pietatis Melica, 421, 536.
Prichard, R. H., 301.
Prys' *Psalter*, 84.
Psalmodia Evangelica, 144, 420.
Psalmodia Sacra, 40.
Psalteriolum Harmonicum, 443.
Psalterium Chorale, 185.
Psalter in Metre, 158.

Quaile, R. N., *App.* 72.

Randall, J., 93, 250.
Ravenscroft, T., 30, 43, 161.
Ravenscroft's *Psalter*, 6, 30, 43, 140, 161, 166, 178, 267, 365, 428, 472.
Redhead, R., 372, 477, 513, *App.* 29.
Reimann, J. B., 406.
Reinagle, A. R., 405.
Rheinhardt MS., 42.
Rogers, B., 328.

INDEX OF COMPOSERS

Roth, H. (?), 248.
Rouen Church Melody, 18, 38, 65, 151, 191, 242, 311, 335, 435, 636, 653.
Russell, S. L., 482, 531, 615.
Ryley, G. C. E., 34.

St. Alban's Tune Book, 216.
St. Gall *Gesangbuch*, 35, 292.
Sankey, I. D., 584, *App.* 22.
Sarum Antiphonale, all Plainsong hymns not otherwise described.
Sarum Gradual, 238.
Scheffler, *Heilige Seelenlust*, 286, 586, 648.
Schein, J. H., 138, 459.
Schicht, J., 119.
Scholefield, C. C., *App.* 16.
Schop, J., 418.
Schulthes, W., *App.* 21.
Schulz, J. A. P., 293.
Schumann's *Gesangbuch*, 17, 462.
Scott-Gatty, A., 346.
Scottish Hymn Melody, 401, 445.
Scottish Psalter, 43, 64, 291, 332, 354, 394, 428, 445, 449, 451, 472, 474, 493, 525, 637.
Selneccer, *Christliche Psalmen*, 126.
Seven Sobs of a Sorrowful Soul, 79, 403.
Shaw, Geoffrey, 535.
Shaw, Martin, 99, 205, 376, 396, 415, 427, 481, 503, 548, 602.
Sheeles, J., 297.
Shrubsole, W., 364.
Silcher, F., 600.
Slater, G., 419.
Smart, G., 502.
Smart, H., 395, 431, 616, *App.* 27.
Smith, I., 369.
Smith, J., 37.

Smith, R. A., 290.
Smith's *Sacred Music*, 367.
Sohren, P., 72, 138.
Solesmes Church melody, 331, 626, 736.
Somervell, A., 522, 566, 590.
Soto, F., *App.* 60.
Speer, D., 280.
Standard Psalm tunebook, 312, 433.
Staniforth, T. Worsley, *App.* 69.
Stanley, S., 320, 530.
Steggall, C., 47, 411.
Steiner, J. L., 253.
Stewart, *see* Hylton Stewart.
Storl's *Wurtemberg Gesangbuch*, 195.
Stralsund Gesangbuch, 536.
Students' Hymnal, 227.
Stubbs, S., 472.
Sullivan, A. S., 26, 643, *App.* 17.
Supplement to the New Version, 240, 450, 558.
Swiss Traditional Melody, 243, 399.

Tallis, T., 3, 78, 92, 153, 267, 453, 496.
Tans'ur, W., 300.
Tears or Lamentations of a Sorrowful Soul, 180.
Teschner, M., 622.
Thrupp, F. J., *App.* 9.
Tochter Sion, 71.
Tours Breviary (?), 350.
Traditional Melody, 91.
Troyte, A. H. Dyke, 494, *App.* 59.
Turle, J., 441.

Van Damme, Canon, 308.
Vaughan Williams, R., 152, 273, 368, 524, 541, 624, 641.
Vehe's *Gesangbüchlein*, 35.
Vetter, D., 36.

Viner, W. L., 523.
Vulpius, M., 101, 187, 232, 360.
Vulpius, *Gesangbuch*, 67.

Waghorne, W. R., *App.* 66.
Wagner, R., 313, 629.
Wainwright, J., 21.
Wainwright, R., 168.
Walther's *Gesangbüchlein*, 110.
Warrell, A. S., 509.
Weale, W., 83.
Webb, G. J., 581.
Webbe, S., the elder, 155, 260, 631.
Webbe, S., the elder, *Motetts or Antiphons*, 31, 63, 469, 623, 626.
Webbe, S., the younger, 107, 375, 471.
Weisse, M., 314, 436, 652.
Welsh Hymn Melody, 75, 108, 116, 207, 222, 324, 334, 349, 407, 430, 437, 439, 514, 539, 556.
Welsh Traditional Melody, 233, 268, 423.
Wesley, J., *Foundery Collection*, 135, 381.
Wesley, S. S., 244, 489, 496, *App.* 28.
Whinfield, W. G., 409, 642, *App.* 56.
Whitwell, W. J., 592.
Wilkes, J., 532.
Wilkins' *Psalmody*, 158.
Williams, A., *New Universal Psalmodist*, 11.
Williams, R., 143.
Wise, M., 312.
Woodbury, I., *App.* 51.
Wood, T., 271.
Wright, T., 82.
Wurtemberg Gesangbuch, 195.

Yoakley, J., *App.* 57.
York Breviary, 249.

Zions Harfe, 218, 321.
Zundel, J., *App.* 68.

INDEX OF AUTHORS, ETC.

[*The numbers in brackets refer to translations.*]

Abelard, Peter, 465.
Adam of St. Victor, 172, 179, 200.
Adams, Sarah Flower, 444.
Addison, Joseph, 92, 297, 491, 511, 542.
Ainger, Arthur Campbell, 548, 559.
Alderson, Eliza Sibbald, 119.
Alexander, Mrs. Cecil Frances, 106, 112, 117, 132, 205, (212), 227, 493, 587, 589, 590, 605, 610.
Alford, Henry, 210, 289, 337, 486, 642.
Ambrose, St., Bishop of Milan, 14, 49, 52, 164, 192, 255, 261, 262, 271.
Anatolius, 32, 388.
Anon., 4, 22, (59), (130), (317). (*Before 6th Cent.*) 60, 123, 124, 141, 142, 150, 151, 254, 269. (*6th–10th Cent.*) 1, 2, 3, 5, 10, 17, 51, 56, 57, 58, 59, 61, 62, 63, 65, 69, 81, 125, 128, 144, 153, 154, 159, 160, 169, 170, 174, 175, 176, 180, 181, 182, 183, 188, 189, 191, 213, 214, 215, 234, 249, 264, 276, 307, 633, 636. (*11th–15th Cent.*) 22, 31, 67, 89, 97, 155, 184, 228, 229, 233, 237, 238, 250, 252, 311, 350, 419, 431, 438, 459, 507, 630, 634. (*16th–19th Cent.*) 8, 28, 37, 71, (89), 99, 103, 251, 280, 321, (342), 413, 480, 512, 560, 614, 625, 626, 629, 632, 649, 653, 654.
Anstice, Joseph, 13, 457.
Antoniano, Silvio, 193.

Aquinas, St. Thomas, 317, 326, 330, 331.
A. R. (*See* Riley, Athelstan).
Auber, Harriet, 157, 461.
Austin, John, 296.

Bahnmaier, Jonathan Friedrich, 552.
Baker, Sir Henry Williams, (177), (413), 436, 490, 496, 508, 537, (623).
Baring-Gould, Sabine, 136, (503), 568, 592, 603, 643.
Baxter, Richard, 401, 433, 517.
Bede, The Venerable, 35, 146, 225.
Bell, Maurice Frederick, (60), (68), 604, (624), (634).
Benson, Arthur Christopher, 539.
Benson, Richard Meux, (189).
Bernard of Cluny (or Morlaix), 371, 392, 412, 495.
Besnault, Sebastien, 36.
Bickersteth, Edward Henry, Bishop of Exeter, 468.
Bigg, Charles, (2), (49).
Birkbeck, William John, (621).
Blacker, Maxwell Julius, (10), (636).
Blake, William, 506.
Blew, William John, (27), (629).
Bliss, P. P., *or* Philipp, 570.
Bode, John Ernest, 577.
Bonar, Horatius, 312, 361, 505, 556, 574, 575.
Bourne, George Hugh, 319.

Bowring, Sir John, 409.
Brady, Nicholas (*see* Tate, N.).
Bramley, Henry Ramsden, 29.
Bridges, Matthew, 341, 381.
Bridges, Robert (*see* Y. H.).
Bright, William, 240, 256, 302, 327, 340.
Brooke, William Thomas, (614).
Brooks, Phillips, Bishop of Massachusetts, 15.
Browne, Thomas Browne 534.
Brownlie, John, (349), (454), (650), (652).
Bryan, Joseph, 90.
Bryant, William Cullen, 550.
Buckoll, Henry James, 523.
Bullock, William, 508.
Bunyan, John, 402.
Burke, Christian, 530.
Burkitt, Francis Crawford, (12), (194).
Burleigh, William Henry, 482.
Butler, Henry Montagu, 429.
Byrom, John, 21, 443.

Calverley, Charles Stuart, (225).
Campbell, Jane Montgomery, (293).
Campbell, Robert, 128, (139), 246.
Canton, William, 403, 609.
Carlyle, Joseph Dacre, 79.
Carlyle, Thomas, (362).
Carney, Mrs. Julia A., 600.

1014

INDEX OF AUTHORS

Caswall, Edward, (5), (40), (57), (71), (80), (99), (280), (326), (330), 382, (419), (512).
C. B. (*see* Bigg, Charles).
Celano, Thomas of, 351, 487.
Cennick, John, 7, 373.
Chadwick, John White, 384.
Chambers, John David, (62), (633).
Chandler, John, (9), (36), (37), (44), (46), (144), (265), (453), (623).
Chatfield, Allen William, (77).
Chesterton, Gilbert Keith, 562.
Clark, John Haldenby, (480).
Claudius, Matthias, 293.
Clephane, Elizabeth Cecilia, 567, 584.
Coffin, Charles, 9, 11, 27, 44, 64, 265, 398, 453.
Coles, Vincent Stucky Stratton, 190, 218, 334.
Collins, Henry, 416, 417.
Collyer, William Bengo, 4.
Conder, Josiah, 304.
Contes, Jean-Baptiste de, 253.
Cooper, Edward, 387.
Coote, Mrs. Maude, 222.
Copeland, William John, (81).
Cosin, John, Bishop of Durham, 153.
Cotterill, Thomas, 4, 143.
Cowper, William, 332, 394, 400, 422, 445.
Cox, Frances Elizabeth, (134), (204), (455), (478).
Coxe, Arthur Cleveland, Bishop of Western New York, 108, 551.
Creighton, Mandell, Bishop of London, 347.
Crossman, Samuel, 411.

Cummins, James John, 75.
C.W.H. (*see* Humphreys, C. W.).
Damascene, St. John, 131, 137, 138, 360.
Davis, Roby Furley, (613).
Daye's Psalter, 365.
Dearmer, Percy, (38), (95), 126, (150), (160), (165), (180), (215), 221, (237), 313, (329), (352), 353 (Part 2), 531, 543, 598, (628).
Denton, William, 109, 206.
Dix, William Chatterton, 39, 292, 301, 379, 596.
Doane, George Washington, Bishop of New Jersey, 546.
Doddridge, Philip, 6, 320, 447, 518.
Donne, John, 515.
Downton, Henry, 286.
Dryden, John, 156.
Duffield, George, 581.
Duncan, Mary Lundie, 599.

Edmeston, James, 426.
Ellerton, John, (18), 116, 207, 209, 248, (271), 273, 277, 345.
Elliott, Charlotte, 316, 374, 440.
Elliott, Ebenezer, 566.
Elliott, Emily Elizabeth Steele, 585.
Elpis, 226.
Ephraim the Syrian, St., Deacon of Edessa, 194.
Everest, Charles William, 484.

Faber, Frederick William, 101, 111, 161, 275, 315, 399, 441, 451, 499, 571.
F. B. P., 638.
F. C. B. (*see* Burkitt, Francis Crawford).

Fletcher, Phineas, 98.
Fortunatus, Venantius Honorius Clementianus, Bishop of Poitiers, 94, 95, 96, 624, 628.
Foundling Hospital Collection, 535 (Part 1), 631.
F. P. (*see* Pott, Francis).
Franck, Johann, 306.
Fulbert, St., Bishop of Chartres, 122, 139.
Fuller-Maitland, Frances Sara, 467.

Gellert, Christian Fürchtegott, 134.
Gerhardt, Paulus, 102, 278.
Germanus, St., Patriarch of Constantinople, 19.
G. G. (*see* Gillett, Gabriel).
Gillett, Gabriel, (58), 118, (172), (630).
Gladstone, William Ewart, 322.
Grant, Sir Robert, 87, 466.
Greek Service Books, 3, 310, 318, 349, 650, 652.
Gregory the Great, St., Patriarch of Rome (*ascribed to*), 50, 66, 68, 165.
Grève, Philippe de, 230.
Guiet, Charles, 171.
Gurney, John Hampden, 290, 509, 517.
Gurney, Mrs. Dorothy Frances, 346.

Hanby, Benjamin Russell, 612.
Hankey, Arabella Catherine, 583, 586.
Hartsough, Lewis, 573.
Havergal, Frances Ridley, 285, 572, 582.
Haweis, Thomas, 85.
Hawker, Robert Stephen, 606.
Heber, Reginald, Bishop

INDEX OF AUTHORS

of Calcutta, 41, 162, 202, 244, 268, 299, 305, 323, 547, 557, 640.
Heermann, Johann, 70.
Hensley, Lewis, 554.
Herbert, George, 93, 424, 427, 485.
Herrick, Robert, 410.
Hewett, John William, 86.
Hickson, William Edward, 560 (Part 2).
Holland, Henry Scott, 423.
Holmes, Oliver Wendell, 434.
Hort, Fenton John Anthony, (271).
Hosmer, Frederick Lucian, 463, 504, 538.
Housman, Laurence, 16, (142), (188), (191), 219, 220, (228), (229), (230), (231), (234), 611.
How, William Walsham, Bishop of Wakefield, 294, 514, 522, 565, 578, 588, 597, 641.
H. P. (see Packer, Harriett).
Hughes, Thomas, 449.
Humphreys, C. W., (310), (329).
Hupton, Job, 380.

Ingemann, Bernhardt Severin, 503.
Irons, William Josiah, (351).

J.B. (see Brownlie, John).
Jervois, William Henry Hammond, 308, 328, 335.
Johnson, Samuel, 375.
Jones, John Samuel, 282.
Joseph the Hymnographer, St., 187, 245.
Julian, John, 386.
Justinian, Emperor, 325.

Keble, John, 33, 140, 158, 216, 244, 260, 274, 348, 370, 497.
Kelly, Thomas, 147, 281, 510, 627.
Ken, Thomas, Bishop of Bath and Wells, 217, 257, 267.
Kethe, William, 365.
Kingsley, Charles, 525.
Kipling, Rudyard, 558.

Lacey, Thomas Alexander, (8), (66), (67), (69), (104), 114, (123), (124), (174), (208), (226), (249), (325), 544.
Laufenberg, Heinrich von, 338.
Leeson, Jane Elizabeth, 602.
L. H. (see Housman, Laurence).
Littledale, Richard Frederick, (152), (183), 291, (350), 355, 359, (632), 647, 655.
Logan, John, 447.
Longfellow, Samuel, 288, 295, 406.
Lowell, James Russell, 563.
Löwenstern, Matthäus Apelles von, 435.
Lowry, Somerset Corry, 529.
Luke, Mrs. Jemima, 595.
Luther, Martin, 362.
Lynch, Thomas Toke, 555.
Lyra Davidica, 133.
Lyte, Henry Francis, 363, 395, 432, 469, 470.

Maclagan, William Dalrymple, Archbishop of York, 113, 120.
Madan, Martin, 24.
Malabar, Liturgy of, 329.
Mant, Richard, Bishop of Down & Connor & Dromore, 110, (115), (176), 196, 372.
Marckant, John, 84.
Marriott, John, 553.

Mason, Jackson, (179).
Mason, John, 404.
Maude, Mrs. Mary Fawler, 344.
M. D., 656.
Meinhold, Johann Wilhelm, 353 (Part 1).
Metrophanes, Bishop of Smyrna, 163.
M. F. B. (see Bell, Maurice Frederick).
Midlane, Albert, 607.
Miller, Emily, 594.
Milman, Henry Hart, 83, 513, 620.
Milton, John, 492, 532.
Monro, Edward, 656.
Monsell, John Samuel Bewley, 42, 88, 389, 579.
Montgomery, James, 45, 78, 100, 167, 201, 300, 391, 474, 481, 549.
Moore, Thomas, 298.
Morison, John, 43.
Moultrie, Gerard, (3), (318), 358, 619.
Muirhead, Lionel B.C.L., 488.

Neale, John Mason, (1), (14), (17), (19), (31), (32), (35), (51), (53), (56), (61), (63), (64), (65), (72), (94), (96), (103), 109, (122), (125), (131), (137), (138), (141), (155), (159), (163), (164), 166, 168, (169), (170), (175), (181), (182), (184), (187), (192), (214), (238), (241), 243, (245), (250), (252), (254), (255), (261), (262), (264), (276), (307), (326), (330), 339, 366, (371), 380, (388), 392, (412), (418), (431), 452, (465), (494), (495), 500, (507), (622), (626).
Neander, Joachim, 536.
Newell, Ebenezer Josiah, 211.
Newman, John Henry, 390, 425, 471.

INDEX OF AUTHORS

Newton, John, 287, 377, 393, 405.
Nicolai, Philipp, 12.
Noel, Caroline Maria, 368.
Notker, Balbulus, 494.

Oakeley, Frederick, (28), (614).
Olivers, Thomas, 646.
Osler, Edward, 535 (Part 2).
Oswald, Heinrich Siegmund, 455.
Owen, Mrs. Frances Mary, 430.
Oxenham, Henry Nutcombe, (311).

Packer, Harriett, (11).
Palgrave, Francis Turner, 464.
Palmer, Edmund Stuart, 356, (356).
Palmer, Ray, 421, 439.
Palmer, William, (253).
Parnell, Thomas, 314.
Patrick, St., Bishop of Armagh and Apostle of Ireland, 212.
Paulinus, St., Bishop of Nola, 195.
Paulus Diaconus, 223, 224.
P. D. (*see* Dearmer, Percy).
Pentecostarion, 454.
Perronet, Edward, 364.
Pestel, Thomas, 20.
Pierpoint, Folliott Sandford, 309.
Plumptre, Edward Hayes, 458, 526, 545, 644.
Pollock, Thomas Benson, 647, 648, 651.
Pope, Robert Martin, (54), (55).
Pott, Francis, 73, (625).
Prudentius, Aurelius Clemens, 34, 40, 53, 54, 55, 104, 185, 352, 613.
Prynne, George Rundle, 415.

Purchas, John, 569.
Pusey, Philip, 435.

Quarles, John, 432.

Rabanus Maurus, St., Archbishop of Mainz, 208, 241, 242.
Rankin, Jeremiah Eames, 524.
Rawnsley, Hardwicke Drummond, 247, 357.
R. E. R. (*see* Roberts, Richard Ellis).
R. F. D. (*see* Davis, Roby Furley).
Richter, Mrs. Anne, 509.
Riley, Athelstan, (34), (97), (185), 186, (193), (195), (213), 239, (242), (321), (360), 519.
Rinkart, Martin, 533.
R. M. B. (*see* Benson, Richard Meux).
R. M. P. (*see* Pope, Robert Martin).
Roberts, Richard Ellis, (151), (223), (224), (233).
Robinson, Joseph Armitage, 236.
Robinson, Richard Hayes, 270.
Romanis, William, 232, 272.
Rorison, Gilbert, 501.
Rossetti, Christina Georgina, 25, 203.
Russell, Arthur Tozer, 148.
Santeüil, Claude de, 623.
Santeüil, Jean-Baptiste de, 46, 177, 178.
Sarum Processional, 617, 618, 621, 622, 624, 628.
S. B.-G. (*see* Baring-Gould, Sabine).
Scheffler, Johann, 460.
Schenk, Heinrich Theobald, 204.
Schmolck, Benjamin, 336.
Schütz, Johann Jakob, 478.
Scott, Sir Walter, 487.

Scottish Psalter (1650), 472.
Sears, Edmund Hamilton, 26.
Sedulius, Coelius, 18, 38.
Shirley, Walter, 105.
Shuttleworth, Henry Cary, 528.
Siena, Bianco da, 152.
Simpson, Mrs. Jane Cross, 473.
Smith, Isaac Gregory, 121.
Smith, Walter Chalmers, 407.
Smyttan, George Hunt, 73.
Spenser, Edmund, 283.
Stanley, Arthur Penrhyn, 48, 235.
Stevenson, Isabella S., 520.
Stone, Samuel John, 91, 489.
Synesius, Bishop of Ptolemais, 77.

Tailour, F. R., 564.
T. A. L. (*see* Lacey, Thomas Alexander).
Tate, Nahum, 30.
Tate, Nahum, *and* Brady, Nicholas, 74, 367, 502.
Taylor, Jane, 601.
Tennyson, Alfred, Lord, 483.
Tersteegen, Gerhard, 637.
Theoctistus, of the Studium, St., 418.
Theodulph, Bishop of Orleans, 621, 622.
Thring, Godfrey, 279, 448, 516, 527, 541, 615, 645.
Todi, Jacopone da, 115.
Toke, Mrs. Emma, 149, 206.
Toplady, Augustus Montagu, 477.
Trevelyan, William Bouverie, 308.
Turton, Lt.-Col. William Harry, 324.

INDEX OF AUTHORS

Tuttiett, Lawrence, 462.
Twells, Henry, 266.

Van Alstyne, Frances Jane, 580.
Vere, Aubrey de, (115).
V. S. S. C. (*see* Coles, V. S. S.).

Watts, Isaac, 107, 197, 199, 354, 376, 420, 442, 450, 498, 635.
W. B. T. (*see* Trevelyan, W. B.).
Webb, Benjamin, (146), (459).
Weisse, Michael, 129.
Wesley, Charles, 7, 23, 24, 82, 135, 143, 258, 259, 303, 333, 343, 378, 414, 428, 437, 446, 476, 479, 591, 639.

Wesley, John, 635, (637).
Whately, Richard, Archbishop of Dublin, 268.
White, Henry Kirke, 467.
Whitefield, George, 24.
Whitfield, Frederick, 576.
Whiting, William, 540.
Whittier, John Greenleaf, 173, 383, 408, 456.
Williams, Isaac, 76, (171), (178), (251), 369.
Williams, Peter, (397).
Williams, William, 397.
Willis, Mrs. Love M., 385.
Winkworth, Catherine, (129), (306), (336), (338), (353, Pt. 1), (460), (533), (536), (552).
Wipo, 130.
W. J. B. (*see* Birkbeck, W. J.).

Woodd, Basil, 616.
Woodford, James Russell, Bishop of Ely, (331).
Wordsworth, Christopher, Bishop of Lincoln, 47, 127, 145, 198, 284, 396, 521, 593.
Wordsworth, William, 263.
Wreford, John Reynell, 561.

Y. H. (*Yattendon Hymnal*, by Robert Bridges), (50), (52), (70), (102), (154), (200), (269), (278), (398), (438), 442, 475, 564.
York Processional, 630, 634.
Young, Andrew, 608.

INDEX OF ORIGINAL FIRST LINES OF TRANSLATED HYMNS

GREEK

	HYMN
Ἄισωμεν πάντες λαοί	131
Ἀναστάσεως ἡμέρα	137
Ἀντιλαβοῦ, σῶσον, ἐλέησον	652
Ἀπὸ δόξης εἰς δόξαν πορευόμενοι	310
Αὕτη ἡ κλητή	138
Βασιλεῦ οὐράνιε, Παράκλητε	454
Ζοφερᾶς τρικυμίας	388
Ἰδοὺ ὁ Νυμφίος ἔρχεται	3
Ἰησοῦ γλυκύτατε	418
Μέγα καὶ παράδοξον θαῦμα	19
Μετὰ τῶν ἁγίων ἀνάπαυσον, Χριστέ	744
Μνώεο, Χριστέ	77
Ὁ μονογενὴς Υἱός	325
Ποία τοῦ βίου τρυφὴ διαμένει λύπης ἀμέτοχυς	360
Σιγησάτω πᾶσα σάρξ βροτεία	318
Ταχὺς εἰς ἀντίληψιν, μόνος ὑπάρχων Χριστέ	349
Τὴν ἡμέραν διελθών	276
Τριφεγγὴς μονὰς θεαρχική	163
Τῷ Βασιλεῖ καὶ Δεσπότῃ	32
Τῶν ἱερῶν ἀθλοφόρων	187
Ὑπὲρ τῆς ἄνωθεν εἰρήνης	650
Φῶς ἱλαρόν	269
Φωστῆρες τῆς ἀΰλου	245

LATIN

	HYMN
A solis ortus cardine	18
Ad cenam Agni providi	125
Ad regias Agni dapes	128
Adeste, fideles	28, 614
Adesto, sancta Trinitas	159
Adoro te devote	331
Aeterna caeli gloria	56
Aeterna Christi munera	175
Aeterna Lux, Divinitas	632
Aeterne Rex altissime	141
Ales diei nuntius	53
Alleluya, dulce carmen	63
Amor Patris et Filii	438
Angularis fundamentum	170
Anima Christi, sanctifica me	89
Annue Christe, saeculorum Domine	174
Antra deserti	224
Attolle paulum lumina	103
Audi, benigne Conditor	66
Aurea luce	226
Aurora jam spargit polum	57
Aurora lucis rutilat	123
Ave, colenda Trinitas	633
Ave, maris Stella	213
Ave, rex noster	App. 3
Ave, verum Corpus natum	311
Beata nobis gaudia	151
Beate Martyr, prospera	185
Caelestis aulae principes	177
Caelestis formam gloriae	233
Caelestis O Jerusalem	251
Caeli Deus sanctissime	60
Cantemus cuncti melodum	494
Chorus novae Jerusalem	122, 139
Christe cunctorum Dominator alme	636
Christe qui lux es et dies	81
Christe Redemptor omnium	17
Christe, sanctorum decus Angelorum	242
Clarum decus jejunii	68
Collaudemus Magdalenae	230
Conditor alme siderum	1
Corde natus ex Parentis	613
Crux fidelis	737
Cultor Dei, memento	104
De profundis exclamantes	350
Deus Creator omnium	49
Deus ignee fons animarum	352
Deus, tuorum militum	181
Dies irae, dies illa	351, 487
Dignare me, O Jesu, rogo te	413
Divine, crescebas Puer	46
Ecce dies nobis	195
Ecce tempus idoneum	67
Ex more docti mystico	65
Exultet caelum laudibus	176
Exultet cor praecordiis	237
Felix dies quem proprio	36
Festum Matris gloriosae	228
Finita jam sunt praelia	625
Fortem, virili pectore	193
Gloria, laus et honor	621, 622
Gloriosi Salvatoris	507
Hic breve vivitur	371
Hora novissima	495
Hostis Herodes impie	38
Hymnum canamus gloriae	146
Hymnum canentes martyrum	35

1019

INDEX OF ORIGINAL FIRST LINES

	HYMN
Immense caeli Conditor	58
In domo Patris	252
Instantis adventum Dei	11
Iste Confessor	188
Jam Christus astra ascenderat	150
Jam desinant suspiria	27
Jam lucis orto sidere	254
Jerusalem et Sion filiae	172
Jerusalem luminosa	431
Jesu, Corona Virginum	192
Jesu, dulcis memoria	238
Jesu, dulcis memoria	419
Jesu nostra redemptio	144
Jesu, quadragenariae	69
Jesu, Redemptor omnium	189
Jesu, Salvator saeculi	249
Jordanis oras praevia	9
Labente jam solis rota	265
Laetabundus	22
Lauda, Sion, Salvatorem	317
Laudate Dominum	534
Lucis Creator optime	51
Lustra sex qui jam peracta	96
Lux ecce surgit aurea	55
Magnae Deus potentiae	61
Martyr Dei qui unicum	180
Mundi salus affutura	229
Nocte surgentes	165
Nox et tenebrae et nubila	54
Nunc, Sancte, nobis, Spiritus	255
O Amor, quam ecstaticus	459
O beata beatorum	184
O bona patria!	392
O Deus, ego amo te	80
O Esca viatorum	321
O Fons amoris, Spiritus	453
O filii et filiae	626
O gloriosa Femina	215
O Lux beata Trinitas	164
O Maria, noli flere	231
O nata Lux de lumine	234
O Pater sancte	160
O quam juvat fratres	398
O quanta qualia sunt illa Sabbata	465
O sola magnarum urbium	40
Pange, lingua, gloriosi Corporis mysterium	326
Pange, lingua, gloriosi proelium certaminis	95
Patris aeterni suboles coaeva	171
Plasmator hominis, Deus	62
Plausu chorus laetabundo	179

	HYMN
Praecursor altus luminis	225
Primo dierum omnium	50
Prome vocem, mens, canoram	623
Pugnate, Christi milites	480
Quae stella sole pulchrior	44
Quem terra, pontus, aethera	214
Quicumque certum quaeritis	71
Quisquis valet numerare	250
Quod chorus vatum	208
Rector potens, verax Deus	261
Rerum Deus tenax vigor	262, 271
Rex gloriose Martyrum	183
Salus aeterna	10
Salve, festa dies	624, 628, 630, 634
Salvete, flores martyrum	34
Sancte Dei pretiose	31
Sancti, venite, Christi Corpus sumite	307
Sanctorum meritis	182
Sermone blando Angelus	124
Si vis vere gloriari	97
Sol praeceps rapitur	280
Sponsa Christi quae per orbem	253
Splendor paternae gloriae	52
Stabat Mater dolorosa	115
Supernae matris gaudia	200
Supreme, quales, Arbiter	173
Supreme Rector caelitum	629
Te laeta, mundi Conditor	64
Te lucis ante terminum	264
Telluris ingens Conditor	59
Tibi, Christe, splendor Patris	241
Tu Christe nostrum gaudium	142
Urbs beata Jerusalem	169
Urbs Sion aurea	412
Ut queant laxis	223
Veni, Creator Spiritus	153, 154, 156
Veni, Redemptor gentium	14
Veni, sancte Spiritus	155
Veni, veni, Emmanuel	8
Verbum supernum prodiens	2
Verbum supernum prodiens, nec Patris	330
Vexilla Regis prodeunt	94
Victimae Paschali	130
Victus sibi cognomina	37
Virginis Proles	191
Vox clara ecce intonat	5

SYRIAC

ܢܒܝܐ ܐܚܢܢ ܐܬܪܐ ܘܦܓܪܗ . . . 329

ܡܚܠ ܡܚܐ ܚܕܘܬܗ ܚܠܡ . . . 194

INDEX OF ORIGINAL FIRST LINES

GERMAN

	HYMN
Ach lieber Herre, Jesu Christ	338
Beim frühen Morgenlicht	512
Christe du Beistand	435
Christus ist erstanden	129
Ein' feste Burg	362
Gott ist gegenwärtig	637
Guter Hirt, du hast gestillt	353
Herzliebster Jesu	70
Jesus lebt, mit ihm auch ich	134
Liebe die du mich zum Bilde	460
Liebster Jesu, wir sind hier	336
Lobe den Herren	536
Nun danket alle Gott	533
Nun ruhen alle Wälder	278
O Haupt voll Blut und Wunden	102
Schmücke dich	306
Sei Lob und Ehr' dem höchsten Gut	478
Wachet auf	12
Walte fürder, nah und fern	552
Wer sind die vor Gottes Throne	204
Wem in Leidenstagen	455
Wir pflügen und wir streuen	293

RUSSIAN

	HYMN
Со святыми упокой, Христе	744

WELSH

Arglwydd arwain trwy'r anialwch	397

IRISH

Ατομπυιζ ιη'οιυ	212

ITALIAN

Discendi, Amor santo	152
Viva! Viva! Gesù	99

DANISH

Igjennem Nat og Trængsel	503

SWAHILI

Yesu Bin Mariamu	356

GENERAL INDEX

First Line	Hymn	Name of Tune
A brighter dawn is breaking	126	Nun lasst uns Gott dem Herren.
A few more years shall roll	361	Leominster.
A great and mighty wonder	19	Es ist ein' Ros' entsprungen.
A safe stronghold our God is still	362	Ein' feste Burg.
Abide with me; fast falls the eventide	363	Eventide.
According to thy gracious word	300	Bangor.
Advent tells us Christ is near	586	Welt, Keine Schönheit hat die
Ah, holy Jesu, how hast thou offended	70	1. Herzliebster Jesu. 2. [Alternative version.]
Alleluya! Alleluya! Hearts to heaven and voices raise	127	1. Würzburg. 2. Everton (*App.* 27).
Alleluya, sing to Jesus	301	Hyfrydol.
Alleluya, song of sweetness	63	Tantum ergo.
All glory, laud, and honour	622	St. Theodulph (Valet will ich dir geben).
All hail, adorèd Trinity	633	Mont Richard.
All hail the power of Jesu's name	364	Miles Lane.
All hail, ye little Martyr flowers	34	Sarratt.
All people that on earth do dwell	365	1. Old Hundredth. 2. [Alternative version.] 3. [Simpler Alternative version.]
All prophets hail thee, from of old announcing	208	1. Plainsong. 2. Diva Servatrix.
All things are thine; no gift have we	173	Herr Jesu Christ.
All things bright and beautiful	587	1. Royal Oak. 2. Greystone (*App.* 66).
All ye who seek a comfort sure	71	St. Bernard.
Almighty God, who from the flood	61	1. Plainsong. 2. Illsley.
An image of that heavenly light	233	1. Plainsong. 2. Nostre Dieu. 3. Vom Himmel hoch (*App.* 35).
And did those feet in ancient time (*p.* 984)	656 A	
And now, belovèd Lord, thy soul resigning	119	Zu meinem Herrn.
And now, O Father, mindful of the love	302	Song 1.
Another year completed	195	Bremen.
Another year is dawning	285	Cherry Tree.
Around the throne of God a band	243	Solothurn.
Art thou weary, art thou languid	366	1. Cuttle Mills. 2. Bullinger (*App.* 18).
As now the sun's declining rays	265	St. Nicholas.
As pants the hart for cooling streams	367	Martyrdom.
As with gladness men of old	39	Dix.
At even when the sun was set	266	Angelus (Du meiner Seelen).
At the Cross her station keeping	115	1. Stabat Mater. 2. Christi Mutter stund vor Schmerzen. 3. Stabat Mater Dolorosa (Plainsong).

1023

GENERAL INDEX

First Line	Hymn	Name of Tune
At the Lamb's high feast we sing.	128	Salzburg.
At the name of Jesus.	368	King's Weston.
At thy feet, O Christ, we lay	256	Voller Wunder.
Author of life divine	303	Lovely.
Ave Maria! blessèd Maid	216	St. Alban.
Awake, my soul, and with the sun	257	Morning Hymn.
Be present, Holy Trinity	159	1. Plainsong. 2. Adesto Sancta Trinitas.
Be thou my Guardian and my Guide	369	Abridge.
Before the ending of the day	264	1, 2. Plainsong. 3. Te Lucis Ante Terminum.
Behold a little Child	588	Wesley.
Behold the Bridegroom cometh	3	1. Second Mode Melody. 2. [Tallis' Original version.]
Behold the great Creator makes	20	This Endris Nyght.
Behold us, Lord, before thee met.	340	Lambeth.
Beneath the Cross of Jesus.	567	1. Gloria. [(*App.* 22). 2. Beneath the Cross
Bethlehem, of noblest cities	40	Stuttgart.
Blessèd City, heavenly Salem.	169	1. Plainsong. 2. Urbs Coelestis.
Blessèd Feasts of blessèd Martyrs	184	Alta Trinita Beata.
Blessèd Jesu! here we stand	336	Liebster Jesu.
Blest are the moments, doubly blest	263	Warrington.
Blest are the pure in heart	370	Franconia.
Blest Martyr, let thy triumph-day	185	Beata Nobis Gaudia.
Bread of heaven, on thee we feed.	304	1. Christopher (Ihr Gestirn'). 2. Bread of Heaven (*App.* 43).
Bread of the world in mercy broken.	305	Rendez à Dieu.
Brief life is here our portion	371	Thule.
Bright the vision that delighted	372	Redhead No. 46.
Brightest and best of the sons of the morning	41	1. Liebster Immanuel. 2. Epiphany (*App.* 9).
By Jesus' grave on either hand	121	O Mensch sieh.
Captains of the saintly band	177	Harts.
Children of the heavenly King	373	Melling.
Christ, enthroned in highest heaven	350	Ad Perennis Vitae Fontem.
Christ is gone up; yet ere he passed	166	St. David.
Christ is made the sure Foundation.	170	1. Plainsong. 2. Urbs Coelestis.
Christ, the fair glory of the holy Angels	242	1. Plainsong. 2. Coelites Plaudant.
Christ the Lord is risen again	129	1. Orientis Partibus. 2. Wirtemburg (*App.* 12).

GENERAL INDEX

First Line	Hymn	Name of Tune
Christ, whose glory fills the skies	258	Ministres de l'Éternel.
Christian, dost thou see them	72	Gute Bäume bringen.
Christian, seek not yet repose	374	Morgenglanz der Ewigkeit.
Christians, awake, salute the happy morn	21	Yorkshire or Stockport.
Christians, to the Paschal Victim	130	Plainsong. (Sequence.)
City of God, how broad and far	375	Richmond.
Come down, O Love divine	152	Down Ampney.
Come, faithful people, come away	619	Come Faithful People.
Come, Holy Ghost, our souls inspire	153	Veni Creator.
Come, Holy Ghost, with God the Son	255	Plainsong.
Come, let us join our cheerful songs	376	1. Cheerful. 2. Nativity (*App.* 48).
Come, let us join the Church above	186	Balfour.
Come, my soul, thy suit prepare	377	Louez Dieu.
Come, O Creator Spirit, come	154	1. Plainsong. 2. Veni Creator (*App.* 30).
Come, O thou Traveller unknown	378	David's Harp.
Come rejoicing	22	1. Plainsong. (Christmas Sequence.) 2. Laetabundus.
Come sing, ye choirs exultant	179	Ach Gott von Himmelreiche.
Come, thou holy Paraclete	155	1. Plainsong. (Golden Sequence.) 2. Veni Sancte Spiritus.
Come, thou Redeemer of the earth	14	1. Plainsong. 2. Puer Nobis Nascitur.
Come unto me, ye weary	379	Rusper.
Come, ye faithful, raise the anthem	380	Neander.
Come, ye faithful, raise the strain	131	Ave Virgo Virginum.
Come, ye thankful people, come	289	St. George.
Conquering kings their titles take	37	Innocents.
Creator of the earth and sky	49	1. Plainsong. 2. St. Gregory (Zeuch meinen Geist).
Creator of the stars of night	1	Plainsong.
Creator Spirit, by whose aid	156	Veni Creator (Attwood).
Crown him with many crowns	381	1. Milites. 2. Corona. [49]. 3. Oliva Speciosa (*App.*
Daily, daily sing the praises	568	Daily, daily.
Day of wrath and doom impending	351	Plainsong. (Sequence.)
Days and moments quickly flying	382	Goldschmidt (O der Alles).
Dear Lord and Father of mankind	383	1. Repton. 2. Hammersmith (*App.* 50).
Deck thyself, my soul, with gladness	306	Schmücke dich.
Dismiss me not thy service, Lord	555	Brunswick.
Disposer supreme, and Judge of the earth	178	Old 104th.
Do no sinful action	589	Newland.

GENERAL INDEX

First Line	Hymn	Name of Tune
Dost thou truly seek renown	97	Das ist meine Freude.
Draw nigh, and take the Body of the Lord	307	1. Draw Nigh. 2. The Sacred Heart (*App.* 44).
Drop down, ye heavens, from above	736	Plainsong.
Drop, drop, slow tears	98	Song 46.
Earth's mighty Maker, whose command	59	1. Plainsong. 2. O invidenda martyrum.
E'en in thy childood, 'mid the desert places	224	1. Plainsong. 2. Herr, deinen Zorn.
Eternal Father, strong to save	540	Melita.
Eternal Glory of the sky	56	1. Plainsong. 2. Richard.
Eternal Light, Divinity	632	Montgomery.
Eternal Monarch, King most high	141	1. Plainsong. 2. Gonfalon Royal.
Eternal Power, whose high abode	635	O Jesu mi Dulcissime.
Eternal Ruler of the ceaseless round	384	Song 1.
Evensong is hushed in silence	569	Evening Hymn.
Every morning the red sun	590	Langdale.
Fair waved the golden corn	290	Selma.
Faithful Cross! above all other	737	Plainsong (p. 895).
Father, hear the prayer we offer	385	Sussex.
Father most holy, merciful and tender	160	1. Plainsong. 2. Christe du Beistand.
Father of all, to thee	386	Warsaw.
Father of heaven, whose love profound	387	Das Leiden des Herrn.
Father of men, in whom are one	528	Exeter.
Father of spirits, whose divine control	352	Old 124th.
Father, see thy children bending at thy throne	308	Adoro Te (No. 2).
Father, to thee we look in all our sorrow	538	L'Omnipotent.
Father, we praise thee, now the night is over	165	1. Plainsong. 2. Christe Sanctorum.
Father, who on man dost shower	531	Charing.
Fierce raged the tempest o'er the deep	541	1. White Gates. 2. St. Aëlred (*App.* 62).
Fierce was the wild billow	388	St. Issey.
Fight the good fight with all thy might	389	Shepton-Beauchamp.
Firmly I believe and truly	390	Shipston.
Fling out the banner! let it float	546	Cathcart.
For all the Saints who from their labours rest	641	1. Sine Nomine. 2. Luccombe. [23]. 3. For all the Saints (*App.*
For all thy Saints, O Lord	196	Mount Ephraim.
For ever with the Lord	391	1. Llanllyfni. 2. Montgomery (*App.* 51).
For the beauty of the earth	309	England's Lane.
For thee, O dear, dear country	392	Magdalena.
For thy mercy and thy grace	266	Culbach.
Forgive them, O my Father	112	St. Mary Magdalene.

GENERAL INDEX

First Line	Hymn	Name of Tune
Forsaken once, and thrice denied	227	1. Childhood. 2. Erskine (*App.* 34).
Forth in thy name, O Lord, I go	259	Angel's Song (Song 34).
Forty days and forty nights	73	Aus der Tiefe.
Forward! be our watchword	642	Upwick.
From east to west, from shore to shore	18	1. Plainsong. 2. Rouen.
From foes that would the land devour	557	Isleworth.
From glory to glory advancing	310	Sheen.
From Greenland's icy mountains	547	Calcutta.
From the eastern mountains	615	1. Sutton Valence. 2. Zundel (*App.* 68).
From thee all skill and science flow	525	1. Farnham. 2. Culross.
Gentle Jesus, meek and mild	591	Part 1. Farnaby. Part 2. Lew Trenchard.
Gentle Shepherd, thou hast stilled	353	Jesu meines Glaubens Zier.
Give me the wings of faith to rise	197	Song 67.
Give rest, O Christ, to thy servant	744	Kieff Melody.
Glorious things of thee are spoken	393	Austrian Hymn.
Glory and praise and dominion be thine	621	Plainsong.
Glory be to Jesus	99	Boundary.
Glory to thee, my God, this night	267	1. Tallis' Canon. 2. [Alternative Version.]
Go, labour on; spend, and be spent	556	Llangollen (Lledrod).
Go to dark Gethsemane	100	Nicht so traurig.
God be with you till we meet again	524	Randolph.
God is working his purpose out	548	1. Purpose. 2. Benson (*App.* 63).
God moves in a mysterious way	394	London New.
God of all grace, thy mercy send (*Evening Litany*)	652	1. Michael. 2. Oldbridge (*App.* 72).
God of mercy, God of grace	395	Heathlands.
God of our fathers, known of old	558	Folkingham.
God of our fathers, unto thee	559	Etona.
God save our gracious Queen	560	National Anthem.
God that madest earth and heaven	268	1. Ar Hyd y Nos. 2. Nutfield (*App.* 15).
God the Father, God the Son (*Litany of the Advent*)	647	Tres Magi de Gentibus.
God the Father, God the Son (*Litany of Penitence*)	648	Helfer meiner armen Seele.
God the Father, God the Son (*Litany of the Church*)	651	Litany.
God the Father, God the Son (*Children's Litany*)	654	Farnaby.
God the Father, God the Son (*Commendatory Litany*)	655	Jesu, Jesu du mein Hirt.
God the Father, God the Word (*Litany of the Blessed Sacrament*)	653	Prompto Gentes Animo.
God the Father, seen of none (*Litany of the Passion*)	649	1. Galliard. 2. St. Mark (*App.* 71).
Gracious Spirit, Holy Ghost	396	Dian.

GENERAL INDEX

First Line	Hymn	Name of Tune
Great God, what do I see and hear . . .	4	Luther's Hymn (Nun freut
Guide me, O thou great Redeemer . . .	397	Caersalem. [euch).
Hail, harbinger of morn	225	Hail Harbinger of Morn.
Hail, O Star that pointest	213	1. Plainsong. / 2. Ave Maris Stella.
Hail, our Monarch	App. 3	Plainsong.
Hail the day that sees him rise . . .	143	Llanfair.
Hail the Sign, the Sign of Jesus . . .	592	Groombridge.
Hail thee, Festival Day! (*Easter Procession*)	624	1. Plainsong. / 2. Salve Festa Dies.
Hail thee, Festival Day! (*Ascension-Day Procession*)	628	Plainsong.
Hail thee, Festival Day! (*Whit-Sunday Procession*)	630	Plainsong.
Hail thee, Festival Day! (*Dedication Procession*)	634	Plainsong.
Hail, thou Source of every blessing . . .	616	Rex Gloriae.
Hail to the Lord's Anointed	45	Crüger.
Hail to the Lord who comes	209	Old 120th.
Hail, true Body, born of Mary. . . .	311	Ave Verum.
Happy are they, they that love God . .	393	Binchester.
Hark! a herald voice is calling	5	Merton.
Hark! hark, my soul! Angelic songs are swelling	399	Pilgrims of the Night.
Hark, how all the welkin rings	23	Dent Dale.
Hark, my soul, how everything	296	Lyne.
Hark, my soul! it is the Lord	400	1. White Ladies Aston. / 2. St. Bees (*App.* 52).
Hark the glad sound! the Saviour comes .	6	1. Bristol. / 2. [Alternative version.]
Hark! the herald Angels sing.	24	Mendelssohn.
Hark! the sound of holy voices	198	1. Vision. / 2. Deerhurst (*App.* 32).
Have mercy, Lord, on me	74	St. Bride.
Have mercy on us, God most high . .	161	1. St. Flavian. / 2. [Alternative version.]
He is risen, he is risen	132	Gott des Himmels.
He sat to watch o'er customs paid . . .	240	Alfreton.
He wants not friends that hath thy love .	401	Cameronian Midnight
He who would valiant be	402	Monks Gate. [Hymn.
He, whose confession God of old accepted	188	1. Plainsong. / 2. Iste Confessor.
Hear us, O Lord, have mercy upon us .	736	Plainsong.
Hear what the voice from heaven proclaims	354	Wigton.
Heavenly Father, send thy blessing . .	593	Pleading Saviour.
Her Virgin eyes saw God incarnate born .	217	Farley Castle.
Here, O my Lord, I see thee face to face .	312	Congleton.
High Word of God, who once didst come .	2	1. Plainsong. / 2. Verbum Supernum.
His are the thousand sparkling rills . .	117	Saffron Walden.

GENERAL INDEX

First Line	Hymn	Name of Tune
His cheering message from the grave	124	1. Plainsong. Part 1. 2. Plainsong. Part 2. 3. Solemnis Haec Festivitas.
Ho! my comrades, see the signal	570	Hold the Fort.
Hold thou my hands	403	Miserere Mei.
Holy Father, cheer our way	270	1. Ton-Mân. 2. Huddersfield (*App.* 37).
Holy Father, in thy mercy	520	Eastergate.
Holy Ghost, come down upon thy children	571	Bossiney. [kam.
Holy God, we show forth here	313	Da zu dir der Heiland
Holy, Holy, Holy! Lord God Almighty	162	1. Nicaea. 2. [A higher setting] (*App.* 14).
Holy Jesus! God of love	314	Freuen wir uns.
How are thy servants blest, O Lord	542	Kilmarnock.
How bright these glorious spirits shine	199	Ballerma.
How shall I sing that Majesty	404	Old 137th.
How sweet the name of Jesus sounds	405	St. Peter.
I bind unto myself to-day	212	1. St. Patrick. 2. Deirdre.
I could not do without thee	572	Gosterwood.
I hear thy welcome voice	573	I Hear Thy Welcome Voice.
I heard the voice of Jesus say	574	Kingsfold.
I lay my sins on Jesus	575	Prysgol.
I look to thee in every need	406	O Jesu.
I love to hear the story	594	Gosterwood.
I need thee, precious Jesu	576	Prysgol.
I think when I read that sweet story of old	595	East Horndon.
If there be that skills to reckon	250	Lewes.
Immortal, invisible, God only wise	407	St. Denio.
Immortal love for ever full	408	Bishopthorpe (St. Paul's).
In our work, and in our play	596	Lyne.
In Paradise reposing	355	Hambridge.
In stature grows the heavenly child	46	Cornhill.
In the bleak mid-winter	25	Cranham.
In the Cross of Christ I glory	409	Wychbold.
In the hour of my distress	410	Holy Comfort.
In token that thou shalt not fear	337	St. Stephen.
Into thy hands, O Lord	739 740	Plainsong.
It came upon the midnight clear	26	Noel.
It is a thing most wonderful	597	Herongate.
It is finished! Blessèd Jesus	120	Omni Die.
It is finished! Christ hath known	118	Jesu meines Glaubens Zier.
Jerusalem, my happy home	638	Part 1. St. Austin. Part 2. Southill. Part 3. Stalham. Dunstan [Alternative tune]. Jerusalem (*App.* 69).

GENERAL INDEX

First Line	Hymn	Name of Tune
Jerusalem on high	411	Christchurch.
Jerusalem the golden	412	Ewing.
Jesu, gentlest Saviour	315	vv. 1, 3, 5, Eudoxia. vv. 2, 4, 6, Caswall (Wem in Leidenstagen).
Jesu, grant me this, I pray	413	Song 13.
Jesu, Lord of life and glory	75	1. St. Raphael. 2. Llanilar.
Jesu, Lover of my soul	414	1. Hollingside. 2. Aberystwyth.
Jesu, meek and gentle	415	1. Belsize. [53]. 2. St. Constantine (*App*.
Jesu, meek and lowly	416	St. Martin.
Jesu, my Lord, my God, my All	417	1. Gesius (Heut' triumphiret), 417. [19]. 2. St. Chrysostom (*App*. 3. Stella (*App*. 54).
Jesu, name all names above	418	Werde Munter.
Jesu, Son of Mary	356	1. Dun Aluinn. [47]. 2. Corpus Domini (*App*.
Jesu, tender Shepherd, hear me	599	Shipston.
Jesu, the Father's only Son	17	1. Plainsong. 2. Vom Himmel hoch.
Jesu!—the very thought is sweet	238	1. Plainsong. 2. Jesu Dulcis Memoria. 3. The Rosy Sequence (Parts 1 and 3).
Jesu, the very thought of thee	419	1. St. Botolph. 2. Parts 2, 3. King's Norton. 3. St. Agnes (*App*. 55).
Jesu, the Virgins' Crown, do thou	192	1. Plainsong. 2. St. Ambrose (193).
Jesus calls us!—o'er the tumult	205	Herald.
Jesus Christ is risen to-day, Alleluya	133	1. Easter Hymn. 2. [Original Version.] 3. [A higher setting] (*App*. 13).
Jesus, good above all other	598	Quem Pastores laudavere.
Jesus lives! thy terrors now	134	1. Christ ist erstanden. 2. St. Albinus.
Jesus shall reign where'er the sun	420	Truro.
Jesus, these eyes have never seen	421	Nun danket all.
Jesus, where'er thy people meet	422	St. Sepulchre.
Joy and triumph everlasting	200	Psalm 42.
Judge eternal, throned in splendour	423	Rhuddlan.
Just as I am, without one plea	316	Saffron Walden.
Kindly spring again is here	287	Da Christus geboren war.
King of glory, King of peace	424	Gwalchmai.
Laud, O Sion, thy salvation	317	Plainsong. (Sequence.)
Lead, kindly Light, amid the encircling gloom	425	Lux Benigna.

GENERAL INDEX

FIRST LINE	HYMN	NAME OF TUNE
Lead us, heavenly Father, lead us	426	Mannheim.
Let all mortal flesh keep silence	318	Picardy.
Let all the world in every corner sing	427	1. High Road. 2. Universal Praise (*App.* 56).
Let our choir new anthems raise	187	Weimar.
Let saints on earth in concert sing	428	Dundee.
Let sighing cease and woe	27	St. Michael (Old 134th).
Let the round world with songs rejoice	176	1. Plainsong. 2. Auctoritate Saeculi.
Let thine example, holy John, remind us	223	1. Plainsong. 2. Herr, deinen Zorn.
Let us, with a gladsome mind	532	Monkland.
Lift up your heads, ye gates of brass	549	Praetorius (Für dein empfangen Speis und Trank).
Lift up your hearts! We lift them, Lord	429	1. Birmingham. 2. All Souls (*App.* 57).
Lighten the darkness of our life's long night	430	Erfyniad.
Light's abode, celestial Salem	431	Regent Square.
Little drops of water	600	Gott ein Vater.
Lo! God is here! let us adore	637	Old 117th.
Lo! golden light rekindles day	55	1. Plainsong. 2. Gaude, regina gloriae.
Lo! he comes with clouds descending	7	Helmsley.
Long did I toil, and knew no earthly rest	432	Battle.
Lord, behold us with thy blessing	523	Dismissal.
Lord, enthroned in heavenly splendour	319	Bryn Calfaria.
Lord God of hosts, within whose hand	219	Falkland.
Lord, I would own thy tender care	601	Eardisley.
Lord, in this thy mercy's day	76	1. Heiliger Geist. 2. St. Philip (*App.* 10).
Lord, in thy name thy servants plead	140	1. Lincoln. 2. [Alternative version.]
Lord, in thy presence dread and sweet	342	Advent.
Lord, it belongs not to my care	433	Dibdin.
Lord Jesu Christ, our Lord most dear	338	In einem Kripplein lag ein Kind.
Lord Jesus, think on me	77	Southwell.
Lord Jesu, who at Lazarus' tomb	357	Song 18.
Lord of all being, throned afar	434	Uffingham.
Lord of Creation, bow thine ear, O Christ, to hear	174	1. Plainsong. 2. Annue Christe.
Lord of life and King of glory	530	Calvary.
Lord of our life, and God of our salvation	435	Iste Confessor (2).
Lord, teach us how to pray aright	78	First Mode Melody.
Lord, the wind and sea obey thee	543	Quem Pastores laudavere.
Lord, thy word abideth	436	Ravenshaw.
Lord, to our humble prayers attend (*Litany of Rogationtide*)	650	Beatus.
Lord, when thy kingdom comes, remember me	113	Song 4.

1031

GENERAL INDEX

First Line	Hymn	Name of Tune
Lord, when we bend before thy throne	79	Hunnys.
Lord, while for all mankind we pray	561	Aberdeen.
Lord, who shall sit beside thee	232	Christus der ist mein Leben.
Love Divine, all loves excelling	437	Moriah.
Love of the Father, love of God the Son	438	Song 22.
Love's redeeming work is done	135	Savannah (or Herrnhut).
Loving Shepherd of thy sheep	602	1. Gentle Jesus. 2. Buckland (*App*. 67).
Maker of earth, to thee alone	64	Dunfermline.
Maker of man, who from thy throne	62	1. Plainsong. 2. Illsley.
Martyr of God, whose strength was steeled	180	1. Plainsong. 2. Leighton.
Mary, weep not, weep no longer	231	Plainsong.
Most glorious Lord of life, that on this day	283	Farley Castle.
Most Holy Lord and God of heaven	60	1. Plainsong. 2. O invidenda martyrum.
My faith looks up to thee	439	1. Denbigh. 2. Olivet (*App*. 58).
My God, accept my heart this day	341	St. James.
My God and Father, while I stray	440	1. Layriz (Ins Feld geh). 2. Troyte No. 1 (*App*. 59).
My God, and is thy Table spread	320	Simeon.
My God, how wonderful thou art	441	Westminster.
My God, I love thee; not because	80	Solomon.
My God! My God! and can it be	101	Der Tag bricht an.
My Lord, my Life, my Love	442	Song 20.
My spirit longs for thee	443	Maria jung und zart.
Nearer, my God, to thee	444	Horbury.
New every morning is the love	260	Melcombe.
Now in holy celebration	228	1. Plainsong. 2. Oriel.
Now is the healing time decreed	67	1. Plainsong. 2. Jena (Das neugeborne Kindelein).
Now my soul, thy voice upraising	623	St. Thomas.
Now thank we all our God	533	Nun danket.
Now that the daylight fills the sky	254	Plainsong.
Now the busy week is done	282	Ratisbon (Jesu meine Zuversicht).
Now the day is over	603	Eudoxia.
Now the labourer's toils are o'er	358	Pressburg (Nicht so traurig).
O blest Creator of the light	51	1. Plainsong. 2. Lucis Creator.
O boundless Wisdom, God most high	58	1. Plainsong. 2. O invidenda martyrum.
O Christ, our hope, our hearts' desire	144	1. Bromsgrove. 2. Metzler's Redhead No. 66 (*App*. 29).

GENERAL INDEX

First Line	Hymn	Name of Tune
O Christ, our joy, to whom is given	142	1. Plainsong. 2. Gonfalon Royal.
O Christ, who art the Light and Day	81	1. Plainsong (*App.* 1). 2. St. Bartholomew.
O come, all ye faithful	28 614	Adeste Fideles.
O come and mourn with me awhile	111	1. St. Cross. 2. Das Leiden des Herrn (*App.* 11).
O come, O come, Emmanuel	8	Veni Emmanuel.
O day of rest and gladness	284	Herzlich thut mich erfreuen.
O dearest Lord, by all adored	604	Mit Freuden zart.
O Faith of England, taught of old	544	Psalm 68.
O Father all creating	345	Dank sei Gott in der Höhe.
O Food of men wayfaring	321	In allen meinen Thaten.
O for a closer walk with God	445	1. Caithness. 2. Stracathro.
O for a heart to praise my God	82	Stockton.
O for a thousand tongues to sing	446	O God of Love.
O gladsome light, O grace	269	Nunc dimittis.
O glorious King of Martyr hosts	183	1. Plainsong. 2. Rex Gloriose.
O glorious Maid, exalted far	215	1. Plainsong. 2. O Amor Quam Ecstaticus.
O God, Creation's secret force	262	Plainsong.
O God of Bethel, by whose hand	447	Burford.
O God of earth and altar	562	Kings Lynn.
O God of mercy, God of might	448	Fitzwilliam.
O God of truth, O Lord of might	261	Plainsong.
O God of truth, whose living word	449	Martyrs.
O God, our help in ages past	450	St. Anne.
O God the Son eternal, thy dread might	244	St. Michael New.
O God, thy power is wonderful	451	Melrose.
O God, thy soldiers' crown and guard	181	1. Plainsong. 2. Deus Tuorum Militum.
O happy band of pilgrims	452	Knecht.
O happy day, when first was poured	36	Das walt' Gott Vater.
O heavenly Jerusalem	251	Paderborn.
O help us, Lord; each hour of need	83	Bedford.
O Holy Spirit, Lord of grace	453	Tallis' Ordinal.
O Jerusalem, look toward the East	618	Plainsong.
O Jesu Christ, from thee began	69	1. Plainsong. 2. Plaistow.
O Jesu, thou art standing	578	1. In der Wiegen. 2. St. Catherine (*App.* 65).
O Jesus, I have promised	577	Missionary Hymn.
O kind Creator, bow thine ear	66	1. Plainsong. 2. Cannons.
O King enthroned on high	454	Temple.
O King most high of earth and sky	629	Parsifal.
O lead my blindness by the hand	322	Leicester (or Bedford).
O let him whose sorrow	455	Clewer.

GENERAL INDEX

First Line	Hymn	Name of Tune
O let the heart beat high with bliss	237	1. Plainsong. 2. Cromer.
O Light of light, by love inclined	234	1. Plainsong. 2. Whitehall.
O little town of Bethlehem	15	Forest Green.
O Lord, and Master of us all	456	Blackbourne.
O Lord, how happy should we be	457	Magdalen College.
O Lord of heaven, and earth, and sea	521	Es ist kein Tag.
O Lord of hosts, all heaven possessing	458	Neumark.
O Lord of hosts, who didst upraise	539	Llangoedmor.
O Lord, to whom the spirits live	359	South Cerney.
O Lord, turn not away thy face	84	St. Mary.
O love, how deep, how broad, how high	459	Eisenach.
O Love, who formedst me to wear	460	Christchurch.
O Master, it is good to be	235	Tallis' Lamentation.
O, most merciful! O, most bountiful	323	Schönster Herr Jesu.
O my people, what have I done unto thee?	737	Plainsong.
O North, with all thy vales of green	550	Auch jetzt macht Gott.
O perfect Love, all human thought transcending	346	Welwyn.
O praise our great and gracious Lord	461	Old 81st (Old 77th).
O quickly come, dread Judge of all	462	Vater unser.
O sacred head, sore wounded	102	1. Passion Chorale. 2. [Alternative version.]
O Saviour Jesu, not alone	249	1. Plainsong. 2. Deo Gracias.
O Shepherd of the sheep	190	Carlisle.
O sing to the Lord, whose bountiful hand	291	67th Psalm.
O sinner, raise the eye of faith	103	Allein Gott in der Höh sei Ehr.
O splendour of God's glory bright	52	1. Plainsong. 2. Wareham.
O Strength and Stay, upholding all creation	271	School House.
O thou from whom all goodness flows	85	Harington (Retirement).
O thou in all thy might so far	463	Crowle.
O thou not made with hands	464	Old 120th.
O thou, who at thy Eucharist didst pray	324	Ffigysbren.
O thou who camest from above	343	Affection.
O thou, who didst with love untold	206	Crediton.
O thou who dost accord us	86	Innsbruck.
O thou who gavest power to love	347	Kent.
O thou who through this holy week	109	Cheshire.
O thou whose all-redeeming might	189	Plainsong.
O Trinity of blessèd light	164	1. Plainsong. 2. Hilariter (Die Ganze Welt).
O Unity of threefold light	163	Old 22nd.
O what their joy and their glory must be	465	Regnator Orbis.
O Word immortal of eternal God	325	Song 24.
O Word of God above	171	St. Edmund.
O worship the King	466	Hanover.
O worship the Lord in the beauty of holiness	42	Was lebet, was schwebet.
Of the Father's heart begotten	613	Divinum Mysterium.
Of the glorious Body telling	326	1. Plainsong. 2. Pange Lingua. 3. Tantum Ergo (No. 2).

GENERAL INDEX

First Line	Hymn	Name of Tune
Oft in danger, oft in woe	437	University College.
On Jordan's bank the Baptist's cry	9	Winchester New.
On the Resurrection morning	136	1. Resurrection Morning. 2. Hornsey (*App.* 28).
Once in royal David's city	605	Irby.
Once, only once, and once for all	327	Albano.
Once to every man and nation	563	Yn y Glyn.
Only-Begotten, Word of God eternal	636	Iste Confessor (2).
Onward, Christian soldiers	643	1. Haydn. 2. St. Gertrude.
Our blest Redeemer, ere he breathed	157	1. Wicklow. 2. St. Cuthbert (*App.* 31).
Our Father's home eternal	252	Au fort de ma détresse.
Palms of glory, raiment bright	201	1. Boyce. 2. Palms of Glory (*App.* 33).
Peace, perfect peace, in this dark world of sin	468	Song 46.
Pleasant are thy courts above	469	1. Benevento. 2. Maidstone (*App.* 20).
Portal of the world's salvation	229	1. Plainsong. 2. Collaudemus.
Pour out thy Spirit from on high	167	Duke Street.
Praise, my soul, the King of heaven	470	Praise my Soul.
Praise the Lord of heaven	534	Laus Tibi Christe.
Praise the Lord! ye heavens, adore him	535	Praise.
Praise to the Holiest in the height	471	Richmond.
Praise to the Lord, the Almighty, the King of creation	536	Hast du denn, Jesu.
Pray that Jerusalem may have	472	1. York. 2. [Alternative version.]
Pray when the morn is breaking	473	Meirionydd.
Prayer is the soul's sincere desire	474	Wigton.
Receive, O Lord, in heaven above	194	St. Ambrose.
Rejoice, O land, in God thy might	475	Wareham.
Rejoice, the Lord is King	476	Gopsal.
Rejoice! the year upon its way	151	1. Plainsong. 2. Aeterna Christi Munera (Rouen).
Rejoice to-day with one accord	537	Ein' feste Burg.
Rejoice, ye pure in heart	644	Ich halte treulich still.
Rest of the weary	579	Fortunatus.
Ride on! ride on in majesty	620	Winchester New.
Rock of ages, cleft for me	477	Redhead No. 76.
Round me falls the night	272	Seelenbräutigam.
Safe in the arms of Jesus	580	Arms of Jesus.
Saint of God, elect and precious	31	1. Plainsong. 2. St. Thomas.
Saints of God! Lo, Jesu's people	239	Sussex.

GENERAL INDEX

First Line	Hymn	Name of Tune
Saviour, again to thy dear name we raise	273	1. Magda. 2. Ellers (*App.* 38).
Saviour, blessèd Saviour	645	1. Nous allons. 2. Goshen (*App.* 70).
Saviour eternal	10	Plainsong. (Sequence.)
Saviour, sprinkle many nations	551	Hope.
Saviour, when in dust to thee	87	Aberystwyth.
Saviour, who didst healing give	247	Jesus ist das schönste Licht (Meine Liebe lebet noch).
See, Father, thy belovèd Son	328	Hymnus Eucharisticus.
See him in raiment rent	656	1. Bridgwater (Parts 1, 2, and 5). 2. Langport (Pts. 3 and 4).
See the Conqueror mounts in triumph	145	In Babilone.
See the destined day arise	110	Nun komm, der Heiden Heiland.
Servant of God, remember	104	1. Plainsong (*App.* 2). 2. Nun lasst uns geh'n.
Sinful, sighing to be blest	88	Tunbridge.
Sing, my tongue, the glorious battle	95	Plainsong.
Sing praise to God who reigns above	478	Wittenberg (Es ist das Heil).
Sing to the Lord the children's hymn	606	St. Hugh.
Sing we all the joys and sorrows	230	1. Plainsong. 2. Collaudemus.
Sing we triumphant hymns of praise	146	Tugwood.
Sion's daughters! Sons of Jerusalem	172	1. Plainsong (Sequence). 2. Sion's Daughters (*App.* 7) (Plainsong).
Soldiers of Christ, arise	479	St. Ethelwald.
Soldiers, who are Christ's below	480	Orientis Partibus.
Son of a Virgin, Maker of thy mother	191	1. Plainsong. 2. Ut Queant Laxis.
Son of God, eternal Saviour	529	Lugano.
Songs of praise the Angels sang	481	Riley.
Songs of thankfulness and praise	47	St. Edmund.
Soul of Jesus, make me whole	89	Anima Christi.
Spirit of mercy, truth, and love	631	Melcombe.
Spouse of Christ, in arms contending	253	1. Plainsong. (All Saints' Sequence.) 2. Gott will's machen.
Spread, O spread, thou mighty word	552	Gott sei Dank.
Stand up!—stand up for Jesus	581	Morning Light.
Stars of the morning, so gloriously bright	245	Quedlinburg.
Still will we trust, though earth seem dark	482	1. Stanstead. 2. Langa (*App.* 60).
Strengthen for service, Lord, the hands	329	Ach Gott und Herr.
Strong Son of God, immortal Love	483	Song 5.
Sun of my soul, thou Saviour dear	274	1. Birling. 2. Herr Gott Vater. 3. Hursley (*App.* 39).
Sweet Saviour, bless us ere we go	275	Lodsworth.
Sweet the moments, rich in blessing	105	Batty.

GENERAL INDEX

FIRST LINE	HYMN	NAME OF TUNE
Take my life and let it be	582	Ives.
Take up thy cross, the Saviour said	484	Breslau.
Teach me, my God and King	485	Sandys.
Tell me the old, old story	583	Tell me the Old, Old Story.
Ten thousand times ten thousand	486	Komm, Seele.
That day of wrath, that dreadful day	487	Babylon's Streams.
The advent of our God	11	St. Thomas.
The children of the Hebrews	617	Plainsong.
The Church of God a kingdom is	488	Capel.
The Church triumphant in thy love	639	Eatington.
The Church's one foundation	489	Aurelia.
The dawn is sprinkling in the east	57	1. Plainsong. 2. Richard.
The day draws on with golden light	123	1. Plainsong. Part 1. 2. Plainsong. Part 2. 3. Solemnis haec Festivitas.
The day is past and over	276	1. Hominum Amator. 2. St. Anatolius (*App.* 40).
The Day of Resurrection	137	Ellacombe.
The day thou gavest, Lord, is ended	277	1. Les commandemens de Dieu. 2. St. Clement (*App.* 16).
The duteous day now closeth	278	Innsbruck.
The dying robber raised his aching brow	114	1. Old 124th. 2. [Alternative version.]
The earth, O Lord, is one great field	168	Manchester.
The eternal gifts of Christ the King	175	1. Plainsong. 2. Aeterna Christi Munera.
The fast, as taught by holy lore	65	1. Plainsong. 2. Jesu Corona.
The glory of these forty days	68	1. Plainsong. 2. Erhalt' uns, Herr.
The God of Abraham praise	646	Leoni.
The God of love my Shepherd is	93	University.
The God whom earth, and sea, and sky	214	1. Plainsong. 2. O Amor quam Ecstaticus.
The great God of heaven is come down to earth	29	A Virgin Unspotted.
The head that once was crowned with thorns	147	St. Magnus (Nottingham)
The highest and the holiest place	210	Jackson.
The hymn for conquering Martyrs raise	35	Wer da wonet.
The King, O God, his heart to thee upraiseth	564	Donne Secours.
The King of love my Shepherd is	490	St. Columba.
The Lamb's high banquet we await	125	1. Plainsong. 2. Rex Gloriose. 3. Jesu Redemptor Saeculi (*App.* 26).
The Lord and King of all things	32	Wohlauf, thut nicht verzagen.

GENERAL INDEX

First Line	Hymn	Name of Tune
The Lord ascendeth up on high	148	Nun freut euch.
The Lord is come! On Syrian soil	48	Cantate Domino.
The Lord is risen indeed	627	Narenza.
The Lord my pasture shall prepare	491	Surrey.
The Lord will come and not be slow	492	Coleshill.
The Maker of the sun and moon	16	Newbury.
The merits of the Saints	182	1. Plainsong. 2. Das herrlich hohe Fest.
The praises of that Saint we sing	193	St. Ambrose.
The race that long in darkness pined	43	1. Dundee. 2. [Alternative version.]
The radiant morn hath passed away	279	1. Gaza. 2. St. Leonard (*App.* 41).
The roseate hues of early dawn	493	Old 107th.
The royal banners forward go	94	Plainsong.
The Saint who first found grace to pen	220	Brockham.
The Son of Consolation	222	Rhyddid.
The Son of God goes forth to war	202	Stettin (Nun seht).
The spacious firmament on high	297	London (or Addison's).
The strain upraise of joy and praise	494	Troyte No. 2.
The strife is o'er, the battle done	625	Victory.
The summer days are come again	288	Soll's sein.
The sun is sinking fast	280	1. Speer (Sag was hilft). 2. St. Columba (*App.* 42).
The voice that breathed o'er Eden	348	St. Alphege.
The wingèd herald of the day	53	1. Plainsong. 2. Wareham.
The winter's sleep was long and deep	221	King's Langley.
The Word of God, proceeding forth	330	1. Plainsong. 2. O Salutaris. 3. Part 2. O Jesu Christ Pearsall. [(*App.* 46).
The world is very evil	495	
The year is swiftly waning	294	Devonshire.
Thee, O Christ, the Father's splendour	241	1. Plainsong. 2. Neander.
Thee we adore, O hidden Saviour, thee	331	Adoro Te.
There is a blessèd home	496	1. 7th Mode Melody. 2. Hawarden.
There is a book who runs may read	497	Relief.
There is a fountain filled with blood	332	Windsor.
There is a green hill far away	106	Horsley.
There is a happy land	608	Happy Land.
There is a land of pure delight	498	Mendip.
There's a Friend for little children	607	Ingrave.
There's a wideness in God's mercy	499	Zum Frieden.
There were ninety and nine that safely lay	584	The Ninety and Nine.
They come, God's messengers of love	246	1. Daniel. 2. St. Crispin (*App.* 36).
They whose course on earth is o'er	500	Vienna.
Thine arm, O Lord, in days of old	526	St. Matthew.
Thine for ever! God of love	344	Horsham.
Thirty years among us dwelling	96	Plainsong.
This day the first of days was made	50	1. Plainsong. 2. Andernach.

GENERAL INDEX

First Line	Hymn	Name of Tune
Thou art gone up on high	149	Old 25th.
Thou art, O God, the life and light . . .	298	New 113th.
Thou didst leave thy throne and thy kingly crown	585	Margaret.
Thou hallowed chosen morn of praise . .	138	{ 1. Mach's mit mir Gott. 2. Dies ist der Tag.
Thou, Lord, hast power to heal	349	Dolgelly.
Thou to whom the sick and dying . . .	527	{ 1. St. Leonard. 2. Requiem (*App.* 21).
Thou who sentest thine Apostles . . .	248	Bryntirion.
Thou whose almighty Word	553	Moscow.
Three in One, and One in Three	501	Capetown.
Throned upon the awful Tree	116	Arfon.
Through all the changing scenes of life .	502	Wiltshire.
Through the day thy love has spared us .	281	Dretzel.
Through the night of doubt and sorrow .	503	{ 1. Marching. 2. St. Oswald (*App.* 61).
Through the night thy Angels kept . .	609	Peacefield.
Thy hand, O God, has guided	545	Thornbury.
Thy kingdom come, O God	554	{ 1. Kingsland. 2. St. Cecilia (*App.* 64).
Thy kingdom come! on bended knee . .	504	Irish.
Thy way, not mine, O Lord	505	Psalm 32.
'Tis good, Lord, to be here	236	Carlisle.
'Tis winter now; the fallen snow . . .	295	Danby.
To Mercy, Pity, Peace, and Love . . .	506	Epsom.
To my humble supplication	90	De Profundis.
To the name that brings salvation . . .	507	Oriel.
To thee, O Lord, our hearts we raise . .	292	{ 1. St. Gall. 2. Golden Sheaves (*App.* 17).
To thee our God we fly	565	Croft's 136th.
Victim Divine, thy grace we claim . . .	333	Coleraine (Vicenza).
Virgin-born, we bow before thee . . .	640	{ 1. Mon Dieu, prête-moi l'oreille. 2. Urquell aller Seligkeiten.
Wake, O wake! with tidings thrilling . .	12	Wachet auf!
We are but little children poor	610	Puer Nobis Nascitur.
Weary of earth and laden with my sin .	91	{ 1. Valor. 2. Dalkeith (*App.* 25).
We give thee but thine own	522	Windermere.
We love the place, O God	508	Quam Dilecta.
We plough the fields, and scatter . . .	293	Wir pflügen.
We praise thy name, all-holy Lord . . .	211	Old 44th.
We pray thee, heavenly Father	334	Caerlleon.
We saw thee not when thou didst come .	509	Farmborough.
We sing the glorious conquest	207	Llangloffan. [uns).
We sing the praise of him who died . .	510	Calvisius (Ach bleib bei
What are these that glow from afar . .	208	Ymdaith Mwngo (Monk's March).

GENERAL INDEX

First Line	Hymn	Name of Tune
What star is this, with beams so bright	44	Ein Kind gebor'n.
What sweet of life endureth	360	Christus der ist mein Leben.
When all thy mercies, O my God	511	Belgrave.
When came in flesh the incarnate Word	13	Walsall.
When Christ our Lord had passed once more	150	1. Plainsong. 2. Monte Cassino
When Christ was born in Bethlehem	611	Rodmell.
When God of old came down from heaven	158	Stroudwater.
When I survey the wondrous Cross	107	Caton (or Rockingham).
When morning gilds the skies	512	O Seigneur.
When our heads are bowed with woe	513	Redhead No. 47.
When, rising from the bed of death	92	1. Third Mode Melody. 2. [Tallis Original version.]
When spring unlocks the flowers	299	Gosterwood.
When wilt thou save the people	566	Kendal.
Wherefore, O Father, we thy humble servants	335	Christe Fons Jugis.
While shepherds watched their flocks by night	30	1. Winchester Old. 2. [Alternative version]. 3. Northrop (*App.* 8).
Who are these, like stars appearing	204	All Saints.
Who is he, in yonder stall	612	Resonet in Laudibus.
Who is this so weak and helpless	514	Llansannan.
Who is this with garments gory	108	Ebenezer (Ton-y-Botel).
Why, impious Herod, shouldst thou fear	38	1. Plainsong. 2. St. Venantius.
Wilt thou forgive that sin, by man begun	515	So giebst du.
With Christ we share a mystic grave	339	Farrant.
With golden splendour, and with roseate hues of morn	226	Plainsong.
Word supreme, before creation	33	Grafton.
Work is sweet, for God has blest	516	Voller Wunder.
Ye choirs of new Jerusalem (L.M.)	122	1. Plainsong. 2. Montesano.
Ye choirs of new Jerusalem (C.M.)	139	St. Fulbert.
Ye clouds and darkness, hosts of night	54	1. Plainsong. 2. Gaude, regina gloriae.
Ye holy Angels bright	517	Darwall's 148th.
Ye servants of the Lord	518	Narenza.
Ye sons and daughters of the King	626	1. O Filii et Filiae (1). 2. O Filii et Filiae (2).
Ye watchers and ye holy ones	519	Lasst uns erfreuen.
Ye who own the faith of Jesus	218	Den des Vaters Sinn geboren.